Information Security Management Handbook

Sixth Edition

Volume 5

OTHER INFORMATION SECURITY BOOKS FROM AUERBACH

A Practical Guide to Security Assessments
Sudhanshu Kairab
ISBN 978-0-8493-1706-4

Adaptive Security Management Architecture
James S. Tiller
ISBN 978-0-8493-7052-6

Assessing and Managing Security Risk in IT Systems: A Structured Methodology
John McCumber
ISBN 978-0-8493-2232-7

Asset Protection through Security Awareness
Tyler Justin Speed
ISBN 978-1-4398-0982-2

Cyber Security Essentials
James Graham and Ryan Olson, Editors
ISBN 978-1-4398-5123-4

Data Mining and Machine Learning in Cybersecurity
Sumeet Dua and Xian Du
ISBN 978-1-4398-3942-3

Defense against the Black Arts: How Hackers Do What They Do and How to Protect against It
Jesse Varsalone and Matthew McFadden
ISBN 978-1-4398-2119-0
Publication Date: September 09, 2011

FISMA Principles and Best Practices: Beyond Compliance
Patrick D. Howard
ISBN 978-1-4200-7829-9

Information Security Risk Analysis, Third Edition
Thomas R. Peltier
ISBN 978-1-4398-3956-0

Information Technology Control and Audit, Third Edition
Frederick Gallegos and Sandra Senft
ISBN 978-1-4200-6550-3

Introduction to Security and Network Forensics
William J. Buchanan
ISBN 978-0-8493-3568-6

Machine Learning Forensics for Law Enforcement, Security, and Intelligence
Jesus Mena
ISBN 978-1-4398-6069-4

Managing an Information Security and Privacy Awareness and Training Program, Second Edition
Rebecca Herold
ISBN 978-1-4398-1545-8

Mobile Device Security: A Comprehensive Guide to Securing Your Information in a Moving World
Stephen Fried
ISBN 978-1-4398-2016-2

Practical Risk Management for the CIO
Mark Scherling
ISBN 978-1-4398-5653-6

Secure and Resilient Software: Requirements, Test Cases, and Testing Methods
Mark S. Merkow
ISBN 978-1-4398-6621-4

Secure Java: For Web Application Development
Abhay Bhargav and B. V. Kumar
ISBN 978-1-4398-2351-4

Secure Semantic Service-Oriented Systems
Bhavani Thuraisingham
ISBN 978-1-4200-7331-7

The Security Risk Assessment Handbook: A Complete Guide for Performing Security Risk Assessments, Second Edition
Douglas Landoll
ISBN 978-1-4398-2148-0

Security of Mobile Communications
Noureddine Boudriga
ISBN 978-0-8493-7941-3

Security Patch Management
Felicia Nicastro
ISBN 978-1-4398-2499-3

Security Strategy: From Requirements to Reality
Bill Stackpole and Eric Oksendahl
ISBN 978-1-4398-2733-8

AUERBACH PUBLICATIONS
www.auerbach-publications.com
To Order Call: 1-800-272-7737 • Fax: 1-800-374-3401
E-mail: orders@crcpress.com

Information Security Management Handbook

Sixth Edition

Volume 5

Edited by

Harold F. Tipton, CISSP · Micki Krause Nozaki, CISSP

CRC Press
Taylor & Francis Group
Boca Raton   London   New York

CRC Press is an imprint of the
Taylor & Francis Group, an **informa** business

AN AUERBACH BOOK

CRC Press
Taylor & Francis Group
6000 Broken Sound Parkway NW, Suite 300
Boca Raton, FL 33487-2742

© 2012 by Taylor & Francis Group, LLC
CRC Press is an imprint of Taylor & Francis Group, an Informa business

No claim to original U.S. Government works

Printed in the United States of America on acid-free paper
Version Date: 20110707

International Standard Book Number: 978-1-4398-5345-0 (Hardback)

Visit the Taylor & Francis Web site at
http://www.taylorandfrancis.com

and the CRC Press Web site at
http://www.crcpress.com

Contents

Introduction ix

Editors xi

Contributors xiii

DOMAIN 1: ACCESS CONTROL
Access Control Techniques

1   Whitelisting for Endpoint Defense 3
    ROB SHEIN

2   Whitelisting 15
    SANDY BACIK

Access Control Administration

3   RFID and Information Security..21
    SALAHUDDIN KAMRAN

4   Privileged User Management 37
    GEORGES J. JAHCHAN

5   Privacy in the Age of Social Networking..55
    SALAHUDDIN KAMRAN

DOMAIN 2: TELECOMMUNICATIONS AND NETWORK SECURITY
Communications and Network Security

6   IF-MAP as a Standard for Security Data Interchange 69
    DAVID O'BERRY

Internet, Intranet, Extranet Security

7   Understating the Ramifications of IPv6.. 117
    FOSTER HENDERSON

Network Attacks and Countermeasures

8 Managing Security in Virtual Environments..137
E. EUGENE SCHULTZ AND EDWARD RAY

DOMAIN 3: INFORMATION SECURITY AND RISK MANAGEMENT
Security Management Concepts and Principles

9 Do Your Business Associate Security and Privacy Programs Live Up to HIPAA
and HITECH Requirements?...153
REBECCA HEROLD

10 Organization Culture Awareness Will Cultivate Your Information Security
Program..163
ROBERT PITTMAN

Risk Management

11 Role-Based Information Security Governance: Avoiding the Company Oil
Slick 179
TODD FITZGERALD

12 Social Networking Security Exposure..193
SANDY BACIK

13 Social Networking, Social Media, and Web 2.0 Security Risks 199
ROBERT M. SLADE

14 Applying Adult Education Principles to Security Awareness Programs...................207
CHRIS HARE

Security Management Planning

15 Controlling the Emerging Data Dilemma: Building Policy for Unstructured
Data Access..215
ANNE SHULTZ

16 Governance and Risk Management within the Context of Information Security ...229
JAMES C. MURPHY

17 Improving Enterprise Security through Predictive Analysis....................267
CHRIS HARE

Employment Policies and Practices

18 Security Outsourcing 283
SANDY BACIK

DOMAIN 4: APPLICATION DEVELOPMENT SECURITY
System Development Controls

19 The Effectiveness of Access Management Reviews 293
CHRIS HARE

20 Securing SaaS Applications: A Cloud Security Perspective for Application
Providers...301
PRADNYESH RANE

21 Attacking RFID Systems...313
PEDRO PERIS-LOPEZ, JULIO CESAR HERNANDEZ-CASTRO,
JUAN M. ESTEVEZ-TAPIADOR, AND ARTURO RIBAGORDA

DOMAIN 5: CRYPTOGRAPHY
Cryptographic Concepts, Methodologies, and Practices

22 Cryptography: Mathematics vs. Engineering...337
RALPH SPENCER POORE

23 Cryptographic Message Syntax 343
JEFF STAPLETON

DOMAIN 6: SECURITY ARCHITECTURE AND DESIGN
*Principles of Computer and Network Organizations, Architectures, and
Designs*

24 An Introduction to Virtualization Security 367
PAUL HENRY

DOMAIN 7: OPERATIONS SECURITY
Operations Controls

25 Warfare and Security: Deterrence and Dissuasion in the Cyber Era 391
SAMUEL CHUN

26 Configuration, Change, and Release Management..403
SEAN M. PRICE

27 Tape Backup Considerations..423
SANDY BACIK

28 Productivity vs. Security 429
SANDY BACIK

DOMAIN 8: BUSINESS CONTINUITY AND DISASTER RECOVERY PLANNING
Business Continuity Planning

29 Continuity Planning for Small- and Medium-Sized Organizations 435
CARL JACKSON

DOMAIN 9: LEGAL, REGULATIONS, COMPLIANCE, AND INVESTIGATIONS
Information Law

30 The Cost of Risk: An Examination of Risk Assessment and Information
Security in the Financial Industry 447
SETH KINNETT

31 Data Security and Privacy Legislation 455
SALAHUDDIN KAMRAN

Incident Handling

32 Discovery of Electronically Stored Information 473
SALAHUDDIN KAMRAN

DOMAIN 10: PHYSICAL (ENVIRONMENTAL) SECURITY
Elements of Physical Security

33 The Layered Defense Model and Perimeter Intrusion Detection 489
LEO KAHNG

Index 505

Information Security Management Handbook, Sixth Edition:
Comprehensive Table of Contents..521

Introduction

From the earliest editions of the *Handbook*, we recognized a growing need for professionals who are qualified to meet the challenges of complex technologies and escalating threats to information security.

However, as risks mount and information technology becomes that much more complicated, certified information security professionals must increasingly partner with skilled staff from sister disciplines such as risk management, business continuity, and law.

Today, maintaining information technology security, as well as keeping pace with competing standards, onerous regulations, and competitive markets, requires a village—a well-trained, well-educated, and well-informed team.

And so we offer our current edition of the *Handbook of Information Security Management*, with its virtual toolset of essays and dissertations addressing the whole of risk management, including people, processes, and technologies.

The information provided is practical, useful, and hands-on. The pieces are written by dedicated and committed persons who seek to share their "been there, done that" stories with those who may benefit from them. Within each of the chapters, you will find personal histories and problem solving that each author has been gracious enough to share.

It takes teamwork ...

The *Handbook*'s mission is to be used by a wide audience. Yes, the chapters are of substantial value to the information security professional; nevertheless, they also address issues applicable to managers, executives, attorneys, risk managers, technology operators, and beyond. So, read heartily. If you learn one thing or find one idea to apply, we have succeeded.

As always, we wish you the best.

Hal Tipton
Micki Krause Nozaki

Editors

Harold F. Tipton is an independent consultant and past president of the International Information System Security Certification Consortium, and has been a director of computer security for Rockwell International Corporation, Seal Beach, California, for about 15 years. He initiated the Rockwell computer and data security program in 1977 and then continued to administer, develop, enhance, and expand the program to accommodate the control needs produced by technological advances until his retirement from Rockwell in 1994.

Tipton has been a member of the Information Systems Security Association (ISSA) since 1982. He was the president of the Los Angeles chapter in 1984 and president of the national ISSA organization (1987–1989). He was added to the ISSA Hall of Fame and the ISSA Honor Roll in 2000 and elected an ISSA Distinguished Fellow in 2009. Tipton was a member of the National Institute for Standards and Technology (NIST), the Computer and Telecommunications Security Council, and the National Research Council Secure Systems Study Committee (for the National Academy of Science). He received his bachelor of science in engineering from the United States Naval Academy and his master of arts in personnel administration from George Washington University, Washington, District of Columbia; he also received his certificate in computer science from the University of California, Irvine, California. He is a Certified Information System Security Professional, an Information Systems Security Architecture Professional, and an Information Systems Security Management Professional.

He has published several papers on information security issues for Auerbach Publishers in the *Handbook of Information Security Management and Data Security Management,* and other publishers, in the *Information Security Journal,* the National Academy of Sciences' *Computers at Risk,* DataPro Reports, various Elsevier publications, and the *ISSA Journal.*

He has been a speaker at all the major information security conferences, including the following: Computer Security Institute, the ISSA Annual Working Conference, the Computer Security Workshop, MIS Conferences, AIS Security for Space Operations, DOE Computer Security Conference, National Computer Security Conference, IIA Security Conference, EDPAA, UCCEL Security & Audit Users' Conference, and Industrial Security Awareness Conference.

He has conducted/participated in information security seminars for International Information Systems Security Certification Consortium [(ISC)$^{2\circledR}$]; Frost & Sullivan; University of California, Irvine; California State University, Long Beach; System Exchange Seminars; and the Institute for International Research. He participated in the Ernst & Young video, "Protecting Information Assets." He is currently serving as the editor of the *Handbook of Information Security Management* (Auerbach). He chairs the (ISC)^2 CBK committees and the QA committee. He received the Computer Security Institute's Lifetime Achievement Award in 1994 and the (ISC)^2's Harold F. Tipton Lifetime Achievement Award in 2001.

Micki Krause Nozaki, MBA, CISSP, has held positions in the information security profession for the past 20 years. Nozaki was named one of the 25 most influential women in the field of information security by industry peers and *Information Security* magazine as part of their recognition of "Women of Vision" in the field of information technology security. She received the Harold F. Tipton Lifetime Achievement Award in recognition of sustained career excellence and outstanding contributions to the profession.

She has held several leadership roles in industry-influential groups, including the ISSA and the (ISC)^2, and is a passionate advocate for professional security leadership.

She is also a reputed speaker, published author, and coeditor of the *Information Security Management Handbook* series.

Contributors

Sandy Bacik, CISSP-ISSMP, CISM, CGEIT, CHS-III
Bacik Consulting Service

Samuel Chun, CISSP
Hewlett-Packard Company

Juan M. Estevez-Tapiador, PhD
Carlos III University of Madrid

Todd Fitzgerald, CISSP, CISA, CISM, CGEIT, PMP, HITRUST, ISO27000, ITILV3
National Government Services

Chris Hare, CISSP, CISA, CISM
Verizon

Foster Henderson, CISSP, CISM, SRP, NSA IEM
United States Government

Paul Henry, CISSP
Forensics & Recovery LLC

Julio Cesar Hernandez-Castro, PhD
Carlos III University of Madrid

Rebecca Herold, CIPP, CISSP, CISM, CISM, FLMI
The Privacy Professor®

Carl Jackson, CISSP
Pacific Life Insurance Company

Georges J. Jahchan, CISA, CISM and BS7799-2 Lead Auditor
Quattro Associates

Leo Kahng, CISSP
Cisco Systems, Inc.

Salahuddin Kamran, CISSP, CISA, CFE
Alvarez & Marsal

Seth Kinnett, CISSP
The Goldman Sachs Group, Inc.

James C. Murphy, CISSP-ISSMP, GSEC, CISA, CISM
North Carolina Office of Medicaid
   Management Information System Services

David O'Berry, CSSLP, CRMP, CISSP-ISSAP, ISSMP, MCNE
The South Carolina Department of Probation,
   Parole, and Pardon Services (SCDPPPS)

Pedro Peris-Lopez, PhD
Carlos III University of Madrid

Robert Pittman, CISSP
County of Los Angeles

Sean M. Price, CISA, CISSP
Independent Security Researcher and Consultant

Ralph Spencer Poore, CISSP, CFE, CISA, CFE, CHS-III, CTGA, QSA
Cryptographic Assurance Services, LLC

Pradnyesh Rane
Persistent Systems Limited

Edward Ray, CISSP
NetSec Consulting

Arturo Ribagorda, PhD
Carlos III University of Madrid

E. Eugene Schultz, PhD, CISSP
Emagined Security Consulting

Rob Shein, CISSP
Hewlett-Packard Company

Anne Shultz
Illinois Institute of Technology

Robert M. Slade, CISSP
Consultant

Jeff Stapleton, CISSP
Bank of America

ACCESS CONTROL

DOMAIN
1

Access Control Techniques

Chapter 1

Whitelisting for Endpoint Defense

Rob Shein

"Whitelisting" refers to an approach for control whereby a list of "known good" activities is maintained. Any actions that correspond to that list are permitted, while all others are blocked or disallowed. A classic example of this is proper firewall configuration, whereby only predefined "acceptable" traffic is allowed to pass, and all other traffic is dropped by a default rule. There is little debate that, given the numerous and ever-expanding ways in which attackers learn to overcome defensive measures, a whitelisting approach is far superior to blacklisting. The challenge, however, is in producing an all-encompassing list of precisely what behavior constitutes "acceptable," and doing so in advance with enough reliability that the security function in question will not break or hinder continuing operations. For networking traffic, this is relatively simple, since there are a finite number of protocols (either as defined by Internet Engineering Task Force Requests for Comments (IETF RFCs) or by port numbers), a finite number of endpoints that receive inbound connections, and simple methods by which the activity of existing systems may be observed and categorized in advance. In other realms, whitelisting has proven more challenging and thus only now has become feasible. This chapter will examine application whitelisting including differing approaches, the overall maturity of the industry, benefits and disadvantages over traditional antimalware approaches, and considerations when considering adoption of the technology.

Ashes to Ashes, Bytes to Bytes: The Malware Life Cycle

A useful construct in discussion of antimalware solutions is the "malware life cycle," which starts with the creation of a variant of malware and ends with the termination of the last remaining instance of that malware in the wild. For some forms of malware (such as custom-developed instances, intended for targeted use against a specific organization) the life cycle may be quite short. For others, such as worms with broad infection footprints and highly effective counterdetection mechanisms (like Conficker), the life cycle may be extremely long.

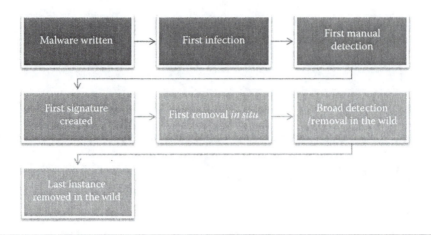

Figure 1.1 Malware life cycle.

The first three steps of the life cycle relate to the period of time when the malware is developed, released, and first detected. This period preludes the existence of any signatures by which organizations may protect themselves using blacklist-based solutions. The second period begins with the establishment of automated means for detection and (if possible) removal of the malware variant. During this period, the overall threat of the malware declines steadily. Finally, in the last step of the life cycle, the malware variant reaches extinction. It should be noted that this final step may be delayed for years, simply due to the presence of infected machines that are neither cleaned (due to limited use of the systems or a user with limited expertise who has come to accept the impact of virus infection) nor retired until long after obsolescence (Figure 1.1).

During the first three steps, blacklisting offers no protection whatsoever. In the absence of detection by manual means, there can be no signature to detect the malware; in the absence of a signature, there can be no automated, broad-ranging detection that would prevent further infection by the malware. Symptoms may manifest themselves boldly, but until detection of the malware itself (and the isolation of the offending file or files that must come with it), few options exist to address the threat effectively on any manner of scale.

During the next three steps, risk to the general populace (resulting from the malware variant) decreases fairly rapidly. Once a first signature is created by one vendor, others are certain to follow shortly thereafter. In fact, there is a fair amount of what could arguably be called plagiarism in the antivirus industry, as demonstrated by Kaspersky Labs in early 2010. Kaspersky put out signatures for nonmalicious files. When other antivirus vendors quickly followed suit, Kaspersky revealed that the binaries in question were entirely innocuous and were in fact developed by Kaspersky as nothing more than innocent applications intended as the basis for their own deliberately fraudulent signatures, to illustrate the degree to which antivirus companies copy each others' work with no validation of the work being copied. And thus, once a single antivirus vendor has issued a signature and malware classification, others are close to follow.

How Traditional Antivirus Fails

When talking about a new approach to a problem, it is useful to first discuss old approaches and why a new method is worth considering. In the end, all innovation must be weighed against the status quo. Traditional antimalware approaches (most commonly referred to as "antivirus" solutions, although they typically protect against more than just viruses) use a blacklisting approach, in the form of signature-based detection of malicious executable files. This approach is often bolstered by a behavioral system of some form, which consists of a blacklist of suspect behaviors commonly used by malware. The challenge posed by the first approach is that only files known to be malicious are detectable. As a result, it follows that at some point in the life cycle of detection, any new form of malware is undetectable using a blacklisting approach. It is the viral equivalent of a zero-day exploit. At the level observed within a single endpoint, this period of time extends not only to the point where a signature has been developed for the specific instance of malware, but also to the point where a signature is available for the brand of antivirus software it uses and the point in time when that signature has been downloaded. This is an important point, as it explains both the race for antivirus software vendors to keep current with their competitors and the necessity for frequent updates to their software.

There is an additional challenge to antivirus, where the life cycle is circumvented. Some malware employs tactics like polymorphism or self-encryption/decryption to evade detection in combination with other tactics (like kernel hooking) to interfere with the ability of antivirus solutions to block their activity. In the worst cases, each new infection is like its own standalone release of a virus, undetectable by any signature that is based upon a different instance of that virus. This kind of malware is the digital equivalent of human immunodeficiency virus (HIV); the core payload is the same, but the surrounding shell of data is sufficiently unpredictable to make immunization infeasible using current technology. Approaches exist to detect such malware based upon behavior, but this results in a specialized approach for each worm or virus, and is not a scalable or feasible approach.

The manifestation of this problem with blacklisting is well documented. Looking at the statistics provided by VirusTotal (a free, open-to-the-public service to analyze suspicious files using existing antivirus engines), two interesting facts appear side by side. The first statistic relates to how many files submitted within the last 24 hours had malicious content that went undetected by one or more of the antivirus engines (39 of them at the time this was written) that are used. At the moment this sentence was written, that statistic showed that only 2,764 out of 73,016 files were detected as malicious by every antivirus engine. The second statistic is the number of updates that have occurred within the last 24 hours. At the time of writing, that period of time showed an average of 9.2 updates per hour combined across the entire spectrum of products. That amounts to an average of 5.7 updates each day for each of the software products. At this rate, it is impossible to perform any meaningful kind of change control or quality testing at a customer site before deploying a signature update; before the testing for one update was complete, the next one would have arrived, restarting the cycle. This would not be a problem if the signatures could be relied upon to be accurate or safe.

Unfortunately, signatures are regularly released that incorrectly flag innocuous (and often critical) software components as being viruses. In some instances, system binaries of Microsoft Windows have been affected, causing machines to crash or even become unbootable. (In a turn of irony, the submission of this chapter to the publisher was actually delayed by the release of a faulty signature in early 2010, which rendered the author's laptop unbootable until it could be fixed. Unfortunately, whitelisting is not nearly as widely deployed in enterprise environments as traditional antivirus and no home-user version of whitelisting exists as of yet.) *Virus Bulletin* did a test of 60 different antivirus products in early 2010; of these, 20 were said to have failed the test due to false positives, in many cases related to software from Google, Microsoft, Adobe, and Sun Microsystems. While some that failed the test were from smaller and less mature vendors, solutions by Microsoft, Norman, and Fortinet also failed. The operating system upon which the solutions were tested was Windows XP, which is hardly a new platform.

So, with these problems, it seems natural to hold the entire industry at fault for such failings. The approach taken, after all, is akin to setting up security guards around a military base that are supposed to let everyone in except the bad guys. Such an approach is foolhardy at best, and destined to fail, yes? Perhaps, but it's important to take note of the fact that until recently, technology hadn't reached the point where another method was feasible. This point will arise later on, but in short the antivirus industry has evolved around a blacklisting approach because for most of the time since the PC became commonplace, blacklisting was the only workable approach to malware detection.

Another Way: How (and Why) Whitelisting Works

Whitelisting takes an opposite approach to malware prevention. Instead of trying to block only that which is known to be bad, it allows only that which is known to be good. There are several benefits to this approach. But to understand the benefits, first it is important to understand the underlying mechanisms of whitelisting itself.

There are effectively two forms of whitelisting: file-based and system call-based. The first focuses on the actual executables that are called into memory (either from disk or network I/O), while the second focuses on specific system calls at a very low level that are executed by software. The second approach is now frequently referred to as a form of Host-based Intrusion Prevention System (HIPS), but in reality is another form of whitelisting. In both cases, there is a learning period, during which the whitelisting application undergoes "supervised learning," and is essentially told what the definition of "good" is. For most file-based whitelisting applications, this is a matter of having the software recursively search the file system to find every executable present and add them to the policy for that machine. This policy governs the list of applications that are allowed to execute and what they are permitted to do. For call-based whitelisting, the process is more involved. A test system is set up and run with the whitelisting application in a mode whereby it will alert on policy violations, but not block the activity behind the alerts. Much like the tuning of a firewall, the alerts become the basis for policy rules, and after a time all normal executable activity is accounted for, after which point the policy can be deployed safely to endpoints.

For file-based whitelisting, the typical identification of executables revolves around a tuple of hash, filename, file size, and file location. In combination, these characteristics provide for robust identification of specific files and serve to detect tampering as well. For call-based whitelisting, these components come into play, along with specifics related to low-level activity by the file in question (such as what directories it reads from/writes to, what network activity it engages in, and so on). One benefit of this method over traditional antivirus is that all the software needs to do when an executable runs is to hash it. This is less demanding in both memory and processing power than the task of checking an executable's entire length (the primary executable for Microsoft Outlook 2007, for example, is over 12 megabytes in size) against a long list of signatures (which range into the millions). The relatively static nature of both approaches lends itself to proper change control, while preventing the kinds of issues that faulty antivirus signatures tend to cause. Even more importantly, this approach requires no system-wide scans past the initial learning phase, as opposed to the necessary but nonetheless extremely annoying scans that are typically needed on a weekly basis by other antivirus products, just to ensure that no malicious content has slipped onto a system.

There are other benefits as well, based around business processes. For example, when a corporate laptop is out of touch (such as when a consultant is traveling) from the corporate network, it is unable to receive updates to its antivirus signatures or the policy that controls antivirus software. However, it is at greater-than-normal risk from viruses and other malware, as it connects to Wi-Fi networks in hotels and coffee shops without the same protections that defend it while on a corporate network. On the other hand, whitelisting products require no interaction with the central management point to maintain a steady state of protection. For most products, approved changes can even be made to the endpoint's policy without the ability to communicate back to the central management point. So in this way whitelisting also trumps antivirus for protection based upon its "accept known good, reject all else" methodology, and the simplicity that comes with it.

In terms of the malware life cycle, everything changes. Instead of being released into an environment that is hospitable until otherwise decided, malware is unable to gain any foothold whatsoever. Even tactics such as polymorphism are turned on their head; if a piece of malware should somehow accidentally be added to the whitelist, and thus allowed to run, the very nature of its polymorphic routine would make it unable to infect other machines. The evasive tactics that help it evade detection by traditional antivirus would render additional instances of the malware unmatchable by the permissive policy setting. In the context of an environment with whitelisting on every endpoint, the path goes directly from malware creation to simultaneous detection and extinction, with no interim steps. Additionally, whatever executable content exists is still preserved, but in a form of stasis, unable to run even to clean up after itself. This, along with the detailed information provided by the whitelisting application, makes for powerful forensics tools (Figure 1.2).

Once described in light of other methods, this approach seems like an obvious choice, particularly given the way such paradigms work in the real world. For example, we control access to our homes with keys, and only give copies of those keys to people we know and trust. We don't attempt to build doors that will let everyone in except burglars, or distribute keys widely but forbid select untrustworthy individuals from owning copies. And the same philosophy works well in the world of computer security as well. Programmers are taught to sanitize inputs not by blocking characters that are known to be problematic, but instead by only allowing those which would be used for valid purposes. So why hasn't this approach been adopted long ago?

The answer lies in the challenge of defining "good," managing that definition, and enforcing it. For file-based whitelisting, the challenge is a bit easier, since all that is needed is the identification of the executable itself, but for call-based whitelisting it can be more challenging. Every possible valid behavior of every piece of valid software on the system must be accounted for, in advance, or significant problems will result. In addition, issues can be introduced as a result of the added interaction with regard to network or disk I/O. One product, when tested on a Domain Name System (DNS) server system intended for heavy use, introduced failures this way; the network shim acted as a stateful firewall, but did not have sufficient buffer to maintain state for the 3000+ connections per second (even though User Datagram Protocol (UDP) is stateless, any good firewall will maintain a sense of which inbound responses to expect) and, therefore, caused failures in

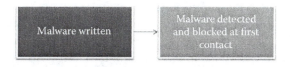

Figure 1.2   Malware life cycle under whitelisting.

the server. The vendor, with assistance from the project that performed the testing, modified and improved their whitelisting product to address this problem, but it demonstrated the peculiar ways in which such low-level interaction can negatively impact applications.

Considerations When Implementing Whitelisting

Whitelisting products work quite differently from traditional antivirus solutions, and as such they have radically different challenges with regard to selection and implementation. While it is important with all technologies to prepare adequately before rollout, this is especially true when it comes to whitelisting. The first set of challenges relates to the process by which system policies are created for the endpoints. If a policy is created on a single system for rollout to other systems, then two things need to exist. One, there needs to be a reasonable assurance of the homogeneity of the environment to which that policy is being deployed, as each variation will result in adverse or unexpected behavior. Two, there needs to be a process for addressing such variances. It's also important to recognize that there will almost inevitably be systems that are infected with some form of malware and that these will cause variances as well.

Whitelisting is obviously best suited for environments with mature controls over endpoint configuration and use. When end users have been given control over what is installed on their own systems, their configurations drift from the original deployed definition. Some of these deviations are relatively harmless (like addition of valid search bars to web browsers) while others are more dangerous (free screensavers, anyone?). Either way, they will all add to the complexity and difficulty of a whitelisting solution, both during deployment and immediately after. In such environments, there needs to be a fundamental shift in user behavior. A standard user login must not be permitted to make changes to endpoint policy configuration. If it can, then any malware that executes will execute in that user's context, and thus will be allowed to alter the endpoint. This nullifies the point of whitelisting entirely, and renders it absolutely useless. Even for power users, who can be (or, for business reasons, need to be) trusted with the ability to install new applications, there needs to be an alternate login that they use, so that they know precisely when they are (and more importantly, are not) adding new approved executables to their desktop configuration. It is worth noting that this approach works well with most file-based whitelisting, but does not work with call-based systems.

Challenges When Deploying Whitelisting

The deployment of whitelisting can provide extraordinary insight into the current state of an environment, as variances from the expected norm will almost always be found in surprising places. So in the exception handling process during rollout, a distinction must be made between innocuous (but unaccounted for) executables and malicious ones, or else those performing the rollout will simply lump any viruses or trojans in with other applications that will be allowed to exist on the network. This approach works best in environments where there is a standard desktop build, and especially well where end users do not have local administrator privileges, for obvious reasons. An accounting should be made for add-ons to existing valid applications (like browsers, which will have both good and bad search bars and helpers, plus add-ons like Flash, which will exist in multiple versions in any environment). A decision should be made whether temporarily accepting old versions or forcing updates will be the normal operating procedure during rollout as well.

If, on the other hand, policies will be autogenerated for each system, then there needs to be assurance in advance that every system is clean from malicious content. It is tempting to plan for manual inspection of the policies after the fact, to search for anything that seems unusual; this method is doomed to failure. A policy for file-based whitelisting will have thousands of entries at the very minimum; every .exe, every .dll, every driver will be listed there. Examining a policy like this quickly makes one aware of just how little they know of the underlying software that drives any desktop or server, and there is no human way possible to spot a malicious file with any degree of assurance whatsoever. When looking at a policy for call-based whitelisting, it's even worse, as you're not looking at a list of files but a list of specific granular behaviors. In the future, analytic tools will probably exist to determine delta between multiple systems to find what is and is not the common norm for a specific form of desktop, but in the meantime systems must be proven clean prior to autogeneration of whitelisting policies. Obviously, given the shortcomings of other antimalware approaches, this is a challenge for endpoints that have been in use for any length of time (particularly desktops). So, there's an added benefit to deploying whitelisting during a rollout of new systems, a switch to virtual desktops/thin clients, or establishment/implementation of a standard core desktop deployment. In each of these cases, endpoints are freshly deployed from a "known good" image or definition, and can be assumed to be free of harmful content. In this case, however, even more care must be taken to ensure that the deployment is properly planned, or else the whitelisting may cause complications during rollout and initial testing (or be blamed incorrectly for problems that stem from other causes). Still, this is a case of trading one kind of assurance (making sure endpoints are clean prior to policy generation) for another (planning a clean and well-supported whitelisting rollout), and the latter form of assurance is one that should be performed to a fair degree anyway.

Postdeployment Challenges to Whitelisting

Once a whitelisting solution has been fully deployed, activities switch to maintaining the solution, which is comprised of four things. One, the policies on the endpoints will need to change over time, as new applications are deployed and existing ones are updated/patched. Two, the processes and procedures around the whitelisting solution will need to be refined as exceptions to user behavior and rights as well as special requirements for specific business purposes come to light. (There will be more on that later.) Three, updates to the central management points of the whitelisting solution must be performed, and in such a way as to maintain continuity of the solution. And four, updates to the end-point agents must be performed as well. Whitelisting is a relatively new technology and as such the vendors tend to make frequent and valid improvements, resulting in many software updates over the course of a year. Even more importantly, these updates provide significant improvement, driven by the observations and experiences of the vendors' customer base.

Policies on the endpoints will require updates for a number of reasons, but the most frequent changes will result from patches to applications and operating systems. At the bare minimum, "Patch Tuesday" will result in a number of alterations as .dlls and .exes are replaced on Windows-based devices. For file-based whitelisting, there needs to be a means to identify the source of the changes and identify it as a trusted source. For most applications, this can be done either by identifying the service (when automated patching is used) that is implementing the patch or by doing patching with credentials that are authorized to make changes to the whitelisting policy. The first approach is often called "trusted agent," while the second is known as "trusted user."

For call-based whitelisting, changes to application behavior must be enumerated and added to the end-point policy before the patch can be deployed, or such changes must be provided by the whitelisting vendor (where they've done the fingerprinting for their customer base) in advance. The first approach is time-consuming and must precede the normal testing cycle for patches (thus elongating the patch cycle), while the second approach leaves the environment vulnerable to errors by the vendor in their fingerprinting, or at the mercy of any subtle differences from the vendor's test systems. This is another of the reasons that file-based whitelisting has been more rapidly accepted than call-based whitelisting.

In most environments, culture must change with regard to user behavior when whitelisting is implemented. As stated earlier, users must not be allowed to operate with administrator rights and the ability to alter the whitelisting policies as a matter of normal operations. For most users, the ability to alter whitelisting policies should not be granted; for those users that are the exception to this, alterations to those policies should not be possible with their normal login. This is, in effect, another way of ensuring that end users cannot install or update their own applications, and represents a shift in how things are done for most environments. The effects of this will manifest in unexpected ways, and the best thing that can be done is to provide a means to quickly and easily respond to requests from users for new or updated applications. The most unexpected form of this need may be in the need to install or update applets or other web-based controls; most online collaboration tools, for example, rely upon such components, and the end user will tend to discover their inability to install them at the worst possible moments. The ability to quickly intercede, install the applet/ActiveX/plugin on short notice, determine the change to policy, and then push that policy out to all endpoints is usually the best way to address this, but different whitelisting solutions will provide different options to address short-turn requests of this sort. And on the other hand, the fact that all software installation needs to go through a review process, no matter how short, helps maintain control over desktop configurations and prevent not only the introduction of malware but also work-inappropriate or pirated software as well.

When Not to Employ Whitelisting

There are several types of users and user environments where whitelisting is not an effective or feasible approach. Home users are not well suited for whitelisting; in fact, there is no consumer-oriented whitelisting product on the market today. The dual challenges of determining a starting policy and maintaining it (including both patching and using proper diligence in vetting changes to that policy) are beyond the scope of nearly all home users. Additionally, the principle of using dual logins (one for normal use and another for making changes to whitelisting policy) is not only not likely to be followed by a typical user, it also is not in conformance with the way that home-oriented versions of Windows operate. Added to this are the challenges with troubleshooting the effects of incorrect policy settings, and the basic familiarity with how applications function that is needed in order to administer properly a whitelisting system. In comparison, normal antivirus products need only be installed and left alone, from the perspective of a casual user. (Until a flawed signature is released, that is.)

Other environments that are ill suited for whitelisting are ones where development work is being performed. Every new build of an executable will have a different signature and so the developer will be unable to perform much (or any) testing without either constantly running as a trusted user (which breaks the whole point of whitelisting) or constantly adding the new executables to the existing policy of allowed applications. It is potentially possible to configure whitelisting so that it will recognize the compiler as a trusted agent, but this is sometimes easier said than done.

Evaluating Whitelisting Products

At the time of writing, the whitelisting product space was remarkably mature, despite being (in terms of years) relatively young. A recent comparison of file-based whitelisting products by a major publication gave high marks to every product reviewed, and while one product did stand out above the others, none were considered to be inferior. (For the most part, call-based whitelisting seems to have fallen to the side and is used for cases where extreme security and assurance are required, for reasons described earlier here.) It is worth noting that, with the advent of Windows 7, there is a whitelisting capability native to Windows: AppLocker.

Before choosing (or even evaluating) any technical solution, it is absolutely essential to identify requirements. This cannot be stressed enough and is particularly true with regard to whitelisting. Unless it is known what capabilities, characteristics, and features are needed or desired (and the difference between the two), it is impossible to properly meet those needs or desires. This is particularly true with whitelisting, where initial planning and preparation are even more important than with most other technologies. That said, there are a number of components/attributes to whitelisting products that can be compared when evaluating against those requirements.

The first aspect of whitelisting functionality that can be evaluated is manageability. The endpoint agents have the ability to utterly nullify systems or applications; without a means of properly administering the entire whitelisting solution, there is the potential to wreak havoc throughout an environment. Also, as policies evolve, there should be a way to track changes or break them out into components. One example would be a specific policy that prohibits the execution of certain applications (like iTunes, or other applications that are forbidden by a company's acceptable use policy), but which can stand apart from the individual policies that govern each individual endpoint. Other important things to consider are reporting and the ability to get reliable visibility into the overall state of end-point agents. In very large environments, it's crucial to have the ability to organize information (like the list of endpoints under control) into manageable groups. Imagine what it would be like sorting through a list of thousands or tens of thousands of systems, looking for a particular one, when doing troubleshooting. When determining requirements for the management capabilities, think about what information will be needed or desirable to gather, and what forms of control should be centralized.

Deployment is another factor. The best solutions will have the ability to deploy to endpoints remotely, from the management console. The question then becomes one of determining which agents have failed to deploy properly (since all whitelisting solutions hook the kernel, kernel-hooking malware that has already infected an endpoint can be a cause of this) and addressing the problem. Automatic discovery (either through network discovery or pulling information from Active Directory) is enormously helpful; make sure that there is a way to identify systems that should not have whitelisting agents installed, if there is reason to believe that such systems will exist. Otherwise, the same capability that makes for a simple and rapid rollout will also cause problems when machines that are not intended for whitelisting control (such as development systems) have it imposed upon them by an overzealous or inattentive administrator. This could be accomplished either by placing such systems into a special organizational unit within the management system or by applying a policy whereby whitelisting control is not enforced.

A related but separate thing to consider is the way the policies themselves are defined. Each system will, in effect, have its own policy. That said, there is a need for the ability to define policies that will govern entire groups of systems, much like the way Group Policy Objects operate in Active Directory. While better solutions will have the ability to define policies in this manner, this also results in the potential for confusion (also, as can happen in Active Directory with Group Policy Objects). The management system should allow not only for the definition of policies in multiple contexts, but also the ability to see precisely which policies affect which systems, and the ability to view the effects of inheritance. If one policy allows an application to run and another prohibits it, which one wins?

The last set of considerations relate to end-user experience. For the most part, whitelisting applications are transparent to the end user, with two exceptions: when an application is blocked and when the user is permitted to override or modify that prohibition. When looking at this functionality, it's important to consider the user base, and both the percentage of users who will interact with the whitelisting endpoint agents (for example, as trusted users) and how technically savvy they are. The amount of information displayed to them in a notification will have an effect on troubleshooting and should also be sufficient to make a sensible determination as to whether or not something that has been blocked is hostile, or simply an executable that needs to be permitted. In short, think about the different types of users that you will have (from the context of the whitelisting application) and be sure to get a feel for how the end-user experience will play out for each of those user types.

Summary

In closing, the important things to remember about application whitelisting are as follows:

- Whitelisting operates under a "Permit Good, Deny All Else" philosophy.
- There are fundamentally two approaches:
  - Whitelisting that looks at specific granular behaviors at the system level (call-based).
  - Whitelisting that looks at the specific executables that want to load into memory and operate (file-based).
- File-based whitelisting has come into prominence, mostly due to greater ease of implementation and management.
- Whereas traditional antivirus (which uses a blacklisting approach) incurs significant processor and I/O performance hits (especially during a full system scan), whitelisting is relatively lightweight.
- There is reduced risk to using whitelisting, owing to its better coverage with regard to new forms of malware and the ability to maintain it using proper change control methods. In comparison, traditional antivirus signatures are prone to false negatives and come out so frequently that change control is infeasible; this problem is all the more alarming given that on a fairly regular basis incorrect signatures are released by vendors with harmful effects.
- Any whitelisting deployment must be carefully planned and executed; whitelisting has the potential to cause significant disruption if it is improperly implemented.
- The vendor space for whitelisting is still evolving, but the products already show a high degree of functionality and usability.
- As yet, no feasible options exist for home users who wish to use application whitelisting.

- Whitelisting works best in environments where end users are not normally allowed to install applications and where there is a high degree of standardization among endpoints.
- Requirement gathering and development is a must when evaluating whitelisting solutions.

About the Author

Rob Shein, CISSP, is a cyber security architect for HP. During the past 30 years—starting with writing his first program at age 11—Rob has focused almost exclusively on security. His role at HP has spanned the utility, outsourcing, financial, government, and manufacturing sectors in the Americas and Asia. Rob's areas of specialization range from policy work to penetration testing, implementation/architecture, C2 systems, pure consulting related to security processes, and development of security solutions and standards around Smart Grid and SCADA systems. He has authored a novel and contributed to numerous publications, and is a frequent presenter at conferences.

Chapter 2

Whitelisting

Sandy Bacik

Access control consists of permitting or denying the use of a particular resource. Within networking environments, particularly at the network perimeter, enterprises have used blacklisting. Blacklisting consists of banning a list of resources from access. As the unauthorized and invalid access attempts increased, the blacklist continued to grow. This method allowed everything unless explicitly denied, i.e., default allow. Enterprises are now doing the reverse, only allowing authorized access, i.e., whitelisting, the "known good." Whitelisting turns blacklisting upside down, categorizing everything as bad except for a small group. Whitelisting is listing entities that are granted a set of privileges (access, services, validity, etc.) within an environment. A whitelist is solely used to define what is allowed to be executed, whereas anything that is not included on the whitelist cannot be executed.

Due to compliance, audit, and regulatory requirements, the enterprise resources and assets function should be documenting assets and resources. Resources can be groups, services, applications, computers, servers, routers, websites, etc. In small enterprise environments, a general purpose server is used for all manner of things (surfing the Web, reading e-mail, running enterprise applications, evaluating new software, etc.) and it is very difficult to keep whitelisting restrictions up to date for access. On the other hand, when a server has very few functions (like one used for just reading e-mail), using whitelisting can greatly improve security. Unfortunately, most enterprise systems fall somewhere near the middle between these two extremes. There are many types of whitelists an enterprise can utilize to assist in implementing whitelisting over blacklisting:

- *E-mail*: An e-mail whitelist is a list of contacts that the user deems are acceptable to receive e-mail from and should not be sent to the trash folder, similar to spam filters.
  - Internet Service Providers (ISPs): ISPs receive requests from legitimate companies to add them to the ISP whitelist of companies.
  - Noncommercial whitelists: Noncommercial whitelists are operated by various nonprofit organizations, ISPs, and other entities interested in blocking spam.
  - Commercial whitelists: Commercial whitelists are a system by which an internet service provider allows someone to bypass spam filters when sending e-mail messages to its subscribers in return for a prepaid fee, either an annual fee or a per-message fee.

- *Local Area Network (LAN) whitelists*: Many network admins set up Media Access Control (MAC) address whitelists, a MAC address filter, or subnets to control who is on their networks. This can be used when encryption is not a practical solution or in tandem with encryption. However, it's sometimes ineffective because a MAC address can be faked. Many firewalls can be configured to only allow data traffic from/to certain (ranges of) Internet Protocol (IP) addresses.
- *Program whitelists*: Enterprises should keep a list of valid software within the network. If an organization keeps a whitelist of software, only titles on the list will be accepted for use. The benefits of whitelisting in this instance are that the school administration can ensure itself that students will not be able to download and/or use programs that have not been deemed appropriate for use.
- *Application whitelists*: Enterprises should do regular application inventories for license agreements. One approach to combat viruses and malware is to whitelist software which is considered safe to run, blocking all others.

Let's compare using blacklists and whitelists for access control (see Table 2.1). There are more advantages and fewer disadvantages in using whitelists. Yet, there are two potential glaring issues with whitelisting. First, most organizations are apprehensive about going the whitelist route because the IT department does not want to increase the resources needed to manage the impact of keeping track of valid resources and impacting users. On the other hand, many organizations see explicitly denying things via a blacklist is not the most effective or productive way to manage and protect the environment. So it boils down to: What to do and why? The best approach depends on the solution to prevent execution of applications, services, and code. For example, if the implemented solution contains a very basic enforcement method that uses the "yes" or "no" to determine executability, then the enterprise might want to look elsewhere. Trying to use a

Table 2.1 Whitelist and Blacklist Advantages and Disadvantages

Blacklist Advantages	Whitelist Advantages
Easy to manage	More secure
Easy to install	More accurate
Can download updates quickly	Minimizes false positives
	Can be created at various levels within the enterprise
	Easy to customize
Blacklist Disadvantages	Whitelist Disadvantages
Exponential growth	More time to manage
Many false positives, potentially denying valid access	Requires additional time to install
Continual updates are required	
Hard to switch to whitelisting	

whitelist with this logic could turn into a management nightmare while also dramatically impacting end-user productivity. Another example would be a solution using the methodology by defining rules. This methodology is flexible enough to effectively balance enforcement, management, and productivity. This is definitely not the endgame in endpoint protection. It does have a built-in target solution and can be easily maintained.

In looking at today's enterprise, there are many requirements, standards, and policies that require access control to be implemented and reviewed on a regular basis for governance, audit and compliance. Implementing whitelisting will assist in making the audit and compliance reviews simpler to complete. Enterprises should have a list of valid applications, network equipment, customers, partners, sites/locations, employees, roles/groups, contractors, consultants, services, and ports. If an enterprise has these documented, they have a start on implementing a whitelisting solution for access control. See Table 2.2 for a sample listing of how whitelisting can be implemented for access control using some of the list above.

Using the information in Table 2.1 and the examples in Table 2.2, an enterprise can better manage access control of resources and limit the risk to those resources.

In conclusion, documenting all network resources and being able to use whitelisting will give the enterprise more control over those resources and lessen the risk to the enterprise. The upfront work for implementing whitelisting will require a larger effort. Once completed, the whitelisting will enable the enterprise to specifically know what resources are available and who has access to what resources. Overall, implementing whitelisting will reduce the risk of findings during a compliance audit.

Table 2.2   Using Whitelists

Asset List	Whitelisting Use
Applications	This allows an enterprise to track what application can and cannot be used within the network. Along with assisting in access control, this can reduce viruses and malware, and assist with license compliance
Network equipment	This allows an enterprise to be able to segment and route traffic based on network devices. It can allow or limit the access from partner, customer, and Internet sites to stop unauthorized access to finding unsecured resources
Groups	This allows an enterprise to have easier access control to applications and network resources by maintaining group memberships rather than have separate access control lists for each application or network resources
Ports	By knowing which ports an application or service uses, a perimeter firewall can be locked down to only permit the required ports to required network devices, again limiting the security risk to the network environment
Contractors or Consultants	By knowing who the contractors and consultants are within the enterprise, contract audits and access can be reviewed more quickly and removed, if necessary

About the Author

Sandy Bacik, CISSP-ISSMP, CISM, CGEIT, CHS-III, author and former CSO, has over 14 years of direct development, implementation, and management information security experience in the areas of audit management, disaster recovery and business continuity, incident investigation, physical security, privacy, regulatory compliance, standard operating policies and procedures, and data center operations and management. Ms. Bacik has managed, architected, and implemented comprehensive information assurance programs and managed internal, external, and contracted and outsourced information technology audits to ensure various regulatory compliance for state and local government entities and Fortune 200 companies. She has developed methodologies for risk assessments, information technology audits, vulnerability assessments, security policy and practice writing, incident response, and disaster recovery.

Access Control Administration

Chapter 3

RFID and Information Security

Salahuddin Kamran

Introduction

This chapter provides an overview of radio frequency identification (RFID) technology and some thoughts on privacy and security issues concerning RFID systems, and highlights some of the areas that have to be considered in designing and deploying RFID systems.

RFID is a technology that facilitates the automated identification of objects. While people are generally skillful at visual identification of a range of objects, computers are not. The task of identifying a coffee mug as a coffee mug is one that many bleary-eyed people perform naturally and effectively every morning in a variety of contexts. For computing systems, this same task can pose a challenging exercise in artificial intelligence. The simplest way to ease the process of automated identification is to equip objects with computer-readable tags. This is essentially what happens in a typical supermarket. Through a printed barcode on its packaging, a box of cereal identifies itself automatically to a checkout register. While a checkout clerk must manually position items to render them readable by a scanner, printed barcodes alleviate the overhead of human categorization and data entry. Over the course of decades, they have proven to be indispensable timesavers and productivity boosters.

The purpose of an RFID system is to enable data to be transmitted by a portable device, called a tag, which is read by an RFID reader and processed according to the needs of a particular application. The data transmitted by the tag may provide identification or location information, or specifics about the product tagged, such as price, color, date of purchase, etc. The use of RFID in tracking and access applications first appeared during the 1980s. RFID quickly gained attention because of its ability to track moving objects. As the technology is refined, more pervasive and invasive uses for RFID tags are in the works.

In a typical RFID system, individual objects are equipped with a small, inexpensive tag that contains a transponder with a digital memory chip that is given a unique electronic product code (EPC). The interrogator, an antenna packaged with a transceiver and decoder, emits a signal activating the RFID tag so it can read and write data to it. When an RFID tag passes through the electromagnetic zone, it detects the reader's activation signal. The reader decodes the data encoded in the tag's integrated circuit and the data is passed to the host computer for processing.

RFID tags promise in the near future to become the most numerous computational devices in the world. Their impending pervasiveness owes much to the power and flexibility that they achieve through starkly minimalist design. These tags come in a wide variety of shapes and sizes. Some tags are easy to spot, such as the hard plastic antitheft tags attached to merchandise in stores. Animal tracking tags that are implanted beneath the skin of family pets or endangered species are no bigger than a small section of pencil lead. Even smaller tags have been developed that can be embedded within the fibers of a national currency.

While barcodes have historically been the primary means of tracking products, RFID systems are rapidly becoming the preferred technology for keeping tabs on people, pets, products, and even vehicles. One reason for this is because the read/write capability of an active RFID system enables the use of interactive applications. Also, the tags can be read from a distance and through a variety of substances such as snow, fog, ice, or paint, where barcodes have proved useless. Developments in RFID technology are yielding systems with larger memory capacities, wider reading ranges, and faster processing. In response, the market for RFID tags is growing explosively and is projected to reach $10 billion annually within the decade.

History

RFID systems have gained popularity, and notoriety, in recent years. A driving force behind the rapid development of RFID technology has been the rise of pervasive commerce, sometimes dubbed the quiet revolution. Pervasive commerce uses technologies such as tracking devices and smart labels embedded with transmitting sensors and intelligent readers to convey information about key areas where consumers live and work to data processing systems. To gather this data, retailers can choose from a range of options.

RFID systems may be roughly grouped into four categories:

1. *Electronic Article Surveillance (EAS) systems*: Generally used in retail stores to sense the presence or absence of an item. Products are tagged and large antenna readers are placed at each exit of the store to detect unauthorized removal of the item.
2. *Portable Data Capture systems*: Characterized by the use of portable RFID readers, which enables this system to be used in variable settings.
3. *Networked systems*: Characterized by fixed position readers that are connected directly to a centralized information management system, while transponders are positioned on people or moveable items.
4. *Positioning systems*: Used for automated location identification of tagged items or vehicles.

These RFID systems enable businesses to have real-time access to inventory information, as well as a broader, clearer picture of consumers' buying habits. RFID technology also enables retailers and corporations to peek into the lives of consumers in ways that were, until recently, off limits. Products embedded with RFID tags can continuously transmit information ranging from an EPC identifier, to information about the item itself, such as consumption status or product freshness. Data processing systems read and compile this information, and can even link the product information with a specific consumer.

This composite information is vastly superior—and more invasive—than any data that could be obtained from scanning bar codes, or even loyalty cards. Frequent shopper cards link consumers to their purchases, but this limited information gives retailers only a narrow view of a consumer's in-store purchasing trends. In contrast, RFID systems enable tagged objects to speak to electronic readers over the course of a product's lifetime—from production to disposal—providing retailers with an unblinking, voyeuristic view of consumer attitudes and purchase behavior.

Technology

RFID systems can be very complex, and implementations vary greatly across industries and sectors. For purposes of discussion in this document, an RFID system is composed of up to three subsystems:

- An *RF subsystem* performs identification and related transactions using wireless communication.
- An *enterprise subsystem* contains computers running specialized software that can store, process, and analyze data acquired from RF subsystem transactions to make the data useful to a supported business process.
- An *interenterprise subsystem* connects enterprise subsystems when information needs to be shared across organizational boundaries.

Every RFID system contains an RF subsystem and most RFID systems also contain an enterprise subsystem. An RFID system supporting a *supply chain* application is a common example of an RFID system with an interenterprise subsystem. In a supply chain application, a tagged product is tracked throughout its life cycle, from manufacture to final purchase, and sometimes even afterwards (e.g., to support targeted product recalls).

The characteristics of RFID enterprise and interenterprise subsystems are very similar to those of any networked IT system in terms of the types of computers that reside on them, the protocols they support, and the security issues they encounter.

RF Subsystem

To enable wireless identification, the *RF subsystem* consists of two components:

- RFID *tags* (sometimes referred to as *transponders*), which are small electronic devices that are affixed to objects or embedded in them. Each tag has a unique identifier and may also have other features such as memory to store additional data.
- RFID *readers*, which are devices that communicate with tags to identify the item connected to each tag and possibly associate the tagged item with related data.

Both the tag and the reader are two-way radios. Each has an antenna and is capable of modulating and demodulating radio signals. Figure 3.1 shows a simple RF subsystem configuration.

Tags

Most RFID tags contain at least two components: an integrated circuit for storing and processing information, modulating and demodulating a radio-frequency signal, and other specialized functions; and an antenna for receiving and transmitting the signal. Figure 3.2 shows samples of tags.

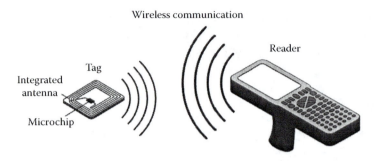

Figure 3.1   Simple RF subsystem.

The market for RFID tags includes numerous different types of tags, which differ greatly in their cost, size, performance, and security mechanisms. Even when tags are designed to comply with a particular standard, they are often further customized to meet the requirements of specific applications. Understanding the major tag characteristics can help those responsible for RFID systems identify the tag characteristics required in their environments and applications. Major characteristics of tags include identifier format, power source, operating frequencies, functionality, and form factor.

Tags are categorized into four types based on the power source for communication and other functionality:

1. *Passive*: A *passive tag* uses the electromagnetic energy it receives from a reader's transmission to reply to the reader. The reply signal from a passive tag, which is also known as the *back-scattered signal*, has only a fraction of the power of the reader's signal. This limited power significantly restricts the operating range of the tag. It also means that passive tags can only support data processing of limited complexity. On the other hand, passive tags typically are cheaper, smaller, and lighter than other types of tags, which are compelling advantages for many RFID applications.

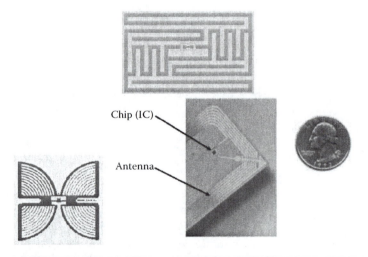

Figure 3.2   RFID tags.

2. *Active*: An *active tag* relies on an internal battery for power. The battery is used to communicate to the reader, to power on-board circuitry, and to perform other functions. Active tags can communicate over greater distances than other types of tags, but they have a finite battery life and are generally larger and more expensive. Since these tags have an internal power supply, they can respond to lower power signals than passive tags.

3. *Semiactive*: A *semiactive tag* is an active tag that remains dormant until it receives a signal from the reader to wake up. The tag can then use its battery to communicate with the reader. Like active tags, semiactive tags can communicate over a longer distance than passive tags. Their main advantage relative to active tags is that they have a longer battery life. The waking process, however, sometimes causes an unacceptable time delay when tags pass readers very quickly or when many tags need to be read within a very short period of time.

4. *Semipassive*: A *semipassive tag* is a passive tag that uses a battery to power on-board circuitry, but not to produce return signals. When the battery is used to power a sensor, they are often called *sensor tags*. They typically are smaller and cheaper than active tags, but have greater functionality than passive tags because more power is available for other purposes. Some literature uses the terms "semipassive" and "semiactive" interchangeably.

Readers

The tag and the reader must comply with the same standard in order to communicate. If a tag is based on a proprietary design, a reader must support the same communication protocol to communicate with that tag. In many cases, if proprietary tags are used, only proprietary RFID readers from the same vendor can be used.

A reader's interface with an enterprise subsystem may be wired or wireless. Most wired readers are in fixed locations and support applications in which the tags approach the reader. Some wired readers offer limited mobility using cables. Figure 3.3 shows a reader portal that reads tags on a pallet of boxes moving through the portal.

Figure 3.4 shows reader antennas mounted above each toll lane in a series of toll booths. As vehicles pass through one of the toll lanes, the reader reads a transponder that is attached to that vehicle's windshield.

In contrast, wireless readers support applications in which personnel must move around to read tags. Figure 3.5 shows an example of a mobile handheld reader.

Tag-reader communication is achieved by using a common communications protocol between the tag and the reader. Tag-reader communication protocols are often specified in RFID standards. Prominent international standards include the ISO/IEC 18000 series for item management and the ISO/IEC 14443 and ISO/IEC 15693 standards for contactless smart cards. The most recent EPCglobal Class-1 Generation-2 standard is essentially equivalent to the ISO/IEC 18000-6C standard.

Enterprise Subsystem

The *enterprise subsystem* connects readers to computers running software that can store, process, and analyze data acquired from RF subsystem transactions to make the data useful to a supported business process. For example, an RFID system in a retail clothing store has an RF subsystem that can read the identifier associated with each tagged garment. The enterprise subsystem matches the identifier to the garment's record in a database to determine its price and the number of other items of a similar type that remain in inventory. Some simple RFID systems consist of an RF

Figure 3.3   Reader portal.

subsystem only (e.g., RFID-based key systems in which a reader can make an access control decision without access to other computers). However, most RFID systems have both an RF subsystem and an enterprise subsystem.

The enterprise subsystem consists of three major components, which are shown in Figure 3.6.

Middleware: RFID *middleware* is responsible for preparing data collected from readers in the RF subsystem for the analytic systems that directly support business processes. Middleware hides the complexity and implementation details of the RF subsystem from the analytic systems.

Analytic systems are composed of databases, data processing applications, and Web servers that process the data outputs of middleware based on business requirements and user instructions. They contain customized business logic for each business process they support.

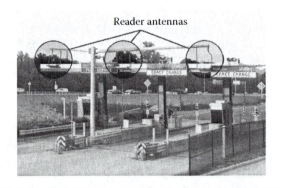

Figure 3.4   Reader antennas.

Figure 3.5   Mobile handheld reader.

Network infrastructure enables communication between the RF and enterprise subsystems, as well as among components of the enterprise subsystem.

Interenterprise Subsystem

The *interenterprise subsystem* connects enterprise subsystems together when information needs to be shared across geographic or organizational boundaries, such as in a supply chain application. Not all RFID systems contain interenterprise subsystems. The largest government interenterprise subsystem is currently the US Department of Defense's (DoD) Global Transportation Network. The DoD improves its logistics and operational efficiency by tracking DoD assets and personnel from their origin to their destination.

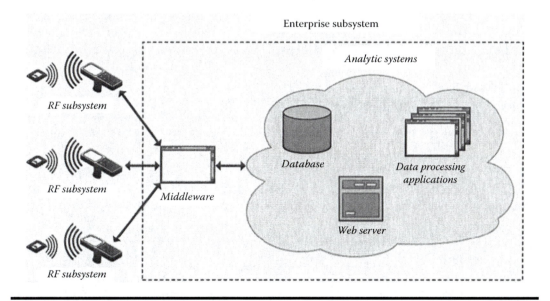

Figure 3.6   Enterprise RFID subsystem.

Open and Closed RFID Systems

RFID systems are either open or closed. Closed RFID systems are systems that do not have links with an outer environment. According to the intention of the designer, data that are collected within the system do not trespass the system's boundaries and remain entirely within the system. Data from outside the system will not trespass the system's boundaries either. Open systems are systems in which data that are collected within the system may be shared with other systems.

An example of a closed system is a logistics system that uses proprietary solutions for dealing with the data it collects from its tags. An example of an open system is a public transport ticketing system which is used in conjunction with an electronic shopping system, for instance by adding e-payment functionality to the transport ticketing card for shopping at shopping malls.

Keeping track of the collected data becomes more problematic in an open situation; relations may exist with third parties outside the system who use the information collected for other purposes.

Applications

RFID Application Types

There are many types of RFID applications, of which some of the most common are asset management, asset tracking, automated payment, and supply chain management. The key characteristic differentiating one RFID application from another is the purpose of identifying the tagged items. Table 3.1 lists reasons why an organization might want to identify an item and the general application type that best corresponds to those reasons.

Application types are not mutually exclusive; an implementation can combine elements of several application types. For example, both access control systems and sophisticated asset management systems include tracking features. Supply chain management is a tracking application that spans organizational boundaries and often includes process control and payment transactions.

Personnel responsible for designing and implementing RFID systems should understand what application types apply to their implementation so that they can select appropriate security controls. For example, the security controls needed to protect financial transactions in automated payment systems are different from those needed for tracking applications. The personnel should

Table 3.1 RFID Application Types

Identification Purpose	Application Type
Determine the presence of an item	Asset management
Determine the location of an item	Tracking
Determine the source of an item	Authenticity verification
Ensure affiliated items are not separated	Matching
Correlate information with the item for decision-making	Process control
Authenticate a person (holding a tagged item)	Access control
Conduct a financial transaction	Automated payment

also understand that an adversary may leverage RFID technology for an unintended purpose. For example, a warehouse may use RFID technology to determine what items it has in its current inventory, but an adversary may use the same system to track an item's whereabouts after it leaves the warehouse. In this case, an asset management system is later used to enable an unauthorized tracking application, perhaps used by an adversary to locate high-value targets.

Risks

RFID technology enables an organization to significantly change its business processes to:

- Increase its efficiency, resulting in lower costs
- Increase its effectiveness, improving mission performance and making the organization more resilient and better able to assign accountability
- Respond to customer requirements to use RFID technology to support supply chains and other applications

As described earlier, the RFID technology itself is complex, combining a number of different computing and communications technologies to achieve the desired objectives. Unfortunately, both change and complexity generate risk. For RFID implementations to be successful, organizations need to effectively manage that risk, which requires an understanding of its sources and its potential characteristics.

Privacy Aspects

In relation to RFID, privacy and security are two sides of the same coin and require an approach in which they are both tackled together and it might be possible to include security safeguards that may have positive implications on privacy. The double-sidedness of privacy and security requires attention, since it deals with embedding privacy regulations in the standards that are being developed on the various aspects of the RFID system (tags, readers, middleware, and the back-end information systems).

RFID is a means for identification. This identification can be of products, services, or persons. In most cases, RFID tags are related to products. When, however, a person is correlated to specific products by means of a token, an index, or another pointer, the identified information becomes personal information (or information that enables the identification of a person). Due to the 'enabling' characteristics of RFID tags the threat to privacy is a major concern, for the general public, companies, and governments alike.

In Figure 3.7, two direct privacy threats are identified: one in relation to the tag-reader system, and one in relation to the information that is collected and disseminated outside the tag-reader system.

The first kind of threat is the one that is most directly related to RFID. It focuses on the privacy implications of the tag-reader system itself. The second kind of threat relates to the use of data collected by means of an RFID system. The data that are disseminated by the tag-reader system may be collected in a database, for instance to monitor pallets in a supply chain management system. This kind of threat is not uniquely determined by the RFID system, but due to RFID the threats may be aggravated and have very specific dimensions.

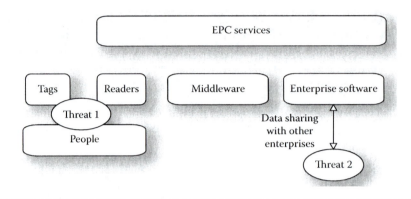

Figure 3.7   RFID privacy threats.

Privacy Threats within the Tag-Reader System

A tag may contain personal information. Passports, identity cards, and specific forms of public transport cards contain identifiable information. They may contain directly identifiable information on the card such as name and birth date. They also may contain data that functions as a key for a database in which personal information is stored. The privacy threat in the first case is obvious. In case a card holds indirectly identifiable information (a pointer that may refer to information about an identifiable person in a database), the privacy threat is indirectly present. Only when the intruder is able to link the pointer to the real person will privacy be invaded.

The unauthorized reading of tags is considered to be the most prominent privacy threat. Unauthorized reading is possible, especially in case of using UHF-based tags with reading ranges of approximately 20–30 ft.

Using tags to track persons is usually identified as being the second biggest threat to privacy. Tracking of persons via objects presupposes the linkage of identification data with individual track movements. Identification data can be acquired on the basis of electronic payments, loyalty cards, electronic ticket cards in public transport, etc. When a person carries an object that is linked to that person (such as a wristwatch) the data of the tag attached to the wristwatch may be used as identifiable information for the person carrying the wristwatch. It is possible to track the movements of this person by surveying the movement of the object for which the tag data are known. The information can for instance be used to retrieve personal preferences.

Privacy Threats at the Backend of the RFID System

The threats mentioned above correlate directly with the RFID reader to tag communication and the direct use of these data. Most privacy threats, however, refer to the collection and subsequent use of information outside the tag-reader system. Tags with unique IDs can easily be associated with a person's identity and smart cards with their own processing capacities may contain sensitive personal information.

There are three privacy threats related to the use of data outside the tag-reader system:

1. Using data for aggregating personal information
2. Using data for purposes other than originally specified
3. Using data to monitor specific behaviors

By means of data-mining techniques it is possible to find correlations between hitherto separated objects (and subjects). Deducting social networks may be especially interesting for intelligence agencies, for instance in trying to discover social networks of criminals: if one criminal can be traced, it is possible by data mining and pattern recognition techniques to sort out who else has a similar pattern of movement. This privacy threat is closely related to the following one.

RFID data may be collected for use in specific settings, but subsequently used in other settings. This is an example of "function creep": though originally not perceived, data collected for a specific purpose turns out to be useful for other purposes as well.

Monitoring can be done in real time, but it also can be done on the basis of aggregated data, that are subsequently analyzed in order to deduct specific patterns of behavior. An example of using RFID technology for individual monitoring is the business that uses an identifiable token (such as a loyalty card) to collect information on shopping behavior and uses this information to base decisions related, for example, on pricing without the consent of the customer.

Solutions that are more directly related to RFID are the ones that try to keep control over the data flow to the user (by means of killer and blocker tags, for example) in order to prevent information being disseminated against the user's wishes, and offer the users an "opt-in" choice. These solutions are based on the technical functioning of the RFID system, especially in the communication of RFID tag and reader. Other proposed solutions in this vein are using a Faraday cage to shield the tag from being read and reducing or removing the antenna (in the first case as a means to reduce the read range, while in the latter as a means to disable the tag). "Privacy by design" means that compliance with the privacy principles is sought by means of appropriate technical measures.

Another problem is the fact that low-cost RFID devices do not have the computational resources to use selected cryptographic methods. The kill tag, though appealing through its radical approach, may kill beneficial uses of the information that is hidden on the tag as well.

Security Aspects

This section contains a general overview of security threats of an RFID system, consisting of an RFID tag and a reader. The security threats are classified as either threats for the tag, or the wireless interface between the tag and the reader, or the reader.

Security Threats for the Tag

Falsification of Contents

Data can be falsified by unauthorized write access to the tag. This type of attack is suitable for targeted deception only if, when the attack is carried out, the ID (serial number) and any other security information that might exist (e.g., keys) remain unchanged. This way the reader continues to recognize the identity of the tag correctly. This kind of attack is possible only in the case of RFID systems that, in addition to ID and security information, store other information on the tag.

Falsification of Tag ID

The attacker obtains the ID and any security information of a tag and uses these to deceive a reader into accepting the identity of this particular tag. This method of attack can be carried out using a device that is capable of emulating any kind of tag or by producing a new tag as a duplicate of the old one (cloning). This kind of attack results in several tags with the same identity being in circulation.

Deactivation

These types of attack render the tag useless through the unauthorized application of delete or kill commands. Depending on the type of deactivation, the reader can either no longer detect the identity of the tag, or it cannot even detect the presence of the tag in the reading range.

Physical Destruction

Tags could be physically destroyed by chemical or mechanical means, or by using strong electro-magnetic fields (like in a microwave oven). Active tags could also be shut down by removing or discharging the battery.

Detaching the Tag

A tag is separated physically from the tagged item and may subsequently be associated with a different item, in the same way that price tags are "switched." Since RFID systems are completely dependent on the unambiguous identification of the tagged items by the transponders, this type of attack poses a fundamental security problem, even though it may appear trivial at first sight.

Security Threats for the Wireless Interface

Eavesdropping

The communication between reader and transponder via the wireless interface is monitored by intercepting and decoding the radio signals. This is one of the most specific threats to RFID systems. The eavesdropped information could, for example, be used to collect privacy-sensitive information about a person. It could also be used to perform a replay attack, i.e., the attacker records all communicated messages and later on can either simulate this tag towards the reader or simulate this reader towards the tag.

Blocking

So-called blocker tags simulate to the reader the presence of any number of tags, thereby blocking the reader. A blocker tag must be configured for the respective anticollision protocol that is used.

Jamming

Jamming means a deliberate attempt to disturb the wireless connection between reader and tag and thereby attacking the integrity or the availability of the communication. This could be achieved by powerful transmitters at a large distance, but also through more passive means such as shielding. As the wireless interface is not very robust, even simple passive measures can be very effective.

Relay Attack

A relay attack for contactless cards is similar to the well-known man-in-the-middle attack. A device is placed in between the reader and the tag such that all communication between the reader and the tag goes through this device, while both tag and reader think they communicate directly to each other. Smartly modifying this communication could, for example in payment systems, lead to charging the wrong electronic wallet (a smart card with an RFID tag). To make this attack more practical one could increase the distance between the legitimate card and the victim's card by splitting the device into two components: one communicating with the reader and one with the victim's card. The communication between these two components could be implemented by any kind of fast wireless technology.

Security Threats for the Reader

Falsifying Reader ID

In a secure RFID system the reader must prove its authorization to the tag. If an attacker wants to read the data with his own reader, this reader must fake the identity of an authorized reader. Depending on the security measures in place, such an attack can be "very easy" to "practically impossible" to carry out. The reader might need access to the backend in order, for example, to retrieve keys that are stored there.

Security Threats for Other Parts of RFID Systems

When considering the security challenges of RFID in a broader perspective, one has to take into account the infrastructure, including a back office where additional information of all tags is stored, and the aspect of convenience in use. A general RFID architecture is depicted in Figure 3.7.

RFID readers are generally connected to the middleware using modular drivers, much like Windows uses device drivers to communicate with a graphics card. This allows different readers to be used with the middleware, without having to modify the middleware. In addition to event processing, the middleware handles different kinds of user interfaces. A user interface is generally provided for system-management purposes, for example to modify the series of filters through which an event is passed. There will also be user interfaces that allow regular users to access the system and use it. For example, in a supermarket distribution center, there will be a user interface that provides information on the current stock levels.

The middleware also communicates with other software systems, which implement the application's business logic. To stay with the supermarket example, it is likely that the supermarket RFID system is connected to a stock management system, which orders new stock from suppliers before it runs out. When considering the broader RFID architecture, new security risks and countermeasures come to mind:

Tag-Borne Attacks at Back Office

One could foresee an attack at the back office through information stored at the tag, which was recently shown by a few Dutch students. Basically there are three types of RFID malware, which are listed in increasing complexity of implementation:

1. *RFID exploits*: Just like other software, RFID systems are vulnerable to buffer overflows, code insertion, and SQL injection.
2. *RFID worms*: A worm is basically an RFID exploit that downloads and executes remote malware. A worm could propagate through the network or through tags.
3. *RFID viruses*: An RFID virus starts with malicious content of a tag. When the tag is read out, this initiates a malicious SQL query that would disturb a database in the back office. Although such an attack has not yet been performed in practice, this type of threat cannot be excluded.

Misuse of Gateway Interface

The user interface to the gateway could be misused by unauthorized individuals to attack the integrity of the filters and to misguide the product management system.

Corrupted Drivers

The drivers that are used by RFID readers to communicate with the middleware could be corrupted. This could be done either by modifying the driver of a legitimate reader or by replacing the legitimate reader with a fake reader that has a corrupted driver. A corrupted driver could be used to attack and misguide the gateway.

Attacking the Reader-Gateway Communication

The communication between reader and gateway could be eavesdropped or modified.

Security Measures for the Tag

Security Measures to Prevent Unauthorized Modification of Tag Data (Contents and ID)

An obvious security measure to prevent modification of tag data is to use read-only tags for which unauthorized modification is intrinsically impossible. Another effective measure, also recommended for reasons of data management, is to shift all data except the ID to the backend. Some types of tags dispose of an authentication method (like the ISO-9798 standard), through which the reader can be authenticated by the tag such that only authorized readers can modify the tag contents.

Security Measures for Deactivation

Unauthorized application of delete commands or kill commands can be prevented by using an authentication method (when available).

Security Measures for Physical Destruction

A countermeasure for physical destruction of the tag would be a close mechanical connection between the tag and the tagged item to make it difficult to destroy the tag without damaging the item. To prevent discharging the battery of an active tag one could implement a sleep mode in the tag.

Security Measures for Detaching the Tag

A countermeasure for detaching the tag from the tagged item would be a tight mechanical bond between the tag and the tagged item to ensure that removing the tag will also damage the product. In the case of active tags, an alarm function is conceivable: a sensor determines that the tag has been manipulated and transmits the alarm to a reader as soon as it comes within range. For high-value items an option would be to manually check whether the tag is attached to the correct item.

Security Measures for the Wireless Interface

Security Measures for Eavesdropping

An effective measure to reduce the effect of eavesdropping is to shift all data to the backend. More advanced tags have a module to encrypt the communication with the reader, which also prevents eavesdropping. Such advanced tags cannot be read out by intruders and are still available for legitimate use. Another measure would be to design the RFID system such that tags are used within a small range, which is just sufficient for the legitimate readers (and thereby shutting out a class of unauthorized readers).

Security Measures for Blocking

There are no technical measures to prevent the use of blocker tags, but a solution is to ban their use in the standard terms and conditions of business.

Security Measures for Jamming

It is possible to detect jamming transmitters by performing random measurements or by using permanently installed field detectors.

Security Measures for Relay Attacks

One way to guard against relay attacks is to shield the tag when it is not used, e.g., by putting the tagged card in a Faraday-like cage. Another way is to require an additional action by the user (push a button, type in a PIN code, or use a fingerprint) to activate the tagged card, although this solution eliminates some of the convenience of the contactless system.

Security Measures for the Reader

Security Measures for Falsifying the Reader ID

To prevent readers from falsifying their ID to obtain unauthorized access to a tag, an authentication method (when available at the tag) can be used to authenticate the reader towards the tag. This risk can be further reduced when the reader has to access the backend during the authentication procedure, e.g., to retrieve cryptographic keys. Note that these measures are designed to assure the integrity of a reader that is about to communicate with the tag. For measures like shielding, which prevent an unauthorized reader from communicating, see "Security measures for eavesdropping".

Security Measures for Other Parts of RFID Systems

Security Measures for Tag-Borne Attacks at Back Office

To avoid such attacks, the content of tags should be checked by the reader and regular security measures should be taken to protect the gateway. A typical countermeasure against RFID viruses is to improve the software in the gateway that is able to distinguish a regular tag ID from an SQL query such that these attacks can be prevented from entering a database.

Security Measures for Misuse of Gateway Interface

To prevent such an attack the user interface should be provided with some kind of authentication mechanism such that only authorized users are able to access the gateway. Another measure would be to place the gateway and the user interface in a physically protected room such that only authorized employees that have access to this room can access the user interface.

Security Measures for Corrupted Drivers

A possible solution to this problem is to use only signed drivers, i.e., each legitimate driver should be digitally signed such that the gateway can check that communicating readers contain a legitimate driver. The use of drivers enables the fact that different readers can be used to communicate to the gateway. From a security point of view the use of different readers should be encouraged because an attack is likely to be specific for one type of reader or one type of driver, so a diversification of types lowers the impact of a possible attack.

Security Measures for Attacking the Reader-Gateway Communication

The communication between reader and gateway could be eavesdropped or modified.

Security Measures against Cloning

When considering one tag and one reader as a system, which has been done in the previous sections, the risk of cloning (duplication of the tag ID in a new tag) has been identified. Only in the broad view of the complete architecture, such a risk could be handled: in the database where all the different tag IDs (with respect to a specific application) are collected, a duplicate ID could be detected and in some cases even the clone could be recognized (i.e., be distinguished from the original tag).

Conclusion

This document presented an overview of some of the technical facets of RFID. The most striking lesson here is that even though RFID is a conceptually simple technology, it engenders technological questions and problems of formidable complexity. For this reason, it is unwise to view RFID privacy and security as a technological issue alone. Policymaking will also have a vital role to play in the realm of RFID. They must not only supplement the protections that technology affords, but must prove sensitive to its novelties and nuances. To be most effective, RFID security controls should be incorporated throughout the entire life cycle of RFID systems—from policy development and design to operations and retirement. A delicate balance between privacy and utility is needed to bring RFID to its high pitch of promise.

Chapter 4

Privileged User Management

Georges J. Jahchan

Introduction

On June 22, 2008, Terry Childs made national headlines when he locked access to the city of San Francisco's Fiber Wide Area Network (WAN) by resetting administrative passwords to its switches and routers and then declining to hand over those passwords.[*]

On October 24, 2008, an employee at Fanny Mae's Urbana, MD, data center was let go from his contract, almost two weeks after erroneously creating a computer script that changed the settings on the Unix servers without the proper authority of his supervisor.[†] Within 90 minutes of being told his contract was terminated, and several hours before his access to the Fannie Mae network was disabled later that evening, he embedded a malicious script inside a legitimate script that ran on Fannie Mae's network every morning. The malicious script was to trigger on January 31, but was discovered by chance by another engineer on October 29. The malicious script was planted after a page of blank lines intended to conceal it. Had that script run, it would have disabled monitoring alerts and all log-ins, deleted the root passwords to the approximately 4000 Fannie Mae servers, then erased all data and backup data on those servers by overwriting with zeros. It would have caused millions of dollars in damage and reduced or shut down operations for at least a week.

March 17, 2009: An IT contract employee was indicted on charges of sabotaging a computer system he helped set up, because the company did not offer him a permanent job.[‡] He was charged with affecting the integrity and availability of an offshore platform monitoring computer system designed to detect oil leaks. While working as a contract employee, he had set up multiple accounts that he used to illegally gain access to the system after he stopped working for the company.

---

[*] http://www.computerworld.com/s/article/9110470/Questions_abound_as_San_Francisco_struggles_to_repair_locked_network.

[†] http://www.computerworld.com/s/article/9127040/Fannie_Mae_engineer_indicted_for_planting_server_bomb.

[‡] http://www.computerworld.com/s/article/9129933/IT_contractor_indicted_for_sabotaging_offshore_rig_management_system.

In the three cases, had appropriate privileged user controls been implemented, the incidents could have been prevented, or at least detected in a timely manner so as to minimize damage. In the second and third case, dame luck averted disaster, but organizations should not count on their lucky star to safeguard their information assets.

With the job cuts and corporate belt tightening, resulting from the faltering economy, companies are advised to be especially vigilant with disgruntled employees.[*]

A disgruntled administrator is not the only threat to an organization. Outsiders who manage to steal legitimate privileged users' credentials and then use them to gain access to high-value targets pose an even greater threat. Hackers who band together in across-the-globe virtual communities and share knowledge are the most dangerous as they combine their diverse skills to mount innovative and highly sophisticated targeted attacks. They will typically carefully plan their attacks and break into a system outside working hours, when they are most likely to go unnoticed, plant a back door that subsequently grants them root access, and leave as quickly as possible, erasing their tracks.

Computer Emergency Response Team (CERT's) published analysis of 150 insider attack incidents[†] classified the attacks into three categories: fraud, theft of information, and IT sabotage, and identified the typical perpetrators' profiles. Following is a summary table of the results.

Type of Incident	Typical Insider's Profile	Method of Attack	What was the Motive?	How was the Incident Detected?	How was the Insider Identified?	What was the Impact?
Fraud	Nontechnical nonmanagement positions with privileged access Nontechnical means	Used their own credentials Acted during business hours from within workplace	Greed	System irregularity Nontechnical means	System logs	Financial impacts on employer Impact on innocent victims
Theft of confidential information	Male employees Half had accepted other position Half were in technical positions	Used own credentials Half compromised an account	Disgruntled Financial gain Did not know it was wrong	Half by system irregularity Nontechnical means	System logs	Financial impacts on employer Organization and customer confidential information revealed Trade secrets stolen Innocent victim murdered Insider committed suicide

---

[*] http://www.computerworld.com/s/article/9117138/Tough_economic_climate_can_heighten_insider_threat.

[†] A Risk Mitigation Model: Lessons Learned From Actual Insider Sabotage; Dawn M. Cappelli, Andrew P. Moore, and Eric D. Shaw. November 7, 2006.

15

Type of Incident	Typical Insider's Profile	Method of Attack	What was the Motive?	How was the Incident Detected?	How was the Insider Identified?	What was the Impact?
IT sabotage	Former employees Male Highly technical positions	Disgruntled Revenge for negative work-related event	No authorized access Backdoor accounts, shared accounts, other employees' accounts, insider's own account Many technically sophisticated Remote access outside normal working hours	Manually by nonsecurity personnel System failure or irregularity	System logs Most took steps to conceal identity and/or actions	Inability to conduct business, loss of customer records, inability to produce products Negative media attention Private information forwarded to customers, competitors, or employees Exposure of personal or confidential information Website defacements Many individuals harmed

CERT recommends that management must recognize the technical precursors and have the "ability to disable access on demand in the absolute, particularly for administrators and privileged users" when demoting or firing. In practice, that requires an understanding of the access paths available to insiders, which "depends on rigorous access management practices." Access management must be proactive and ongoing, as "practices tend to degrade over time without regular enforcement" and "it takes time to recover from poor access management practices."

Effective privileged user controls need to combine policies, procedures, and technologies that address the particular environment and needs of organizations. Though there may be similarities, no two organizations' environments are alike. Consequently, what works very well for one organization may not for another in the same line of business. In security, there is no such thing as "one solution fits all." While the administrative and operational controls are particular to a company, the technology controls are licensed for a variety of tools available from specialty security vendors.

At a high level, organizations use technology solutions to come as close as possible to the goal of consistently granting and controlling rights based on the principle of least privilege (or access on a need-to-know and/or need-to-do basis). Furthermore, auditors come to expect organizations to prove it. Regulations further complicate matters with regulation-specific control/audit/reporting requirements.

The technical controls to manage privileged users fall in three main categories: privileged password management, privileged user access controls, and identity and access management suites. Some vendors have products that fall into more than one category, others are platform specific (Windows-only or *nix-only), while others are cross-platform. This paper explores some of the products that help automate and enforce rigorous privileged account management practices. The content of this article is based on published information from vendors and independent sources.

The information is reported "as is"; no attempt was made to validate vendor claims, as product evaluations are beyond the scope of this article.

Full management of privileged accounts requires organizations to not only control who has access to privileged credentials, but also, once access is granted, restrict use exclusively to perform specific tasks, and maintain an audit trail of user actions. As we will see, none of the solutions reviewed meet all of the goals.

The solutions are categorized, but they are not sorted in any particular order.

Privileged User Audit Solutions

Centrify DirectAudit

Centrify DirectAudit helps comply with regulatory requirements, perform in-depth troubleshooting, and protect against insider threats for UNIX and Linux systems. DirectAudit's detailed logging strengthens compliance reporting and helps spot suspicious activity by showing which users accessed what systems, what commands they executed, and what changes they made to key files and data. With DirectAudit one can also perform immediate, in-depth troubleshooting by replaying and reporting on user activity that may have contributed to system failures. And its real-time monitoring of current user sessions enables spotting of suspicious activity.

The DirectAudit Agent continuously communicates user session activity in an encrypted, compressed format to a DirectAudit Collector Service. The Collector Service in turn stores the data in a central SQL Server repository, providing enterprise-scale performance and scalability. For increased reliability, the DirectAudit Agent continues to record session data even when there is no network connection and subsequently forwards it to a DirectAudit Collector Service when the network is available. Centrify also supports load balancing among multiple DirectAudit Collector Services when deployments of DirectAudit Agents range in the 100s or 1000s.

In the DirectAudit Console, a right-click can replay any user session on any audited system to see what commands were executed, what changes were made to key files and data, and what system output appeared. Pause, rewind, or fast-forward are similar to using a VCR. This playback feature gives a tool for monitoring activity, troubleshooting changes that may have led to a system failure, or documenting system configuration tasks.

The DirectAudit Console's out-of-the-box views provide visibility into active sessions and historical sessions, or custom-built views that show sessions by specific users, machines, time periods, or other criteria. They can also perform full-text searches to find, for example, all instances of a password command across all sessions. DirectAudit adopts a non-proprietary SQL data format, enabling reporting and querying through third-party tools.

The DirectAudit Console gives a centralized, real-time view of every user session on every audited UNIX and Linux system. For each session one can see who is logged on and one can immediately drill down to see what they are currently doing. The console allows spotting of suspicious activity and aids in troubleshooting system issues.

IBM Tivoli Compliance Insight Manager

Consul Insight Suite integrates log management, rules- and policy-based monitoring, and reporting. It normalizes, analyzes, and reports on privileged user activity.

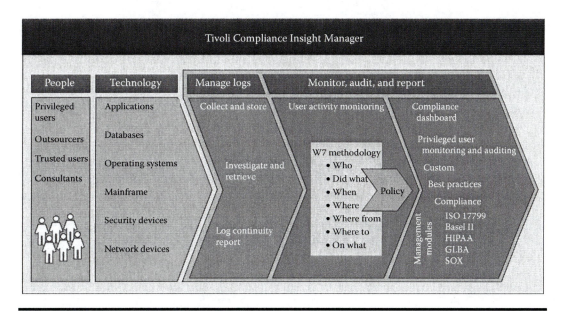

Figure 4.1 Tivoli Compliance Insight Manager captures security information about people and technology for audit and compliance reporting.

Tivoli Compliance Insight Manager provides an easy-to-use security compliance dashboard that summarizes billions of log files. Through this dashboard, you can quickly gain an overview of your security compliance posture, understand user activities and security events in comparison to acceptable-use frameworks, and monitor privileged users and related security events (Figure 4.1).

IBM Tivoli Consul Manager Highlights:

- Collects, stores, investigates and retrieves logs through automated log management
- Performs privileged user monitoring and audit (PUMA) on databases, applications, servers, and mainframes
- Helps automate audit reporting through an enterprise compliance dashboard and flexible report distribution
- Creates custom compliance modules through advanced policy and report definition engines.
- Supports auditing needs by translating captured native audit log data into easily understood language
- Eases addition of new log collectors and parsers through an advanced toolkit
- Leverages a full audit and compliance infrastructure through integration with numerous IBM Tivoli identity and access management products and advanced databases

Privileged User Control Solutions
e-DMZ Total Privileged Access Management (TPAM) Suite

The TPAM suite is a modular solution that consists of the following individually licensed modules based on two appliances: Password Auto Repository and eGuardPost™ (Figure 4.2 and Figure 4.3).

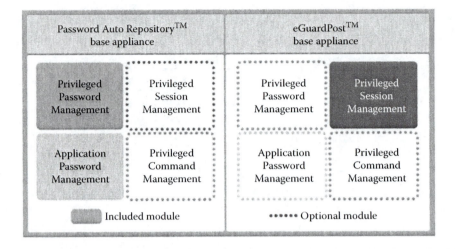

Figure 4.2   TPAM Suite.

- Privileged Password Management (PPM)
- Application Password Management
- Privileged Session Management
- Privileged Command Management

Privileged Password Management Module

Provides secure storage, release control, and change control of privileged passwords across a heterogeneous deployment of systems and applications. e-DMZ's Password Auto Repository (PAR) provides enterprise class features, functions, and scalability.

Application Password Management Module

Through a robust CLI/API supported by PAR, hard-coded passwords can be replaced with a simple call script or program calls into PAR, meeting the needs of application-to-application (A2A), application-to-database (A2DB), and application-to-system (A2S) requirements.

Figure 4.3   Total privileged access management.

Privileged Session Management Module

eGuardPost provides full session management and controls including fine-grain resource access control, active session monitoring, and full session recording in an efficient format for future replay. Extensive session proxy types supported include: SSH, RDP, http/https, ICA, telnet, x5250, and VNC.

Privileged Command Management Module

Provided through eGuardPost™, this supports privileged access control down to the privileged command level. It is able to control, record, and monitor sessions and can limit a user's connection to a specific command for both Unix/Linux and Windows systems.

Cyber-Ark Privileged Identity Management (PIM) Suite

Cyber-Ark's Privileged Identity Management (PIM) Suite is an enterprise-class, full life-cycle solution for securing, managing, automatically changing, and monitoring all activities associated with privileged accounts. This includes the Root account on UNIX/Linux, Administrator in Windows, Cisco Enable, Oracle systems/sys, MSSQL SA, SAP Application Server, and many more such as Emergency or "Firecall" Ids.

The PIM Suite includes the following products:

■ Enterprise Password Vault
■ Application Identity Manager
■ Privileged Session Manager

Enterprise Password Vault (EPV) enables organizations to secure, manage, automate, store, protect, and log all activities associated with privileged, shared, and elevated accounts. EPV supports over 50 operating systems, databases, firewalls, network devices, business suites, and key systems.

Application Identity Manager (AIM) offers a comprehensive suite of software and services to securely manage embedded, privileged application, and script accounts, and to eliminate the use of hard-coded credentials. AIM v5.5 contains secure and robust authentication methods.

Privileged Session Manager (PSM) allows organizations to secure, control, and monitor privileged access to sensitive systems and devices while leveraging privileged single sign-on capabilities. PSM also helps to streamline the control and management around who is entitled to access the sensitive devices and networks, how to secure and manage the underlying privileged credentials required to initiate these sessions, as well as perform audit reports of all activities within these privileged sessions.

Irdeto Cloakware Password Authority

Password Authority automates the life-cycle management of passwords on the target systems (servers, applications, workstations, routers, etc.) and provides an intuitive web interface for authorized users to quickly obtain current target account passwords. Credentials remain protected at every stage of their use. Critical information like passwords, keys, and business logic are protected while on disk, in memory, and on the network.

External Directory (LDAP) integration for management and authentication of users provides dynamic access to Password Authority and leverages the current directory administration process.

This has enabled the creation and enforcement of complex password composition policies and scheduled password change frequency. It has built-in capability to change password on view, password check-out/in, trouble-ticket system integration, dual-authorization workflow and auto-login to target the system via SSH or RDP (password is never in plain sight), dual authorization with Password Authority's workflow, and require a reason code through integration with the help desk.

Password Authority server can be deployed on Microsoft Windows, Linux, or Solaris operating systems. A wide range of Password Authority target connectors are standard, or users can build their own custom connectors with Password Authority's extensible connector framework. For programmatic access, a wide range of both 32- and 64-bit operating system types are supported. A Java API and CLI provides automation and customization.

The server-based component architecture and extensible connector technology allows integration with virtually any back-end process. Out of the box, Password Authority supports a wide variety of common datacenter systems such as databases, servers, and routers. Easy to use templates make it easy to add plug-and-play support for other systems. Data and control flow transformations in Password Authority help protect against static and dynamic analysis attacks.

Password Authority can be deployed as a single server instance, as a cluster (e.g., for high transaction rates), or in multisite primary-secondary (or primary to multiple secondary) arrangement for geographically dispersed organizations. Password Authority has the flexibility to fit various IT architectures and is licensed to allow scaling when needed. Its multi-instance license option ensures disaster recovery (DR) planning flexibility.

The Password Authority's programmatic access client is multihome capable and additionally provides a secure local cache. In the event access to the Password Authority server(s) is not available, requests can continue to be served securely from the local client cache.

NetWrix Privileged Account Manager

Privileged Account Manager (PAM) maintains and protects privileged shared accounts of all types, from Active Directory and servers to routers and database systems. The product provides a secure facility for provisioning, accessing, automatic updating, and de-provisioning of shared administrative accounts, to enable centralized control and auditing of all privileged accounts.

NetWrix Privileged Account Manager enables:

- *Protection of Privileged Accounts*: All devices, servers, and workstations have powerful built-in accounts with unlimited rights, such as enable on Cisco, Administrator on Windows, and root on UNIX. PAM provides secure storage for all privileged accounts and their passwords within your organization.
- *Centralized Management*: Stores all privileged accounts in a central location, enabling designated members of your IT team to access them according to established role-based security policies. PAM provides one unified workflow for accessing and updating all privileged accounts.
- *Regulatory Compliance*: The product controls and audits the use of privileged shared accounts to enable security and compliance with Sarbanes-Oxley, GLBA, HIPAA, PCI, and others. At every single point, you can determine who knows an account password today and who knew it, for example, a month ago. PAM includes audit reports on operations with shared accounts.
- *Automated Password Management*: Automatically updates account passwords according to password expiration policies. It changes the account itself and updates all affected services and applications that use this account.
- *Account Checkout*: Must be done by every user who wants to gain access to the password. Once the password has been used, the system creates a new random password to prevent further use until the next check-out.

- *Automatic Discovery*: Provides an automatic scanning engine to import the current set of privileged shared accounts into the system during initial setup. Scheduled rediscovery ensures that no shared privileged accounts are used while bypassing centralized auditing and control.
- *Automated Password Resets*: Automates routine password maintenance according to effective password policies. The system changes the password and updates all associated services, scheduled tasks, etc—everything that uses the password being updated, preventing service disruptions, account lockouts, and related issues.
- *Encrypted Information Storage*: All passwords are stored and transmitted in encrypted form (AES encryption and SHA-1 algorithm) to prevent unauthorized disclosure.
- *Web-based Console*: For management of all privileged accounts.
- *Role-based Entitlement Management*: Flexible security rules to define the systems and accounts to which an employee can have access. As soon as a specific person moves to another department or retires, the product makes sure that he or she no longer has access to specific accounts and systems.
- *Extensive Auditing*: All operations performed with accounts and systems are logged into the audit database to enable creation of detailed reports and real-time alerting. Audit records track the times, user identities, and changes made to privileged accounts.

Identity and Access Management Suites

CA Access Control

CA Access Control is a multiplatform (Windows, Unix, Linux, and virtualized environments: VMware ESX, Solaris 10 Zones and LDOMs, Microsoft Hyper-v, IBM VIO and AIX LPAR, HP-UX VPAR, Linux Xen and Mainframe x/VM) that combines access control with privileged user management. It is one of the components of the vendor's Identity and Access Management (IAM) suite (Figure 4.4).

CA Access Control:

- *Provides comprehensive access controls on operating systems*: It is designed to control access to system resources, programs, files, and processes through a stringent series of criteria: time, login method, network attributes, and access program. These controls enforce separation of administrative duties on the servers. For example: separating system administration from application administration or virtualization administration, providing controlled rights to developers or support personnel, etc.
- *Privileged User Password Management (PUPM)*: By carefully segregating their duties and securely protecting the recording of their activities, organizations can protect against a privileged user making a mistake or committing a malicious act. PUPM provides secure access to privileged accounts and helps provide the accountability of privileged access through the issuance of passwords on a temporary, one-time use basis, or as necessary while providing user accountability of their actions through secure auditing. PUPM is also designed to allow applications to programmatically access system passwords and, in so doing, remove hard-coded passwords from scripts. Support for PUPM is available for a multitude of servers, applications (including databases), and devices in a physical or virtual environment.

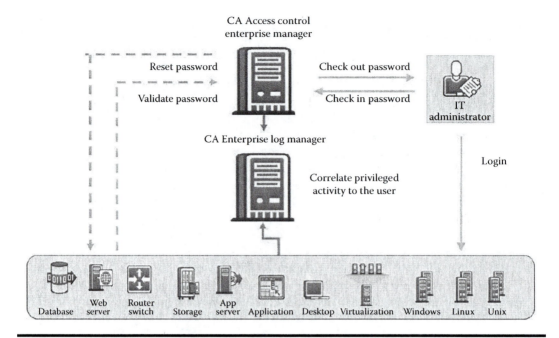

Figure 4.4 CA Access Control enterprise manager.

CA Access Control: Privileged User Password Management

■ *Unix Authentication Broker (UNAB)*: Authenticating UNIX/Linux users typically means maintaining records separate from Windows users. This complicates password synchronization and can get in the way of deprovisioning privileged users by adding time or errors. UNAB allows the management of UNIX users in Microsoft Active Directory (AD), which allows the consolidation of authentication and account information into the enterprise AD as opposed to having UNIX credentials on various systems (Figure 4.5).

■ *Entitlements Reports*: Policy-based reports provide proactive views of who has access to what across distributed and virtual server environments. These reports rely on the effective policy being enforced and allow the generation of reports required by auditors, such as User and Group Entitlement Reports, Policy Compliance Reports, and Orphan Account Reports. These proactive reports complement existing event-based auditing by allowing administrators to monitor compliance requirements and highlight existing discrepancies, before incidents occur.

BeyondTrust Privilege Manager and PowerKeeper

BeyondTrust Privilege Manager is a Windows-only solution that enables organizations to remove administrator rights and allow end users to run all required Windows applications, processes, and ActiveX controls.

Privilege Manager is implemented as a Group Policy extension. One specifies the application and which permissions and privileges should be added to the process token when the application is launched. By setting Privilege Manager policy, end users without administrative privileges will be able to run desired applications.

BeyondTrust PowerKeeper is an automated password management (APM) solution for access control, manageability, and audit of privileged accounts such as shared administrative accounts, application accounts, and local administrative accounts. PowerKeeper offers complete device support for any operating system, account, or device. All encryption in PowerKeeper is provided by commercially supported, FIPS 140-2 validated software (Figure 4.6).

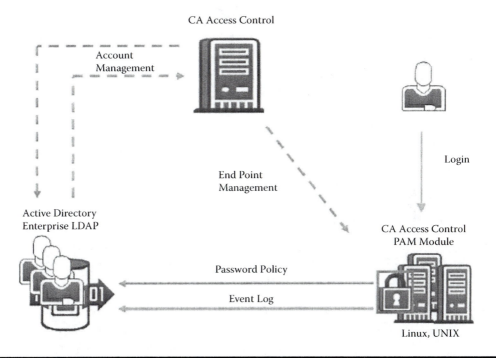

Figure 4.5   CA Access Control: Unix authentication broker.

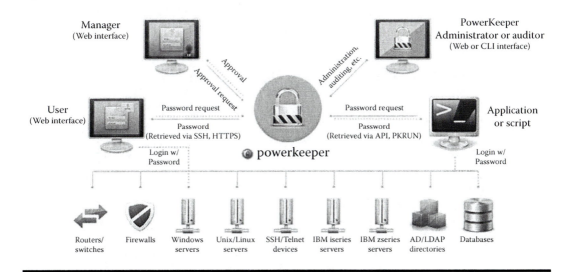

Figure 4.6   BeyondTrust PowerKeeper.

PowerKeeper is available as Physical and Virtual Solutions:

- Runs on Windows 2008/SQL Server 2008
- Hardware appliances are 64-bit
- Virtual machines are 32-bit
- Virtual machine runs on VMware virtualization platforms

and includes multiple layers of security:

- No direct access to the sealed operating system
- Employs commercially supported FIPS 140-2 validated components for all encryption
- Supports authentication methods (i.e., LDAP, AD, SecureID, Safeword)
- Program Factors to validate authenticity of application/script that is requesting credentials (i.e., User, Host, OS, Program)

PowerKeeper provides client libraries to enable existing and new application programs or scripts to securely retrieve current credentials from PowerKeeper.

ScriptLogic Privilege Authority

ScriptLogic Privilege Authority is a *free* Windows-only solution which enables organizations to run users with the least privileges possible, and elevate applications and ActiveX controls only when needed. It is supported by the Privilege Authority community of users.

- Privilege Authority uses elevation rules to determine what applications, features, or controls are elevated to higher privileges. These rules can include the common rules included with Privilege Authority, customized versions of the common rules, or completely custom, user-defined rules. Rules can be copied, shared, and moved easily between test and production networks.
- Privilege Authority elevation rules are attached to group policies, to ensure reliable delivery to clients. This gives administrators the flexibility to assign rules where needed by attaching them only to the group policies going to the intended clients.

Lieberman Software Enterprise Random Password Manager

Lieberman Software products help organizations control privileged account access through a four-part I.D.E.A. process (Figure 4.7):

- *Identify* and document all critical IT assets, their privileged accounts, and their interdependencies.
- *Delegate* access to privileged credentials so that only appropriate personnel, using the least privilege required, can log in to IT assets.
- *Enforce* rules for password complexity, diversity, and change frequency, and synchronize changes across all dependencies.
- *Audit* and alert so that the requester, purpose, and duration of each privileged access request is documented.

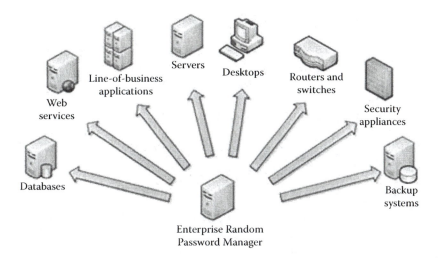

Figure 4.7   Lieberman Software Enterprise Random Password Manager.

Enterprise Random Password Manager stores privileged credentials with default AES 256 encryption. Optionally, a FIPS 140-2 validated module and PKCS#11 hardware encryption are available.

Enterprise Random Password Manager secures Windows, Linux, Unix, OS/390, and AS/400. It instantly enrolls new systems as they are brought online.

It handles:

- Continuous detection, securing, and propagating interdependent service accounts.
- Continuous discovery, synchronization, and propagation of:
  - Windows tasks login credentials.
  - Windows COM+/DCOM/MTS applications.
  - Embedded accounts in scripts, binary files, applications, agents, Web services, and others.
  - SQL Server, Microsoft SCOM Run As accounts, SharePoint, automatic logon accounts, logon cache.
- Management and protection of privileged identities in clustered services.
- Direct authentication with Active Directory, Oracle Internet Directory, Novell eDirectory, IBM Tivoli Directory Server, and OpenLDAP.
- Automatic enforcement of organizational policies as staff roles change.
- Expanded access to management and to auditors. They can authorize requests, configure access, and view comprehensive reports from a secure Web interface.
- An unlimited number of concurrent users accessing the web-based password checkout application.
- Temporary access to vendors and contractors.
- Auto-rolling of passwords after each access.
- User, system, and account histories alongside operational reports & KPIs.
- Detailed auditing and compliance reports.
- Configurable immediate notification of password checkouts and unusual requests.

- Scalable zone processing architecture enables policy enforcement across high-latency or unreliable WAN links.
- Discovery and mitigation of unsecured privileged access across domain security boundaries and inside DMZs.
- Pulling of real-time system configuration data from BMC Atrium CMDB, CA CMDB, and IBM CCMDB.
- Out-of-the-box integration with Microsoft Systems Center, HP Operations Center, HP NMC, and ArcSight.
- SDK included at no charge.

Verdasys Privileged User Management

With Verdasys Digital Guardian, automated compensating controls can be enforced across different types of privileged users with centrally managed security polices defined at the group or individual user level. Digital Guardian's agent-based architecture mitigates the risk of potential data loss or compromise by privileged or inside users, while enabling these same users to have greater access to the sensitive data required to complete their tasks.

Digital Guardian has the following features:

- Host-based monitoring, both on and offline: takes action before data is compromised
- All users are monitored and all activity is recorded and auditable: even privileged user activity, including real-time alerting to appropriate managers
- Segregation of duties through access and usage controls
- Complete audit records of all privileged users
- Invisible, hardened, very difficult to defeat agent architecture
- Deterrence of risky activity through real-time warning and justification prompts
- Privileged user monitoring on older legacy, mainframe, or custom applications utilizing the Digital Guarding Application logging and masking module

Novell Privileged User Manager

Novell Privileged User Manager provides a UNIX Super User Privilege Management (SUPM) system that minimizes exposure to unauthorized transactions and information access by delegating access to the root account and providing centralized activity logging across mixed UNIX/Linux environments. This enables administrators to lock down user privileges by configuring rules based on the command executed, the user who executed it, and the location. The account delegation feature removes the need to grant common access to the root account on any system (Figure 4.8).

Novell Privileged User Manager sits between the user and the operating system, intercepting typed commands and sending them to a central authorization database for approval. According to policy, it can record single commands or entire user sessions. It extracts full keystroke data, storing it in secure, redundant databases. The collected commands are automatically analyzed and graded according to activity risk level.

Whether or not a command executes depends entirely on the policies defined by the organization. Novell Privileged User Manager provides an intuitive, graphical interface that allows organizations to create granular controls that govern command authorization based on the context of who the user is, what the command is, where it's being executed, and when it's being executed. The policies also provide separation-of-duty verification and accountability of user actions.

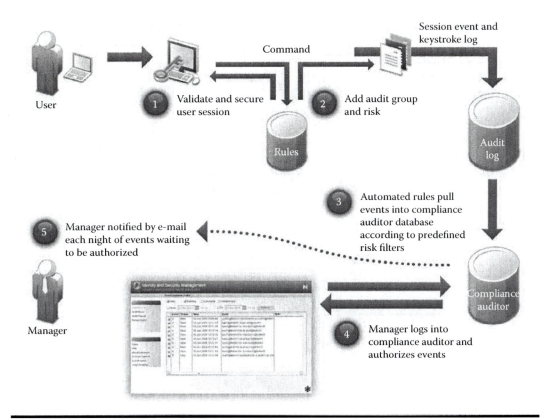

FIGURE 4.8 Novell Privileged User Manager.

If Novell Privileged User Manager determines by policy that a command should be authorized, the command is remotely executed on the target machine under a privileged account's credentials, such as root. It can also provide real-time alerts of any anomalies or command attempts that don't adhere to policy. Additionally, the solution can log all keystroke command activity to distributed databases, based on policy.

Novell Privileged User Manager utilizes business-defined rules to pull filtered log events into its Compliance Auditor according to preset risk criteria. It automatically alerts managers via e-mail of any activities that require internal auditing and sign-off. The solution performs audits using an intuitive, color-coded interface, enabling the fast identification of high-risk commands. It provides for the review of any suspicious activities, and if sanctioned by the organization's management, electronically signs them as authorized.

Novell Privileged User Manager Process Workflow

Novell Privileged User Manager integrates seamlessly with Unix and Linux platforms, allowing lockdown user privileges and providing centralized logging of activity across mixed Unix/Linux environments. It also supports select Microsoft Windows and XP systems. Supported platforms include:

- AIX 4.2, 4.3.x, and 5.x
- HP-UX (PA-RISC) 10.20, 11, 11i v1, v2, v3
- HP-UX (Itanium) 11i v1, v2, v3

- Linux kernel 2.4: SUSE 9.x, 10, Red Hat 9, Ent Srv v3, v4, and Fedora
- Solaris (Sparc) 2.6, 2.7, 8, 9, and 10
- Solaris (Intel) 8, 9, and 10
- Tru64 4.x, and 5.x
- Microsoft Windows 2000, 2003, and XP

The Compliance Auditor component of Novell Privileged User Manager provides a comprehensive interface that pulls filtered audit events at hourly, daily, weekly, or monthly intervals. This enables auditors to view prefiltered security transactions, play back recordings of user activity, and record notes for compliance purposes. In an era of increasing regulatory compliance, the ability to provide demonstrable audit compliance at any time provides a more secure system and reduces audit risk.

In addition to the Command Controls and Compliance Auditor, several out-of-the-box tools simplify the deployment and administration of user management and tracking. These include:

- An intuitive drag-and-drop visual interface for creating rules.
- Tools for dragging rules into nested hierarchies which, when used in conjunction with scripting, provide granular control for the most demanding environments.
- All rules and policies are maintained, updated, and edited in a central fashion.
- An integrated test suite that allows administrators to model and test rule combinations before pushing new rules into a production environment.
- Tools for creating account groups that include user accounts and hosts.

Conclusion

With the sheer number of available solutions, how would one choose a solution that is appropriate to his environment? A simplified methodology for selecting a privileged user management solution is provided below. It is by no means the only one and should be adapted to individual situations.

1. *Determine high-level business need*: Are you looking for a privileged user management audit solution, or for a more elaborate audit and control solution?
2. *Determine regulatory requirements*: Are you subject to regulations? If yes, ensure the solutions have tools templates that help you with your compliance efforts.
3. *Establish a detailed functionality checklist, with business benefit and priority*: Must-have, highly desirable, desirable. The functionality should be assessed based on its business benefit, not on technical merit.
4. *Determine the environment the solution will apply to*: Check compatibility against the prospective vendors' published supported platforms. Any unsupported platforms—assuming they can be integrated—will require extra implementation effort. Custom integration effort is not without risks: failure (total or partial), time/cost overruns, and will the integration work through minor/major product revisions or updates? Does the vendor's solution integrate with your in-house service desk or ticketing solution? Is the integration unidirectional or bidirectional?
5. *Reporting requirements*: Does the solution provide out-of-the-box the reports you need? If not, can they be custom-defined? If yes, what is the effort needed?
6. *Implementation*: Will you be relying on the vendor or partner/reseller resources, or will you be implementing using in-house staff? In both cases, education is of prime importance; assess your options. In the first case, ask for references and ensure the implementer has the resources and know-how to handle your environment.

7. Ask for customer references from the vendor and/or from the implementer (if applicable). Ask for customer contact details and do make the effort to contact them (with permission). When contacting them, discuss your concerns.

8. Once you have done your homework regarding steps 1 through 7, and short-listed the solutions down to one or two, it is evaluation time. Is the vendor willing to perform a limited scope on-site proof-of-concept (PoC)? Your expectations from the proof-of-concept should be realistic; you are trying to get a feel for the product and evaluate the out-of-the-box functionality that is important to you, on supported platforms in your environment. Establish a checklist of out-of-the-box (OOTB) functionality you want to see during the PoC, share it in advance with the vendor, and have them include it in a deliverables document. At the end of the PoC, both parties should complete and comment on the deliverables checklist.

There are several other factors to take into account in your decision in order to minimize the risk of selecting the wrong solution for your environment.

About the Author

Graduated in 1980 as an electrical engineer from McGill University in Montreal, Canada, **Georges J. Jahchan** has been in various personal computer-related positions for thirty years, six of which were spent addressing gateway security, three as a security officer in a private university, and four as a senior security and enterprise systems management consultant in Levant, North Africa and Pakistan with CA. He is now Chief Security Officer at Quattro Associates, an IT Market Gateway covering the Middle East, Turkey, and North Africa. He holds CISA, CISM, and BS7799-2 Lead Auditor certifications.

Chapter 5

Privacy in the Age of Social Networking

Salahuddin Kamran

Introduction

The term *social networking* refers to applications and services that facilitate collective action and social interaction on the Internet, such as blogs, wikis, social networks, and discussion forums. In recent years, online social networks have become very popular and many websites have sprung up where one can meet their offline friends in the virtual world of the Internet. Services like Facebook, Orkut, MySpace, etc. allow people to host their online social networks. People create their profiles in such social networks and share this information with their friends and a vast number of strangers.

When people join social networking sites, they begin by creating a profile, then make connections to existing friends as well as those they meet through the site. A profile is a list of identifying information. It can include the user's real name or a pseudonym. It also can include photographs, birthday, hometown, religion, ethnicity, and personal interest. Members connect to others by sending a "friend" request, which must be accepted by the other party in order to establish a link. "Friending" another member gives them access to one's profile, adds them to their social network, and vice versa. Members use these sites for a number of purposes. The root motivation is communication and maintaining relationships. Popular activities include updating others on activities and whereabouts, sharing photos and archiving events, getting updates on activities by friends, displaying a large social network, presenting an idealized persona, sending messages privately, and posting public testimonials.

The success of social computing systems, whose content is created almost entirely by user contribution, depends on the willingness of the participants to share. Individuals' willingness to provide information, in turn, is governed by their privacy concerns. This issue seems to be particularly important given that social networks such as Facebook have been facing increasing criticism over their privacy policies.

Facebook is the largest social network service provider in the United States and is the second most-visited website in the United States after Google. According to Facebook, there are more than 400 million active users, with approximately 120 million in the United States. Around 200 million users log on to Facebook each day. More than 2.5 billion photos are uploaded to Facebook each month. It is the largest photo-sharing site on the Internet, by a wide margin.

In this paper, we have briefly described of some major features and benefits of social networking that have made social networking one of the most popular Internet technologies at this moment. We have also highlighted the crucial privacy and security threats that may arise due to the "almost-anything-goes" ethos of social networking sites. Finally, we have given a few recommendations to enhance the security issues of social networking sites to ensure that users will benefit from the social network sites rather than suffering their downsides.

Structure and Evolution of Online Social Networks

Social networks have received significant interest from researchers in various domains such as psychology, philosophy, education, and recently, computer science. Social networks are a social structure of nodes that represent individuals and the relationships between them within a certain area. Therefore, social networks are usually built based on the strength of relationships and trust between the members. Scrutiny of the ways in which these nodes are connected has resulted in the identification of varying types of ties between nodes. In this context, a strong tie is one established directly between two people in the same network, whereas a weak tie is a relationship between two people connected through another person.

The way social networking has evolved can be linked with the evolution of the Internet itself.

Bulletin Boards

People have been using computers for social communication since the very beginning of the personal computer industry. Long before the Internet became accessible to the general public, people were hosting Bulletin Board Systems (BBS), many of them focused on an interest group or local community; such forums also had profiles, but unlike the online social networks of today they were more limited and usually didn't contain sensitive personal information.

Online Services

Commercial online services reached their peak in the 1990s, first as destinations themselves and later as portals to the Internet. These services provided access to a broad range of services that are now mirrored on the web. News, travel reservations, shopping, and social hubs were all part of the package; much of what we see today on the web existed in some form on these sites. Social communication was one of the big draws for online services, as a major source of their revenue was derived from billing for usage on a per-minute basis. First Prodigy and then America OnLine (AOL), in particular, recognized this and allowed users to create communities about just about any topic.

Web 1.0

From the mid-1990s to 2000, there was an explosion of activity as companies rushed to reproduce existing online services on the web. There were many social services created during this period, notably GeoCities and theGlobe.com. One thing the web did was to eliminate the silo problem that plagued AOL and its brethren. During this period privacy was not a major concern; the Internet was just taking off and services were given more importance than privacy, however the concept of social networking had not fully evolved yet, and people were in full control of their content and what they were posting online. The absence of profiles limited privacy-related risks.

Web 2.0: Profiles and Updates

Social networks make it easy for people to create profiles using standard templates. This makes sense, but this is really no different from a web page. People can share information about themselves, profiles can make it easy for users to share too much information, and even if they do not share too much, the little that they share can also impact their privacy, since there are numerous social networks and information may be distributed over all of them. One of the reasons Facebook is so addictive is because it is a convenient way to track the status of friends. This, too, is something that can be moved onto the open web. Anyone who wants to can publish updates, events, etc. via standard formats like Twitter, RSS, and iCal. Anyone who wants to monitor their friends' updates can do so, via a feed reader or some other way.

Figure 5.1 is a map of the world, showing the most popular social networks by country.

Table 5.1 lists the top websites in the United States with the social networking sites in bold.

The prevalence of social networking sites among the top 20 United States sites indicates their popularity among the public.

The Case about Privacy

In America, we live in a paradoxical world of privacy. On one hand, teenagers reveal their intimate thoughts and behaviors online and, on the other hand, government agencies and marketers are collecting personal data about us. For instance, the government uses driver's license databases to find fathers who are behind on their child support payments. Many government records have been turned into digital archives that can be searched through the Internet. Every time we use a shopping card, a retail store collects data about our consumer spending habits. Credit card companies can create even larger profiles of our shopping behaviors. Locked away on hundreds of servers is every minute detail of our daily lives from our individual buying preferences to personal thoughts. Social networking sites create a central repository of personal information. These archives are persistent and cumulative. Instead of replacing old information with new materials, online journals are archive-oriented compilations of entries that can be searched. While American adults are concerned about how the government and corporations are centrally collecting data about citizens and consumers, teenagers are freely giving up personal and private information in online journals. Marketers, school officials, government agencies, and online predators can collect data about young people through online teenage diaries. Herein lies the privacy paradox. Adults are concerned about invasion of privacy, while teens freely give up personal information. This occurs because often teens are not aware of the public nature of the Internet.

While privacy is well researched in the literature, there has been very little research on the social aspects of privacy in social networks. Most research on online privacy deals with users who share their information with e-commerce websites. In such a context, information sharing is usually mandatory and is part of a purchase process. Online communities, on the other hand, rely on information voluntarily supplied by their members. There has been little research on how privacy concerns impact this

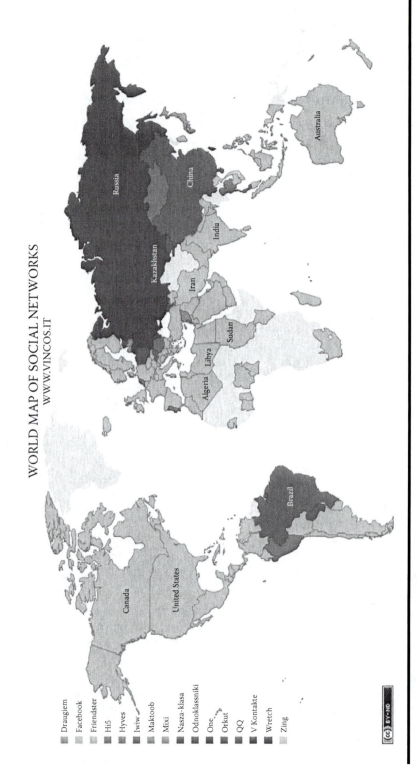

Figure 5.1 World map of social networks. (Created on Many Eyes [http://many-eyes.com] © IBM.)

Table 5.1 Most Visited Websites in the United States

1	Google.com
2	**Facebook.com**
3	Yahoo.com
4	**YouTube.com**
5	Wikipedia.org
6	Craigslist.org
7	**Blogger.com**
8	**Twitter.com**
	…
12	**MySpace**
	…
17	**LinkedIn.com**

Source: From Alexa.com, March 2010.

information sharing. This issue is further complicated by the fact that users in online communities share information not only with firms such as Facebook, but also with other members of their online community. Furthermore, it is well understood that privacy is a relative construct and a significant component of an individual's privacy concern depends on observing the behavior of others. Therefore, actions and intentions of other users are likely to affect users' privacy concerns.

Social networks present us with a unique opportunity to study the background of privacy concerns in a social context. In the context of e-commerce, privacy concerns are associated with decreased willingness to share information. In social computing communities, however, the impact of privacy is not yet clear. One might believe that community users are not highly privacy con-scious, since many of them exhibit the most private information on public venues such as Facebook or Flickr, and appear unconcerned about privacy risks. However, recent public debate suggests that users do attach importance to how the information they share in online communities is used.

Online social networks offer exciting new opportunities for interaction and communication, but also raise new privacy concerns. If online social networks are not carefully used then instead of bringing the blessings to the users, they will become a dangerously powerful tool for spammers, unscrupulous marketers, and others who may do serious harm to the users.

Privacy Revelation

Social networking sites share the basic purpose of online interaction and communication, but the specific goals and usage patterns change across different services. The most common scenario is based on the use of the participant's profile and the presentation of their network of friends. This approach can stretch in different directions. In dating websites, like match.com and Nerve, the profile is the critical component and there is no network of friends. In blogging sites like

LiveJournal and Blogger, profiles become secondary; networks may or may not be visible and blog entries take a central role.

Online social networking thus can change into classifieds in one direction and blogging in another direction. The way people share information on these online social networks is very different and depends on the site under consideration. Using a real name to present an account profile to the members of an online community may be encouraged on sites like Facebook; such networks try to connect a participant's profile to their real-life identities. Other websites like MySpace and Friendster tolerate use of real names; such sites create a thin layer of anonymity between the real-life and online profile by making only a part of the real name visible on the online profiles, i.e., showing only the first name while hiding the last name. Other websites, like match.com, discourage publishing real names and other personal contact information; sites like these attempt to protect the real-life identity of a person by making its link to the online profile more difficult.

Most social networking sites encourage the publication of personal and identifiable personal photos. The type of information revealed or found often revolves around different hobbies and interests, but can go in many other different directions, like information such as current and previous schools and employers; private information such as drinking and drug habits, and sexual and political preferences and orientation.

The visibility of information on online social networks changes all the time. In some sites any member may view any other member's profile. On other social networking sites access to personal information may be restricted to people that are part of the direct or extended network of the profile's owner. However, the visibility control of the information changes across different sites. People generally are happy to disclose as much information as possible to as many people as possible. Gross, Acquisti, and Heinz did an analysis of different fields used in Facebook profiles and the percentage of users filling them.

- 93.8% of users disclose their sex.
- 83.3% of users disclose their hometown.
- 87.1% of users disclose their high school.
- 45.1% of users disclose their home address.
- 59.8% of users filled out the About Me field.
- 67.8% of users disclose their Instant Messaging address.
- 83.8% of users disclose their birthday.
- 92.3% of users disclose their email address.
- 78.5% of users disclose their relationship status.

Privacy Implications

The privacy implications depend upon the amount of information provided, who can access that information, and how accurate that information is. Even if a social networking site protects the identity of a user, it may still be possible to link an online profile with the real-world identity of the person, for example through face identification. Often people have accounts on many social networking sites and usually they use the same picture across different sites, providing more information in their profile on some sites than others. So through face identification, if a link between different profiles can be constructed, then it may be possible to gather more information than would be possible from just one social network. Identification can also be archived. Even if the profile picture information is not used, demographic information can be used or obtained through other overlapping information like special hobbies, interests, etc.

Some social networks have started to expose their application programming interfaces (API) and have made it possible for developers to implement applications—one famous example is Facebook. There are numerous applications available on Facebook: users can play movie trivia, where they can answer questions and be ranked with their friends, and can find how closely their movie tastes match with that of their friends. Then there are some applications where users can mark different cities or countries they have visited, have lived in, or want to visit in the future. These applications can also help in the revelation of different kinds of information about a particular user. Usually when a user installs some application or performs some activity with some application, the user's network of friends are also notified about the activity, the friends are also invited to take part in the activity, and they can comment and share views about such activities.

How can this information be used? Once a third person has access to a social network, risks range from identity theft to even physical stalking, blackmailing, embarrassment, or other people getting to know information not meant to be shared with them. People can get e-mail addresses and identities of different messaging services used by the person, and this information can later be used to stalk the person; female users are especially the target of such kinds of stalking. The profile pictures on display can also be misused by persons with negative agendas. In some cases these are just forwarded to friends, but in other extreme cases these may be posted on inappropriate forums or websites. There have been some reported cases where people have used phone numbers to harass users.

The information shared on social networking websites is always available to the operating staff of the website, and also to the web hosting provider of that online social network. Such information may be stored indefinitely when the site's data is backed up even long after the user has removed his account from the online social network. This information can also be shared by either the social network provider or the web hosting provider with law enforcement agencies upon their request.

Threats of Online Social Networking

The casual posting of personal information on a digital medium might create a permanent record of users' indiscretions and failures of judgments that can be exploited by third-party commentary to produce a number of threats to the users. The potential threats that the users might face can be broadly categorized in four groups:

1. Privacy-related threats
2. Network and information security threats
3. Identity-related threats
4. Social threats

In the following subsections, we have described these threats.

Privacy-Related Threats

Digital Dossier of Personal Information

With the advancement of data mining technology and the reduction of cost of disk storage, the third party can create a digital dossier of personal data with the information revealed on the profiles of social networks. A common vulnerability is that more private attributes than the ones that are directly accessible by profile browsing can be accessed via search (e.g., a person's name and profile image is accessible via search on MySpace, Facebook and others, unless default privacy settings are changed). The information revealed on social networks can be exploited by an adversary to embarrass, blackmail, or even damage the image of the profile holder.

Face Recognition

Users of social networks often tend to add images to their individual profiles that can be used to identify the corresponding profile holders. Thus a stranger can use this data source for correlating profiles across services using face recognition, which is a part of the broader threat posed by so-called mash-ups. For example, a pseudoanonymous dating profile with an identified corporate website profile. As a result, an adversary can gather substantially more information about a user than intended.

Content-Based Image Retrieval

Most of the social networks have not employed any privacy controls over the images of the profiles to prevent the disclosure of information through Content-Based Image Retrieval (CBIR) yet. CBIR is an emerging technology which is able to match features, such as identifying aspects of a room (e.g., a painting) in very large databases of images, and thus increases the possibility of locating users. It opens up the possibility of deducing location data from apparently anonymous profiles containing images of users' homes. This can lead to stalking, unwanted marketing, blackmailing, and all other threats associated with unwanted disclosure of location data.

Image Tagging and Cross-Profiling

Users generally have the option to tag images with metadata such as the name of the person in the photo, a link to their social network profile (even if they are not the owner/controller of that profile), or even their e-mail address. An adversary can use this feature to slander well-known personalities or brands and gain profit from their reputation.

Difficulty of Complete Account Deletion

Users of social networks normally face more difficulty in deleting secondary information than in deleting their user accounts from an online social network. In some cases, such secondary information is almost impossible to remove. For instance the public comments a user has made on other accounts using their identity will remain online even after the poster's account has been deleted. The information that can't be removed can be used as a digital dossier.

Network and Information Security Threats

Spamming

The enormous growth of social networking sites has encouraged spammers to create unsolicited messages known as Social Network Spams to produce traffic overload in social networks. Social Network Spam may cause traffic overload, loss of trust, or difficulty in using the underlying application, as well as phishing and diversion to pornographic sites.

Cross Site Scripting, Viruses, and Worms

Social networks are vulnerable to cross-site scripting (XSS) attacks and threats due to widgets produced by weakly verified third parties. An adversary can use this vulnerability to compromise the account, to perform a phishing attack, and to spread the unsolicited content to e-mail and instant messaging (IM) traffic. Moreover, it can also be used for denial of service and associated loss of reputation.

Social Networking Aggregators

Some of the new applications such as Snag and ProfileLinker provide read/write access to several social networking accounts to integrate the data into a single web application. But such applications use weak authentication methods, resulting in increased vulnerability. The effects of this vulnerability are identity theft, zombification of the accounts, e.g., for XSS attacks or advertising, and loss of privacy for other members of the service by allowing searches across a broader base of data.

Identity-Related Threats

Phishing

A phisher can easily and effectively exploit the information available on social networks to increase the success rate of a phishing attack. Social networks are also vulnerable to social engineering techniques, which exploit low entry thresholds to trusted networks, and to scripting attacks, which allow the automated injection of phishing links.

Information Leakage

The privacy of online social networks is jeopardized, since an adversary can easily become a friend of a member of any restricted group by dissembling his identity and then accessing the private information that belongs to the members of only that group. Moreover, on many social networks such as MySpace, it is even possible to use scripts to invite friends. Some of the potential risks associated with this threat are leakage of private information, phishing for information, and conducting spamming and marketing campaigns.

Profile Squatting

A malicious attacker can create a fake profile to impersonate a famous person or a brand. Such profiles are usually created by people who know the personal details of a user and create a profile to impersonate him or her, thereby causing all sorts of problems for the victim. Profile squatting can do significant damage to the reputation of a person or brand. This may in turn result in financial damages and social embarrassment.

Social Threats

Stalking

Stalking can be a real side effect of using online social networks when not enough attention is paid to sharing information. A participant can reveal personal information including location, schedule, home address, and phone number in their profile, which can be used by an attacker for social stalking (threatening the victim through physical proximity, phone calls, e-mails, instant messages, or messaging on the service). Users generally also share their instant messaging accounts, which may include Yahoo! Messenger, MSN Messenger, Google Talk, and AOL Instant Messenger among others. Some of these services allow users to add friends or buddies to their list without their knowledge or first getting a confirmation from the person being added to the list. Once the person is in the buddy list, it is possible to send messages or track the online presence. The impact of cyber stalking on the victim is well known and can range from mild intimidation and loss of privacy to serious physical harm and psychological damage.

Corporate Espionage

Social engineering attacks using social networks are a growing but often under-rated risk to corporate IT infrastructure. The main risk here is the loss of corporate intellectual property, but gaining access to insiders may also be a component in a broad range of other crimes, such as hacking corporate networks to cause damage, blackmailing of employees to reveal sensitive customer information, and even access to physical assets.

Protecting Privacy in Social Networks

Online communities require you to provide personal information. They ask for at least a user name, e-mail address, and password when registering with these services. In the interest of community building and commercial marketing, later on the social networks might request the user to fill out a user profile that includes much more personal information, such as birth date, home and work addresses, home and work phone numbers, gender, marital status, occupation, instant messaging names, and more. These profiles are usually public, but some social networking sites allow their members to view profiles of any other members even if they are not in their social network of friends. It is usually a good idea not to post information that a person is not comfortable sharing with strangers. The comments posted are permanently recorded on the social networking site. As time goes by and users get to know other members of the community, the community might begin to feel casual and familiar, and users might be tempted to talk about their kids by name, mention where they work or live, or reveal information about valuable collections in their home that might not be listed in the profile or they might have refrained from publishing in their profile. As the discussions get casual, users sometimes may even mention when they plan to be out of town. Its usually a good idea to stay vigilant at all times, even if a member has been involved with a community for a long time. Members should not be fooled into a false sense of security.

What Can Users Do to Protect Privacy?

Some information is so revealing of individual identity that it should never posted on the public area of any website, for example social security number, phone numbers, home address. Social networking sites like Facebook, MySpace, LinkedIn, and similar sites have become incredibly popular because of their social factor as they help people stay in touch with friends or business contacts, and make new ones as well. To take advantage of their benefits, though, these services need people to share some personal information. That is where one should be cautious before sharing any information. People should understand the information that they share with the site, and think about the information the site will share and with whom. Use the privacy controls the site provides to better protect information. It is also important to know how the social networking site itself will use information.

Users should refrain from posting sensitive information on social networks, including details of their private life, work, and employers, even if these are well protected by the site's security mechanisms. There is always a danger of a hacker somehow getting access to the social network's server or just the user's account. Such a hacker may gain access to the private information and might post it on public places, where it may stay for a long period of time if a search engine like Google keeps a copy of said records in its cache.

Online communities offer several ways to ensure privacy, before joining a social network. Some of the things to look for are:

- Privacy policies that explain exactly what information the service will collect and how it might be used.
- User guidelines that outline a basic code of conduct for users on their sites. Sites have the option to penalize reported violators with account suspension or termination.
- Special provisions for children and their parents, such as family-friendly options geared towards protecting children under a certain age.
- Password protection to help keep the user account secure.
- E-mail addresses should be hidden in the profile or at least the social networking site should offer an option to hide or show e-mail addresses and stipulate who can see them. Users should have the option to select if only friends, friends of friends, everyone, or no one can see their e-mail address.
- E-mail address masking: Masking involves inserting a word or phrase in the middle of your regular e-mail address to help foil automated e-mail "harvesting" programs, for example: someone@nospam.example.com. However, as spammers become more sophisticated, their harvesting software might be able to recognize a masked e-mail address.

What Can Technology Do to Protect Privacy?

Social networks can make it easier for users to use privacy controls so that even a novice user can control what other people can see from their profile. When a user creates a new account on a social network the default settings should be such that the private profile entries are hidden or even the whole profile is hidden unless the user chooses to publish his profile to public or his friends later on. Warnings should be displayed and easy to understand. Online help should be available whenever a user chooses to change any of the privacy settings. Captchas can be used by the social networking sites to prevent information harvesting by automated bots. Even though these can be quite useful when guarding against automated scripts, normal users can get annoyed by them.

Conclusion

Social networking is still evolving, and new innovations and ideas are rapidly being implemented. Social networks are now targeting different mediums, and mobile media is one such medium. Online social networks are huge and much more loose than real life; some people in such networks have hundreds of friends in their profiles and may even have thousands through an extended profile, but still personal and sometimes sensitive information is freely and publicly available. Based on the information provided in their profiles, users expose themselves to various physical and online risks; these risks are not unique to just one social network but common to all of the social networks.

When participating in such social networks, users should be vigilant and should take special precautions before they expose their identities. Technology should make it easy for users to protect their privacy and privacy controls should be well placed and easy to use, so anyone can use them. We are watching social networking expand from websites to handheld devices and technologies such as blue-tooth and Global Positioning System (GPS) will play a crucial role in the mobile social networking arena. However it remains to be seen how users' privacy will be handled when such new ideas are implemented.

Social networks and applications have been churning out location-enabled features this year at an alarming rate. It's not just new networks that are playing in the location space—Google Buzz, Twitter, and possibly Facebook are all dipping their feet in the location-enabled pool. The new era in social media is no longer simply knowing *what* your friends are doing—it's knowing *where* they are doing it. As a greater number of location-based features have been rolled out, so too has greater attention been given to the potential privacy ramifications brought on by these new trends in social media.

TELECOMMUNICATIONS AND NETWORK SECURITY

Communications and Network Security

Chapter 6

IF-MAP as a Standard for Security Data Interchange

David O'Berry

"Soon to Be Ripped from the Headlines?"

Date: Christmas Day, 2021
Time: UTC/GMT +14 hours: 00:00:01
Location: Kiritimati, Christmas Island, Kiribati

The Kiribati Digital Modernization Program (KDMP), undertaken in 2021, has been successful and (while still a work in progress) is intended to function as an early warning beacon for significant digital events. This collaborative initiative included a consortium of commercial companies, the governments of several countries, and the participation of a small number of individuals around the world who realized early on the tenuous hold society had on the Techno-Industrial Revolution in the first decade of the twenty-first century. Often derided for their "fatalistic" view of the current digital world, this group of people worked continuously to educate and collaborate in order to attempt to make a difference when the inevitable happened. The purpose of this collaborative group, the Global Information Systems Transformation (GIST), was to protect the Global Information Grid (GIG) with extremely limited assets through application of open standards for autonomic data-sharing and response across all aspects of emergency management and defense. To that end, rather than wasting limited resources and space, the University of Hawaii's research facility on Kiribati was dual-purposed to serve as the very first Beacon Point Sensor (BPS) outpost, aptly named Standard Autonomic Field Engagement One (SAFE1). Quickly, New Zealand, understanding the gravity of the situation and closing window of opportunity, embarked on a massive upgrade of their infrastructure and autonomic digital response capabilities starting with the Chatham Islands and quickly moving to Auckland and beyond. A number of entities followed New Zealand's lead.

The code was innocent enough, tiny really...a couple of lines that had no meaning if executed by themselves. The problem is that the BOTs had done the work over the last decade before the sensor network went into place and now nearly every machine had small pieces of code embedded in flash, firmware, memristor-based machines, SCADA systems, hard-drives, SSDs, robots, toys, prosthetics, Wii v3, Xbox 1000s, old printers, refrigerators, washers and dryers, USB keys, cars, trucks, etc. Anything with space to store information and access to the Global Information Grid (GIG) was now a holding tank for the pieces of code that sought to bring the world back to what the "Luddite Group" (LG) called Previously Acceptable Reality or "PAR," as the press called it. Calling it a new "Decepticon Class" virus, the press release from the LG hits the newswires at 12:01:00.

12:00:02 Kiritimati took the brunt of the initial assault but did get data and a number of messages out using IF-MAP automatically from various dispersed BPSs via a wide assortment of communications channels to "Shepherd Collector Servers" (SCS) in the Chatham Islands. Chatham's entire sensor network went online immediately as it mobilized upstream resources to analyze the current attack from a vulnerability and risk perspective. SAFE1 stopped sending less than 30 seconds from initial communication, which meant that more than likely all available systems for transmission had been neutralized. The repercussions of that type of total failure also meant SCADA systems were at least malfunctioning, which equated to possible total loss of power, communications, water, etc. In the worst case, whatever had done this had corrupted the programs or given control to the terrorists, which in turn could possibly cause large-scale harm to the inhabitants of the island via normally trusted systems like water and electricity. Processing this data along the emergency management branch prediction IF-MAP servers upstream of the Chatham Islands in New Zealand, the system kicks off different processes that quickly alert geo-relevant authorities and aid organizations in order to respond to the potential humanitarian concerns. Profiles are automatically loaded based on standard information exchanged and response scenarios for all participating GIST members are put into action immediately. Using the power of the remainder of the network upstream, the emergency management teams will be constantly fed updated iterative and timely situational awareness information throughout their response efforts.

00:02:15 It's now just over two minutes from the initial catastrophic infection and the Chatham Islands have now gone dark but not before feeding over two minutes and several terabytes of data upstream to Auckland. Systems upstream across the entire world have already begun the process of closing the holes on local hosts via SCAP and XCCDF protocols enabled by IF-MAP transmission of critical information. SCS servers started running petabytes of data through analysis within milliseconds of the initial beacon through the distribution of discrete computing units out to the SETI for Security Cloud Endpoints updating the Distributed Threat Database (DTDB) for all subscribers. Now set to high alert, all endpoints are fully participating in distributed peer review on heightened sensitivity while marshalling additional processing power to shine a spotlight on an entire traffic stream when anomalies even resembling the known attack vector detailed in the DTDB are observed.

00:02:18 The comprehensive analysis and correlation of the attack vector from the network perspective is going through its 50th iteration dynamically attaching grid resources as it needs in order to complete the immense computations. In the same timeframe, New Zealand has leveraged network flowpoints to slow and in some cases stop the malicious catalyst code sequence. Digital circuit breakers upstream trip, shutting down all "unknown state" egress points from the initial infection area of the GIG while cleansing agent profiles from GIST participants outside of New Zealand are sent to inline (wired, wireless, etc.) devices further upstream to cordon off additional infectious behavior.

00:02:25   Circuit breakers slowly reset, allowing help from the external GIST participants to assist New Zealand proper in restoring any and all digital assets lost in the event. Emergency management personnel now have New Zealand as a base of operations in order to respond to Chatham and Kirimati. A joint task force of the military from several countries will be assisting and all of the pertinent information including potential attribution has been transferred to them. Law Enforcement in all potential LG operation zones has been put on alert and will act as soon as possible to begin their investigation and to put the culprits behind bars with all lawfully obtained pertinent information available to them.

00:03:00   The first known human analyst to participate, Thomas Anderson (HA1), makes a phone call to his superiors stating that a significant cyber event has potentially occurred.

00:05:00   HA1 calls back and reports that the incident has been contained and emergency personnel have been dispatched to the affected areas. There are no reports of human casualties but both Kirimati and the Chatham Islands will require extensive repair of digital and mundane assets. He reports that all military and law enforcement personnel have also been communicated the situational awareness information.

00:06:00–00:20:00   Anderson sits down at his console and fires up the collaboration portal. The chatter of the instant messaging scrolls faster and faster as the members of GIST sift through the first reports of SAFE locations worldwide. An air of disbelief permeates the conversation at first, quickly changing to incredulity that something like this could have happened under the noses of the entire world with so little warning. As he finishes the initial after-action report provided by the network, a sigh of relief mixed with fear escapes as he slowly shakes his head. Mr. Anderson feels very lucky.

"Context Matters"

Does the above seem far-fetched to you? While I am taking a bit of artistic license, to include my unfettered admiration of everything New Zealand, both sides of the above scenario are not only probable in the near future, but not that far from possible today. I always suffer over these chapters, and believe me the editor suffers with me, because I try and write on the very edge of current state so that when the books are actually published the information has at least a remote chance of being timely for the readers. That always proves to be a challenge. Of course, if it was easy to write these chapters then I guess it would take the fun out of it, right? Ok, so there is very little fun writing something like this because of the demands it places on you mentally to try and produce something worth reading, but I do believe it is important and, therefore, am here again with my humble offering to the InfoSec Gods. This is my third chapter for this book and I am approaching this a bit differently by only briefly touching on the ten thousand foot view before rapidly descending to actionable standards and plans for medium term-solutions where possible given the current status of the security community and its various participants.

I always want to give credit where it is due, so I want to be clear this chapter is more a compilation of various sources of information than it is groundbreaking in what I bring to you. At the same time, what I often find is that there is amazing work out there, but somehow it continues to stay within silos that hamper its ability to potentially rapidly expand the sphere of influence through reuse and collaboration. For instance, there are a number of people doing amazing work in this field and specifically here I want to thank Dr. Steve Venema, mentors like Steve Hanna and Will Pelgrin, Hal Tipton, John Banghart, Daniel Schmidt, Harley Parkes, Vint Cerf, Glenn Kowack, Rob Dixon, Simon Hunt, and Will Pelgrin's amazing CSIC team, along with various members of the Multi-State Information Sharing and Analysis Center (MS-ISAC), Tony Sager and his great staff, Ian Dobson from The Open Group, as well as a myriad of individuals not named here who as a whole have either directly contributed use cases, information, and ideas or have indirectly contributed over my career by helping me to simply think better in general about the opportunities we have to really make a significant difference in the "Digital Ecosystem" in the near future.

"Perfection is the Enemy of Progress"

From my perspective, this type of flexibility to innovate is critical to the long-term health and welfare and really the survival of the "Digital Ecosystem." The title of this section is a bit deceiving though, because to me true progress is not defined as some tightly locked-in standard controlled by a small number of the larger companies. These alliances look good on paper but the insidious "Open API" verbiage that gets thrown around is deceptive in that practitioners are still, in most cases, writing to their black box. At the same time (as I mentioned in last year's ISMH), smaller companies must kneel at the feet of the larger companies, in some cases begging to do business and working to stay in the good graces of their much larger peers. That is not a sustainable way to progress because smaller innovative companies like Triumfant, SignaCert, Imprivata, or NetWitness (to name a few I have personal knowledge of), as well as noncommercial entities and communities, oftentimes are either slowed or impeded completely from innovating and competing at full speed by the sheer gravity of the requirements of the larger organizations. Remember, "Open API" does not mean "Open Standards," and that is a distinction that has to be made, stressed, and enforced as we progress in order for a real discussion to take place. I have always put my organization's money and my professional reputation where my mouth is at every juncture possible. With the above challenges in mind, in many cases getting to a workable business solution that did not cripple my organization has been less than a direct path just simply based on what I call the "technology dis-innovation life cycle" illustrated in Figure 6.1.

Do I hate commercial companies? Of course not. I believe they must exist to innovate and move things forward at a pace that communities and state entities simply cannot manage. The problem comes in when a few of the larger "T-Rex" vendors decide that innovation is not all that profitable. That has been the current state over the last two decades and only recently have we really seen any sort of change for the better. In fact, for many years I have been stressing this, as one member of the audience at a presentation called it, "Militant Consumerism." This mentality has always been a part of my approach but it became much more tangible and visible a few years back. I supported contract requirements as well as the concept of "Centrally Distributed Computing" in this book series by writing:

> "Basically in this environment, we are watching the sampled data at different points in the system and as heuristics continue to evolve, we can decide whether or not to focus the more intensive capabilities of the forensic aspect of that network on our trouble spots. With the proliferation of headless attack vectors like printers, iPods, and iPhones there has to be a way of distributing the load of the visibility so that we have early warning indicators before things overwhelm the core. It has been proven

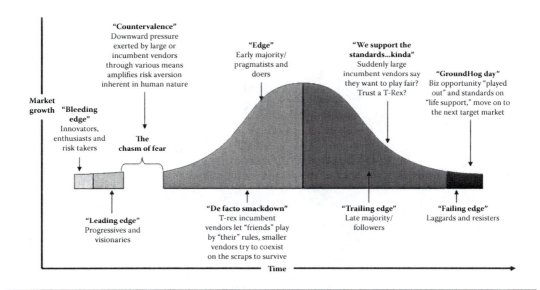

Figure 6.1 Technology dis-innovation life cycle. (Original work by David O'Berry with input from Steve Hanna. Adapted from Moore, G.A., *Crossing the Chasm*, Harper, 1991.)

that core defense simply does not work because of the drastic increase in bandwidth coming from the edge, the huge liability located in the endpoint including what data it sees and what it does with that data, and new valid "malware-like" software that serves valid business purposes while fraying the nerves of the security team. As we continue to move towards the evolution of more transient and distributed network security supplicants on these clients, we need to concern ourselves with network design that allows for the inclusion of this data in real time so that when it does get here we do not have to rip and replace yet again. Buying switches that are sFlow capable should be on the agenda while paying attention to both standards adherence in the past as well as roadmap postures for the future again comes to the forefront. Paying attention to how a router supports NetFlow and whether or not the company is really participating in the standards associated with communications in general should become a main criterion for our discussions. Recognizing how we are going to put that information to use and what we need to do in order to further the evolution of the industry needs to become a prime consideration if we are ever to get ahead of the curve."*

Again, that does not mean it has to be an "us versus them" model. It has to be a true partnership and we have to do our part as well. In fact, many commercial companies have really stepped up to the plate over the last two years and started to realize that building a better mousetrap in a truly open environment allows you to develop not only loyalty from current customers but gives you the ability to potentially leverage the power of the mob to have things created around your

---

* David O'Berry, "Enhanced Security Through Open Standards: The Path to a Stronger Global Digital Ecosystem," in *Information Security Management Handbook*, 6th ed. (Boca Raton: Auerbach Publications, 2007), Vol. 3.

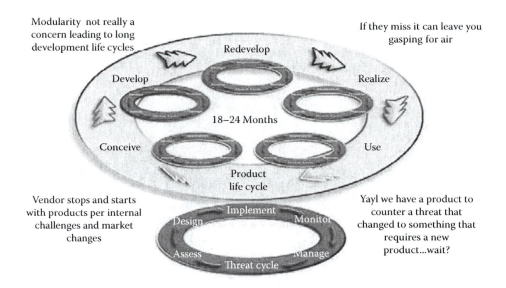

Figure 6.2 Product cycle versus threat cycle: an illustration of gaps.

framework that otherwise would simply not have occurred or would have taken much more time than made them business feasible to weaponize. This directly correlates to the "product versus threat cycle diagram" illustrated in Figure 6.2.

Revisiting "Centrally Distributed Computing," "Threat State Databases," and "SETI for Security"

You would be amazed at how the comments on the simple idea of a "centrally distributed computing model" have changed over the last half a decade. It was not that long ago that operating expenses ruled the day and security was still an afterthought. What that management philosophy promoted was single homogenous vendor solutions that appeared on the surface as a more cost-effective, enterprise-friendly path to take. The rapid changes in both the attack vectors and the seeming inability of commercial-only solutions to fill the huge and rapidly evolving gaps have truly created an environment where innovation, with the support of the community of consumers, can be reintroduced into the equation. It is not unlike the communities that have grown up around certain code or open source projects and within it we see the real power of the mob. We get an indication of what is possible when rework is minimized and open collaborative initiatives are given true support. The only real way from both a technological and societal aspect to begin to harness this power is to have loosely coupled but potentially tightly integrated control at the center while leaving power at the edge. This will allow each subsequent addition to the GIG to potentially contribute to the system load required to diminish risk, thereby possibly averting a collapse under the weight of the rapidly proliferating number of nodes.

Last year in the Information Security Handbook, 6th edition, Volume 4, I wrote:

"Deployment of protections coupled with correlation of the information coming back from our increasingly complicated environments is pretty much make or break going forward. In a previous chapter, published in the 6th Edition Volume 3 of the Information Security Management Handbook, I mentioned and defined the flexible "Endpoints and Flowpoints" concept in a fairly generic way. This type of flex defense concept can adapt as you go to attempt to combat the increasingly intense evolution of threat and attack vectors in the next few years. The Mississippi River analogy still holds here as the sheer size and the overwhelming flood of information combine to overwhelm most if not all typical castle and moat type defenses. You cannot dam the Mississippi River but you can dam some tributaries while you watch the Mississippi and that type of thinking needs to be heavily considered for future deployments in networks. Single go/no go calls on endpoints as they come in to the network are far less valuable in this new environment. At a rapidly accelerating pace, various pieces of information need to be collected and then combined and assessed to provide access control and monitoring adapted to a myriad of situations. Again while this has existed in some form for years, the changes possible when enabled via an agile scalable framework like IF-MAP are very powerful. By sharing this information freely amongst various devices from all of the companies in your network, activity can be correlated with users to identify behavior that is anomalous for that user, eventually allowing the administrator or an automated system to decide the best course of action and then to enable it to take that action. Watching this diverse information stream with concepts from the past would have been nearly impossible based on both false positives as well as simply the inability of many of the practitioners in the field to fully grasp the nuances of the required skill-sets for sometimes incredibly intricate manipulation of the interfaces necessary to be successful. I remember having this conversation with several of my friends and colleagues and we always came back to the question of why IF-MAP was necessary and why it mattered so much. I would bring up threats and use cases and they would detail the various things they had to approximately do the same thing. We would venture into harder core concepts and they would detail the sometimes fairly complicated data extracts and imports, the array of custom filters, the various pieces of command and control within their networks most of the time from the same company, and invariably we would broach the amount of care they had to take to make sure anything they bought fit with their management model. After this exercise with several friends, it became painfully clear to most of them that while they could do this it could not be and should not be an assumed skill-set or even valid method of operation for our profession going forward. It simply did not scale.

As we move to drastically increase the visibility points throughout, that scalability becomes critical. As the next iterations of NBAD evolve we need to be able to truly innovate in the development of our strategies in order to enable the network to trigger responses to stimuli that begin to capture a lot more information at the first hint of trouble. The increased participation of both traditional and non-traditional endpoints in the security environment around them will allow, through IF-MAP, for the profession to potentially graduate to a "Threat State Database" as one manifestation. IF-MAP is a cornerstone of this type of concept but is only one of the tools in the box. As things like Common Uniform Driver Architecture evolve, projects like SETI can be imitated with the goal of thousands of individual clients participating in a grid working on the distributed task of a more secure ecosystem. Open source clients that serve various functions would all be IF-MAP enabled and could then possibly fill dual roles of both subscribing to information to strengthen their overall posture as well as publishing what they see around them. Effectively they each become individual sensors in their own right. This in turn allows for a weighting of input and potentially a furtherance of the vetting of information going into the repositories. This is a distributed peer review of sorts and while the input would have to be vetted to ascertain trust levels, it could be another indicator stored in the MAP that gives an additional clue as to the state of the network based more on what the individual clients see around them and less on what they tell the network about themselves. This weighting of input could be adjusted as warranted and would potentially yield an important piece of the equation. The concept of "Federated Security" is not really new but the achievability of it has certainly been a bit of a pipe dream for some time. A truly comprehensive picture of not only your enterprise but of the portions of partner enterprises that matter to you is a potential force magnifier for defense. Real-time information flowing to an open standards-based repository allows you the ability to quickly focus efforts and resources potentially before an area becomes a concern. This on the fly tuning would simply not have been even conceivable in heterogeneous networks a few years ago and yet with the IF-MAP and Trusted Computer Group's newest TNC specifications, it seems like we are finally at the cusp of a true OODA or Boyd's Loop interactive decision-cycle based on timely feedback to each action and decision.*

It is clear from the above, my previous work in this series of books, as well as my work within the community, that I am a huge proponent of completely open standards for a number of reasons. Reiterating, I believe that control of the supply/demand value chain must be a partnership between the producers of technology and the consumers of technology. It has to be so because no single participant in the value chain can take on the responsibility. So how do we get there from here? What are the potential pieces, groups, and solutions that can move us down the path to a more secure, manageable, efficient digital ecosystem? The concept of open standards is a fairly simple one and has been discussed at length in previous chapters. For specifics though, we need to consider organizations and current capabilities that can be weaponized on a large scale. They definitely do not all come from one source, with some taking form as entities like Trusted Computing Group (TCG) and the Open Group (TOG) while others are government entities like the National Security Agency, or National Institute of Standards and Technology (NIST), or Department of Defense (DoD). Still others are part of the communities that have grown up around the tools that practitioners have used to do their jobs (e.g., NMAP and Snort). Of course we cannot leave out formal standards organizations like the IETF, IEEE, etc., because despite drawbacks stemming from a fairly dated approach, they do play an important role. From the commercial side, we have companies both large and small that see the value of an environment where products are capable of working together and the best of the best can be utilized where it is needed. We have companies like Mitre who maintain and push forward on initiatives like OVAL, and we have companies like Google, Juniper, Symantec, Infoblox, etc. that not only participate in critical standards organizations but also sponsor working groups to attempt to really get a handle on the rapidly evolving technology curve and its impact on current state. We have smaller aggressive

---

* David O'Berry, "Achieving Global Information Systems Transformation (GIST) through Standards: Foundations for Standards-Based Network Visibility via IF-MAP and Beyond," in *Information Security Management Handbook*, 6th ed. (Boca Raton: Auerbach Publications, 2007), Vol. 3.

companies like Triumfant and SignaCert that have the technology and the desire to really change the future. Beyond that, we have individuals that care and that want to make a difference. Those are too numerous to name (they know who they are), but my hat is off to each and every one of them. Each of the above participates because they see the potential proliferation of truly agile solutions as a game changer and life saver. My contention is that humanity will participate in its own survival if given the chance, so we must make sure we are inclusive and open minded at every juncture so that the industry and eventually the entire ecosystem become proactive instead of consistently reactive.

The Game Is in Progress: The Current Players Are….

NIST/NSA/DoD/DHS, etc.

The usual suspects when it comes to tinfoil hat theorists (except maybe NIST). I could say more but then I would have to…! In reality these organizations have done some amazing work that stands whole and complete outside of their respective organizations. The critical role they are playing is only going to accelerate as the world gets even more complicated and dangerous. At the same time, the NSA and NIST specifically have gone out of their way to not only be inclusive but to stay as open and transparent as possible. They may not disclose some things, but down this path they have been religiously anything but secretive. They see the storm that is upon us and realize that the worst is far from over and have gone the extra mile to give us something we can really work with in the community without the "black helicopter" syndrome rearing its ugly head.

Trusted Computing Group

Why recreate for the sake of an ego when we can just use industry standards, focused groups/ organizations, and open standards that are already out there? We should not even consider that path, especially considering the current debacle in "cloud" standards organizations. A vehicle that makes sense to start is TCG with now more than 100 member organizations. The organizations vary in size, from the smallest to largest vendors, while also including a growing number of customers. The fruits of this group include accepted, and in some cases ingrained, products and concepts like Trusted Platform Module and recently standards-based full disk encryption, as well as initiatives that should have been accepted as standards years ago like Network Access Control from their Trusted Network Connect (TNC) working group. The group has gone out of its way to be as inclusive as possible and everything published by it, including programs like the certification for standards compliance, is both open and vendor agnostic. The group was founded and has evolved in pursuit of the singular goal of helping users to protect information in any and every form it takes.

In order to accomplish that task, the group has specifically targeted the development, definition, and promotion of open specifications, all targeted towards "Trusted Computing." This includes all facets of the digital interaction including software and interfaces as well as the base hardware platforms covering everything from PCs to printers and peripherals. TCG has done this while maintaining an open architecture and complete vendor neutrality.*

---

* Trusted Computing Group. "about_tcg" About TCG. www.trustedcomputinggroup.org. June 2010 and Dr. Steve Venema, personal communication, May 2010.

The Open Source Community

Per my friend and colleague Rob Dixon, let us not forget open source software, because many of us rely on these tools every day. Rob writes:

> "Specifically within this arena, NMAP – written by Gordon Lyon, known to most as Fyodor Vaskovich, has been the de facto standard for network mapping for many years. Many commercial tools are based on or rely on the output from NMAP. With the recent addition of NSE (NMAP Scripting Engine) the possibilities are endless. NMAP enters the network vulnerability scanner arena. Many believe NMAP will be what NESSUS used to be to the open source community." (Rob Dixon, personal communication, June 12, 2010)

Rob specifically mentions NMAP here and in thinking it through this is exactly the type of open community that is going to be critical for us to leverage as we progress, for a number of reasons, not the least of which is just how powerful something like it becomes in an open SCAP/IF-MAP type world. Separate even from that is just the basic concept of a community that produces without having to get the blessings of larger vendors. The scalability and flexibility to solve current and future problems this can potentially enable in the ecosystem is unparalleled by anything we have witnessed so far in computing history.

Public/Private Cooperative Ventures and YOU!

So the easy part of this is mentioning companies like MITRE who steward incredibly important initiatives like Common Vulnerability and Exposures (CVE) and Open Vulnerability and Assessment Language (OVAL) for the community and do so in an open and transparent manner by involving both the supply and demand side of the equation, including vendors as well as the customers they serve. For instance, MITRE has copyrighted and trademarked both OVAL and CVE in order to ensure they remain free and open standards. It also lends itself to legally protecting the ongoing use of it and any resulting content by the community as a whole. The harder part of this is the involvement by the individual like you or myself, who still seems to almost not know where or when to try and get involved in things that truly affect not only your business enterprise but the very demand-driven economy many of us have grown so fond of throughout the world. How do we even start? After you get to the end of this chapter, I hope you will have an idea of how to reach out to your current partners and start participating.

The Game Pieces or "Where's the Beef?!!?"

The above organizations and a host of others have not been idle over the past decade and so there are a number of things already existing in the body of standards work that can be leveraged as the foundation pieces for progression. There is no way to adequately cover these topics in depth, nor to mention all of the possibilities or even all of the current standards works in progress in the space allotted. Instead, I will concentrate on SCAP as a suite of protocols, OVAL as a key foundation language that is also used within SCAP, IF-MAP as a connector, and the required groundwork practices and procedures enabled by the above such as Secure Configuration Management as well as what I call Standard Secure Configuration Management (S^2CM). I will also work in some base and slightly more advanced use cases before moving on to the reasons and methods the community can and must use to push this initiative forward in a more cohesive manner.

Secure Content Automation Protocol (SCAP)

"Attack of SCAP: The Community Strikes Back"

Daniel Schmidt wrote:

SCAP is a suite of standards that are used to

- Establish common enumerations for software flaws, security-related configuration issues, and product names
- Determine if specific software flaws, configuration issues, patches, or products are present on a system
- Accurately and consistently communicate the impact of security issues while providing transparency regarding how the score was derived
- Enable integration and management of critical Computer Network Defense and IT configuration information.*

That's about as clear as you can get as far as the function of SCAP. As far as form is concerned, the most important aspect to remember is that, although a NIST initiative, SCAP is a synthesis of truly open and interoperable specifications that was developed and continues to incorporate the *community's* ideas and participation. Probably one of the greatest strengths of SCAP is the participation by an incredibly diverse community of participants that truly want to make a difference in the current environment.

At its core, SCAP 1.1 (there may be a new version when this hits) is a suite of technical standards. The seven current specifications within 1.1 are XCCDF, OVAL, OCIL, CPE, CCE, CVE, and CVSS. Yes, I know I need to spell those out and I do below, but I worried I might create a buffer overflow in Word if I did it all on one line! The specifications are divided into three categories: languages, enumerations, and metrics.

For context, it is my expectation that SCAP 1.1 will come out of draft by the time you read this and so I am going to proceed with it instead of rehashing 1.0. In fact, 1.1 is in use currently in some organizations and based on the loosely coupled design, individual protocols within the suite actually progress at their own pace. If for some reason it does not clear draft then the draft can be found at the link below. If it is finalized then the page should link over or be replaced by the current 800-126.†

SCAP Design, Purpose, and Flow

Daniel Schmidt wrote:

"As discussed previously, the volume of vulnerabilities and threats and diverse nature of the typical enterprise IT architecture is beyond the ability of a human to manage on a per-threat, per-asset basis. Machine-consumable standards to uniformly describe asset, vulnerability, and threat data in a fashion that can be consumed and correlated automatically, in near real time is the only realistic option. To start with, all hardware and software assets must share a common naming scheme. This was achieved by

---

* Daniel Schmidt, "Security Automation: A New Approach to Managing and Protecting Critical Information [Electronic version]," *IAnewsletter* 13, no. 1 (2010).
† Steven Quinn, David Waltermire, Christopher Johnson, Karen Scarfone, John Banghart (2009) "The Technical Specification for the Security Content Automation Protocol (SCAP) SCAP Version 1.0," The National Institute of Standards and Technology, http://csrc.nist.gov/publications/PubsSPs.html#SP-800-126-Rev.%201.

development of the Common Platform Enumeration (CPE) specification and CPE dictionary that is now hosted in the NVD, where it is available to the global community."*

Daniel makes a number of valid points in a short paragraph. We know the threat landscape and it is not encouraging. We also know resources are not on the upswing, especially from a security perspective. End-nodes are proliferating and unfortunately software development is not getting all that much better (maybe worse), while evidently fuzzing techniques are rapidly evolving using botnets and grid/parallel concepts. With all of these things bearing down on us, for the "digital ecosystem" to survive we require:

1. Vulnerabilities to be identified in a uniform manner.
2. Risks posed by each vulnerability must be assessed automatically within its own native environment.
3. Assets must be uniformly identified by a group of CPEs.
4. Platform enumeration must enable software flaws (CVE) and configuration settings (CCE) to be uniquely identified for each individual software and hardware component.
5. Configurations (CCE) for a particular platform (CPE) must be able to be tested (OVAL) and packaged in a checklist (XCCDF) that can be consumed by SCAP-validated tools that manage the platforms.
6. Consumption and correlation of data in order to meet compliance requirements must occur.
7. Standards-based feeds that would then supply the data to automatically populate certification and accreditation activities iteratively must be created.

Daniel Schmidt wrote:

[Figure 6.3] "demonstrates the overlapping functionality of the various SCAP components to integrate asset, vulnerability, configuration, and compliance reporting under a comprehensive and interoperable set of standards, consumable by tools, and therefore enabling an automated response to network security threats."[†]

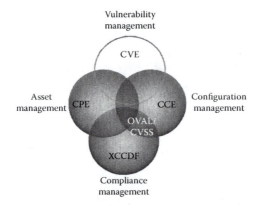

Figure 6.3 SCAP—A new approach.

* Schmidt, "Security Automation."
[†] Ibid.

Languages

SCAP languages provide a standardized means for identifying what practitioners need to evaluate while also allowing us to check the current state of any and all systems that adhere to the standard. The three current language standards within the SCAP suite are:

eXtensible Configuration Checklist Description Format (XCCDF) 1.1.4

XCCDF is a specification language for expressing security configuration checklists, vulnerability alerts, and other related documents. The specification is designed to support information interchange, document generation, organizational and situational tailoring, automated compliance testing, and compliance scoring. An XCCDF document represents a structured collection of system assessment rules for some set of target systems. The specification also defines a data model and format for storing results of assessing an XCCDF benchmark. The intent of XCCDF is to provide a uniform means of expressing security checklists and the results of checklist evaluation.[*]

Open Vulnerability Assessment Language (OVAL) 5.6

OVAL is used to express standardized, machine-readable rules that can be used to assess the state of a system. Under SCAP, OVAL is commonly used to determine the presence of vulnerabilities and insecure configurations. A set of instructions used to check for a security problem, such as an incorrect minimum password length setting, is known as an OVAL Definition. A file containing one or more OVAL Definitions (often hundreds or even thousands) is known as an OVAL Definition file.[†]

Open Checklist Interactive Language (OCIL) 2.0

Open Checklist Interactive Language is officially Part of SCAP 1.1 DRAFT located at http://scap. nist.gov/specifications/ocil/ The Open Checklist Interactive Language defines a framework for expressing a set of questions to be presented to a user and corresponding procedures to interpret responses to these questions. Although the OCIL specification was developed for use with IT security checklists, the uses of OCIL are by no means confined to IT security. Other possible use cases include research surveys, academic course exams, and instructional walkthroughs.[‡]

XCCDF documents are made up of one or more rules. XCCDF rules are usually high-level definitions of technical system (hardware, software, etc.) checks. XCCDF rules are flexible and do not mandate how checks should be performed. In a loosely coupled, tightly integrated design, the rule actually points to other XML documents (e.g., OVAL Definition files) for the granular mechanism and instructions needed to perform the checks. Principally, XCCDF is the list by which everything else runs. It seeks to standardize how security checklists, benchmarks, and related documents are created and then stored. It is the foundation for expression of various checks.

OVAL (as previously mentioned) is a set of definitions broken down into vulnerability, patch, inventory, and compliance. Each defines conditions associated with its realm and are referenced,

---

[*] Steven Quinn, David Waltermire, Christopher Johnson, Karen Scarfone, John Banghart (2009) "The Technical Specification for the Security Content Automation Protocol (SCAP) SCAP Version 1.1," The National Institute of Standards and Technology, http://csrc.nist.gov/publications/drafts/800-126-r1/second-public-draft_sp800-126r1-may2010.pdf.

[†] Trusted Computing Group. "about_tcg" About TCG. www.trustedcomputinggroup.org. June 2010.

[‡] Quinn et al., "Technical Specification, Version 1.1."

within the SCAP suite, by XCCDF. OVAL is the what, the why, and sometimes the how. It allows you, deterministically, to run a series of "standards-based syntax" questions against an asset that should return objective measures of current state. Pretty basic, right? It also does a lot more and I will go into that in more depth later.

OCIL is a method and framework that enables systems to be checked that cannot be evaluated without some human interaction or feedback. It accomplishes this basically by presenting questions to its intended users in a standard language format. It includes standard syntax for the questions posed to users as well as instructions that guide those users towards an answer. Additional processes such as acceptance of responses, transfer of artifacts, and eventually evaluation of results are also included. Extrapolating OCIL's potential, we can easily see that it has far-reaching implications based on the fact that so much of what we do still requires some type of "analog" input from users both within IT and outside of the profession.

Enumerations

The goal of SCAP enumerations is to provide standards-based naming formats to facilitate open-sharing without having to constantly negotiate definitions between systems. The maintenance of an associated dictionary of items associated with those standards is also critical.

Common Configuration Enumeration (CCE)

"The Common Configuration Enumeration, or CCE, assigns unique entries (also called CCEs) to configuration guidance statements and configuration controls to improve workflow by facilitating fast and accurate correlation of configuration issues present in disparate domains. In this way, it is similar to other comparable data standards such as the Common Vulnerability and Exposure (CVE) List, which assigns identifiers to publicly known system vulnerabilities."[*]

Did you get that? Basically, as mentioned above there are hundreds and sometimes thousands of settings associated with configurations of software, hardware, firmware, etc. Manually setting these is quickly growing beyond the ability of any organization of any size and this standardization allows for the consumption of configuration management changes in an automatic fashion using XCCDF checklists or OVAL, etc.

Common Platform Enumeration (CPE) 2.2

"CPE is a structured naming scheme for information technology systems, platforms, and packages. Based upon the generic syntax for Uniform Resource Identifiers (URI), CPE includes a formal name format, a language for describing complex platforms, a method for checking names against a system, and a description format for binding text and tests to a name."[†]

Hand in hand with CCE is the CPE, which enforces a common naming scheme across all hardware and software platforms. The practical application of this is called the CPE dictionary, which is available to the global community. It is currently hosted at the National Vulnerability Database website and is a list of well over 17,000 official CPE product names. The dictionary is in

---

[*] Mitre Corporation, "CCE faqs," About CCE, http://cce.mitre.org/about/faqs.html, June 2010.
[†] Mitre Corporation, "CPE faqs," About CPE, http://cpe.mitre.org/about/index.html, June 2010.

XML format and available to the public via the web. The CPE dictionary is currently generated daily (as needed) to add new products to the dictionary or update existing dictionary entries.

CPE is used by SCAP in the following ways:

- XCCDF – In an XCCDF checklist, CPE Names can be used to identify the hardware or software platform to which an XCCDF object (e.g., benchmark, profile, group, rule) applies.
- CCE – CPE Names can be associated with configuration vulnerabilities to identify platforms covered by CCE technical mechanisms.
- CVE – CVEs are related to one or more product platforms expressed as CPEs. The mapping of CPEs to CVEs is performed by NVD analysts and is published in the NVD vulnerability data feed.*

Common Vulnerabilities and Exposures (CVE)

> "CVE is a dictionary of unique, common names for publicly known software flaws. This common naming convention allows sharing of data within and among organizations and enables effective integration of services and tools."[†]

The CVE was created principally to address the differences in vulnerability names and descriptions. The inconsistency of schemas and naming conventions as well as descriptors in the past had created a great deal of confusion. Anyone that adheres to the CVE naming conventions, which is required to use SCAP effectively, is able to use terms that all security practitioners can agree mean the same thing. While this may seem like a fairly basic concept, believe me it is not. To get an idea of how the profession has communicated in the past, just imagine the Tower of Babel in the Bible, but worse.

A significant practical application of standard naming involving both CPE and CVE is illustrated by the National Vulnerability Database. John Banghart nut-shelled the concept and detailed the actual real-world application, its benefits, and its scope as currently implemented.

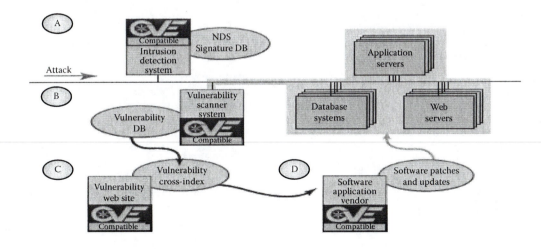

---

* Quinn et al., "Technical Specification, Version 1.1."
† Ibid.

Schmidt wrote:

National Vulnerability Database

The NVD is the federal government repository of standards-based vulnerability management reference data. The NVD contains information regarding vulnerabilities (software flaws and misconfigurations), including impact measurements, detection techniques, remediation assistance, and security control mappings. NVD search and publication capabilities provide access to all publicly available federal vulnerability resources and references to industry resources. NVD also contains a statistics engine to enable users to gain a deeper scientific understanding of the nature of published vulnerabilities and associated trends. NVD supports SCAP by making SCAP standard reference data readily available to industry and government agencies.

Vulnerability Search Engine

NVD currently contains over 38,000 vulnerability advisories with an average of 14 new vulnerabilities added daily. NVD provides basic and advanced online searching capabilities. The basic search allows users to search for vulnerabilities containing specific words or phrases of interest with the ability to limit results to vulnerabilities published within the "Last 3 Months" or "Last 3 Years." The basic search criteria can also be tailored to retrieve vulnerabilities associated with United States Computer Emergency Readiness Team (US-CERT) Technical Cyber Security Alerts or Vulnerability Notes or vulnerabilities for which SCAP automated check content is available. The NVD "Advanced Search" option provides additional search capabilities, including searching by—

- CVE identifier of CPE vendor or product name
- Category (e.g., buffer errors, cross-site scripting, input validation)
- Date of publication or last modification
- CVSS Version 2 Impact Metrics
- NVD CVE Publication.

NVD also provides the ability for Web download of vulnerability XML files that contain the core vulnerability data as well as CVSS impact metrics and CPE identifiers for affected products. The CVE XML files are available by year—

- Vulnerabilities by year (2003–2008)
- Vulnerabilities prior to and including 2002
- All recently published or recently updated vulnerabilities.*

CVE is used in conjunction with other SCAP specifications to satisfy the following use cases:

- *XCCDF*: In an XCCDF checklist, CVEs are used to uniquely identify which software flaw vulnerabilities are of interest (i.e., flaws that are to be checked during the evaluation of the checklist).
- *CVSS*: CVSS scores are associated with CVE entries to uniformly express the fundamental characteristics of the software flaw and to provide a severity score based on these characteristics.

---

* John Banghart, "The Security Content Automation Protocol (SCAP) [Electronic version]," *IAnewsletter* 13, no. 1 (2010).

▪ *OVAL*: Including the specific CVE entry in the OVAL metadata enables a reviewer to accurately understand the basis for a given OVAL definition such as a vulnerability or patch test.

Official Vendor Statements on CVE Vulnerabilities

▪ NVD provides an open forum to industry to allow comments to be submitted regarding CVE vulnerabilities affecting their products. Product vendors possess a great depth of knowledge regarding their products and are uniquely positioned to comment on the nature and scope of these vulnerabilities. Organizations can use the service in a variety of ways. For example, they can provide configuration and remediation guidance, clarify vulnerability applicability, provide deeper vulnerability analysis, dispute third-party vulnerability information, and explain vulnerability impact. The set of "official vendor statements" is available as an XML feed from the NVD Data Feed page.[*]

Metrics

"SCAP vulnerability measurement and scoring systems provide the ability within SCAP to measure and evaluate specific vulnerability characteristics to derive a vulnerability severity score."[†]

Common Vulnerability Scoring System (CVSS) 2.0

▪ Developed by the CVSS Special Interest Group (CVSS-SIG), CVSS 2.0 enables practitioners to get a better picture of total risk through a deterministic metrics-based assessment of vulnerabilities by providing an objective measurement of risks posed by specific vulnerabilities. It is composed of three scores to include base, environmental, and temporal. Base is consistent across all environments and times, environmental is specific to organizations, and temporal is any and all things that affect potential proliferation including "in the wild" aspects of code written or zero day situations disclosed before vendors can mobilize. The flexibility of three scores allow customization of individual events within disparate organizations but with a commonality that can be easily communicated.[‡]

From a practical application perspective, the CVSS has a number of applications, as illustrated by the large repository of scores already in place.

John Banghart wrote:

"The CVSS provides an open framework for communicating the characteristics and impacts of IT vulnerabilities. Its quantitative model ensures repeatable, accurate measurement while enabling users to see the underlying vulnerability characteristics that were used to generate the scores. Thus, CVSS is well suited as a standard measurement system for industries, organizations, and governments that need accurate and consistent vulnerability impact scores. NVD provides CVSS scores for almost all publicly

---

[*] Banghart, "SCAP"; Quinn et al., "Technical Specification, Version 1.1."
[†] Quinn et al., "Technical Specification, Version 1.1."
[‡] Banghart, "SCAP"; First.org, "CVSS faqs," About CVSS, http://www.first.org/cvss, June 2010.

known vulnerabilities. In particular, NVD supports the CVSS version 2 standard for all CVE vulnerabilities. NVD provides CVSS "base scores," which are derived from the innate, immutable characteristics of each vulnerability. NVD does not currently assign 'temporal scores' (scores that change over time due to events external to the vulnerability); however, NVD provides a CVSS score calculator to allow a user to add temporal data and to calculate environmental scores (scores customized to reflect the impact of the vulnerability on an organization). This calculator contains support for government agencies to customize vulnerability impact scores based on FIPS 199 System ratings."*

Again, it will take some work but there is no reason to recreate when we can borrow, especially considering the staggering amount of great work already done in this arena.

SCAP Vulnerability Assessment

As SCAP stands now, vulnerabilities are basically defined as flaws in software. I would add hardware and especially firmware, which create potential attack vectors or security holes through which an attack could happen. It does not mean that an attack occurred; it simply means a vulnerability provides a potential avenue for such an attack. One of the most compelling areas for initial significant gains with SCAP is in the enablement of interoperability among vulnerability scanners and reporting tools. This type of standards-based interworking has the potential to deliver rapid but consistent detection and reporting of any number of flaws. At the same time, working with IF-MAP and other aspects of the suite you could quickly see autonomic remediation capabilities that currently require a great deal of manual work or scripting that is fairly arcane to most practitioners. As an illustration, the below use case is pretty powerful.

Use Case: SCAP Vulnerability Assessment Using XCCDF and OVAL

Effective vulnerability assessment using a combination of SCAP components requires the following data sources:

For an SCAP Vulnerability Assessment to be performed by the appropriate SCAP-validated product, the following conditions SHALL be met:

1. The XCCDF <xccdf:Benchmark> element SHALL contain references to one or more CPEs.
2. XCCDF Vulnerability Scanning SHALL generate an XCCDF Results file. The XCCDF Results document SHALL include a result for each rule that was evaluated during the scan.
3. Each Rule specified in an XCCDF benchmark SHALL include an <ident> element containing a CVE reference, where an appropriate reference exists.
4. Each Rule specified in an XCCDF benchmark SHALL reference a specific OVAL vulnerability, patch, or inventory definition; except in cases where no automated mechanism exists to express a check in OVAL.
5. Each Rule specified in an XCCDF benchmark SHALL reference an OCIL questionnaire ONLY for cases where there is no automated mechanism and the checks require human feedback.

---

* Banghart, "SCAP."

6. If OVAL Results are generated:
   a. OVAL Results SHALL be expressed in compliance with the OVAL Results schema, and
   b. OVAL Results documents SHALL include the results of every OVAL Definition used to generate the reported rule results.
7. If OCIL Results are generated:
   a. OCIL Results SHALL be expressed in compliance with the OCIL schema, and
   b. OCIL Results documents SHALL include the results of every OCIL questionnaire used to generate the reported rule results.
8. If a CVE reference is specified in an XCCDF benchmark rule, then that reference SHALL match the CVE reference found in the associated OVAL Definition(s).*

Real-World Use Case: National Checklist Program

Theory or lab environments are always useful but sometimes do not translate to the real world. With that in mind, NIST set out to attempt to leverage some of the current work the community had done along with their own. The goal was to come up with a program that would not only be a number of steps in the right direction but would also lay the groundwork for automatic consumption of what was produced without being forced to continually rework content. To that end, they established the National Checklist Program. Daniel Schmidt had a solid write-up that I include below.

John Banghart wrote:

National Checklist Program (NCP)

There are many threats to users' computers, ranging from remotely launched network service exploits to malicious code spread through emails, malicious Web sites, and the download of infected files. Vulnerabilities in information technology (IT) products are discovered daily, and many ready-to-use exploitation techniques are widely available on the Internet. Because IT products are often intended for a wide variety of audiences, restrictive security configuration controls are usually not enabled by default, so many out-of-the- box IT products are immediately vulnerable. In addition, identifying a reasonable set of security settings for many IT products is a complicated, arduous, and time consuming task, even for experienced system administrators. To facilitate development of security configuration checklists for IT products and to make checklists more organized and usable, NIST established the NCP. The goals of the NCP are to—

- Facilitate development and sharing of checklists by providing a formal framework for vendors and other checklist developers to submit checklists to NIST
- Provide guidance to developers to help them create standardized, high-quality checklists that conform to common operations environments
- Help developers and users by providing guidelines for making checklists better documented and more usable
- Encourage software vendors and other parties to develop checklists
- Provide a managed process to review, update, and perform maintenance of checklists
- Provide an easy-to-use repository of checklists
- Provide checklist content in a standardized format

---

* Quinn et al., "Technical Specification, Version 1.1."

■ Encourage the use of automation technologies for checklist application such as SCAP.

Checklists can take many forms, including files that can automatically set or verify security configurations. Having automated methods has become increasingly important for several reasons, including the complexity of achieving compliance with various laws, executive orders, directives, policies, regulations, standards, and guidance; the increasing number of vulnerabilities in information systems; and the growing sophistication of threats against those vulnerabilities. Automation ensures that the security controls and configuration settings are applied consistently within an information system, and that the controls and settings can be effectively verified. The SCAP program addresses these needs by enabling standards-based security tools to automatically perform configuration checking using NCP checklists.*

It is clear that NIST really gets it and they are consistently laying the foundation that will enable the efforts we must make, going forward in a way that should scale. It is also worth noting that NIST constantly seeks and incorporates input and content from the community. Leveraging this many-to-many relationship has tangible benefits and is a departure from some historical interactions between government organizations and the community at large. I know this chapter is going to make my editor and publisher want to choke me just based on length, so I am looking for ways to be concise where possible. With that in mind, I only have room to summarize emerging SCAP standards. Currently, as I am writing this, there are also a number of emerging specifications that may or may not be adopted fully by the time this goes to print. From NIST's website:†

Languages

Asset Reporting Format (ARF)

The ARF language (http://scap.nist.gov/emerging-specs/listing.html#arf) is a general security automation results reporting language developed by the DoD in conjunction with NIST and members of the SCAP vendor community. It provides a structured language for exchanging and exporting detailed, per-device assessment data between network assessment tools. ARF is intended to be used by vulnerability scanners, XCCDF (http://scap.nist.gov/specifications/xccdf/scanners), and other tools that collect detailed configuration data about Internet Protocol-based networked devices.

Detailed information about ARF can be found in the ARF specification and data dictionary at http://metadata.dod.mil/mdr/ns/netops/shared_data/arf_index_page/0.41

Open Checklist Reporting Language (OCRL)

Open Checklist Reporting Language is a language for writing machine-readable XML definitions that gather information from systems and present it as a standardized report for human evaluation of policy compliance. Each generated report file corresponds to a single policy recommendation. OCRL complements existing benchmark languages such as eXtensible Configuration Checklist Description Format XCCDF and OVAL—which already provide capabilities for structuring security guidance in a machine-understandable way and describing how to gather and evaluate system information to determine compliance—by addressing those instances where a human is necessary

---

* Banghart, "SCAP."
† National Institute of Standards and Technology, "Emerging Specifications: Emerging-specs listing," http://scap.nist.gov/emerging-specs/listing.html, June 2010.

to determine compliance with a given policy recommendation, or where XCCDF and OVAL do not have the necessary capability to evaluate collected information for compliance with a recommendation. For example, a policy recommendation that states, "The user should disable unnecessary services on the computer," requires human judgment to determine what services are unnecessary. An OCRL Definition could be written to provide a report of all the services running on the computer, which could then be used by a person to determine whether any unwanted services are present.

OCRL was specifically designed to work with the XCCDF and OVAL benchmark authoring languages. While OCRL documents can be used alone by a software program to create one or more reports, by using OCRL in conjunction with OVAL more automation can be called out from an XCCDF document than using OVAL alone, resulting in significantly enhanced capabilities for benchmark automation.

Metrics

Common Configuration Scoring System (CCSS)

CCSS is a set of standardized measures for the characteristics and impacts of software security configuration issues located at (http://scap.nist.gov/emerging-specs/listing.html#ccss).

NIST IR 7502 (http://csrc.nist.gov/publications/PubsDrafts.html#NIST-IR-7502) provides several examples of how CCSS measures and scores would be determined for a diverse set of configuration issues. Once CCSS is finalized, CCSS data can assist organizations in making sound decisions as to how configuration issues should be addressed and can provide data to be used in quantitative assessments of host security.

Common Misuse Scoring System (CMSS)

A set of standardized measures for the characteristics of software feature misuse vulnerabilities. A software feature misuse vulnerability is present when the trust assumptions made when designing software features can be abused in a way that violates security. NIST IR 7517 (http://csrc.nist. gov/publications/PubsDrafts.html#NIST-IR-7517) defines the CMSS specification, and it also provides examples of how CMSS measures and scores would be determined for software feature misuse vulnerabilities. Once CMSS is finalized, CMSS data can be used along with CVSS and CCSS data to assist organizations in making sound decisions as to how their host vulnerabilities should be addressed. CMSS data can also be used in quantitative assessments of host security.

Wow, asleep yet? Jeez…as you can see, SCAP is incredibly robust and has applicability in its current form with great potential to evolve in the future in concert with other standards (more on that later). With that in mind, in the next section, I am going to dig deeper into probably the most mature aspect of the SCAP suite, OVAL. While each protocol within the suite matters, without OVAL it is entirely possible that the entire effort would have been too cumbersome early on to even attempt.

Circle Gets the OVAL?

"Open Vulnerability and Assessment Language (OVAL) is an international, information security, community standard to promote open and publicly available security content, and to standardize the transfer of this information across the entire spectrum of security tools and services. OVAL includes a language used to encode system details, and an assortment of content repositories held throughout the community. The language standardizes the three main steps of the assessment process: representing configuration information of systems for testing; analyzing the system for the presence of the specified machine state (vulnerability, configuration, patch state, etc.); and reporting the results of this assessment. The repositories are collections of publicly available and open content that utilize the language."[*]

Before OVAL there was no common or structured means to determine and share the existence of software vulnerabilities, configuration issues, programs, and/or patches in systems. That is not to say that the information was not out there, but it was mostly text based and housed within tools and knowledge bases of various organizations. The challenge is that it remains incredibly labor-intensive for humans to involve themselves in interpreting what amounts to unstructured information associated with configurations and vulnerabilities. Skill levels differ widely amongst individuals and organizations and, even when perfectly executed, the process tends to be error-prone for system administrators as they attempt to read and interpret this unstructured information in order to make a determination of whether a particular vulnerability or configuration issue exists within the network and/or endpoints. To compound this issue, the very detection of vulnerabilities and misconfigurations had never been standardized and therefore led to the use of exploit code basically as an assessment tool. Using a black box to solve the problems of another black box can drop you and your organization down a black hole of inefficiency and potential liability. How do you know the tool you are using actually works? What level of confidence can you place in it?

Never Fear! OVAL is Here!

As expressed above, the solution to many of these issues can be found within OVAL, based on its ability to promote standardized and structured assessments of vulnerability and configurations. More importantly, the large numbers of eyes on an open standard like this actually brings about increased confidence based on the ability to produce repeatable information assurance metrics. Also, it is not exclusive and so code you are already using to collect information can be OVAL'd, resulting in better overall results in general, with less work, more accuracy, and therefore a lower liability. This, in turn, decreases the attack surface, from a scalability perspective, of the enterprise in a way that no human interaction can. In addition, seemingly arcane security problems are better expressed in concrete, manageable, actionable, and (most importantly) digestible units by the operations groups directly involved with security remediation efforts.

While the above is powerful enough in its own right, the involvement of the community and how it supports the proliferation of reusable solutions amplifies the impact of OVAL. The open and egalitarian nature of OVAL definitions, based on a common XML definition schema, is best expressed by the diverse composition of the OVAL Board as well as deep participation by both the supply and demand sides of the value chain. The involvement of universities, private and public companies, members of the security community, government, etc. in reviewing and commenting on the OVAL schemas in an open collaborative environment where discussion is not only allowed but encouraged tends to reflect the insights and combined expertise of an incredibly broad collection of professionals throughout the various areas of the Information Security Community as a whole. While not a vulnerability scanner, OVAL does enable drastically enhanced sharing of technical details in order to identify the vulnerability state of an endpoint and potentially the

---

[*] Mitre Corporation, "OVAL faqs," About OVAL, http://oval.mitre.org/, June 2010.

network system as a whole. All of this is to the benefit of the end users who may not have the skill set or collaborative network to handle these types of tasks themselves. Reuse, and the repository of skills and knowledge this allows them to leverage, in turn potentially frees resources on their side to explore ways to make their organizations better and in many cases to then give back to the community. Let's just say that OVAL helps us create a measurable and transparent circle of give and take that enhances the entire community whether or not everyone participates. At the same time, growth of participation has the very real potential to yield an exponential growth in capabilities.

> "OVAL enables interoperability between security products by allowing them to exchange information through a standard XML language. It allows products in different vertical markets to leverage other products that accomplish different tasks. For example, a vulnerability assessment product can leverage a vulnerability research service to quickly and automatically check for the latest vulnerabilities. A compliance checking engine can leverage government security guidance to automatically monitor compliance without the need to translate traditional prose based guidance."*

While I generally am concerned with the consumption side of the value chain, I know that things have to make sense from a business perspective for the commercial entities. If you look at it from a vendor perspective, an open standards-based structured vulnerability information format enables them to potentially do what they do best by allowing them to quickly consume data from multiple sources. This commoditization of the more grunt-work aspect of this problem then allows a realignment and focus of resources to product functionality, which may enhance the pace of technological innovations.

Consumers, and particularly nonsecurity steeped practitioners, have a different point of view, and standard content format, for them, has the added benefit of shedding light on the oftentimes arcane vulnerability assessment process. At the same time, a truly objective comparison of features and capabilities of products becomes more practical. As previously mentioned, the community aspect for these initiatives is critical and so a well-documented, open standard format provides the community with the information they need to be able to understand the details of an issue, and to determine how a specific product is conducting its business. It also encourages participation by allowing opportunities for practitioners to generate their own checks in the language and interpret them with any product that allows as such. The outcomes of tests become much more deterministic, which in turn allows for more linear troubleshooting if products give different results. This in turn removes the burden of leveling the field from the consumers, allowing them to expend their resources more on selecting a product with the features that best meet their needs, and less on the more difficult problem of which product does the correct job of detecting vulnerabilities.

OVAL capabilities have been defined to create logical functionality groupings in order to allow for maximum flexibility for the organizations attempting compliance. This ensures only those parts of OVAL that make the most sense for products are used without requiring participants to try to digest some huge onerous list of capabilities all at once. It also serves to make OVAL available/consumable by a wider range of security products, thereby enhancing penetration. OVAL capabilities are mapped to use cases to confirm their validity across the entire implementation in order to ensure greater interoperability within the industry. Clear definition of the capabilities also enables members of the community to better understand how any "compliant" product is using the OVAL Language, which in turn helps them properly satisfy their business needs.

---

* Mitre Corporation, "OVAL Use Cases," About OVAL Adoption, http://oval.mitre.org/adoption/usecasesguide. htm, June 2010.

OVAL Capabilities

- *Authoring Tool*—Vendors may use an Authoring Tool to assist in the development of vulnerability content to provide to their customers. End users may use an Authoring Tool to assist in developing their own checks.
- *Definition Repository*—The logic required to determine the presence of a vulnerability can be expressed in an OVAL Definition, which is machine readable, and published in a Definition Repository along with the original security advisory as soon as the vulnerability is discovered. Providing vulnerability detection information in a structured format allows end users to more quickly assess their systems and take action as needed.
- *Definition Evaluator*—A product that implements the Definition Evaluator Capability can consume vulnerability checks from many Definition Repositories. This will significantly reduce the size of the vendor's content team as well as reduce time it takes to get a vulnerability check out to end users. Additionally, the end user may supply custom developed OVAL Definitions to a Definition Evaluator.
- *System Characteristics Producer*—A product that generates a valid OVAL System Characteristics file based on the details of a system.
- *Results Consumer*—A product that accepts an OVAL Results document as input and either displays the results to the user, or uses the results to perform some action. OVAL is principally concerned with gold standard tests that definitively determine whether the specified software vulnerability, configuration issue, program, or patch is present on a system.*

The high-level summary includes the following: "vulnerable software exists," which states the specific operating system (OS), the name of the file with the vulnerability in it, application version, and patch status; and "vulnerable configuration," which indicates if the service is running or not, specific configuration settings, and workarounds. The detailed portion of definitions provides the logic for checking for the system characteristics to indicate that vulnerable software exists, and configuration attributes to indicate that a vulnerable configuration exists. Each definition is distinguished by a unique identifier. These identifiers are called OVAL-IDs and use a standard format. It is worth not that the OVAL-ID format extends across all of the globally reusable components in the OVAL language to include definitions, objects, states, tests, and variables.

Format

"oval:Organization DNS Name:ID Type:ID Value"
DNS Name
Syntax: 'org.mitre.oval';
ID Type denotes the entity to which the ID is being applied
Acceptable values: def - Definition, obj - Object, ste - State, tst - Test, or var - Variable);
ID Value is an integer that is unique to the DNS name and ID Type pair that precedes it
e.g., oval:org.mitre.oval:def:1115.[†]

---

* Mitre Corporation, "OVAL Use Cases," About OVAL Adoption, http://oval.mitre.org/adoption/usecasesguide.htm, June 2010.
† Mitre Corporation, "OVAL Language Requirements," About OVAL Language Requirements, oval.mitre.org/oval/documents/docs-06/oval_language_requirements.pdf, June 2010.

So how do these pieces complement one another? The Common Vulnerabilities and Exposures (CVE) is a publication that provides common names for known information security vulnerabilities and exposures. CVE uses common names in order to make it easier to share data across separate network security databases and tools that are CVE-compatible. The OVAL Repository is CVE-compatible. This means OVAL actually uses the publicly known vulnerabilities identified in the CVE list as the basis for its vulnerability definitions. Again community participation is critical and they (the OVAL Repository Community) are the ones that actually write definitions against these vulnerabilities, configuration issues, and patches that are then submitted and available for public comment and review before being posted. Below are the OVAL definition classes with short definitions followed by a sample use case that was posted on the MITRE website. Links are also included.

OVAL Definition Classes

- *OVAL Vulnerability Definitions*—Tests that determine the presence of vulnerabilities on systems.
- *OVAL Compliance Definitions*—Tests that determine whether the configuration settings of a system meets a security policy.
- *OVAL Inventory Definitions*—Tests that whether a specific piece of software is installed on the system.
- *OVAL Patch Definitions*—Tests that determine whether a particular patch is appropriate for a system.[*]

Use Case: Security Advisory Distribution

One acknowledged need within the security industry is for application and operating system vendors, and other authoritative organizations, to publish vulnerability information in a standard, machine-readable format. The benefit of this is two-fold. First, it provides scanning products with immediate access to OVAL Content that can be used to assess the security posture of a system. Second, it moves the authoring of the technical details of a vulnerability from the reverse engineering efforts of the scanner-product developer to a more authoritative source: the developer of the vulnerable software. Relevant OVAL Capabilities include:

- *Authoring Tool*—Organizations publishing security advisories may utilize an Authoring Tool to assist in the development of the security advisories as OVAL Definitions.
- *Definition Repository*—Organizations publishing security advisories as OVAL Definitions can be considered a repository of OVAL Definitions.
- *Definition Evaluator*—Products that implement the Definition Evaluator capability can consume OVAL Definitions for the security advisories and report any vulnerabilities found on a set of hosts.[†]

I know you want to ask: "So what does it take to really 'adopt' OVAL and begin making a difference?" The OVAL Adoption Program was established to guide the way. In the process it enables

---

[*] Mitre Corporation, "OVAL Repository," About the OVAL Repository, http://oval.mitre.org/repository/about/overview.html, June 2010.
[†] Mitre Corporation, "OVAL Use Cases."

interoperability among security products, educates vendors on best practices regarding the use and implementation of OVAL, and provides vendors with an opportunity to make formal self-assertions about how their products utilize OVAL. To be an official adopter of OVAL the organization must provide one or more of the five high-level OVAL capabilities that were mentioned and defined above.

- *OVAL Authoring Tool*—A product that aids in the process of creating new OVAL files to include products that consolidate existing definitions into a single file.
- *OVAL Definition Evaluator*—A product that uses an OVAL Definition to guide evaluation and produces OVAL Results (full results) as output.
- *OVAL Definition Repository*—A repository of OVAL Definitions made available to the community either for free or as a paid service.
- *OVAL System Characteristics Producer*—A product that generates a valid OVAL system characteristics file based on the details of a system.
- *OVAL Results Consumer*—A product that accepts OVAL Results as input and either displays those results to the user, or uses the results to perform some action.*

Additional OVAL Use Cases

Patch Management

The needs of patch management vendors are similar to those of vulnerability assessment vendors. There is some amount of reverse engineering that must be done in order to generate content in a format that is readable by a patch management product. Having this information generated by the software vendor, and provided in a standard format, removes the reverse-engineering requirement and allows content to be provided to end consumers in a more timely fashion. Another requirement for this class of products is they must be able to easily consume vulnerability assessment results from a variety of scanning products. If these results are offered in a standard format, interoperability between products is no longer an issue.

Relevant OVAL Capabilities

Authoring Tool—Vendors may utilize an authoring tool to assist in the development of patch applicability content to provide to their customers. End users may utilize an authoring tool to assist in developing their own checks.

Definition Repository—The logic required to determine patch applicability can be expressed in OVAL definitions and published in definition repositories along with the original patch advisory. Vendors can then leverage these definition repositories, from multiple organizations, as input into their products.

Definition Evaluator—A product that implements the definition evaluator capability can consume patch applicability checks from many definition repositories. This will significantly reduce the size of the vendor's content team as well as reduce the time it takes to get a patch check out to end users. Additionally, the end user may supply custom-developed OVAL definitions to a definition evaluator.

---

* Mitre Corporation, "OVAL faqs," About OVAL, http://oval.mitre.org/, June 2010.

Results Consumer—A patch management product that implements the results consumer capability might consume OVAL results from a vulnerability assessment product in order to determine which patches a system might need. In this way, the results of a vulnerability assessment can feed into the patch management process.

System Characteristics Producer—A system characteristics producer might be used to provide detailed system configuration information to a patch management product.

Currently, organizations that develop vulnerability assessment products need to employ a team of content developers. The role of this team is to investigate vulnerabilities as they become known, gather all of the available information for a given vulnerability, and run various tests against live systems to examine the parameters that indicate the presence of a vulnerability. Once a vulnerability is understood, this team must develop the checks in the language of the product in question. All of these tasks must be completed under a very strict time requirement. The final requirement obviously runs counter to those before it, and may result in incomplete analysis and testing before a check absolutely has to be disseminated to the vendor's customers.

Auditing and Centralized Audit Validation

Audit validation is responsible for providing reports about the state of a machine at any given time in the past. There are two basic needs in this area. First and foremost is capturing machine configuration information at a level of granularity that allows an organization to monitor, track, and reconstruct the transition of a system's configuration from one state to another. The second need is that the data be stored in a standardized, data-centric format, thus ensuring that it is not bound to a specific product, which may or may not be available at the time it is necessary to review the data.

Relevant OVAL Capabilities

Authoring Tool—An authoring tool might be used to assist in the development of audit checks.

Definition evaluator—A product that implements the definition evaluator capability can consume audit checks and store their results over time as OVAL results. OVAL results provide detailed system configuration information in a structured format independent of any specific product implementation.

Results Consumer—An auditing product that implements the results consumer capability might consume OVAL results from a number of other products in order to have a complete picture of an enterprise.

System Characteristics Producer—A system characteristics producer might be used to provide detailed system configuration information to an auditing product.

Security Information Management Systems (SIMS)

SIMS rely upon the output of a variety of security, auditing, and configuration products, as well as their own agents, to build a comprehensive view of the security posture of an organization's network. Clearly the fewer data formats the SIM needs to understand, the more flexible and powerful this class of products can be. As with the Patch Management class of products, standardizing the data exchange formats between products greatly simplifies the interoperability requirements and provides end users with a wider array of applications to choose from.

Relevant OVAL Capabilities

Results Consumer—SIMS that implement the results consumer capability might consume OVAL results from any number of other products that could be serving a variety of functions. In this way, the burden of integrating numerous output formats is greatly reduced.

System Inventory

A common issue, not only for security products, but for any product that is trying to conduct some sort of evaluation of a computer system, is determining the attributes of that system (e.g., operating system, patch level, installed applications, etc.), and being able to convey those attributes clearly and consistently. Currently, there is no universally accepted method for gathering the attributes from a system, nor is there a common way to express those attributes such that they can be easily consumed by another application. The need for this capability is widely acknowledged and its use would be widespread.

Relevant OVAL Capabilities

Authoring Tool—An authoring tool might be used to assist in the development of system inventory checks.

Definition Evaluator—A product that implements the definition evaluator capability can consume system inventory checks from a number of definition repositories and report inventory results in the form of OVAL results which could be consumed by other products.

Results Consumer—A central asset database that implements the results consumer capability might consume OVAL results from a number of other products in order to have a complete picture of an enterprise.

Malware and Threat Indicator Sharing

Having a standard format for exchanging low-level system state information will enable cross-organization sharing of malware and threat indicators. Encoding this information in a structured format will allow organizations to more quickly and accurately detect potentially compromised systems. The need for a standard format to support this capability is widely acknowledged and its use by incident coordination centers would be widespread.

Relevant OVAL Capabilities

Authoring Tool—An authoring tool might be used to assist in the development of checks for indications of a threat or particular piece of malware.

Definition Evaluator—A product that implements the definition evaluator capability can consume checks for indications of a threat or particular piece of malware and report results in the form of OVAL results for further analysis.*

---

* Mitre Corporation, "OVAL Use Cases," About OVAL Adoption, http://oval.mitre.org/adoption/usecasesguide. htm, June 2010.

IF-MAP: The Tie That Binds

"Egalitarian Trumps Totalitarian"

Last year I wrote:

> "At the most basic of levels, IF-MAP is a open standards based repository of information about a variety of subjects. Specifically, it provides a standard protocol for real time sharing of information on network users & devices as well as their state and activities. The specification itself initially denoted three different capabilities, including IF-MAP Publish, IF-MAP Subscribe, IF-MAP Poll, and IF-MAP Search. These capabilities run over the wire, using Simple Object Access Protocol (SOAP), against an IF-MAP Server (MAP) which in turn houses but does not validate information from all devices with the ability to publish to it. The initial metadata specifications defined for network devices include IP-to-MAC binding, Layer-2 Location, Security Events, Device Attributes, Authentication Information, and Access Request Information. They were defined and initially published in the Trusted Network Connect (TNC) IF-MAP binding for SOAP specification 1.0 revision 25. Individually they are somewhat significant but when you begin to put them together, they become much more compelling."*

As a brief history update, Trusted Computing Group published IF-MAP v1.0 Standard in April 2008 and then published IF-MAP v1.1 in May 2009. Version 1.1's announcement coincided with Interop'09 with multivendor collaborative demonstrations. Interop'09 demonstrated use cases principally centered around the base use cases of Remote User Access, Security Industrial Controls, Physical Access Security, and Datacenter Management. At the same time significant progress has been made in the IETF NEA-WG and it has published RFCs (standards) compatible with both IF-TNCCS and IF-M.

Since I am a big proponent of reuse and dislike reinventing the wheel, the question as to why I support the creation and proliferation of a newer protocol instead of using existing options (e.g., relational databases or directories) is valid. The answer is in the very nature of the network systems data as compared to the strengths and weaknesses of each possible approach. The vast majority of coordination data within network systems is loosely structured and changes frequently. At the same time, infrastructure elements are often interested in different attributes and patterns that do not necessarily lend themselves to current capabilities. IF-MAP is an extensible highly scalable publication/subscription type (pub/sub) architecture for asynchronous searches purposely built to fit the security coordination use case to include large numbers of real-time data writes, unstructured relationships, diverse interest in changes to the current state as they occur, and distributed data producers and consumers. The design is also predicated on the assumption that you will never find a single data relation schema to satisfy all needs. Additionally, identifiers exist implicitly with no meaning until metadata is attached to them and are defined along with metadata in XML schemas.

First off, from a context perspective, network security metadata describes attributes of network data flows and associated principals. Metadata is data about other data, so a file's name, size, or description is metadata about the file's data (the content of the file). For instance "A picture of a building" is descriptive metadata about a file containing an image of a building. So, effectively, IF-MAP can answer any number of questions such as the following: "Who" is associated with what data flows? What credentials were used? What policy decisions have been made? Were there any recent "unusual" behaviors?

---

* O'Berry, "Achieving Global Information Systems Transformation (GIST) through Standards."

"Loosely Coupled, Tightly Integrated"

IF-MAP is Based on Four Main Operations

Properties of Publish:
Used to create, update, or delete information about a network element
Clients store metadata in Metadata Access Points (MAP) for others to see
Incorporates create, modify, and delete functionality

Properties of Search:
Used to retrieve information (immediately) from the database about network elements
Clients retrieve published metadata associated with a particular identifier and its linked identifiers
Constrained by link-match and result-filter criteria
Constrained by maximum depth and size criteria

Properties of Subscribe:
Used to maintain a list of searches that the IF-MAP client wants to be notified about
Includes instance of clients requesting asynchronous results for searches that match when others publish new metadata
A client's subscription consists of a list of one or more searches
A client names its searches so that asynchronous results are unambiguous

Properties of Poll:
Used by the IF-MAP client to confirm they are ready to receive the results of a subscription
(Steve Hanna, personal communication, May 2010; Dr. Steve Venema, personal communication, May 2010)

Enterprises are occupied by a wide variety of users, including visitors, partners, contractors, employees, and privileged employees. Networking and security devices from multiple vendors interoperate using TNC-based technology to provide appropriate access for each user based on their identity, endpoint compliance, and role. Community involvement is critical. Examples, such as the open-source client XSupplicant, an 802.1x client from the OpenSEA Alliance, that provides cross-platform support for user authentication and endpoint health checking, are very important to the long-term penetration of a market that has always been dominated by a few very large vendors and their proprietary frameworks. IETF adoption of TNC specifications was critical and recently achieved. It ensures industry-wide agreement on standards, providing consistency across products from leading networking and security vendors. TNC interfaces published as IETF RFCs (standards) enable dynamic differentiation and access control enforcement for a wide variety of users in mixed-use environments with the backing of a body considered to be one of the ultimate authorities for internet standards.

- IF-TNCCS (called PB-TNC by the IETF) defines a standard way to perform a health check of a network endpoint such as a laptop computer or printer. If the endpoint is not healthy, it can be fixed or have its network access restricted.
- IF-M (called PA-TNC by the IETF) defines a standard set of health checks that are commonly performed, such as checking firewall status.
- IF-PEP enables provisioning of appropriate access for each user while ensuring consistent access control across wired and wireless connections.

So in the spirit of trying to put my "use cases where my mouth is," I reached out to Dr. Steve Venema and Steve Hanna to make sure I have some practical information to go along with the high-level statements of how awesome IF-MAP is now and can be going forward. (Steve Hanna, personal communication, May 2010; and Dr. Steve Venema, personal communication, May 2010.)

Employee Cubicle: Accessing a Production Network

Business Requirements

An employee comes to work in the morning. When she badges into the building, the physical access control system publishes her location to a central clearinghouse, the Metadata Access Point (MAP). The employee authenticates to the enterprise network and her workstation is checked for compliance with corporate security policies. The policy server provisions appropriate access to network resources for the employee.

At the end of the day, the employee logs out of her PC and badges out to go home. The physical access control system publishes her location to the MAP and the MAP notifies the policy server that she has left the building. The policy server provisions a new access policy for the employee's workstation, and the switch reassigns the workstation to a machine VLAN with restricted access for overnight maintenance and upkeep (such as backups or patch management).

Operational requirements:
    User must be authenticated and authorized with identity management system and AAA services
    User must be badged into building
    Endpoint must be healthy
        Antivirus software running and properly configured
        Recent scan shows no malware
        Personal firewall running and properly configured
        Patches up-to-date
    Behavior must be acceptable
        No port scanning, sending spam

Coordination challenges:
    Security infrastructure is complex, heterogeneous, and usually distributed
    Getting worse
    Large, real-time data flows between infrastructure components occur
    Coordination between sensors, flow controllers, IDPs, etc. that are each interested in different patterns of events
    Timely routing and reliability of delivery of this data is critical

TNC technology:
    IF-PEP enables dynamic admission control and port-based network enforcement for both 802.1X-authenticated and MAC-authenticated endpoints.
    IF-TNCCS-SOH provides integration between TNC and Microsoft NAP, a NAP Agent is enabled to communicate endpoint health information to a TNC PDP without requiring a third-party supplicant.

The CESP defines mechanisms that ensure the ability to dynamically provision appropriate access for endpoints that lack a TNC client and are unable to authenticate to the network and/or demonstrate compliance with security requirements.

IF-MAP enables integration of information from additional security systems, adding behavioral intelligence to the access decision for managed and unmanaged endpoints, and integrating physical security with network access control.

Guest Access: Conference Room

Business Requirements

A guest visits the company using a laptop compliant with IETF/TNC standards. A health check against the guest endpoint ensures it complies with enterprise security policies before allowing it access to the corporate network. The guest is placed in a restricted VLAN, which provides access to appropriate resources, such as the Internet, but blocks access to the internal corporate subnets. His endpoint health and behavior are monitored throughout the duration of his connection to the network.

Operational Requirements:
    Connection must be allowed via restricted VLAN
    Endpoint must be healthy
        Antivirus software must be running and properly configured
        Recent scan shows no malware
        Personal firewall running and properly configured
        Patches up-to-date
    Behavior must be acceptable
        No port scanning, sending spam

TNC Technology:
    IF-PEP enables provisioning of appropriate access for each user while ensuring consistent access control across wired and wireless connections.
    IF-TNCCS and IF-IMC/IMV enable endpoint integrity checking; implementations can range from a full supplicant to a lightweight dissolving agent.
    The CESP defines mechanisms that enable the application of access controls to endpoints without TNC clients that can't provide identity or endpoint health information.
    IF-MAP enables integration of network intelligence from additional security systems to add a behavioral consideration to the access decision.

Contractor Access: Gone Rogue

A contractor arrives to perform maintenance on a protected system. The contractor successfully authenticates and his endpoint passes the health check; the policy server provisions access only to that system and he is also monitored. The contractor plugs in an EVDO device and makes a connection to the Internet, in violation of corporate policy. A network leak prevention sensor detects the leak and publishes a policy violation event to the MAP. The MAP notifies the policy server of the policy violation and the policy server terminates the contractor's access privileges on the network. Comprehensive logging enables the corporate security team to identify what the contractor did and why access was restricted. TNC interfaces enable location, identity, endpoint health, and behavior-based access control decisions for users in an enterprise environment, along with detection and remediation of illicit activity such as data leakage by an endpoint.

Operational Requirements:
    User must be authenticated and authorized with the identity management system (IDMS) and AAA services
    Endpoint must be healthy
        Antivirus software running and properly configured
        Recent scan shows no malware
        Personal firewall running and properly configured
        Patches up-to-date
    Behavior must be acceptable
        No port scanning, sending spam
        No violation of data leak prevention policy

TNC Technology:
    TNC interfaces enable location, identity, endpoint health, and behavior-based access control decisions for users in an enterprise environment.
    Detection and remediation of illicit activity, such as data leakage by an endpoint or unauthorized changes to network device configurations and correlation of physical security with network access privileges.
    IF-PEP enables dynamic admission control and assignment of endpoints to the appropriate VLAN.
    IF-MAP enables data leak prevention, configuration management, and correlation of physical access privileges with network access privileges.

Extensions of the Security Use Case: Advanced Human Resources Use Case

Scenario

An employee leaves the company, which is recorded as a change in status in the HR database from active to inactive. This brings up a number of questions. How are perimeter security services notified? How are all the various enterprise applications and servers notified? How are suppliers and partners notified? In the simplest sense, this is a coordination problem. With that in mind, what business problems are you trying to solve? Can you operationalize those today?

Coordination services:
    Combined physical security and cyber security
    Convergence of IT networks/security and industrial controls security (a.k.a., SCADAnet)
Location services:
    Coordination of supply chains and process flow across one or more enterprises
Process/Event coordination:
    Too many business process today are coordinated synchronously or (worse yet) open loop
    The asynchronous pub/sub notification capability built into the MAP database can give us a new coordination pattern for many business processes.

The "old" way:

> All need-to-know servers and applications manually poll the HR database periodically, often infrequently, to look for changes.
>
> Creates issues related to access control, personally identifiable information, timeliness, and performance.
>
> Requires careful engineering of all interconnected systems.
>
> Changes in HR system ripple out to all others.

What does this imply for future reliability and scalability? The answer to the operations question above, in this scenario, is probably no, or a significantly qualified yes, but with a great deal of effort.

The "new" way:

> HR publishes employee identifiers and status metadata to MAP.
>
> All "interested" applications subscribe to metadata updates that result in "status" changing to "inactive."
>
> Can include suppliers and partners.
>
> HR controls publication of other potentially sensitive information (PII, etc.).
>
> Extensible and scales well in the face of many applications with many changes.

So I ask again, with the new way can you now operationalize what you need in order to take action? Does the task now seem to be more manageable? (Dr. Steve Venema, personal communication, May 2010.)

Standard Secure Configuration Management: Not Just an Endpoint Thing Anymore! OVAL+SCAP+IF-MAP=S^2CM....OMG!?!?!?!

Managing security systems today continues to challenge the organizations on a ridiculously large and growing number of fronts. The sheer volume of complex and disparate operating systems and applications that must be secured is expanding rapidly based on positive traction in areas like open source as well as in open community interaction, even in what has traditionally been closed source only. Enterprises are complex as a general rule, with infrastructure networks holding standard PII, new and scary health information, intellectual property, business knowledge, as well as more mundane everyday data. Confidentiality, Integrity, and Availability (CIA) (regards to Hal Tipton, Dr. Corey Schou, and the other triangle creators/supporters) requirements are not the same for the different data but requirements do exist for each and every piece. When you mix legacy systems with newer systems that include commercial off-the-shelf (COTS), custom developed, and government off-the-shelf (GOTS) software, it is difficult enough to keep up with from a simple operations perspective. Couple that with the many manual processes required to baseline, inventory, and potentially address risks necessary in order to meet compliance and its clear to see how organizations can quickly get overwhelmed. For reference, think about the hundreds and sometimes thousands of settings that must be kept up with and verified as correct each time a patch goes in for some operating systems.

Daniel Schmidt wrote:

> "…manually intensive processes in place today are incapable of supporting accurate tracking and management necessary to truly protect these assets. A component of security automation is achieving a fairly precise understanding of the computing

environment and its compliance with policy. To do so requires the ability to accurately account for installed hardware, software, and more importantly, the actual configuration of these assets. To facilitate this, the SCAP standards were developed. The individual components of SCAP are described in Table 1. SCAP is a collection of open, interoperable standards that support automated vulnerability management, measurement, and policy compliance evaluation. More specifically, SCAP is a suite of standards that are used to-

- Establish common enumerations for software flaws, security-related configuration issues, and product names
- Determine if specific software flaws, configuration issues, patches, or products are present on a system
- Accurately and consistently communicate the impact of security issues while providing transparency regarding how the score was derived

Enable integration and management of critical Computer Network Defense and IT configuration information."*

As mentioned above, organizations have an increasing number of compliance requirements that must be demonstrated as satisfied to an ever-widening number of entities, both governmental and commercial. High-level requirements drive the implementation of security policy and procedure as well as the implementation of individual security controls in some situations. These policies, procedures, and controls require a process to map requirements to each of them, which has historically been a highly subjective exercise. In many cases it has been based on individual interpretation of the intent of the requirement by either someone in management, information technology, or God help us, legal. That in turn means that over the long term, compliance evidence, based on this entirely manual process and interpretation, is more than likely unreliable.

Of course things are getting easier on the vulnerability and malware front so it all balances out…errr…oh wait…just the opposite! Instead, now we contend with the daily emergence of a dizzying array of new vulnerabilities and the malware used to exploit them. Remember that vulnerabilities are more often than not valid attack vectors and the National Vulnerability Database (NVD) contains over 33,000 vulnerabilities with approximately 20 new vulnerabilities added per day. At the same time, networks in general are simply not static entities and their dynamic nature gives static certification and accreditation processes of the past fits. With networks changing in some organizations on an almost daily basis, certification and accreditation of those systems MUST change from static (and hence inadequate) to more dynamic machine-to-machine if enterprises are ever to understand the impact of those changes on the accreditation.

Marcia Weaver wrote:

"As the Global Information Grid (GIG) expands and the number and complexity of devices on it continue to increase, those who manage the enterprise and its networks are challenged to maintain the components of the GIG in secure configurations. There are millions of assets within the DoD installed with numerous types of operating systems and applications—involving thousands of security-related settings—where

---

* Schmidt, "Security Automation."

settings for the same software often need to be secured and configured differently on multiple hosts. Defining and maintaining a secure standard baseline for each application and operating system on the GIG infrastructure is a mammoth task—but even this is not sufficient to protect the GIG. Daily vulnerabilities are publicly announced, and attacks attempting to exploit those vulnerabilities are ever increasing. To win the fight against those vulnerabilities, standardized IA best practices must be consistently implemented, new countermeasures must be rapidly directed, and most critically, secure configuration compliance must be vigilantly verified. The dynamic nature of today's DoD missions means that computers are often disconnected and reconnected to new domains, new software applications are installed, and changing administrators and users may alter security features deemed inconvenient. Organizations require a standardized, automated way of regularly collecting the configuration state of security settings and patches of assets under their authority and producing compliance evidence. Once standardized, configuration information can be easily shared and correlated across disparate domains to enable better situational awareness of the overall security posture of the enterprise. When the information is further correlated with standardized vulnerability information, the DoD is able to rapidly and accurately assess risk posed by new vulnerabilities or non-compliant assets and identify, prioritize, and direct countermeasures. Today, organizations typically employ a variety of tools for security management that use proprietary data formats, nomenclature, and interface—preventing interoperability, creating inconsistencies in reports for the same findings, and causing significant delays in decision making. Increasing interest and adoption of the Security Content Automation Protocols (SCAP) is about to change all of that. SCAP comprises a suite of specifications for organizing and expressing security-related information in standardized ways as well as related reference data such as identifiers for software flaws and security configuration issues. SCAP can be used for maintaining the security of enterprise systems, such as automatically verifying the installation of patches, checking system security configuration settings, and examining systems for signs of compromise. [1] Federal acquisition officials have already begun embedding requirements for SCAP-validated products in their procurements. The DoD is on target to deploy enterprise-wide SCAP assessment tools in early Fiscal Year 2010. This article addresses current security configuration challenges facing the DoD and the strategy to evolve to a SCAP-based Secure Configuration Management (SCM) capability that significantly improves situational awareness of the security posture of the GIG—and ultimately enables well-informed decision making and rapid implementation of changes to that posture."*

She pretty much just nut-shelled the entire problem right there, especially from the DoD perspective. As noted, we also dealt with this in the enterprise space and like our buddies at DoD, our first response to these challenges was to throw a barrage of management tools at it. This was not a bad stopgap, but each tool set was often automated and communicated only within its own area of effect, often creating silos of really good information that other parts of the organization's distributed systems might benefit from, if only they knew it existed and could easily consume it. Often the tools available used proprietary code that unintentionally or intentionally locked users in to certain products. Nonstandard interfaces, data formats, enforcement mechanisms,

---

* Marcia E. Weaver, "Secure Configuration Management [Electronic version]," *IAnewsletter* 13, no. 1 (2010).

outputs, etc. quickly evolved to create substantial inconsistencies in the auditable security state of distributed system assets. Even guidance properly given from organizations meaning well, NIST and NSA for instance, was so complex and manual as to be nearly impossible to implement on a large scale without an unsustainable increase in resources. Couple that with limited automated assistance and little communication outside of areas of effect (for instance vulnerability management and inventory management), and what you eventually get is security teams tasked with the almost impossible. They must determine what systems are affected by new security policies, mandates, and vulnerabilities, and then manually execute remediation actions using existing proprietary mechanisms across a sizable heterogeneous dynamic organism. What does that then lead to? Basically it leads to "head in the sand syndrome," with organizations oftentimes relying on patching and configuring baselines infrequently, then pretty much assuming the settings will be maintained with very little ongoing verification of that assumption.

Death by Console Avoided!

So we realize the challenge revolves mostly around outdated processes on which the industry often relies. These processes are normally heavily scripted, in order to have a degree of automation, by incredibly knowledgeable individuals that unfortunately are not immortal. The knowledge they have cannot be replicated in any real scalable fashion so in effect we either have to find the 'Fountain of Youth" as well as the "Fountain of Eternal Contentment" or we need to go about this a better way. With that in mind, in order to protect their IT systems in the real world, security managers must be able to accurately and consistently assess the security state of their networks and institute consistent and repeatable mitigation policies throughout the enterprise. S²CM is a means to gain greater control over and ensure the integrity of vast distributed systems by providing a standardized, automated way of patching, configuring, and securing hardware, firmware, software, etc. SCAP specifications and content developed by NIST, industry partners, community participants, standards organizations, etc. create that common way of enumerating everything from flaws to simple misconfigurations. SCAP's standard assessment language also removes the guesswork related to communication of what and how software, patches, software flaws, and individual security settings will be checked.

Base Use Case: Secure Configuration Management ver.1

Marcia Weaver writes:
Configuration management products concern themselves with examining a machine's configuration state, comparing it against a known good or mandated configuration state, and reporting the results. There are a number of publicly available best practice configuration guides (e.g., the National Security Agency (NSA) Configuration Guides), and many more developed specifically for individual organizations. In many cases, these guides exist in paper form only, and it is up to the IT Staff to translate the document into something that can be applied and enforced on a consistent basis. There are also automated solutions available, most notably the Center for Internet Security's Benchmark products, which can scan a system for compliance against a given configuration and offer tailoring capabilities to suit the specific needs of an organization. Unfortunately, these products often rely upon proprietary data formats, making it difficult to introduce new policies to the product or move data from one product to another.

Having a standard language for expressing system configuration issues offers many benefits in this area. Firstly, a single configuration specification need only be written once. At this point it can be consumed by any configuration management product. Secondly, organizations can more easily develop and maintain their own configuration standards, as it only requires learning a single language, and not a language specific to a particular product. Finally, as with some of the cases above, divesting the language from the product provides the product vendor with a wider repository of content and allows them to focus more on functionality and features.

Relevant OVAL Capabilities

Authoring Tool—Organizations may utilize an Authoring Tool to assist in the development of configuration checking content. End users may utilize an Authoring Tool to assist in developing their own checks.

Definition Repository—When a best practice configuration is created, or a configuration policy is established, the checking logic that verifies that a given system is configured accordingly can be expressed as a set of OVAL Definitions and published in Definition Repositories. Vendors can then leverage these Definition Repositories, from multiple organizations, as input into their products. IT staff can leverage and tailor best practice configuration checking content for their own organizational needs.*

The above illustrates where the paths are crossing between OVAL and SCAP, and touches on the benefits of what we need to accomplish in the first industry-wide implementation of SCM. Marcia really hits her stride and effectively takes us to S²CM; she just does not call it by name:

"The result is consistent and repeatable checks for configuration concerns such as compliance with policy, evidence of system compromise, and vulnerability to emerging exploits. Where previous IA content was proprietary to the tool, SCAP enables the separation of the IA content from the specific tool implementation to:

■ Improve data correlation
■ Enable interoperability
■ Foster automation
■ Ease the gathering of metrics for use in situational awareness and IT security audits.

Inventory and configuration information from multiple tools can be easily correlated through standard SCAP enumerations and checklists, and emerging standardized reporting capabilities. The correlated results can be aggregated within a single organization or across the entire enterprise to provide uniform, shareable, and consumable decisioning information on what networks exist; what devices, circuits, and people are resident on the networks; and how these assets are configured. The SCM initiative will extend the current SCAP specifications to go beyond collecting the security posture of DoD assets, to identifying and implementing recommended countermeasures. IAVMs, CTOs, and other policy changes will become machine-readable files consumed by configuration assessment tools for automated identification

---

* Ibid.

of affected assets, and consumed by remediation tools for automated implementation of required remediation actions. SCM will be enterprise-deployable and operational in a multi-tiered infrastructure environment. As illustrated in Figure 1, national-level security configuration policies and associated system security checklists such as those embodied in the Office of Management and Budget Federal Desktop Core Configuration will serve as the basis for DoD systems, but will be tailored as appropriate at each tier to meet specific organizational and operational requirements. SCAP checklists are documented in standard XML so checks can be easily added, deleted, or modified. Organizations will employ SCAP-validated tools to use the checklists on a regular basis to confirm that systems are secured as intended. Mappings to high-level security controls are maintained and distributed by NIST, which allow the tools to automatically generate compliance evidence. Compliance evidence and inventory configuration assessment results will flow up through the DoD infrastructure, providing an increasingly broader view of the security posture of DoD systems."[*]

She touches on a critical piece here with the word correlation and although I believe she is initially referring to the interaction between the SCAP suite, it's also clear that she "gets" the importance of aggressive collaboration both in the community and at the higher levels of organizations regarding alignment of standards and practices where possible. Her mention of a loosely coupled, tightly integrated network involving load balancing related to the work that needs to be done illustrates that clearly. She specifically states:

"The SCM initiative will extend the current SCAP specifications to go beyond collecting the security posture of DoD assets, to identifying and implementing recommended countermeasures."[†]

Now that is a pretty powerful statement to make considering the enormous amount of people involved in making that a reality. At the same time, that is exactly where we need to be. When you take those concepts, the SCM use case from the MITRE website, and what we know about IF-MAP and the use cases involving it to the next level, you get something that resembles a continuation of a conversation between Steve Hanna and a member of a government organization critical to the success of the proliferation of this type of standards interaction. They wrote:

"At the moment, I think they can be viewed as complementary. There is some overlap, especially w.r.t. CPE and OVAL, but the overlap is only partial. I can think of several use cases where PA-TNC and SCAP can be used together; sometimes at different levels and sometimes in concert at the same level. I'll just list two such cases:

1. Separate layers: A posture validator could employ OVAL and XCCDF to assess and/or report posture to an overarching enterprise security management framework. The communication to the device would be pure TNC. The only obstacle to this scenario at the moment might be lack of OVAL schemas that allow one to write definitions and convey characteristics from a TNC posture.
2. Interleaved layers: It would be useful to be able to report the results of an OVAL test over PA-TNC. I think it would be valid to consider the state of a client's

---

[*] Ibid.
[†] Ibid.

> compliance to an OVAL test as an attribute of that client. I don't quite see how PA-TNC would convey this, but it certainly looks possible." (Steve Hanna, personal communication, May/June 2010; anonymous government employee, personal communication, May/June 2010.)

Read that again…and realize the impact of the exchange not just from an operational standpoint but from a strategic and then potentially unlimited theoretical capability point of view. Imagine that all of a sudden things that should be commodity actually are, while the shroud of mystery surrounding the "security voodoo" is vaporized. I can hear the joyful gasp from CxOs everywhere. Now wake up, there is still a lot of work to do!

Pushing Forward on Standards Like OVAL, SCAP, and IF-MAP

Allan Paller wrote:

> "Software interoperability is fundamental to automation of security. Without effective interoperability, network defense is a hit-and-miss game that takes too many people, too much money, and too much time—
>
> - If the intrusion detection system cannot communicate with the inventory system, then attacks that are critical (because they are rare but highly targeted) may get too little attention, while harmless attacks (common attacks but aimed at systems without the target vulnerability) may get too much attention.
> - If the vulnerability management system cannot interact fully with the configuration management system, then days or weeks of manual patch testing may be required before patches can be installed. On the other hand, if they can communicate, the configuration management system can verify that the vulnerability being tested is in a system that has a configuration that matches the standard, so it can be patched immediately.
>
> There are many more examples that other writers in this issue illuminate. I include these just to support the theme that security will be far too expensive and ineffective without software interoperability."*

He goes on to illuminate some key reasons that the "status quo" of a lack of true open interoperability has been maintained for so long. His statistics are rather eye-opening, including:

1. Software companies get 90% of their profits from existing customers.
2. When a company creates (or buys) a completely new product it finds that selling to an existing customer costs one fifteenth of what it costs to sell to a new customer.
3. Since holding onto customers is possibly one of the few winning strategies (based on the fact that marketing and sales consumes 50 cents out of every dollar), software companies will look for an "edge" that makes it hard for customers to shift to a replacement product.
4. Academics call this "switching costs" and of course what do standards do? They LOWER "switching costs," which of course makes it easier to switch.

---

* Alan Paller, "Why Industry Needs Federal Government Leadership to Gain the Benefits of Security Automation [Electronic version]," *IAnewsletter* 13, no. 1 (2010).

This man is preaching to the choir in the above quoted text and then goes on to absolutely nutshell possibly THE critical problem that continues to permeate the IT industry, specifically the security discipline at this point, with the following:

> "That means that regardless of the vendors' claims, most software vendors will work diligently to delay the creation, vetting, or deployment of standards for software interoperability that might make it easier for their clients to switch. The vendor representatives may even come to meetings and act as if they are helping, all the while looking for ways to delay the process."[*]

YES! This is exactly what has happened in just about every facet of our profession for as long as I can remember. I have written this very statement in columns for publications, spoke the same words to journalists for articles, preached the gospel from the stages of trade shows, communicated in earnest with vendors that say they care, and published the same concept in the sixth edition, Volume 3, of this very same book. Thank you Allan! At least if I am crazy, I am not alone, and this rock a few of us have been pushing up this hill could use all the extra hands it can get. Allan then goes on to explain how the smaller clients get pretty much blown off and describes a scenario I swear has occurred to me on several occasions. He writes:

> "Software vendors have very limited teams of advanced development engineers, so they jealously guard the priorities placed on those engineers. Clients who ask for new product features that make it easier for them to switch to other vendors' products usually get a friendly "thank you" and a statement something like, "You are the first organization to suggest that, but it is really a good idea. I'll take it back to our development team." They say that even when dozens of customers have asked for the same thing—like interoperability. And you probably will never hear from them again on that topic."[†]

Wow, does that sound familiar? Jeez, it's so accurate it's almost spooky, and the sad part is that we allow ourselves to be controlled and isolated (as I referenced last year in this book) based on these silos created for vendors for the purposes of compensation structures within their own companies. We are not that different as organizations and where we do differ, the percentage of difference is easily no more than twenty to thirty percent, if that. That means there is a commonality of seventy to eighty percent within organizations that often gets cordoned off by our egos and lack of attention to our surroundings and the vendor's desire to both maintain what they have and to keep it as simple as possible for their accounting departments.

How Do We Push Forward with Adoption of SCAP/IF-MAP?

Batter up! Do we NEED a clean-up hitter?!?!

Our new friend Allan goes on to write:

> "When a very big customer comes to a vendor and says, "We need this particular feature in order to buy your product or continue using your product," the natural

---

[*] Ibid.
[†] Ibid.

defenses disappear. The sales staff has direct access to the development staff and those few advanced development engineers are assigned to make it happen. But you have to be an extremely large client in order to have a real impact. Even the largest corporations are, individually, very small buyers of any one product. When they try to gather other users together to speak with one voice, the vendor will offer special incentives (free upgrades or discounts or training, for example) to get them to act individually. It is very hard to hold the line on demanding open standards when a vendor is offering your boss a 40% discount if he agrees to select the current, proprietary product instead. That is why federal leadership, especially Department of Defense (DoD) leadership, is the key to enabling rapid adoption of security automation. The U.S. government is a large enough buyer of technology to provide the incentives for security vendors to adopt open standards. If the DoD establishes a policy that all software licenses after a date certain must include a specific list of open standard capabilities, the vendors will build the interoperable products. Once they are built, industry can buy them, too."[*]

Uh oh! He said a few bad words in that chock-full paragraph. He said "federal leadership" and he mentioned the D word (DoD)! Now, whether I agree with Allan or not on these specific points, which I do, we cannot wait around while governments progress (I hope) towards requiring standards and hope they include us along the way. Yes, even large companies are small in the grand scheme of things but I believe that a collaborative group of companies coupled with the governments of various countries, states, locals, etc., can make an even faster impact. I am currently leading a working group within the Open Group titled "Improving the Digital EcoSystem," which focuses on what I am calling Small and Medium Government and Business (SMGB). While we are first working on the idea of providing actionable standards and procedures to companies that need it, there is no reason a collective like that could not work with its larger partners to help expedite real open standards. At the end of the day, we are all part of the same value-chain in this consumer-driven economy so everyone (even the vendors that sell proprietary solutions) has a vested interest in seeing our digital foundation strengthened and our ability to survive, and eventually thrive, enhanced.

So we know Allan's view on how we get this done, but in the meantime, while Godzilla is mobilizing, what can we do? Well so far we know that the Federal Desktop Core Configuration (FDCC) has been a success for the United States. I am not sure about the current worldwide adoption of it or a similar concept, but I expect that the larger countries have taken many of the same steps. FDCC actually leveraged SCAP but the current ubiquity of similar solutions is not what we need to have even greater capabilities emerge. Most of this has some aspect of commodity so as we go we must make sure to look for the repeatable and see if someone has already been there and done that. The only way we can do that is to make output from various tools consistent and consumable by other tools.

Robert Martin writes:

"We feel that those who buy software products, create organizational security policies, and create security guidance and benchmarks can help us all get to these greater capabilities faster by adopting some of the following practices. We feel that those who buy software products, create organizational security policies, and create security guidance

---

[*] Ibid.

and benchmarks can help us all get to these greater capabilities faster by adopting some of the following practices."*

Specifically regarding software, Robert references an internal government standard but then goes on to include specific requirements that are potentially applicable to any and all purchases within an enterprise.

- Provide a public address (email and/or Web) for reporting security-relevant issues with the provider's software
- Provide a publicly available statement of the time frame and process the software provider's organization follows in addressing reports of security relevant issues with the provider's software
- Provide public advisories of relevant security related issues and their resolution
- Include a CVE Identifier for security-related issues when the issues are related to a software flaw or default setting that constitutes a security shortcoming of the provider's software as part of the initial public advisory
- Include an initial Open Vulnerability and Assessment Language (OVAL) definition(s) as a machine-readable description of how to tell if the flaw, misconfiguration, or incorrect default settings are present and whether any of the known resolutions have been taken as part of the initial public advisory
- Include the base and initial temporal severity score portions of the CVSS rating for the flaw, misconfiguration, or incorrect default settings as part of the initial public advisory.†

He goes on to then refer to government configurations and mentions that systems should be set up for operations use with what he calls a "blessed" configuration. This is pretty much standard fare in many organizations regarding software loads but has never, until recently, extended to configuration of said software in an automatic fashion. Where possible, organizations should consider the following:

- Express policies and guidelines in the XCCDF/OVAL standard languages so that tool technologies can use these machine-readable descriptions directly to evaluate the status of information technology with regards to those policies and guidelines.
- Adopt the use of automated methods to directly use the machine-readable XCCDF/OVAL policies and guidelines for assessing, reporting, and directing action on exceptions to the policies and guidelines.

Procurement Guidance for Security Assessment and Management Tools is also fairly straightforward and is expressly intended to assist in the use of automated tools used to implement and verify security controls across organizations. Martin specifically references SCAP standards but also mentions any similar standardization that uses a defined nomenclature where there are gaps in SCAP.

---

* Robert Martin, "Practicing Standards-Based Security Assessment and Management [Electronic version]," *IAnewsletter* 13, no. 1 (2010).
† Ibid.

■ Include the appropriate CVE Identifier for security-related information that is related to a software flaw or a non-secure default setting.
■ Provide for the searching of security-related information by CVE Identifier
■ Incorporate the machine-readable tests for flaws, patches, and configuration checks written in conformance with the OVAL Definition schema.
■ Generate machine-readable assessment results from tests for flaws, patches, and configuration checks in conformance with the XCCDF and OVAL Results schema.
■ Incorporate the machine-readable results from flaw, patch, and configuration check assessments that are written in conformance with the OVAL Results schema.
■ As appropriate to the functionality of the tool, incorporate support for the different severity score portions of the CVSS rating for the flaw or incorrect default settings.[*]

This type of open-mindedness is required to realize that attack vectors are multiplying way too quickly for any one standards organization, body, or entity to have a shot at keeping up. Instead we need to be loosely coupled but tightly integrated in our push for standards going forward and look for the additional areas of standardization that are emerging that will lend themselves to the total visibility required and in the future will benefit those working to secure their enterprises proactively instead of constantly being in a reactive state.

End Game: "Don't reinvent, reuse. Don't redo, repurpose. Don't resist, realize."

As previously mentioned, I was involved in a pretty interesting e-mail conversation between Steve Hanna and a member of a government organization deeply involved in the SCAP space. It was one of those conversations that I could simply just cheer on for the most part in order to make sure not to disrupt the flow of concepts and ideas that were being shared by two very intelligent individuals.

> Steve wrote: " ...the SCAP and TNC specs are remarkably complementary. SCAP defines the vocabulary and policies. TNC mostly stays out of those areas, with the exception of PA-TNC, which is totally extensible so the SCAP vocabulary can replace or supplement PA-TNC. I agree with your suggestion to keep the SCAP standards transport-independent. Such layering and separation enables faster innovation and greater flexibility.
>
> Still, there is considerable value in agreeing on standard transport and enforcement protocols. By agreeing on those protocols, we greatly improve interoperability and reduce integration complexity and cost.
>
> Our goal is to reach a point where every device can vouch for its own posture (security configuration) when it comes on the network, using interoperable standards that enable instant interoperability, just as DHCP and TCP/IP are built into every network-connected product today. Then customers will be able to unpack a new laptop or network-enabled printer, plug it into the network, and have it interoperate with their network security system. That's not all of the TNC vision (which also encompasses integrating a wide variety of security systems to enable automated security enforcement and response) but it's a big part.
>
> TNC...integrating with SCAP will provide common vocabularies and languages for identifying vulnerabilities, platforms, and configurations and expressing essential assessment concepts like checklists and assessment results." (Steve Hanna, personal communication, May/June 2010)

---

[*] Ibid.

OVAL, SCAP, IF-MAP, SCM, and eventually S²CM begin to resolve many of the current inefficiencies in information security through interoperability, transparency, repeatability, scalability, uniformity, automation, and ultimately autonomic response to threats that occur far faster than anything human-driven can react. The "Techno-Industrial Revolution" has created a vast number of opportunities while at the same time creating exponentially more dangerous terrain which we as practitioners have to navigate. Open standards that lead to machine-to-machine automation are the only way we will keep our organizations above water as the tide rises rapidly over the next decade. We must look to break through the various silos, whether they be intentional or accidental, to bring the various caches of information from disparate countries, companies, communities, and disciplines together to facilitate actionable correlations of things we may not even have thought of yet. Solving this problem with status quo is far beyond the capability of any single company, government, country, or consortium of countries. It will take a unified effort from all of us and those that come after us in order to reestablish the foundation for the next twenty years of technological innovation. I know at times I feel like I am trying to move an elephant with a straw. No matter how hard I blow or how many times I poke it, it moves when it wants to. The exchange I referenced above and the subsequent meeting between the various involved parties was different though, as the conversation progressed down a path that really made me believe (maybe the right word is hope) it was possible to get there from here. As follows:

> Steve wrote: "Beyond the specific technical integration possibilities that we have been talking about (which are very exciting!), I wonder if we should also be talking about a broader, more strategic alignment of our efforts. SCAP and TNC seem to share a common goal of enabling security integration and automation. SCAP has focused on vocabularies and languages. TNC has focused on network protocols and APIs. Both of us have good solid architecture documents. Maybe we should be looking at combining our efforts instead of just aligning them."

> Government participant: "There's definitely a lot of potential for SCAP to gain deployment traction if we can leverage adoption of TNC standard protocols. (I'd be inclined to keep SCAP specs protocol-agnostic, but separately define standard mechanisms, identifiers, and conventions for conveying those artifacts over TNC standard protocols; that's just a gut feeling through. For example, a standard PA-TNC sub-type for OVAL results data.)

> Steve wrote: "I agree with both of your ideas. On item 2, PA-TNC is designed to run over transport and session protocols called PT and PB-TNC. We shouldn't have any trouble carrying the results of an OVAL assessment from the endpoint to a server. I think we could even conduct an OVAL assessment over these NEA protocols. The nice thing about that is we can conduct the assessment or at least check the results before the endpoint gets any network access using EAP over 802.1X as the PT protocol.
> TNC also has another protocol that may be complementary to SCAP: IF-MAP. IF-MAP is a standard network protocol for updating and querying a database (called a MAP) that stores information about the network: which devices are on the network with which users, what attributes are associated with those devices and users (groups, roles, device compliance and vulnerability information, etc.), and what abnormal events have been reported by various sensors. IF-MAP includes real-time notification capabilities so that action can be immediately taken in response to events (e.g.,

automatically quarantine a misbehaving device, if such an action is called for by pol-icy)... I think that TNC and SCAP do not need to be in conflict." (Steve Hanna, per-sonal communication, May/June 2010; anonymous government employee, personal communication, May/June 2010)

YAHTZEE! I actually cannot say it any better than they did. Can this industry with the mammoth challenges ahead of us, with the history of short-cuts, the litany of examples of vendor lock-in and greed, the purposeful proliferation fear uncertainty and doubt, falling budgets, rising expectations, and daily attacks from an increasing number of vectors, actually accomplish this? The world better hope so. With that in mind, I will leave you with one of the things I have said over the years:

> "When confronted with seemingly insurmountable challenges, always ask your-self: If not us, who? If not now, when? Then take that first step..."

Bluntly, it is clear we have the leadership, the vision, the technology, the skill sets, and the people to do what needs to be done. The real question, and it's one that I ask myself a lot, is do we as a community have the fortitude. Only you, as an individual, can answer that, as we all must.

About the Author

David O'Berry, CSSLP, CRMP, CISSP-ISSAP, ISSMP, MCNE, is the director of ITSS at SCDPPPS. He is a strong proponent of the pervasive implementation of open standards and shar-ing of information to facilitate secure code reuse, best practices, and in-depth security and vis-ibility concepts in a collaborative environment as a fundamental requirement for a stronger overall digital ecosystem. Industry engagements include SC's ITSC, MS-ISAC Executive Committee, SC's Security and TOG's "Digital Ecosystem" WG chairs, Midlands ISSA President, GRCSI's cer-tification board, and founding member of McAfee's Cyber-Security Experts Council and TNC's Customer Advisory Council. He was awarded Technologist of the Year for SC's IT Directors' Association in 2008.

Internet, Intranet, Extranet Security

Chapter 7

Understating the Ramifications of IPv6

Foster Henderson

The purpose of this chapter is to provide and discuss the various information assurance issues associated with migrating from the current Internet Protocol version 4 (IPv4) (with features about which most Internet users are said to be subconsciously aware) to Internet Protocol version 6 (IPv6), (i.e., the next generation of the Internet). Prior to discussing the IPv6 information assurance issues or concerns, it is critical to understand the basic concepts of the current version of Internet protocols, otherwise the problems and issues associated with IPv4 will not be fully understood during an eventual migration to IPv6.

In 1962, the United States Air Force requested a study, which was performed by Paul Baran of the RAND Corporation, to determine how the Air Force could maintain command and control over its missiles and bombers in the event of a nuclear war (Kristula, 2001). The proposal was to develop a military research network that could survive a nuclear strike that was decentralized so that if any specific locations were attacked, the Air Force would still maintain control of its nuclear arms (Kristula, 2001). The RAND Corporation wrote

> Consequently, Baran conceived a system that had no centralized switches and could operate even if many of its links and switching nodes had been destroyed. Baran envisioned a network of unmanned nodes that would act as switches, routing information from one node to another to their final destinations. The nodes would use a scheme Baran called "hot-potato routing" [known as packets today] or distributed communications. (RAND, 2007, para 4)

Baran developed the process of dividing messages into separate building blocks, sending those blocks to a remote area, and then having the building blocks reassembled at a remote location (RAND, 2007). In 1969, under the Advanced Research Projects Agency (now known as DARPA, the D is for Defense), the first physical network, called ARPANET, was constructed, linking four nodes (Kristula, 2001). In 1973, DARPA developed the Transport Control Protocol (TCP)/Internet Protocol (IP) (Kristula, 2001).

Baran's previous work is the basis for DARPA's request for comment (RFC) 793, which was published in 1981 (Usenet FAQ, 2010). Due to the success of Department of Defense's (DoD's) TCP/IP on ARPANET, the National Science Foundation (NSF) initiated construction of an Internet backbone and later turned it over for public management (Internet Society, 2010). This is, as everyone knows, the end result today.

TCP and the OSI Reference Model

The Open System Interconnection (OSI) reference model, depicted in Figure 7.1, has seven layers, as shown on the right of the column labeled "Layer." The TCP operates on the Transport layer and to the immediate left is the word "segment." Under the IPv4, the maximum Ethernet data frame that can be sent is 1500 bytes. The TCP is responsible for segmenting large messages or files into smaller Ethernet blocks (i.e., packets) sizes. This process is known as message fragmentation (Heywood, 1997). Each segment that is transmitted to a remote computer is individually labeled with a sequence segment number (Heywood, 1997) before being placed onto the network backbone. It is not uncommon for segments not to be received in the order in which they were originally sent. The remote recipient's computer has to be able to recompile those segments in the correct sequence and inform the original sender which specific segments sent arrived corrupted or simply did not arrive. For example, an individual wants to send this research paper to a colleague. Hypothetically speaking, this paper would be broken into 25 individual segments (i.e., it exceeds the predetermined byte size for transport) by the host computer via the TCP. Using the previous scenario, the recipient's computer during transmission received 23 of 25 original data segments as the result of perhaps data corruption, misrouting, etc. The recipient's remote computer would send a retransmission request message to the host (i.e., sender's) computer regarding the specific missed sequence numbers required to be rebroadcast.

	Data unit	Layer	Function
Host layers	Data	7. Application	Network process to application
		6. Presentation	Data representation and encryption
		5. Session	Interhost communication
	Segment	4. Transport	End-to-end connections and reliability
Media layers	Packet	3. Network	Path determination and logical addressing
	Frame	2. Data Link	Physical addressing
	Bit	1. Physical	Media, signal, and binary transmission

Figure 7.1 OSI reference model. (From Hewitt, J., OSI RM model, Wikimedia Commons, accessed Jan 19, 2011 at http://en.wikipedia.org/wiki/File:Osi-model-jb.png.)

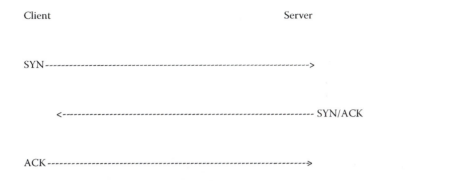

Figure 7.2   Client and server can now send service-specific data. (From Carnegie Mellon, CERT® Advisory CA-1996-21 TCP SYN Flooding and IP Spoofing Attacks. http://www.cert.org/advisories/CA-1996-21.html. 2000.)

The TCP is an error-tolerant and connection-oriented protocol. Specifically, each data segment sent by the host is acknowledged on the remote side (i.e., destination address) whether a data segment was successfully received or requires retransmission. To initiate a communication, a TCP handshake is performed as shown in Figure 7.2. A host sends a synchronous (SYN) packet to the remote computer, which acknowledges the receipt, by sending an acknowledgment message (SYN/ACK) packet to the host source (Harris, 2002). The host computer replies and ends the connection request by acknowledging (ACK) it has received the remote sources SYN/ACK message (Harris, 2002). The TCP takes up a lot of overhead for being such an error-tolerant protocol. The overhead is in the form of communications between two computers before the next packet is sent.

What Is Internet Protocol?

Using the OSI model as a reference, the IP is located on layer three, the network layer. The IP establishes the process that provides an envelope and addresses for each packet (i.e., the source and destination address) in order to be properly routed so that a packet arrives at its intended destination (Harris, 2002). Unlike the TCP, the IP is a connectionless protocol. In layperson terms, packets are simply provided a source and destination IP address and sent across the network, "which means that there is no continuing connection between the endpoints that are communicating" (SearchUnifiedCommunications.com, 2010, para 3). The current IP version most widely used within the Internet is IPv4.

IPv4 Common Attack Methods

"As soon as you have anything of value, you are at risk of losing it – it is just that simple" (Tiller, 2004, 1064). Portions of the Internet are subject to attack on a constant basis. Technology is multifaceted and each technological application has its advantages, disadvantages, and unique limitations (Henderson & Craig-Henderson, 2004). The Internet is not immune to this philosophy and the following passages will briefly discuss the most popular forms of Internet attack methods used, though they should not be considered all-inclusive.

The Internet in its most basic architectural form is a series of routers, gateways, Domain Name Service (DNS) servers, Internet Service Provider (ISP) trunk lines (i.e., Fiber Distributed Data Interface, copper, wireless, cable, etc.) and for the sake of argument we will include a few remote access service (RAS) servers. The ISPs use a database or RAS servers that identify, recognize, and authenticate each individual's computer before allowing access to the ISP's gateway router (Internet access). If this were not the case, everyone within the United States would be surfing the Internet for free. However, there is no telecommunication service in the United States like this today.

The problem with the current Internet is that its original purpose was the command and control of nuclear weapons in the event of a nuclear war. Everyone was one "big happy family" within DoD. That is, "we" all trusted one another within the DoD family. There lies one of the chief problems today.

It is probably safe to say that the original designers had no clue that the Internet would be used in the manner or method it is used today or that it would be so popular. Today's issues include: "who is an individual corresponding to?", "how does one know it is the intended person with whom they want to communicate?", and "Is the IP address spoofed?" Here are some commonly used methods to attack a network segment (not all-inclusive):

1. Viruses
2. Worms
3. Denial of services (DoS)
4. Buffer overflows
5. Malicious code
6. Poorly designed software or implementations
7. Reconnaissance

A virus is a small string of code whose main function is to reproduce and affect an application or file (Harris, 2002). A virus infects a host (i.e., using the "most basic architectural" rule). As mentioned earlier, the Internet foundation pieces are a DNS or RAS server. It doesn't take much technical knowledge to understand the impact if a DNS or a RAS server is compromised by a virus; it is a network disaster! A virus needs the intervention of a user or program in order to spread (Harris, 2002). There are varying degrees and different categories of viruses. However, it is not necessary to discuss those differences at this time.

In contrast, worms do not require outside interventions to propagate and are self-contained programs (Harris, 2002). In recollection, the Nimda worm was one of the worst worms released upon the Internet based upon both the speed to infect a mass number in a short time and the impact it had on systems. The Nimda code was a compact code that used the User Datagram Protocol (UDP) to traverse the Internet to infect nodes (Symantec, 2007). As an example, most streaming audio programs use the UDP protocol because unreliable delivery is an acceptable compromise given the benefit of the speed at which the UDP travels. As a reminder, the UDP is a connectionless protocol and like the IP there are no TCP handshakes to slow the transmission process. Finally, if anyone thinks that worms don't have much effect on the "most basic architectural" Internet pieces (in this case routers), then one should research the impact that the Code Red worm propagation had on older Cisco routers (Cisco, 2001).

The TCP SYN attack is a form of denial of service attack. Many wireless attacks use this method to cause a host to release its IP address and request a new IP address to a rogue wireless access point in the attempt to break the weak encryption algorithms. Carnegie Mellon's

Software Engineering Institute (2001, para 1) states, "a denial-of-service attack is characterized by an explicit attempt by attackers to prevent legitimate users of a service from using that service."

Buffer overflows may be lumped into the DoS category, but hackers use buffer overflows typically to gain root access to a server (i.e., again think DNS or RAS server) by crashing a thread or application being run. A buffer overflow occurs when a program or process attempts to store more data than the address space (i.e., temporary data storage area or RAM) it was intended to hold (Kurtz, McClure, & Scambray, 2005). If the address space isn't well defined (within the programs) and the input and output aren't checked against that finite amount of address space, that extra information, which has to go somewhere, overflows into adjacent buffers and corrupts or overwrites the valid data held in them.

An address space represents the amount of space or memory available to a program. For example, think of address space as filling up an ice tray to place in the freezer. If someone were to overfill one space or cell of that ice tray, the water dumps over into the next adjacent slot. Each slot, for this analogy, represents a single program running in memory.

While both viruses and worms are malicious code, they are not the only forms. There is spyware, and mobile code in the form of Java applets or Active X, VBS scripts, etc., which can bring a network down if they are malicious in nature. Mobile code has been defined on Wikipedia as software transferred between systems (perhaps transferred across a network or via a USB flash drive) and executed on a local system without explicit installation or execution by the recipient. Examples of mobile code include JavaScript, VBScripts, ActiveX controls, and macros embedded within Office documents.

The most commonly used attack method on the Internet is to use an exploit against a known software bug (i.e., vulnerability). Most issues with security come from the application layers software vulnerabilities (i.e., OSI model). One example is the buffer overflows, which is the result of poorly written code. Another, yet different, example is an implementation issue such as the TCP SYN attacks which appeared several years ago for IPv4. This was not a software bug in implementations, but rather an attack against the base specification for TCP. Another similar example includes the vulnerabilities that appeared for the Simple Network Management Protocol (SNMP) several years ago (CERT, 2008).

Finally the most common exploit is to simply scan the network boundaries, gather information on the type of applications, services, hardware used on a particular network segment, and the IP address range for a respective network segment. Specifically, we are discussing the term footprinting (Kurtz, McClure, & Scambray, 2005). Once the network is mapped and cataloged, a hacker simply exposes the security architecture tools that protect a network segment to known vulnerabilities to gain access to an organization.

Address Space Problems

The goal here is not to rehash a very well-documented and published problem but to discuss the address space problems from an IA perspective. Due to the manner in which IP address space has been allocated, "there are routinely over 85,000 routes in the routing tables of Internet backbone routers" (Microsoft, 2008, 1). Network Address Translator (NAT) was developed to mitigate the shrinking address space by mapping multiple "private addresses to a single public IP address" (Microsoft, 2008, 1). Unfortunately, IP-enabled phones attempt to connect to one another (i.e., Voice over IP (VoIP)) and the NAT frequently makes that configuration extremely difficult to manage (Beijnum, 2006). IPv6 introduced the Secure Internet Protocol (IPsec), which was eventually made backwards compatible for IPv4. However, when two endpoints attempt to establish the tunnel, the two ends usually can't agree on IP addresses. This problem results because somewhere in the middle, NAT translated the IP address for one of the endpoints (Beijnum, 2006). Finally, if an individual has experience with attempting to establish an IPsec tunnel and multiple vendors are involved, then one knows it is virtually impossible to use IPsec solutions from various vendors because of the various proprietary IPsec implementations used by vendors.

IPv6 Introduction

A brief history on the Internet was provided in the Introduction. It was stated that the original Internet designers could not have foreseen or planned for the explosive growth of the Internet. The Internet has changed from its original planned use. Routing for the current Internet is very inefficient, Quality of Service (QoS) support is lacking today's requirement for real-time delivery of data, and the IPsec support is a patchwork project—best-case scenario.

IPv6 is the next-generation Internet, which is being designed to address many of the shortcomings of IPv4. The first RFC for IPv6 was published in 1995 and since then there have been revisions (Beijnum, 2006).

Similarities between IPv4 and IPv6

Perhaps the easiest way to understand the similarities is to inspect the internal headers of both IP versions. Figure 7.3 represents the 32-bit IPv4 header next to the 128-bit IPv6 header. The

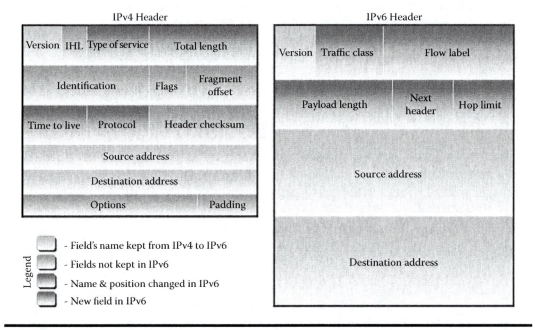

Figure 7.3 IPv4 and IPv6 header comparison. (From Cisco, IPv6 Extension Headers Review and Considerations. http://www.ciscosistemas.org/en/US/technologies/tk648/tk872/technologies_white_paper0900aecd8054d37d.pdf. 2006.)

gold-colored areas are the same with the exception of the increase in bit size for the source and destination address. The "version" designation area is the same and delineates whether an IPv4 or IPv6 datagram is being sent. The areas marked in blue are the same features, but have been moved and have a new name, though they both provide the same basic features. Below are the IPv4 fields marked in blue mapped against the similar field that was moved and renamed in the IPv6 header:

1. Type of service = traffic class
2. Total length = payload length
3. Time to live = hop limit
4. Protocol = next header

An earlier discussion was provided on the various common attack methods for IPv4 under the common attack method subheading. It was also stated that the IP is a connectionless based protocol located on the network layer of the OSI model. If it isn't apparent at this point, then for clarification, the upper-level layers from the OSI model (i.e., 5–7) have the same basic implementations. Hence IPv6 is vulnerable to many exploits currently used on the Internet. IPv6 inherits many of the same challenges. This is an important issue to understand for the remainder of this chapter. The IP is the network layer based upon the OSI model, so most of the common category of attacks mentioned earlier are inherited in IPv6. Think about it: if an application is poorly written, and assuming that there is no IP address embedded in the code for it to run, the TCP and UDP are the same in IPv6. So why is it commonly thought that IPv6 is more secure than IPv4?

IPv6 Misunderstandings

The information security profession must have a good foundation in order to implement successful security architectures (Henderson & Craig-Henderson, 2004). One reason why IPv6 is thought to be more secure than IPv4 is probably because not all the features are fully understood. In addition, this misunderstanding is probably also explained by the fact that whereas IPsec is required in IPv6, it is only an option in IPv4 (Beijnum, 2006). Furthermore, using IPv6 during a transition period will make organizations more susceptible to vulnerabilities due to the fact that those organizations are now susceptible to vulnerabilities by running both protocols (i.e., IPv4 and IPv6). For example, Apple's two most current operating system (OS) releases, X 10.5 and X 10.6, better known as "Leopard" and "Snow Leopard" respectively, and Microsoft's OS, Vista, Windows Server 2008, and Windows 7, share a common default installation configuration (Microsoft, 2010). The TCP/IP stack for IPv4 and IPv6 is installed and enabled by default (Apple, 2008). Many of the current security tools for IPv6 are not mature enough to protect against breaches (GAO, 2006). Finally, with capabilities existing such as automatic configuration, it actually can facilitate attacks on a network if not configured or monitored properly (GAO, 2006).

IPv6 Features and Benefits

The key benefits of IPv6 include:

1. Additional address space
2. Simpler IP header for flexibility and innovation

   3. Improved efficiency (i.e., routing)
   4. Enhanced mobility
   5. Improved QoS
   6. Integrated IPsec
   7. Easier configuration capabilities (GAO, 2005)

Additional Address Space

Beijnum (2010) states that as of January 1, 2010, from the 4,294,967,296 total available IPv4 addresses, approximately 16% or 722.18 million IPv4 addresses remain. In contrast, IPv6's possible IP addresses are approximately 3.4×10^{38} or 340,282,366,920,938,463,374,607,431,768,211,456 (Beijnum, 2006). This staggering number is the result of IPv6's 128-bit addressing scheme vs. IPv4's 32-bit addressing scheme. Put in another manner, IPv6 has enough IP address space that "provides 655,570,793,348,866,943,898,599 (6.5×10^{23}) addresses for every square meter of the Earth's surface" (Microsoft, 2008, 8). The significance of this fact will be discussed later under the security issues section.

   "IPv6 has three types of addresses: unicast, multicast, and anycast" (Beijnum, 2006, 15). Unicast address is a one-to-one communication much like that which is currently used on IPv4 (Beijnum, 2006). Multicast is a one-to-many communications, much like that as broadcast feature in IPv4; though it is now more targeted so only those interested in receiving the communication may listen (Microsoft, 2008). Anycast is similar to multicast except "that the packets sent to an anycast address are only delivered to one system in the anycast group rather than all" (Beijnum, 2006, 15). For clarification, an anycast is defined as the "nearest" interface in terms of routing. An anycast is a one-to-one-of-many transmissions (Microsoft, 2008). There are several issues to consider with anycast and multicast address use and those will be discussed later within the security portions of this paper.

Simpler IP Header for Flexibility and Innovation

A review of Figure 7.3's "IPv4 and IPv6 Header Comparison" indicates that 14 header fields have been reduced to 8 (GAO, 2005). The header size in IPv6 is now fixed, whereas under IPv4 the header sizes could vary. The main reason IPv4 address space hasn't run out is because of the use of NAT and NAT severely restricts peer-to-peer applications (Beijnum, 2006). IPv6 can fully implement technologies such as peer-to-peer applications (Beijnum, 2006). For example, IPv6 can enable gaming, VoIP, video teleconferencing, etc. This is because an IP address can be provided to each IP-enabled application, thereby eliminating the need for NAT.

   A simplified header can provide new features or extensions (GAO, 2005). With new features come unknown issues to address in the future given that the IPv6 technology is still maturing.

Improved Efficiency

A majority of the processors on today's market are 32-bit CPUs and 64-bit CPUs, and corresponding BUS architectures are available from several vendors. IPv6's header is optimized for processing 64 bits at a time vs. 32 bits for the IPv4 header. The IPv4 checksum header was removed to improve efficiency. Under IPv6, routers are not required to fragment oversized packets (Beijnum, 2006). Now they simply signal the "source" to send smaller-size fragments. From its inception IPv6 was designed to support efficient hierarchical routing and addressing. In contrast, IPv4 has three classes of IP addresses and it is well documented that a majority of those IP addresses are not contiguous addresses.

Enhanced Mobility

Each vendor of network interface cards (NIC) has a unique vendor identification number in the world. The machine address code (MAC) is based upon the vendor's unique identification number provided by the Institute of Electrical and Electronics Engineers (IEEE) and the serial number on each NIC (generated during the manufacturing process by the vendor). The traditional IPv4 MAC address is a 48-bit address. Under IPv6, RFC 3513 for unicasts, the new network interface address or extended unique identifiers (EUI-64) address is a new standard.

The EUI-64 is IPv6's lower unicast 64-bit address space that is comprised of the vendor's identification number, which remains the same length (24 bits). However, the vendor's serial number is now expanded to 40 bits (Microsoft, 2008). This was done to gain a much larger serial number and hence larger physical address space. This standard provides wireless or wired devices with a unique IP address that is independent from the current Internet point of presence attachment (GAO, 2005). The interface doesn't change while roaming and a constant IP address is maintained (i.e., in this example the interface identification (ID) was autoconfigured, but to be clear, an interface ID may also be autogenerated, provided by DHCP, or manually inputted). While autoconfiguration greatly supports mobility, it naturally raises privacy issues. Warfield (2003, 8) states,

> a system could be tracked or identified between networks or across renumbering… There exists the possibility of mapping network infrastructure or connectivity through EUI mapping. Mappings of EUI between networks can reveal underlying subnet structures and subnet mappings (SLAs) between networks.

Right now a normal IT professional should be thinking: a 2003 reference is a Smithsonian ancient archeological "find" for IT. Not so, if the information is still valid! For example, NIST (2010, 6–7) states, "the use of the MAC address in EUI-64 addresses theoretically makes it easier for an attacker to scan a network." NIST (2010) recommends blocking scanning at the network perimeter and generating addresses using a nonpredictable function such as a cryptographic feature. Finally, Microsoft takes its shots in the form of criticism from security professionals and the public at times, but it has to be commended for making the "permanent interface identifier that is randomly generated to mitigate address scans of unicast IPv6 addresses on a subnet. This is the default behavior for IPv6 in Windows Vista and Windows Server 2008" (Microsoft, 2008, 19).

Improved QoS

IPv6's header has introduced a new feature called the flow label (i.e., reference Figure 7.3). "Packets belonging to the same stream, session, or flow share a common flow label value, making the session easily recognizable without having to look 'deep' into the packet" (Beijnum, 2006, 153). The flow size is 20 bits and uses "non default quality of services connections" (Microsoft, 2008, 30). While this feature is still very much undefined between vendors, it also raises unknown possibilities and establishes possible developing back-door issues.

Integrated IPsec

It has been stated several times within this article that IPv6 requires IPsec. With IPv6 there are two IPsec headers: the Authentication Header (AH) and the Encapsulating Security Payload (ESP) header (Beijnum, 2006). The AH protects the entire header and also provides authentication (Beijnum, 2006). The ESP header "provides either authentication, or encryption or both" (Beijnum, 2006, 200). Importantly, the ESP header only protects the data following the ESP extension header.

As a reminder, the IPv6 header has a fixed length and as a result "option fields" cannot be tagged into the IP header as they were previously in IPv4. However, this does not exclude the use of extension headers. The AH and ESP extension headers are part of IPsec (Beijnum, 2006). Other extension headers (e.g., hop by hop, destination, etc.) are nestled between the IPv6 header (i.e., layer 3) and the TCP and UPD (i.e., layer 4 the transport layer) headers (Beijnum, 2006). The significance of this is that the extension headers have no standard format (Beijnum, 2006).

Stateful and Stateless Autoconfiguration

Dynamic Host Configuration Protocol (DHCP) "is a communications protocol that lets network administrators centrally manage and automate the assignment of Internet IP addresses in an organization's network" (Whatis.com, 2008, para 1). Without DHCP, a network administrator would have to manually configure each host computer in an organization with an IP address, which would be manpower intensive, and from a management view nearly impossible.

> One of the most useful aspects of IPv6 is its ability to automatically configure itself, even without the use of a stateful configuration such as DHCP for IPv6 (DHCPv6). An IPv6 host performs stateless address autoconfiguration by default and stateful address autoconfiguration as indicated by the following fields in the Router Advertisement message sent by a neighboring router. (Microsoft, 2008, 74)

In IPv6, the "router" takes on much more importance and more critical functions. Stateless autoconfiguration is in effect, and in order for a host to obtain an IP address the host listens for a router's router advertisement (RA) (Beijnum, 2006). The RA communicates the top 64 bits (i.e., address space) and for those hosts connected to the same subnet the bottom 64 bits are based upon the EUI-64-derived (i.e., MAC) values (Beijnum, 2006). "Even in the absence of a router, hosts on the same link (i.e., subnet) can automatically configure themselves [neighbor discovery] with link-local addresses and communicate without manual configuration" (Microsoft, 2008, 3). Hosts may request a router solicitation, which under the Internet Control Message Protocol (ICMP) is supported in IPv6 by ICMPv6. Finally RAs can inform hosts which router to use to gain access to the Internet (Beijnum, 2006).

Renumbering

Imagine the poor system administrators at Time Warner when Time acquired America Online, which at that time was the world's largest business merger (Guinness, 2006). One can only imagine the monumental tasks merging two networks into one network (i.e., under IPv4). Under IPv6, routers simply stop advertising their old prefix and simply advertise the new ones (Beijnum, 2006). Communication interruptions are minimized because newly created sessions, which use the new

IP addresses for hosts and routers and the existing communication sessions after the switch is made, are allowed to continue until existing communication sessions are naturally terminated (Beijnum, 2006).

A Preface of IPv6 Security Issues

IPv6 brings several new features, benefits, and future innovations yet to be seen. Unfortunately, it is also still susceptible to many of the higher-level protocol attack (OSI model) methods that plague IPv4. It's ironic that IPv6 is commonly thought of as being more secure than IPv4 because from earlier discussions an informed individual can reasonably argue IPv6 may be considered less secure than IPv4. However, it is probably wiser to state that IPv6 is no more or less secure than IPv4.

"As a region, Asia controls only about 9 percent of the allocated IPv4 addresses, and yet has more than half of the world's population" (GAO, 2005, 8). At some point in the near future, due to globalization forces, running out of IPv4 address space, IPv6 is going to have to be supported. "The long term solution is to deploy IPv6. IPv6 is not backward compatible with IPv4" (NIST, 2010, 6-1). The point here is not to determine whether the IPv4 address space will be exhausted in 2011 but rather to remind an individual that running both IPs makes respective organizations susceptible to vulnerabilities from running both protocols during a transition process.

Under the Address Space section, the terms anycast (one to one "nearest" communication) and multicast (one to many) were quickly mentioned with the promise to discuss the associated security issues later. Pardon the euphemism, but it's time to "pay the Piper." Anycast addresses cannot be used as source addresses and are reserved for routers. The issue is that there is no defined method, registration, or validation process in place. Someone may be impersonating an anycast server (NIST, 2010).

Multicast may be used for a denial of service attack vectors. IPv6's current multicast implementation method hasn't incorporated IPsec or Internet Key Exchange and thus is not fully protected (IPsec is between two specific points as in unicast communications, however this concept is invalid because of multicast's one to many communications) (NIST, 2010). The concern with the multicast is that it actually supports "footprinting," discussed under IPv4's common attack subheading. Multicasts "can enable an adversary to identify key resources on a network and then attack them" (Convery & Miller, 2004, 6). In addition, routers and DHCP servers have site-specific addresses (i.e., FF05::2 and FF05::3 respectively) (Convery & Miller, 2004). Specifically, by listening to a multicast an individual can more easily identify critical resources by the default site address prefixes.

The flow label, which was discussed in the Improved QoS section, has a security issue with its use. The issue is that the flow label may be used to establish a back-door channel. Beijnum (2006, 153) wrote the following regarding the flow label values: "making the session easily recognizable without having to look 'deep' into the packet". Because the flow label is new, it is not clear whether routing vendors have uniform codes or standard, nor was any documentation discovered to determine if any testing was done to validate any vendor claims (i.e., includes firewall vendors' ability to inspect this area also).

Transition Methods

In order to send an IPv4 transmission to an IPv6 network or vice versa, there are three methods to implement the procedure: Dual Stack Transition Mechanism (DSTM), tunneling, and translation.

At the risk of "stealing the Mitigation section's thunder," in DSTM the "dual stack" is the preferred transitioning method to IPv6 (GAO, 2005). The security issue is that an organization is more susceptible to vulnerabilities because both IP stacks are being run simultaneously. Consequently, the second issue is how much available router resources are available when running a dual stack? Specifically, both IP routing tables and routes have to be maintained.

There are several tunneling methods currently available.

1. *Automatic tunneling*: An IPv4 address maps to one IPv6 address (Beijnum, 2006).
2. *6over4*: RFC 2529 "Transmission of IPv6 over IPv4 domains without explicit tunnels," which uses port 41 (Shelton, 2006).
3. *Intra-Site Automatic Tunneling Addressing Protocol (ISATAP)*: Uses Non-Broadcast Multiple Access (NBMA) and is a mechanism to automatically interconnect an IPv6 host with a site to an IPv4 network (Beijnum, 2006).
4. *6to4*: A process to automatically interconnect IPv6 sites to an IPv4 network (similar to ISATAP but allows tunneling between sites) (Beijnum, 2006).
5. *Teredo*: A Microsoft implementation which uses the UDP (i.e., port 3544) (Microsoft, 2007).

The issue with automatic tunneling is that it accepts packets from anyone and everyone from the global IPv6 network. The majority of "host" computers sit behind the perimeter network defenses (i.e., Intrusion Detection System (IDS), firewall, proxy, etc.) and automatic tunneling simply allows a "back-door" channel directly to a host computer. Chapple (2005, para. 7) wrote the following concerning tunneling:

> However, one of the greatest risks inherent in the migration is the use of tunneling protocols to support the transition to IPv6. These protocols allow the encapsulation of IPv6 traffic in an IPv4 data stream for routing through non-compliant devices. Therefore, it's possible that Users on your network can begin running IPv6 using these tunneling protocols before you're ready to officially support it in production.

Another note on tunneling issues: Cisco developed a tunneling protocol called Generic Route Encapsulation (GRE) (Beijnum, 2006). This protocol allows the transmission of protocols other than the IPv6 over IP tunnels (Beijnum, 2006).

Teredo is particularly worrisome because it allows UDP packets to a host computer and basically turns it into a router in the IPv6 world; in other words: "open sesame" (Microsoft, 2007). It should also be mentioned that under Windows XP, with IPv6 installed, "the system automatically sets up a 6to4 pseudo interface if a public IPv4 address is available" (Beijnum, 2006, 36).

Translations technologies "introduce automatic tunneling with third parties and additional DoS vectors" (Convery & Miller, 2004, 20). Beijnum (2006) states that translation between IPv4 and IPv6 is the most controversial of the three transition techniques and presents the same problems as NAT, which IPv6 is supposed to eliminate.

Routing/Protocol Issues

IPv6 presents a few security challenges for both the router and hosts. IPv6 has eliminated IPv4's Address Resolution Protocol (ARP) with a similar procedure performed by ICMPv6's neighbor discovery (ND) feature (Convery & Miller, 2004). When a system or host wants to send a message on the same subnet, it requires the "link address" (i.e., MAC for IPv4 but has a new name) (Beijnum, 2006). ND allows hosts to discover other "link addresses," but at the "source." IPv6 also introduces "stateless autoconfiguration," hence it is imperative to allow some ICMPv6 traffic to transverse in order to obtain some reasonable functionality (Convery & Miller, 2004). "This decentralized [stateless autoconfiguration] approach may be easier from a system administration perspective, but it raises challenges for those of us charged with tracking the use (and abuse!) of network resources" (Chapple, 2005, para 8). Stateless autoconfiguration messages can be "spoofed," which is a form of DoS (Convery & Miller, 2004). Finally, another feature to be made aware of is that "IPv6 host performs stateless address autoconfiguration by default and stateful address autoconfiguration as indicated by the following fields in the Router Advertisement message sent by a neighboring router" (Microsoft 2008, 78).

Beijnum (2006) stated the RFC 2461 devised a method to circumvent the ICMPv6 messages being sent by remote hackers. The process involves ND and other ICMPv6 messages on a single subnet to set the hop limit to 255 from the originating host (Beijnum, 2006). It is impossible for a remote user to send an ICMPv6 message with a hop count of 255 to a destination because the routers would decrease the number during routing (Beijnum, 2006). The issue is that the other IPv6 protocols, such as RIPng, OSPFv3, and DHCPv6, did not implement the RFC 2461 procedures.

Given the concerns that the "link local addresses" present, which were discussed earlier, it is possible to have a system join on the local subnet without an administrator's knowledge. ND has other key services that present security concerns (e.g., prefix discovery where a host can learn what IPv6 prefixes are active on the local subnet, or the use of "redirection" to point a host to a different router because a better path is provided to a destination) (Microsoft, 2008). Furthermore, with introduction of extension headers, there isn't a standard and IPv6 firewalls are not capable of processing the various extension headers. Firewalls and routers configured to filter IPv6 would be faced with the dilemma to either "allow the packet" or to discard it because it's an unknown entity (Beijnum, 2006).

Reconnaissance

Warfield (2003) and Convery and Miller (2004) state that because of the IPv6's rather large address space and associated subnet sizes (i.e., default 2^{64}) it is nearly impossible to scan IP ranges. However, scanning a /64 subnet, based upon a specific vendor's EUI-64 value (i.e., think MAC value) narrows the field and requires a matter of hours with a DSL modem connection to perform the drastically scaled down scan (Beijnum, 2006).

Lack of Training

Warfield (2003) wrote that network administrators often overlook IPv6, don't recognize its presence when running an IPv4 network, and lack the skill, training, and expertise required to manage IPv6. Security is best implemented in a layered process. The analogy of "don't put all of your eggs in one basket" has significant implications and an understanding to network security professionals. Naturally, not having trained personnel to recognize the risks or capabilities that IPv6 presents is a risk because it is these same individuals that organizations typically rely on (i.e., the network administrators and IA tools) to support an organization's network and its IT goals.

Viruses/Worms etc.

Most of the viruses that exist in IPv4, those that don't scan for vulnerabilities, present the same issues and problems in IPv6. This is because the upper layer (i.e., OSI model) security issues from IPv4 are nearly the same in IPv6. One slight difference is that the scanning techniques for vulnerable systems are more likely to slow the propagation of a virus spreading (i.e., due to the IPv6 large address space) (Beijnum, 2006). In addition, the application vulnerabilities that trouble IPv4 are also the same in IPv6. Finally, the existing IDS (i.e., same functionality as IPv4), firewalls, and other IA tools necessary to support a system administrator responsible for running IPv6 are still sparse, and this presents various concerns in managing an IPv6 network.

Mitigations

The level of risk one is willing to accept will vary between organizations or even individuals. As no IT system connected to the Internet can be made totally secure, there will always be some sort of exposure to a risk, threat, or vulnerability. As long as an individual is informed of the particular circumstances and the risks, then an informed responsible decision can be made. This section will discuss several common mitigation strategies for the security issues previously discussed (not intended to be an all-inclusive list by any nature).

Among the three transition processes discussed earlier (i.e., DSTM, tunneling, or translation), DSTM or "dual stack" is the preferred transitioning method to use when transitioning to IPv6 (Convery & Miller, 2004). It is recommended to block all automatic tunneling services because tunneling bypasses the entire network security perimeter defense and is difficult to detect. If tunneling is used, then using a 6to4 static route is preferable. This provides network administrators the ability to establish a trust with the endpoints while maintaining the egress and ingress security configuration policy (Convery & Miller, 2004). If using tunneling, it is highly recommended to use a DMZ to inspect the traffic in the neutral zone by using stateful inspection rather than allowing the tunnel to simply terminate on a key asset bypassing a firewall. In addition, it is recommended to block the following ports at the firewall on native IPv4 networks:

- Port 47 (i.e., GRE)
- Port 41 (i.e., 6 over 4)
- Port 3544 (i.e., Teredo)
- Block all UDP traffic (except the DNS port 53)
- Conduct outbound filtering only for authorized static tunnels' destination endpoints

Routing/Protocol Recommendations

Routers are particularly vulnerable to attacks. Below is a list of recommended actions (Convery & Miller, 2004) to perform to configure routers:

1. Use authentication for BGP and IS-IS.
2. Use IPsec to secure protocols (AH & ESP).
3. Use IPv6 hop limits (set internal host on same subnet to use 255, prevent SNMP outside the domain to be spoofed).

4. Screen ICMPv6 (block echo and echo reply inbound Internet traffic).
5. Allow ICMPv6 traffic listed below (if running IPv6 and to have use functionality).
   a. ICMPv6 Type 1 Code 0: no route to destination
   b. ICMPv6 Type 3: time exceeded
   c. ICMPv6 Type 128 and Type 129: echo request and echo reply (internal to edge boundary router)
   d. ICMPv6 Type 2: packet too big required for Path MTU Discovery to function
   e. ICMPv6 Type 4: parameter problem—this is required as an informational message to an IPv6 node
   f. ICMP Type 130-132: multicast listener messages
   g. ICMPv6 Type 133/134: router solicitation and router advertisement
   h. ICMPv6 Type 135/136: neighbor solicitation and neighbor advertisement
6. Ingress filter multicast and check for authentication of source (via AH) (Convery & Smith, 2004). Also filter inbound TCP headers with the SYN and ACK bit cleared (Beijnum, 2006). It is not possible to establish a TCP session from the outside to the inside, and those sessions would have initiated from the inside boundary router (Beijnum, 2006).
7. Block anycast addresses unless they are for DNS or NTP purposes, then filter using IPsec using AH.
8. Drop fragments less than 1280 except the last bit. The reason for this is because IPv6's minimum MTU size is 1280 bits, which was not addressed earlier in the paper (Convery & Miller, 2004).
9. Egress filter internal local link or site-specific addresses from leaving the network perimeter bound for the Internet (Convery & Smith, 2004).
10. Use IPsec to secure protocols and use an IDS at the end of the destination tunnel to monitor the traffic and a DMZ to open the traffic for inspection.

Many of the same application threats in IPv4 exist in IPv6 (i.e., policies in place, patch management, harden configurations, etc.). It is critical to use host and network IDS for IPv6, though the author is not aware of any host IDS software for IPv6 at this time. Network administrators should use best practices such as proxies for host requests (e.g. Apache 2.0 as a Web proxy [Beijnum, 2006]) and stateful inspection firewalls. In addition, network administrators should use the principal of least privilege and determine which nodes require "global unicast addresses" (i.e., communication with the Internet) so that all other nodes are assigned site local addresses or link local addresses (i.e., subnet) (Convery & Smith, 2004). Finally, an inventory of all IT assets (yes, this includes software), to include which specific protocols are required to support each asset, should be performed. Then, an individual can simply use only those protocols required to support a business requirement.

Provide Training

If it isn't readily apparent by now, before any transition to IPv6 is performed, it is highly recommended that network administrators and security managers receive IPv6 training. IPv6 introduces many new changes and challenges. In order to understand these challenges, changes, and benefits users must be made aware of the technology and be made aware of its limitations to properly support an organization.

Software Hardware Support Recommendations

The application and hardware support for IPv6 is "spotty" at best. Research for this article reveals that the traditional popular monitoring tools for the IPv4 network, HP's "Openview" and Aprisma's "Spectrum," do not support the SNMPv3 and the only way to manage routers is by using secure shell remotely (Gunsch & Beech, 2005). Windows 2003 Server active directory does not work with IPv6 (i.e., allow a host to register to the active directory domain) (Gunsch & Beech, 2005). DNS and DHCpv6 are still issues that have not been totally resolved at this time. While looking for some IDS capable of supporting IPv6, conflicting information was received.

Recommended Proposed Implementation

Unless organizations are planning to place some information on an IPv6-accessible Web server, it is not recommended to proceed forward with an IPv6 transition until DNS and some additional networking monitoring tools have further matured to support business operations. Windows 2003 server does not support active directory, and in order to run Exchange 2003, active directory is required for it to work. Windows Vista, 7, and Server 2008 have dual TCP/IP communication stacks enabled by default (Microsoft, 2008). Until additional research is performed to determine the configuration management and risks (i.e., Windows Server 2008 currently is undergoing Common Criteria testing), along with industry providing some IA tools to verify some of the recommended settings (i.e., filtering outbound Internet traffic), it is not recommended to pursue an IPv6 migration at this time. It is prudent to follow the rest of the United States government to plan for the future and continue to purchase IPv6-capable products and continue in disabling IPv4. "Current Windows operating systems lack many basic features to support IPv6 networking. Many networking hardware devices can support basic IPv6 operation but lack features such as management and security" (Gunsch & Beech, 2005, 4). Unless an individual is privileged to work for "early adopter" organizations (i.e., running Windows 7 and or Server 2008, which still has not completed its Common Criteria testing) then it's a safe assumption that Gunsch and Beech's work is still relevant and valid.

Conclusion

In order to implement a migration to IPv6, it is recommended that a full migration from IPv4 to IPv6 transition occurs when there is an equivalent functionality as IPv4. This is not the case at this time. According to Gunsch & Beech (2005, 4), "The IPv6 is not ready for production use at this time." Most businesses that are not part of the gaming industry, music, or other entertainment businesses will find that the current state of IPv6 does not meet their business needs. For organizations supporting the Department of Defense and other U.S. government entities, vendors will have to mature their products to successfully support a migration to IPv6; otherwise proprietary and other sensitive information is at risk of being compromised due to the lack of support.

About the Author

Foster Henderson, CISSP, CISM, SRP, NSA IEM, is a senior information assurance engineer consultant to the United States government. He is currently a member of the chief information officer team covering a wide range of IA issues.

References

Apple. (2008). Mac OS X: Security Configuration for Version 10.5 Leopard 2nd Edition. Retrieved March 27, 2010, from http://images.apple.com/support/security/guides/docs/Leopard_Security_Config_2nd_Ed.pdf.

Beijnum, I. V. (2006). *Running IPv6*. New York, NY: Apress.

Beijnum, I. V. (2010). 2009 IPv4 Address Use Report. Retrieved March 24, 2010, from http://www.bgpexpert.com/addrspace2009.php.

Carnegie Mellon Software Engineering Institute. (2008). CERT® Advisory CA-2002-03 Multiple Vulnerabilities in Many Implementations of the Simple Network Management Protocol (SNMP). Retrieved March 21, 2010, from http://www.cert.org/advisories/CA-2002-03.html.

Carnegie Mellon Software Engineering Institute. (2001). CERT® Denial of Service Attack. Retrieved March 13, 2010 from http://www.cert.org/tech_tips/denial_of_service.html.

Carnegie Mellon Software Engineering Institute. (2000). CERT® Advisory CA-1996-21 TCP SYN Flooding and IP Spoofing Attacks. Retrieved May 26, 2006 from http://www.cert.org/advisories/CA-1996-21.html.

Chapple, M. (2005). Get Ready for IPv6: Five Security Issues to Consider. Target Search. Retrieved April 29, 2006, from http://searchnetworking.techtarget.com/tip/0,289483,sid7_gci1101877,00.html.

Cisco. (2001). Cisco Security Advisory: "Code Red" Worm - Customer Impact. Retrieved March 14, 2010, from http://www.cisco.com/warp/public/707/cisco-code-red-worm-pub.shtml.

Cisco. (2006). IPv6 Extension Headers Review and Considerations. Retrieved March 25, 2010, from http://www.ciscosistemas.org/en/US/technologies/tk648/tk872/technologies_white_paper-0900aecd8054d37d.pdf.

Convery, S., & Miller, D. (2004). IPv6 and IPv4 Threat Comparison and Best-Practice Evaluation. Retrieved April 21, 2006, from http://www.cisco.com/web/about/security/security_services/ciag/documents/v6-v4-threats.pdf.

Guinness World Records. (2006). Largest Company Merger. Retrieved May 28, 2006, from http://www.guinnessworldrecords.com/content_pages/record.asp?recordid=53969.

Gunsch, T., & Beech, B. (2005). IPv6 Transitioning: Not Ready for Prime Time. Shelton, C. Provided Email, May 18, 2006.

Harris, S. (2002). *All in One: CISSP Certification Exam Guide*. Berkeley, CA: McGraw-Hill/Osborne.

Henderson, F., & Craig-Henderson, K. (2004). Security architecture and models. In Krause, M., & Tipton, H., *Information Security Management Handbook*, Fifth Edition (pp. 1531–1554), Auerbach Publications.

Heywood, D. (1997). *Novell's Guide to TCP/IP and IntranetWare*. San Jose, CA: Novell Press.

Hewitt, J., OSI RM model, Wikimedia Commons, accessed Jan. 19, 2011 at http://en.wikipedia.org/wiki/File:Osi-model-jb.png.

Internet Protocol Version 6: Federal Agencies Need to Plan for Transition and Manage Security Risks. (2005). Washington: Government Accounting Office.

Internet Protocol Version 6: Federal Government in Early Stages of Transition and Key Challenges Remain. (2005). Washington: Government Accounting Office.

Internet Society. (2010). A Brief History of the Internet and Related Networks. Retrieved March 20, 2010, from http://www.isoc.org/internet/history/brief.shtml.

Kristula, D. (2001). The History of the Internet. Retrieved March 20, 2010, from http://www.davesite.com/webstation/net-history2.shtml.

Kurtz, G., McClure, S., & Scambray, J. (2005). *Hacking Exposed*, Fifth Edition. Berkeley, CA: Osborne/McGraw-Hill.

Microsoft. (2008). IPv6 Security Considerations and Recommendations. Retrieved March 21, 2010, from http://technet.microsoft.com/en-us/library/bb726956.aspx.

Microsoft. (2007). Teredo Overview. Retrieved March 21, 2010, from http://technet.microsoft.com/en-us/library/bb457011%28printer%29.aspx.

Microsoft. (2008). Windows 2008 Server: Introduction to IP Version 6. Retrieved March 21, 2010, from http://technet.microsoft.com/en-us/library/bb726944.aspx.

Microsoft. (2010). The Cable Guy: Support for IPv6 in Windows Server 2008 R2 and Windows 7. Retrieved March 27, 2010, from http://technet.microsoft.com/en-us/magazine/2009.07.cableguy.aspx.

NIST. (2010). Guidelines for the Secure Deployment of IPv6 (Draft). Retrieved March 23, 2010, from http://csrc.nist.gov/publications/drafts/800-119/draft-sp800-119_feb2010.pdf

RAND Corporation. (2007). Paul Baran and the Origins of the Internet. Retrieved March 20, 2010, from http://www.rand.org/about/history/baran.html.

Search Unified Communications. (2010) Internet Protocol. Retrieved May 13, 2010, from http://searchunifiedcommunications.techtarget.com/sDefinition/0,,sid186_gci214031,00.html.

Shelton, C. Personal Communication, April 20, 2006.

Symantec. (2007). W32.Nimda.A@mm. Retrieved March 13, 2010, from http://www.symantec.com/security_response/writeup.jsp?docid=2001-091816-3508-99&tabid=2.

Tiller, J. S. (2004). Outsourcing security. In Krause, M., & Tipton, H., *Information Security Management Handbook*, Fifth Edition (pp. 1061–1072). New York: Auerbach Publications.

Usenet FAQ. (2010). RFC 793 - Transmission Control Protocol. Retrieved March 20, 2010, from http://www.faqs.org/rfcs/rfc793.html.

Warfield, M. H. (2003). Security Implications of IPv6. Internet Security Systems. Retrieved April 29, 2006, from http://documents.iss.net/whitepapers/IPv6.pdf.

Whatis.com. (2008). DHCP. Retrieved March 21, 2010, from http://searchunifiedcommunications.techtarget.com/sDefinition/0,,sid186_gci213894,00.html.

Wikipedia.org. (2009). Mobile code. Retrieved March 21, 2010, from http://en.wikipedia.org/wiki/Mobile_code.

Network Attacks and Countermeasures

Chapter 8

Managing Security in Virtual Environments

E. Eugene Schultz and Edward Ray

Introduction

Few issues in the IT arena are regarded with more interest and zeal than virtualization. Virtualization refers to technologies that provide a layer of abstraction between computer hardware systems and the software that runs on them. By supplying a logical instead of a physical view of computing resources, virtualization solutions deliver several extremely useful functions. Most basically, they in effect make an operating system (OS) recognize a set of servers as a single pool of computing resources. They can also allow multiple operating systems (OSs) to run simultaneously on a single physical machine.

The beginnings of virtualization are in partitioning, which separates a single physical server into multiple logical servers. Once a physical server is divided, each logical server can run an OS and applications independently. In the 1990s, virtualization was used mainly to re-create end-user environments on a single piece of mainframe hardware. IT administrators who wanted to roll out new software, but first wanted see how it would work on a Windows NT or a Linux machine, used virtualized environments to create different test environments.

With the introduction of the x86 architecture and inexpensive PCs, virtualization lost much of its popularity and seemed to be little more than a passing fad of the mainframe era. The recent rebirth of virtualization on x86 platforms is more to the credit of the current market leader, VMware, than anything else. VMware developed the first hypervisor (a special type of virtual machine monitor) for the x86 architecture in the 1990s, serving as a strong impetus for the current virtualization boom.

Types of Virtualization

There are four basic categories of virtualization: storage, network, application, and server virtualization, all of which are described in the following section.

Storage Virtualization

Storage virtualization melds physical storage from multiple network storage devices so that they appear to be a single storage device. A good example of storage virtualization is Storage Area Networks (SANs), which typically use a large number of high-capacity storage devices to provide a large amount of virtualized storage space. They are a good example of storage virtualization.

Network Virtualization

Network virtualization combines computing resources in a network by splitting the available bandwidth into independent channels that can be assigned to a particular server or device in real time.

Application Virtualization

In application virtualization, an application is encapsulated and separated by the OS through a virtualization layer that intercepts the application's file and other operations and redirects them to a virtual location.

Server Virtualization

Server virtualization hides the physical nature of server resources, including the number and identity of individual servers, processors, and OSs, from the software running on them. This type of virtualization is by far the most common application of the technology today and is widely considered the primary driver of the market. When most individuals use the term "virtualization," there is a good chance that they are referring to server virtualization.

Benefits of Virtualization

The industry buzz around virtualization is just short of deafening. This "must-have" capability has fast become "gonna-get-it" technology, as new vendors enter the market and enterprise software providers weave it into the latest versions of their product lines. The reason is that the more virtualization is used, it continues to demonstrate additional tangible benefits, thereby augmenting its value.

Server Consolidation

Server consolidation is the sweet spot in this market. Virtualization has become the cornerstone of just about every organization's favorite money-saving initiative. Survey after survey show that between 60% and 80% of IT departments are pursuing server consolidation projects. The main reason is obvious—by reducing the numbers and types of servers that support their business applications, organizations are obtaining significant cost savings.

Dynamic Load Balancing

Another major benefit of virtualization is dynamic load balancing capacity across multiple file systems and machines. Applications slow down or even come to a halt when processing bottlenecks occur on conventional machines. Dynamic load balancing helps ensure that such bottlenecks do not occur, thereby enabling applications to run continuously and without disruption. This is especially important for business-critical applications.

Still another benefit of virtualization is lowered power consumption, both from the servers themselves and the facilities' cooling systems. Fuller use of existing, underutilized computing resources translates into a longer life for the data center and a fatter bottom line. Additionally, a smaller server footprint is simpler to manage.

Information Security Benefits

Many potential benefits from an information security perspective also exist. These include the following:

Process Isolation

Virtualization's benefits go far beyond efficiency, functionality, and continuity in that virtualization offers much for information security. Virtual machines (VMs) can be used to isolate processes from attackers and malware, making systems and applications more difficult to successfully attack or infect. User access to applications can be tightly controlled in that virtualization allows special applications to be isolated from end-user applications, making unauthorized access to the former very difficult. Even if a system or application that runs in a virtualized environment is successfully attacked, any impact resulting from the attack is usually attenuated. The ability of attackers and malicious code to spread attacks (particularly malware-based attacks) is thereby reduced.

A good example of the usefulness of virtualization-supplied process isolation in information security is the way Java applets run in a "sandbox" environment in the Java VM. A sandbox is used when executable content has come from an external source that is not completely trusted. The sandbox restricts capabilities such as reading or writing to files on each local computer, starting or calling programs on each local computer, and obtaining network connectivity to the same computer from which applets have been loaded. Restrictions may include keeping a downloaded executable from being able to connect to the network from the machine to which it has been downloaded and from being able to reach the file system of the machine on which it runs. Most sandboxes place more restrictions on executables that have been remotely downloaded than those that have been locally downloaded.

Use in Business Continuity and Disaster Recovery

Yet another benefit of virtualization is that it can greatly increase the efficiency and can greatly reduce the cost of business continuity and disaster recovery operations. Using virtualization in these arenas is still in its relative infancy. Still, virtualization can greatly reduce the cost of setting up and maintaining a duplicate data center in that fewer pieces of hardware need to be purchased. In addition, virtualization decreases procurement-related risks during outages and disasters. New VMs can be quickly created to support rapid recovery of business operations. Not to be overlooked also is that virtualization can greatly reduce electrical power demands when electricity is at a premium.

Honeypot Support

Virtualization also supports honeypots: computers, services, or applications designed to serve as a decoy that attracts perpetrators. Not intended for legitimate users, honeypots appear to have something of value to attackers, behave as if vulnerable to a wide range of attacks, and appear to belong to a network, but are actually isolated. Almost every current honeypot tool is based on virtualization.

Virtualization makes "high-interaction honeypots," honeypots that have an extremely similar "look and feel" as real systems, possible in the following ways:

- *Full virtualization*: All major honeypot components are virtualized
- *Partial virtualization*: Applications, but not other honeypot components, run on VMs
- *Paravirtualization*: Only OS device drivers support a virtual environment

Virtualization can also be used in creating and running "low-interaction honeypots," honeypots that do not have the "look and feel" of a real system.

Honeyd is one of the many honeypot tools that use virtualization. Honeyd is a small service that creates VMs on a network. It can be configured to run arbitrary services, answer pings and traceroutes, appear to be running certain OSs and services, send proxy service requests to other systems, have multiple IP addresses on a single platform, allow or deny scans, deceive others in appearing to use certain network routes when it in reality does not, and to create massive honeynets, virtual networks for honeypots that make network traffic flow look as if it were real. honeyd offers a sandbox using a function called systrace to stop an attacker from being able to exploit bugs in honeyd scripts.

Cloud Computing Support

Another benefit of virtualization is that it supports cloud computing. There is no general agreement concerning exactly what the term "cloud computing" means. Wikipedia provides as good a definition as there is by defining cloud computing as "the provision of dynamically scalable and often virtualized resources as a service over the Internet on a utility basis. Users need not have knowledge of, expertise in, or control over the technology infrastructure in the 'cloud' that supports them." Cloud computing and virtualization go hand in hand. Cloud servers are often highly distributed and virtualized, e.g., the Amazon Elastic Computer Cloud (EC2) has massive data center virtualization. Virtualized storage is another kind of cloud service that typically depends on virtualization.

Other Benefits

Other significant benefits of virtualization include failover functionality, ability to maintain systems without taking them down, the ability to pool computing resources, the ability to have custom VMs, each of which serves as a container for application delivery, and many others.

Virtualization-related Security Risks

Virtualization also creates a number of security risks, some of which are serious. This section discusses these risks.

Interactive Risks among VMs on the Same Physical Machine

Secure isolation, confining a program to a virtualized environment, which should guarantee that any action performed inside the VM cannot interfere with the system that hosts it, is basic to virtualization. Consequently, VMs have seen rapid adoption in situations in which separation from a hostile or hazardous program is critical. If the physical host server's security becomes compromised, however, all of the VMs and applications residing on that particular host server are impacted. In addition, a compromised VM might also wreak havoc on the physical server, which may then have an adverse effect on all of the other VMs running on that same machine.

Other Interactive Risks

Too often interactive risks in virtualized environments are viewed solely as host (VM)-based risks. Interactive risks also occur when there is a virtualized server and a virtualized network. In this case, the total risk exceeds the sum of the individual risks. Any vulnerability in any virtualized OS or application can be the weak link that causes multiple compromises in virtualized components.

Hyperjacking

Another security-related risk is "hyperjacking," in which an attacker creates and then runs a very thin hypervisor that takes complete control of the underlying OS. A good example of how this risk might present itself is the Blue Pill rootkit developed by security researcher Joanna Rutkowska. A rootkit is a Trojan program designed to hide all evidence of its existence from system administrators and others who look for anomalies and security breaches in systems. The Blue Pill rootkit bypasses the Vista integrity-checking process for loading unsigned code into the Vista OS's kernel. This code uses Advanced Micro Devices's (AMD's) secure VM, designed to boost security, to masquerade itself from detection, and becomes a hypervisor, taking control of the OS without system administrators and others detecting its presence.

Sniffing-Related Risks

Virtual environments, like conventional ones, are vulnerable to unauthorized sniffing. It is, for example, possible to capture data from layer 2 of the network by configuring a network interface card in a certain manner.

Network Defense Controls May Not Work as Expected

Network defense controls that information security managers assume are in place may not work in virtual environments. Network traffic in virtual networks may not be protected by the types of barriers (e.g., firewalls) commonly used in physical networks. Perimeter security appliances generally cannot see inter-VM traffic, and traffic flows in virtualized environments are typically different (involving bridged connections between VMs within the same physical machine) from in conventional network environments. The fact that virtualization results in a restricted view into inter-VM traffic exacerbates this problem.

Vulnerabilities in Virtualization Products

A surprising number of vulnerabilities have been identified in virtualization software, the software that enables VMs and virtual applications to run. Examples include vulnerabilities that allow unauthorized users to escape a VM to gain superuser access on a physical machine, vulnerabilities that allow perpetrators to gain unauthorized access from a guest OS to the host OS, a vulnerability that allows attackers to enter a particular sequence of characters in an SSL-encrypted remote administration session to gain unauthorized superuser access to the guest and all host OSs, and numerous vulnerabilities related to buffer overflow conditions.

The problem that the existence of so many vulnerabilities in virtualization products has caused has been exacerbated by the fact that vendors of these products have not always been forthright and prompt in acknowledging and fixing vulnerabilities in their products. A startling growth in types of attacks in which vulnerabilities in virtual servers are the focus has occurred in recent years. Additionally, because of previously discussed differences between virtual and conventional networks, intrusion detection and intrusion detection technology in virtual networks is likely to identify a lower percentage of attacks. Lack of visibility and controls on internal virtual networks created for VM-to-VM communications also blinds existing security policy enforcement mechanisms.

Malicious Code

The Black Hat community has increasingly turned its attention towards vulnerabilities and exploits in virtualized environments. Not surprisingly then, malicious code that runs in virtualized environments is becoming considerably more sophisticated. The previously discussed Blue Pill rootkit is one of the best examples. Malicious code (malware) that creates its own hypervisor poses the greatest risk. Malware can exploit bugs in virtualization products, resulting in buffer overflows, ability to tamper with code that controls power consumption, and more. Additionally, malware authors can now detect VM software and change their malicious code to disguise its purpose when it runs on this software.

Data Storage-Related Risks

Virtualized storage presents another group of risks of which "data comingling" is one of the most serious. Data comingling means that a hard drive contains data for different organizations such that one sector might store data for company A and a neighboring sector might store data for a competitor of that company. Furthermore, vulnerabilities that allow a hostile VM to gain access to disk space used by other VMs exist.

Denial of Service-Related Risks

Denial of service attacks are another major source of risk in virtualized environments. Denials of service-related risks are of particular concern, because multiple VMs typically run on a single physical machine. If a denial of service attack against the machine is successful, all VMs become unavailable. Shared IP addresses among multiple VMs increases the likelihood of success of network traffic flooding attacks. A vulnerability in a major virtualization product allows a malicious user on the guest OS to cause denial of service in both the host and guest OSs.

Physical Security Risks

Physical theft of or physical damage to the hardware that houses multiple VMs can be catastrophic. In contrast to a conventional computing environment in which one OS runs on one physical machine, the loss of a physical machine that houses multiple VMs and/or virtualized applications can seriously disrupt business and other operations.

Patching Barriers

VM state changes occur constantly in many virtualization products. A VM that is online at one point in time may be offline soon afterwards and then online again sometime later. Patch management tools cannot patch an offline VM. Additionally, VM cloning can result in VMs about which patch management tools are unaware. The result is VMs that are not up-to-date with respect to patches.

VM Migration Risks

VM migration in which a VM is moved from one physical machine to another introduces several vulnerabilities. Although the most fundamental problem is a lack of inherent migration security mechanisms in a number of virtualization products, man-in-the-middle (MITM) attacks in which an attacker is able to capture traffic between two physical machines while a VM is being migrated is a special concern. Additionally, full access to whatever state a VM is in is potentially available to anyone with access to the VM during migration.

Time Synchronization-Related Risks

Time synchronization among VMs is a potentially major security concern. Clock drift can be a major problem in nonvirtual environments. In a virtual environment, timer ticks that VMs need for timekeeping may be delayed, suddenly delivered all at once, or missed entirely. VM clock drift plus normal clock drift can result in tasks (including security tasks) running at the wrong time, wrong times for log entries, and failure of log-in restrictions (e.g., data/time restrictions) to work as expected.

Control of Physical Devices

The virtualization layer enables each individual VM to directly or indirectly control physical devices such as CD-ROMs on a computing system. This functionality can be configured for every VM and can generally be altered for a VM when it is running. If more than one VM requests access to a device during the boot process, the remaining VMs may go dormant until the first has released the device, unnecessarily delaying the boot process.

Lack of Uniformity of Mechanisms

Virtualized environments are typically characterized by great diversity, something that can interfere with IT standardization, change control, and compliance efforts. Consider, for example, virtualization in the Java applet environment. Although Java applets are typically run as part of a Web page, they can be downloaded and then run locally as a file independently of the sandbox's restrictions. The sandbox does not always function as intended either. Applets can, for example, send information from computers on which they execute to other network-connected systems, thereby substantially raising the risk of unauthorized disclosure or theft of stored data and programs.

Approaches to Risk Mitigation

Given all of the previously mentioned considerations and vulnerabilities, determining the best and safest way to leverage security virtualization may seem daunting. So how does an organization that uses virtualization mitigate virtualization-related risk? As with everything else in information security, risks have to be weighed against rewards. Using Parallels on a Macintosh to run Windows applications in a VM environment is normally very justifiable from a security risk perspective because the benefits far outweigh the risk. Running a VM that has known vulnerabilities to show how easy it is for real attackers to attack a system and how little skill is required to execute a program that gives an attacker complete control of the target system is perfectly acceptable in the context of teaching, but not in the context of mainstream IT operations. In malicious code research, analyzing the risk to benefit ratio is not nearly as easy as it might seem. Malicious code *can* break out of the VM and compromise the physical machine's OS. Attackers could then start to build malicious code capable of breaking out of the segregated environment. It is thus extremely expedient to realistically analyze the risks that may present themselves in virtualized environments and to avoid having a false sense of security with respect to virtualization.

Organizations that buy more hardware that is redundant and run multiple VMs together on a shared hardware platform also need to be especially cautious concerning the particular types of servers that reside on a single physical machine. For example, it would be a bad idea to put the firewall, an intrusion detection system, a public Web server, and database server all on one shared physical machine. In the VM world, if one VM is compromised, all VMs on the same physical machine can generally be more readily compromised. In fact, it would be easier to compromise multiple VMs in this hypothetical case, because the hardware that each VM uses is on the same platform. Even if all the VMs are equally secure against attacks, risk is nevertheless escalated due to the fact the VMs can talk among themselves without passing information through the network layer. The bottom line is that it is prudent to be careful about the architecture used and the VMs that are mixed together on the same physical platform.

Finally, if an organization has air-gapped networks that carry differently classified information (e.g., proprietary and nonproprietary information), migrating the machines that store this information to a virtualized environment all for the sake of making it easier for users to access both types of information would be very unwise from a risk management perspective. It would be far better to instead use a KVM (Keyboard, Video, and Mouse) switch.

Securing Virtualized Environments

Securing virtualized environments and, in particular, VMs must start before VMs are deployed, and ideally before vendors and products are selected. The reason is that security and securability must be factored into the evaluation and selection process; otherwise, security in virtualized environments must be retrofitted, something that is likely to not only lead to unidentified risks, but also to practical difficulties and escalating cost over time. Questions to be asked and answered before deployment include the following:

■ Where and how does your organization use virtualization and cloud computing?
■ What business drivers in particular are tightly linked with virtualization and cloud computing?
■ What security risks exist and which ones translate to business risk?

- Is your organization (in particular, senior management) aware of the security and business risks associated with virtualization and cloud computing?
- If not, what might you be able to do to promote awareness of these risks?
- What security standards does your organization have regarding the use of virtualization and cloud computing?
- Are there restrictions on the use of virtualization and/or cloud computing? If so, what are they, and are compliance checks being done?
- Is the effort to implement controls adequately integrated into your organization's change control process?
- Is there a patch management policy in place for VM OSs and cloud services? If so, is there a patch management tool or system in place?
- Does your organization have a plan for reducing these risks? If so, what control measures have been prescribed/implemented?
- Are you thinking in terms of defense in depth for virtualized and cloud environments?
- Does your organization have a mechanism for enforcing security standards in both environments?
- Does your organization's security training and awareness program address virtualization and cloud computing issues? If not, do you plan to include these issues sometime in the future?

Developing an Approach

After basic questions about how virtualization is currently being used in your organization and how current security controls apply to virtualization-related risk, a good next step is to develop an approach for securing virtualized environments. In most organizations, the approach taken for securing virtual environments is to use current configuration standards and tools that were used in the past for securing any OS, network device, or application. Although this approach has some merits, it fails to address the security ramifications of having multiple platforms on the same physical machine. Simply applying the same controls used in securing physical servers will not, for example, provide sufficient protections for VMs. Securing VMs must start before the VMs are deployed, and ideally, before vendors and products are selected, so that security and securability can be factored into the control evaluation and selection process. The first focus should thus be physical security. All the logical protections that a virtualized environment can have will be in vain if anyone can walk into a data center and steal disk drives from any machine. This scenario can easily happen if a service console is not afforded strong levels of physical protection.

Policies and Standards for Virtualized Environments

Policies and standards for virtualized environments should for the most part *not* be radically different from those for conventional environments. Areas such as separation of duties in virtualized environments, back-ups, auditing and monitoring, business continuity, and disaster recovery planning in virtualized environments should be addressed at a high level in an organization's information security policy and also in more technology-specific ways (including required parameters and configuration settings) in information security standards. Areas also to be addressed in standards for virtualized environments include baseline configuration, special security measures (including physical and logical controls for consoles used to administer VMs and special controls for mobile VMs), patch management, change management (particularly with respect to creation of VMs), placement and configuration of firewalls, required intrusion detection, and possibly also intrusion prevention mechanisms and required configurations for each, antimalware software, and other controls. Finally, standards should also require that a library of trusted virtualized server builds be created and stored in a safe place.

Selection and Implementation of Controls

Once the necessary changes to the information security policy and standards are made, approved, and implemented, technical control measures should be selected and implemented. One important caveat should be considered—many security and system and network management tools have significant limitations (including inability to sufficiently mitigate security risk) when used in conventional computing and networking environments. Using them in virtualized environments is bound to only compound these problems.

A sound control selection and implementation process will help ensure that a suitable set of controls will be in place. All of the following components of virtualized environments must be carefully considered.

The VM OS

The VM OS must be secured in accordance with the standards that the information security organization adopts for the OS in question. Failing to secure the VM OS cannot only make compromising it trivial, but can also substantially elevate the probability of a network compromise. The reason is that once compromised, the VM OS can readily serve as a springboard for attacks against the network.

The VM

Security of the VM is dependent on the OS and should follow the same processes already developed by the information security practice for these OSs as if each VM were a physical host. A VM and a physical server do not differ from a security perspective. Besides using the service console's access to the VM File System (VMFS), the only other way to access another VM is through its network connections. Securing the network is therefore of primary importance. Because the Console Operating System (COS) hypervisor can access the VM disk files, securing the service console is even more important.

VM Networks

All externally initiated VM network connections should be shielded by a properly configured, well-maintained firewall. Additionally, as just mentioned, the OS in the VM must be properly secured.

The VMkernel

The VMkernel is by its nature much more secure than any other component in virtualized environments. With no publicly accessible Application Programming Interfaces (APIs), possible ways of hacking or cracking this crucial software dwindle to almost none. This does not mean that it is impossible to compromise this software, however. Regularly patching the VMkernel with vendor updates in accordance with an organization's information security policy and standards is imperative in avoiding VMkernel compromises.

VM-Server to VM-Server Traffic and VMkernel Traffic

Communication between servers (i.e., VMware VMotion) passes memory data between VM servers to help manage each VM host and to facilitate performance balancing. The VMkernel network is also used to perform NFS mounts and Internet Small Computer System Interface (iSCSI) access. The data are passed unencrypted; access to the network that passes these data should thus be adequately controlled at all times.

The COS

The COS has access to everything that the VMkernel can access, namely hardware as well as the data stores for the VM disk files. The COS is thus another crucial security consideration. At a minimum, to limit possible attack origin points, VMs not used in system and network administration should have no access to the COS network. Additionally, placing the COS properly within an organization's network is necessary. At a minimum, keep the COS out of a demilitarized zone (DMZ) where it can more easily fall prey to externally initiated attacks. Placing it at a point within a network where a firewall shields it from such attacks is far better from a security perspective.

VM Deployment

There are many different tools for deploying VMs that use the COS network connection. Typically, these tools send unencrypted information to the target VM Server. Securing the deployment network by ensuring that such traffic is encrypted with strong encryption (e.g., Advanced Encryption Standard encryption) is thus a necessary part of any sound defense-in-depth solution.

VM Backup

Typically, VMs are backed up in one of two ways. The first is to back up from within the VM, which uses the network connections of the VM. The second method is externally via the COS (i.e., VMware Consolidated Backup). In either case, backup data traversing the network should be encrypted with strong encryption and the backup server should be adequately secured through the use of strong authentication and access control lists (ACLs) for file access.

Data Security

Data in virtualized environments need to be protected in the same manner a data center should be protected. Although each VM is separate and distinct, the service COS is part of the VM Server and it has access to critical data. Properly configured ACLs and applying the least privilege principle will both minimize the likelihood of data security breaches.

Patching and Updating

Ensuring that recent patches and updates are promptly tested and, if found suitable, installed is an essential part of securing virtualized (as well as conventional) environments. Additionally, it is important that patches and signature updates are kept up to date for offline VM and "VM appliance" images. This includes patching and security configuration management of VM appliances in which the underlying OS and configuration are not accessible. Protection from tampering is also essential.

Auditing

Finally, it is important to ensure that sufficient auditing (coupled with procedures that require regular and systematic inspection of audit log output) is enabled and continuously running on the VM server service console. Network monitoring is also necessary. The ultimate goal should thus be to provide as much preventative protection as needed while at the same time to allow for auditing and monitoring the OS with minimal impact on the operation of the system applications.

Other Controls

Additionally, understanding that eventually a wider variety of attacks, some of which may be successful, will surface in virtualized environments is imperative; necessary adjustments must be made and necessary additional security controls must continually be considered and, if justified in terms of costs versus benefits, implemented to minimize the likelihood of successful attacks in these environments. Candidate controls include (but are not limited to) network firewalls, application firewalls, strong authentication, antivirus/antispyware tools, denial of service (DoS) protection through fault tolerance or other mechanisms, forensic tools, remote logging, periodic vulnerability scans, and patch management.

Conclusion

Information security managers as well as other information security professionals need to thoroughly understand virtualization and its advantages and disadvantages from information security, information technology, and business viewpoints. They also need to keep up with changes in virtualization. With the ever-increasing popularity of virtualization, one thing is certain—virtualization and computing will continue to converge well into the future. Unfortunately, virtualization is also likely to provide a disproportionately increasing number of targets for attackers and malicious code. It thus behooves information security managers to be as proactive as possible in their approach to managing virtualization-related security risk.

About the Authors

Dr. E. Eugene Schultz, CISM, CISSP, is the chief technology officer at Emagined Security, an information security consultancy based in San Carlos, California. He is the author/coauthor of five books, one on Unix security, another on Internet security, a third on Windows NT/2000 security, a fourth on incident response, and the latest on intrusion detection and prevention. He has also written over 120 published papers. Gene was the editor-in-chief of *Computers and Security* from 2002 to 2007, is currently on the editorial board for this journal, and is an associate editor of *Network Security*. He is also a certified SANS instructor, senior SANS analyst, member of the SANS NewsBites editorial board, coauthor of the 2005 and 2006 Certified Information Security Manager preparation materials, and is on the technical advisory board of three companies. Gene has previously managed an information security practice as well as a national incident response team. He has also been professor of computer science at several universities and is retired from the

University of California. He has received the NASA Technical Excellence Award, the Department of Energy Excellence Award, the ISACA John Kuyers Best Speaker/Best Conference Contributor Award, the Vanguard Conference Top Gun Award (for best presenter) twice, the Vanguard Chairman's Award, and the National Information Systems Security Conference Best Paper Award. Named a distinguished fellow of the Information Systems Security Association (ISSA), Gene has also received the ISSA Hall of Fame Award as well as the ISSA's Professional Achievement and Honor Roll Awards. While at Lawrence Livermore National Laboratory, he founded and managed of the U.S. Department of Energy's Computer Incident Advisory Capability (CIAC). He is also a cofounder of FIRST, the Forum of Incident Response and Security Teams. He is currently a member of the accreditation board of the Institute of Information Security Professionals (IISP). Dr. Schultz has provided expert testimony before committees within the U.S. Senate and House of Representatives on various security-related issues and has served as an expert witness in legal cases.

Edward Ray is currently the chief information security officer for MMICMAN, a defense contractor based in Clearwater, Florida. He is currently involved in malware research as it pertains to virtualization. He has written extensively on virtualization security issues as well as malware detection. Mr. Ray possesses extensive knowledge of tracing and debugging Windows and Unix processes in the context of malware reverse engineering, deep understanding of network flow data analysis, deep packet inspection, and network behaviors of malicious software. Mr. Ray also has comprehensive knowledge of antidebugging and anti-instrumentation techniques as well as packing and antireverse engineering techniques, including data obfuscations that employ cryptography.

Mr. Ray has worked as both a manager and technical staff member in information security for more than fifteen years. Moreover, he has been involved in the design of intrusion detection systems for insider and outsider threats for more than eight years. Edward Ray holds the Certified Information System Security (CISSP), GIAC Certified Intrusion Analyst Gold (GCIA Gold), and GIAC Certified Incident Handler Gold (GCIH Gold) professional security certifications. Mr. Ray's principal research for his GCIH practical involved malware analysis of the SQL Slammer worm. Mr. Ray has held prior positions at the Naval Research Laboratory, Hughes Aircraft (now Raytheon), and TRW (now Northrop Grumman).

INFORMATION SECURITY AND RISK MANAGEMENT

Security Management Concepts and Principles

Chapter 9

Do Your Business Associate Security and Privacy Programs Live Up To HIPAA and HITECH Requirements?

Rebecca Herold

The "Health Information Technology for Economic and Clinical Health Act," otherwise known as the "HITECH Act" portion of the American Recovery and Reinvestment Act of 2009 (ARRA), effectively widened the requirements for the Health Insurance Portability and Accountability Act (HIPAA) Privacy Rule and Security Rule to include the business associates (BAs) of covered entities (CEs), making CEs accountable for more active validation of BA security and privacy program compliance beyond just having a BA contract in place. It is more important than ever for CEs to take proactive measures to ensure BAs establish and maintain effective and appropriate information security and privacy policies and other supporting actions. Simply depending upon a security questionnaire answered once (or even less often) a year, with no validation that the information provided is even accurate, is not effective. CEs must take a more proactive approach to ensuring BAs have effective and compliant programs in place. After all, CEs are ultimately responsible for ensuring the security and privacy of the information they collect from their own clients, patients, customers, and employees.

There Are Many Business Associates

I've done a great amount of HIPAA compliance work for CEs over the past decade, since just before HIPAA went actively into effect. In the past few years I've done around 200 BA information security and privacy program reviews.

There are many different types of BAs that perform work for CEs. A large portion of them do business in other industries in addition to the healthcare industry. In the BA information security and privacy program reviews I've performed, the BAs were of all sizes, providing a very wide range of services (some I had never even thought of before) to many different industries.

I've been asked if a comprehensive list of BAs exists. Not only do I doubt a comprehensive list of BAs exists, I doubt if one even could exist; the companies that become a BA and leave being a BA is constant.

The numbers of BAs used by CEs can be huge. As just one example, one CE I did BA security and privacy program review work for (with approximately 15,000 employees) had identified over 2,000 business partners, and of these they identified around 600 "high-risk" BAs, those with access to protected health information (PHI).

Consider the statistics within the HHS Breach Notice Rule. They help to reveal the very wide-spread impact of the HITECH Act. The HHS has determined that the HITECH Act impacts over 734,178 "Small Business" HIPAA CEs alone, not even taking into consideration the medium and large CE businesses.

Consider the following data taken from the HHS web site, based on US business census data provided to the Small Business Administration Office of Advocacy, which looks at how many "small" CEs will be impacted by the HITECH Act:

- 605,845 physicians, dentists, ambulatory care centers, hospitals, and nursing facilities
- 107,567 suppliers of durable medical equipment and prosthetics (that are CEs)
- 3,266 insurance firms and third-party administrators
- 17,500 independent pharmacy drugstores

This represents a total of 734,178 small CEs. However, a large section of clearinghouses are missing from this list. There are more types of clearinghouses than what would fall under those shown.

Now think about how many more thousands of medium-to-large CEs there are. The total number of CEs, as defined by HIPAA, in the U.S. is well over one million.

So then, think about how the HITECH Act has expanded HIPAA to effectively require all BAs to comply with the Security Rule and the Privacy Rule, and how many BAs are used by each CE. Consider a few numbers:

- One small CE I'm working with has 5 employees, and they have 5 BAs.
- A slightly larger CE I've helped, with around 50 employees, has 15 BAs.
- A large CE I did over 150 BA security and privacy program reviews for has over 2,000 business partners, of which 600 are identified as being BAs that have access, in some way, to PHI.

Based upon just these limited examples, the HITECH Act has effectively expanded the reach of HIPAA by five to 600 times! The HITECH Act will be impacting literally millions of organizations. This demonstrates how the HITECH Act is impacting healthcare information security and privacy compliance much more widely than even HIPAA did. Each CE now must widen their compliance purview significantly to help ensure all their many BAs are appropriately safeguarding information and providing appropriate—and required—security and privacy protections.

BA Services

BAs perform a very wide range of services. An example of just some of the activities performed by the 200 BAs I've reviewed include:

- Call center work
- Application development
- Archiving
- Backup vaulting
- Physical files maintenance
- Employee background checks
- Job candidate background checks
- Test data creation
- Transcriptionist services
- Contracted laboratory and radiology departments
- Software development
- Hot site hosting
- Billing
- Document disposal and shredding
- Facilities security
- Payment processing
- Home care services
- And many, many more...

So what is a "business associate"? HIPAA defines a business associate as follows within § 160.103 Definitions:

"Business associate:

1. Except as provided in paragraph (2) of this definition, business associate means, with respect to a covered entity, a person who:
   On behalf of such covered entity or of an organized health care arrangement (as defined in §164.501 of this subchapter) in which the covered entity participates, but other than in the capacity of a member of the workforce of such covered entity or arrangement, performs, or assists in the performance of:
   a. A function or activity involving the use or disclosure of individually identifiable health information, including claims processing or administration, data analysis, processing or administration, utilization review, quality assurance, billing, benefit management, practice management, and repricing; or
   b. Any other function or activity regulated by this subchapter; or
   Provides, other than in the capacity of a member of the workforce of such covered entity, legal, actuarial, accounting, consulting, data aggregation (as defined in §164.501 of this subchapter), management, administrative, accreditation, or financial services to or for such covered entity, or to or for an organized health care arrangement in which the covered entity participates, where the provision of the service involves the disclosure of individually identifiable health information from such covered entity or arrangement, or from another business associate of such covered entity or arrangement, to the person.
2. A covered entity participating in an organized health care arrangement that performs a function or activity as described by paragraph (1)(i) of this definition for or on behalf of such organized health care arrangement, or that provides a service as described in paragraph (1)(ii) of this definition to or for such organized health care arrangement, does not, simply through the performance of such function or activity or the provision of such service,

become a business associate of other covered entities participating in such organized health care arrangement.
3. A covered entity may be a business associate of another covered entity."

Think about all the possible types of organizations you outsource different types of business activities to. If they have access in any way to PHI, then they are most likely considered to be BAs.

Ten Common Indicators of BA Security and Privacy Program Problems

During the course of performing BA security and privacy program reviews I have repeatedly come across recurring problems when reviewing the completed questionnaires and other documentation, such as policies, website information, and so on. The following provides a high-level listing of the ten most common indicators that a BA information security and privacy program has some problems at best, and completely insufficient and risky programs at worst.

Indicator 1: Incomplete Response

When a BA does not completely answer the information security and privacy questionnaire used during a review it may indicate there is not an acceptable program in place. It may also indicate that the appropriate person did not provide the questionnaire responses. I have often had the BA's marketing contact try to answer the questions him- or herself. The best areas to answer the questions are the information security and privacy areas. I have also found BAs also often choose not to answer a question at all if it will look negative for them; perhaps they think not responding at all looks better.

Indicator 2: Inconsistencies Between Policy and Response

There have been many times when I have found the responses in the BA's completed questionnaire did not match the documentation provided. For example, the respondent for the questionnaire may indicate the passwords used are a minimum of six alpha characters, but the actual policy may indicate passwords must all be a minimum of eight alphanumeric characters. This shows that the BA is likely not enforcing their policies, that the systems are not configured to support the security policies, that compliance audits are not performed, and/or that there is no training or awareness provided for the policies.

Indicator 3: No Assigned Security or Privacy Responsibility

The responsibility of security and privacy may be delegated to a "Jack/Jane-of-all-trades" or performed ad hoc. Information security and privacy responsibilities need to be formally assigned and documented. Not only is this a requirement under multiple rules and regulations, including HIPAA, it is also good business practice to ensure personnel know their responsibilities with regard to security and privacy practices. A formally documented responsibility must be in place to ensure security is appropriately and consistently addressed.

Indicator 4: Response Is Provided by Another Company

Be sure to verify that the questionnaire responses apply to your BA and are not provided by some other entity. I have come across many instances when a completely different organization filled out the security and privacy questionnaire instead of the BA. For example, there have been multiple times the BA used an outsourced managed services provider to take care of their network, and got them to answer the questionnaire based upon the managed services security and privacy program, not upon the BA's program. It is important to know if your BA uses a managed services provider, but your BA still needs to answer the questionnaire and tell you about their own security and privacy program. Your BA needs to have an information security and privacy program in place to address all the operational, physical facilities, and human issues, even if they have outsourced the network management.

Indicator 5: Subcontracting

There have been many times when the BA was subcontracting the processing of my client (CE's) data to yet another company and that subcontracted company did not have good security practices. In fact, in some instances the subcontractor had basically no security practices! There have also been times when the subcontracted company was located in a different country. Be sure to cover the issue of having your BA subcontract within your organization's contract with the BA. In one very interesting case I discovered that the company that my client's BA had been subcontracting PHI management and processing to employed an ex-employee of my client who had left under very hostile terms. This was certainly a high risk to have such a person handling such sensitive information for a company against which he had a vendetta!

Indicator 6: No Mobile Computing Controls

One of the most common ways in which security incidents and privacy breaches occur is through lost or stolen mobile computing devices, such as BlackBerrys, laptops, notebooks, smart phones, and so on. An alarmingly large number of the BAs I've reviewed did not have security policies or controls in place for these types of mobile computing devices or for their employees who work from remote locations. However, they often allowed the CE's data to be stored on the mobile devices or allowed personnel who used these types of computers to process the CE data. Make sure BAs have appropriate security in place for such situations.

Indicator 7: No Use of Encryption

Another type of incident reported weekly, and sometimes daily, is the loss or theft of personal information, including large amounts of PHI, that was not encrypted. I have found most of the BAs do not use encryption to protect information in storage, in transit, or on mobile computing media and devices, such as laptops, backup tapes, USB drives, and so on. This is slowly changing, but in most cases the BA will not spend the time and resources to encrypt data unless required contractually or by law to do so. Now laws in Massachusetts and Nevada require encryption of such personal information. Plus, the HIPAA security rule, which BAs must now be in compliance with, requires encryption to be used based upon risk. Be sure encryption is used by BAs to mitigate the risk involved in such situations.

Indicator 8: Missing, Incomplete, or Outdated Business Continuity and Disaster Recovery Plans

I never cease to be surprised when I find a BA does not have any documented business continuity or disaster recovery plans! It seems like such a common sense type of protection to have. However, in far too many cases business continuity and disaster recovery plans are often either missing or were written several years ago and never tested. Recently I actually found a BA with a very well-documented and detailed business continuity plan…from 1995! The plan had never been updated or tested! Needless to say, most of the BA systems and applications had been either replaced or changed dramatically since 1995. Be sure the BAs have up-to-date plans in place and that they test them regularly.

Indicator 9: No Corrective Actions for Prior Breaches

Has your BA had an information security or privacy breach? This is definitely something you need to check on. Check multiple places. Use the time your BA is completing the security and privacy questionnaire to do research to see if they have had any publicized security incidents or privacy breaches. There are multiple services you can use to check on this, in addition to dozens to hundreds of good websites to search for news about the BA and any security breaches for which it was involved. I have found that some BAs indicated on their security questionnaire that they had never experienced a security incident or privacy breach, after I had found through my own research that they have had significant incidents and breaches! If you find the BA has had a breach, be sure to ask the company about it and find out what actions they have taken to prevent such a breach from occurring again.

Indicator 10: No Independent Assessment

If a BA has never had an independent security or privacy assessment of their organization, it is a warning sign. It could be indicative of many possible problems, such as:

- *Lack of funding for the security and privacy program*: Most organizations serious about security and privacy have an independent audit or assessment to ensure their controls and safeguards are appropriate.
- *A false sense of security*: Many of the BAs I've reviewed have indicated that they believed things were fine, so they didn't need someone to do a review. Ignorance is definitely not bliss when it comes to security, privacy, and compliance.
- *Independent assessments have been done but are not being shared*: I've run across two very large BAs who did not want to share the results of their security and privacy program audit because it had so many significant findings.

Of course, it is also possible that you will find upon investigation that the BA simply did not know that doing an independent assessment was advantageous, or they simply didn't want to spend the money to do one. However, it is still worth checking on.

Be HIPAA/HITECH Compliant or Pay a Hefty Penalty

Besides expanding HIPAA to apply to BAs and adding breach notice requirements, HITECH also upped the ante on what noncompliance can cost organizations. The HHS released HITECH

Table 9.1   Categories of Violations and Respective Penalty Amounts Available

A. Did Not Know it was a violation: $100–$50,000 per violation to a maximum $1,500,000 for all violations of an identical provision.
B. Reasonable Cause violation: $1,000–$50,000 per violation to a maximum $1,500,000 for all violations of an identical provision.
C. Willful Neglect violation: $10,000–$50,000 per violation to a maximum $1,500,000 for all violations of an identical provision.

Act Enforcement Interim Final Rule* on October 29, 2009. The revised penalty scheme differs significantly from its predecessor by its establishment of several categories of violations that reflect increasing levels of culpability, as shown in the table they provided (Table 9.1).

These HITECH fines are significantly higher than the original HIPAA penalties. It is worth noting that the interim final rule indicates that HHS will not impose the maximum penalty amount in all cases, but will determine penalty amounts based on the nature and extent of the violation, the nature and extent of the resulting harm, as well as the other factors.

The Office of Civil Rights (OCR) started hiring more HIPAA/HITECH enforcement officers around the same time as the rule was published, leading many compliance experts to state that there will be many more penalties applied now under HITECH regulations than there were since HIPAA went into effect up through 2009.

Here's the text of the HHS announcement:

HITECH Act Enforcement Interim Final Rule

The Health Information Technology for Economic and Clinical Health (HITECH) Act, enacted as part of the American Recovery and Reinvestment Act of 2009, was signed into law on February 17, 2009, to promote the adoption and meaningful use of health information technology. Subtitle D of the HITECH Act addresses the privacy and security concerns associated with the electronic transmission of health information, in part, through several provisions that strengthen the civil and criminal enforcement of the HIPAA rules.

Section 13410(d) of the HITECH Act, which became effective on February 18, 2009, revised section 1176(a) of the Social Security Act (the Act) by establishing:

Four categories of violations that reflect increasing levels of culpability;
Four corresponding tiers of penalty amounts that significantly increase the minimum penalty amount for each violation; and
A maximum penalty amount of $1.5 million for all violations of an identical provision.

It also amended section 1176(b) of the Act by:

Striking the previous bar on the imposition of penalties if the covered entity did not know and with the exercise of reasonable diligence would not have known of the violation (such violations are now punishable under the lowest tier of penalties); and

---

* See the full text at http://edocket.access.gpo.gov/2009/pdf/E9-26203.pdf.

Providing a prohibition on the imposition of penalties for any violation that is corrected within a 30-day time period, as long as the violation was not due to willful neglect.

This interim final rule conforms HIPAA's enforcement regulations to these statutory revisions that are currently effective under section 13410(d) of the HITECH Act. This interim final rule does not make amendments with respect to those enforcement provisions of the HITECH Act that are not yet effective under the applicable statutory provisions.

This interim final rule will become effective on November 30, 2009. HHS has invited public comments on the interim final rule, which will be considered if received by December 29, 2009.

To avoid these much higher fines, it is important for not only CEs to be diligent in their compliance efforts, but also for them to make sure their BAs are also in compliance.

Benefits of Active BA Compliance Management

If you depend upon doing BA security and privacy program reviews through the use of questionnaires, as is typically done, you will likely reveal a very wide range of risks. As I've described, I've done around 200 of these, and while they've been very beneficial to identify concerns within BA information security and privacy programs, they also have their drawbacks. Some of these include:

- Each review typically takes around four to eight weeks to complete, depending upon how timely the BA completes the questionnaire, provides documentation, and makes key contacts available for interviews.
- The review is an assessment of a point in time for the BA. As soon as the review is over, if anything within the BA operations, systems, networks, administration, or other signification factor changes, it will likely also change the information security and privacy posture for the BA.
- Most of the answers on the questionnaires are not validated. Many organizations answer the questionnaires in the way that will be most beneficial for them to "pass" the review, and they do not truly represent the reality of the BA information security and privacy program.

As I did increasingly more of these BA security and privacy program reviews, I became increasingly more convinced that there must be a better, more effective, accurate, and efficient way for CEs to ensure, on an ongoing basis, that BAs have good information security and privacy programs in place. To meet this need, I partnered with Jack Anderson, of Compliance Helper (http://www.compliancehelper.com), to create an automated way to allow CEs to see the documentation for their BAs at any time, on an ongoing basis, to validate that appropriate documents, forms, and activities exist for BA security and privacy program compliance. By having a window into the key BA security and privacy program components, CEs are able to ensure BAs:

- Are in compliance with legal and regulatory requirements and/or expectations
- Perform due diligence efforts during the contracting process or other risk management activities
- Are in compliance with CE contractual security and privacy expectations
- Resolve security and privacy issues promptly and appropriately

This is an effective and cost-efficient alternative to performing the more time-and-resource intensive reviews based upon point-in-time questionnaires and documentation reviews. It also helps to quickly and effectively address and eliminate the ten BA security and privacy program problems discussed earlier in this paper.

There are many benefits for CEs performing BA information security and privacy program reviews, or choosing to use ongoing compliance monitoring capabilities. They include, but are not limited to:

- They meet compliance with multiple laws and regulations.
- They demonstrate due diligence by the CE organization.
- The resulting reports clearly detail for the BA what the CE wants them to do to protect the information and system that the CE has entrusted to them.
- Having such documentation also helps to motivate the BA and ensure the risks are resolved in a timely manner.
- Ongoing monitoring, or doing point-in-time reviews, aid in a reasonable and appropriate evaluation of the BA's security and privacy program.
- Security and privacy expectations for the BA are aligned with the CE's requirements.
- Reviews and/or monitoring helps both CE and BA organizations define within their contract the issues and activities that are considered as grounds for termination of a business relationship.
- Vulnerabilities and threats can be identified and mitigated before bad things happen.

Following formal information security and privacy review methodologies or using an ongoing program monitoring service will help CEs to ensure BA compliance, which also helps CEs to ensure they are appropriately demonstrating due diligence, complying with all their compliance obligations and doing all they can to safeguard information, and, as a result, prevent privacy breaches.

About the Author

Rebecca Herold has over two decades of information security, privacy, and compliance experience. She was named a *Computerworld* "Best Privacy Advisor" multiple times, and an *IT Security* magazine "Top 59 Influencer in IT Security." Rebecca has been an adjunct professor for the Norwich University MSIA program since 2004. She has led the NIST Smart Grid standards committee privacy subgroup since June 2009. Rebecca has had her own business providing information security, privacy, compliance, and education services and products since 2004 (http://www.privacyguidance.com) and created all the content for, and is a partner in, Compliance Helper (http://www.compliancehelper.com). Reach Rebecca at rebeccaherold@rebeccaherold.com.

Chapter 10

Organization Culture Awareness Will Cultivate Your Information Security Program

Robert Pittman

Throughout life many of us have commuted to and from our occupation, traveled during vacation to other states and perhaps other countries, and spent quality time with the family, as well as found time for entertainment at a sporting event, play, beach, or concert. Many of these trips and activities place you in an environment where people exist. People are unavoidable regardless of where your commute or travels take you. When the gathering of people exists, so does a culture that requires a keen knowledge and insight to ascertain how you should approach that individual(s). To identify an appropriate approach is warranted but challenging when establishing or cultivating an information security program; regardless of what sector (e.g., public, private, and nonprofit) you are employed in.

There are many well-known theorists like Douglas McGregor (created Theory X and Y model), Edgar Schein (created Organization Culture model), psychologist Abraham Maslow, who created the Hierarchy of Needs five-level model, and numerous others in the field of organizational behavior and culture research. These individuals have brought this topic to the forefront because of their immense research and the value it brings to organizations worldwide.

The worldwide sprawl of organizations use government businesses essentially supported by the public. The public is comprised of its citizens, constituents, businesses such as nonprofits and corporations, and government agencies at all levels. A relationship amongst everyone involves citizens in terms of governments and associated organizations coordinating their programs and services on behalf of the public. At least, this is one of the goals of government, since they are providing services that a corporate business would not even consider. The plethora of services being provided to the public and its citizens include social services, general government, health care, and public safety.

Some of the countless government social services programs are those addressing and supporting low-income families, foster care, emancipated youths, and general relief payments for food and housing for the disadvantaged. Other services consist of property value assessment, property tax payment, requests for a birth certificate, marriage license, or a death certificate, as well as simply registering to vote. Our citizens, from the time they are brought into this world and throughout their lives will require health-care services. Medical and mental health care, including public health issues, will always be of the highest concern to all levels of government, involving all ages. It may seem obvious that public safety services are at the top of the list along with health care. The security of our homeland, border and port protection, law enforcement, and protection of our loved ones is an area where government visibly plays a significant role.

All of the aforementioned government services are provisioned externally to citizens. The perspective on services provided internally would be different than those provided by corporate, in terms of the existence and loyalty of a significant amount of employees' labor unions (i.e., Civil Service Rules), attractive sustained retirement packages, consistent health and dental benefits, career and job advancements within the same government level where opportunities exist at different departments, branches, and agencies, and are knowingly supporting a cause or the greater good.

Regardless of what lens we use to view government and corporate, the lens illustrates that obvious differences do exist. Many of the services to the public are intangible where government employees have a fond appreciation for the internal services they receive.

By viewing government from the eighty-thousand-foot level and viewing through the Looking Glass, differences exist from an employee and organization perspective. Local government (i.e., county and city) organizations have differences with respect to corporations. Obviously, corporate stock shares and job security are some of those differences. However, establishing an information security program has significant differences in local governments as compared to corporations.

To establish an information security program in local government involves an array of focal points that must be addressed within the initial eighteen months by the chief information security officer (CISO), chief security officer (CSO), or information security manager (ISM). In some recent information security forums and industry writings, the term chief risk officer (CRO) may have a significant role as well. It is imperative that these focal points are addressed in terms of having them established and adopted by the organization:

- Enterprise information security policies
- Information security steering committee
- Enterprise information security program
- Enterprise information security strategy
- Identify the organization health level based on an information security risk assessment
- Enterprise and departmental (or agencies) computer emergency response teams
- Enterprise security engineering teams

Each of the above focal points can be categorized as your "Lucky 7." Throughout this chapter these points will be referred to as Lucky 7. The information security professional that addresses these points will be "lucky" and the others will not be as "lucky" in terms of continued employment with that particular organization, since the primary responsibility exists in the information security unit. This may sound harsh. However, at the end of the day, the citizens and constituents that the organization is providing business and services to have the expectation that their confidential, sensitive, and personally identifiable information (PII) is secured and protected. It is the job of the information security professional to accept the challenge and responsibility to ensure that the organization stays away from any press or media release announcing a data breach or perhaps a breach of trust. As information security practitioners are aware, there has been a plethora of announcements in the press and media on organizations (public and private sectors) that have experienced computer security breaches. These are in corporate America, colleges and universities, health-care organizations, as well as the 26 million veterans' records with PII that were the responsibility of the federal government Veteran's Administration (public sector) and T.J. Maxx's 45.7 million credit and debit card owners (private sector), whose confidentiality was breached in 2005. However, the all-time record breach occurred four years later, during 2009, with Heartland Payment Systems. This incident is now the leading hack to have hit or affected the financial services industry (private sector), with 130 million credit and debit card account numbers.

Organizational Governance

It seems more apparent that the public sector leverages a security-related event to promote an information security program or, at the minimum, obtain a funding source to support a project or initiative. Despite the consequences of failure or compromise, security governance is still a muddle. It is poorly understood and ill defined and, therefore, means different things to different people. Essentially, security governance is a subset of enterprise or corporate governance. Moreover, one could identify governance as security responsibilities and practices, strategies and objectives for security, risk assessment and management, resource management for security, and compliance with legislation, regulations, security policies, and rules.

Information security governance is "the establishment and maintenance of the control environment to manage the risks relating to the confidentiality, integrity, and availability of information and its supporting processes and systems."

From a local government perspective, counties are governed by a five-member board of supervisors and the chief executive officer (CEO). The CISO, departmental information security officers (DISOs), and the Information Security Steering Committee (ISSC) or a security council comprise the information security governance.

A federated organizational structure is the norm for the majority of local government organizations. In a county or city government, numerous business units or departments serve unique and differing business purposes. Because of these unique business units, comprehensible governance is vital to the success of any information security program. This governance involves a strategic organization framework (Figure 10.1) that provides a clear illustration of the involved players. The

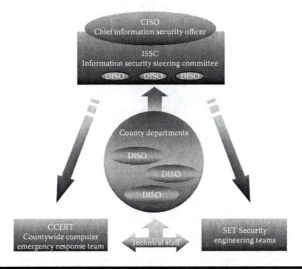

Figure 10.1 Information security strategic framework.

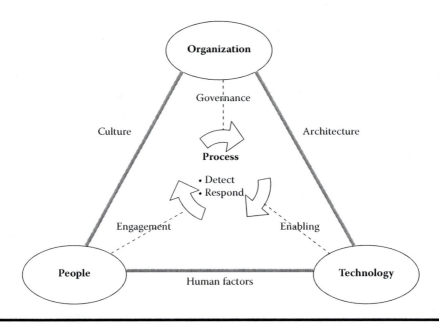

Figure 10.2 Information security strategic organization "security triangle."

"Security Triangle," shown in Figure 10.2, is a framework that is doable for CISOs' organization regardless of whether their information technology is decentralized, centralized, or a managed-security service. Additionally, a local government organization can be deemed as an organization with 30 or more corporations, in terms of having 30+ county departments with distinct businesses as they serve their respective constituents (Figure 10.3).

The Security Triangle must be supported by the organization's senior management; however, articulation of this support should be achieved by the development of board-adopted policies. These policies are similar to the corporate world where the board of directors and CEO can adopt policies. However, information standards and procedures can be approved by an information security council.

Public-Sector	*Private-Sector*	*Public Corporation*
Director	Owner	Board of Directors
Deputy director/Branch manager	Vice President	Executive management
Division chief	Manager	Middle management
Section manager	Manager	Supervisory management
Associate	Employees	Employees

Figure 10.3 Public sector versus private sector and corporate organizations.

Organizational Culture and Behavior

Bruce Schneier is an internationally renowned security technologist and author, as well as the go-to security expert for business leaders and policy makers. Currently, he is the chief security technology officer for BT Managed Security Solutions. He states, in his book *Beyond Fear: Thinking Sensibly about Security in an Uncertain World*, that security is all about people: not only the people who attack systems, but the people who defend those systems. If we are to have any hope of making security work, we need to understand these people and their motivations. We have already discussed attackers; now we have to discuss defenders.

Schneier also states that good security has people in charge. People are resilient. People can improvise. People can be creative. People can develop on-the-spot solutions. People are the strongest point in a security process. When a security system succeeds in the face of a new or coordinated or devastating attack, it is usually due to the efforts of people.

If it was not obvious prior to reading this chapter, it should be obvious now that people play a significant role as part of any information security program. Moreover, those same people at times can bring about challenges as well. However, it is the culmination of people that defines organizational behavior and its culture. Organizational culture is the culture that exists in an organization, something akin to a societal culture. It is composed of many intangible phenomena, such as values, beliefs, assumptions, perceptions, behavioral norms, artifacts, and patterns of behavior. The unseen and unobserved force is always behind the organizational activities that can be seen and observed. Organizational culture is a social energy that moves people to act. "Culture is to the organization what personality is to the individual—a hidden, yet unifying theme that provides meaning, direction, and mobilization."

Organizations are assumed to be rational-utilitarian institutions whose primary purpose is the accomplishment of established goals (i.e., information security strategy and initiatives). People in positions of formal authority set goals. The personal preferences of organization employees are restrained by systems of formal rules (e.g., policies, standards, and procedures), authority, and norms of rational behavior.

These patterns of assumptions continue to exist and influence behaviors in an organization because they repeatedly have led people to make decisions that "worked in the past." With repeated use, the assumptions slowly drop out of people's consciousness but continue to influence organizational decisions and behaviors even when the environment changes and different decisions are needed. They become the underlying, unquestioned, but largely forgotten, reasons for "the way we do things here"—even when the ways may no longer be appropriate. They are so basic, so ingrained, and so completely accepted that no one thinks about or remembers them.

In the public sector it seems that almost every employee has worked at least twenty years or more. In retrospect, they may have only worked many years less. Reality is when many employees consistently echo the aforementioned phase, "the way we do things here." If you are the CISO attempting to implement one of your many information security initiatives, this phrase seems to echo loudly, increasing exponentially with the number of employees that will be affected by implementing a change to their environment. This type of behavior illustrates the presence of a strong organizational culture.

A strong organizational culture can control organizational behavior. For example, an organizational culture can block an organization from making changes that are needed to adapt to new information technologies. From the organizational culture perspective, systems of formal rules, authority, and norms of rational behavior do not restrain the personal references of organization employees. Instead, they are controlled by cultural norms, values, beliefs, and assumptions. In order to understand or predict how an organization will behave under varying circumstances, one must know and understand the organization's patterns of basic assumptions—its organizational culture.

Organizational cultures differ for several reasons. Some organizational cultures are more distinctive than others. Some organizations have strong, unified, pervasive cultures, whereas others have weaker or less pervasive ones; some cultures are quite pervasive, whereas others may have many subcultures existing in different functional or geographical areas.

In contrast, there are some "prescriptive aphorisms" or "specific considerations in changing organizational cultures." When this occurs, your information security program (i.e., Lucky 7), along with its processes and practices, will flourish with positive outcomes:

- Capitalize on propitious moments
- Combine caution with optimism
- Understand resistance to culture change
- Change many elements, but maintain some continuity and synergy
- Recognize the importance of a planned implementation
- Select, modify, and create appropriate cultural forms
- Modify socialization tactics
- Locate and cultivate innovative leadership

Altered organizational culture is merely the first—but essential—step in reshaping organizations to become more flexible, responsive, and customer driven. Changing an organizational culture is not a task to be undertaken lightly, but can be achieved over time.

Organizational cultures are just one of the major tenets that constrain the establishment and building of an information security program. As a CISO, or an information security practitioner within your organization, you should have had at least some interaction with the various target groups (i.e., stakeholders) to grasp an awareness of their behavior. Figure 10.4 illustrates the expected behavior of the target groups and desired behavior to assist in driving your program. This chart will provide benefits when you rate each stakeholder from your perspective.

Organizational Target Group	*Desired Behavior*
Board of supervisors / city council	Endorsement
Executive management	Priority
Middle management	Resources
Supervisory management	Support
Employees	Diligence
Constituents / consumers	Trust
Security program	Execution

Figure 10.4 Stakeholders desired behavior.

The Information Security Executive in the Organization

The University of California at Los Angeles (UCLA) legendary men's head basketball coach John Wooden, wrote "there is a choice you have to make in everything you do, so keep in mind that in the end, the choice you make makes you." Nowhere is this more evident than the relationships that are established throughout your organization, as well as external to the organization. Surround yourself with people who add value to you and encourage you. At the minimum, having photographs or prints hanging from your office walls of individuals that have achieved greatness, regardless of what industry, will provide an added psychological benefit when tough decisions must be made. If the opportunity presents itself where you are able to visit my home or business office, this psychological benefit is apparent. In plain sight you will see the memories and fondness of greatness from the first African-American athletic to enter and play major league baseball, Jackie Robinson, Muhammad Ali (former name Cassius Clay), who changed the culture of boxing to a style, business, and character (e.g., charisma) that had not previously been seen, and Louis Armstrong (nicknamed Satchmo), once proclaimed the greatest musician ever to have lived, and the first jazz musician to appear on the cover of *Time Magazine*, on February 21, 1949. Having established strong relationships is an excellent indicator of a strong CISO; however, staying visible in the organization is equally important.

People can trace the successes and failures in their lives to their most significant relationships. Establishing relationships is part of our livelihood in terms of family, personal life, professional life, and business. Moreover, as the CISO, when establishing an information security program and chairing an information security steering committee meeting with your security peers or colleagues in your organization, those relationships are imperative to your success. Effective CISOs have learned how to gain the trust and confidence of the executive team. The CISO must remember that security is easier to sell if the focus is on the benefits to the company. Sometimes while selling security, analogies associated with personal and home practices can provide some clarity and additional reinforcement.

The CISO is the information security executive (i.e., senior management) regardless of whether in public or private (i.e., corporate America) sector organizations. Regardless of what sector, an organization's CISO must address the big picture and must rely on timely and actionable risk information that enhances their ability to make decisions that will drive local government efficiencies and operational effectiveness.

In local government, many CISOs are using a matrix reporting structure and either report to the chief information officer (CIO) or the CEO, and ultimately the city manager, board of supervisors (Board), or city council (Council). Actually, this matrix model can only function in this fashion as long as no operations responsibilities are incorporated. In other words, the daily operational activities and tasks would collide, at the minimum, with the strategic and tactical mindset of the information security practitioner. This model has brought this author numerous successful implementations of information security projects and initiatives.

However, there are many other ways to organize the security function and they all have advantages and disadvantages. Strong CISOs understand it is not important how security is organized or the hierarchical structure. The key to success is the support structure the CISO is able to build among the executive team. However, the manner in which security is organized will change the methods and processes a CISO will use to be successful. Effective CISOs will adapt their approach to the most advantageous organizational structure. The two most common primary organization structures are (1) matrix structure, in which the CISO is an enterprise-level (or corporate-level for private sector) organization and the security staff report in the business lines or (2) the CISO has direct or indirect (e.g., dotted-line organizational structure model) responsibility for the implementation and operation of security.

Smart CISOs understand that they do not need to have all the security staff in their direct reporting line. Be ready for decentralization. Being a strong CISO is not about how many staff you manage; it is about how many staff you can influence. Drive the difference of security any way you can—through direct staff, matrix staff, and supporting staff—to reach the security program goals and initiatives. Large organizations have already implemented a matrix organization or are seriously reviewing how to manage the business lines more effectively. Be prepared to manage in a matrix organization.

Regardless of the reporting structure, decisions must be made to eliminate press clippings in tomorrow's local newspaper, or perhaps the national news. The CISO cannot be risk-adverse. All information security practitioners should think quantitatively. This does not necessarily mean doing calculations. Rather, it means thinking about things in terms of the balance of arguments, the force of each of which depends on some magnitude.

Some local government organizations are forward-thinking companies that have recognized that business and IT executives (e.g., CIO, CISO, or chief technology officer) need to establish standardized, repeatable ways to identify, prioritize, measure, and reduce business and technology risks, both collaboratively and effectively. Moreover, security executives who were accustomed to working in their own silo must now consider all business-related risk areas to align initiatives (e.g., business and applications system migration projects, and customer-based applications to enhance e-government/e-services) properly with exposures.

Collaboration and communication is sunshine on its brightest day. Team relationships and/or team meetings are training gold nuggets. If the opportunity exists, inviting individuals to attend selected meetings within your security program can go a long way to helping them understand the scope and breadth of security. Make them an honorary member of the team. This has been done on several occasions to break through the myopia barrier. In addition, if other groups will let you attend a team meeting or two, go for it. This seems very simple, and is, but can be unbelievably powerful.

It is very true that there is success in numbers from an empirical perspective, where teams can drive your information security program. Two types of teams should be implemented to support an information security program: proactive and reactive.

The proactive measures teams we call the security engineering teams (SET). All of these teams develop and review policies, standards, procedures, and guidelines. These teams are usually experienced and knowledgeable in terms of the technical, culture, and organizational perspectives. These teams address host strengthening and isolation, policy and operating procedures, malware defense, and application security, to name a few. However, there will be opportunities where a proactive team will be formed to address a point-in-time project. For example, our implementation of an Internet content filter was a win-win because of the formulation of a SET from development of the technical specifications to enterprise deployment. Once deployed throughout the organization, the team was no longer required.

A reactive team addresses an enterprise-wide computer emergency response team (CERT). This team reacts to situations that potentially impact or have impacted the enterprise network, servers, applications, workstations, etc. This is reactive in nature. However, use of a structured methodology while responding, resolving, and reporting the incident is vital. Use of well-maintained and clearly written documentation (e.g., narratives, matrixes, and diagrams) for responding to incidents, and using a standardized incident reporting form are crucial. It may be obvious that by defining the various types of information security incidents to report will provide one of the

Stage	Dominant Assumption	Socioemotional Focus
Group/Team formation	*Dependence:* "The leader knows what we should do."	*Self–orientation:* Emotional focus on issues of: a) Inclusion, b) Power and influence, c) Acceptance and intimacy, and d) Identity and role.
Group/Team building	*Fusion:* "We are a great group/team; we all like each other."	*Group/Team as idealized object:* Emotional focus on harmony, conformity, and search for intimacy. Member differences are not valued.
Group/Team work	*Work:* "We can perform effectively because we know and accept each other."	*Group/Team mission and tasks:* The emotional focus is primarily on accomplishment, teamwork, and maintaining the group in good working order. Member differences are valued.
Group/Team maturity	*Maturity:* "We know who we are, what we want, and how to get it. We have been successful, so we must be right."	*Group/Team Survival and Comfort:* The emotional focus is preserving the group/team and its culture. Creativity and member differences are seen as threats.

Figure 10.5 Stages of group/team evolution. (From Schein, E.H., *Organizational Culture and Leadership*, 3rd edition, Jossey-Bass, San Francisco, 2004.)

numerous performance metrics that can be established to measure a portion of the operational aspects of your program (Figure 10.5).

Information Security Policies, Standards, Procedures, and Guidelines

One of the major components of an information security program is the formulation, collaboration, and adoption of information security policies. These written policies cannot survive without associated supporting standards, procedures (some private sector organizations use standard operating procedures or SOP), and guidelines. Personally, having clear, distinct, and physically separated policies, standards, and procedures would provide benefits to your overall information security program.

Charles Cresson Wood, well known in the information security industry as a leader for information security policy development, has emphasized segregating information that has different purposes. Specifically, one should formulate different documents for policy, standards, procedures, and guidelines. This structure provides numerous benefits to the responsible owner of these documents in terms of ease of modification to maintain currency and relevance, more efficient reviews and approvals, and the ability to distribute requests for any single type of document on a need-to-know basis that protects the security and privacy of the written information, where applicable.

Policy is defined as the rules and regulations set by the organization. Policies are laid down by management in compliance with applicable law, industry regulations, and the decisions of enterprise leaders and stakeholders. Policies, standards, and procedures are mandatory; guidelines are optional. However, policies can be used to clearly define roles and responsibilities of the information security program, including the CISOs, steering committee, etc. Moreover, policies are written in definite language and require compliance. Failure to conform to policy can result in disciplinary action, termination of employment, and even legal action.

Information security policy governs how an organization's information is to be protected against breaches of security. Familiar examples of policy include requirements for establishing an information security program, ensuring that all laptops are deployed with automatic hard disk encryption software, employees' Internet usage, security awareness and training, malware (e.g., antivirus, antispam, and antispyware) defense, and computer incident reporting for employees, to name a few.

Information security standards can be an accepted specification for software, hardware, or human actions. These standards can be de facto, as well, when they are so widely used that new applications routinely respect their conventions. However, the written format is preferred and recommended from the perspective of an information security professional and information technology professionals, including auditors.

A software standard can address a specific vendor's solution for antivirus software protection. In fact, from a defense-in-depth perspective an organization may be standardized on two vendor's solutions. If a particular organization has implemented all Cisco Systems, Incorporated (Cisco) network devices, they could conclude that their hardware standard for network infrastructure is Cisco. There are many standards to address human actions or even their behavior. For example, to address a potential computer security breach a standard will address actions to be performed by specific employees' roles, responsibilities, and time lines for an appropriate response.

Procedures prescribe how people are to behave in implementing policies. For example, a policy might stipulate that all confidential and private data network communications from employees who are working or traveling and desire to connect externally to the enterprise network must be encrypted. This would constitute previously identified software and hardware (perhaps an adopted standard for communicating externally) required to be implemented based on policy. The corresponding procedure (the "how-to") would explain in detail each step required to initiate a secure connection using a particular virtual private network (VPN) or some other technology.

Policies, standards, and procedures, as previously stated, are mandatory. However, guidelines are not mandatory. Guidelines could be used in the absence of a documented standard or procedure and in the future they could be transformed and adopted into a standard or procedure. Establishing guidelines assists in identifying the usefulness and the trial of specific security controls for future adoption. For example, an organization prefers the use of Windows Mobile operating system for all mobile devices, but there is a small community within the organization that prefers the proprietary BlackBerry device. Therefore, one may have to satisfy both communities. A guideline would be feasible to address appropriate security controls for the BlackBerry device, whereas a standard would address appropriate security controls for all Windows Mobile devices. Eventually, the BlackBerry security controls guideline would be transformed into a standard after a greater acceptance within the organization was achieved. This eliminates use of a de facto standard in this example.

All documents should use suitable policy resources, including the aforementioned Charles Cresson Wood's Information Security Policy Made Easy, government (e.g., National Institute of Standards and Technology [NIST], National Security Agency [NSA] Security Guidelines, and RFC 2196), industry bodies (e.g., International Standards Organization [ISO] 17799/27002, Control Objectives for Information and related Technology [COBIT], and Committee of Sponsoring Organizations [COSO]), and commercial (e.g., Microsoft) organizations, in preparing to formulate policies and standards.

The writing style should state what employees can do and what they cannot do, use short sentences, written at a tenth-grade level similar to the model newspapers use, review and improve (i.e., Sunset date) or adapt policies regularly, circulate drafts showing changes in policies to stakeholders and interested participants prior to adoption, and articulate major changes to senior management (e.g., department heads, counsel, CIOs, and privacy officers) within the enterprise.

The Information Security Organization

The organizational culture and behavior, the CISO as the information security executive, and the organization structure are the dependent variables in establishing an information security program. The framework that has been proved at numerous local governments west of the Mississippi River, regardless of workforce size, is the "Security Triangle" (Figure 10.2). This framework has paid dividends in having clearly defined roles and responsibilities, while addressing defense and offense strategies. In other words, these strategies are the previously stated reactive and proactive teams that allow for continual collaboration with stakeholders vertically and horizontally throughout the public sector organization.

The information security strategic organization diagram shown in Figure 10.1 (i.e., Security Triangle) depicts an example from a local government (i.e., county government). It illustrates the CISO at the top of the organization that may report to a CIO or CEO, as previously stated. The ISSC is composed of the DISOs. This will provide a forum for all information security-related collaboration and decision making. This deliberative body will weigh the balance between heightened security and departments performing their individual business. The ISSC responsibilities will be to:

- Develop, review, and recommend information security policies
- Develop, review, and approve best practices, standards, guidelines, and procedures
- Coordinate interdepartmental communication and collaboration
- Coordinate countywide education and awareness
- Coordinate countywide purchasing and licensing
- Adopt information security standards

The DISOs are responsible for departmental security initiatives and efforts to comply with countywide information security policies and activities. They also represent their departments on the ISSC. To perform these duties, the DISO must be established at a level that provides management visibility, management support, and objective independence. DISO responsibilities include:

- Represent their department on the ISSC
- Develop departmental information security systems
- Develop departmental information security policies, procedures, and standards

- Advise the department head on security-related issues
- Devise department security awareness programs
- Conduct information security and privacy self-assessments/audits

The countywide computer emergency response team (CCERT) will respond to information security events that affect several departments within the county with actions that must be coordinated and planned. The CCERT is comprised of members from the various departments that are often members of the departmental computer emergency response team (DCERT). The CCERT team meets biweekly to review the latest threats and vulnerabilities, and ensure that membership data is kept current. The CISO participates in their activities, as well as leading the response to cyber-related events. Efforts include improved notification and communication processes, and ensuring that weekend and after hour response is viable. Additionally, training will be conducted to provide forensic capabilities to the CCERT team members, but will be specific to incident response in terms of maintaining the chain-of-custody of electronic evidence.

The information security strategic framework (Figure 10.1) developed to support a local government is designed to address organization, people, processes, and technology, as they relate to information security. The strategy is based on the principle that security is not a one-time event, but must be a continuously improving process, an emergent process that addresses changes in business requirements, technology changes, new threats and vulnerabilities, and a need to maintain currency with regard to software release at all levels within the security network, server, and client arena. It also is based on the realization that perfect security is an impossible goal and that efforts to secure systems must be based on the cost of protective measures versus risk of loss.

As the CISO or ISM, many of these protective measures are identified in an information security strategy, as a necessity. A documented strategy that is annually reviewed is imperative to ensure currency of the projects and initiatives for that particular fiscal year. It is prudent that as the information security practitioner you align your security projects, initiatives, and activities with the annual budget process of the organization. This will provide a means and awareness to senior management that funding is mandatory to sustain a true information security program that will reduce risk. This strategy must clearly articulate the mission and vision of the program. Additionally, information security program goals and objectives are articulated in the strategy, in terms of short- and near-term timelines. For example, your high-level goals can be derived from the twelve information security domains that are articulated in the ISO 27002 standard. The objectives will support the stated goal that should apply to your organization's required level of security protections. The strategy will assist in the CISO's ability to achieve the stated goals and objectives over a defined period.

Conclusion

Today's information security professional is increasingly being challenged by the numerous fronts, based on the numerous threats and vulnerabilities that exist in the world. Government organizations also exist throughout the world. Rather, we are discussing local government or private sector organization challenges. Some specific areas are unique to government, such as the diversity of businesses and services under a single organization (i.e., county or city government), the types of business that warrant differing security and privacy protections, multiple legislations and regulations that sanctions departments within a local government organization, and perhaps most of all the culture issue, because of the Civil Service Rules that cause difficulty when employee termination is being considered.

The CISO responsibilities range through establishing and sustaining relationships with executive management, learning about the organization's culture and behavior, constantly being visible and communicating the security message throughout the organization, having formulated, clearly defined policies, standards, and procedures, and establishing a governance structure that comprises and establishes a successful information security program.

In today's global society, a career path definitely exists for information security practitioners that would ultimately lead to holding a position as a CISO or CSO. This chapter, as well as other chapters in this book, should provide dividends throughout your career as a practitioner. However, having a business acumen, information technology (IT) experience, and strong leadership skills are a few of the major tenets in striving to be an outstanding and successful CISO. On the other hand, IT training curricula do not usually include managerial skills such as leadership, team building, collaboration, risk assessment, and communication skills, including negotiating, or psychology and philosophy courses.

Risk Management

Chapter 11

Role-Based Information Security Governance: Avoiding the Company Oil Slick

Todd Fitzgerald

There was a massive oil spill in the Gulf of Mexico, spewing approximately 200,000 of gallons of oil each day, as the result of an explosion from an oil rig, possibly eclipsing the size of the 11 million gallon Exxon Valdez oil spill in 1989. Lawyers will most likely spend several years litigating over whether or not the well was properly capped or "cemented" by the oil services contractor. The destruction of wildlife and the disruption to people's lives will be enormous. By the time this article is read, the well will have been capped and cleanup efforts will be well underway. Based upon the Exxon Valdez oil spill, the cleanup effort could take years, and even then, toxic remnants will be the result.

So what does this have to do with information security governance? Plenty. Let's think for a moment what happens whenever something in our lives goes wrong. We are likely to (1) jump to an immediate determination or conclusion of what went wrong, (2) determine who is responsible, (3) figure out how to contain the problem and keep it from spreading/continuing to cause more damage, and (4) implement changes to minimize the potential for reoccurrence. After we have answered these questions, we then figure out how to get on with our lives and have some sense of peace until the next challenge is presented to us! We also start to ask ourselves: How did this happen in the first place and could it have been avoided? Monday morning quarterbacking is a self-perceived right that each of us will invoke on some situation at some point in our lives. Information security governance unfortunately follows a similar path within many organizations—the incident that "should never have happened" occurs, the organization quickly mobilizes to resolve the issue, finds the person to accept responsibility for the problem, attempts to limit the damage, and then, and only then, decides that maybe there is a fundamental problem with the way information security is being managed and exercised within the organization. This then leads to reviewing how information security is being governed and changes begin to occur. Recent history has numerous examples of where the information security officer was asked to leave the organization following a major incident, however the reality is that many times the issue is a governance issue involving shared responsibility across the organization. In the case of the oil spill, while it is currently unclear as to who was at fault, early media reports are faulting cleanup efforts for not being swift enough to contain the oil spill. Not every business will experience an incident of this magnitude and if the incident is not very significant, business may occur as usual until a large incident negatively impacting the organization's reputation or financially occurs.

Information Security Governance Defined

The word "governance" comes from Latin origins meaning to steer or have power over something. Organizations enable information assurance by granting specific powers to different departments and individuals to protect the information assets. Along with this authority granted by charters, policies, management structure, and the rules by which the business agrees that they will operate, there is an expectation imposed and subsequent performance that must be measured. The goal is to avoid undesirable consequences by coordinating and controlling the information security activities to support the mission of the business. Controls are put in place to ensure that activities are adequately performed to provide comfort that the activities are being completed with sufficient accuracy and effectiveness to achieve the intended result. The subsequent sections will walk through the necessary roles that should be in place to increase the likelihood that a security-affirming culture will be present to reduce the likelihood of losses due to the lack of information security.

Security Governance Starts with Defining Roles

Information security governance needs to be addressed from the board of directors to the end users of the organization. Each individual has a "role" that must be played with respect to governance, and the following sections will define what the roles are and how they work together to provide information assurance for the organization. It is not enough to define what the policies, standards, procedures, and various functions of information security are, without employing the appropriate management structures to ensure that these same policies, standards, and procedures are adhered to across the organization. It is equally dangerous to limit the role of information security to the information security department (which may be as few as a couple of people to hundreds for a medium-large sized organization), as this would leave large organizational gaps of where security is actually being exercised within the company.

Role-based access is typically focused on the access granted to end users through the use of standardized "profiles" that provide access to various information systems resources needed by the end user to perform their jobs. Prior to the implementation of role-based access control, each user was granted access to each resource that was requested, often regardless of the specific job of the individual. Even if the job role was considered when approving the access, there was little control over the long term, when each user in the same department and job function could potentially end up with a different set of accesses. Auditors typically like to audit the accesses provided as part of a segregation/separation of duties review, particularly if there is no concept of a role-based architecture due to the high likelihood that individuals will have acquired more access than necessary over the term of their employment. Role-based access can mitigate this risk by ensuring that standard profiles are created for the majority of the users based upon their job function. For example, a "claims processor" or "bank teller," would have a predefined set of access to physical and logical resources within a particular department or company. When a new claims processor or bank teller is hired, the model profile access can be provided immediately to the associate. This provides a consistent set of access vs. assigning "whatever Joe had." Joe may have been a 30-year employee with the company that moved from organization to organization, picking up access along the way (because the new manager typically has little incentive to "remove access" as long as Joe can perform his job with the access he already has). Thus, the entire organization, without role-based access, could end up with significantly more access than required. Under the role-based access model, when "Joe" transfers to another department or job function, access is provided for his new role under the role-based access profile, and the old access is removed or overlaid with the new role profile.

Once a standardized set of roles are developed, it becomes much easier to maintain the access. For systems which have many different applications within one environment, such as a mainframe application with multiple security settings inside the application to read and/or update certain fields, a macro could be written to populate the base role profile to the new or transferred employee that needs the role. This greatly simplifies the administration by reducing the number of combinations of security setting to the one defined in the role vs. possibly a different set for each user. It also provides for better control because changes to the role can be agreed to and made in one place, at the role profile level.

Even with using a role-based approach, over time there may be users that acquire multiple profiles (for different systems), and now no longer need access to a particular system or resource and the manager has not informed the information security department. For this reason, it is advisable to minimally recertify the role profile content on an annual basis (quarterly on high-risk systems) and to recertify that each end user assigned to that role profile still is performing a job function which needs access to that particular role. Another benefit of utilizing standardized roles is that when the role profile changes for one user for a particular job function, then this change can be applied to all individuals within the same job function. This again promotes consistency of access.

Establishing a role-based profile and assigning the profile to end users to perform their jobs is an important aspect of information security governance, however there is much more to governance that extends beyond the provisioning of access. An organization can spend millions on the implementation of an identity management system to receive requests and provision access, which is all for naught if the roles are not defined to sufficiently segregate duties, vetted by the functional areas responsible for the access, assigned to the correct individuals, or the roles for and support for promoting information security are not clearly defined. Authorized system access is just one component of the information security program. The subsequent sections delineate the various roles within the organization that are essential to ensuring information security governance.

Information Security Officer's Role

The Chief Information Security Officer (CISO), Information Security Officer, Director Information Security, Manager of Information Security, or whatever title is bestowed upon the individual responsible for information assurance, should really be regarded as the 'facilitator' of information security for the organization. The security officer's role is to identify the risks, obtain the impacts of the risks, and guide the management of the organization to make educated determinations of what security investments should be made to mitigate the risk. The business management of the organization are the only ones that can really accept the risks within the organization.

Without an information security governance model that clearly defines what the expectations are of the board of directors, the C-level suite (chief executive officer, chief information officer, chief financial officer, chief operations officer, chief compliance officer, chief technology officer, etc.), executive management (vice presidents of the business units), middle management (directors/managers), first-line management (supervisors/leads), and the nonmanagement end users, it will not be clear who is actually supposed to accept the risks. Executives accept all kinds of risks, financial, operational, technical, external, and other business risks, each day. Risks identified through the CISO's facilitation of the security risk assessment are just another set of risks that the senior management must address. Whether or not the information security officer communicates the risks clearly or not, the organization is implicitly "accepting" risks through the normal course of business. So, the better approach is for the information security officer to actively facilitate discussion of the risks with the appropriate parties.

In the facilitation context, the information security officer may be likened to an orchestra leader, bringing together all of the instruments in the company, each making their own distinct sound and different methods to create their sounds, into one, unified great sounding symphony. Alternatively, it may sound like the third-grade violin section, with each part trying to perform at their best level. It is well accepted that that first elementary school concert will be full of squeaks, out-of-place sounds, and the knowledge that the band "will get better over the years." Both orchestras are attempting to produce the same music, with the main difference being complexity of the methods and the experience of the group. Companies are not much different: as they mature in information security governance, they become more structured with who is responsible to perform and approve which activity according to a predefined procedure.

The governance role of the information security officer is to build the information security strategy to meet the business needs, develop and implement information security policies, develop appropriate managerial, technical, and operational controls, ensure that security is provided on an ongoing basis through monitoring programs, and communicate failures of the security controls to the senior management. The typical security organization will manage the functions or some aspects of security policy and administration, business continuity and disaster recovery, security operations, identity and access management, audit/risk management liaison, and security architecture. Organizations may have a small number of individuals in the CISO function reporting to business line management with a component in IT security reporting to the chief information officer (CIO), a combined model with all functions reporting to one security officer, or a variation. The tools of information security governance used by the security officer include the policies themselves, standard operating procedures, risk assessments, systems security plans, corrective action plans, audits, logging and monitoring, vulnerability scanning, penetration testing, security awareness, and identity management systems to name a few. The proactive planning utilizing these tools identifies areas needing increased attention to protect the information assets. The information security officer must be able to "translate" the current status and the issues found by these activities into digestible terms that will be understood by whatever audience is being addressed. The level of detail or information deemed necessary will vary across the managerial and technical groups, as well as the level of the individual within the organization.

Security Officer Reporting Relationships

There is no "one size fits all" for the information security department or the scope of the responsibilities. The location of where the security organization should report has also been evolving. In many organizations, the information security officer still reports to the CIO or the individual responsible for the information technology activities of the organization. This is due to the fact that many organizations still view the information security function as an information technology problem and not a core business issue.

Alternatively, the rationale for this may be due to the necessity to communicate in a technical language, which is understood by information technology professionals and is not typically well understood by the business. Regardless of the rationale for the placement, placing the individual responsible for information security within the information technology organization could represent a conflict of interest, as the IT department is motivated to deliver projects on time, within budget, and of high quality. Shortcuts may be taken on the security requirements to meet these constraints if the security function is reporting to the individual making these decisions. The benefit of having the security function report to the CIO is that the security department is more likely to be engaged in the activities of the IT department and aware of the upcoming initiatives and security challenges.

A growing trend is for the security function to be treated as a risk management function and, as such, be located outside of the IT organization. This provides a greater degree of independence as well as providing the focus on risk management vs. management of user IDs, password resets, and access authorization. Having the reporting relationship outside of the IT organization also introduces a different set of checks and balances on the security activities that are expected to be performed. The security function may report to the chief operating officer, chief executive officer, general counsel, internal audit, legal, compliance, administrative services or some other function outside of information technology. The function should report as high in the organization as possible, preferably to an executive-level individual. This ensures that the proper message is conveyed to senior management, the company employees view the appropriate authority of the department, and that funding decisions can be made while considering the needs across the company.

Security Planning

Strategic, tactical, and operational plans are interrelated and each provides a different focus towards enhancing the security of the organization. Planning reduces the likelihood that the organization will be reactionary towards the security needs. With appropriate planning, decisions on projects can be made with respect to whether or not they are supporting the long-term or short-term goals and have the priority that warrants the allocation of more security resources.

Strategic

Strategic plans are aligned with the strategic business and information technology goals. These plans have a longer-term horizon (3–5 years or more) to guide the long-term view of the security activities. The process of developing a strategic plan emphasizes thinking of the company environment and the technical environment a few years into the future. High-level goals are stated to provide the vision for projects to achieve the business objectives. These plans should be reviewed minimally on an annual basis or whenever major changes to the business occur, such as a merger, acquisition, establishment of outsourcing relationships, major changes in the business climate, introductions of new competitors, and so forth. Technological change will be frequent during a 5-year time period, so the plan should be adjusted. The high-level plan provides organizational guidance to ensure that lower-level decisions are consistent with executive management's intentions for the future of the company. For example, strategic goals may consist of the following:

- Establish security policies and procedures
- Effectively deploy servers, workstations, and network devices to reduce downtime
- Ensure all users understand the security responsibilities and reward excellent performance
- Establish a security organization to manage security entity-wide
- Ensure that risks are effectively understood and controlled

Tactical

Tactical plans provide the broad initiatives to support and achieve the goals specified in the strategic plan. These initiatives may include deployments such as the establishment of electronic policy development and distribution process, implementing robust change control for the server environment, reducing the likelihood of vulnerabilities residing on the servers, implementing a "hot site" disaster recovery program, or implementing an identity management solution. These plans are more specific and may contain multiple projects to complete the effort. Tactical plans are shorter in length, such as 6–18 months to solve a specific security weakness of the company.

Operational/Project Plans

Specific plans with milestones, dates, and accountabilities provide the communication and direction to ensure that the individual projects are being completed. For example, establishing a policy development and communication process may involve multiple projects with many tasks:

- Conduct security risk assessment
- Develop security policies and approval processes
- Develop technical infrastructure to deploy policies and track compliance
- Train end users on policies
- Monitor compliance

Depending upon the size and scope of the efforts, these initiatives may be steps of tasks that are part of a singular plan, or they may be multiple plans managed through several projects. The duration of these efforts is short term to provide discrete functionality at the completion of the effort. Traditional "waterfall" methods of implementing projects spent a large amount of time detailing the specific steps required to implement the complete project. Executives today are more focused on achieving some short-term or at least interim results to demonstrate the value of the investment along the way. Demonstration of value along the way maintains organizational interest and visibility for the effort, increasing the chances of sustaining longer-term funding. The executive management may grow impatient without realizing these early benefits.

Board of Directors' Role

The primary role of the board of directors in relation to information security governance is to set the proper direction. The board understands the risk appetite of the organization. For example, a financial institution may follow a very conservative, risk-adverse approach towards the implementation of security controls, requiring more granular access requests for information and the restriction of local administrative rights, whereas a creative marketing company may want their graphic designers to have more open access and the ability to download certain types of software to their development machines. Alternatively, an organization may be a technology leader or an early adopter and allow projects to take risks on new, unproven, beta-tested quality software, while another may prefer to implement new software after it has been proven in the marketplace with multiple version releases and is also adopted by major corporations first. These are decisions that are set based upon the tone-at-the-top established by the board of directors.

The internal audit department typically has a dotted-line relationship to the audit committee, which in turn provides the necessary information to the board of directors. This can provide valuable insight to the board as to the level of internal and external audit issues that the company is facing, some of the issues being a direct reflection on the information security governance activities being performed. Are there many audit findings? Are they being closed promptly? Could these audit findings have been avoided? Does the quantity of audit findings indicate the absence of a good information security governance program? These are all questions that the board of directors should be asking so that they can set the direction to ensure that risks are properly assessed and managed, policies and standards are being implemented to reduce the risks, and there is some accountability by standardized periodic measurements.

The information security officer should ensure that the board of directors is informed of the current state of security and the compliance with the appropriate external laws and regulations impacting the business. This may be through direct contact, via the audit committee, or another C-level executive carrying the message forward. Information should be at a high enough level that the board can grasp the issue and recommended solutions very quickly, without having to have in-depth knowledge of information security practices. The board is very busy and explaining what port 443 is or the latest vulnerability in Adobe is most likely not a good use of their time. Explaining how the implementation of an identity management system may benefit the organization or how a virtual private network investment would reduce the facilities costs substantially would be of more interest to the board of directors.

Boards of directors have paid much more attention to information security in recent years due to the increasing number of laws and regulations, damage to business reputations in the news, cost of incidents, and the potential for large fines or criminal prosecution. Boards do not necessarily want "the best" security, unless it will provide some competitive advantage. As with many other business decisions, they typically want "just enough" security where the margin return = marginal benefit. They are concerned with what their competition is spending on security, as less may mean not enough is being spent, thus leaving our systems more vulnerable; more may mean we are spending too much, money that could be made available for deployment in other areas of the company.

C-Level Suite Role

The C-level (CEO, CIO, CFO, CTO, etc.) suite are critical players to ensure the longevity of the security program. If they are not visibly brought in to the role of the security department and provide tacit support for or vocalize the notion that "security is a necessary evil," it will be difficult for the security officer to get the support of the other executives. On the other hand, the C-level individual can be a tremendous resource to move the program forward. They have the ability by their positional authority as well as their influencing power to bring together executives of different business units that may disagree on the need for stronger security controls. As with the board of directors, the security officer must recognize that the C-level has limited time, and "expects" that the security officer is managing security as a business and implementing what is minimally necessary to get the job done.

Senior/Middle Management Role

Senior/middle management maintains the overall responsibility for protection of information assets. The business operations are dependent upon information being available, accurate, and protected from individuals without a need to know. Financial losses can occur if the confidentiality, integrity, or availability of the information is compromised. They must be aware of the risks that they are accepting for the organization, either through explicit decision-making or the risks that they are accepting by failure to make decisions or understand the nature of the risks inherent in the existing operation of the information systems.

This level communicates their support for the program by their actions. If they are not onboard with the security policies, the likelihood is that their middle and first-line management will not feel the need to adhere to the security policies. When push comes to shove, the decisions will be made in favor of the business implementation imperative, potentially bypassing the rules seen as "issued by the security department." Just as the board of directors and the C-level suite are demonstrating the tone-at-the-top, so are these executives in their daily actions.

Security executives that are engaged in the information security practices ensure that risks are appropriately identified within all of their material projects, security is integrated across the organization, and business cases include the security requirements. Senior management frequently relies upon the judgment and feedback of the middle management team. If the middle management is not supportive of the security changes, it becomes much harder for the senior management to embrace the security department's security practices. This can be dangerous for the long-term support of the security program. One way to build the support is through the establishment of a security council.

Security policies should only be issued by the senior management/C-level of the company, or if issued by the security officer, should have the endorsement of these levels. The policies then are no longer seen as only the security department's desires, but rather are interpreted to be the company management's intentions. Investment decisions can then be made in consideration of the approved company security policies.

Steering Committee/Security Council Role

Security councils or security steering committees are typically made up of managerial and technical representatives of the different line and staff units within the company. Chaired by the information security officer, the council may include legal, human resources, information technology, internal audit, risk management, compliance, physical security/facilities, and representatives of the business units such as marketing, finance, operations, and so forth. The role of the council is to review the security policies, investments, and status and come to agreement. Once the council has vetted the policies, then, and only then, should the policies be provided to the senior management for approval. Why? The council builds the "grassroots support" that is very beneficial in influencing the senior management to accept the policies. The other benefit is that there is often now a greater understanding of why the security policy is necessary amongst the middle/first-line management, as they were involved in crafting the recommendation. The council also may surface issues with the proposed security policy or investment in the early stages of development, thereby saving the organization considerable resources and rework. Once this process is well instituted within the company as a key information security governance role, departments will begin to surface issues to their representatives on the council to bring forward, providing business input. The senior management over time can begin to trust the collective decision-making process from the council, thereby speeding up the senior management approval process. Decisions are more likely to be supported in the long run since they have received the review and broad support of the security council and subsequent senior management approval.

End Users' Security Role

Many different individual contributors within an organization contribute to successful information protection. As the often-expressed cliché goes, security is the responsibility of everyone within the company. Every end user is responsible for understanding the policies and procedures that are applicable to their particular job function and adhering to the security control expectations. Users must have knowledge of the responsibilities and be trained to a level that is adequate to reduce the risk of loss. While the exact titles and scope of responsibility of the individuals may vary from organization to organization, the following roles support the implementation of security controls. An individual may be performing multiple roles when the processes are defined for the organization, depending upon the constraints and organizational structure. It is important to provide clear assignment and accountability to designated employees for the various security functions to ensure that the tasks are being performed. Communication of the responsibilities for each function, through distribution of policies, job descriptions, training, and management direction provides the foundation for execution of security controls by the workforce.

- *End User*: The end user is responsible for protecting the information assets on a daily basis through adherence to the security policies that have been communicated. The end users represent many "windows" to the organization and through their practices the security can either be strengthened through compliance or compromised through their actions. For example, downloading unauthorized software, opening attachments from unknown senders and falling prey to phishing attacks, or visiting malicious websites could introduce back doors or Trojans into the environment. End users should also be the front-line eyes and ears of the organization and report security incidents for investigation. Creating this culture requires that this role and responsibility is clearly communicated and understood by all. End users may be assigned multiple roles inheriting the security attributes of the role profiles previously discussed. Hence, the term "end user" is an oversimplification of the role provided to an end user. End user in this context represents a broad category of individuals for the purpose of ensuring that they have (1) adequate general understanding of information security (presystem access training, annual refresher training, and interim training on targeted subjects), (2) know how to recognize an incident, (3) know where to report the incident, (4) obtain the appropriate access for their jobs, and (5) follow appropriate security policies.

▪ *Information Systems Security Professional*: Development of the security policies and the supporting procedures, standards, baselines, guidelines and subsequent implementation and review are performed through these individuals. Guidance is provided for technical security issues and emerging threats are considered for the adoption of new policies. Interpretation of government regulations and industry trends, and determining the placement of vendor solutions in the security architecture to advance the security of the organization is performed.

▪ *Data/Information/Business Owners*: A business executive or manager that is responsible for an information asset. These are the individuals that assign the appropriate classification to the asset and ensure that the business information is protected with the appropriate controls. Periodically the data owners need to review the classification and access rights associated with the information asset. Depending upon the formalization of the process within the organization, the data owners or their delegates may be required to approve access to the information from other business units. Data owners also need to determine the criticality, sensitivity, retention, backups, and safeguards for the information. Data owners or their delegates are responsible for understanding the policies and procedures used to appropriately classify the information.

▪ *Data Custodian*: Individual or function that takes care of the information on behalf of the data owner. These individuals ensure that the information is available to the end users and is backed up to enable recovery in the event of data loss or corruption. Information may be stored in files, databases, or systems whose technical infrastructure must be managed, typically by systems administrators or operations.

▪ *Information Systems Auditor*: Determines whether or not systems are in compliance with the security policies, procedures, standards, baselines, designs, architectures, management direction, and other requirements. The auditors provide independent assurance to management on the appropriateness of the security objectives. The auditor examines the information systems and determines whether they are designed, configured, implemented, operated, and managed in a way that the organizational objectives are being achieved. The auditors provide top company management with an independent view of the controls that have been designed and their effectiveness. Samples are extracted to test the existence and effectiveness of the controls. Auditors can be a critical resource and partner to the security organizations as they examine the implementation of security controls to determine if the controls are really effective and are working as designed. Well-governed organizations regard their efforts as an essential feedback mechanism and leverage the insights of the auditors to enhance the security program.

▪ *Business Continuity Planner*: Develops contingency plans to prepare for the occurrence of a major threat with the ability to impact the company's objectives negatively. Threats may include earthquakes, tornadoes, hurricanes, blackouts, changes in the economic/political climate, terrorist activities, fire, or other major actions potentially causing significant harm. The business continuity planner ensures that business processes can continue through the disaster and coordinates those activities with the information technology personnel responsible for disaster recovery on specific platforms. Senior management typically plays a critical role during the crisis, where an emergency crisis team may be engaged for a significant event, such as a bomb scare or planning testing the response for a pandemic.

▪ *Information Systems/Information Technology Professionals*: Responsible for designing security controls into information systems, testing the controls, and implementing the systems in production environments through agreed-upon operating policies and procedures. The information systems professionals work with the business owners and the security professionals to ensure that the designed solution provides security controls commensurate with the acceptable criticality, sensitivity, and availability requirements of the application. This role may have elevated access rights, such as administrative rights permitting access to servers and databases, which need to be managed to limit exposure. Some IT professionals may be granted rights to move source code to production status in a client-server program library, while other developers may only have access to the code in the test environment. Clearly documenting who is supposed to have what access is necessary to ensure that excessive privileges are not granted, thus reducing the comfort level that the appropriate change control policies issued are being followed and thereby weakening the overall information security governance.

- *Security Administrator*: Manages the user access request process and ensures that privileges are provided to those individuals that have been authorized for access by the proper management. This individual has elevated privileges and creates or deletes accounts and access permissions. The security administrator also terminates access privileges when individuals leave their jobs or transfer company divisions. The security administrator maintains records of approvals as part of the control environment and produces these records to the information systems auditor to demonstrate compliance with the policies. The security administrator is the one who utilizes the role profiles to grant the appropriate access in response to the request, either through the automated mechanisms of the identity management system or manual processes.

- *Systems Administrator*: Configures the hardware and operating systems to ensure that the information can be available and accessible. The administrator runs software distribution systems to install updates and tested patches on the company computers. The administrator tests and implements system upgrades to ensure the continued reliability of the servers and network devices. Periodic usage of vulnerability testing tools, either through purchased software or open source tools tested in a separate environment identifies areas needing system upgrades or patches to fix the vulnerability.

- *Physical Security*: The individual(s) assigned to the physical security role establish relationships with external law enforcement, such as the local police agencies, state police, or the Federal Bureau of Investigations (FBI) to assist in the investigations. Physical security personnel manage the installation, maintenance, and ongoing operation of the Closed Circuit Television (CCTV) surveillance systems, burglar alarm systems, and card reader access control systems. Guards are placed where necessary as a deterrent to authorize access and to provide safety for the company employees. Physical security personnel interface with systems security, human resources, facilities, legal, and business areas to ensure that the practices are integrated.

- *Administrative Assistants*: This role can be very important to information security, as in many companies of smaller size this may be the individual who greets visitors, signs packages in and out, recognizes individuals that want to enter the offices, and serve as the phone-screener for executives. These individuals may be subject to social engineering attacks, whereby the potential intruder attempts to solicit confidential information that may be used for a subsequent attack. Social engineers prey on the good will and good graces of the helpful individual to gain entry. A properly trained assistant will minimize the risk of divulging useful company information or providing unauthorized entry.

- *Help Desk Administrator*: As the name implies, the help desk is there to service the questions from users that report system problems through a ticketing system. Problems may include poor response time, potential virus infections, unauthorized access, inability to access system resources, or questions on the use of a program. The help desk individual would contact the Computer Incident Response Team (CIRT) when a situation meets the criteria developed by the team. The help desk resets passwords, resynchronizes/reinitializes tokens and smart cards, and resolves other problems with access control. These functions may alternatively be performed through self-service by the end user (i.e., Intranet-based solution that establishes the identity of the end user and resets the password) or by another area such as the security administration, systems administrator, etc., depending upon the organizational structure and separation of duties principles. Care must be taken to ensure that the help desk administrator authorized to reset passwords does not also have the capability to modify user access, delete accounts, or perform other security functions.

An organization may include other roles related to information security to meet the needs of the particular organization. Individuals within the different roles will require different levels of training. The end user may require only security awareness training including the activities that are acceptable, how to recognize that there may be a problem, and what the mechanism is for reporting the problem to the appropriate security personnel for resolution. The security administrator will need more in-depth training on the access control packages to manage the log-on IDs, accounts, and log file reviews. The systems/network administrator will need technical security training for the specific operating system (Windows, UNIX, Linux, etc.) to competently set the security controls.

Establishing Unambiguous Roles

Establishing clear, unambiguous security governance roles has many benefits to the organization beyond providing information regarding the responsibilities and who needs to perform them. The benefits may also include:

- Demonstrable executive management support for information security
- Increases employee efficiency by reducing confusion about who is expected to perform which tasks
- Team coordination to protect information as it moves from department to department
- Lower risks to company reputation damage due to security problems
- Provides capability to manage complex information systems and networks
- Establishes personal accountability for information security
- Reduces turf battles between departments
- Balances security with business objectives
- Supports disciplinary actions for security violations up to and including termination
- Facilitates increased communication for resolution of security incidents
- Demonstrates compliance with applicable laws and regulations
- Shields management from liability and negligence claims
- Provides roadmap for auditors to determine whether or not necessary work is being performed effectively and efficiently
- Enables the continuous improvement efforts (i.e., ISO9000)
- Provides a foundation for determining the security and awareness training required

Information security is a team effort requiring the skill sets and cooperation of many different individuals. The executive management may have overall responsibility and the security officer/director/manager may be assigned the day-to-day task of ensuring the organization is complying with the defined security practices, however every person in the organization has one or more roles to ensure appropriate protection of the information assets.

Conclusion

Information security governance is comprised of much more than just the development and issuance of an information security policy. Role-based access is more than just the creation of a role that specifies access to system resources and then assigning those roles to different end users. Effective information security governance requires each person within the organization to know what their role is with regard to protecting the information assets within their purview and to act accordingly. The board of directors has a specific role with respect to the security program (i.e., setting direction), which is very different from that of the information security officer (i.e., provide risk assessments, systems security plans, vulnerability scanning, high-level status to the board), and from the various types of previously illustrated management levels and end users. Failure at any one of these roles, not just through inappropriate assignment of access, but also by not contributing to the protection of information assets according to their expected position within the organization, serves to threaten the overall information security governance.

Oil slicks shouldn't happen, but they do. Security exposures shouldn't happen, but they do. In either case, with the right forethought, catastrophic problems can be avoided with the appropriate roles-based governance structures and controls put in place.

About the Author

Todd Fitzgerald is responsible for external technical audit and internal security compliance for one of the largest processors of Medicare claims. Todd has led the development of several security programs and actively serves as an international speaker and author of information security issues. Todd coauthored the 2008 (ISC)² book entitled *CISO Leadership: Essential Principles for Success*. Todd graduated from the University of Wisconsin–Lacrosse, serves as an advisor to the College of Business Administration, and holds an MBA with highest honors from Oklahoma State University.

Chapter 12

Social Networking Security Exposure

Sandy Bacik

Did you get my tweet? Can I join your LinkedIn? Did you see my updates on Facebook or MySpace? Some people with limited knowledge of computers might think "What language are you talking?" Social networking is continuing to creep into all arenas of people using computers, even the corporate environment. Does your enterprise permit access to social networking sites during business hours or does your enterprise have a policy that states what can and cannot be posted to a social networking site? Many enterprises do not have guidelines or education programs for their staff and the enterprise does not know what information may be being disclosed and what staff is posting about themselves or the enterprise. In the age of social networking, what are the enterprise risks with using social networking internally and not guiding employees on information disclosure?

What exactly is social networking? A social network is a social structure made of people that are tied by one or more specific types of interconnections, such as values, ideas, friendship, or professional connections; similar to the game six degrees of separation. Our network of social relations has been expanded and moved to the Internet and organized. Online social networking exploded during 2003 and 2004. All online social networking sites allow people to provide information themselves and whatever other information they would like to share. The types of communications within social networking sites include forums, chat rooms, e-mail, and instant messenger. Social networking sites allow browsing based on certain criteria. Some social networking sites have communities and subgroups for particular interests. So what are some of the security implications of online social networks?

- Some people may not exercise caution when disclosing information, as they would when they are in person.
- There is a perception of anonymity when online.
- Lack of physical interaction provides a false sense of security.

- Many Internet sites are now tailoring information for those they are connected to without realizing who else may see it.
- A person may offer insights to impress friends and colleagues.

For the most part, people using these sites do not pose any threats, yet malicious people may be drawn to these sites because of the freely available (personal) information. The more information available about you, the more someone might be able to use it for malicious reasons. Malicious people can attempt to form relationships and eventually perform a social engineering attack using the information a person has provided about the enterprise they were or are employed by. Social networking sites, depending upon the site, store a person's personal information. What is the largest global enterprise you can think of? Now think of the number of accounts and images that global enterprise stores. It does not matter which one you choose, because you can bet that Facebook or MySpace contains many more accounts and images. And what is used for security of those social networking accounts?—yes, a simple user ID and password. For many security professionals, their social networking accounts probably have strong passwords, but what about the millions of other accounts that have no security background. Today, many enterprise users prefer to manage their personal information on a social networking site to keep acquaintances abreast of their activities and accomplishments.

OK, so we share personal information. What type of privacy and security issues and threats are present with social networking sites to the enterprise?

- *One of the larger enterprise risks is social engineering attacks*: Social engineering is a means of attack frequently used by hackers to bypass security mechanisms and access sensitive enterprise data—not by using technology (although technology may be involved), but by using enterprise employees. Data is collected subtly and is gathered gradually piece by piece. Some information is necessary to create an account or to enter an online community but often the privacy settings are neglected and, therefore, the threshold for gaining information to be used in a social engineering attack is low.
- *Spam*: Social networking sites enable various types of messaging. These messaging services allow others to provide unsolicited emails to members, even though site policies are in place.
- *Spear phishing*: With the social networking messaging, members are potentially opening themselves to an e-mail spoofing fraud attempt that targets a specific enterprise, seeking unauthorized access to confidential data.
- *Information leakage*: Some information is only available to "friends" or a member of a restricted group within a social networking site and this is the first line of defense in protecting privacy. Since it is easy to become linked to another, someone may be linked under false pretenses. Some users do not intend to release information about their enterprise, yet it is part of the details of their profile.
- *Reputation slander*: Fake profiles are created in the name of well-known personalities or brands or in order to slander people who are well known within a particular network of linked profiles. Not all profiles are necessarily an accurate portrayal of the individual posting the profile.
- *Stalking and bullying*: This is repeated and purposeful acts of harm that are carried out using technology against individuals.
- *Information aggregation*: Profiles on social networking sites can be downloaded and stored over time and incrementally by third parties. This information can be used by third parties for purposes and contexts not intended by the original person.

- *Secondary data collection*: Personal information knowingly disclosed in a profile can be seen by the site operator using the network itself (data such as time and length of connections, location (IP address) of connection, other users' profiles visited, messages sent and received, and so forth).
- *Face recognition*: Personal information on social networking sites can include user-provided digital images that are an integral and popular part of a profile.
- *Linkability from image metadata, tagging, and cross-profile images*: Many social networking users tag images with metadata, such as a link to their profile or e-mail address.
- *Social network aggregators*: This is a relatively new breed of applications that try to consolidate all your various social networking profiles into one. Many social network aggregators have not had much success to date.
- *Creating an account*: Many of the social networking sites require a birth date as part of the registration to ensure the member is over a certain age. Other information requested is phone number, address, likes, dislikes, favorite things, family. While this information is simple, what can happen if it falls into the hands of a malicious person?
- *Difficulty of complete account deletion*: Trying to delete an account from a social networking site is difficult to completely remove. It is easy to remove the primary pages and information, but secondary information such as public comments made to others within the social network sites remain online and linked to the original account.

From a business point of view, there are benefits to various social networking sites that start with recruitment and go through staff termination and trying to find resources to acquire staff for a project. Many human resource recruitment processes now include Internet and social networking site searches to find prospective employees and contractors. Social networking sites can reveal how professional a person can potentially be and the various activities the recruit is involved with, and can validate information on their résumé. Prospective employees can also do research on enterprises for which they are applying for a position. On the other hand, when an employee is exhibiting anomalous behavior and is reported for disciplinary actions, the human resource department can again use a social networking site to see if the enterprise is possibly being slandered or discussed by the employee in question. The results can determine to what extent the employee is disciplined. During a professional career, we meet many people; we lose touch and want to reconnect for an opportunity or resource. Professional networks allow enterprises to research and connect with potential resources and business partners for technology projects. With caution and validation of information researched, social networking sites can benefit an enterprise.

Trying to adequately control employee use of public social networking by simply telling them to stop is futile. The employee behavior can be modified somewhat by awareness training, but behavior is what it is. Some employees will continue to act in either careless or malicious ways, especially if motivated to do so. These recommendations should be implemented based on business need, risk, and availability of resources. Here is a list of a few enterprise recommendations to limit the risk of social networking sites within the enterprise:

- Block use of social networking sites from the enterprise network. This will help protect your data or social engineered information, about your company or network, from finding its way directly from the employee's desk or your network.
- Strengthen or implement a data leakage prevention program. Know where and how your data is moving.

■ *User awareness training*: User awareness is one of the better defenses against any type of technological or nontechnological attack. Within the use of awareness training, information awareness should be discussed from a business and personal point of view for a better understanding of the risk of information disclosure. Information awareness should also include social engineering attack awareness. Promote the idea that the more information is given out, the more vulnerable you are, and that the Internet is a public resource.

■ Establish a security policy architecture that includes a security policy on information and a standard or guideline on the use of social networks. Topics for the security policy architecture include accounts, passwords, information handling, and disclosure.

■ Set up processes to routinely search social networking sites for enterprise (and employee) information.

■ Set up processes to report and detect abuse. Possible techniques for detecting abuse can include the following:
  - Filtering of malicious or spam comments
  - Filtering by websites or providers
  - Filtering comments by quality to increase content quality
  - Filtering on enterprise or staff names

If the enterprise decides the use of social networking sites is permitted, then the enterprise needs to define guidance for the enterprise employees while connected to the enterprise network and when not connected to the enterprise network. Benefits of a social networking enterprise statement may shield the enterprise from defamation lawsuits and can limit the potential disclosure of company proprietary information. An enterprise could make a policy statement like "Be mature, be ethical, and think before you type and press Enter." A statement like that will leave much interpretation up to the enterprise employee. As the enterprise decides to incorporate a social networking policy, standard, or guideline into the employee handbook, the enterprise might want to consider the following questions:

1. How far should the statements reach? Should the statements be meant only for employees while at work or connected to the enterprise network? And/or are the statements meant for employees when they are not at work? For liability reasons, the statements should cover both scenarios.

2. Does the enterprise want to permit social networking while connected to the enterprise network? It is not realistic to ban all social networking at work. The enterprise will lose the benefit of business-related networking, such as LinkedIn.

3. If the enterprise prohibits social networking, how will social networking be monitored? Turning off Internet access, installing software to block certain sites, or monitoring. Employees' use and disciplining offenders are all possibilities, depending on how many resources the enterprise has or how aggressive the enterprise monitoring is intended to be.

4. If the enterprise permits employees to social network while connected to the enterprise network, does the enterprise limit the access to work-related conduct or permit limited personal use?

5. Does the enterprise want employees to identify with the enterprise when networking online? Enterprise employees should be made aware that if they post as an employee of the enterprise, the enterprise can hold them responsible for any negative portrayals. Or the enterprise can simply require employees to not affiliate with the enterprise and, potentially, lose the networking and marketing potential.

6. How does the enterprise define "appropriate behavior"? The enterprise needs to understand that what is posted online is public and they have no privacy rights in what they put out for the world to see. Another note is that anything in cyberspace might be used as grounds to discipline an employee, no matter whether the employee wrote it from work or outside of work.

Information that should be included in enterprise guidance for social networking is as follows:

- *Notice*: Make sure that the statements are easily accessible by all employees and that the statements are included in orientation, awareness, and employee manuals. The enterprise may also want to consider whether employee acknowledgements of the statements are required.
- *Competence*: Inform the enterprise employees that they should not use any social media tool unless they really understand how it works. Offer social networking awareness training regarding these technologies.
- *Purpose*: Remind the enterprise that enterprise assets are designed and intended for business, not for personal use. Make sure that the enterprise employee knows that social networking must not interfere with their work obligations.
- *Respect*: Inform the enterprise employees that social networking sites are not to be used to harass, threaten, malign, defame, or discriminate against anyone within the enterprise, customers, or anyone else.
- *Employment decisions*: Include counsel to determine what steps the company may legally take to obtain information from social networking sites as part of hiring, promotion, and other employment decisions.
- *Integrity*: Remind the enterprise employees of the enterprise ethics statements.
- *Appropriate content*: Remind the enterprise employees that any electronic communications for work-related purposes must maintain and reflect the enterprise's standards for professionalism.
- *Confidential information*: The enterprise must state that employees must comply with all company policies covering confidential information and trade secrets.
- *Disclaimers*: Remind the enterprise employees to state in any social media environments that what they write is their own opinion and not that of the enterprise.
- *No right to privacy*: Remind the enterprise employees that they have no right to privacy with respect to any information sent, received, created, accessed, obtained, viewed, stored, or otherwise found at any time on the enterprise network and assets.
- *Penalties/Discipline*: The enterprise needs to state that any violations of the policy will subject the employee to discipline, up to and including termination.
- *Modifications*: The enterprise should state that they reserve the right to modify, discontinue, or replace the policy or any terms of the policy.
- The enterprise statement should include examples of content that should not be permitted for posting, such as
  - Comments not topically related to the resource being commented upon
  - Content that promotes, fosters, or perpetuates discrimination against the enterprise
  - Content that promotes, fosters, or perpetuates discrimination on the basis of race, creed, color, age, religion, gender, marital status, status with regard to public assistance, national origin, physical or mental disability, or sexual orientation
  - Profane language or content
  - Sexual content or links to sexual content

- Solicitations of commerce
- Conduct or encouragement of illegal activity
- Information that may tend to compromise the safety or security of the public or public systems
- Content that violates a legal ownership interest of any other party

Social networking sites have business benefits and risks. Yes, social networking sites can be blocked through filtering software, but will it help or hurt the enterprise business model. It is up to the enterprise to protect assets and intellectual property through awareness, technology, and processes. As with any technology, the enterprise needs to document business requirements and perform a risk assessment before implementing or allowing the use of specific technology within the enterprise network.

About the Author

Sandy Bacik, CISSP-ISSMP, CISM, CGEIT, CHS-III, author and former CSO, has over 14 years of direct development, implementation, and management information security experience in the areas of audit management, disaster recovery and business continuity, incident investigation, physical security, privacy, regulatory compliance, standard operating policies and procedures, and data center operations and management. Ms. Bacik has managed, architected, and implemented comprehensive information assurance programs and managed internal, external, and contracted and outsourced information technology audits to ensure various regulatory compliance for state and local government entities and Fortune 200 companies. She has developed methodologies for risk assessments, information technology audits, vulnerability assessments, security policy and practice writing, incident response, and disaster recovery.

Chapter 13

Social Networking, Social Media, and Web 2.0 Security Risks

Robert M. Slade

Social networking has become extremely popular recently. Given the fact that a great deal of network and Internet use and applications have been social, this is hardly surprising. What is more surprising is that the traditional media and technology pundits seem to feel that we need to have a special term for this type of application. Activities that have always gone on in networked environments, even before the creation of the Internet, now have to be identified as social networking, social media, Web 2.0, or related terms and jargon.

Much of the risk involved in social media relates to social engineering. In security, of course, we have had to deal with social engineering in many ways, and for a long time. While the popularity of social media increases the amount of this activity, it doesn't alter the type. People are people, and they like to be sociable. Instant messaging, mailing lists, Usenet newsgroups, and even the old finger program all related to this type of activity. The social functions have, at various times, been used for commercial purposes as well, and this disparity in approach and usage has frequently led to conflict, such as the rise of spam, dating back to the "Green Card Lawyers" and even earlier.

Businesses are, again, attempting to make use of social media, such as Facebook and Twitter, for corporate purposes, primarily marketing.

While these applications are, at the moment, more projected than proven, it is undeniable that many enterprises are either examining Web 2.0 technologies or are facing rogue use of these systems by employees. In either case it is best to become informed about the concerns and security dangers related to such use.

Make yourself informed. Study up on Web 2.0. Make sure you have relevant policies in place, and that your employees know about them, and why they are in place.

To attempt to structure an examination of this topic, let us use the standard Confidentiality, Integrity, and Availability (CIA) triad.

Confidentiality

Your own social networking can lead to improper disclosure of information in a huge variety of ways. The first such hazard is disclosure of one's own information. When creating an account on a social system, there is an extremely strong temptation to provide a lot of information. You can disclose details about yourself, such as birth and anniversary dates, family members, pet names, and other items that people, all too frequently, use as passwords. Even if you don't use your cat's name as your password, you may betray sufficient information for someone to try to steal or misuse your identity. Be careful. Don't disclose too much about yourself. Don't get caught up in the excitement when you first approach social networking. It might be an idea to view some accounts and think about whether these people have said too much about themselves. Then think it over, sleep on it, and prepare what you are willing to say about yourself before you create your own account. Tomorrow.

I am not even going to stress, here, the perils of posting pictures of yourself doing silly or embarrassing things. OK, maybe you did get drunk enough to pose, half-naked, getting into a frosting wrestling match with That Other Person on top of the cake at the last release party. And maybe it was just your luck that a number of your friends caught different angles with their camera phones. But posting it on Flickr is your own fault.

Oh, you had an embarrassing shot on your account, but you've deleted it? It may still be there. Many social networking sites have usage agreements (you didn't read it when you electronically "signed" it, by clicking on it, did you?) stating that anything you provide to the site now belongs to them. Partly for technical reasons, they find it easier simply to remove a pointer, but leave the material in place.

(While I was writing this article, I came across a site called Blippy. I'm still not quite sure that I believe this. Supposedly it is a site for listing what you buy. Users are encouraged to link their account to a credit or debit card, and then the purchases are automatically listed, as well as cash advances and withdrawals. Even without displaying the credit card number, this provides a wealth of information to identity thieves and fraudsters.)

If you note details about your work, and coworkers, someone can try and use that information in order to try a social engineering attack against the company. (Usually while you are away, if you provide a vacation message on your e-mail and an itinerary of your trip on LinkedIn.) Be more careful, not less, when it is not your information. I am not a particularly private person and have accounts on Flickr, Twitter, Facebook, and LinkedIn, as well as blogs and websites. You will notice, though, that they don't provide much information about friends and family, unless they want to provide it themselves.

As well as outright disclosure, there is also the issue of aggregated information. There are already systems using data from social media sites (and even Web search engines) to gather weather information and forecast epidemics. This is not done on the basis of reporting from a number of trained volunteers, but simply searching the mass of chatter for certain keywords. The sheer volume provides a high degree of accuracy to the data, even if someone knows what is going on and tries to skew the curve.

However, it is also possible to track an individual over time and find out a great deal. Twitter is now providing location information from those posting via cell or mobile phones. Over time this will build up a reliable pattern of where you are at a given time of the day, week, or month. (An attacker can then launch the aforementioned social engineering attack while you are at home or lunch, or burgle your home while you are at work.)

(Remember that embarrassing photo? Even if you took it off your page, and even if the site actually did delete it, there are systems that regularly take "snapshots" of the Internet. The material may still be in one of those archives.)

There is, in addition, the fact that information can be aggregated over different social systems. You may provide some information on one site, and different, perhaps complementary, data on another. (The greatest problem in this regard is the practice of using the same password on all your different sites. There was a recent case where attackers were able to crack passwords on a site with little protection and then use these passwords to hijack accounts on systems like Facebook.)

(By the way, don't rely on your ability to create an "anonymous" account with a cute [and fake] name, or even using an anonymizing system. Simply by posting you start to give away information about yourself: even the choice of words you use can identify you. I am a member of security communities and discussion groups and have seen numerous instances where individuals have tried to annoy the communities under the guise of an alias. This is perhaps the most foolish choice of venue to try such a thing: these are people with skills and contacts to do a lot of tracking in cyberspace. In one case the collective members got annoyed enough to find out not only the identity, name, residence, and phone number of the anonymous poster, but some actually went out and got pictures of his workplace and school. People from other communities may not have training in digital forensics, but there are bound to be some with enough technical savvy to start putting together the clues you leave behind. You give away a lot more information about yourself than you think, on Web 2.0.)

(While in the final stages of writing this article, I was introduced to a site that allows you to create your own cards, and then have them printed and mailed. One of the suggested uses is to have your Christmas cards done this way: it's fast, and a reasonable price, in comparison to the purchase of commercial cards and normal postage. The site has multiple levels of "membership" you can purchase, in a style similar to multilevel marketing systems. Do you *really* want to give pyramid sellers your entire contact list?)

Corporate

Another danger is of providing too much information about the company. We mentioned the possibility of attackers mounting social engineering attacks, fueled by disclosures about coworkers, superiors, subordinates, and corporate activities and policy. However, there is also the risk of divulging sensitive information about products, services, pricing, customers, or even trade secrets. Social media sites have always pursued function over security. Many are now starting to take security more seriously, but these systems simply do not have the same level of protection that you may give to your own enterprise resources.

Social networking sites do have protections in place, but it can be extremely difficult to find out exactly what certain settings actually do. A great deal of trial and error may be necessary before you know whether your information is actually protected. If you are going to use Web 2.0 systems, make sure you do your homework.

(If you use "applications" on Facebook, any applications at all, you should be aware of the fact that *all* of your information is available to the application, regardless of how private and confidential you think you have made it. Not all applications do read all your data, but any application can. Think about it next time you want to send someone a cute pink jellyfish…)

As with e-mail, you should probably have policies clearly stating what your employees can, and cannot, say on social sites. It probably isn't a good idea to have blanket prohibitions against using social networking sites. A better idea is to make your staff aware of the dangers, and the reasons that you want them to be careful.

(Something you should be very careful about posting is material that is covered by copyright. This can get you in legal trouble. However, be particularly cautious of posting any material from your company that is covered by copyright. Many sites have policies stating that once you post something on the system it becomes theirs, or at least they are free to use it in any way they see fit. By posting content that your company holds copyright on, you may be releasing that material from copyright and destroying value for the company.)

Others

There is yet another peril in regard to personal information on social systems and that one comes from your friends. You, frequently, create pieces of information about your friends and family, in ways as simple as tagging them in photographs on picture-sharing sites. Others do the same with regard to you. It may surprise you to find out how much information there is about you on the Internet, even if you, yourself, do not participate in social networking activities. It's probably a good idea to do an "ego search" every once in a while and find out what other people have posted about you. An ego search is simply a search on your name, or any nickname you commonly use, with any search engine. There are also now services that automatically search on a variety of search engines, specifically aimed at finding this sort of information about people.

I did such a search on "Robert Slade." On Altavista, the first result was the Wikipedia article that someone did on me. The second result was http://www.robertslade.com, which I hadn't known existed. As well as correctly listing my published books, this page informed me that I was mentioned on the Wikipedia entry for the RISKS-Forum Digest. It also provides a photograph of someone else. (A professor of chemistry at the University of Surrey with the same name, but not a member of the "Robert Slade Internet Club.") Searching for images, I also found the church in which I am buried, so perhaps I can be forgiven if this article gets turned in a bit late.

There is a further danger related to this one. Privacy laws frequently relate to the duty a company has to protect data you provide to them about yourself. The same duty may not always apply if someone else has provided that information. Information provided about you may not always be accurate and this is a major danger in social networking. There have been so many instances of people deliberately providing misinformation about people on Wikipedia, that there is now a policy stating that changes to entries about living people must be approved by a qualified editor.

(A sales representative got wind of a merger deal between two competitors, but could not confirm one of the parties, based on personal contacts and knowledge of the industry. Using social networking the rep was able to identify the company, plus personnel issues creating significant business problems for the one company and the new combined enterprise. The employees of the company had protected their profiles and properly avoided disclosing too much information. However, friends and relatives, who could be identified from profiles or last names, had posted comments that, together, provided vital clues and confirmation.)

(OK, you deleted the embarrassing photo, made sure the site deleted it too, and you even missed getting archived by one of the way back sites. By the way, did any of your friends download a copy of that picture while it was still there?…)

Employers may now be estimating your likelihood of being a problem drinker by how much your (social networking) friends drink.

Integrity

Research

You undoubtedly have an "all news" radio or TV channel in your area. You probably have an "all traffic" radio station as well. On your regular commute this may be helpful, alerting you to traffic jams so that you can take an alternate route. (Or, if you get well and truly stuck in traffic, you can call and tell people you'll be late.)

However, if you are using this information to plan more extensive driving, you'll find it isn't quite so helpful. A large metropolitan area has a huge complex of routes and not all may be covered by the reports. The reports, even though rattled off at machinegun speed, take some time to cover the aspects they do cover. Information from roadworks and closures, traffic cameras, and other sources needs to be collated, and this takes time. The radio reports go out in a set sequence, so that unless information about a problem is received at the right time, it probably won't get sent out over the air until later. In the meantime, modern traffic is so close to the maximum capacity that traffic jams can happen in an instant, and, within a few minutes, create backups and bottlenecks miles away. If you do listen to traffic radio, you will undoubtedly have experienced situations of running into a massive traffic jam that has not been reported at all. Or you've been told of a huge problem, only to sail through that area and see nothing. Part of this has to do with the timing issue just mentioned. But another part has to do with the fact that much of the information relayed in the traffic reports comes from people calling in (or sending text messages) from cell phones. Not all of these reports are reliable. Sometimes people are reporting what they see, without understanding the implications. Sometimes people are reporting what they think is happening. (And, unfortunately, these days sometimes people are just messing with the system…)

Social networking can be used for a number of helpful purposes. Governments and relief agencies have used them to warn people in disasters or to get reports out to a large number of people. Businesses use social media for advertising and market research. For quick research on opinion and public perception they can be very useful.

I did research into the use of social networks in different situations. During the forest fires that threatened Kelowna, British Columbia, it was possible to use Twitter to find reports, and even video, providing information on aspects of the fires that were not being reported in the major media. (This material did have to be extracted from a great many messages simply directing people to major media reports and also a number of postings simply sending messages of sympathy to those in the affected areas.) However, it is unlikely that the Twitter system could have been of help to those closest to the affected areas: the type of data was fine for those who could safely analyze from a distance. (On the other hand, it could be that this might be of help to those directing emergency response and overall disaster planning.)

Earlier, it was interesting to see the Twitter traffic regarding the Conficker infections. In that case, the information was almost completely useless. Much of the traffic consisted solely of jokes and comments. Some postings suggested ways to prevent or check for the infection: these were almost uniformly mistaken and, therefore, unhelpful.

Wikipedia is famous as the encyclopedia that anyone can edit and add to. For items or general knowledge it is quite good. For entries in specialized areas it is less reliable. I have written two major texts on computer viruses, and checked out the Wikipedia article on the topic. It averages roughly two major errors per paragraph.

"The irony of the Information Age is that it has given new respectability to uninformed opinion." (John Lawton)

In any case of research using social media, be very careful to test the results you get. You will have to sift a lot of chaff to get at the wheat, if, indeed, there is any wheat to be had. Try to confirm what you find out by checking with other sources (and beware if those sources use exactly the same wording: other people are reading Twitter, too). If the information cannot be confirmed, be aware that you may be taking a significant risk by acting on unconfirmed data.

(By the way, for those of you who are keen on hiring through LinkedIn or Facebook, remember that one thing you can be certain of if you hire people who are very active in updating their accounts is that they will be extremely active users of social networking, possibly while they are supposed to be working for you.)

Your Info

Stalkers are annoying and possibly frightening, but, unless they physically attack you, that's generally about it. Cyberstalkers can be much worse. They frequently post misinformation about their targets. Often they will engage in identity theft and pretend to be the target, sometimes by taking over accounts, but more often simply by creating accounts and using the target's name and personal information. This has been happening on the net for years, but it is happening a lot in social networking systems.

This is the worst form of misinformation about you, but it is far from the only type. Do you have an account on a social site that you abandoned before you met your present Significant Other? Some information is simply out of date, but seems current because, after all, it's on the Internet.

There are lots of ways that "false" information can be posted about you. Sometimes people don't know you as well as they think they do, but post about you anyway. Some pieces of data may be posted out of context. Sometimes it isn't even about you. Unless your name is really unusual, there is probably any number of people with the same name.

(Rob Slade started the "Robert Slade Internet Club" way back when the net was much smaller than it is now. [Ah, yes, but *which* Rob Slade?] With the increase in population on the net, any net "ego search" on Robert Slade will probably turn up more people who weren't in the club.)

Again, it is probably a good idea, every once in a while, to do an "ego search" and find out what has been posted about you. Remember that it is unlikely that you will be able to "correct" the information. However, forewarned is forearmed.

Company

Is your company website up to date? Did your corporation start up an area in MySpace, only to abandon it? Did someone from your marketing department start up all kinds of interesting discussions on business-related mailing lists and discussion groups, and then get bored? What information about your company is out there? What have people said about you? What *are* they saying about you? If it is wrong, maybe you'd better correct it. (Of course, you have to be careful. Sometimes the information isn't incorrect. Social networking allows people to complain about you worldwide, and sometimes in very creative ways.)

Once you have found out what is being said about your company on the net, you may have to choose your battles. Do you want to get a reputation like that of a certain entertainment company, which seems to be willing to sue someone any time the name of one of their characters gets mentioned?

System

Social networking sites are popular, and all the rage. New ones keep popping up all the time. In order to keep new and fresh, social media vendors keep adding functions and adding to the existing sites. Therefore, security takes a back seat to "time to market" and new operations.

The sites and systems have had numerous weaknesses and faults, and a number of these can affect you.

Sometimes these problems can result from code that is used by a large number of social networking systems, creating loopholes and weaknesses that are common to a variety of popular systems.

Availablity

Twitter is hugely successful. It is the fastest growing site on the Internet at the moment. (Of course, this being the Internet Age, by the time you read this, Twitter may be old hat, visited only by a few nostalgia buffs. But …). That being the case, Twitter is, inevitably, a victim of its own success. With the huge numbers of new users, parts of Twitter bog down so regularly that Twitter bought a special image to present to users when the system was not working properly: the now famous "Fail Whale." (It's possible you may not have actually seen the Fail Whale. Twitter now fails in so many different ways that often the Fail Whale image itself is unavailable.)

The failure of suddenly popular websites or pages is now so common that it's been given a name: the slashdot effect. The popular Slashdot website was responsible for many sites being overloaded once noted there and so now any site that has been deluged by a sudden rush of fans is said to have been slashdotted.

There is another aspect in relation to availability and that is the type of access to a site. Twitter users, for example, can post messages to Twitter and receive postings from those they follow, through text messages or short service messages on their cell or mobile phones. This can sometimes create a disconnect between those posting and those reading. For those using Twitter via the Web interface, a few dozen messages within the period of an hour is no big deal. For those dealing with the service primarily via cell phone, such a volume can be extremely annoying.

Twitter is also accessible via specialized programs and through feeds on other websites. Again, those who use Twitter in one format may see it completely differently from those who view it through another.

Twitter provides an almost ridiculously simple service, for which people have found an enormous number of uses. Facebook, on the other hand, has a huge number of functions. Use, however, may be restricted, since you can't see much of anything posted on Facebook unless you are a member and signed in. (This is in spite of the fact that certain Facebook settings seem to imply that the information can be see by anyone, even those not on the system.) In this way, some of the social networks are actually antisocial, creating division of the net world on the basis of certain technologies. Facebook is a major factor in this hiving off of the Internet, but Google is following closely with Google Apps and other related services.

Certain related technologies may also factor in. One of the major activities you will see on all social networking sites is mention or note of some other website or page. With this constant referencing has come a desire to shorten the URLs that are used to get to a site. A huge number of shortening and redirecting sites are now being used for that purpose.

This is particularly true on Twitter. Twitter initially used TinyURL and it was top of the redirectors when Twitter used it. Now Twitter uses bit.ly and it has become the leader. (This also implies that the leading redirection site may, in turn, become a victim of its own success and be unavailable to do the redirection if swamped.) (Note that there is an additional danger with redirectors: they can be used to hide the fact that you are being forwarded to a malicious site.)

Last Advice

Remember that social networking is social. Try to maintain civility. Remember the suggestions about network etiquette (netiquette) you were formerly given for e-mail.

About the Author

Robert M. Slade, a security specialist, malware researcher, and author, published *Robert Slade's Guide to Computer Viruses*, coauthored *Viruses Revealed*, prepared the world's first course on forensic programming, wrote *Software Forensics*, and maintained a glossary of security terms, now published as *Dictionary of Information Security*. More information than anyone would be interested in is available at http://victoria.tc.ca/techrev/rms.htm.

Chapter 14

Applying Adult Education Principles to Security Awareness Programs

Chris Hare

Security awareness is one of those topics many security professionals shudder at. Not because they don't believe it is worthwhile, but more so because of the challenges in getting a security awareness program off the ground and measuring its success.

The goal of security awareness programs is to raise the level of knowledge and understanding of the user's role in a security program. Organizations want their employees to understand how the decisions and actions they take affect the organizational security program. Likewise, they want their employees to understand how those same actions can result in weakening or compromising the organization's security.

There has been much research on the development of a good security awareness program. This chapter discusses how the success of a security awareness program could be enhanced through the application of adult education philosophies to the program's design and implementation.

Being faced with the daunting challenge of designing a security awareness program, practitioners need to ask themselves what they are trying to achieve. The question is not only the goal for their security awareness program, but do they understand the learning context which needs to exist before change can really take place.

Is Education Applicable to Security Awareness?

Education is widely used in various formats to convey information and knowledge to students. There have been studies about the effectiveness of education programs in many settings including medical awareness (Healton, 1993) and cultural awareness (Nieto, 1999), just to name two examples. The application of social science has also been widely studied, especially the impact of human behavior as it relates to advertising (Chun, 2007).

Security awareness programs must be aware of the attitudes and belief systems of the users in the community of interest or organization. Chun (2007) identifies why knowledge of these attitudes and beliefs is important:

- *They are predictors of behavior*: "If you can determine the target population's attitudes toward information security issues such as privacy and confidentiality, you can use that information to predict how secure your environment will be."
- *They are targets for change*: "If you can change someone's attitude toward something, you can change their behavior."
- *They are a source of risk*: "Extreme attitudes toward someone or something can lead to irrational cognitive function and behavior."

Just as Chun (2007) has indicated the value of understanding attitudes, these same factors are also important in an educational setting. If someone has a poor attitude toward something, it may be a result of not understanding or having the knowledge to make an informed decision. People are often afraid to admit they do not know something, especially to peers. We can change the first two reasons to illustrate an educational approach to understanding attitudes:

- *They are predictors of behavior*: If you understand the attitudes of the target population to the desired subject matter, in this case information security issues, then you can identify the types of information which will be important to communicate.
- *They are targets for change*: Changing someone's attitude and behavior can be as simple as providing them the information they don't want to admit they do not know, in a manner which they can understand and process.

Even though you can provide people with the information and knowledge to make good decisions about their behaviors and actions, sometimes people will behave irrationally. No amount of education can eliminate this possibility.

Chun (2007) presented the Tripartite Model regarding attitudes in the sixth edition of the *Information Security Management Handbook*. We can summarize the three points of the Tripartite Model, shown in Figure 14.1 (Chun, 2007), as follows:

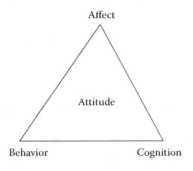

Figure 14.1   Tripartite model. (From Chun, S.W., *Information Security Management Handbook,* **Sixth edition., Auerbach Press, Boca Raton, 2007.)**

- The emotional or affective state of our attitude play an important part in how we feel toward something.
- Changing behaviors can sometimes lead to changes in our attitudes.
- Attitudes can be formulated by thinking about them.

These three points are important to consider when the security practitioner focuses on the business perspective of the security awareness puzzle: "informed and trained employees can be a crucial factor in the effective functioning and protection of the information system" (Hansche, 2007, p. 546).

In Hansche's presentation, she follows an almost educational model in arranging her security awareness program. Setting goals, deciding on content, delivery, and beyond, venturing into the formal aspects of training.

The question then, is can including the principles of adult education impact a security awareness program? The answer to this question can be both yes and no, depending upon your perspective.

Understanding the Adult in Adult Education

How does adult education have anything to do with information security? If we consider for a moment that our security awareness program is a set of activities to educate the user community about information security in the organization, then a security awareness program has some degree of similarity with a training program.

Before we examine the principles, let's first establish some common definitions. Education is the process of receiving or providing systematic instruction. When thinking about the definition, it sounds much more formal than most security awareness programs. Education, however, is not always in a structured setting. Everyone experiences some form of informal education almost every day. That being said, the security practitioner is looking more for learning to occur as a result of the security awareness program, than education. Learning involves the acquisition of knowledge through a variety of methods to influence the attitudes and behaviors of the learner.

That does not mean the security awareness program needs to be as intensive or as structured as a training program, but it does have some similar elements. There are three primary formats where training or educational activities occur: formal, informal, and nonformal. The distinction between these types may at first seem insignificant, but understanding their differences highlights how each contributes to an information security awareness program.

Formal education is "highly institutionalized, bureaucratic, curriculum driven and formally recognized" (Merriam, Caffarella, & Baumgartner, 2007). Formal education conjures images of lectures, professors, educational institutions, and graduation ceremonies. Except for those programs specializing in information security, few educational institutions address information security within their specific disciplines. Consequently, even the most educated and experienced employees still need and can benefit from information security awareness programs.

Nonformal education is structured education that occurs outside a formal education institution. Nonformal education situations are often short-term, voluntary, and have fewer prerequisites (Merriam, Caffarella, & Baumgartner, 2007). Organizations offer training for their employees using classroom or online, computer-based delivery methods providing a nonformal learning environment. Security awareness programs are typically structured on their own, often short-term, have a defined set of objectives, and are often voluntary to some degree, even though organizations would like all employees to participate in the program.

The final type of education, informal education, is "spontaneous, unstructured learning that goes on daily in the home and the neighborhood…and in the workplace" (Merriam, Caffarella, & Baumgartner, 2007). Because of the variety regarding where informal education occurs, it is difficult to identify as it is embedded in our activities, discussions, analyses, and interpersonal exchanges. The primary difference between nonformal and informal education is the planning and structure associated with the former and the lack of "externally imposed curriculum" (Merriam, Caffarella, & Baumgartner, 2007) in the latter.

Why Is Adult Education Different?

Teaching adults is different from teaching children and brings with a set of unique challenges. Understanding the differences is critical to success when teaching adults. Since the issue is a security awareness program, why is understanding how adults learn important? A major objective in an information security awareness program is to influence the audience into changing their behavior as a result of the awareness program. Educational programs are striving to make similar changes as a result of the information conveyed to the student in the course.

Successful adult learning programs pay attention to six key principles first proposed by Malcolm Knowles. Knowles is considered the father of adult learning. These principles are as follows:

1. "Adults need to know why they need to learn something before undertaking to learn it.
2. Adults have a self-concept of being responsible for their own lives…they develop a deep psychological need to be seen and treated by others as being capable of self-direction.
3. Adults come into an educational activity with both a greater volume and a different quality of experiences from youth.
4. Adults become ready to learn those things they need to know … to cope effectively with their real life situations.
5. In contrast to children's and youth's subject-centered orientation to learning (at least in school), adults are life-centered or task centered or problem centered) in their orientation to learning.
6. While adults are responsive to some extrinsic motivators (better job, promotions, salary increases, etc.), the more potent motivators are intrinsic (the desire for increased self-esteem, quality of life, responsibility, etc.)" (Knowles in Merriam & Brockett, 1997).

Even a brief examination of these adult learning principles suggests a correlation with the Tripartite Model. B.F. Skinner proposed that behavior could be learned and unlearned. Therefore, the employee who forgets to engage their screen saver when they leave their desk can also unlearn that behavior. It is more likely that they will learn a new behavior though, once they understand why they need to learn a new one.

The emotional or affective state of our being affects our attitudes, as noted by Chun (2007). This is important because it speaks to more intrinsic motivators, as our emotional state is after all an internal one. Similarly, adults want to be seen and treated fairly by others and as being able to do things on their own.

How do these principles affect out security awareness program? More often than not, the security practitioner or security leader says a security awareness program is needed and everyone sits around trying to come up with neat and catchy phrases which will get the attention of the employees.

Unfortunately, they are focusing on the delivery phase of the program, instead of starting at the goal as suggested by Hansche (2007). Without a goal, it is impossible to explain to the adult employee why they need to learn something. Of course, education has been used as a driving force in social settings and is essentially an "apparatus for social control" (Merriam, Caffarella, & Baumgartner, 2007). Indeed, when you think about it, the security practitioner is trying to change or control the social fabric of the enterprise through the awareness program.

Establishing the goal(s) of the security awareness program helps put the program into the contexts that appeal to the employee population. "This is a good thing to learn because…" and "I am responsible for information security" are phrases which take on new meaning because they set the basis for the adult understanding why they need to learn something and appeal to them on an emotional level.

Once the goals are decided, Hansche suggests focusing on the content. The content is what the learner will be exposed to and hopefully will be assimilated into their consciousness. One of the challenges here is that adults have a lot and highly varying ranges of experiences in the security arena. Some topics will be very familiar to them and others will not. Engaging a cross-section of employees to find out what is important from an information security perspective in their area of the company and their familiarity with the identified topics is important. This is what Stephen Covey calls "seeking to understand first." While possibly taken out of context, the point is it is necessary to understand where you are going and use the resources you have available to get there.

Using employees to assist in content selection and development engages the adult in some level of responsibility for the learning process. While you can't do this with the entire employee population, the ideas, both content and delivery, from this employee cross-section will be valuable to the practitioner.

When it comes time to consider the implementation of the selected content, a variety of delivery methods is key. It isn't just mouse pads and slogans, although they help. There is much evidence that people learn new information in a variety of ways, including visual, auditory, and kinesthetic.

Visual learners benefit from mouse pads, screen savers, and written material because they prefer to learn through reading and other visual stimuli. Auditory learners, however, prefer information delivery through hearing, so speeches, lectures, and information delivered through voice mail broadcasts are of importance to them. Finally, the kinesthetic learner wants to do it. They want their hands on it. Squeeze balls and security games are great ideas for these learners.

During the planning for the implementation of the program, it is important to remember that adults are task- or problem-centered learners. Not only do you have to present the information in a format they will accept it in, but you also have to do it a way where some problem they are experiencing can be solved or made easier as a result.

Following Hansche's model, evaluation of the program is necessary, just as in a formal education setting. The program planners should take stock of the feedback they receive. The employee cross-section used during the content development should be surveyed to find out their view of the program's success or what they would do differently. Finally, the participating employees should also be surveyed. Did the program assist them in some fashion? Will they or have they done things differently that were influenced by the program?

Evaluation is often left out of security awareness programs because attempting to measure the program's success is nebulous and hard to do. Just because it is hard, doesn't mean we shouldn't try to figure out how to do it. Planning for evaluation should be just as important as planning the content and delivery, because content is what we want the employees to remember. We don't care if they remember the survey they did right after a presentation, but we do want them to remember the key messages from the program.

Can adult education principles be used to provide a better security awareness program? I think the answer is yes. That being said, following a development method such as Hansche's, while coupling it with the Chun's Tripartite Model and the adult education principles, has the potential to yield an effective awareness program grounded in social science, education theory, and information security.

About the Author

Chris Hare, CISSP, CISA, CISM, has over 23 years in the computing industry and is the coauthor of New Riders Publishing's *Inside Unix, Internet Firewalls and Network Security, Building an Internet Server with Linux* and *The Internet Security Professional Reference.* His book credits also include the *General Linux II Examination Guide* and the *Official CISSP Study Guide.* Chris holds a master of arts degree in adult education from Northwestern State University of Louisiana and a bachelor of arts and science degree in information systems from Dallas Baptist University.

References

Carnegie Mellon University (2007, September 28). Online Game Helps People Recognize Internet Scams. ScienceDaily. Retrieved January 3, 2009, from http://www.sciencedaily.com/releases/2007/09/070925110204.htm.

Chun, S. W. (2007). Change that Attitude: The ABCs of a Persuasive Security Awareness Campaign. In H. Tipton (Ed.), *Information Security Management Handbook*, Sixth edition (pp. 521–530). Boca Raton: Auerbach Press.

Covey, S. (1990). *The Seven Habits of Highly Effective People.* New York: Simon & Shuster.

Cranton, P. (2000). *Planning Instruction for Adult Learners,* Second edition. Toronto: Wall & Emerson Inc.

Cranton, P. (2003). *Finding Our Way: A Guide for Adult Educators.* Toronto: Wall & Emerson.

Hansche, S. (2007). Making Security Awareness Happen. In H. Tipton, & M. Krause (Eds.), *Information Security Management Handbook*, Sixth edition (pp. 541–554). Boca Raton: Auerbach Press.

Healton, C. G., & Messerri, P. (1993). The Effect of Video Interventions on Improving Knowledge and Treatment Compliance in the Sexually Transmitted Disease Clinic Setting. *STD Journal.* Retrieved December 29, 2008, from http://scholar.google.com/scholar?hl=en&lr=&q=info:f1L8ggyCrQIJ:scholar.google.com/&output=viewport&pg=1.

Merriam, S. B., & Brockett, R. G. (1997). *The Profession and Practice of Adult Education.* San Francisco: Jossey-Bass.

Merriam, S. B., Caffarella, R. S., & Baumgartner, L. M. (2007). *Learning in Adulthood,* Third edition. San Francisco: Jossey-Bass.

Nieto, S. (1999). *The Light in Their Eyes: Creating Multicultural Learning Communities.* Multicultural Education Series. New York: Teachers College Press. Retrieved December 29, 2008, from http://eric.ed.gov/ERICWebPortal/custom/portlets/recordDetails/detailmini.jsp?_nfpb=true&_&ERICExtSearch_SearchValue_0=ED440164&ERICExtSearch_SearchType_0=no&accno=ED440164.

Tennant, M., & Pogson, P. (1995). *Learning and Change in the Adult Years.* San Francisco: Jossey-Bass.

Security Management Planning

Chapter 15

Controlling the Emerging Data Dilemma: Building Policy for Unstructured Data Access

Anne Shultz

It's everywhere. It's saved blatantly on the desktop of a coworker's unattended computer, just waiting to hop onto the next flash drive and head out of the company. It lingers just a click away, ready to be uploaded and e-mailed to a competing company. It lies nakedly on a manager's desk, eager to be picked up by criminal hands. It lurks in an unsecured network drive, hoping to be discovered by someone with malicious intentions. It's unstructured data and it's demanding attention.

What Is Unstructured Data?

In general, unstructured data can be defined as any electronic information without a specific structure. Depending on the context, this definition can indicate data that is stored outside of a database as well as documents where the contents can take any shape, much like the text in a Word document. This includes documents, blueprints, presentations, image files, video files, etc. However, it is important to remember that whether or not the data is considered structured depends on the context. For example, although spreadsheet data can be structured in cells and arranged in rows and columns, like those created with Excel, this is not controlled by the application (Dorian, 2007). For this reason, spreadsheets should be considered unstructured data.

Unstructured data makes up over 85% of all business information, as estimated by Merrill Lynch (Atre & Blumberg, 2003). To make matters worse, the amount of unstructured data within companies is still growing. With e-mail and file services being the biggest contributors, more and more information is becoming available electronically and easy to share (Dorian, 2007). According to a study by the Aberdeen Group, a yearly increase in the amount of unstructured data generated throughout the organization was reported by 86% respondents (Aberdeen Group, 2009). As it comprises such a large percentage of business information, one would assume that management of unstructured data and unstructured data access would be a priority for most organizations. However, a survey developed by the Ponemon Institute and Varonis System Inc. indicates differently. According to this study, which surveyed 870 IT operations professionals, 91% of organizations do not have a process for establishing ownership of unstructured data. Further, 76% of respondents were not able to determine who can access unstructured data, while almost 70% felt that employees in their organization had unnecessary access to unstructured data. Lastly, 89% of respondents surveyed by the Ponemon Institute and Varonis acknowledged that controlling access to unstructured data is very difficult for their organization (StorageNewsletter.com, 2008).

Why Is Unstructured Data Access a Problem?

The looming beast of unstructured data is a serious issue for companies from a legal standpoint. More specifically, businesses lacking control over unstructured data access may be ill prepared when it comes to legal discovery. In the event of a lawsuit, all related documents must be held as potential evidence. If there is no control over unstructured data in general, required documents may be difficult to find in the time allotted by the court (Dorian, 2007). Searching for documents may be challenging if it has not been determined who is responsible for the information. Further, "chain-of-custody" must be verified for any documents held during the litigation process (Murchison, 2009, 9). To verify chain-of-custody, a company must prove that the documents are authentic and are what they claim to be (p. 31). This means that there needs to be documented proof of when the documents were created, who created them, what was done with the documents, and who accessed or viewed the documents. Verifying chain-of-custody may prove to be nearly impossible with no control over unstructured data access. In addition to maintaining chain-of-custody, any retention policy mandated by the company will be difficult to enforce if it has not been determined who is accountable for maintaining the data. If the retention policy is not applied evenly, documents may be deleted prematurely or kept longer than the retention policy requires. Either of these situations will point to an inconsistent retention policy and could cause serious trouble for a company faced with providing documents in a court of law.

Lack of control over unstructured data is also a problem for businesses when it comes to compliance. In light of today's corporate compliance requirements, such as Sarbanes-Oxley, Payment Card Industry Act (PCI), and Health Insurance Portability and Accountability Act (HIPAA), many businesses must tighten controls on their processes and systems. This also involves tightening controls for systems that handle unstructured data. For example, the Sarbanes-Oxley Act requires strong access controls to ensure that financial information is not corrupted (Lambert, 2009). This includes strong access controls for financial systems, as well as for unstructured financial data. The (PCI) Data Security Standards also require strong access controls in order to ensure sufficient protection for customer credit card information (Burton et al., 2007). Most specifically, the PCI requirement 7.2 maintains that access to cardholder information must be denied for all employees unless access is absolutely needed for their job (Burton et al.). Like Sarbanes-Oxley, this rule applies not only to credit card systems, but to unstructured credit card data as well. Yet another act which requires tighter access controls around unstructured data is the Health Insurance Portability and Accountability Act (HIPAA). HIPAA sets security standards in order to maintain "confidentiality and integrity of individual health information" (Infotechadvisor, n.d.). These security standards require strong access control over any information systems that handle individual health information, including those that handle unstructured information, such as file systems (Infotechadvisor, n.d.). Without the ability to control unstructured data, a business will find any of these regulations difficult to comply with.

In addition to any legal and compliance implications, lacking control over unstructured data access is also a problem from a general security standpoint. As the Ponemon Institute and Varonis survey demonstrated, 76% of respondents were not able to determine who can access unstructured data and nearly 70% of respondents felt that employees in their organization had unnecessary access to unstructured data (StorageNewsletter.com, 2008). With no control over the access to unstructured data, highly confidential information could easily fall into the wrong hands and possibly leak to the public. Depending on what type of highly confidential information is leaked, this could impact the company's ability to be competitive in its transactions or even damage the company's ability to execute its business.

Whether the lack of control over unstructured data access is a problem for legal and compliance reasons or simply general security reasons, it is obviously something that must be addressed. Fortunately, more and more solutions are surfacing in the area of unstructured data. Unfortunately, none of these seems to have completely solved the problem. Throughout this paper, I will review available methods for controlling unstructured data access and propose a strategy for developing a foundation for unstructured data access policy.

Available Unstructured Data Access Solutions

Upon first consideration of any problem relating to information, it is typical for businesses to look first to technology solutions. This idea seems to have held true for unstructured data access as well. As the problem of unstructured data access has gained momentum, more and more technology solutions have surfaced with the promise to improve organization and productivity. These technologies have many different names but can generally be referred to as content management systems or document and record management systems. Throughout this paper, they will be referred to as content management systems. Content management systems can be used as unstructured data repositories, which allow the information to be organized and controlled. Basic components of content management systems include document repository, integration with desktop applications, check-in and check-out, versioning, auditing, classification and indexing, search and retrieval, and security (Adam, 2008).

The most relevant component of content management systems in the context of unstructured data access is security. Adam (2008) explains that "security should be tightly integrated with the system, allowing for security access permissions to be applied at different levels within the system." To specify, an adequate content management system may allow security to be assigned to groups or individuals as well as to groups of documents or individual documents. For example, an administrator should have the ability to assign one group of users the ability to read and edit a specific document while assigning another group of users the ability to read the document only. Still another group of users may not have access to see that specific document at all. As another example, an administrator should be able to assign access so that all users have the ability to read documents stored in a specific folder while only one user has the ability to edit them.

Content management systems handle access differently with unique options for securing data at multiple levels of granularity. An example of a content management system with growing popularity is Microsoft Office SharePoint. SharePoint users can be granted access in two ways. First, as with most content management systems, access permissions can be granted to a user or group of users (Curry & English, 2008). Second, SharePoint makes use of collaboration sites which are essentially websites used to organize display groups of documents (Microsoft, 2007). By way of inherited permissions, collaboration sites can be used to allow for more creation with less access management overhead. If a group of users have read-only access to a collaboration site and the site is configured to inherit permissions, that same group of users will have read-only access to all subsequent sites as well (Curry & English, 2008). Another example of a content management system with unique security capabilities is Laserfiche. In addition to offering security permissions at a group or individual user level, Laserfiche also allows for users to control access to specific documents through the use of security tags (Laserfiche, 2008). For example, if a user is assigned to a security tag titled "Confidential," that user will have access to all documents that have the "Confidential" tag applied to them. Further, if that user is creating or saving a document in Laserfiche, they will also have the ability to apply the "Confidential" tag to their own documents. These are just two examples of the many diverse content management systems available. Regardless of the specific functionalities offered by the software, any content management system will no doubt propose a unique solution to the problem of unstructured data access.

At first take, it seems that content management systems should be the perfect solution to the problem of unstructured data access. However, contrary to the claims of content management system vendors, this is not likely to be the case. The fundamental issue with content management systems lies in the establishment of policy. In other words, these content management systems cannot be used effectively if it is not first established how the access should be set up. The authors of *Integrative Document and Content Management* explain that development, communication, and acceptance of a policy framework should be completed before even beginning requirement specifications for a content management system (Asprey & Middleton, 2003). To further emphasize this, the authors state, "the development of a policy framework is not dependent on an investment in [content management systems]. The policy framework can be developed to apply improved practices for managing documents using existing tools" (Asprey & Middleton, 2003). This is an extremely important point for any technology solution. A policy must be established first to support the needs and fundamental requirements of the organization. Only after the policy has been developed and accepted should an organization turn to a technology solution for the possible automation of controls required by the policy.

Further, since the policy serves as a cornerstone for any technology configurations, it is imperative to realize that the effectiveness of the content management system depends on the effectiveness of the policy. As an example, to ensure that the importance of policy is taken into account for SharePoint deployment, the following is stated in Microsoft Office SharePoint Server 2007 Best Practices, "SharePoint Server 2007 provides a multitude of security features which, when implemented in concert with well-understood information security policies, provide significant protection of confidential information" (Curry & English, 2008). This statement clearly emphasizes the point that the security functions offered in the software are only effective when implemented with comprehensive policy. This is an important basis of information for any content management system deployment, which brings about another dilemma: What makes an effective policy for unstructured data access?

Guidance for building unstructured data access policy for use with content management systems is still lacking. Furthermore, until it is established, content management systems may never be used effectively for unstructured data access. However, it is helpful to remember that the wheel does not need to be completely reinvented in this situation. Standard access structuring methods have already been developed and may prove useful if applied to unstructured data. Examples of these methods include discretionary access control, mandatory access control, role-based access control, and attribute-based access control.

First, discretionary access control (DAC) is based on information ownership and delegating rights (Department of Defense, 1985). In a DAC model the creator of the information is also considered the owner and administrator of the information (Department of Defense, 1985). More specifically, the creator is responsible for granting or revoking access to their information (Department of Defense, 1985). This also means that the creator has the ability to grant administrative access to other users so that they may grant or revoke access to the information as well (Department of Defense, 1985). Compared to other access control model categories, DAC is considered to be the most simple (Lopez et al., 2008). Because of its simplicity, many security conditions are not taken into account with DAC. For example, since users are responsible for granting and revoking access, any security requirements are also the responsibility of the users and cannot be easily managed by organization authorities (Lopez et al., 2008). Another condition unaccounted for is the possibility of cascading revocation chains where one user removes access from someone immediately after the access has been granted by a different user (Lopez et al., 2008). Most fundamentally, however, is the lack of control over the flow of information with DAC (Lopez et al., 2008). Access can be granted whenever and to whomever at the discretion of the user.

Next, mandatory access control (MAC) is centered around the idea that access is set up based on predefined, mandatory rules. There is no notion of ownership involved with MAC. Instead, in order to access information protected by MAC, the user must possess the appropriate security clearance required for accessing the information (Department of Defense, 1985). MAC strategies are considered to form "lattice" access control systems (Department of Defense, 1985). The flow of information in a lattice-based access-control system is predetermined by the mathematical structure of that specific model. Each MAC model uses a specific mathematical formula to govern how access will be structured (Department of Defense, 1985). The development of the MAC concept was driven by policies created for military environments (Benantar, 2006). While these static control methods work well in a hierarchical military context, they are typically too rigid for use in enterprise organizations (Benantar, 2006). This is due to the fact that MAC controls cannot be changed unless amended by an administrative authority and thus do not permit sharing of information across the organization (Benantar, 2006).

Role-based access control (RBAC) is used most widely in large enterprise organizations and originates from the concept of grouping users by job function (Sandhu, Ferraiolo, & Kuhn, 2000). The idea is that users who share the same job functions will require similar access rights (Sandhu et al., 2000). For example, a role would be created with the access permissions required by a particular job function and that role would be granted to all users performing that job. Two categories of RBAC include hierarchical RBAC and constraint RBAC. Hierarchical RBAC is the idea of roles having an order based on access levels (Sandhu et al., 2000). With hierarchical RBAC, roles may be inherited to acquire the access permissions of lesser or greater roles (Sandhu et al., 2000). Constraint RBAC is an RBAC concept used to accommodate segregation of duty constraints required and can be accomplished through static or dynamic separation of duties (Sandhu et al., 2000). Static separation of duty is the method of ensuring segregation of duties by using a separate role for each job function (Sandhu et al., 2000). Dynamic separation of duty is the method in which roles are only activated if the situation permits (Sandhu et al., 2000). For any role-base access control method, any users joining the organization, changing job functions, or leaving the organization must be accounted for and have their access updated accordingly (Benantar, 2006). In addition, roles must be reviewed and updated on a regular basis to catch any access rights that may need to be removed or added to any particular role (Benantar, 2006).

Finally, attribute-based access control (ABAC) was developed to accommodate security requirements of larger, dispersed systems (Li, Mitchell, & Winsborough, 2002). In this method, access is determined by user attributes and is granted in a role style, similar to RBAC (Li et al., 2002). Examples of attributes could be position, department, age, location, etc. Depending on an individual user's specific attributes, they will be granted specific predetermined access permissions. The idea is that a user's access permissions will be changed as their attributes change. For example, if a user changes departments, they will be granted access specific to their new department while access specific to their old department will be removed. It is important to note that although ABAC is considerably more flexible, this method does imply greater complexity in the creation and maintenance of policy (Li et al., 2002).

The fact that access structuring methods have already been established is comforting in light of the unstructured data access dilemma. However, the question now remains: Why haven't these access structuring methods been applied successfully to enterprise unstructured data? Although these methods exist, there is no guidance available to help organizations decide which method will work best. In the context of unstructured data, how is a business to decide which structure should be used or how their information should be organized within that structure? Although access structuring methods have been established, understanding on how to effectively incorporate these methods into an unstructured data access policy is still lacking.

Fortunately, there is one emerging concept that appears to be filling the position as the next fundamental puzzle piece in the development of unstructured data access policy. This is the concept of data governance. With data governance, organizations are learning to step back and develop data access strategies from an enterprise point of view. Gwen Thomas, of The Data Governance Institute, describes data governance as, "a system of decision rights and accountabilities for information-related processes, executed according to agreed-upon models which describe who can take what actions with what information, and when, under what circumstances, using what methods" (Thomas, n.d., 3). More simply, data governance can be considered the concept of making decisions about what should be done with information. Most importantly, data governance promotes the idea that security of information is no longer the sole responsibility of the information technology department, but that it should involve the enterprise as a whole. The organization of information security must be conceived with the entire organization in mind so that rules and access philosophies are applied consistently throughout. To explain this fundamental data governance concept, Thomas uses the analogy that information technology is like a plumbing system with pipes, pumps, and storage tanks. Thomas explains further that, "data is like the water flowing through those pipes" (p. 4). Using this analogy, the goal of data governance is to addresses issues specific to what is "flowing through the pipes" (p. 5). In order to address these issues, input is required from management and subject matter experts who understand the data, not from the "plumbers" of the system (p. 4).

Depending on the goals of the company, data governance projects may focus on different areas, or may even focus on two or three areas at once. These different categories of data governance focuses include policy/standards/strategy, data quality, privacy/compliance/security, architecture/integration, data warehouses/business intelligence, and management support (Thomas, n.d., 7). The data governance focus that sets the stage most effectively for the creation of unstructured data policy is that which focuses on privacy, compliance, and security. This type of data governance program usually originates from data privacy or access management concerns (p. 8). New regulatory compliance, contractual, or internal requirements may also play a role in inspiring a program of this type (p. 8). Thomas explains that a data governance program with this emphasis is likely to include initiatives for a number of tasks focused on securing the information. One of these tasks would be to support the use of access management and security requirements to safeguard sensitive data (p. 9). Assisting the risk assessment and development of risk management controls is one more task involved with a data governance program of this nature (p. 9). Another task involved with securing information is to ensure the enforcement of compliance requirements

(p. 9). Aligning initiatives and frameworks will also be done as part of such a program, along with identifying stakeholders, determining decision privileges, and clarifying responsibilities (p. 9).

It is important to realize that although initiatives for a data governance program may be similar, the details of the program will be specific to the organization. The purpose of data governance is to understand the information in the context of the organization and develop a method for governing the information based on the specific needs of that enterprise. Due to the subjective nature of the project, outcomes and deliverables of a data governance project may differ from organization to organization.

Proposed Solution for Unstructured Data Access Policy

At this point, I would like to introduce a strategy for using data governance in combination with access structuring methods to develop a foundation for unstructured data access policy. In this proposed method, data governance can be utilized as an essential prerequisite for the development of unstructured data access policy. While data governance deliverables will vary depending on the goals of the organization, I believe that some deliverables are crucial if the organization has plans to establish an adequate policy for unstructured data access. The first step in this proposed strategy is to ensure that essential data governance deliverables have been completed sufficiently. Deliverables should include an established governing body for information security related matters, a document retention series, clear establishment of information owned by each department, as well as clear sensitivity handling levels and procedures.

To explain the essential deliverables further, the governing body, which should be established as part of the data governance program, must include at least one knowledgeable representative from each department. These representatives will be needed to lead the development of unstructured data access procedures within their own departments. An unstructured data access policy lead must also be established to be the overall organizer of the policy. This individual should be well versed in the data governance project as a whole, which includes a basic knowledge of business functions and processes for each department. This person should also be capable of leading and organizing subject matter experts from each department in order to facilitate the development of unstructured data access structures and practices for the entire enterprise. It is important to remember that the role of the unstructured data access policy lead as well as the roles of the department subject matter experts is ongoing. These positions will be necessary not only for the creation of the policy but for the continuous maintenance of the policy as well.

Next, a document retention series must be established as part of the Data Governance program. While the actual retention periods specified on the series will not be used directly for the development of an unstructured data access policy, the categories of data content listed on the series are extremely important. Since the effectiveness of the unstructured data access policy depends on the accuracy of the content categories, it is of utmost importance that these categories be considered thoroughly. Content categories should accurately reflect all types of information content handled at the organization (S. Murchison, personal communication, January 2009). However, it is also important that content categories be broad enough that they will not need to be constantly modified (S. Murchison, personal communication, January 2009). In general, categories should represent types of data content found in the organization and should overlap to some degree with the main business processes found in the organization as well (S. Murchison, personal communication, January 2009). The document retention series on the whole should be well understood throughout the company with content categories being easy to recognize by all employees. To ensure this understanding, it is helpful for each department to identify which of their documents will fit into each content category. This will provide solid examples as well as demonstrating how the record retention series will relate to employees' day-to-day work.

Clear establishment of information owned and used by each department is another important deliverable which should be used in the development of unstructured data access. This may be added as an addendum to the document retention series and should list three groups of content categories for each department. More specifically, these three groups should include content categories (a) owned by that specific department, (b) owned by all departments, and (c) used by that specific department. A department that owns a content category should also be the department responsible for retaining or destroying documents within that content category according to the document retention series. Content categories that are owned and used by a department can be distinguished by considering "whose lap the document falls into" (S. Murchison, personal communication, January 2009). For example, suppose a human resources department creates a business case showing estimated costs for a specific project. Once the business case is approved, perhaps it is standard practice within the company for the purchasing department to keep the final, signed copy for budgeting purposes. In this case, the business case "falls into the lap" of the purchasing department. In this situation, purchasing would be the owners of the business case content category while the human resources department would simply use the category. Still, other documents seem to fall into every department's lap and would be considered as being owned by all departments. Documents owned by all departments may include polices, forms, as well as other nondepartment specific types. An example of content category groupings for an information technology (IT) department within an organization may resemble that which is listed in Figure 15.1.

Finally, in order to develop a comprehensive unstructured data access policy, clear sensitivity handling levels and procedures should be established as part of the data governance program. These are levels of classification used to define the sensitivity of documents as well as how such documents should be handled as part of a data classification model (Whitman & Mattord, 2008, 270). Well-understood sensitivity handling levels are necessary to guide employees on the acceptable use of confidential information within the organization, aiding proper use of an unstructured data access structure. One simple example of a data classification model could include levels such as "public," "for official use only," "sensitive," and "classified". In this type of model, specification for "public" documents would be any document acceptable for release to the public, such as a press release. "For official use only" may indicate documents that are not especially sensitive but that should be kept within the organization, such as internal communications. "Sensitive" documents may signify documents that are considered to hold important information, potentially embarrassing the company or damaging market share if leaked to the public. Lastly, "classified" information may indicate extremely confidential information that could significantly harm the interests of the company (Whitman & Mattord, 2008, p. 271).

Once the data governance program has been launched and all deliverables essential for development of an unstructured data access policy have been completed, the second step of policy development can begin. The second step is to determine all access situations that must be accounted for. Since access requirements for each type of information will be best understood by people working with that information, this step should be completed by each department individually. Department representatives established as part of the data governance program should be responsible for coordinating this step for their departments. Further, although each department will complete the step individually, all departments should use the same methods to complete the task to ensure consistency throughout the enterprise.

Owned–Department Specific:

System development documents

System maintenance documents

Owned–Department Non-Specific:

Form masters, templates

Policies, procedures, manuals

Research, reference materials

Projects, subject matter working files

Calendars, appointment books

Training class educational materials, handouts

Used–Owned by Another Department:

Organizational charts, employee lists (owned by Human Resources)

Personnel files (owned by Human Resources)

Budgets & forecasts (owned by Accounting)

Business cases, vendor bids, proposals, quotations (owned by Purchasing)

Audit final reports, collateral workpapers (owned by Internal Controls)

System monitoring, access, audit trails (owned by Internal Controls)

Figure 15.1   Example of content category groupings for an IT department.

Determining access requirements for information can be difficult in a collaborative business culture. Information must be shared across many departments but also secured appropriately. Rather than beginning with known access structuring methods such as DAC, MAC, RBAC, or ABAC, I suggest examining the information to understand what type of security each type of document actually requires. Determining all access requirements can be accomplished by asking the following questions: What information needs to be accessed by who? For how long? A matrix may be helpful in determining all possible access situations. A matrix example that I would like to suggest for determining what data needs to be accessed by who is one that examines the information in both vertical and horizontal access planes within the organization. In this type of matrix, management levels of the organization could be listed vertically while departmental groupings could be listed horizontally, as in Figure 15.2. Throughout this paper, this matrix will be referred to as an Access Requirement Matrix.

Using an Access Requirement Matrix, content categories can be mapped according to the access levels they require, similar to an attribute-based access control (ABAC) method in which access is determined by attributes. Of course, the vertical and horizontal access levels listed in the matrix will vary, depending on the organization structure of the company. To limit complexity, a separate Access Requirement Matrix should be used for each department. To demonstrate this concept, I will use the IT department exemplified previously. Remember that the content categories owned by the example IT department included system development documents and system

Horizontal access levels

	Individual personnel only	Individual sections of the department only	This department only	This department and other individual departments only	All departments
President					
Vice president (over this dept.)					
General manager (over this dept.)					
Assistant general manager (within this dept.)					
Manager (s) (within this dept.)					
Assistant manager (within this dept.)					
Specialist (within this dept.)					
Contractors (within this dept.)					

Vertical access levels

Figure 15.2 Access Requirement Matrix demonstrating vertical and horizontal access levels.

maintenance documents. Suppose that both of these content categories are shared between all sections and all individuals within the IT department. Further, suppose it is acceptable for all levels within and above the department to access these categories. Suppose that in addition to system development and system maintenance documents that are shared within the department, system maintenance documents also exist which must be accessed by employees from other departments. For example, documents used for maintaining financial applications may need to be accessed by employees from the organization's finance department. To satisfy both of these access requirements, system development and system maintenance documents could be placed in the matrix as illustrated in Figure 15.3. The gray arrows in Figure 15.3 have been added to demonstrate the vertical and horizontal levels which should have access to these content categories, according to the placement on the matrix.

In order to complete an Access Requirement Matrix for a department, each of the content categories should be entered into the appropriate cell according to the access requirements for documents within the category. Clearly established sensitivity handling levels along with an understanding of information owned and used by different departments will help to guide the placement of content categories within the matrix. For example, documents associated with higher sensitivity levels will be placed higher on the vertical access plane. In addition, documents that are owned or used by different departments will be placed farther out on the horizontal access plane. A completed Access Requirement Matrix for the exemplified IT department may look similar to that illustrated in Figure 15.4.

Once an Access Requirement Matrix has been completed, each cell of the matrix indicates a different unstructured data access configuration, which must be accounted for in the unstructured data access policy. However, it is important to understand that this matrix is developed primarily for determining access requirements that do not change often, similar to a mandatory

	Individual personnel only	Individual sections of the department only	This department only	This department and other individual departments only	All departments
President					
Vice president (over this dept.)					
General manager (over this dept.)					
Assistant general manager (within this dept.)					
Manager (s) (within this dept.)					
Assistant manager (within this dept.)					
Specialist (within this dept.)					
Contractors (within this dept.)			System development documents System maintenance documents	System maintenance documents	

Figure 15.3 Access Requirement Matrix demonstrating content category access for system development and system maintenance documents.

access control (MAC) method. Since access requirements established through use of an Access Requirement Matrix are considered primarily static, additional processes may need to be considered to account for possible temporary situations. One common example of a temporary access situation would be that of a cross-departmental project. This is a situation in which nonstandard groups of individuals may require access to particular documents during the life of the project.

	Individual personnel only	Individual sections of the department only	This department only	This department and other individual departments only	All departments
President					
Vice president (over this dept.)					
General manager (over this dept.)					
Assistant general manager (within this dept.)					
Manager (s) (within this dept.)				Personnel Files Budgets and Forecasts	
Assistant manager (within this dept.)					
Specialist (within this dept.)				Audit Final Reports, Collateral Workpapers System Monitoring Access, Audit Trails	
Contractors (within this dept.)			System Development Documents System Maintenance Documents Form Masters, Templates Policies, Procedures, Manuals Research, Reference Materials Projects, Subject Matter Working Files Calendars, Appointment Books Training Class Educational Materials, Handouts	System Maintenance Documents Organizational Charts, Employee Lists Business Cases, Vendor Bids Proposals, Quotes	Form Masters, Templates Policies, Procedures, Manuals Training Class Educational Materials, Handouts

Figure 15.4 Access Requirement Matrix using IT department example.

One suggested method of handling this type of situation is to create a process in which the project manager is responsible for determining the access. In this case, the project manager would determine which individuals should have access to the project file as well as when the access should expire. This type of process may resemble a discretionary access control (DAC) method in which a user is responsible for granting and removing access. However, for temporary situations such as projects, it is important that the start and end dates be respected. Once a project comes to a definite end, all documents to be retained according to the retention series should be moved from the temporary project file to appropriate locations, based on content category.

Once unstructured data access requirements have been developed, procedures must be developed for the granting, revoking, and changing access. Whether it is possible for these processes to be automated or whether they must be monitored and completed manually, it is vital that these procedures be developed and documented. Without establishment of these procedures, unstructured data access will be unenforceable and the policy will quickly become ineffective. In addition, it is critical that each department review their unstructured data access requirements on a regular basis to ensure that needs are still being met. If any changes have occurred to the content categories or the organizational structure, Access Requirement Matrices must be updated accordingly. Any file access configurations developed from the Access Requirement Matrices must also be updated accordingly.

Finally, after all unstructured data access requirements, processes, and procedures have been developed, the writing of the policy may begin. Many effective policy writing guides exist and can be applied to the development of an unstructured data policy. Whitman and Mattord offer a framework for an issue-specific policy type, which could be used for the development of an unstructured data access policy. Using an issue-specific framework should allow for the unstructured data access policy to roll up to a general information security policy for the enterprise (Whitman & Mattord, 2008, 119). This framework includes statement of purpose, authorized uses, prohibited uses, systems management, violations of policy, policy review and modification, and limitations of liability. In order to create an unstructured data access policy, the content of these sections should be based on the processes and requirements established specifically for the control over unstructured data access. This will include requirements specified through the Access Requirement Matrices or any other processes developed to account for temporary access situations. Processes and procedures developed for the granting, reviewing, revoking, and changing of access should also be included as a foundation for the unstructured data access policy.

Perspectives

The strategy for unstructured data access policy foundation provided in this paper has been developed through research in combination with experiences gained through implementation of a data governance program at New United Motors Manufacturing Inc. (NUMMI). NUMMI operated for 26 years as a privately owned auto manufacturing plant, located in Fremont, California, until its closure in April, 2010. It is important to note that the strategy proposed has not been formally tested or evaluated. However, since this strategy is based so closely on unique access needs associated with the information, it can be implemented in almost any organizational setting. Many other approaches, including content management systems and known access structuring methods, begin with a solution and then attempt to apply that solution to the data. In these scenarios, it is likely that the solution will not always answer the problems posed by the information. Conversely, the primary goal of this proposed strategy is to begin with an understanding of the access needs associated with the information. By understanding these needs first, a solution can be developed which caters to the unique access needs of that specific information. This will potentially enable successful implementation of the strategy in organizations of all different sizes and industries. Results will always be unique and subject to the individual access needs of the organization. As long as the organization has unstructured data and subject matter experts who understand the information contained in the data, the organization has the basic means to implement this strategy. If implemented properly, this unstructured data access policy strategy could result in an access structure that enables appropriate security and effective collaboration simultaneously. Organizations could use this strategy to move from a state of disorganized, uneven security to a standard unstructured data access structure that consistently satisfies all security needs. Such a structure could then be used to form specific requirements for configuration of content management software. This will ensure that content management software is used appropriately in a way that accommodates the needs of that organization.

Future areas of research could incorporate assessment of this strategy along with other Unstructured Data Access Policy solutions. Methods for effectively managing unstructured data access after it has been established could also be included in future research. In general, unstructured data access control methods must be developed further if organizations hope to harness the full potential of unstructured data. Unstructured data has become extremely easy to share and controls must be established to ensure that sharing is done appropriately within an enterprise setting. Further, with growing legal, compliance, and security issues, unstructured data will only become a greater issue if not addressed. With solid development of unstructured data access management and policy, this information may finally receive the attention it deserves.

About the Author

Anne Shultz is a graduate student in the Information Technology and Management degree program at Illinois Institute of Technology (IIT). Ms. Shultz was previously employed at New United Motors Manufacturing, Inc. (NUMMI), a Toyota/GM auto manufacturing plant in California. During her employment at NUMMI, Ms. Shultz held a position in information security compliance and was deeply involved in the design of the company's data governance program. Since her enrollment at IIT, Ms. Shultz has been awarded a "50 For the Future Technology Talent Award" from the Illinois Technology Foundation. Ms. Shultz holds a bachelor degree from the University of California, Santa Cruz.

References

Aberdeen Group. (2009, July). *Securing Unstructured Data: How Best-in-Class Companies Manage to Serve and Protect.* Retrieved from http://www.rsa.com/products/DLP/ar/10399_5877-RA-Unstructured_Data-DB-06-SPD.pdf.

Adam, A. (2008). *Implementing Electronic Document and Record Management Systems.* Boca Raton, FL: Auerbach Publications.

Asprey, L., & Middleton, M. (2003*). Integrative Document & Content Management: Strategies for Exploiting Enterprise Knowledge.* Hershey, PA: IGI Global.

Atre, S., & Blumberg, R. (2003, February). The problem with unstructured data. *Information Management Magazine,* February 1, 2003. Retrieved from http://www.information-management.com/issues/20030201/6287-1.html.

Benantar, M. (2006). *Access Control Systems: Security, Identity Management and Trust Models*. New York, NY: Springer.

Burton, Jr., J. D., Chuvakin, A., Elberg, A., Freedman, B., King, D., Paladino, S., & Shcooping, P. (2007). *PCI Compliance: Implementing Effective PCI Data Security Standards*. Burlington, MA: Syngress Publishing.

Curry, B., & English, B. (2008). *Microsoft Office SharePoint Server 2007 Best Practices*. Redmond, WA: Microsoft Press.

Department of Defense. (1985, December). *Department of Defense Trusted Computer System Evaluation Criteria* (DoD Standard No. 5200.28). Retrieved from http://csrc.nist.gov/publications/history/dod85.pdf.

Dorian, P. (2007, March). *FAQs: Unstructured Data FAQ*. Retrieved from http://searchstorage.techtarget. com/guide/faq/category/0,,sid5_tax306615_idx0_off10,00.html.

Infotechadvisor. (n.d.). *HIPAA: Comprehensive Guide*. Retrieved from http://trygstad.rice.iit.edu:8000/ HIPAA/HIPAA%20Guide%20Part%20I%20-%20infotechadvisor.mht.

Lambert, L. K. (2009, February 4). *Access Management and SOX Compliance*. Retrieved from http://www. securityinfowatch.com/root+level/1296049.

Laserfiche. (2008). Laserfiche 8 (Version 8.0) [Software]. Available from Datanet Solutions: http://www. datanet-solutions.com/content/enterprise-content-management.html.

Li, N., Mitchell, J. C., & Winsborough, W. H. (2002, May). *Design of a Role-Based Trust Management Framework* (Proceedings of the 2002 IEE Symposium on Security and Privacy). IEEE Computer Society Press. Retrieved from http://www.isso.sparta.com/documents/rt_oakland.pdf.

Lopez, J., Furnell, S. M., Katsikas, S., & Patel, A. (2008). *Securing Information and Communications Systems: Principles, Technologies, and Applications*. Norwood, MA: Artech House.

Microsoft. (2007). *Microsoft Office SharePoint Server* (Version 2007) [Software]. Available from Microsoft: http://sharepoint.microsoft.com/how-to-buy/Pages/default.aspx.

Murchison, R. S. (2009). *Retention Management for Consistency & Compliance* [PowerPoint slides]. Available from http://www.matchps.com/training.html.

Sandhu, R., Ferraiolo, D., & Kuhn, R. (2000). *The NIST Model for Role-Based Access Control: Towards a Unified Standard* (NIST RBAC model). Retrieved from http://csrc.nist.gov/rbac/sandhu-ferraiolo-kuhn-00.pdf.

StorageNewsLetter.com (Ed.). (2008, July 1). *Organizations Lack Control of Their Unstructured Data Assets* [Press release]. Retrieved from http://www.storagenewsletter.com/news/miscellaneous/ varonis-ponemon-institute-unstructured-data.

Thomas, G. (n.d.). *The DGI Data Governance Framework*. Retrieved from http://datagovernance.com/dgi_ framework.pdf.

Whitman, M. E., & Mattord, H. J. (2008). *Management of Information Security*, Second edition. Boston, MA: Thomson Course Technology.

Chapter 16

Governance and Risk Management within the Context of Information Security

James C. Murphy

Introduction

The twenty-first-century view of risk management is of an industry that has blossomed worldwide with standards and certification organizations supported by national regulations, conferences (in the best of locations), and supporting consulting and audit enterprises. The message is heard far and wide of the importance of efficient risk management, and more critically, the price to be paid for poor or absent risk management. The appropriate term is *governance*, which broadly addresses establishing, managing, and monitoring business processes towards the organizational goals [1]. Virtually every executive at and above "C-level" understands the significance and has been exposed to risk management governance frameworks and implementation schemes. In this century, which began with the post-year 2000 (Y2K)/post-September 11, 2001 (9-11)/post-modern-internet decade (*all rolled into one!!*), the recognition that *information* is an organization's second most important asset—its human resource is first!!—began to dawn on those executives and leaders. Many had assumed that the worst was over after correcting dates because of Y2K—or really over after the response to the assaults on our nation on 9-11—or *really* and *truly* over after HIPAA privacy and/or Sarbanes/Oxley requirements had been checked off, only to find out that all vital records had been stolen/altered/destroyed and posted for sale or ransom on an untracked foreign website [2].

Scenarios like this—altogether too real and too frequent—highlight an additional awareness: *information* is the primary target of those intending ill will towards organizations and individual persons for monetary gain [3]. Managing the organizational information resource is no longer to be taken for granted (something that information security (IS) professionals had been shouting into the wind for many years!!) (a personal observation). Though it had begun in earnest years before, the maturation of the governance and risk management industry was driven by the circumstances of the past two decades, and it is now addressing the importance of protecting information in this new century that began so precipitously. One of the most significant initiatives has been to demonstrate that careful governance and risk management has a positive benefit to organizations [4], not simply in reducing the potential for adverse events, but actually adding value to the organization as it grows and changes.

Information technology (IT) professionals in general, and IS professionals in particular, have long been engaged in *providing protection for* and *controlling access to* data and information [5]. In this century, IT and IS professionals are challenged to embrace the governance concept and help structure a risk management process within the organizational setting and governance structure. This will necessarily affect the tactical and strategic planning of IT change management, because information security and technology practices and processes can no longer be crafted and implemented in isolation. The basis for efficiency in the usage (acquisition, implementation, maintenance, and disposal) of information technology (IT) infrastructure [6] has become careful IT risk management, including initial and ongoing assessments, analyses, controls implementation, audits, and corrective mitigation. Fortunately, there is no lack of resources—white papers and standards documentation from the international standards bodies; and experienced consultancies from organizations and individuals in broad range of industry categories (Table 16.1 [7]).

In the face of this abundance, the challenge for IT and IS professionals is actually how to break the historic isolation and fit IT risk efforts into the organizational governance structure. The difficulty is, despite the fact that "everyone knows about risk management," there are puzzling if not troubling inconsistencies in the definitions of risk and its associated terms and concepts. As governance became part of the organizational structure, the business management groups began to set the tone for risk management. Unfortunately, many advocates of specific standards organizations often appear to assume that their own definitions and usages are understood and accepted by everyone else without appreciating the differences. Most of the risk governance comes from the domain of business financial accounting and auditing, with focal organizations such as the Information Systems Audit and Control Association (ISACA) (see Table 16.1).

Within manufacturing, chemical, and certain research organizations that use or generate hazardous (to humans and the environment) materials, safety and physical security organizations began to identify emergency management and risk governance appropriately within their industrial settings. And IT and IS professionals within all organizations began to develop responsible processes and practices around the protection of information and the recovery of information processes after major crises. All of this has led to differing views (even if only slightly) of the implementation of risk assessment and management, and has resulted in conflicting, if not redundant, efforts to address the problems.

IS professionals are also challenged to respond to the increasing trend towards a related concept, *convergence*, which has justified and defined the collaboration and cooperation with organizational physical security/safety (PS/S) units [8]. Convergence concepts can bring some clarity to the overall discussion of organizational risk management by providing a context for removing barriers and crafting relationships among organizational units.

Chapter Preview

In this chapter, I will explain how the concept of convergence actually represents a positive move towards an appropriate contextual understanding of the roles and responsibilities of not

Table 16.1   Selected List of Risk Management Organizations

ASIS International, Alexandria, VA, USA Risk Assessment Standard	http://www.asisonline.org/guidelines/committees/ra_std.htm
Contingency Analysis, international consulting, Boston, MA, USA	http://www.contingencyanalysis.com/
European Institute of Risk Management (EIRM), Copenhagen, Denmark.	www.EIRM.net
Federation of European Risk Management Associations (FERMA), Brussels, Belgium	www.ferma.eu
Global Association of Risk Professionals (GARP), Jersey City, NJ, London, UK	www.GARP.com
Institute for Risk Research (IRR), Network for Environmental Risk Assessment and Management, Waterloo, CA	http://www.irr-neram.ca/
The Institute of Internal Auditors, Altamonte Springs, FL, USA, standards and guidelines	http://www.theiia.org/guidance/standards-and-guidance/
The Institute of Risk Management, London, UK, Risk Management Standard	http://www.theirm.org/publications/PUstandard.html
Information System Audit and Control Association (ISACA), Rolling Meadows, IL, USA	http://www.isaca.org/
IT Governance Institute (ITGI), Rolling Meadows, IL, USA	http://www.itgi.org/
Risk Management Institution of Australasia (RMIA), Melbourne, AU	www.RMIA.org.au
RiskWorld, news and views about risk, Knoxville, TN, USA	http://www.riskworld.com/
The Risk Digest, forums on risk, Menlo Park, CA, USA	http://catless.ncl.ac.uk/Risks
The Risk Doctor, international consulting, Petersfield, UK	http://www.risk-doctor.com/index.asp

only the IS and PS/S professionals, but the rest of the organization's participants—executives, privacy/regulatory professionals, auditors, software developers, IT professionals—in addressing governance and risk management. I plan to describe how clarifying *context* will lead to better understanding of the participants—and ultimately to increased efficiency and effectiveness—in the processes or risk management. I intend to present governance and risk management in this chapter from the perspective of information security, and will address how IS professionals can effectively contribute to the overall organizational structure. From this chapter, IS professionals should better understand the terms and frames of reference, and also be able to identify and describe to the rest of the organization how IS tactical and strategic information management practices are vital to the optimal efficiency of organizational risk management.

For the further discussions in this chapter, I consider IT risks and IS risks to be so closely aligned as to be synonymous, and may frequently interchange the two concepts. Though the risks themselves may be synonymous, IS and IT professionals have different, but collaborative responsibilities in the overall management of risk, as I will explain.

In the first section of this chapter after the introduction, I will briefly review the history of risk and how its usage and frames of reference have evolved, and I will also demonstrate some of the conflicts in definitions, the challenges to risk measurement, and how they interfere with the organizational processes from the IS/IT perspective. To that end, I will offer suggestions for resolving some of the misunderstandings to enable better organizational collaboration for more efficient governance. This section is not intended to be an evaluation or critique on the risk industry as a whole, but an attempt to bring context to the challenges for managing risk within IT and the contributions from IT to organizational risk management.

In the second section, I describe collaborative risk management, which clarifies the separate but cooperative responsibilities among organizational units—IS, IT, PS/S, and the privacy/compliance/audit units—and I will indicate how this creates the context for the participants. Understanding how the various unit responsibilities fit together is vital to gaining efficiency in the overall governance structure. And I will indicate how such collaboration reinforces the importance and value of risk governance for the organization as a whole.

In the third section, I will address risk assessment from the IS perspective. I intend to distinguish (but not completely separate) the IS processes from the classic risk assessment processes and identify the added value based on the distinction. I will also introduce a model for IS management that offers a disciplined, cyclical approach to addressing IS responsibilities, which will continue to insure the IS contribution to organizational risk assessment and management.

Finally, in the last section, I will identify the IS component of risk governance based on the introduced model. I will describe how the disciplined approach addresses tactical and strategic planning and implementation of IT technical support security procedures. This will include documenting the required governance attention necessary for several specific technologies that can affect the targeted data/information.

Clarification Needed!

> *"security based on risk management, risk reduction, and risk assessment is a failed concept."*
> Donn Parker, 2006, my emphasis

In the face of abundant resources, years of momentum, reinforcement from industry peers, and strong encouragement from government agencies, organizations are actively building and refining risk management and governance structures. As with most IS professionals, I have been caught up in the same spirit and sweat of risk assessment and analysis! My objective in information security consulting has always been to seek and recommend efficiency in the usage of IT infrastructure. I have been persuaded that the basis of efficiency is careful IT risk management, including the initial and ongoing assessments, analyses, control audits, and corrective mitigation. I have also participated in several assessment efforts, large and small, across a variety of organizations.

However, despite the abundance and momentum, I have observed during my assessment opportunities that different organizational units have found themselves in disagreement over the leadership and administration of risk management. In the past decade, for better or for worse, risk governance has become associated with the compliance activities in response to the Sarbanes-Oxley regulations, which, towards the middle of the last decade, required unexpected increases in time and resources to fulfill (Claburn, 2007), often several months each year to collect the audit evidence necessary. Many have questioned the need for such expense and question the overall benefit of the effort (O'Sullivan, 2006).

My own struggle with this problem began with attempts to infer aspects of IT and IS risk from the overall concepts of business risk. I have long considered IS risk management to be distinct from, but nonetheless a subset of, business risk management. Yet I have struggled to clarify exactly that relationship, especially in the face of other non-IT/IS professionals who tend to associate all risks as variations on the overall theme of business decisions and probabilities of success or failure from those decisions. Even within the same organization, I have observed a lack of consistency among definitions and documentation of roles and responsibilities among the organizational groups—executives, auditors, security professionals, IT management and staff, and the general user community. Unfortunately, the differences among frames of reference and term definitions have not always been acknowledged, and this has contributed to a lack of appreciation for organizational risk management efforts that do not quite seem to fit the IT environment. Understandably, Donn Parker's recent suggestion, quoted at the beginning of this section, certainly caught my attention.

I suggest that this inconsistency and imprecision of term usage contributes to the lack of appreciation for the distinction between IS risk and business risk. And I suggest that this dilemma contributes greatly to the inefficiency (in time and money) in IS and IT risk management and the difficulty in relating IT spending to overall business expense, as related by Parker (2006) and Carr [9], who question the need for such IT spending.

History of Risk Definitions

I have never sought to challenge the definitions among groups of business and financial risk experts, who have been engaged in the process for decades. I have simply sought the definitions and appropriate terms that applied within IT and IS settings in hopes for a basis of better communication. I began with a search for clear definitions of risk itself and its associated terms, and I have discovered that I am not alone in this search, nor am I the only one concerned about the confusion of the definitions. In discussing financial activities, Holton (2004) expressed concern:

> Practical applications…all depend on the measurement of risk. In the absence of a definition of risk, it is unclear what, exactly, such measurements reflect….A search of the financial literature yields many discussions of risk but few definitions.

Recently, Saner [10], wrote on behalf of the Canadian Institute on Governance:

> The key to a successful discussion on risk Management is the careful handling of terminology—one should neither ignore the importance of semantics nor be paralyzed by it.

and

> The situation gets even worse if one includes additional standards into the comparison. Semantic disagreement of this magnitude can become a serious obstacle to effective analysis and communication.…It becomes essential to be precise about meaning at all times (and especially when comparing frameworks or when communicating interdepartmentally).

Parker (2006) also said:

> The debate about security risk is obscured and confusing because supporters mix together risks and certainties that are not risks.

In this chapter, it is not possible to address all available definitions of terms and concepts, but I offer a selection for comparison and discussion, and to highlight some of the inconsistencies and precision problems. To facilitate reading and subsequent discussion of the chapter, I have sequentially numbered the definitions of risk and other associated terms throughout the chapter.

I begin with my favorite definition of risk, from Neumann [11]:

1. risk. Intuitively, the adverse effects that can result if a vulnerability is exploited or if a threat is actualized. In some contexts, risk is a measure of the likelihood of adverse effects or the product of the likelihood and the quantified consequences. *There is no standard definition.* (my emphasis)

Notwithstanding Neumann's assertion, there are certainly many standard definitions, which is part of the problem. The history of risk and risk management has roots in centuries past, evolving through discussions about gambling, number theory, nascent statistical analysis, insurance, and investments. An accurate and dated historical view of the history of risk is beyond the scope of this chapter, however a most excellent and enjoyable review for risk-takers and -assessors across all organizational lines and roles is Bernstein's (1998) book, *Against the Gods: The Remarkable Story of Risk*. This book has supplied much of the following historical perspective.

Up to the early twentieth century, business risk primarily involved the assessment of major business decisions, such as sending out merchant ships to and from remote ports, expansions such as acquisitions or mergers, developing new product lines, etc. Risk management, therefore, involved evaluating the success or failure of the outcome of the decision and seeking ways and means to avoid the consequences of the failure. Arguably, the earliest definition of risk addressing this is from de Moivre, in 1711 [12]:

2. The risk of losing any sum is the reverse of Expectation; and the true measure of it is, the product of the Sum adventured multiplied by the Probability of the Loss.

Bernstein indicated the historical significance of de Moivre's work "in using samples to estimate the total population established the basis for the concepts of the normal distribution (bell curve) and the dispersion around the mean (standard deviation) [12]."

In more recent times, this concept has been reflected in other definitions of risk [13]:

3. The probability of harmful consequences, or expected losses (deaths, injuries, property, livelihoods, economic activity disrupted or environment damaged) resulting from interactions between natural or human-induced hazards and vulnerable conditions. www.adrc.or.jp/publications/terminology/top.htm
4. [risk:] The chance that the value of an investment could decline in the marketplace. www.johnsontrust.com/news_resources_glossary.asp
5. The probability of harm or injury (physical, psychological, social, or economic) occurring as a result of participation in a research study. Both the probability and magnitude of possible harm may vary from minimal to significant. www.virginia.edu/vprgs/irbsbsterminology.html
6. Risk is an album by the metal band Megadeth released in 1999 [14].

These definitions reflected an early understanding that risk involved estimating and avoiding *harmful* (adverse, loss, negative, etc.) consequences of a process. Through the years, students and scholars of risk debated the importance of likelihood or *probability* of outcomes based on measurements of events past vs. making efforts to minimize *uncertainty* about the outcomes [15]. In the early twentieth century, proponents of game theory introduced the concept of an "other player" (competitor, rival, or enemy) who affected the outcome of business decisions:

The true source of uncertainty lies in the intentions of others [16]. (author's emphasis)

This meant that besides estimating uncertainty and probability, a goal of risk management involved reducing the effects of the "other player(s)." This has interesting implications for addressing risk within the IS context, which I will address in a later section. Holton (2004) also relates additional factors of *exposure* or *preference* to risk and, more importantly, the concept of an *operational* definition of risk, which involves perception. In other words, risk is only *perceived* (and therefore managed) if it is *relative* and *relevant* to the decision or process at hand:

> Operational definitions, by construction, apply only to that which can be perceived. At best, we can hope to operationally define only our *perception* of exposure… Consequently, it is impossible to operationally define risk. At best, we can operationally define our *perception* of risk. There is no true risk. (Hillson, 2005, author's emphasis)

Dr. Hillson (the Risk Doctor – see Table 16.1) makes a similar assertion:

> A more complete definition of risk would therefore be "an uncertainty that if it occurs could affect one or more objectives". (Hillson, 2006)

In other words, defining a risk in an operational context is much the same as relating a risk to a particular business objective.

Summarizing this brief historical overview, the definitions and characterizations of risk include:

- Assessing and avoiding an *adverse* or *negative* outcome
- *Probability* of failure, or negative outcome
- *Uncertainty* of the outcome
- Uncertainty based on *competitor/opponent* influence
- *Exposure*, or *perception* of exposure, and/or *preference* of risk factors
- Risk within *operational* contexts or affecting a particular *business objective*

As the explanations or definitions of risk broadened into operational or business objective contexts, risk management processes were no longer restricted to single grand organizational decisions and began to be defined within day-to-day organizational management. All aspects of the business are now viewed under the risk lens, resulting in categories and subcategories of risk aligned to the business, e.g., investment risk, project management risk, financial risk, technology risk, environment risk, etc., virtually touching every process of every organizational unit (Hillson, 2007).

As risk began to be scrutinized more carefully, descriptive models emphasized the components of risk that enabled more accurate estimates of risk and enabled comparisons across business units through time. The most widely accepted terms associated with risk include "Threat" (Threat Source, Threat Vector), "Vulnerability" (Weakness, Exposure), "Hazard" (Danger to

Humans), and "Asset" (or more pertinently, the value or cost of replacement of the Asset) [17]. "Asset Value" may be the only concept that has a fairly consistent definition: expenses incurred from the loss or replacement of services, products, capital equipment, or personnel. The definitions of the other terms share colorful inconsistencies, exacerbating the overall confusion. To illustrate, here are a selected set of definitions:

7. [risk] hazard: a source of danger; a possibility of incurring loss or misfortune; "drinking alcohol is a health hazard." http://wordnet.princeton.edu/perl/webwn?s=risk
8. [risk] This term must not be confused with the term "hazard." It is most correctly applied to the predicted or actual frequency of occurrence of an adverse effect of a chemical or other hazard. www.bio.hw.ac.uk/edintox/glossall.htm
9. [Hazard] Set of inherent properties of a substance,…that,…make it capable of causing adverse effects to organisms or to the environment,…in other words, a source of danger. RELATED TERM risk. www.biomonitoringinfo.org/glossary/glossary.html
10. [Hazard] A source of potential harm or damage, or a situation with potential for harm or damage. www.peercenter.net/glossary/
11. [Threat] An indication or source of impending danger; declaration of an intention to harm, injure, etc. www.wpi.edu/Pubs/Policies/Judicial/sect16.html
12. [Threat] A combination of the risk, the Consequence of that risk, and the Likelihood that the negative Event will take place. Often used in analysis in place of risk. www.mc2consulting.com/riskdef.htm
13. [risk] A threat that exploits a vulnerability that may cause harm to one or more assets. http://www.symantec.com/avcenter/refa.html
14. [Vulnerability] Weakness in an information system, system security procedures, internal controls, or implementation that could be exploited. www.tecrime.com/0gloss.htm
15. [Vulnerability] (1) A system limitation or weakness (may not be exploitable); (2) the openness of a system to exploitation by countermeasures; (3) the practicality and probability of an adversary exploiting a susceptibility in combat. appl.nasa.gov/resources/lexicon/terms_v.html
16. [Vulnerability] The extent to which an individual, community, sub-group, structure, service, or geographic area is likely to be damaged or disrupted by the impact of a particular disaster hazard. www.cwserp.org/training/CWSEMT/KCmodulea.php
17. [Vulnerability] A design, implementation, or operation flaw that may be exploited by a threat; the flaw causes the computer system or application to operate in a fashion different from its published specifications, and to result in destruction or misuse of equipment or data. www.flashback.se/archive/BT/btcsmg.html

From all these, we observe with complete clarity (!) that:

- "Risk" is a "Hazard."
- "Risk" is not a "Hazard."
- "Hazard" is a source of a probability of harm.
- "Hazard" and "Threat" are virtually synonymous.
- "Threat" and "Risk" are also synonymous.
- "Vulnerabilities" are "weaknesses," "flaws," or "susceptibilities" that are or are not exploitable.
- "Vulnerabilities" may be exploited by "countermeasures," "adversaries," "hazards," and "threats" (which may lead one to conclude that "countermeasures," "adversaries," "hazards," and "threats" are equivalent).

Although these lists are hardly representative of the complete population of definitions, they do highlight the current problems in discussing risk and risk assessment or measurement across lines of business context.

Measuring Risk

The challenge that confronted the owners of the merchant ship sailing across the globe in centuries past still confronts business owners and decision makers today: How much will accepting and managing risk cost? In order to find the cost and determine how to manage risks in general business contexts, risk must be assessed or measured. Again, abundant resources are available for descriptions, methodology, and models addressing risk assessment and measurement (see Table 16.1 for a running start). Defining risk in a formula or equation format is used for rating and ranking risk situations. If values are applied, even in a relative sense (e.g., high, medium, and low) for Threat, Likelihood, Vulnerability, and Asset Value, then risk situations can be compared across the organization [18].

Most are variations on the theme for defining the components of risk and assessing the contribution of each of the components to the overall summation of risk itself. This characterization of the components has come to mean that "risk" itself does not stand alone, but is a *derived* term. This means that "risk" is not directly measured, but is a formulation of the measurements or estimates of the component terms. The significance of this is that risk itself is not able to be directly measured. Though it is generally accepted throughout the practice of risk governance to describe risk as directly measured, it is functionally imprecise, since only the *components* of risk are directly measured. This does not affect the need for the responsible units at the executive level to assess risk, derived as it may be, and be in a position to make comparisons of the value of risk over time as a means of contributing to organizational strategy.

The most comprehensive expression of IT risk as a formula or an equation is as follows [19]:

1. $R = (L)T*V*A,$

where **R** is Risk, **L** is Likelihood (or Probability), **T** is Threat, **V** is Vulnerability, and **A** is (Information) Asset Value. The Value of the Information Asset is usually considered negatively, i.e., the loss of all (or part) of the asset in question. This is typically expressed as:

18. The potential that a given threat will exploit vulnerabilities of an asset or group of assets to cause loss and/or damage to the assets. It is usually measured by a combination of impact and probability of occurrence [20].

The references for analyzing risk are too numerous to cite, but are certainly available from web searches. In given contexts, some references may omit the Asset Value, some omit Likelihood (or Probability) of Threat, and some offer measurements for single instances of loss, annualized rates of occurrence, and therefore annualized costs of the loss. Some researchers also attach probability estimates to vulnerabilities [21]. However, Equation 1 expresses all requisite components of IT risk. From such an operation, a numeric (qualitative or quantitative) value of risk can be determined by plugging in assessed values for Threat, the Likelihood of that Threat, Vulnerability, and, if appropriate, a quantitative or qualitative monetary value of the asset loss and/or replacement.

The simple logical implication of this formula is that if any one of the components of risk are not present—i.e., no threats, no vulnerabilities, or assets with no value—then there is no risk to be assessed. If the physical protection structure is completely without vulnerabilities, then there is no risk. If an unlocked warehouse has no stored assets, then there is no risk. If global peace reigns, and there are no more threats, then there is no risk! These statements are naïve, but illustrate perspectives to consider when determining some risk management strategies, as discussed in later chapter sections.

Recently, characteristics or definitions of risk have suggested neutrality to the outcome. While the predominant view of risk involves a negative outcome, this view advocates that risk be defined as either a negative or a positive outcome [22]. From Hillson (2008):

> From the late 1990's project management professionals began to realise that there were other types of uncertainty that mattered. Sometimes good things might occur on a project which would result in saved time or reduced cost, or which would enhance productivity or performance. Such "opportunities" could be brought under the existing definition of risk by simply expanding the types of impact to include positive as well as negative effects. This resulted in a change in approach by a number of organisations, including the Project Management Institute (PMI®). The *Guide to the Project Management Body of Knowledge* (PMBoK® Guide, 2000 Edition) adopted a definition of project risk as "an uncertain event or condition that, if it occurs, has a positive or negative effect on a project objective." (Project Management Institute, 2000). This broader definition has been retained in the current PMBoK Guide and PMI's *Combined Standards Glossary* (Project Management Institute, 2004, 2005). It is also reflected in a number of other leading standards, both in the project management area (for example Association for Project Management, 2004, 2006) as well as in more general risk standards (Australian/New Zealand Standard, 2004; Institution of Civil Engineers et al., 2005; Institute of Risk Management et al., 2002; Office of Government Commerce, 2007). The forthcoming ISO risk management standard is also expected to adopt a similar position.

Though I have no identifiable reference, I suggest that this might be related to a business management or assessment concept prevalent in the second half of the twentieth century: strengths, weaknesses, opportunities, and threats (S.W.O.T.) [23]. This concept was used to provide structure for business assessment and decision making. "Strengths" and "weaknesses" referred to internal corporate characteristics, and "opportunities" and "threats" pertained to the decision or venture at hand. In this process, the consequences of making a major business decision could have a positive or a negative outcome, based on the assessments of the factors.

The application of neutrality of outcome to risk analysis can be represented in the following formula:

2. $R = (L)T*V*C(A)$,

where **C** stands for Consequences, and expressed as:

19. Risk is the likelihood of a threat operating through a vulnerability to produce consequences regarding an asset [24].

I suggest that this concept is problematic for IT or IS risks. When the historical single-event concept of risk is viewed abstractly, the outcome of choosing a single event can only have two consequences: positive or negative (success or failure). As described above, historical risk assessment is an attempt to ascertain the probability of the negative. If a given outcome can have only two consequences, then the probability of one is the inverse of the probability of the other, therefore pursuing the probability of both success and failure is redundant.

Nonetheless, this definition can make sense within general business risk contexts, especially if it is associated with the SWOT concept. From a strict project management perspective, it does make sense to structure any business assessment endeavor or major decision—where the outcome could be positive or negative—in the same project management framework, providing consistency and comparability through time. Also, within the breadth of all business processes, it would be possible to conceive of a particular process, decision, or venture that could have many possible successful or unsuccessful outcomes, so determining all possible successes and failures is important. This hearkens back to the original concept of risk as described by Bernstein (above) regarding the investment in the voyage of a merchant ship, hoping for positive, successful returns, while attempting to protect the possible loss by purchasing insurance. However, in terms of measuring or assessing the outcome, one could argue that each individual outcome is associated with a specific success-failure ratio, so that on a case-by-case assessment of the potential outcomes, the same argument of redundancy (described above) applies.

Information Security Risk

As businesses became more dependent on IT solutions, business risk and risk management concepts and practices began to be applied to the management of IT resources (see Table 16.1, above, for several sources, e.g., ISACA, ITGI). IT risk management has received increasing attention in the last two decades, gaining steam as the preparations for Y2K subsided across industries and the response to financial fraud exploded. In this new century, IT and IS professionals have watched in dismay at the dramatic increase in network threats [25], while the ability (and unfortunately, the willingness) to protect resources has lagged behind. On the near horizon is the looming expectations of healthcare information sharing [26], bringing reinforced regulations to penalize loss or disclosure of personal healthcare information, and appropriate increased scrutiny to data protection. The activities served to highlight the close relationship between IT and IS processes, which, though often regarded as distinct, if not competing, areas of responsibility, are actually complementary, especially regarding aspects of risk management. Several important international standards organizations have produced documentation and implementation details for IT and IS risk management (see Table 16.1). The definition of risk continued to evolve as its scope expanded within IT and the various IT subprocesses, e.g., information risk, application risk, continuity risk, access risk; although these are concepts that have arisen from the business-oriented risk management units, and may not directly relate to IT risk.

As I have described above, risk is clearly not a term that stands on its own, rather it is a *derived* concept based on measurements or assessments of probability, uncertainty, context, choice, and outcome. Related to the other historical business risk concepts, risk in the IT domain is within the *context* of IT management of technology and infrastructure, and continues to take *probability* and *choice* into account. Though general business risk characterizations also include concepts of "threat" and "vulnerability" within the context of business decisions, it is apparent that this pair of concepts optimally and definitively characterize IT risk.

Within IS and IT, "threat" and "vulnerability" are understood in the context of *providing protection of and controlling access to data and information* (as related above). IS threats have clearly become associated with the hostile Internet-based malicious software tools that have evolved from nuisance exploration to theft of data for monetary gain. Other threats to the organization's physical structures are important as they impinge on the repositories of organizational information. IS vulnerabilities can be associated with the openness of organizational networks and infrastructure, which arise from errors of omission and poor installation and management. Network and infrastructure hardening schemes address the complete network, and not just the specific components containing private information. Decisions about asset value are made by the upper management layers of the organization and lie beyond the IT units, apart from understanding the replacement cost of the technology resources. Assessments of probability of threats also have to take into account the attackers (the "intentions of others" as described by Bernstein [1998]). With the increasing black market value, identity-based information is a prominent target.

I do suggest that the definition (19, above) that includes a neutral, or possibly positive, outcome is at best a distraction from the pursuit of maximally efficient IT risk assessment and management. Quite simply, assessing risks within an IS/IT setting only involves preventing loss of information assets (directly inferring financial loss). Restating Equation 2:

20. Consequences are the result (good or bad) of a Threat penetrating a Vulnerability impacting a particular Asset.

This definition of Consequence is essentially identical to many definitions of risk itself, as exemplified by restating Equation 1:

21. Risk is the result of a Threat penetrating a Vulnerability impacting a particular Asset.

This puts "risk" and "consequences" on a common plane. In that case, with substitution of terms, Equation 2 (above) describes a circular argument:

22. Risk is the likelihood of a threat exploiting a vulnerability to produce a risk

Therefore, within the IS context, assessing for anything but a negative outcome makes no practical sense. A term with a relatively new definition has brought some clarity. "Breach" is a term that has been used to describe an event that penetrates security defenses. One definition found in the North Carolina Identity Theft Act (GS75-2A Identity Theft Protection Act) is as follows:

23. Breach: An incident of unauthorized access to and acquisition of unencrypted and unredacted records or data containing personal information where illegal use of the personal information has occurred or is reasonably likely to occur or that creates a material risk of harm to a consumer.

This definition does not involve any quantification of the components, including the valuation of the assets. In other words, a "breach" is the actuality of a negative outcome. For government purposes (as well as IT and IS), "risk" is necessarily an activity with a negative—not occasionally positive—consequence.

In summary, I suggest that the most appropriate IS/IT context definition for risk can be simplified from Definition 22:

24. Risk is the probability of a monetary loss related to information assets.

This simple definition does highlight an inherent problem in measuring risk: it is an inexact science! Because of the (increasing) probabilities of threats, the unpredictable reliabilities of the controls or countermeasures to vulnerabilities, and the challenge for assigning value to assets and cost to their replacements, producing any exact measurement of the components and therefore to risk itself is highly unlikely. Donn Parker (2006) articulated my struggle in his main conclusion:

> "no matter how elaborate…the risk assessment methodology is,…there are no sufficiently valid frequency and impact data that will make the results valid."

The measurements of the risk components will best be considered inexact and relative, especially when comparisons across the organization or between organizations are attempted.

Collaborative Risk Management

"The essence of risk management lies in maximizing the areas where we have some control over the outcome while minimizing the areas where we have absolutely no control over the outcome and the linkage between effect and cause is hidden from us." (P. L. Bernstein, 1998, 197, author's emphasis)

The classic risk management process has been a centralized effort led by a top-level delegated group charged with documenting risks from a business perspective, gathering data from the business units, compiling, over time, a summary document that identified the risks and the active controls, and made recommendations for mitigating the controls over the ensuing months. The process has been hastened into the spotlight by the challenges of the past decade, focusing more attention on the responsibility for managing (and liability for mismanaging) data. The process has been challenged by the annual frequencies demanded, often resulting, for large organizations, in a nearly continuous risk management process all year round. Many have questioned the need for or overall benefit from such efforts [27].

We do live in a world where organizational assets are invaluable to the long-term existence of the organization, where technology is persistently flawed or incomplete, and where complete trust among individuals and organizations is incomplete (if not dangerous). The need for managing risks surrounding the data underlying business processes is clear, in light of the increasing demand for protecting organizational financial data from fraud and protecting personally identifiable data—especially healthcare data. That makes efficient risk management mandatory. To accomplish this, I suggest a collaborative process instead of a top-down process. The impetus for the concept of collaborative risk management came from the quote from Bernstein at the beginning of this section. Bernstein was actually addressing the need to attend to organizational responsibilities and place external factors on the back burner. However, I believe the statement makes efficient sense in addressing risk within the organization, where "linkages" can be established among the collaborators. In a classic, top-down scheme, a centrally situated unit (e.g., risk management office) drives the whole process, mandating a common framework and context for assessing "risks" throughout the other units, producing reports that disclose "risks" at every level of the organization. The results are a comparable set of documents, but at the questionable cost of time and efficiency.

In a collaborative scheme, the difference is that though the executive-based unit may drive the effort—establishing the plans and processes—every other business unit can contribute to the measurement of the risk components in a contextual way, potentially reducing redundancy and increasing efficiency. This is where each organizational unit "maximiz[es] the areas where we have some control over the outcome while minimizing the areas where we have absolutely no control over the outcome". The "outcome" is the governance and risk management posture of the organization. The setting for introducing the collaborative concept begins with the organizational human factor.

Human Factor

Information is certainly the most significant organizational resource and is the basis for economic health. Though organizations sell products and/or services, nothing would be created or sold without the information resource. As important as information is, people are nonetheless the most important resource any organization has. Humans gather, interpret, store, and utilize the information in order to produce the organizational product or service. People also communicate the service or product to appropriate markets and complete the transactions that enable economic growth. Within the organizational units, people contribute differentially to the process of risk management, from the executives who make spending decisions to the experts who implement the technical solutions, and all those in between who make nested business decisions about the products and services based on the executive leadership decisions and utilizing the technical resources and information at hand.

People also are the most predominant sources of threats and vulnerabilities. Internally, accidental and deliberate actions may exploit the information resource through legitimate and authorized pathways. Legitimate external human activities may become illegitimate pathways for gaining access to organizational data and information. The increasingly hazardous Internet "threat space" has a human being behind every threat. Vulnerabilities in the physical or technical protection of information may have arisen by human error in the design of the structure or the infrastructure, or from human acts of omission or commission in setting up the structures and infrastructures. The ultimate challenge for collaborative risk management efforts is to recognize the human factor in the causes and the solutions of the risk components.

Organizational Responsibilities

Responsibility for risk management (as with IS management) is found throughout the organization: top to bottom. Each unit, and each worker in the units, has responsibilities for ensuring that risk (as a possibility of asset financial loss) is reduced by taking proper care within the unit and collaborating with the other units for the complete result of proper governance.

Every organization potentially has different names for the following units and, based on size, some of the units may be combined or otherwise reoriented. Each unit has a contribution to make toward protecting information and data. The organizational executive unit starts the process.

Organizational Executives

This group consists of the organizational decision makers responsible for spending time and money in the appropriate directions on behalf of the organization. This unit defines the core business values within the selected industry sector, and from that the executives also define the services or products for marketing and generating income. This unit holds the ultimate responsibility for organizational integrity regulatory and legal compliance, and consequences of loss from risks. As a major collaborator in the risk governance process, the executive unit makes three primary decisions in the collaborative model:

- Delegating the organizational management of risk in an appropriate unit, usually with top-level reporting status. This unit will lead the process and planning, and account for all contributions from all other business units and produce the appropriate reports.
- Defining the business processes and authorizing the business rules for how the processes are crafted based on the decisions for products and services. This is for existing activities as well as major new business decisions involving direction or growth. Though some of the detailed processes may be delegated, the responsibility and initiation is with this unit.
- Determining the overall value of the various organizational assets in terms of current standing value and replacement cost: physical structures, capital equipment, proprietary information stores, reputation, and (most importantly) personnel. This is the foundation for determining risk, especially at the organizational level. This unit has the fiscal stopping point for value and cost, even if some asset expenses are delegated to other units.

Risk Management Unit

This unit can be a single-purpose entity or it may be combined with several related organization-wide management efforts, such as privacy, regulatory compliance, internal audit, and/or quality control, primarily based on organizational size and industry sector. This is the group that will design the governance and risk management structure, and set the plans in place for organizational collaboration. It is the final collecting point and repository for data and reports involved in assessing and determining organizational risk. This unit initiates the periodic (annual or otherwise) processes within the organization and interacts with all other units based on their assigned risk responsibilities. Towards risk management, this unit

- Addresses regulatory compliance vulnerabilities that have potential monetary penalties, which can contribute to the overall picture of asset loss in determining risk. This unit crafts policies, procedures and other documentation for privacy and regulatory issues, and monitors the internal compliance.
- Arranges for internal assessments and external audits, based on industry sector and regulatory requirements. This unit is able to provide the organizational-wide risk posture to internal reviewers and especially to external auditors and other regulators.
- Is the focal point for classifying data based on business rules (confidential, proprietary information) or regulatory requirements. This is most important where protection mechanisms may have to be varied, depending on differences in the importance or value of the information requiring protection. From the human standpoint, private information is that which identifies the individual or that which enables a thief to defraud an individual for financial gain. From the information perspective, private information is that which has been classified as "private", usually as a response to business or regulatory requirements.

General Business Units

These are the units established to address the major business processes as set by the executive unit. These high-level processes are tailored to the service or product or support effort for other units as defined by the organizational direction and industry. In most organizations, the directors/managers of these units are assigned the responsibility of data owners for the sector of information related to their organizational function. The directors/managers address internal threats and vulnerabilities by

- Determining the business rules and information resource requirements—external data, software products, system requirements—for business process. This is with tight collaboration with the executive units to ensure that the business processes are properly defined and articulated and undergirded with the right information.
- Hiring appropriately experienced workforce and insuring that all are trained and made aware of individual responsibilities, both for work assignments and for protecting data.
- Approving and authorizing access of workforce members to organizational systems and applications. Managers also must initiate access deactivation as soon as workforce members are terminated from the organization.
- Reviewing access and other activity reports around the unit-based systems and applications and relaying any reports of potential incidents that might lead to system interruptions and/or data loss.
- Reviewing and authorizing changes made to unit-based production data systems.

The users within the business units are not only the largest source of threats and vulnerabilities to the organizational information resource, but they are potentially the largest part of the solution. It is not difficult to understand that if the workforce staff are enabled to own part of the solution, they will take more care and responsibility for the circumstances within their control. As part of the workforce training for information security (as a major component of risk), users can be enabled to

- Obtain and read context-related policies and procedures.
- Understand the consequences of an open, unattended workstation as well as visible work-related papers and files, and understand the personal consequences and sanctions for deliberate misdeeds.
- Feel confident about addressing strangers or unattended visitors within the work space.
- Identify and report circumstances that could lead to crises, such as anomalous office smoke, impending weather changes, and unusual workstation behavior related to malicious software.
- Identify and report unusual or unexpected employee behavior.
- Understand how to respond in crisis situations requiring evacuation.

Information Security/Information Technology/Physical Security

Many mid-sized to small organizations do not have the luxury of separate IS, IT, and PS/S units. Nonetheless, the roles for contributing to risk management represented by these units require clarification, because there are some important distinctions, as alluded to earlier in the chapter. The IT unit is the backbone of the larger organization. This unit acquires, implements, and manages the architecture and infrastructure as mandated and determined by the executive unit. Increased threats, rapid changes in technology, and the need for information on-demand has begun to provide justification for stable, central IT units who participate in, rather than simply respond to, business decisions as organizations attempt to gain efficiencies in technology costs.

In many organizations, large and small, the need to separate IS from the historical IT units has become more and more apparent. IS increasingly has a role that addresses security from an organizational point of view rather than just the technology view, since challenges to information security are being recognized throughout the organization. Increasingly, IS units are taking on more of a strategic planning role for security, and just as financial audit does not (should not!) report to the organizational finance unit, the IS unit should not be part of IT. There is obvious collaboration, but the IS unit is evolving to be the information security planning and assessment function, while the IT unit implements and manages the technical aspects of security. Some IS units are combined with the larger risk/privacy/audit units, but the role for IS is distinct in that the privacy/audit unit determines which data is private and IS designs the most effective protection structure for private information. From that, the IT unit determines and implements the appropriate technology for the protection structure. Therefore, the IS function has become a catalyst for collaboration among other organizational business units.

Many large organizations have a PS/S unit that addresses the physical structure—buildings and property—establishing access control at entry points and implementing safety practices for fire and emergency circumstances. Some large manufacturing or chemical production organizations have robust PS/S units that address human hazard protection as well as access control. Where such units are present, the IS and IT units can collaborate on structural access control, providing consistency with the organizational network and system access control. IS and IT units will play a collaborative but subordinate role with the PS/S units within crisis response management.

IS units contribute to risk management by

- Planning the information protection response to business process and business rule determination; and determining organizational compliance responsibilities to information security regulations, in collaboration with the privacy unit and privacy regulations.
- Articulating information security strategy in policy and standards documentation and provide training for organizational workforce.
- Participating in hardware and software acquisition/design and change management efforts for information security vulnerability implications; documenting and monitoring vulnerability control efforts.
- Working with IT and PS/S units to track threats from all sources—Internet, hazards, weather, and/or external human activities; determining vulnerabilities and vulnerability controls; participating in internal and external incident response.
- Working with IT and PS/S units to prepare for emergency response and business recovery to major service interruptions or major crisis events.

As these distinct responsibilities are highlighted, the basis for collaboration may begin to be apparent. Based on the risk definitions and formulae described in the previous section:

- Executive units determine the *value or cost of asset loss*, including information. Executives also set the tone and example of risk management.
- Risk governance units determine the *processes* and periodicity for risk governance.
- Privacy units determine the most important (private, proprietary) data/information and the associated *penalties (monetary loss)* for failed compliance. They also craft the *policy statements* that identify organizational posture and sanctions.
- Business unit managers *authorize users* to access the systems and services within the units and *monitor system access* over time.
- Workforce staff take part in the *reduction of internal threats* by becoming participants in the process.
- IS units craft *policies and standards* for information security and set plans for the organizational security structure, and subsequently monitor and assess the security implementation.
- IT units (with IS and PS/S) monitor *threats* from multiple sources.
- IT units (with IS and PS/S) determine structural and infrastructural vulnerabilities and associated controls.

Therefore,

■ *Asset values and associated costs* are determined by the executive units, with assistance from regulatory compliance units.

■ *Threats* (and their probabilities) to organizational integrity, reputation, and business process continuity are addressed by the executive unit with assistance from the risk/privacy/audit units.

■ *Threats* (and their probabilities) to structural and human resources are identified and monitored by PS/S, with assistance from the general organizational workforce.

■ *Threats* (and their probabilities) to information and technology resources are identified and monitored by IT and IS, with assistance from the general organizational workforce.

■ *Organizational and business process vulnerabilities* are addressed by process definition, policies, standards and procedures.

■ *Structural and human resource vulnerabilities* are identified and mitigated by IT and IPS/S with assistance from IS.

■ *Technical and information vulnerabilities* are identified and mitigated by IT and PS/S with assistance from IS.

From those assessments,

■ Controls and countermeasures to organizational and business process vulnerabilities are addressed by executive and risk management units by defined processes, policies, standards, and awareness training.

■ Controls and countermeasures to structural and human resource vulnerabilities are addressed by the PS/S unit by policies, standards, awareness training and implementing well-designed safety practices.

■ Controls and countermeasures to technical and information vulnerabilities are addressed by IS processes, policies, standards, and awareness training; IS and IT planning design and monitoring, and with IT implementation.

Depending on the size and complexity of an organization, the various described roles and efforts are never as exclusively delineated as stated. Nonetheless, this listing begins to indicate the divergent responsibilities among the organizational units. From the assembled sets of threats and vulnerabilities, plus the valuation of asset loss, the overall organizational risk profile can be derived. The picture presented above begins to offer clarity in the areas of focus.

Assessment of Risk

Discipline is any training intended to produce a specific character or pattern of behavior, especially training that produces moral or mental development in a particular direction. (Wikipedia, 2005)

Based on an understanding of the different unit approaches to identifying the risk components, the collaborative model allows the organizational units to identify appropriate threats and vulnerabilities separately and contribute their results to the risk management unit, who combine the results from the units with the valuation to determine the overall risk profiles.

Classic Risk Assessment

In the classic, top-down scenario of risk assessment, the risk management unit will direct an organization-wide effort to identify threats, vulnerabilities, asset valuation, and countermeasures. This unit crafts the plan and defines all terms and processes.

The process begins with the organizational business criticality/impact analysis, to determine, for each of the critical business processes, the monetary value and other costs of the loss of the process, and the cost of restoring or replacing the process, including a measure of priority among the processes to the continuation of the business as a whole. For each process, threats (including probabilities) and vulnerabilities are identified, as well as the controls or countermeasures for each vulnerability and associated threat. From that, the individual and collective risks can be determined. If controls or countermeasures are incomplete, then a gap analysis addresses the incompleteness and leads to a mitigation plan. Ideally, this becomes an annual effort, documenting criticality, assessing threats, vulnerabilities, and controls, filling the gaps in the controls, and redetermining risks. Each organizational unit is directed to assess risks within the scope of the unit, determining threats, vulnerabilities, asset values, and controls, deriving risks, and identifying mitigation plans—a grand, recursive scheme throughout the organization. This would mean that IS and IT units would follow the script and determine risk components and derive risks within the technical infrastructure.

The assembled risk reports provide a measure of the effort undertaken, but as Parker (2006) has observed, the overall outcome for enhancing data protection is questionable. From the assembled reports, the gaps in controls will logically provide the basis for ongoing management of the identified and uncontrolled risks. Depending upon the details and volume of documentation, the overall risk management effort becomes a pursuit of gaps in controls and countermeasures, sometimes apart from the context of managing technology and information security. The previous introduction to collaborative risk management should begin to provide clues for gains in efficiency and enhanced data protection. Based on Bernstein's quote (at the beginning of the second section), I suggest that each of the major contributing organizational units concentrate on "areas of control," specifically, efforts that address the unit-specific components of risk. The executive unit can provide cost estimates for loss of assets and private data. The risk/audit/privacy unit can coordinate the risk management process and document threats and vulnerabilities in the areas of regulatory compliance and organizational policy statements. Business unit managers can administer access control practices and track the protection of systems within their domain. Workforce members can become more aware and active in preventing accidental incidents and observing and reporting potential deliberate incidents. IS and IT units can focus on internal and external threats to information, and the technology vulnerabilities that allow the threats to become actualized. The PS/S unit can focus on external threats to the physical structures and to human safety.

The concept of convergence offers an additional perspective on the collaboration model. Initially, convergence addressed the relationship between IS (including IT) and PS/S, emphasizing the need for the two groups to collaborate on security issues. For convergence to be most effective, it requires *context*. Simply merging the two units into one does not achieve the intended goals; in fact, such an arbitrary merger could dilute the important efforts and process of the separate units. IS and PS/S can converge on the context of access control by combining the technologies for building entry control with data center-administered servers and databases that track the entry of an individual into the building and the subsequent authorized entry into data systems. Divergences in patterns of access derived from both sets of access logs could indicate a threat to the information resource. An additional context for convergence is for incident management up to and including crisis response and business continuity. Security and safety professionals are trained to place human safety as the highest priority during crisis response, and the two units can assist each other in plans for evacuation and verification of workforce staff during a crisis response. In organizations with an emphasis on safety and hazard prevention, such as manufacturing or chemical processing organizations, PS/S units often have robust employee training and awareness programs. IS and IT can benefit from collaborating in such programs, expanded to include information security awareness. Convergence contexts can also be established between IS and the privacy/audit units for tracking and planning the response to regulations and industry standards initiatives, which often include overlapping privacy, security, and audit requirements.

Information Security Context of Risk Assessment

Hopefully, it is more clear that the primary role for IS units within risk assessment is the identification of information-oriented threats and the vulnerabilities that offer potential for exploitation. Characteristically and historically, this has been and still is what IS and IT units do on a daily basis. It is apparent that as the executive and risk/privacy/audit units crossed over the threshold of risk management, IS and IT units were already there. Based on direction from the executive and risk/privacy/audit units, IS and IT manage the technology and processes that provide protection of and control access to data and information. Nonetheless, it is important for IS and IT units and management to understand how to fit within the context of the corporate risk management and governance strategy in collaboration with the other units, not in isolation. When the processes and practices of IS are properly assessed, documented, and managed, the results can be crafted to align with any regulatory requirement and any organizational expectations of risk assessment.

In reality, not all IS/IT units are in a position to collaborate in the organizational risk management processes. Creditably, most IS/IT units provide a reasonable service for data access and protection, but many still act in an isolated way, creating technical environments that often become ends instead of means, and operating separately from the organizational decision-making processes. Many units do not appreciate the data classification and regulatory requirements that directly affect the larger organization. Unfortunately, many still manage in a piecemeal fashion, addressing most problems as they arise, unless interrupted by more serious problems. Many have correctly asserted that information security is not simply a set of repeated tasks, but a process, meaning that it continues through time. I suggest that efficient management of information security is a *discipline*, more than the tasks and the defined processes, it requires a disciplined approach to address the changes in threats, vulnerabilities, technology, and business direction. For this context the best definition of discipline is the one quoted at the beginning of this section.

In the case of IS, organizations and IS professionals are seeking a consistent pattern of behavior based on documented policies and standards towards a direction of data and information protection. Even a disciplined approach requires a structure or framework within which to operate. I suggest the following model, based on the research of Col. John R. Boyd, USAF (1927–1997) [28], which offers a unique perspective of the activities involved in managing IS. Such a disciplined approach will enable the IS unit to converge in context with other units, especially with the central risk/privacy/audit efforts to provide organizational governance and risk management.

The Discipline of Information Security Management: The Boyd Model

Col. Boyd was a U.S. Air Force fighter pilot whose military career spanned from late in the Korean War, through the Vietnam War, and as a military consultant in the Pentagon until his retirement in 1975. He was considered a visionary by many for his designs of efficient, maneuverable fighter planes validated by mathematical proofs and for his research into military warfare strategy. His warfare strategy was based on extensive historical research, probing the writings and experiences of battle leaders from centuries in the past. It introduced smaller, more maneuverable fighting units, speed in decision-making and evasiveness, and some of his concepts were actually implemented in the first Gulf War, 1990–1991. He published very few documents, but he developed several presentations and a massive "briefing" for his military warfare strategy, which he refined over several years, and copies of his presentation are available [29]. Boyd's concept of warfare strategy addressed interaction with an enemy force that actively intended harm and pursued the defeat and/or destruction of the forces Boyd instructed. He strongly urged his audience to understand the nature and behavior of the enemy and to be able to use that as an advantage.

His military warfare strategy has been succinctly summarized by his own diagram (Figure 16.1), the OODA Loop. OODA is an acronym for "Observe", "Orient", "Decide", "Act," and the diagram indicates the contingencies on each of the major phases. This model was developed for active warfare engagements; essentially, this model defines the process that a military leader in the field might use to make decisions based on observations about the enemy; orientation, or context of the activity; and then be able to act on the decisions. The loop is repeated after each decision process, and the ultimate goal is to make decisions and actions more rapidly than the enemy, becoming more maneuverable and elusive, and ultimately achieving dominance if not victory over the enemy. The OODA loop has been widely acclaimed by military and business professionals alike, and has been used to model a number of studies in the military (Schechtman, 1996), in business (Richards, 2004), and even in IT/IS settings (Kovacich, 2003).

When I first learned of Boyd and began researching his career and theories, I readily saw the applicability of the OODA Loop within information security. In Figure 16.2, I have modified the contents towards the information security domain, but retained the flow of the cyclical process. An IS unit (or at least an IS officer) will be constantly observing the IS scene for information on threats, vulnerabilities, regulatory decisions, and standards. Those observations may possibly affect

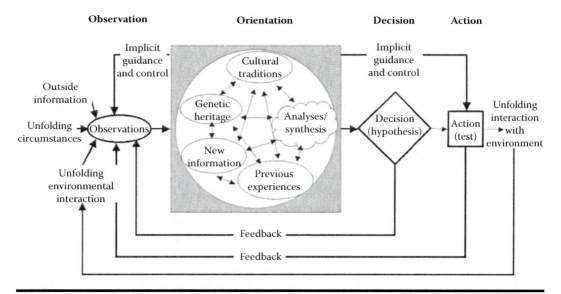

Figure 16.1   The OODA loop. (Adapted from Boyd, J. R., The essence of winning and losing, Air Power Australia, 1996. www.ausairpower.net/APA-Boyd-Papers.html.)

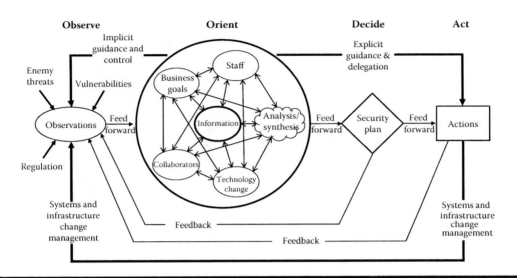

Figure 16.2   The OODA loop adapted for information security.

the overall orientation of organizational information security towards the business goals regarding staffing, technology changes, and interaction with collaborators. The internal information will be synthesized and will influence the IS plans for responding to the changes. With plans in hand, the IS unit makes appropriate decisions to adjust the technical information protection capabilities. The IS plan and the actions taken feed the next cycle of observations. The effort is constantly cycling, because the IS environment, within and without the organization, is constantly changing.

The contributions to risk assessment are from the "Observe" stage of the cycle. New threats are identified, new vulnerabilities are discovered and all are documented and ranked for potential impact on information assets. Within the "Orient" stage, the threats and vulnerabilities are positioned within the control and countermeasure structures, based on input from existing collaborators and staff. The sets of information about the threats, vulnerabilities, and existing control structures are synthesized and analyzed for completeness. As suggested by the quote from Col. Boyd at the introduction to this section, the orientation efforts are the most important portion of the cycle. This is where the experience and knowledge of the IS professionals are utilized to synthesize a complete and up-to-date picture of the existing protection mechanisms and processes. This synthesis feeds the "Decide" stage of the potential changes within the information security plan and documentation that support the protection schemes. It can also be formatted appropriately and supplied to the risk/privacy/audit unit for compilation in periodic updates to impact assessments and the risk management process. Any new changes for the IS function are brought through the change management process within the "Act" stage, and new control structures and other supporting activities are activated. Feedback from the "Decide" and "Act" activities are passed on to the next level of observations.

Based on the size of the IS unit, these processes may overlap as different IS professionals incorporate observations and make new decisions. This effort cannot be carried out in isolation—activities within all phases of the cycle mandate collaboration and convergence with other organizational units. Unfortunately, IS professionals may find themselves where the ability to change a corporate structure is restricted by lack of support at the executive levels and lack of commitment by the organizational workforce. Nonetheless, IS professionals can develop personal discipline and commitment to IS principles and ethics, and need always be in the position to offer and implement a structure in the expectation that opportunities will arise. In the following section, I will illustrate the use of the Boyd cyclical model for managing IS and make the case that the disciplined management of IS is in fact identical to IS risk management.

Management of IT/IS Vulnerabilities

"Note how orientation shapes observation, shapes decision, shapes action, and in turn is shaped by the feedback and other phenomena coming into our sensing or observing window." (John R. Boyd, 1996)

A complete IS management plan for protecting data and information addresses four primary areas: *hardware and network infrastructure*, including clients, servers, networks, and their operating systems and tools; the *software environment*, including application system development and implementation, and all work-enhancing tools and interfaces; *incident response and management*, addressing system or service interruptions up to and including crisis response and recovery; and *human activities*, including internal and external people involved in interacting through the organizational structures with the data and information. Each of these areas has components that are tactical, within an operational calendar year, and strategic, spanning two or more operational calendar years. Each of these primary areas can be addressed within the four stages of the OODA Loop, as demonstrated by Figure 16.2. Establishing a disciplined IS structure is obviously more difficult in an existing organization than in a start-up business, but an IS review and reorganization can begin within any setting. For the best description of the management details within each primary area, it is most appropriate to begin with the "Orient" stage. In new or old organizations, this stage presents the opportunity to examine the current status and begin plans for modification. Much of what is addressed within the "Orient" stage will be examined with a strategic perspective; tactical approaches will be addressed within the "Decide" and "Act" stages. The "Observe" stage represents a never-ending process of reflection on recent activities and potential challenges. Listed below are activities and/or responsibilities of the IS unit and IS professionals within each of the stages.

Orient

This stage is the most important stage for an IS professional, whether starting within a new organization or simply seeking to improve IS circumstances and processes in an existing organization. It is prudent to make detailed assessments before initiating changes that may affect existing services and processes. Below, the IS responsibilities are detailed, but as Figure 16.2 indicates, the assessment is not made in isolation. Input must be accepted from additional units within the organization and external resources as well before decisions can be finalized.

Human Resource

A prudent IS professional, at any level within the organization, will take the time to understand the organization's industry setting, regulatory context, products and services, and active business relationships with external organizations. This is the foundation for the organizational IS plan, which must be crafted around the organizational industry setting, corporate posture, and core values. This demonstrates a difference between IS, which has a broader, enterprise view beyond (but including) technology, and IT, which, though not isolated from the organizational context, primarily addresses the technical resource. It is vital to understand the external organizational relationships, especially those that are involved in information exchange. Most information privacy and security regulations mandate carefully crafted agreements regarding the exchange. Healthcare organizations will soon face tighter scrutiny since the recent enactment of the HITECH Act [30] has not only increased the penalties for loss of private data, but also increased the scrutiny of these organizations. Vendors who supply vital resources and materials should also be noted and tracked, and all external organizations should be documented as part of the organizational business continuity planning efforts.

Having strong interpersonal skills is an asset to IS professionals, because the most significant challenge will be to communicate the serious importance of proper information protection mechanisms and the vital roles that each workforce member plays in the overall protection scheme. Unfortunately, most of the rank-and-file workforce, from top to bottom, have an incomplete or even misdirected understanding of IS concepts. Many security practices and processes are inconvenient for end users, and may give the misunderstood impression of inhibiting work flow. It will pay benefits to develop strong listening skills and it will be significantly important to be able to communicate IS challenges in varieties of settings, from formal presentations to hallway conversations (Murphy, 2009).

As I mentioned earlier, Col. Boyd's model has been used within business settings, but I suggest that it is not a perfect fit. It has been used to attempt a model of business competition for market share of products or services, but in reality, business competitors are not enemies who seek the defeat and destruction of each other, as with military fighting forces from rival nations. Within the IS setting, organizations do have enemies who intend harm, if not destruction of targeted individuals and organizations. Internet-based attackers began as individuals with technical skills whose early intent was curiosity and bragging rights. Recently, these individuals have become much more skillful and organized in pursuit of the monetary value of stolen information, whether proprietary organizational information or personally identifiable information. The efforts of these enemies have increased dramatically in recent years, along with the value of the stolen information.

IS professionals are not ignoring these enemies, and the Boyd model provides a structure that emphasizes knowledge of the enemy and crafting plans to distract, deter, or even defeat these enemies. This calls to mind the historical aspect of risk management concerning uncertainty based on game theory, which attributes aspects of uncertainty to the activities of the "other player" [16]. For IS, the other player is the attacker, and attacker activities are increasing. In this time of the dangerous Internet, IS and IT professionals cannot continue to be passive and fail to take even minimal protection precautions. Technology infrastructures and software environments must be designed with the enemy attacker in mind! We must not only consider whom we choose to allow access, but whom we deliberately choose to block. IS professionals can serve by learning about attack methods and attacker characteristics and consider the design of the hardware and software environments from the perspective of an attacker. We need to assess the environments to see how someone might choose to break our structures, gain access to our systems, and capture or destroy our data.

In dealing strategically with the human resource, IS professionals must

- Learn the commitment and support within the organizational senior levels for disciplined IS processes and practices.
- Understand the process for hiring workforce staff, assigning responsibilities, documenting access permissions to software systems, and the process for terminating staff and deactivating all accounts.

- ■ Determine the level of awareness about information security within the workforce, including responsibilities, privileges, and sanctions for improper use.
- ■ Assess confidentiality agreements for internal workforce and business agreements with partners and associates involved in information exchange.
- ■ Determine the tolerance or acceptance of visitors and other strangers by the organizational workforce.
- ■ Examine organizational practices and physical structures from the perspective of an attacker, probing for vulnerabilities that allow penetration into the information resource.

Technology Infrastructure

The technology infrastructure—servers, workstations, networks, and communications nodes—is the primary domain of the IT unit. The infrastructure is also the primary target for threats against data and information, especially in large organizations with an active history of several years. More recently, IS has become compelled to assess the storage capabilities of internal devices such as printers, scanners, and fax machines (Radcliffe, 2007). These are becoming popular targets of attackers who can take advantage of any and all access for wider exploitation. In the current state of technology, managing the infrastructure is primarily a tactical effort, especially for small-footprint servers and desktops. Changes often occur several times a year based on unit additions, component additions to units, upgrades, and turnover of old equipment, and these changes frequently provide opportunities for threat exploits, especially if the change management process is ill-defined. The primary control suggestion for aged, complex infrastructures is to initiate simplification, reducing the complexity of devices and systems requiring unique service and support.

Many organizations are expanding their network perimeters by configuring virtual private networks (VPNs) for use by telecommuters and travelers. Essentially all of this traffic is wireless, requiring increased network access scrutiny as remote users and their personal workstations become attacker targets. Opportunities for unauthorized access to data is much simpler for experienced attackers within the organizational network perimeter than outside it. By far the biggest challenge to organizational infrastructures and the resident data is the explosion of portable computing devices, including laptops, notebooks, netbooks, multipurpose hand-held devices (especially with cameras), and portable storage devices. The accessibility of these devices will be the source of untold numbers of vulnerabilities in the coming months and years. Personal acquisition has exceeded the management capability of most organizations and policies blocking the use of portable storage devices are essentially unenforceable without investments in workstation management software.

IS professionals who are independent of IT can assist in planning and assessing architecture design changes that enhance data protection, prevent data leakage, and reduce opportunities for malicious software exploits. Creative architecture design that includes multiple tiers, decoupling of service processes, redundancy of components, and remote servers and data storage can enhance the *changeability* of the infrastructure and reduce the complexity of information recovery after crisis interruptions. One possible strategy for gaining control over network access is to shrink the actual perimeter of the organizational network to the central servers and storage units, treating all internal workforce users as external actors. Another consideration is to encrypt all centrally stored data and restrict access pathways (automated key management and implementation) to authorized devices, such as organizational workstations and properly authorized and configured portable devices. This means that all users and all devices will undergo the same access control scrutiny as external users, eliminating the inside-the-perimeter advantage.

IS professionals can strategically assess the current organizational infrastructure by documenting

- A complete network map of all internal addressable nodes; also a clear definition of the network perimeter, both physical (within buildings, campuses, and remote locations) and logical (through VPNs)
- Breadth of hand-held and portable computing devices, usage of portable storage devices, and wireless capability of existing network
- Single points of failure in the operational server architecture, e.g., unpaired servers, network nodes, storage units; out-of-date, out-of-service, or single-purpose hardware
- Storage characteristics of networked printers, faxes, and scanners
- Current state of malware exploits, e.g., logs of malware penetrations, service disruption due to malware, from internal and external sources
- Status of operating system upgrades, patches; documentation of processes
- Status and location of system change and error logs; availability and archival capacity
- Documented processes for posting operational system changes, insuring separation of responsibilities
- Controls for hardware change management, e.g., properly staged, tested, and authorized
- Status of backup and archive processes, e.g., distance from production environment, capabilities of recovery systems
- Desktop workstation management, e.g., control over workstation administration and access to external networks

Software Environment

Administration of software and workstation office technology and tools is frequently a part of the IT unit, but occasionally business units may have developers for targeted systems and applications. IT typically provides support for workstation installation and problem-solving resources for the internal workforce. IS professionals can offer an independent review of development practices to insure that systems and applications reduce or eliminate vulnerabilities that allow for data exposure or unauthorized access. IS together with the risk/privacy/audit unit can document the data retention and archival requirements established by government regulations. There are maximum retention specifications for certain types of legal and personally identifiable information and it is possible that these maxima become the minima for compliance with electronic discovery regulations [31]. With a carefully crafted policy of compliance with retention requirements, organizations can also define data destruction policies that fulfill the expectations of legal discovery challenges.

Development of large systems—usually projects that span months or years—requires rigorous attention from IS professionals. All phases of major system development projects, planning, design, development, testing, acceptance, and operations, present opportunities for vulnerabilities without proper review. In many cases, asking the right questions about data protection and access control at the right time can forestall expensive problems later. Careful testing can identify simple errors and logic errors, and vulnerabilities for data exposure. Planning is the most important phase for introducing security concerns, because once systems are designed and developed, changes can add to the cost in money and time. Even if applications are commercial off-the-shelf (COTS) products, IS can ask appropriate questions about the design and protection capabilities before investments are finalized. Most notably, the *weakest link* in all software environment activities is the human resource. Humans make errors in all phases of software development, and organizational users fail to follow instructions and guidelines (accidentally or deliberately) and inadvertently can leave system sessions active, allowing unauthorized access to anyone wanting to take advantage.

One of the most important design issues for any system or sets of systems is access control. Organizational users must be

- *Identified*: validating the user's identity, usually by the hiring process and/or by personal possessions, e.g., photo ID or other papers
- *Authenticated*: verifying the identity of the user, usually by a combination of a user ID and a password (single-phase) or usage of additional pin number technologies and/or biometric capabilities (two- or multiphase); implemented as a login process to a network or system
- *Authorized*: two phases, management permission to access a system or a portion of a system, and the system-based implementation of that permission

IT units carry out the *provisioning* process, or activation of access after proper authentication and authorization. There are sufficient tools that enable the access control process to be designed as a workflow process, eliminating the need for paper documents and formal signatures. Users will be able to enter requests on-line, and the request can be reviewed and authorized by management also on-line. Finally, the authorized request can be transferred to the systems administrative group for provisioning. The complete process of access control includes mandatory *assessment* of the process of identification, authentication, authorization, and provisioning, including logging of all initial access requests and provisioning responses, logging of access activity (successful and appropriate attempts, and more importantly, unsuccessful and inappropriate attempts), and periodic *audits* of the overall process.

As with any IT-related topic, acronyms and "buzz words" prevail. Many organizations have targeted the concept of *single sign-on*, for the promise of easing the access process across organizational systems for both users and IT systems administrators. This implies that a single ID and password (and other qualifier) can be used to access any or all organizational systems and services. It can also ease the administrative burden of the access control processes. However, abuses may arise if users fail to disconnect from sessions, allowing open access to other individuals. Some IT and IS professionals prefer a concept of *simplified sign-on*, which employs a single ID and password combination for all systems, but separate authentication steps for each system. A single- or simplified-sign-on mechanism can be a component of an organizational identity management scheme, where central control of a large user population is vital. Again, human activity is the most prevalent point of failure for any authentication scheme.

Another access mechanism that can be used to segregate access to separate components of a large system is role-based access control. This process was developed by Dr. Ravi Sandhu (http://profsandhu.com/), his students, and associates, and has become refined and more widely used in recent years (see Figure 16.3). It now exists as an ANSI standard (American National Standard for Information Technology, 2004).

From the ANSI INCITS Standard
Core RBAC model element sets and relations are defined in Figure 16.3. Core RBAC includes sets of five basic data elements called **users** (USERS), **roles** (ROLES), **objects** (OBS), **operations** (OPS), and **permissions** (PRMS). The RBAC model as a whole is fundamentally defined in terms of individual users being assigned to roles and permissions being assigned to roles. As such, a role is a means for naming many-to-many relationships among individual users and permissions. In addition, the Core RBAC

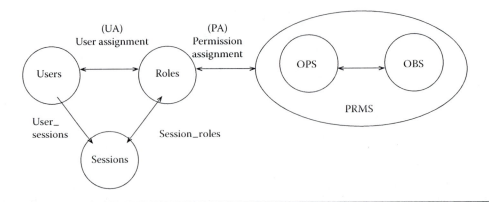

Figure 16.3   Core RBAC. (From American National Standard for Information Technology. 2004. Role based access control. ANSI• INCITS 359-2004. Copyright 2004 by Information Technology Industry Council.)

model includes a set of **sessions** (SESSIONS) where each session is a mapping between a user and an activated subset of roles that are assigned to the user.

Central to RBAC is the concept of role relations, around which a role is a semantic construct for formulating policy. [Figure 16.3] illustrates *user assignment* (*UA*) and *permission assignment* (*PA*) relations. The arrows indicate a many-to-many relationship (e.g., a user can be assigned to one or more roles, and a role can be assigned to one or more users). This arrangement provides great flexibility and granularity of assignment of permissions to roles and users to roles. Without these conveniences there is an enhanced danger that a user may be granted more access to resources than is needed because of limited control over the type of access that can be associated with users and resources. Users may need to list directories and modify existing files, for example, without creating new files, or they may need to append records to a file without modifying existing records. Any increase in the flexibility of controlling access to resources also strengthens the application of the principle of least privilege.

The model (Figure 16.3) itself is fairly straightforward, but the implementation can be difficult in large organizations and complex systems, e.g., a single implementation mechanism may not be adaptable to all COTS systems. The Organization for the Advancement of Structured Information Standards (OASIS) [32] has developed an implementation mechanism using an XML adaptation called XACML [33], specifically for access control systems. RBAC provides tighter control over user access and authorization, and reduces the opportunity for network roaming, which often happens in organizations, such as hospitals and other healthcare centers, where personal information is a major component of the information resource. Adaptations to the core model include usage control (restriction over how data is collected and used) and time constraints (preventing access within specific daily time periods or beyond specific calendar time frames).

More and more, systems are being developed with web-based or web portal interfaces, both for internal and external users of the systems. This adds an additional area of concern for data leakage, since poorly designed web interfaces can introduce abundant vulnerabilities, especially when naïve developers use rapid development tools that produce stock interfaces. IS must insist on appropriate web interface security practices to close opportunities for passing SQL commands through a number of potential vulnerabilities—URL fields, and entry fields for data entry and database queries. Proper review of web design for consistent attention to web vulnerabilities is mandatory [34].

Increasingly, internal workforce staff make use of social network tools and capabilities for personal interactions, short-distance connectivity and file transfer (e.g., Bluetooth), and even personal shopping opportunities—the so-called "Web 2.0" technology. The types are increasing and replacing outmoded technology faster than reference lists of names and methods can keep up! Users are transmitting and displaying personal identity information and many are not aware of the opportunities present for identity theft or incidental disclosure of private information [35]. Even e-mail systems are rife with vulnerabilities for malicious software and data loss. IS professionals must take the initiative to discourage the use of e-mail for distributing organizationally sensitive information directly or as attachments, especially since there are increasingly abundant choices for collaboration software that offer secure means (encryption, redirection) for sharing files and records. Also, e-mail is becoming increasingly the target of legal investigations as a record of activities, and some states are mandating retention policies of all e-mails within specific organizations and conditions. Workforce users must be made aware of the legal rights for management scrutiny of e-mails and other messaging systems within the organization. Executives will need to determine the limits for such activities within the organizational setting.

The array of IS and web-based threats is increasing dramatically, to the extent that it requires nearly full-time, active review and research to keep up. Regardless of the changing attack tools and scenarios, IS staff can contribute to planning workforce office technology by keeping abreast of common Internet threat and vulnerability tracking services [36] and the appropriate defense mechanisms and processes for reducing or eliminating the vulnerabilities.

IS can review and assess the

- Current documentation on licensed software and service accounts
- Alignment of software systems with business processes; identification of out-of-date or little used systems; extent of social media and applications
- User access control mechanisms for critical systems and networks, methodology for access to wireless networks
- Current design of software development process, from in-house staff, commercial off-the-shelf (COTS) products, or service agents
- Current usage and design of web interfaces for internal and external users
- Current usage of e-mail; also methods of collaboration and/or file and report sharing
- Status of software system change management process and logs of changes; e.g., authorizations, testing for known exploits, separation of duties, process for submitting to production
- Data storage, e-mail, and records retention requirements; plans for compliance with electronic discovery requirements

Incident Response and Management

Identifying and tracking incidents that indicate unacceptable activities, accidental or deliberate, which may lead to service interruptions or full-blown crisis interruptions is an organization-wide shared responsibility. IS professionals must be able to communicate the indications and signs of incidents to the workforce members and to design a reporting and response function to receive the varieties of reports and assess the immediate and long-term consequences. In general, this is becoming the most difficult part of data protection, because new exploitation pathways inside the organizational network are increasing exponentially because of the hardware and software challenges detailed above. Also, the increase in fraudulent access and use of organizational information may require a broad range of evidence to identify and thwart the source of the fraud.

Many organizations separate the pathways for reporting problems and system interruptions among desktop support, network management, central mainframe/server support, and business continuity notification. An appropriately designed incident management environment can accept calls about various problems, including malware recognition, triggered log messages about system problems, and personal observations. The incident management structure is best designed and administered jointly by the IS, IT, and PS/S units, with appropriate input from executive leadership. A centrally functioning group can evaluate each call and determine the appropriate target group for the best response. Incidents may be simple enough for a quick solution, or serious enough to trigger a formal disaster or crisis response, but all incidents can be useful in tracking patterns of problems that may have led to attacker invasions and data loss if they are centrally collected and collated.

The IS professional can assess

- Current processes and practices of the existing incident management group, e.g., staffing, staff training, forensics capabilities, documentation, procedures, past response logs
- Current leadership support, including legal and compliance representation
- Current awareness of incident reporting and response in the general workforce
- Characterization of the threat sources pertinent to the industry position and nature of the organization's information resource
- Status of business continuity management planning, e.g., documentation, training, testing, and reports
- Status of plans for control center, pandemic emergencies, hazard response, evacuation, information recovery, temporary location, return to full service
- Contact information for partners, vendors, suppliers, community neighbors, etc.

Decide

During the "Orient" stage, IS professionals analyze and synthesize the information accumulated from the four primary areas of concern. In this stage of the OODA Loop, the synthesized information is crafted into plans for explicit action requiring some delegation to IS staff and other collaborators. Accumulating and interpreting the information is necessary but careful plans set the framework for the disciplined approach to managing IS and documenting threats and vulnerabilities for determining risk. All plans and processes must ultimately contribute to the two-fold goal of controlling access to and providing protection of the organizational data and information.

IS professionals must design plans and policy structures under the direction and oversight of the executive unit. It is conceivable that not all IS plans derived from synthesis of the previous stage will be permitted or affordable. Some plans may be crafted as strategic targets for the longer view or perhaps crafted to be implemented in stages, based on strategic budget considerations. IS professionals are nonetheless encouraged to develop the "big picture" scheme and be prepared to implement processes and plans in a sequence determined by importance and affordability.

Human Resource

As mentioned earlier, human activity is the greatest source of problems for data protection. Therefore, the cornerstone to a robust IS plan is the organizational policy for IS. Such a policy provides the foundation for the IS posture within the organization and sets the expectations for compliance for each workforce member. Though it can be crafted by the IS unit, it must be owned and signed by the executive who is the ultimate backstop for the organization. This becomes the legal justification for all other IS plans, policies, and process documentation. All other policy documents must be directly tied to business processes as a clear indication of business as the driving force behind information usage and protection. All standards documents must be aligned with policies, and procedures and guidelines must be tied to specific standards and policies.

IS professionals must decide to

- Craft policies, standards, and procedure documentation that represent the organization's intent involving its data and information resource. These include
  - Organizational security policy
  - Access control and authorization requirements and responsibilities
  - Confidentiality agreements as a condition of employment
  - IS responsibilities for different categories of users, e.g., executives, managers, general workforce
  - Equipment use and information use policies, defining practices not permitted and sanctions for violations
  - Characteristics of organization data protection and retention, based on regulatory requirements
  - Response to visitors and other non-workforce staff within the organization
- Create the organizational IS plan that documents the data protection perspective for the information resource. The plan
  - Frames the IS posture within the industry, regulatory, and community settings.
  - Defines the scope, responsibilities, and goals for IS within the organization.
  - Delimits collaboration and convergence relationships for specific contexts.
- Implement a workforce awareness and training program, ideally in conjunction with PS/S, IT and privacy units. These will address
  - Policies, standards, and plans
  - Regulatory settings and requirements
  - Personal responsibilities
  - Incident and emergency response

Technology Infrastructure

Decisions about the synthesized technology information result in IS process definitions and refinements. Where there are gaps in the existing controls and countermeasures, the IS unit will plan a mitigation strategy for resolving the problems. One easily controlled gap is data stored on portable laptops and other access devices. The solution can be simply to encrypt all data—hardware-based encryption systems are becoming more available and may afford a more complete protection than software encryption. The process can include mechanisms for encrypting authorized mobile storage devices as well. Finally, if expensive, powerful laptops are targets of theft regardless of the information stored, consider two solutions: acquire inexpensive, simple laptops that have minimal components and tools, and require that users carrying laptops away from the organization remove all organizational data onto a separate, encrypted mobile storage device, carried separately from the laptop.

Many large installations with combinations of mainframes and several mid-range servers become challenging to maintain and difficult to change. Hardware inflexibility becomes a bottleneck for infrastructure change and older devices become drags to innovative opportunities.

Newer environments are built to be more easily changed and modified, a measure of maneuverability and flexibility. It will not be possible or advisable for existing infrastructures to be "ripped and replaced"—active organizations will not be able to suspend systems and services for such a dramatic change. This means that major changes may have to be planned for minor implementation stages.

An extreme change for any environment could be the recommendation to outsource the servers and network infrastructure and administration. Such a decision must be based on a cost-benefit assessment, as well as a risk/security assessment. Recently, storage service organizations have begun to offer varieties of services from simply offsite backups to offsite active data, and even offsite server and storage of all organizational data. This would eliminate the capital expense of organizational equipment and possibly reduce the staffing requirements. "Cloud computing" is another buzzword that essentially addresses the same type of services, but with the possible addition of application and desktop environment support. In either case, organizational data would be stored and managed on remote servers, and all consideration must be given to the vulnerabilities from such an arrangement. Cost savings are important, but the service contract for availability, network protection, business continuity, incident management, performance, and termination of services must be carefully scrutinized.

If an IS professional is beginning with an existing environment, perhaps the most important efforts potentially with positive results will be in closing the most obvious and crucial gaps in controls and countermeasures. As all the changes are implemented, it will also be beneficial for IT groups to design architectures with audit and assessment in mind, beginning with documenting the current status and its limitations and the expectations and benefits of the recommended changes.

IS can assist the IT groups by helping to

- Design hardware and network infrastructure implementation that enhance data protection.
  - Simplified server architecture, reduced complexity of devices and systems.
  - Decoupled architecture, e.g., multitiered servers, and storage arrays to create indirect access to data and services.
  - Server and storage array component redundancy for high availability and service resilience.
  - Data redundancy to facilitate data recovery after major interruptions, e.g., mirroring, file shadowing at local and remote sites, virtual servers for reduced footprints.
  - Processes for protecting central print/fax/scanning devices from capture, periodic cleanup of stored data.
  - Desktop workstation simplification to tighten the weakest link for external malicious software, e.g., centrally controlled, uniform desktop design, "blade" workstations, inexpensive laptops, etc.
  - Hardware-based workstation/laptop encryption and automatic encryption of authorized mobile storage devices.
  - Network access devices and packet filters/inspectors for identifying and reducing unauthorized users and unwanted network traffic.
  - Tighten logical network perimeter to require all access to be scrutinized as remote.
  - Implement internal security management system that potentially allows central administration of workstation setup, inventory, collection of activity logs and malware incidents, etc.
- Assess change management practices to insure that controls and countermeasures are implemented and persist.

- Establish architecture to be more easily changed and audited, expect periodic assessments and reviews.
- Document production activities to ensure separation of responsibilities.
- Establish device retirement process, including data destruction.
- Institute audit processes for infrastructure changes.

Software Environment

The review of the software environment in the previous stage should highlight the problem areas. The challenge for IS is to prioritize the areas of concern and persuade the business units and software developers to consider improvements in the protection schemes. Arguably, the most important starting point will be the desktop workstation environment. Simplification of the services, central management, and removal of personal administrative accounts will reduce the opportunity for weakening the desktop protection schemes. Access control to the existing systems and services can be staged, but it will require careful planning to prevent service interruption. The software development processes are for the most part organizationally unique and will take time to understand the local specifics, although a few simple recommendations can resolve most web interface development vulnerabilities. The most difficult target will be the areas of social interactive systems, and mobile access and storage devices. This area is still a highly vulnerable moving target and will be a challenge for years to come. Potentially, the best avenue for protection might be shrinking the network perimeter so that all users are treated as remote users and all access from mobile devices is not easier inside the organization. We may not stem the flood of personal portable devices, but we can examine ways to shrink and tighten access to the core data systems and storage.

IS can recommend processes for the

- Workstation environment
  - Implement central administration of desktops, e.g., blade PCs, standard configurations with minimal flexibility.
  - Initiate security management system for central administration of software inventory.
  - Implement collaboration software to eliminate file transfer by e-mail.
  - Establish policies/standards for social media and systems within work environment, setting clear expectations for unacceptable activity.
- System access control
  - Unified authentication/authorization/assessment/provisioning and audit processes; ideally workflow-based, logged for review.
  - Consistent and responsive deactivation process for departed and/or reassigned users.
  - Consideration of role-based access control.
  - Encrypt centrally stored data and employ carefully authorized key distribution among devices and users.
- Software development, web interface development
  - Align systems to business processes, and develop deactivation processes for aged-out systems and services.
  - Implement secure web development, e.g., validating input.
  - Establish awareness of web and Internet threats, and maintain contact with appropriate resources for updates and impending problems.
  - Assess development plans for large systems and participate in design/development/test reviews.

- Implement software change management that mandates segregation of responsibilities for authorization, testing, approval, and transfer to production.
- Develop archival processes that attend to regulations for preservation and electronic discovery, e.g., data retention, data destruction, and data deduplication.
■ Mobile devices
- Establish policies for use within organizational settings; establish procedures for evaluating and authorizing/configuring devices to use for organizational data access.
- Establish policies and procedures for authorizing portable storage devices.

Incident Response and Management

Within the "Decide" stage, IS professionals plan for initiating or upgrading the incident response (IR) capability. After synthesizing the organizational posture for IS in general, the IR processes become the primary means for detecting problems and determining the pace and intensity of the response. Plans and processes are being developed for the human resource, the technology infrastructure, and the software environment. IR becomes the eyes and ears for the other workforce units and will be the main source of feedback to the other units and to IT and IS for continuing the OODA loop cycles. IS and IT will have the bulk of the expertise for understanding the threats and vulnerabilities of the environments; the PS/S unit will be able to define the threats from organizational hazards, and the IR team will likely include representation from all groups.

IS professionals assist the incident response activities by

■ Initiating response teams, providing appropriate training as necessary, and preparing workforce awareness programs and presentations.
■ Documenting the response plan with appropriate organizational review and seeking legal advice as necessary.
■ Creating and refining the threat model for the organization.
- Based on organizational information as target.
- Based on organizational application systems and network architecture devices.
- Characterize attack patterns observed within similar organizations.
■ Establishing network perimeter defense to detect exposures, document internal and external network traffic patterns, and thwart potential attacks.
■ Defining and announcing unacceptable network traffic within the organization perimeter and establishing workstation scanning for malware.
■ Documenting environmental and non-network threats.
■ Reviewing and rehearsing emergency response plans with IS, IT, and PS/S.
■ Initiating contact with partners, suppliers, community neighbors, and government-based emergency response programs and efforts.

Act

Where processes and plans are approved and announced, it is finally time to activate the IS practices. It is doubtful that all plans and reviews will be fully implemented, but as much as organizational approval will permit can be initiated. Many of the activities will be long processes, such as software development or hardware/software change management, and many will occur on periodic cycles, during the business calendar. Ideally, the new and revised activities will be preceded by an awareness program or presentation to ensure that the workforce population are not only informed, but are enabled to be part of the solution processes. Initiation of the new activities requires executive approval, but the success of an IS program is based on the acceptance and participation of the human resource.

Hardware and software technology will not cease changing, but it helps to have a program of initiating change that minimizes service disruptions and demonstrates benefits to all levels of the organization. Changes within the workstation environment may be the most challenging to implement and gain acceptance, especially if the changes result in loss of personal flexibility with the desktop environment. This mandates clear training and awareness to keep users abreast and involved, and to provide feedback on the change process itself and the results. It will be difficult to demonstrate benefits, e.g., fewer attacks, fewer malware incidents, etc., without appropriate statistics and comparisons with baselines. Many organizations have top-down management that implements decisions with little fanfare and less opportunity for feedback, but success at the point of information gathering, use, and dissemination means that changes must be announced, demonstrated with pilots, and communicated down the hallways, and the expected benefits must be documented. IS professionals are often evangelists of proper care and feeding of the information resource.

For the IR team, this stage of the cycle represents their busiest time because it will be inevitable that even stable environments will suffer service interruptions, and it may not take too many for the IR team to prove its worth, or (hopefully not) demonstrate its inadequacy. As with all else, planning and preparation are key to this perspective. Success breeds success, and as incidents are thwarted before causing serious problems, the value of the IR team and its abilities will be celebrated. It is always hoped that no incident develops into a full-blown crisis, but many external and environmental threats can often not be avoided. A plan without an incident is a fortunate circumstance; an incident without a plan is a failure.

Observe

This stage in the OODA loop provides the opportunity for the IS professional to reflect on the feedback of the earlier stages, the processes and plans designed and implemented. New information from external and internal sources may affect how the plans and processes are refined and/or modified for the next cycle. Feedback from the IR team provides vital clues to the success or failure (or somewhere in between) of the overall changes in the protection schemes. Collaboration and convergence with other organizational units brings context for specific activities, such as summarizing threats and vulnerabilities for inclusion in periodic risk analysis reports. The sharing and discussion of logs and reports with the IT, PS/S and privacy units ensures that regulatory compliance is met. This time of observation also allows workforce staff feedback on the success of the awareness and training, and the necessary disruption of the status quo within the desktop workspace. Though observation is constant within the continuously changing organizational environment, it will always be appropriate to take time deliberately to observe the aftereffects of major efforts or after major business cycles. Each of the major plans addressing information protection—security plan, incident response plan, change management plans, business continuity plans—requires updates based on recent implementations or testing.

Plans and procedures are designed to be changeable, and the opportunity for observation allows time to reflect and summarize the complete cycle. The dual foundation of an IS program is to *provide protection of* and *control access to* organizational information. Such an effort requires IS professionals with experience and training to implement the discipline of an IS program:

- Orientation brings the observations into the existing setting and kicks off the review and assessment processes, whether they are staged on a calendar basis or spontaneous as incidents indicating vulnerabilities arise. Advances in technology will affect strategic planning; changes in staffing resources will affect tactical planning. In most cases the organization will change within industry settings and not make major cultural changes, barring acquisition and merger issues. It takes experience and discipline to analyze how the input from the various sources affect the overall security posture and plans and synthesize the information into the existing plans.

- From the orientation on the recent observations, the IS unit makes decisions about changes in processes or structures, and reworks plans and process statements appropriately. Major decisions will require appropriate review and approval, but as the IS unit achieves success, opportunities to make selected decisions may increase.

- Action requires decisiveness and speed regarding incidents that threaten the integrity of the information protection resources. The IR team will need to have the technical capability and authorization to respond. Other actions based on tactical and strategic decisions will be implemented on a different timetable.

About the Author

James C. Murphy, CISSP-ISSMP, GSEC, CISA, CISM, is the information security architect for OMMISS, with more than 30 years of experience, predominantly in healthcare IT. Jim plans and designs enterprise-wide information security for major development projects, including the claims processing system for Medicaid and related plans, and the State Health Information Network. For the projects, he documents information security and technical architecture requirements and reviews security throughout project design and development: regulatory compliance, access control, data and network protection, business continuity, operational security, process documentation, and project audit. Jim has written, taught, and spoken on information security management, service continuity, security auditing, and security certification training to diverse audiences.

Notes

1. The IT Governance Institute (http://www.itgi.org) has expanded the concept to include managing the resources of information technology.
2. The stories are too many to list—or avoid! See Gorman, 2010, and Kumar and Helderman, 2009. Also see the Privacy Rights website for a chronology of recent data breaches: http://www.privacyrights.org/ar/ChronDataBreaches.htm
3. See BreachShield's statistics on a 2009 study: http://www.breachshield.com/data-security-breach-statistics.html
4. This is the basic principle behind the ValIT program of the Information System Audit and Control Association (ISACA): http://www.itgi.org/Template.cfm?Section=Val_IT3&Template=/TaggedPage/TaggedPageDisplay.cfm&TPLID=80&ContentID=51867.
5. As identified in the author's recent paper (Murphy, 2009).
6. In its broadest sense, IT infrastructure includes the servers, network, desktop, and portable devices, and the comprehensive arrangement or architecture that supports organizational information management, as well as the software that enables the capture, storage, manipulation, presentation, and sharing of the organizational data and information.
7. Table 16.1 is not intended to be an exhaustive list nor representative of all Internet risk resources.

8. See Crowell et al., 2007; also many articles available from web searches.
9. Carr, 2003, 2004. In his book, Carr addresses IT spending in Chapter 6, where he states: "but at the moment the greatest [IT management risk] of them all is overspending."
10. Saner, 2005. Saner's paper addresses inconsistencies in the characterization of risk management and related concepts, not actually risk itself. His quote is nonetheless applicable to this discussion.
11. Neumann, 1995, Glossary, p. 348. Obviously, I resisted the temptation to stop this article at this point!
12. de Moivre, 1711. de Moivre's work in using samples to estimate the total population established the concepts of the normal distribution (bell curve) and the dispersion around the mean (standard deviation).
13. There are certainly many glossaries—try entering "define:Risk" in a Google search.
14. Apologies, I couldn't resist!
15. Bernstein, 1996, chapters 12, 13. Also, Holton, 2004, and Kloman, 1999.
16. Bernstein, 1996, chapter 14, p. 232.
17. See examples from the Department of Homeland Security: http://www.homelandsecuritydialogue.org/dialogue2/risk-assessment/ideas/use-the-universal-risk-formula.
18. Several sources, e.g., Stoneburner et al. (NIST SP 800-30).
19. Several sources—see DHS link, note 17 above.
20. See COBIT 4.1. 2007. IT Governance Institute, glossary, p. 193: http://www.isaca.org/Template.cfm?Section=COBIT6&Template=/TaggedPage/TaggedPageDisplay.cfm&TPLID=55&ContentID=7981.
21. Several sources, e.g., Jones, 2005.
22. See Hillson, 2008: http://www.Risk-doctor.com/, also Cohen, 2003.
23. See The Origin of S.W.O.T.: http://www.marketingteacher.com/SWOT/history_of_swot.htm and the Use of SWOT: http://www.netmba.com/strategy/swot/.
24. E.g., from Hillson, 2008; Cohen, 2003.
25. See SANS Internet Storm Center http://isc.sans.org/, Symantec Threat Report: http://www.symantec.com/business/theme.jsp?themeid=threatreport.
26. See Health IT plans and documentation: http://healthit.hhs.gov/portal/server.pt.
27. See Claburn, 2007, O'Sullivan, 2006, Parker, 2006.
28. See http://www.aviation-history.com/airmen/boyd.htm.
29. See http://www.ausairpower.net/APA-Boyd-Papers.html.
30. See http://hitechanswers.net/.
31. See http://www.ediscoverylaw.com/.
32. Organization for the Advancement of Structured Information Standards (OASIS): http://www.oasis-open.org/home/index.php.
33. See http://www.oasis-open.org/committees/tc_home.php?wg_abbrev=xacml.
34. The Open Web Application Security Project (OWASP): http://www.owasp.org/index.php/Main_Page.
35. Help Net Security: http://www.net-security.org/.
36. Common Vulnerabilities and Exposures (CVE): http://cve.mitre.org/, Common Weakness Enumeration (CWE): http://cwe.mitre.org/.

References

American National Standard for Information Technology. (2004). Role based access control. ANSI® INCITS 359-2004. Copyright © 2004 by Information Technology Industry Council (ITI).

Bernstein, P. L. (1998). *Against the Gods: The Remarkable Story of Risk*. John Wiley & Sons, USA.

Boyd, J. R. (1996). The essence of winning and losing. Air Power Australia, http://www.ausairpower.net/APA-Boyd-Papers.html.

Carr, N. G. (2003). IT doesn't matter. Harvard Business Review, Harvard Business School Press.

Carr, N. G. (2004). *Does IT Matter? Information Technology and the Corrosion of Competitive Advantage.* Harvard Business School Press.

Claburn, T. (2007). Sarbanes-Oxley costs drive companies away from being public. *InformationWeek*, August 2, 09:00 AM: http://www.informationweek.com/news/global-cio/showArticle.jhtml?articleID=201202504.

Cohen, F. (2003). Risk management: Concepts and frameworks, version: 1.0. *In Depth Research Report*, Burton Group.

Crowell, W. P., DeRodeff, C., Dunkel, D., & Cole, E. (2007). *Physical and Logical Security Convergence.* Syngress Publishing Co., Elsevier Science.

de Moivre, A. (1711). *De Mensura Sortis* (On the Measurement of Lots). – Cited in Bernstein, 1998, p. 126.

Ferris, N. (2007). Foreign hackers seek to steal Americans' health records, *Government Health IT*, http://www.govhealthit.com/online/news/350177-1.html.

Gorman, S. (2010). Broad new hacking attack detected. *Wall Street Journal*, 02/18/2010: http://online.wsj.com/article/SB10001424052748704398804575071103834150536.html.

Hillson, D. (2008). Risk management, Maslow and memetics. Proceedings of the PMI Global Congress 2008 EMEA, Malta.

Hillson, D. (ed). (2007). *The Risk Management Universe — A Guided Tour*, BSI, London.

Hillson, D. (ed). (2006). When is a risk not a risk? *Project Management Practice* 1, p. 6–7.

Hillson, D. (ed). (2002). What is risk? Towards a common definition. *InfoRM*. Institute of Risk Management, April, p. 11–12.

Holton, G. A. (2004). Defining risk. *Financial Analysts J*. v.60, 6. CFA Institute.

Jones, J. (2005). *An Introduction to Factor Analysis of Information Risk (FAIR).* Risk Management Insight.

Kloman, H. F. (1999). Milestones: 1900 to 1999. *Risk Management Reports*, v.26, 12. Seawrack Press, Inc.

Kovacich, G. L. (2003). *The Information Systems Security Officer's Guide.* Elsevier Press, USA.

Krebs, B. (2008). Hundreds of stolen data dumps found. *Washington Post*, December 18, 2008: http://voices.washingtonpost.com/securityfix/2008/12/hundreds_of_stolen_data_dumps.html.

Kumar, A., & Helderman, R. S. (2009). Va. pays dearly for computer troubles. *Washington Post*, 10/13/2009: http://www.washingtonpost.com/wp-dyn/content/article/2009/10/13/AR2009101303044.html.

McManus, R. (2007). Hacking 2.0: Today's hackers target web, for money. *ReadWriteWeb* (2007), http://www.readwriteweb.com/archives/hacking_20.php.

Murphy, J. C. (2009). No one is listening! *ISSA Journal*, May, 2009.

Neumann, P. G. (1995). *Computer-Related Risks.* ACM Press, NY.

O'Sullivan, K. (2006). The case for clarity. *CFO Magazine*, September 1, 2006: http://www.cfo.com/article.cfm/7851741?f=related.

Parker, D. B. (2006). Making the case for replacing risk-based security, *ISSA Journal*, May, 2006. Technical Enterprises, Inc.

Radcliff, D. (2007). The surprising security threat: Your printers. *Computerworld*, January 15, 2007: http://www.computerworld.com/s/article/277746/Smart_Printers_Scary_Printers.

Richards, C. (2004). *Certain to Win.* Xlibris Corporation.

Saner, M. (2005). Information brief on international risk management standards. Institute On Governance, Ottawa, Ontario, Canada.

Schechtman, G. M. (1996). Manipulating the OODA loop: The overlooked role of information resource management in information warfare. Master's Thesis, Air Force Institute of Technology.

Stoneburner, G., Goguen, A., & Feringa, A. (2002). *Risk Management Guide for Information Technology Systems.* NIST Special Publication 800-30.

Chapter 17

Improving Enterprise Security through Predictive Analysis

Chris Hare

On any given day an information security manager reviews information from a multitude of detection systems: intrusion detection sensors, virus infections, trouble tickets, investigations, and web, application, and network scanners. All of this information provides value on its own. But what if the information viewed in a holistic and cohesive fashion could provide additional information including suggesting possible weak areas and where your next attack might be focused?

The Traditional Security Assessment

Many audit and security publications describe audit and assessment techniques involving the identification and assessment of control objectives, requirements and methods for testing, and interpreting the results. Traditional security assessments review and determine the effectiveness of security controls at a given point in time. Assessments and audits are generally time consuming and resource intensive. Teams of specialists are assigned to design, implement, and review security solutions using documented and accepted security standards.

Assessments typically involve requirements from

- The Software Capability Maturity Model
- ISO 27001 and 27002
- OSSTM
- CoBIT
- Technology-specific audit programs
- The reviewer's individual knowledge and experience

These assessments are generally effective at identifying the concerns and focus areas for corrective action. These models and methods, however, only provide a view of the object under review at a given point in time. They do not allow the security professional to maintain an ongoing view of their systems or identify potential risk areas as new vulnerabilities and threats emerge.

Enhanced assessment processes can include the following process elements:

1. Determine the specific function, application, component, or element to be assessed.
2. Review all available documentation describing the desired or intended operation of the item being assessed.
3. Determine the potential threats or risk to the application using the STRIDE model.
4. From the threat and risks, review the required controls to address the risks and threats.
5. Determine methods to assess each of the controls.
6. Establish a sample size, should there be a considerable number of items to assess.
7. Perform the tests identified in step 5.
8. Review and interpret the results. Clearly document the test procedures, methodologies, and results.
9. If there is any uncertainty regarding the test results for the sample assessed, perform additional tests until the uncertainty is removed.
10. Assemble the results and report on the current state of the evaluated controls.

Predictive vulnerability analysis provides an ongoing view of the systems and devices connected to the network based upon data collected through various techniques allowing the security professional to identify possible areas of concern as new threats and vulnerabilities emerge. For example, by maintaining device and application inventories, new vulnerabilities and requirements for exploiting those vulnerabilities can be compared with the collected data to identify specific systems and applications that may be at risk. This knowledge allows the security professional to initially focus targeted analysis on those areas. In doing so, the security organization can mitigate potential problem areas which may be exploited by an attacker.

Predictive vulnerability analysis does not remove the need for security assessments. Rather, it supports the focused assessment and provides current information regarding the system, application, and environment the focused assessment requires. This current database of information can be used by internal or external audit and the enterprise security organization to maintain current risk mitigation plans, which may include recommended system or application upgrades or other protections such as network design considerations and network security appliances.

The Nature of Predictive Vulnerability Analysis

Computer security in most corporations combines policy development, technology selection, implementation, awareness, compliance, and training. Policy states senior management's expectations of the employees. Despite implementation of policy controls, many corporations still experience a high rate of computer security incidents including theft of resources, loss of intellectual property, viruses and other malware,* and system vulnerabilities due to application and operating system software weaknesses.

Figure 17.1 shows attack type data from the 2003 Computer Security Institute/FBI Annual Security Study. For example, the number of virus attacks in 2003 has decreased to 254 from 318

---

* Malware is used in this document to mean any form of malicious software including viruses, worms, Ttrojan horses, and backdoor and remote control programs.

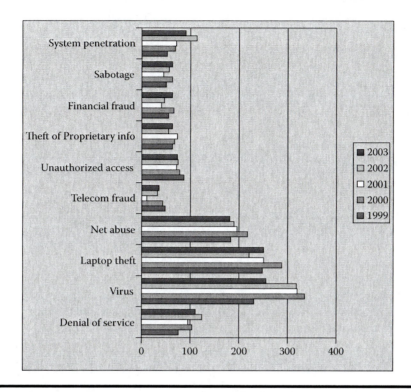

Figure 17.1   CSI/FBI data on types of attack. (Data from 2003 Computer Security Institute CSI/ FBI Annual Security Survey.)

in 2002. This is likely due to better and more prevalent antivirus detection software and more diligent employees.

Despite the reported decrease, the number of viruses in "the wild" continues to increase at an alarming rate. While the number of events may be decreasing in some categories, the financial impact resulting from an attack or compromise is significant.

To effectively manage the wide range of attack types and methods, corporations must deploy analysis and detection tools to identify issues and correct them. The common types of analysis tools include:

- Network-based intrusion detection systems such as ISS, Network Flight Recorder, Snort
- Host-based intrusion detection systems
- Network vulnerability analysis tools including Nessus, ISS, Retina
- Database vulnerability and application scanners
- Web application analysis tools such as WebInspect and AppScan
- Antivirus tools
- Trouble ticketing systems
- Log file analysis and event correlation tools

Most of this technology is passive or active only in a short-term sense. For example, conducting a system or network vulnerability analysis requires corrective action in a short time frame or the value of the analysis decreases. Detection systems require further analysis and review of the collected data to verify the existence of a problem. Finally, corrective action is required to alleviate the issues identified by the tools.

However, these tools on their own do not provide remediation or correction of the vulnerability. Nor do they offer any predictive capability to determine if a system could be affected by a newly discovered vulnerability without the release of "signatures" or checks from the vendor and additional scanning of the organization's systems.

Scanning systems on their own can be a time-consuming process, depending upon a number of factors, including:

- The size of the organization
- The number of systems
- The geographical location of the systems
- The network capacity between the scanner and the target system
- The system type

If an organization has a global network and has implemented good filtering and other security measures, it can take weeks for a reasonably large sample to be obtained. In a recent analysis of 148 systems from an Internet-based scanner, it was found to take 46 hours to complete the analysis, or 19 minutes per system on average.*

The process of scanning systems for a new weakness can consequently take an unreasonable amount of time. The answer, therefore, lies in predictive vulnerability analysis.

Predictive vulnerability analysis uses an approach based upon knowledge of a given system and the specific exploit or vulnerability. Table 17.1 lists the specific knowledge requirements of a given system.

When a new vulnerability is made public, a security analyst can review the known information about the specific vulnerability or exploit and then compare it with the known system profiles. The information shown in Table 17.1 must also be available for the known weakness or vulnerability to determine if a system may be susceptible.

Working from the set of known systems, and the set of elements known about the vulnerability, the security analyst can join the two sets together. Wherever there is a commonality between the two sets, there is a potentially vulnerable system.

Vulnerability information comes from many different sources including:

- The Computer Emergency Response Team at Carnegie Mellon University (CM-CERT/CC)
- National Infrastructure Protection Center (NIPC)
- National Institute of Standards and Technology (NIST)
- The BugTraq mailing list at SecurityFocus.com
- The Common Vulnerabilities and Exposures dictionary†

An example is beneficial to illustrating the concept of predictive vulnerability analysis. Consider the latest remote procedure call exploit against Microsoft operating systems, as reported in CERT Advisory CA-2003-19. The text of the advisory says

---

* The actual scanning time per system is difficult to determine unless scanning one system. Because most network-based scanners are multithreaded, many systems are scanned at once. For example, in the test of the 148 systems, Nessus was used as the vulnerability scanner, which processes 32 systems at a time.
† The CVE dictionary is located at http://cve.mitre.org. The goal of CVE is to "make it easier to share data across separate vulnerability databases and security tools," as stated on the CVE website. It is not a database of vulnerabilities, but rather a dictionary to establish common language across the various databases.

Table 17.1 Required System Knowledge

Element	Description
Hardware platform	Some vulnerabilities are based upon an application or operating system running on a specific type of hardware. Other types are not vulnerable.
Operating system	Some vulnerabilities affect a class of operating system implementation regardless of the version.
Operating system version	Some vulnerabilities are specific to a given operating system version.
Application software	Systems are used to run applications. The specific applications operating on a system can expose other vulnerabilities.
Application software version	Like operating system software, some vulnerabilities are applicable only to a specific version of application software.
Location of the system	Is the system is located within the corporate network or on the Internet.
Available network services	How it is possible to connect to the system over the network.
Filters or security controls	Are there additional security controls used to protect the system?

"Systems Affected
Microsoft Windows NT 4.0
Microsoft Windows NT 4.0 Terminal Services Edition
Microsoft Windows 2000
Microsoft Windows XP
Microsoft Windows Server 2003
…
Known exploits target TCP port 135 and create a privileged backdoor command shell on successfully compromised hosts. Some versions of the exploit use TCP port 4444 for the backdoor, and other versions use a TCP port number specified by the intruder at run-time."

Given the information from the CERT advisory,* a security analyst could establish a query within the predictive model to determine what systems were potentially at risk. Arguably, this is not the best example, since most Microsoft Windows operating system platforms were vulnerable. However, the systems in the environment may have the latest patches already applied, making them

---

* The information in the CERT advisory is substantially more complex and thorough, including references to other CERT Vulnerability Notes and Microsoft Knowledgebase articles. The content has been abbreviated here.

invulnerable to this specific attack. Additionally, since systems visible to the Internet may be a more accessible target, security analysts can refine their search to only those specific systems. The result is a list of systems which are potentially vulnerable to an exploit and which may require attention. If the enterprise must conduct a vulnerability assessment of the systems, an exploit may have already occurred, costing the enterprise in financial, productivity, and potentially reputation losses.

While many security professionals conduct cursory assessment of their environment based upon what they know of the configuration, the real solution and implementation of predictive vulnerability assessment is done using automated tools to collect and manage the large amounts of data an enterprise will accumulate.

Designing the Solution

A predictive vulnerability assessment solution must consider all elements of the enterprise network:

- Systems on the corporate network and protected by network security tools
- Systems on the protected Internet segment and protected by network security tools
- Research and development systems
- Mission-critical application systems
- Systems on the Internet that are not protected by network security tools

Each of the systems in the previous list have their own specific and unique issues from a vulnerability perspective.

Most organizations implement specific network security controls to mitigate the risks associated with connecting their enterprise network to the Internet. Such controls include router filters, firewalls, installation of demilitarized zone (DMZ) networks, service networks, and other appliances to perform protocol and packet analysis and filtering. The end result is to minimize the number of possible attack vectors an intruder has to gain access to the organization's systems, network, and data.

Senior management of many organizations also consider themselves "protected" from attack once these countermeasures are in place. However, security management strategies such as "defense-in-depth" show the security and maintenance of the end node—the system—is an important element to overall network security.

Manual Predictive Analysis

Security professionals around the work perform manual predictive analysis on a daily basis without realizing it. When a report is received from a reporting agency such as NIPC or CERT™, the security analyst reviews the report and determines what course of action must be taken to minimize the threat of the vulnerability. However, the security analyst must deal in generalities and overall actions for the enterprise. This is because the security analyst cannot know the intricacies of each machine, their patch level, applications that are running on the system, or any additional controls for that system mitigating the vulnerability. The manual approach essentially follows the process illustrated in Figure 17.2.

Using this manual process, the security analyst can only deal in generalities unless the process is repeated for each machine and application instance in the enterprise. Consequently, the security analyst is forced to make broad statements including "patch every system," "shoot off that portion of the network," and "implement these filters to block that traffic," without knowing if the

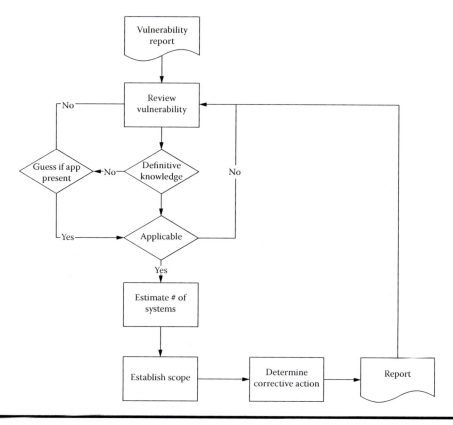

Figure 17.2   Manual analysis process.

actions are warranted. In many cases, the end result of an automated predictive analysis system may indeed result in those same directives in the case of a widespread vulnerability. However, in other situations the automated system may be able to identify specific problem areas due to reliance upon existing information and implemented security controls.

Automated Predictive Analysis

On the other hand, automated predictive analysis is possible and highly efficient. There is a vast amount of data to be collected and collated, as discussed in Chapter 3, however it is possible for the security analyst in the end to quickly make recommendations about the far-reaching actions relevant to the entire enterprise as well as identifying those specific systems which may be vulnerable in other instances.

The heart of an automated assessment and predictive analysis process will be data collection. Data is required from a variety of sources including system assessment tools, and both system and network databases to provide information required in the predictive analysis process.

The objectives for an automated predictive analysis process are:

■ The ability to perform consistent and repeatable assessments of all network devices, regardless of where they are located and their function.
■ Track the location of analyzed systems.

- Record specific controls in place at various locations in the network (i.e., firewalls, protocol and packet filtering).
- Establish automated vulnerability assessment tools and a data transfer method to the assessment engine.
- Record the specific vulnerability tests applied.
- Collect information about the systems including operating systems and applications installed.
- Identify the purpose of the systems and their criticality to the business.
- Initiate tickets for cleanup and remediation of the vulnerabilities (if desired).
- Provide reporting on vulnerability assessment results.
- Provide trend reports.

Achieving these goals is critical to reducing the monthly man-hours in analysis and tracking of the vulnerability. The Figure 17.3 elements are required to achieve these objectives.

The process is largely the same, however it involves much more automated system involvement and data processing than the manual process. The automated process also allows for faster data retrieval, analysis, and decision making than use of the normal manual process.

The functional implementation is based upon data sources from a variety of sources. For some enterprises, these data elements will be already in place through system databases. Other organizations will not have the required data in place and will need to develop a source of this data. This chapter presents a proposed architecture and discusses each element in the architecture, and the data and transport requirements regarding how the system works.

The system analysis of existing vulnerabilities to establish system profiles and identify changes in the environment is done using a vulnerability assessment tool. Exactly which tool or tools the enterprise uses is an enterprise decision. Obviously, the enterprise will also have to develop the custom components to interface their data source into the predictive analysis database. A possible architecture is illustrated in Figure 17.4.

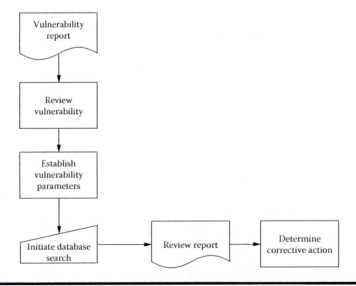

Figure 17.3 Automated analysis process.

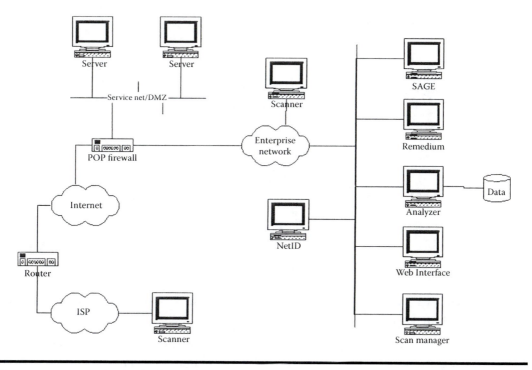

Figure 17.4 Sample physical architecture.

The components illustrated in Figure 17.4 include:

- Network, host and application vulnerability scanners
- Scan manager
- Analyzer
- Web interface
- Interface to trouble ticketing system (if desired)
- Interface from system and application inventory database
- Interface from network inventory database (if desired)

Each element in the architecture is discussed in detail.

Scan Manager

The scan manager provides most of the back-end processing and is capable of managing multiple vulnerability scanners and data collection points. Scans are queued from the scan manager and the jobs are dispersed across the available scanners as configured in the scan manager control files. Scans can be configured to run on a periodic basis, with additional capability providing ad hoc scanning and analysis for specific targeted system. Once the scan is completed, the scan manager accepts the data, processes the jobs to complete the scan, and performs whatever processing is required on the incoming data to normalize to the database format. Finally, the scan manager uploads the data into the database where it is analyzed (Figure 17.5).

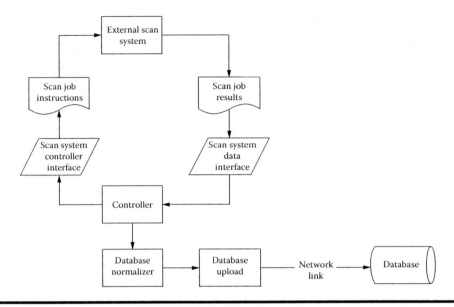

Figure 17.5   Scan manager.

The scan manager is a software controller that accepts scan requests, spools them to the various scanners, monitors the devices, and accepts the resulting output. The scan manager also takes the scan output, normalizes it to the database format, and uploads the data to the database.

Network, Host, and Application Vulnerability Scanners

Predictive vulnerability analysis requires two things: knowledge of the current environment and knowledge of the vulnerability. Since most security teams perform periodic network vulnerability assessments using vulnerability scanners, it is important to include this data in the analysis.

Much of the challenge with the scanner technology is getting the data from the scanner into a machine-readable format. The ability to do this is dependent upon the scanner involved. Ideally, the scanning engine sends its data back to the scan manager for further processing (Figure 17.6).

The role of the scanner is to execute the scan job that has been sent. The scanner requires

- A list of IP addresses to scan
- The policy to use for scanning those systems
- The report format

The scanning software is started using a command line and executes until completion. The scan results are then transferred back to the scan manager for processing.

Analyzer

As scan data is received by the scan manager, the data is uploaded into the database and a command is passed to the analyzer engine to initiate analysis of the incoming data. The actions taken by the analyzer are configurable. These actions include:

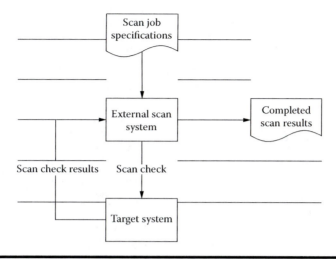

Figure 17.6 External scan system.

- If this is a new vulnerability for the given host, classify it as new and open a trouble ticket for processing.
- If this is an uncorrected vulnerability and a ticket is already open, raise the severity level on the ticket.
- Generate system-specific, region-specific, risk-specific, and trending reports.

The versatility of the analyzer and the variety of data collected allows the number and variety of analysis questions to improve over time (Figure 17.7).

The analyzer is started after the new data is loaded into the database by the scan manager. Using the provided parameters, the newly imported data is analyzed using the configured rule sets. The rules define the actions to be taken based upon the incoming data. For example, if a scanned system has a new vulnerability that has never been ticketed for this system before, the corresponding system data is pulled out of the server application inventory (if it is a server) and the

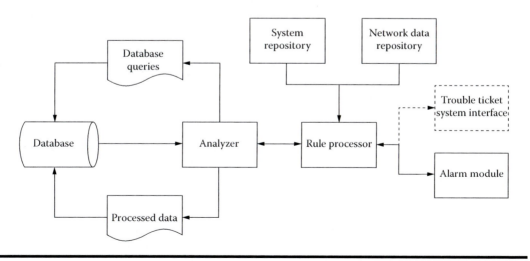

Figure 17.7 Analyzer.

relevant subnet information is pulled from the network inventory database. The data is then used to create a trouble ticket within the enterprise help desk system for remediation. If the issue already has an open ticket, the ticket severity is increased one level.

Tracking on an issue-by-issue rather than purely a system-by-system basis means a greater level of granularity can be achieved on trending and identification of consistent issues within the environment.

Predictive Analysis Engine

The analyzer is also the intelligence that is used to perform the predictive analysis. The web interface discussed later is the primary interface to the analysis engine. The user provides the details of the vulnerability to be compared against the database. The result is a list of potentially affected systems that should be analyzed by the security team (Figure 17.8).

The predictive process involves taking specific information from a new vulnerability and entering it into a query engine, which then works through the collected data to identify systems that may be affected by the vulnerability or have a specific service enabled.

If necessary, targeted scanning could be performed against the systems identified by the database to determine if the issue is positive. Additionally, immediate remediation can be activated on those identified systems while additional queries are made or the environment scanned, looking for new information.

Regardless, the environment must be scanned often and scanned regularly to keep the current data fresh and of value to the decision making, vulnerability remediation, and incident response processes.

Database

Integral to the analyzer is a high-speed SQL database used to store the scanned and analyzed data. The database is required to handle the massive quantity of data forecasted to be collected and for quick retrieval of that data when required for analysis purposes.

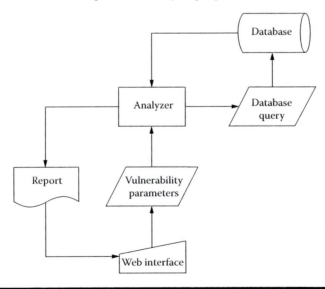

Figure 17.8 Predictive analysis engine.

Web Interface

Like any application, there has to be an interface. In this case, interaction with the user will be through a web interface. The user will submit scan requests through the web and review analysis.

The web interface must be capable of the following tasks:

- Authenticating the user and implementing restrictions on available commands, requests, and retrieved output.
- Report on vulnerabilities identified for a given system.
- Report on ticket status, driven from Remedium.
- Trend reports for a given system or POP.
- Identify potential affected systems when a new vulnerability is announced, based upon past scan data and the specifics of the vulnerability.
- Graphically display POP vulnerability status.
- Repeat offenders for a given system and vulnerability.

The components built to support the web interface can also be used to provide additional information to the CSIRT teams, including information on most available ports, etc.

Interface to Trouble Ticketing System

Remedium is a trouble ticket system based upon the remedy action request system. Performing the scan is the easy part of the work to be done. The harder part is analyzing the data, which can be somewhat automated with the analyzer, and then getting the issues corrected. As the analyzer processes the report, it issues a trouble ticket through Remedium for each item to be corrected.

Interface from System and Application Inventory Database

The analyzer connects with the SAGE database to get information about the machine. This information can assist in routing tickets because it identifies the support level of the system and who supports it.

Interface from Network Inventory Database

Likewise, the NetID network database can also provide information on the physical location of the system. This can be useful for identifying a region that may have a higher level of occurrence for a given configuration or item identified in the scan.

Entire Logical Architecture

The entire logical architecture is illustrated in Figure 17.9.

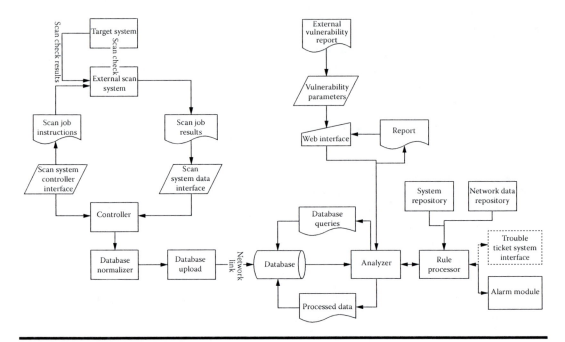

Figure 17.9   Logical architecture view.

Summary

The goal of predictive vulnerability analysis is to help the organization quickly determine the scope of their risk footprint when a new vulnerability is announced. By taking the collected inventory data and the requirements to determine if a machine may be vulnerable, the organization can quickly find out where their potentially affected systems are. Once known, the security teams can make decisions regarding which systems will be patched first, etc., based upon the risk to organization, based upon the inventory data, systems location in the network, and the criticality of the system to the business.

About the Author

Chris Hare, CISSP, CISA, CISM, has over 23 years in the computing industry and is the coauthor of New Riders Publishing's *Inside Unix, Internet Firewalls and Network Security, Building an Internet Server with Linux,* and *The Internet Security Professional Reference.* His book credits also include the *General Linux II Examination Guide* and the *Official CISSP Study Guide.* Chris holds a master of arts degree in adult education from Northwestern State University of Louisiana and a bachelor of arts and science degree in information systems from Dallas Baptist University.

Employment Policies and Practices

Chapter 18

Security Outsourcing

Sandy Bacik

As enterprise risks and threats change almost daily, it is critical for the enterprise to achieve a reliable security program. An investment in security outsourcing needs to be considered in the context of managing business risk. As we know, risks can be accepted, mitigated, avoided, or transferred. Outsourcing occurs when an enterprise secures/purchases products and/or services from a third party, as opposed to producing them in-house. Security outsourcing, whether it is long or short term, has pros and cons; depending on how and what the enterprise has security outsourced, it can turn out to be good or bad. One thing to remember with security outsourcing is that cost is only a short-term leverage for security outsourcing, because everyone moves toward limiting costs. Some of the benefits that will be discussed are that security outsourcing can focus attention on critical issues, more-predictable costs, and, potentially, greater flexibility and adaptability for your security services. Selecting a security outsourcer can combine advanced technology with expert human analysis, enabling an enterprise to cost-effectively strengthen its security posture, and provide a level of technology and expertise that ensures rapid response to real threats. While a cost decision may make it easy to select a security outsourcer, any notion that security is a matter of simply protecting the network perimeter is hopelessly out of date. Enterprises now recognize the importance of "defense in depth," which involves a comprehensive approach to securing critical assets, networks, and information systems while implementing robust defenses against hackers, viruses, and other online threats.

As the enterprise begins to consider security outsourcing, the enterprise needs to understand their environment, the vital assets, and why there is a need to protect the assets. The enterprise needs to establish a security direction before being able to consider outsourcing any of their security services. Prior to selecting what security services to outsource or selecting a security outsourcing firm, the enterprise must consider the following:

- What is the enterprise mission and how does that fit into a security program?
- What are the vital assets and information within the enterprise?
- Where are the vital assets located and who has access to them?
- What are the vital asset interfaces with other enterprise staff, systems, and applications?
- What are the priorities of the organization?

- How does securing resources fit into the enterprise?
- What security services are currently being performed within the enterprise?
- What security services would the enterprise like to have included in the security program?
- What are the business reasons for outsourcing security?

And in reviewing the above questions, it is similar to setting up a security program based on evaluating the existing risk. As the enterprise considers security outsourcing, the range of security services to reduce costs and gain access to skilled staff whose full-time job is security can make an enterprise security program more efficient and effective. Some security services to consider can include:

- Network boundary protection, including managed services for firewalls, intrusion detection systems (IDSs), and virtual private networks (VPNs)
- Security monitoring
- Incident management, including emergency response and forensic analysis
- Vulnerability assessment and penetration testing
- Security control development, maintenance, and testing
- Antivirus and content filtering services
- Information security risk assessments and, potentially, management
- Data archiving and restoration
- On-site consulting for trending, recommendations for improvement or training

Pros/Benefits of Security Outsourcing

Security outsourcing can have many benefits for the enterprise. Some of these benefits include the following:

- Security outsourcing your non-core security activities will give the enterprise more time to concentrate on core security business processes.
- With security outsourcing the enterprise can experience increased efficiency and productivity in non-core security business processes.
- Security outsourcing can help you streamline your security operations.
- Security outsourcing can make the enterprise more flexible to change.
- The enterprise can, if organized, experience an increased set of security controls.
- The enterprise might be able to save on investing in the latest technology, software, and infrastructure as the security outsourcing partner would be investing in these.
- Security outsourcing can give the enterprise assurance that security services are being carried out efficiently, proficiently, and within a fast turnaround time.
- Security outsourcer can cater to the new and challenging demands of the enterprise.
- Security outsourcing might be able to give the enterprise a competitive advantage, because of the increased security service productivity.

There are definitely many advantages to selecting a security outsourcing providers. On the other hand…

Cons of Security Outsourcing

While the pros may outweigh the cons for security outsourcing, the cons definitely need to be considered and measured against the enterprise risk appetite.

- It may be more cost-effective to conduct particular security services in-house, rather than outsourcing them.
- The security outsourcer will be able to see the enterprise's potentially confidential information and hence there is a threat to security and confidentiality.
- When starting to use the security outsourcer, the enterprise might find it difficult to manage and communicate with the security outsourcer when compared to managing the security services within the enterprise.
- The security outsourcer may create potential redundancies for the enterprise.
- In case the security outsourcer goes bankrupt, goes out of business, or is purchased, the enterprise will have to immediately move the security services in-house or find another security outsourcer.
- The security outsourcers may not only be providing security services for the enterprise. The security outsourcers provide services to other companies and there might not be complete devotion to your enterprise and information may be comingled with that of other companies.
- With security outsourcing, the enterprise might lose control over the security services outsourced.
- Security outsourcing, though cost-effective, might have hidden costs, such as the legal costs incurred while signing a contract between companies.
- There can be several disadvantages in security outsourcing, such as renewing contracts, misunderstanding of the contract, lack of communication, poor quality, and delayed services amongst others.

The disadvantages of security outsourcing give the enterprise an opportunity to think about what risks they may be getting into. However, often the disadvantages of outsourcing are less than the advantages of offshore outsourcing. When outsourcing, the enterprise might not experience any of these disadvantages of security outsourcing if a reliable security outsourcing partner is found.

Performing Enterprise Due Diligence

Before selecting security outsourcing, the enterprise must also take the interests of its customers and employees into consideration and then make an informed decision. If the enterprise is genuinely interested in security outsourcing, do not let the disadvantages of security outsourcing stop the decision. Moving on to the next steps, the enterprise needs to perform its analysis of risks and related benefits of using a security outsourcer with considerations, such as

- Erring on the side of caution and only providing administrative access to those systems that are directly related to the security services that the security outsourcer is providing.
- Compiling a list of all relevant systems the security provider will require access to and reviewing this list carefully with the security outsourcer.
- Providing dedicated usernames and passwords to the security outsourcer.
- Dedicating a dead-end or separate network for the security outsourcer access.
- Helping to foster an environment of security service outsourcing success and considering the security outsourcer to be an extension of your team.
- Establishing a good relationship and trust with the security outsourcer can be a challenging process.

■ If a security outsourcer is chosen, the enterprise may become operationally dependent on the security outsourcer. The enterprise may want to consider multiple security outsourcers.
■ Determining who retains ownership of work product and data during the contract process and when the contract is terminated.
■ Initiating the process of security outsourcing may require a complex transition of processes, hardware, software, and assets from the enterprise to the security outsourcer.
■ Often a security outsourcer has done marketing well and the contract is signed, but then the greatest risk comes when there is inadequate and incomplete services and communications from the security outsourcer.
■ As an enterprise outsources anything, there are times when certain costs are overlooked or hidden issues may arise. Some of these internal costs could be giving up experience, knowledge, and skills, and bringing the security services back in-house.

In looking at the types of security services the security outsourcer will provide, the enterprise must also consider the type of metrics the security outsourcer should provide to the enterprise:

■ Technical metrics with statistics on
    – Vulnerabilities, events, systems affected
    – Vulnerabilities patched
    – Critical assets at risk
    – Statistics by application, Operating System (OS)
■ Process metrics with statistics on
    – Cumulative/ongoing processes
    – Time to remediate problems
    – Systemic, recurring problems, areas, or groups
    – Effectiveness of current process and method in providing the desired level of security
    – Whether changes to the process have improved results
■ Risk impact metrics with statistics on
    – Risks and impact to organization
    – Critical assets to the organization
    – Results-oriented views that identify outcomes
    – Potential dollars lost
    – Customer numbers
    – Trade secrets

As the metrics are defined, the type and frequency of reporting need to be considered and included as service-level items.

Part of the due diligence when looking at a security outsourcer is to ensure they can assist the enterprise in maintaining an acceptable risk attempt and limit the threats to the enterprise. Other things to consider when looking at a security outsourcer are as follows:

■ Products and services that are on the right technology/market trends trajectory
■ Products and services that have the right infrastructure story
■ Products and services that sell clearly into budget cycles and budget lines
■ Products and services whose impact is quantitative
■ Products and services that do not require fundamental changes in how people behave or major changes in organizational or corporate culture

- Products and services that, whenever possible, represent total end-to-end solutions
- Products and services that have multiple "default" exits
- Products, services, and companies that have clear horizontal and vertical strategies
- Products and services that have high industry awareness recognition
- Products, services, and companies that have the right technology development, marketing, and channel alliances and partnerships
- Products and services that are politically correct
- Serious people recruitment and retention strategies
- Products and services that have compelling "differentiation" stories
- Company executives that have wide and deep experience
- Products, services, and companies that have persuasive products/services packaging and communications

Decided to Outsource Security

The enterprise has decided that using a security outsourcer will assist in managing business risk. As the enterprise starts looking for a security outsourcer, the contractual agreement needs to include the following:

1. *Service-level agreement* (*SLA*): This is a contractual agreement outlining a specific service commitment made between contract parties. SLAs include language describing the overall service, financial aspects of service delivery, including fees, penalties, bonuses, contract terms and conditions, and specific performance metrics governing compliant service delivery.
2. *Service-level objectives* (*SLOs*): These are individual performance metrics. Some examples of SLOs would include: system availability, help-desk incident resolution time, and application response time.

When considering a security outsourcer, the following identifies certain business issues, among others, that need to be reviewed and considered before selecting a security outsourcer. This list is not intended to identify all issues to be considered when selecting security outsourcers, but is merely representative of some of the more common issues. The facts and circumstances are specific and unique to the transactions contemplated in the outsourcer selection process.

1. A detailed description of the work to be performed by the security outsourcer, and the frequency and general content of the related reports. A description of "support services" is too broad and could result in unsatisfactory performance from the vendor. Some items to request and document include:
   a. The obligations of each party (i.e., identify any responsibilities and important response times of each party to the contract).
   b. The times and days on which the services being provided will be available (if necessary, take fallback facilities into account and/or require other backup coverage or support).
   c. The right to supervise the activities of users (and the right to revoke this right).
   d. A requirement that the security outsourcer keep the software current by incorporating all telecommunication and public company regulatory changes and updates.
   e. Responsibilities for installing and maintaining equipment and software.

  f. Permitted methods of access and the management and use of user identification (IDs) and passwords.

  g. Security outsourcer's obligation to keep a list of authorized persons and a corresponding authorization procedure for user access rights.

2. An outline of the training to be provided for enterprise personnel, including the type and number of personnel to be trained and the related costs, if training is needed or requested.

3. Established time schedule for receipt and delivery of work products or services.

4. The availability of on-line communications, security related to access controls, transmissions, and alternate data entry considerations.

5. A detailed description of liability responsibilities for source documents while in transit to and from the security outsourcer.

6. Maintenance of adequate insurance by the vendor for fidelity and fire liability, reconstruction of physical properties, data reconstruction and resumption of normal operations, as well as for data losses resulting from errors and omissions.

7. Confidentiality of information. Measures to ensure that all information learned about the enterprise, including names and addresses and any internal data, is treated as confidential. The security outsourcer and its agents shall be prohibited from using or disclosing this information except as necessary to provide the contracted services. The security outsourcer is responsible for maintaining appropriate security measures (e.g., policies, procedures, and practices) to ensure confidentiality of all the enterprise information. The security outsourcer will fully disclose breaches in security resulting in unauthorized intrusions into the security outsourcer that may materially affect the enterprise information. Measures to ensure that confidential information is returned to the enterprise after the security outsourcer contract's expiration.

8. Ownership of software, intellectual property, and related documents, if the security outsourcer is writing or selling software and documentation for the enterprise. If a security outsourcer is providing source code, access to security outsourcer's source code and maintenance documentation via escrow agreement for turnkey operations.

9. Ownership of master and transmission data files and their return in machine-readable format upon the termination of the contract.

10. Processing priorities for normal and emergency situations.

11. Mandatory notification of the enterprise by the security vendor of all systems changes that affect the enterprise.

12. A guarantee that the security outsourcer will provide necessary levels of transition assistance if the enterprise decides to convert to other automation alternatives.

13. The management process for information security at the security outsourcer, such as a recent SAS 70 Type II audit report or a third-party risk assessment report.

14. Covenants regarding the reporting and investigation of any security incidents, including contact persons for urgent security incidents.

Conclusion

A few key things to remember when using security outsourcing are as follows:

■ Know what the enterprise is outsourcing.
■ Assess internal controls and policies and decide what level of risk management needs to be extended to the outsourced process.
■ Understand risks and dependencies, and learn about regulations and compliance controls.

- Assess security outsourcer's risk management level.
- Assess experience level of the security outsourcer employees.
- Ensure data is protected appropriately.
- Create clear and explicit SLAs and have a legal review of them.
- Reserve "right to audit" (physical/logical) clauses, escalation path, and altering process, and quantify remuneration for data loss or service down time.

If the enterprise wants to employ outsourcing vendors because they want to wipe their hands clean of regulatory compliance or hand over a messy environment in the hopes the security outsourcer will fix it, this is not a good reason to use security outsourcing. The enterprise must remember that they are still accountable for protecting the vital assets. And if the enterprise does have a messy or insecure environment, the security outsourcer does not have any incentive to fix it and may make it worse. An enterprise should carefully perform their due diligence on security outsourcers. The enterprise needs to evaluate whether their security architecture can operate within an island environment rather than a strong moat, like a castle approach to security architecture. When and if the decision is made to go with a security outsourcer, the enterprise needs to define ways to hold the security outsourcer accountable for its activities.

About the Author

Sandy Bacik, CISSP-ISSMP, CISM, CGEIT, CHS-III, author and former CSO, has over 14 years of direct development, implementation, and management information security experience in the areas of audit management, disaster recovery and business continuity, incident investigation, physical security, privacy, regulatory compliance, standard operating policies and procedures, and data center operations and management. Ms. Bacik has managed, architected, and implemented comprehensive information assurance programs and managed internal, external, and contracted and outsourced information technology audits to ensure various regulatory compliance for state and local government entities and Fortune 200 companies. She has developed methodologies for risk assessments, information technology audits, vulnerability assessments, security policy and practice writing, incident response, and disaster recovery.

APPLICATION DEVELOPMENT SECURITY

System Development Controls

Chapter 19

The Effectiveness of Access Management Reviews

Chris Hare

A major challenge to security practitioners is the need for ongoing access reviews and audits. The reason for this ongoing concern is the frequency at which auditors examine access management. From systems to applications, auditors like access management because it forms a basic control to limit authorized connections to a system and it is a key control identified in CoBIT.

CoBIT,* or Common Objectives for Information Technology, is a product of Information Systems Audit and Control Association (ISACA) and a recognized standard for identifying and classifying IT controls. The CoBIT control specifically relevant to access reviews is DS5, Ensure Systems Security. The goal of the control is to identify access control breakdowns, such as inappropriate access, dormant accounts, or terminated users.

What is an access review? Access reviews must be a repeatable process, which is engaged in periodically as required by CoBIT. The process must determine if the users with access under review should have that access. The problem facing many organizations today is the lack of a centralized solution.

The advances in directory technologies have created the opportunity for access information and user profiles to be stored in a directory. That being said, access is often left to the system or application administrator. This makes it difficult to perform an access review because of the myriad of permissions and roles that exist and because it is difficult to demonstrate to the auditors that access reviews are being conducted.

Additionally, if access reviews are left to the technical staff to perform, they are unaware of and unfamiliar with the business requirements for the access. Similarly, business staff may not have the knowledge to fully understand the capacity of the identified access. Consequently, making it simple benefits the organization.

The use of centralized solutions has typically not been the case, as organizations have relied upon less structured solutions such as discretionary access control to establish the limits of what the user can do. The problem of access is not new, stemming back to the development of the

---

* See ISACA online at http://www.isaca.org.

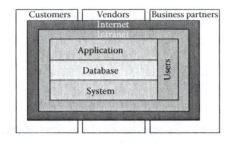

Figure 19.1 Access relationships.

earliest multiuser computers, which lead to the development of access control systems like ACF2 and Resource Access Control Facility (RACF).

If an organization is going to embark on a centralized solution, where should they start? What are the important aspects of access management and the ever-required access review that are necessary for them to consider? Before answering that question, let's look at the relationships illustrated in Figure 19.1.

The problem is that access management spans across the IT infrastructure, and out into the Internet and the realms of our customers, vendors, and business partners. It means that anyone who has access to any of our systems or applications must fall into the access review process, although there may be different requirements across the different user types.

This means the solution must be capable of spanning the infrastructure as well. One possible solution is illustrated in Figure 19.2.

In the example shown in Figure 19.2, the users interact with the specific resource they are interested in, but that resource then queries a centralized access management system to determine if the user has authenticated and is authorized for the resource.

This sounds simple, and in some environments it is, while in others it is exceedingly difficult and complex. If the environment is heterogeneous, including Microsoft Windows, mainframes, and UNIX, then finding a solution like that in Figure 19.2 will require custom programming to provide the services necessary. Each system itself does, however, offer differences and advantages.

Take mainframe computing platforms for example. Because of the nature of the platform, users are assigned privileges and roles using technology such as RACF. This isn't new, as RACF and systems like it have been in existence since the mid 1970s.

What makes the mainframe platform successful is the integrated manner in which RACF operates across the mainframe platform and the applications running there. This, however, is a lot more difficult to achieve on distributed systems such as UNIX and Microsoft Windows. Of

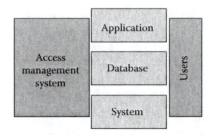

Figure 19.2 Spanning the infrastructure.

course, the more homogeneous your environment, the easier it becomes. Difficulties aside, the question is how can we take an old concept and learn from it to establish new paradigms and opportunities.

If we steal a page from the RACF playbook, users have profiles that consist of privileges and roles. Each user in the centralized system has a profile consisting of every role and privilege. Because of the nature of the information and the rate at which it could grow, using a data representation format such as the eXtensible Markup Language (XML) is highly recommended as new privileges can easily be added to a profile without the need for changing a database structure. One such possible framework could be expressed as illustrated in Figure 19.3.

The main reasons for using an XML-based representation is the plain text representation and the ability to use English-language-like structures, which makes it easy to read.

It is, unfortunately, less of a trick in either creating or buying the centralized directory approach, as it is to get the various infrastructures to use it. For example, Microsoft Windows will want to interrogate an Active Directory forest to get its authentication and authorization information, Mac OS uses Open Directory, and UNIX is quite content with a Lightweight Directory Access Protocol (LDAP)-compliant directory.

Organizations could choose to build their own authentication and authorization environment, or take advantage of commercial products such as eTrust and Siteminder. Both of these products offer centralized authentication and authorization albeit for different purposes.

If user profiles and access controls are not new, then why do organizations struggle with performing periodic access reviews as mandated by CoBIT? Part of the problem is manpower. Access reviews are effectively a detective control, meaning they will detect the existence of a problem because someone found it.

Detective controls are not bad, but moving the access review into a continuous monitoring framework where the routine work is done by the system reduces the manual labor surrounding the task, and can be used to demonstrate to the auditors that problems are identified and remediated quickly.

Detective controls find errors when the preventive system does not catch them. Consequently, detective controls are more expensive to design and implement as they not only evaluate the effectiveness of the preventive control, they must be used to identify potentially erroneous data, which cannot be effectively controlled through prevention. Detective controls include reviews and comparisons, audits, bank and other account reconciliation, inventory counts, passwords, biometrics, input edit checks, check sums, and message digests.

```
<user>
        <uid>e0510510</uid>
        <jobcode>G60</jobcode>
        <platform>
                <name>hostname</name>
                <role>Administrator</role>
                <domain>US1</domain>
                <domainrole>user</domainrole>
        </platform>
        <application>
                <name>Oracle GL</name>
                <instance>PROD-1</instance>
                <role>approver</role>
        </application>
</user>
```

Figure 19.3 Sample XML authorization description.

Preventive controls establish mechanisms to prevent the undesirable activity from occurring. Preventive controls are considered the most cost-effective approach of the preventive-detective-corrective cycle. When a preventive control is embedded into a system, the control prevents the errors and minimizes the use of detective and corrective techniques. Preventive controls include trustworthy, trained people; segregation of duties; proper authorization; adequate documentation; proper record keeping and physical controls.

Regardless of whether the organization uses a single centralized directory or many, the same process can be used to perform an automated validation against the systems. The process is illustrated in Figure 19.4.

Execution of the process assumes two very significant things. First, there is a "golden" source of users or employees available from an HR system. If not, then a more fundamental problem exists that requires action. Assuming there is, the second is a list of systems (applications, databases, etc.) and processes to acquire the list of users from that system for comparison. In many cases, this step will require customization by the IT staff.

Once the list of users is available from the system, it becomes a simple matter of determining if the user is in the HR file and an active employee. If they are not in the HR file or are no longer an active employee, then the access is removed.

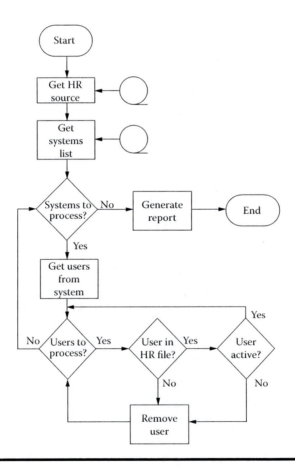

Figure 19.4   Access review process.

This process will only identify terminated users. Since it becomes an automated, continuous monitoring process, any terminated user is removed from the appropriate systems and, therefore, it forms a good preventive control. It will prevent that user from being able to access the organization's systems after they have left, or from anyone else using that user's credentials for some nefarious purpose.

Aside from terminated users, what other tests should be integrated into the access review process? Some include:

- Users who have changed jobs or departments and therefore do not need the same access
- Users who have never used the access they have (dormant accounts)
- Profile appropriateness: Is the access level appropriate?
- Segregation of duties checks

Users who have changed jobs or departments are much more difficult to find than terminated users. It requires the process to keep track of the previous department and job code, and then identify when they have changed. Because associating applications to a specific job code or department is often not done within an organization, some form of manual intervention is typically required. The main point is that if the applications have not been mapped to specific job codes or departments, then are access reviews really being done? Is it enough to simply "rubber stamp" the access by saying the user needs it?

This is where job profiling comes into play. Like user profiles we described earlier, jobs can be profiled to determine what access and applications are required for the user to perform the common tasks within that job. Notice that we are discussing jobs, not departments, because there can be a variety of jobs within a given department, not all of them requiring the same privilege level.

Figure 19.5 illustrates the relationship between users and profiles. Users have jobs. The job is a collection of tasks, assignments, and responsibilities. Each user also has a manager, who themselves have a job.

Every job has a job code, which maps to at least one job profile, because it may take more than one profile to provide the user with the access and privileges necessary to perform their assigned duties.

A side benefit from job profiling is establishing what the base access is for all employees. For example, we could define that all employees have e-mail access and Internet access through the network proxy servers, and access to specific applications, such as employee self-service applications. If an employee changes jobs, they can be assured the automated systems would not remove the basic access.

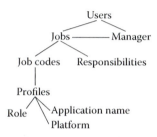

Figure 19.5 User and profile relationships.

Getting to job profiles requires a more in-depth analysis of the specific job. This means being able to uniquely identify the applications, access, and functions the employee needs to fulfill their job responsibilities.

For large organizations, this can be difficult because of the wide variety of positions and job types. Making the problem more difficult is when there are varying degrees of authority or privilege within the same job code. Consequently, it would be highly recommended for organizations to minimize the number of levels within a defined job code.

What would a process for job transfers and department changes look like? One possibility is illustrated in Figure 19.6.

This process is a continuation of what we examined in Figure 19.4. In this part of the process, the user's job code and department are checked. If there is a job profile, then the access the user no longer requires is removed and the new access is added. If there is no job profile, then notification is sent to the old and new managers to perform an access review where they would remove or add access as appropriate for the user's new position.

The notification is sent to both the old and new managers as the old manager will know what access should be removed and the new manager will know what access needs to be added.

Thus far we have established a method for performing an automated and sustainable access review process. There are some significant requirements for the methodology described here to work. To summarize, these requirements are:

1. An available "golden" source of employees from an HR system
2. A list of systems, applications, and databases, collectively referred to as platforms
3. Program code to retrieve the user details from the platform
4. Job codes and job profiles
5. Program code to remove or add access on the platform as required

If these requirements cannot be satisfied in your particular organization, then implementing a periodic manual review by the manager for the employees under their supervision could also be used to satisfy the CoBIT requirements.

Periodic manager reviews also require some form of centralized system where the user's access privileges are recorded. The system would have to notify the manager of the pending access review,

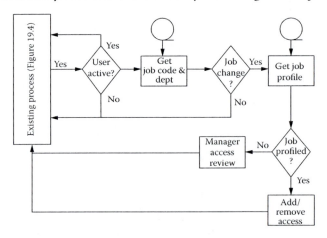

Figure 19.6 Transferred users.

keep track of the completed review, sign off for each employee, and provide reporting for the manager, HR, IT security, and audit. Figure 19.7 illustrates the process of notifying managers when access reviews for their employees are due.

In our example manager notification process, we are assuming the access review must be performed once a year, although the manager's directory is notified if the access review is not done at 13 months, as this would indicate noncompliance with the once per year requirement. Managers could perform the access review more often if they so desired.

Even with the discussion presented here, should access reviews be considered effective? Unless the systems and process have been constructed to break the most complex information down into understandable bits, it is more likely that the manager will "rubber stamp" the access review because they either don't understand what is being displayed to them or they are apathetic to the reasons why the review is required. Like so many things, access reviews are a necessary evil—people understand they are necessary, but that doesn't mean they have to like doing them.

As mentioned previously, the effectiveness of the review is affected by who is doing the review. The technical staff will not understand the business requirements for specific access and the business teams will likely not understand the technical nature or full extent of the granted access. Consequently, the access review must be done by someone who has knowledge of the access and the impact of its existence or removal to the employee and their ability to perform their job. Similarly, the access review system must break down the access succinctly enough for the manager to understand it and make good decisions regarding the access.

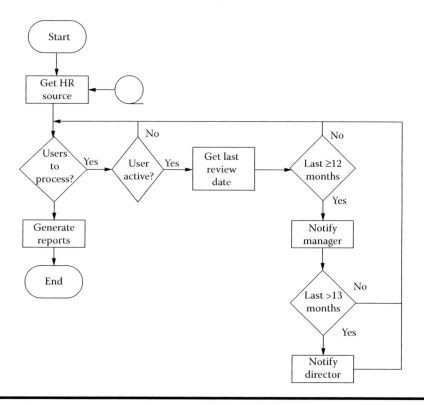

Figure 19.7   Manager notification.

Finally, the system must be tolerant enough to not force the manager to perform the access review for every employee at the same time. Creating the need for simultaneous reviews will only serve to increase the likelihood of rubber stamp reviews and lower the review effectiveness.

The design and implementation of the processes described in this chapter would require back-end code and user interface code. The back-end code would do the invisible, daily processing routines, while the user interface code is what the user interacts with.

This has been a brief look at how an organization can automate access reviews and improve the overall security posture of their organization. Access management is a tricky suite of processes due to the cross-platform, infrastructure-wide nature. This doesn't mean organizations cannot tame the access monster and bring their environment under control.

Rather, it should serve as impetus to solve the problem given the vast benefits to the operational management of the company. Remember, what can be used to remove access could also be used to add it, and create a comprehensive access management product suite.

About the Author

Chris Hare, CISSP, CISA, CISM, has over 23 years in the computing industry and is the coauthor of New Riders Publishing's *Inside Unix, Internet Firewalls and Network Security, Building an Internet Server with Linux* and *The Internet Security Professional Reference.* His book credits also include the General Linux II Examination Guide and the Official CISSP Study Guide. Accredited with the CISSP, CISA, and CISM designations, Chris holds a master of arts degree in adult education from Northwestern State University of Louisiana and a bachelor of arts and science degree in information systems from Dallas Baptist University.

Chapter 20

Securing SaaS Applications: A Cloud Security Perspective for Application Providers[*]

Pradnyesh Rane

Software as a service (SaaS) is rapidly emerging as the dominant delivery model for meeting the needs of enterprise IT services. However, most enterprises are still uncomfortable with the SaaS model due to lack of visibility about the way their data is stored and secured. According to the Forrester study, "The State of Enterprise Software: 2009," security concerns are the most commonly cited reason why enterprises aren't interested in SaaS. Consequently, addressing enterprise security concerns has emerged as the biggest challenge for the adoption of SaaS applications.

This chapter focuses on security considerations, while architecting SaaS applications and mitigation strategies for meeting the security challenges. The adoption of these security practices can help SaaS providers instill enterprises with a degree of confidence in their security by eliminating security vulnerabilities and ensuring the safety of sensitive data.

Overview of SaaS

SaaS is a software deployment model where applications are remotely hosted by the application or service provider and made available to customers on demand, over the Internet. Enterprises can take advantage of the SaaS model to reduce the IT costs associated with traditional on-premise applications like hardware, patch management, upgrades, etc. On-demand licensing can help customers adopt the "pay-as-you-go/grow" model to reduce their up-front expenses for IT purchases.

SaaS lets software vendors control and limit use, prohibits copies and distribution, and facilitates the control of all derivative versions of their software. SaaS centralized control often allows the vendor to establish an ongoing revenue stream with multiple businesses (tenants) and users.

---

[*] Copyright 2010 Persistent Systems.

The tenants are provided a protected sandbox view of the application that is isolated from other tenants. Each tenant can tune the metadata of the application to provide a customized look and feel for its users.

The SaaS software vendor may host the application on its own private server farm or deploy it on a cloud computing infrastructure service provided by a third-party provider (e.g., Amazon, Google, etc.). The use of cloud computing coupled with the pay-as-you-go (grow) approach helps the application service provider reduce the investment in infrastructure services and enables it to concentrate on providing better services to customers.

Security Challenges for SaaS

Over the past decade, computers have become widespread within enterprises, while IT services and computing have become a commodity. Enterprises today view data and business processes (transactions, records, pricing information, etc.) themselves as strategic and guard them with access control and compliance policies.

However, in the SaaS model, enterprise data is stored at the SaaS provider's data center, along with the data of other enterprises. Moreover, if the SaaS provider is leveraging a public cloud computing service, the enterprise data might be stored along with the data of other unrelated SaaS applications. The cloud provider might, additionally, replicate the data at multiple locations across countries for the purposes of maintaining high availability.

Most enterprises are familiar with the traditional on-premise model, where the data continues to reside within the enterprise boundary, subject to their policies. Consequently, there is a great deal of discomfort with the lack of control and knowledge of how their data is stored and secured in the SaaS model. There are strong concerns about data breaches, application vulnerabilities, and availability that can lead to financial and legal liabilities.

Figure 20.1 illustrates the layered stack for a typical SaaS vendor and highlights critical aspects that must be covered across layers in order to ensure security of the enterprise data.

High-Level Security Considerations

The following key security elements should be carefully considered as an integral part of the SaaS application development and deployment process:

- SaaS deployment model
- Data security
- Network security
- Regulatory compliance
- Data segregation
- Availability
- Backup
- Identity management and sign-on process

SaaS Deployment Model

The SaaS security challenges differ depending upon the deployment model being used by the vendor. SaaS vendors may choose to deploy the solution either by using a public cloud vendor

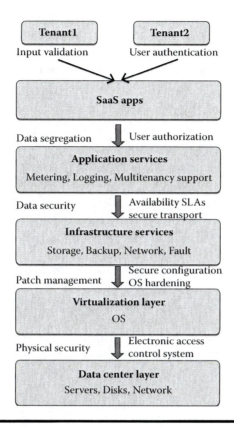

Figure 20.1   Security for the SaaS stack.

or hosting it themselves. Dedicated public cloud providers such as Amazon help to build secure SaaS solutions by providing infrastructure services that aid in ensuring perimeter and environment security. This involves the use of firewalls, intrusion detection systems, etc. A self-hosted SaaS deployment, however, requires the vendor to build these services and assess them for security vulnerabilities.

Data Security

In a traditional on-premise application deployment model, the sensitive data of each enterprise continues to reside within the enterprise boundary and is subject to its physical, logical, and personnel security and access control policies. However, in the SaaS model, the enterprise data is stored outside the enterprise boundary, at the SaaS vendor end. Consequently, the SaaS vendor must adopt additional security checks to ensure data security and prevent breaches due to security vulnerabilities in the application or through malicious employees. This involves the use of strong encryption techniques for data security and fine-grained authorization to control access to data.

In cloud vendors such as Amazon, the Elastic Compute Cloud [EC2] administrators do not have access to customer instances and cannot log into the Guest Operating System (OS). EC2 administrators with a business need are required to use their individual cryptographically strong Secure Shell (SSH) keys to gain access to a host. All such accesses are logged and routinely audited. While the data at rest in Simple Storage Service (S3) is not encrypted by default, users can encrypt their data before it is uploaded to Amazon S3, so that it is not accessed or tampered with by any unauthorized party.

Network Security

In a SaaS deployment model, sensitive data is obtained from the enterprises, processed by the SaaS application, and stored at the SaaS vendor end. All data flow over the network needs to be secured in order to prevent leakage of sensitive information. This involves the use of strong network traffic encryption techniques such as Secure Socket Layer (SSL) and the Transport Layer Security (TLS) for security.

In case of Amazon Web Services (AWS), the network layer provides significant protection against traditional network security issues, such as Man-in-the-Middle (MITM) attacks, IP spoofing, port scanning, packet sniffing, etc. For maximum security, Amazon S3 is accessible via SSL encrypted endpoints. The encrypted endpoints are accessible from both the Internet and from within Amazon EC2, ensuring that data is transferred securely both within AWS and to and from sources outside of AWS.

Regulatory Compliance

The SaaS deployment needs to be periodically assessed for conformance to regulatory and industry standards. The SAS 70 standard includes operating procedures for physical and perimeter security of data centers and service providers. Access, storage, and processing of sensitive data needs to be carefully controlled and is governed under regulations such as ISO-27001, the Sarbanes-Oxley Act (SOX), Gramm-Leach-Bliley Act (GLBA), and Health Insurance Portability and Accountability Act (HIPAA), and industry standards like the Payment Card Industry Data Security Standard (PCI-DSS).

Data privacy has emerged as another significant challenge. Different countries have distinct privacy regulations about how data needs to be secured and stored. These might lead to conflicts when the enterprise data of one country is stored in data centers located in another country.

Data Segregation

In a mature multitenant SaaS architecture, the application instances and data stores may be shared across multiple enterprises. This allows the SaaS vendor to make more efficient use of resources and helps achieve lower costs. At the same time, sufficient security checks need to be adopted to ensure data security and prevent unauthorized access to data of one tenant by users from other tenants. This involves hardening the data store as well as the application to ensure data segregation.

In case the SaaS application is deployed at a third-party cloud vendor, additional safeguards need to be adopted so that data of an application tenant is not accessible to other applications.

In the case of Amazon, the S3 Application Program Interfaces (APIs) provide both bucket-level and object-level access controls, with defaults that only permit authenticated access by the bucket and/or object creator. Write and Delete permission is controlled by an Access Control List (ACL) associated with the bucket. Permission to modify the bucket's ACL is itself controlled by an ACL and it defaults to creator-only access. Therefore, the customer maintains full control over who has access to their data. Amazon S3 access can be granted based on AWS Account ID, DevPay Product ID, or open to everyone.

Availability

The SaaS application needs to ensure that enterprises are provided with service around the clock. This involves making architectural changes at the application and infrastructural levels to add scalability and high availability. A multitier architecture needs to be adopted, supported by a load-balanced farm of application instances, running on a variable number of servers. Resiliency to hardware/software failures, as well as to denial of service attacks, needs to be built from the ground up within the application.

At the same time, an appropriate action plan for business continuity (BC) and disaster recovery (DR) needs to be considered for any unplanned emergencies. This is essential to ensure the safety of the enterprise data and minimal downtime for enterprises.

With Amazon, for instance, the AWS API endpoints are hosted on the same Internet-scale, world-class infrastructure that supports the Amazon.com retail site. Standard Distributed Denial of Service (DDoS) mitigation techniques such as syn cookies and connection limiting are used. To further mitigate the effect of potential DDoS attacks, Amazon maintains internal bandwidth that exceeds its provider-supplied Internet bandwidth.

Backup

The SaaS vendor needs to ensure that all sensitive enterprise data is regularly backed up to facilitate quick recovery in case of disasters. Also, the use of strong encryption schemes to protect the backup data is recommended to prevent accidental leakage of sensitive information.

In the case of cloud vendors such as Amazon, the data at rest in S3 is not encrypted by default. The users need to separately encrypt their data and backups so that it cannot be accessed or tampered with by unauthorized parties.

Identity Management (IdM) and Sign-On Process

The SaaS vendor can support identity management and sign-on services using any of the following models.

Independent IdM Stack

The SaaS vendor provides the complete stack of identity management and sign-on services. All information related to user accounts, passwords, etc. is completely maintained at the SaaS vendor end.

Credential Synchronization

The SaaS vendor supports replication of user account information and credentials between enterprise and SaaS application. The user account information creation is done separately by each tenant within the enterprise boundary to comply with its regulatory needs. Relevant portions of user account information are replicated to the SaaS vendor to provide sign-on and access control capabilities. The authentication happens at the SaaS vendor end using the replicated credentials.

Federated IdM

The entire user account information including credentials is managed and stored independently by each tenant. The user authentication occurs within the enterprise boundary. The identity of the user as well as certain user attributes are propagated on-demand to the SaaS vendor using federation to allow sign-on and access control.

Table 20.1   IdM and SSO Model Advantages, Disadvantages, and Security Challenges

IdM and SSO Model	Advantages	Disadvantages	Security Challenges
Independent IdM stack	Easy to implement No separate integration with enterprises directory	The users need to remember separate credentials for each SaaS application	The IdM stack should be highly configurable to facilitate compliance with enterprising policies, e.g., password strength, etc.
Credential Synchronization	Users don't need to remember multiple passwords	Requires integration with enterprise directory Has higher security risk value due to transmission of user credentials outside enterprise perimeter	The SaaS vendor needs to ensure security of the credentials during transit and storage and prevent their leakage
Federated IdM	Users don't need to remember multiple passwords No separate integration with enterprise directory Low security risk values as compared to credential synch	Relatively more complex to implement	The SaaS vendor and tenants need to ensure that proper trust relationships and validations are established to ensure secure federation of user identities

Table 20.1 highlights the security challenges for adopting these models and the relative advantages and disadvantages.

Securing SaaS Applications

We have identified the following key mitigation strategies for addressing the above critical security challenges and improving the robustness of the SaaS applications:

- Secure product engineering
- Secure deployment
- Governance and regulatory compliance audits
- Third-Party SaaS security assessment

Secure Product Engineering

Product vendors are always rushing to meet market release deadlines. Consequently, product security is often given lesser precedence. This can result in buggy software that is prone to security vulnerabilities. It is a known fact that leakage of sensitive data due to security exploits can result in heavy financial loss to enterprises and expose the SaaS vendor to potential liability issues along with lost credibility.

It is highly recommended that software vendors treat security as part of the product engineering life cycle. At each phase of development (architecture, design, coding), a security review should be performed. This will help with faster identification of any security issues and lower rework costs for any security fixes that need to be implemented. The coding and testing guidelines should similarly be revised while keeping security considerations in perspective.

Secure Deployment

As discussed, SaaS solutions can either be hosted by the SaaS vendor or they can be deployed on a public cloud. In a self-hosted deployment, the SaaS vendor needs to ensure that adequate safeguards are adopted to combat against network penetration and DoS attacks. Dedicated cloud providers such as Amazon and Google help facilitate building secure SaaS applications by providing infrastructure services that aid in ensuring data security, network security, data segregation, etc. The SaaS applications that are deployed on these public clouds should ensure that they harden their application security settings to conform to the best practices recommended by the public cloud vendor.

Governance and Regulatory Compliance Audits

Third-party governance and regulatory compliance (GRC) audits can help validate the conformance of the SaaS vendors to government regulations and industry standards such as ISO27001, SOX, GLBA, HIPAA, and PCI-DSS. Additionally, they can validate that appropriate BC and DR plans are in place and followed meticulously.

GRC audits help the SaaS vendor to identify and fix any deviations from regulations to ensure compliance to industry standards. They also help the SaaS provider ease customer concerns about the security, privacy, and availability of the enterprise data, and help build credibility. It is recommended that SaaS vendors periodically conduct a third-party GRC audit to ensure compliance.

Third-Party SaaS Security Assessment

Third-party SaaS security assessments help validate the security and integrity of the SaaS application and its deployment. It is recommended that SaaS vendors periodically conduct a SaaS security assessment to ensure the security of their solutions.

The standard tools and techniques used for web application vulnerability assessments (VA) as captured by Open Web Application Security Project (OWASP) do not provide sufficient coverage for SaaS-specific concepts such as multitenancy, data segregation, etc. The Cloud Security Alliance (CSA) captures the critical areas for SaaS applications in their CSA security guide. A security assessment specifically tailored for SaaS solutions that incorporates these critical areas is essential for detecting security vulnerabilities and fixing them before they can be exploited by malicious hackers.

The SaaS security assessment should be comprised of both the application VA and network VA for complete coverage. Figure 20.2 gives an overview of the security threats and vulnerabilities that should be covered as part of the security assessment.

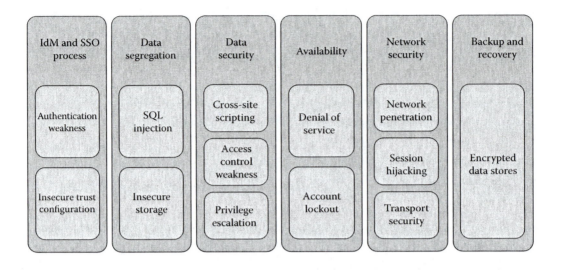

Figure 20.2 Security considerations and vulnerabilities.

Application Vulnerability Assessment

The application VA helps validate application security in a SaaS deployment. This is generally independent of the SaaS deployment model used by the vendor. However, dedicated cloud providers such as Amazon help facilitate building secure SaaS applications by providing infrastructure services that aid in ensuring data security, network security, data segregation, etc.

Data Security

Malicious users can exploit weaknesses in the data security model to gain unauthorized access to data. The following assessments test and validate the security of the enterprise data stored at the SaaS vendor.

- Cross-site scripting (XSS)
- Access control weaknesses
- OS and SQL injection flaws
- Cross-site request forgery (CSRF)
- Cookie manipulation
- Hidden field manipulation
- Insecure storage
- Insecure configuration

Any vulnerability detected during these tests can be exploited to gain access to sensitive enterprise data and lead to a financial loss.

Network Security

Malicious users can exploit weaknesses in network security configuration to sniff network packets. The following assessments test and validate the network security of the SaaS vendor.

- Network penetration and packet analysis
- Session management weaknesses
- Insecure SSL trust configuration

Any vulnerability detected during these tests can be exploited to hijack active sessions, and gain access to user credentials and sensitive data.

Data Segregation

A malicious user can use application vulnerabilities to handcraft parameters that bypass security checks and access sensitive data of other tenants. The following assessments test and validate the data segregation of the SaaS vendor in a multitenant deployment.

- SQL injection flaws
- Data validation
- Insecure storage

Any vulnerability detected during these tests can be exploited to gain access to sensitive enterprise data of other tenants.

Availability

These assessments test and validate the availability of the SaaS vendor.

- Authentication weaknesses
- Session management weaknesses

Many applications provide safeguards to automatically lock user accounts after successive incorrect credentials. However, incorrect configuration and implementation of such features can be used by malicious users to mount denial of service attacks.

Backup

The following assessments test and validate the security of the data backup and recovery services provided by the SaaS vendor.

- Insecure storage
- Insecure configuration

Any vulnerability detected during these tests can be exploited to gain access to sensitive enterprise data stored in backups.

Identity Management and Sign-On Process

The following assessments test and validate the security of the identity management and sign-on process of the SaaS vendor.

- Authentication weakness analysis
- Insecure trust configuration

Any vulnerability detected during these tests can be exploited to take over user accounts and compromise sensitive data.

Network Vulnerability Assessment

Network vulnerability assessment helps validate the network/host security in the cloud used for deploying the SaaS application in a self-hosted model.

SaaS Deployment Model

The following assessments help test and validate the security of the infrastructure used to deploy the SaaS application.

- Host scanning
- Penetration testing
- Perimeter separation for dev/production systems
- Server hardening
- Firewall testing
- Router testing
- Domain name server testing
- Mail server testing

The above assessments help ensure security of the SaaS deployment against external penetration and breaches, and prevent loss of sensitive data.

Availability

The following assessment helps test and validate the availability of the infrastructure used to deploy the SaaS application.

DoS Testing

The above assessment helps test and validate the resilience of the SaaS deployment to denial of service attacks and helps ensure availability of the service to end users.

Conclusion

The SaaS model offers customers significant benefits, such as improved operational efficiency and reduced costs. However, to overcome customer concerns about application and data security, vendors must address these issues head-on.

When it comes down to it, most enterprises' security concerns are centered on the lack of control and visibility into how their data is stored and secured with SaaS vendors. There is strong apprehension about insider breaches, along with vulnerabilities in the applications and systems' availability that could lead to loss of sensitive data and money. Such challenges can discourage enterprises from adopting SaaS applications.

The adoption of SaaS security practices—secure product engineering, secure deployment, GRC audits, and regular SaaS security assessment—is vital to securing SaaS solutions. These can help identify any security issues up front and ensure the safety of the data. SaaS vendors will benefit from the improved security of the solution and third-party validation of their security in the form of shortened sales cycles and reduced operational risk. These measures will help them better answer any sales and marketing queries about security and address customer concerns. Customers will further be benefited and assured about the security of their sensitive data and have higher confidence in the SaaS vendor.

Thus, adoption of the above SaaS security strategies and regular SaaS security assessment can enable SaaS vendors to boost customer confidence in the security of their solution and enable its faster and wider adoption.

About the Author

Pradnyesh Rane is a domain expert at the Security Competency Center, Persistent Systems. To learn more about Persistent Systems and its experience with building secure applications in the Cloud, please visit them on the web at www.persistentsys.com or e-mail them at security_info@persistentsys.com.

Disclaimer: The trademarks or trade names mentioned in this chapter are property of their respective owners and are included for reference only and do not imply a connection or relationship between the author and these companies.

Chapter 21

Attacking RFID Systems

Pedro Peris-Lopez, Julio Cesar Hernandez-Castro,
Juan M. Estevez-Tapiador, and Arturo Ribagorda

A great number of hackers end up working in the security departments of IT and telecommunications companies. In other words, the best way of making a system secure is knowing how it can be attacked. Radio-frequency identification (RFID) is no different from any other technology, so the possible attacks on it should be studied in depth. The extent of an attack can vary considerably; some attacks focus on a particular part of the system (e.g., the tag), whereas others target the whole system. Although there are references to such attacks in a number of publications, a rigorous study has not been made of the subject until now. We examine, in this chapter, the main threats to RFID security. First, we look at data and location privacy. Although these are the risks most often referred to in the literature, there are other equally important problems to consider too. RFID systems are made up of three main components (tag, reader, and back-end database), so we have grouped the threats according to the unit involved in the attack. First, we examine those related to tags and readers such as eavesdropping, cloning, replay, and relay attacks. Then we look at the threats to the back-end database (e.g., object name service [ONS] attack, virus). By the end of this chapter (and with the opportunity to consult the extensive bibliography for further details), we hope the reader will have acquired a basic understanding of the principal security risks in RFID.

Introduction

Background

Press stories about RFID often give inaccurate descriptions of the possibilities that exist for abuse of this technology. They predict a world where all our possessions will have a unique identification tag: clothes, books, electronic items, medicines, etc. For example, an attacker outside your house equipped with a commercial reader would be able to draw up an inventory of all your possessions, and particular information such as your health and lifestyle could also be revealed. Also, it is said that this technology allows "Big Brother" to know when you are in public places (office, cinemas, stores, pubs, etc.), tracking all your movements and compromising your privacy in terms of your whereabouts (location).

RFID technology is a pervasive technology, perhaps one of the most pervasive in history. While security concerns about the possibility of abuse of this pervasive technology are legitimate, misinformation and hysteria should be avoided. One should be aware that ways of collecting, storing, and analyzing vast amounts of information about consumers and citizens existed before the appearance of RFID technology. For example, we usually pay with credit cards, give our names and addresses for merchandizing, use cookies while surfing the Internet, etc.

In this chapter we give an overview of the risks and threats related to RFID technology, helping the reader to become better acquainted with this technology. Although the privacy issues are the main focus in the literature [1–12], there are other risks that should be considered when a RFID system is designed.

Attack Objectives

The objectives of each attack can be very different. It is important to identify the potential targets to understand all the possible attacks. The target can be the complete system (i.e., disrupt the whole of a business system) or only a section of the entire system (i.e., a particular item).

A great number of information systems focus solely on protecting the transmitted data. However, when designing RFID systems, additional objectives, such as tracking or data manipulation, should be considered. Imagine the following example in a store: an attacker modifies the tag content of an item, reducing its price from €100 to €9.90. This leads to a loss of 90 percent for the store. In this scenario, the data may be transmitted in secure form and the database has not been manipulated. However, fraud is carried out because part of the system has been manipulated. Therefore, to make a system secure, all of its components should be considered. Neglecting one component, whatever the security level of the remaining components, could compromise the security of the whole system.

The objectives of the attacks are very different. As we see in the above example, the attack may be perpetrated to steal or reduce the price of a single item, while other attacks could aim to prevent all sales at a store. An attacker may introduce corrupt information in the database to render it inoperative. Some attacks, such as the Faraday cage or active jamming, are inherent in the wireless technology employed. Other attacks are focused on eliminating physical access control and ignore the data. Other attacks even involve fraudulent border crossings, identity stealing from legitimate e-passports, etc.

Security Needs

As any other mission-critical system, it is important to minimize the threats to the confidentiality, integrity, and availability (CIA) of data and computing resources. These three factors are often referred to as "The Big Three." Figure 21.1 illustrates the balance between these three factors.

However, not all systems need the same security level. For example, not all systems need 99.999 percent availability or require that its users be authenticated via retinal scans. Because of this, it is necessary to analyze and evaluate each system (sensitivity of the data, potential loss from incidents, criticality of the mission, etc.) to determine the CIA requirements. To give another example, the security requirements of tags used in e-passports should not equal those employed in the supply chain (i.e., tag compliant to EPC Class-1 Generation-2).

Figure 21.1 Three pillars of security: the CIA triad.

Confidentiality: The information is accessible only to those authorized for access. Privacy information, such as the static identifiers transmitted by tags, fits into the confidentiality dimension. Both users and companies consider this issue of utmost importance. Furthermore, RFID technology allows the tracking of items. From a user perspective, tracking should be avoided. However, companies may control the movements of materials in the supply chains, increasing the productivity of their processes.

Integrity: The assurance that the messages transmitted between two parties are not modified in transit. Additionally, some systems provide the authenticity of messages. The receipt is able to prove that a message was originated by the purported sender and is not a forgery (nonrepudiation). An example of this kind of attack is the spoofing attack.

Availability: System availability is whether (or how often) a system is available for use by its intended users. This factor will determine the performance and the scalability level of the system. Denial-of-service (DoS) attacks are usual threats for availability (i.e., active jamming of the radio channel or preventing the normal operation of vicinity tags by using some kind of blocker tag).

Each time a new technology is implanted, contingency plans for various points of failure should be designed. We recommend periodical security audits to review the security polices, procedures, and IT infrastructures. As has been frequently mentioned, RFID technology may be a replacement for bar-code technology. Nevertheless, new risk scenarios should be considered with its implantation. For example, consider the repercussions of a bar-code reader failing or an RFID reading going down. When a bar-code reader fails, an operator can manually enter the codes into the terminal and the system works, albeit relatively slowly. On the other hand, if the RFID reader is processing high volumes of items and these items are moving at high speed, the consequences will be much worse. Security needs should therefore be considered a priority.

Main Security Concerns

Privacy

No one shall be subjected to arbitrary interference with his privacy, family, home, or correspondence, or to attacks on his honor and reputation. Everyone has the right to the protection of the law against such interference or attacks [13].

Data-processing systems are designed to serve man; they must, whatever the nationality or residency of individuals, respect their fundamental rights and freedoms, notably the right to privacy, and contribute to economic and social progress, trade expansion, and the well-being of individuals [14].

Privacy has no definite boundaries and its meaning is not the same for everyone. In general terms, it is the ability of an individual or group to keep their lives and personal affairs out of public view, or to control the flow of information about themselves.

The invasion of privacy by governments, corporations, or individuals is controlled by a country's laws, constitutions, or privacy laws. For example, taxation processes normally require detailed private information about earnings. The EU Directive 95/46/EC [14] on the protection of individuals with regard to the processing of personal data and the free movement of this limits and regulates the collection of personal information. Additionally, Article 8 of the European Convention of Human Rights identifies the right to have private and family life respected. Within this framework, monitoring the use of e-mails, Internet, or phones in the workplace without notifying employees or obtaining their consent can result in legal action.

RFID technology is a pervasive technology, and seems destined to become more and more so. As Weiser already predicted in 1991, one of the main problems that ubiquitous computing has to solve is privacy [15]. Leakage of information is a problem that occurs when data sent by tags reveals sensitive information about the labeled items. Products labeled with insecure tags reveal their memory contents when queried by readers. Usually, readers are not authenticated and tags answer in a transparent and indiscriminate way.

As an example of the threat this could pose, consider the pharmaceutical sector, where tagged medication is planned for the immediate future. Imagine that when you leave the chemist's with a given drug—say an antidepressive or acquired immune deficiency syndrome (AIDS) treatment— an attacker standing by the door equipped with a reader could find out what kind of medication you have just bought. In a similar scenario, thieves equipped with tag readers could search people, selecting those with multiple tagged bank bills to rob, and they would know how much they would earn with each robbery.

Advanced applications, where personal information is stored in the tags, have appeared recently. E-passports are a good example of this sort of application. As part of its U.S.-VISIT program, the U.S. government mandated the adoption of e-passports by the 27 nations in its Visa-Waiver Program. A combination of RFID technology and biometric technology is employed [7,16,17]. The RFID tags store the same information that is printed on its first page (name, date of birth, passport number, etc.) as well as biometric information (facial image). In phase 2 of the European e-passport project [18], the biometric data from two fingerprints, which is very sensitive information, will also be stored.

Several organizations like CASPIAN [19] and FOEBUD [20] are strongly against the massive deployment of RFID technology. They believe that RFID technology will lead to a significant loss of citizens' privacy. Some of CASPIAN's activities include successful boycott campaigns against important companies like Benetton [21,22], Tesco [23], and Gillette [24], to name but a few. Additionally, a book titled *SPYCHIPS: How Major Corporations and Government Plan to Track your Every Move with RFID*, published in 2005 [25], has contributed to promoting suspicion about RFID technology.

Another example of objection to RFID technology is the case of California State Senator Joe Simitian (Senate Bill 682), who planned to restrict the use of identification systems based on RFID technology: "The act would prohibit identity documents created, mandated, or issued by various public entities from containing a contactless integrated circuit or other device that can broadcast personal information or enable personal information to be scanned remotely" [26]. Due to significant industry opposition, Bill 682 was stalled in the Assembly Appropriations Committee and an important missed deadline resulted in the expiry of the Bill. Legislative maneuvering allowed the resurrection of the case by means of Bill 768 [27]. This bill was finally vetoed by California Governor Arnold Schwarzenegger. In particular, Bill 768 proposed to

1. Criminalize the "skimming" of personal data from RFID-enabled identification documents.
2. Implement specific provisions to ensure the security of data contained in such identification documents.
3. Impose a three-year moratorium on the use of RFID technology in certain types of government-issued identification documents.

In 2002, Garfinkel proposed a set of rights that should be upheld by any system that uses RFID technology [28]. Consumers should have the:

1. Right to know whether products contain RFID tags
2. Right to have RFID tags removed or deactivated when they purchase products
3. Right to use RFID-enabled services without RFID tags
4. Right to access an RFID tag's stored data
5. Right to know when, where, and why the tags are being read

These rights are not necessarily considered as the basis for a new law, but as a framework for voluntary guidelines that companies wishing to deploy this technology may adopt publicly.

Tracking

Location information is a set of data describing an individual's location over a period of time [29]. The resolution of the system (time and localization) depends on the technology used to collect data.

Indeed, location privacy can be viewed as a particular type of privacy information [30]. A secondary effect of wireless communication is that information can be made public and collected. In a mobile phone context, the regions are divided up into cells. Each time a phone enters a new cell, the mobile is registered. Mobile phone operators record handset location information and supply it to third parties (i.e., police, the company that subscribed the localization service, etc.). Other techniques such as triangulation can be used to increase the precision of the system. The new localization services (i.e., third-generation mobile phones) allow an accuracy of a few meters by means of the incorporation of a global positioning system (GPS) receiver. In data network contexts, Wireless 802.11 Ethernet cards obtain connectivity by registering with access points which could be used to locate a network device.

RFID technology is not a high-tech bugging device. It does not possess GPS functionality or the ability to communicate with satellites. RFID tags do not have the storage and transmission capability for large quantities of information. An RFID system is normally composed of three components: tags, readers, and a back-end database. Readers are connected, using a secure channel, to the database. When a database is present in the system, tags might only transmit an identifier. This identifier is used as an index-search in the database to obtain all the information associated with the tag. Therefore, only people with access to the database can obtain the information about the labeled item.

Most of the time, tags provide the same identifier. Although an attacker cannot obtain the information about the tagged item, an association between the tag and its holder can easily be established. Even where individual tags only contain product codes rather than a unique serial number, tracking is still possible using an assembly of tags (constellations) [31]. To clarify the potential risks of tracking, some examples are given:

Wal-Mart: This is an American public corporation, currently one of the world's largest. It has concentrated on streamlining the supply chain, which is why it encourages all its suppliers to incorporate RFID technology in their supply chains. The substitution of bar codes by RFID tags allows an increase in the reading rate of the pallets as they move along the conveyor belt. RFID readers can automatically scan these as they enter or leave the warehouse, saving time and improving product flow. Right now, RFID technology is used at pallet level. Individual packaging is the next logical step.

Individual product packaging: Imagine that your Tag Heuer bifocals possess a tag and this tag stores a 96-bit static identifier, allowing an attacker to establish a link between the identifier and you. On association, an attacker could know when you passed through a given place, for example when you enter or leave your home, when you arrive at or leave your office, etc. Even worse, the attacker could locate several readers in your favorite mall. He could collect data over a long time (data, time, shop, etc.), acquiring a consumer profile of you. Finally, he could send you personalized advertising information depending on your shopping habits.

E-passports: Since October 2006, the United States has required the adoption of e-passports by all the countries in its Visa-Waiver Program. The International Civil Aviation Organization (ICAO) standard specifies one mandatory cryptographic feature (passive authentication) and two optional cryptographic features (basic access control and active authentication). Passive authentication only demonstrates that tag content is authentic but it does not prove that the data container is secure. Basic authentication ensures that tag content can only be read by an authorized reader. Additionally, a session key is established, encrypting all the information exchanged between the tag and the reader. Active authentication is an anticloning feature, but it does not prevent unauthorized readings. Independent of the security mechanism used, tracking is possible. The electronic chip required by the ICAO must conform to ISO/IEC 14443 A/B already adopted in other applications [32,33]. The collision avoidance in ISO 14443 uses unique identifiers that allow readers to distinguish one tag from another [17]. However, this identifier will allow an attacker to unequivocally identify an e-passport's holder. One simple countermeasure is to generate a new random identifier each time the tag is read.

As has been shown, RFID is not the only technology that permits the tracking of people (i.e., video surveillance, mobile phone, Wireless 802.11 Ethernet cards, GPS, etc.). Nevertheless, the equipment used to track people holding RFID tags is not very expensive. If we return to the example of tracking in a mall, we will understand one of the principal differences between RFID and other localization technologies. The great majority of malls have a video surveillance system. You can be filmed in all the supermarket sections in which you buy an item. Then, the information obtained by the system (images) has to be processed to obtain your consumer profile. However, if RFID technology was employed, data could be automatically collected without the need for subsequent data processing as in video systems.

Tags and Readers

Operating Frequencies and Reading Distances

RFID tags operate in fotlur primary frequency bands [34]:

1. Low frequency (LF) (120–140 kHz)
2. High frequency (HF) (13.56 MHz)

3. Ultrahigh frequency (UHF) (860–960 MHz)
4. Super high frequency/microwave (μW) (2.45 GHz and above)

The characteristics of different frequencies are summarized in Table 21.1.

LF tags: These tags operate at 120–140 kHz. They are generally passive and use near-field inductive coupling. So they are suited for applications reading small amounts of data at relatively slow speeds and at short distances. Their read range varies from 1 to 90 cm, typically below 45 cm. LF tags do not support simultaneous tag reads. LF tags are relatively costly because they require a longer, more expensive copper antenna. They penetrate materials such as water, tissue, wood, and aluminum. Their common applications are in animal identification, automobile security, electronic article surveillance, commerce, and other areas.

HF tags: These tags operate at 13.56 MHz. They are typically passive and typically use inductive coupling. HF tags penetrate materials well, such as water, tissue, wood, aluminum, etc. Their data rates are higher than LF tags and their cost is lower due to the simple antenna design. Their read ranges varies from 1 to 75 cm, typically under 40 cm. HF tags are used in smart shelf, smart cards, libraries, baggage handling, and other applications.

UHF tags: UHF active and passive tags can operate at different frequencies. UHF active tags operate at 433 MHz, and UHF passive tags usually operate at 860–960 MHz. Generally, passive UHF tags are not very effective around metals and water. They perform well at distances greater than 90 cm. UHF passive tags usually reach about 9 m. UHF tags have good non-line-of-sight communication, a high data rate, and can store relatively large amounts of data.

Super high frequency/microwaves tags: These tags operate at frequencies of 2.45 GHz and above (also 5.8 GHz) and can be either active or passive. Their characteristics are similar to those of UHF tags. However, they have faster read rates and are less effective around metals and liquids than tags of lower frequencies. These tags can be smaller in size compared to LF, HF, and UHF tags and are used for electronic toll collection as well as for the tracking of shipping containers, trains, commercial vehicles, parking, etc. The read range varies from 0.3 to 0.9 m for passive tags and is very dependent on design. Active systems also use microwave frequency.

Table 21.1　Tag Frequencies and Reading Distances

Frequency Band	Frequency	Distance	Energy Transfer
Low (LF)	125 kHz	1–90 cm, typically around 45 cm	Inductive coupling
High (HF)	13.56 MHz	1–75 cm, typically under 40 cm	Inductive coupling
Ultrahigh (UHF)	865–868 MHz (Europe) 902–928 MHz (United States) 433 MHz (active tags)	Up to 9 m	Electromagnetic coupling
Microwave (μW)	2.45 GHz 5.8 GHz	Typically 0.3–0.9 m	Electromagnetic coupling

Eavesdropping

RFID technology operates through radio, so communication can be surreptitiously over-heard. In [35], the possible distances at which an attacker can listen to the messages exchanged between a tag and a reader are categorized (see Figure 21.2).

Forward channel eavesdropping range: In the reader-to-tag channel (forward channel) the reader broadcasts a strong signal, allowing its monitoring from a long distance.

Backward channel eavesdropping range: The signal transmitted in the tag-to-reader (backward channel) is relatively weak and may only be monitored in close proximity to the tag.

Operating range: The read ranges shown in "Operating Frequencies and Reading Distances" section are the operating read range using sales-standard readers.

Malicious scanning range: An adversary may build his own reader-archiving longer read ranges, especially if regulations about radio devices are not respected. A conversation between a reader and a tag can be eavesdropped over a greater distance than is possible with direct communication. For example, tags compliant to ISO 14443 have a reading distance of around 10 cm (using standard equipment). However, Kfir et al. showed that this distance can be increased to 55 cm employing a loop antenna and signal processing [36].

Eavesdropping is particular problematic for two reasons:

1. *Feasibility*: it can be accomplished from long distances.
2. *Detection difficulty*: it is purely passive and does not imply power signal emission.

Eavesdropping attacks are a serious threat mainly when sensitive information is transmitted on the channel. To give an example, we consider the use of RFID technology in payments cards (RFID credit cards) [37]. In an eavesdropping attack, information exchanged between the credit

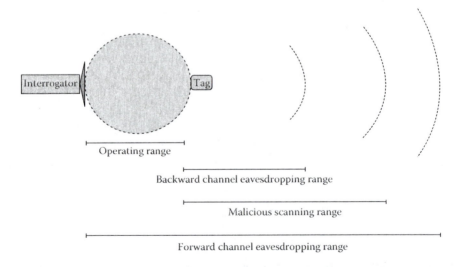

Figure 21.2 Eavesdropping range classification. (From Ranasinghe, D.C. and Cole, P.H., Confronting security and privacy threats in modern RFID systems. In *Proceedings of ACSSC 06*, 2006, pp. 2058–2064.)

card reader and the RFID credit card is captured. Heydt-Benjamin et al. showed how this attack can be carried out [38]. An antenna was located next to an off-the-shelf RFID credit card reader. The radio signal picked up by the antenna was processed to translate it into human readable form. In particular, the following pieces of data were captured: cardholder name, complete credit card number, credit card expiry date, credit card type, and finally information about software version and supported communications protocols. As the above example shows, eavesdropping attacks should therefore be considered and treated seriously.

Authentication

Entity authentication allows the verification of the identity of one entity by another. The authenticity of the claimed entity can only be ascertained for the instant of the authentication exchange. A secure means of communication should be used to provide authenticity of the subsequent data exchanged. To prevent replay attacks, a time-variant parameter, such as a time stamp, a sequence number, or a challenge may be used. The messages exchanged between entities are called tokens. At least one token has to be exchanged for unilateral authentication and at least two tokens for mutual authentication. An additional token may be needed if a challenge has to be sent to initiate the protocol.

In RFID context, the first proposals found in the literature are based on unilateral authentication [39–41]. However, the necessity of mutual authentication has been confirmed in many publications [42–45]. In ISO/IEC 9784, the different mechanisms for entity authentication are described [46]:

- Part 1: General model
- Part 2: Entity authentication using symmetric techniques
- Part 3: Entity authentication using a public key algorithm
- Part 4: Entity authentication using a cryptographic check function

Use of a cryptographic check function seems to be the most precise solution for RFID. Due to the fact that standard cryptographic primitives exceed the capabilities of a great number of tags, the design of lightweight primitives is imperative, at least for low-cost RFID tags.

The two entities (claimant/verifier) share a secret authentication key. An entity corroborates its identity by demonstrating knowledge of the shared key. This is accomplished by using a secret key with a cryptographic check function applied to specific data to obtain a cryptographic check value. This value can be recalculated by the verifier and compared with the received value. The following mechanisms, as shown in Figure 21.3, are possible.

Skimming

Takashimaya, one of the largest retailers in Japan, now sells antiskimming cards called "Sherry" at their department stores. Consumers can just put the cards in their wallets to protect their RFID-chipped train passes, etc. from skimming attacks.

The antiskimming card functions by creating a reverse electromagnetic field like Taiyo's technology [47].

Eavesdropping is the opportunistic interception of information exchanged between a legitimate tag and legitimate reader. However, skimming occurs when the data stored on the RFID tag is read without the owner's knowledge or consent. An unauthorized reader interacts with the tag to obtain the data. This attack can be carried out because most of the tags broadcast their memory content without requiring authentication.

One pass—unilateral authentication

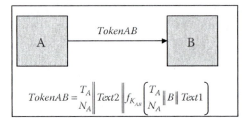

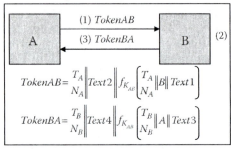

$$TokenAB = \frac{T_A}{N_A} \left\| Text2 \right\| f_{K_{AB}} \left(\frac{T_A}{N_A} \| B \| Text1 \right)$$

Two pass—unilateral authentication

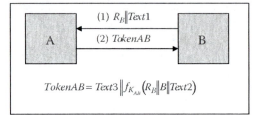

$$TokenAB = Text3 \left\| f_{K_{AB}} (R_B \| B \| Text2) \right.$$

Two pass—mutual authentication

$$TokenAB = \frac{T_A}{N_A} \left\| Text2 \right\| f_{K_{AB}} \left(\frac{T_A}{N_A} \| B \| Text1 \right)$$

$$TokenBA = \frac{T_B}{N_B} \left\| Text4 \right\| f_{K_{AB}} \left(\frac{T_B}{N_B} \| A \| Text3 \right)$$

Three pass—mutual authentication

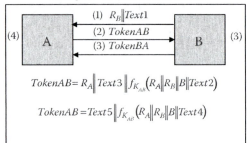

$$TokenAB = R_A \left\| Text3 \right\| f_{K_{AB}} (R_A \| R_B \| B \| Text2)$$

$$TokenAB = Text5 \left\| f_{K_{AB}} (R_A \| R_B \| B \| Text4) \right.$$

FIGURE 21.3 Entity authentication mechanisms.

One interesting project is Adam Laurie's RFIDIOt project [48]. Specifically, RFIDIOt is an open-source library for exploring RFID devices. Several experiments with readers operating at 13.56 MHz and 125/134.2 kHz are shown. The number of standards supported by the library is around 50. Some examples of the attacks carried out are the following:

Nonauthentication example: In 2004, Verichip received approval to develop a human-implant RFID microchip [49]. About twice the length of a grain of rice, the device is typically implanted above the triceps of an individual's right arm. Once scanned at the proper frequency, the Verichip answers with a unique 16-digit number which can correlate the user to the information stored on a database. The type of tag used by Verichip appears to be an EM4x05. This kind of tag can be read simply with the program "readlfx.py," obtaining the following information: card ID, tag type, application identifier, country code, and national ID.

Password authentication example: Since 2003, the Oyster card has been used on Transport for London and National Rail services. The Oyster card is a contactless smart card, with a claimed proximity range of about 8 cm, and based on Philips's MIFARE® standard [50]. A code for attacking this kind of card is included. The sample program "bruteforce.py" can be run against it, and it will try to log in the sector 0 by choosing random numbers as the key.

Nowadays, the security of e-passports has aroused great interest [16,17,51,52]. Skimming is problematic because e-passports possess sensitive data. The mandatory passive authentication mechanism demands the use of digital signatures. A reader will be able to verify that the data came from the correct passport-issuing authority. However, digital signatures do not link data to a specific passport. Additionally, if only passive authentication is supported, an attacker equipped with a reader could obtain sensitive information such as your name, birthday, or even your facial photograph. This is possible because readers are not authenticated; in other words, the tag answers indiscriminately. Certain projects exist which give the code needed to read e-passports: RFIDIOt

(Adam Laurie) [48], OpenMRTD (Harald Welte) [53], and JMRTD (SoS group, ICIS, Radbound University) [54].

Cloning and Physical Attacks

Symmetric-key cryptography can be used to avoid tag cloning attacks. Specifically, a challenge-response like the following can be employed. First, the tag is singulated from many by means of a collision-avoidance protocol like the binary tree walking protocol. The tag (T_i) shares the key (K_i) with the reader. Afterward, the following messages are exchanged:

1. The reader generates a fresh random number (R) and transmits it to the tag.
2. The tag computes $H = g(K_i, R)$ and sends it back to the reader.
3. The reader computes and checks its equality with H.

The g function can be implemented by a hash function or, alternatively, by an encryption function. Note that if the g function is well constructed and appropriately deployed, it is infeasible for an attacker to simulate the tag. Because standard cryptographic primitives (hash functions, message authentication codes, block/stream ciphers, etc.) are extravagant solutions for low-cost RFID tags on account of their demand for circuit size, power consumption, and memory size [55], the design of new lightweight primitives is pressing.

For some kinds of tags, resources are not so restricted. However, their cost is much higher than low-cost RFID tags (i.e., tags used in supply chain). An example of these sorts of tags are e-passports. The active authentication method is an anticloning feature. The mechanism relies on public cryptography. It works by having e-passports prove possession of a private key:

1. The tag generates an 8-byte nonce and sends it to the tag.
2. The tag digitally signs this value using its private key and transmits it to the reader.
3. The reader can verify the correctness of the response with the public key supposedly associated with the passport.

Tamper-resistant microprocessors are used to store and process private and sensitive information, such as private keys or electronic money. The attacker should not be able to retrieve or modify this information. To achieve this objective, chips are designed so that the information is not accessible using external means and can only be accessed by the embedded software, which should contain the appropriate security measures.

Making simple electronic devices secure against tampering is very difficult, as a great number of attacks are possible, including [56]:

- Mechanical machining
- Laser machining
- Energy attacks
- Temperature imprinting
- Probe attacks
- Active or injector probes
- Energy probes

- Manual material removal
- Clock glitching
- Electronic beam read/write
- Imaging technology
- Water machining
- Shaped charge technology
- Radiation imprinting
- High-voltage imprinting
- Passive probes
- Pico probes
- Matching methods
- High or low voltage
- Circuit disruption
- IR laser read/write

As sensitive information such as cryptographic keys are stored on the chips, tamper-resistant devices may be designed to erase this information when penetration of their security encapsulation or out-of-specification environmental parameters is detected. Some devices are even able to erase all their information after their power supply has been interrupted.

In the RFID context, we have to distinguish between low-cost RFID tags and tags used in applications without severe price restrictions. Low-cost RFID tags are very constrained resources (storing, computing, and energy consumption). These kinds of tags are usually nonresistant to physical attacks. An example of these kinds of tags are tags compliant with the EPC Class 1 Generation 2 specification [57]. High-cost tags, sometimes called contactless chips or smart cards, are not so restrictive regarding resources. However, price increases from €0.05 to several euros. For example, the chips used in e-passports have an EAL5+ security level, the highest security level for chips [58]. Therefore, an attacker will not be able to acquire the private key used in private authentication to avoid cloning attacks. The plusID tag, manufactured by Bradcom, is another example of tamper-resistant tags [59]. Initially, its security level was 2 (tamper evidence) according to Federal Information Processing Standards (FIPS), but it was finally increased to level 3 (tamper resistant).

Replay and Relay Attacks

A replay attack copies a stream of messages between two parties and replays it to one or more of two parties. A generalized definition of a replay attack could be the following: an attack on a security protocol using replay of messages from a different context into the intended (or original and expected) context, thereby fooling the honest participant(s) into thinking they have successfully completed the protocol run [60]. An exhaustive classification of replay attacks can be found in [61].

Common techniques to avoid replay attacks are incremental sequence number, clock synchronization, or a nonce. In [62], a set of design principles for avoiding replay attacks in cryptographic protocols is presented. In a RFID context, clock synchronization is not feasible because passive RFID tags cannot make use of clocks, as these kind of tags do not have an on-board power source. Incremental sequence such as session token may be a straightforward solution if tracking is not considered a threat. Therefore, the use of a nonce is the most suitable option for RFID tags.

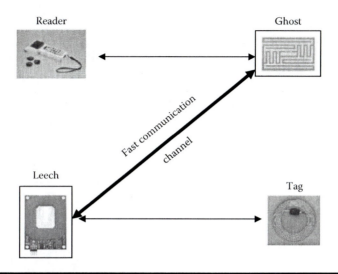

Figure 21.4 Relay attacks.

A number of factors combine to make relay attacks on RFID technology possible. Tags are read over a distance and are activated automatically when close to a reader. Therefore, an attacker could communicate with a tag without the knowledge of its owner.

Two devices, as shown in Figure 21.4, are involved in the relay attack: the ghost and the leech [36]. The ghost is a device which fakes a card to the reader and the leech is a device which fakes a reader to the card. A fast communication channel between the legitimate reader and the victim card is created by the ghost and the leech:

1. Legitimate reader sends a message (A) to the ghost.
2. Ghost receives it and forwards this message (A) to the leech through the fast communication channel (minimum delay).
3. Leech fakes the real reader and sends the message (A) to the legitimate tag.
4. Legitimate tag computes a new message (B) and transmits it to the leech.
5. Leech receives it and forwards this message (B) to the ghost through the fast communication channel.
6. Ghost forwards this message (B) to the real reader.

This sort of attack dispels the assumption that readers and tags should be very close to communicate. Additionally, even if communications are encrypted, the attack is feasible because messages are only relayed through a fast communication channel, without requiring knowledge of its content. In [63], a practical relay attack against ISO 14443 compliant tags is described.

Hiding

RFID technology uses electromagnetic radio waves. Labeled items can be therefore protected by insulating them from any kind of electromagnetic radiation:

Faraday cage: A Faraday cage or shield is a container made of conducting material, or a mesh of such material. This blocks out radio signals of certain frequencies. There are currently a number of companies that sell this type of solution [64,65].

Passive jamming: Each time a reader wants to interact with a single tag, the tag will have to be singulated from a population of tags. A collision-avoidance protocol such as Aloha or binary tree walking protocol may be employed. To conceal the presence of a particular tag, this could simulate the full spectrum of possible tags in the singulation phase, hiding its presence. This concept was first introduced by Juels et al. as the "blocker tag" [66]. In 2004, a variant of the blocker concept, named "soft blocking," was introduced [67]. This involves software (or firmware) modules that offer a different balance of characteristics from ordinary blockers.

Active jamming: Another way of achieving isolation from electromagnetic waves is disturbing the radio channel known as active jamming of RF signals. This disturbance may be effected with a device that actively broadcasts radio signals, so as to completely disrupt the radio channel, thus preventing the normal operation of RFID readers. However, in most cases, government regulations on radio emissions (power and bandwidth) are violated [68].

Deactivating

Some methods exist for deactivating tags and rendering them unreadable. The most common method consists of generating a high-power RF field that induces sufficient current to burn out a weak section of the antenna. The connection between the chip and the antenna is cut off, rendering it useless. This method is usually chosen to address privacy concerns and to deactivate tags that are used to label individual items or prevent thefts in stores.

The benefits of using RFID technology in a store are clear. However, the deactivation of tags may be malicious. The necessary technology can be available to anyone. The usual range of a "kill" signal is only a few centimeters. However, designing and building a high-gain antenna with a high-power transmitter is easy. Using batteries, it could probably fit into a backpack. Then an attacker entering a store could kill all the tags, causing widespread retail chaos. A practical implementation of this sort of attack is the RFID-Zapper project [69,70].

Karjoth and Moskowitz proposed the use of physical RFID structures that permit a consumer to disable a tag by mechanically altering the tag [71]. In "clipped tags," the consumer can physically separate the body (chip) from the head (antenna) in an intuitive way. Such separation provides visual confirmation that the tag has been deactivated. Then the tag can be reactivated by means of physical contact. The reactivation requires deliberate actions on the part of its owner. Indeed, reactivation cannot be carried out without the owner's knowledge unless the item was stolen.

To avoid wanton deactivation of tags, the use of kill passwords has been proposed. Tags compliant to the EPC Class 1 Generation 2 implement this feature [57]. When an electronic product code (EPC) tag receives the "kill" command, it renders itself permanently inoperative. However, to protect tags from malicious deactivation, the kill command is PIN protected. One of the main problems linked to solutions based on password is its management. Employing the same password for all tags could be a naive solution. Nevertheless, if a tag is compromised, all the tags would be at risk. Another straightforward solution is that each tag has a different password with the associated management and scalability problems.

The potential benefits of RFID technology usage are reduced if tags are permanently deactivated. Instead of killing tags, they could be put to sleep, rendering them only temporarily inoperative. As with the killing process, sleeping/waking up tags will not offer real protection if anyone is able to accomplish these operations. So some form of access control, such as PINs, will be needed. To sleep/wake up a tag, a PIN has to be transmitted.

Cryptographic Vulnerabilities

In the nineteenth century, Kerckhoffs set out the principles of cryptography systems [72]:

1. The system must be practically, if not mathematically, indecipherable.
2. It must not be required to be secret and it must be able to fall into the hands of the enemy without inconvenience.
3. Its key must be communicable and retainable without the help of written notes, and changeable or able to be modified at the will of the correspondents.
4. It must be applicable to telegraphic correspondence.
5. It must be portable, and its usage and function must not require the concourse of several people.
6. Finally, it is necessary, given the circumstances that command its application, that the system be easy to use, requiring neither mental strain nor the knowledge of a long series of rules to observe.

RFID tags are very constrained devices, with restrictions on power consumption, storage, and circuitry. Due to these severe limitations, some commercial RFID tags support weak cryptographic primitives, and thus vulnerable authentication protocols. Additionally, some of these cryptographic primitives are proprietary. The use of proprietary solutions is not really inadequate if algorithms are published to be analyzed by the research community. However, time has shown, the security of an algorithm cannot reside in "obscurity." A system relying on security through obscurity may have theoretical or actual security vulnerabilities, but its owners or designers believe that the flaws are unknown and that attackers are unlikely to find them [72].

Texas Instruments manufacture a low-frequency tag, named digital signature transponder (DST). The DST executes a challenge-response protocol. The reader and the DST share a secret key K_i. The reader sends a challenge R to the DST. The DST computes an encryption function of the challenge $C = e_{Ki}(R)$ and sends this value to the reader. The reader computes $C' = e_{K'_i}(R)$ and compares this value with the received value. The challenge is 40 bits in length and the output of the encryption function is 24 bits in length. The length of the K_i is only 40 bits. It is a very short length. In 2005 the National Institute of Standards and Technology [73] and the ECRYPT EU Network of Excellence on cryptography [74] recommended a key length of 80 bits for a minimal level of general purpose protection and 112 bits for the following ten years. The most common uses of DST are the following:

1. DST is employed as a theft-deterrent (immobilizer keys) in automobiles, such as Ford and Toyota vehicles.
2. DST serves as a wireless payment device (speedpass), which can be used by more than seven million individuals in around 10,000 Exxon and Mobile gas stations.

Texas Instruments has not published details of the encryption algorithm, basing itself on security through algorithm obscurity. A team of researchers at Johns Hopkins University and RSA Laboratories discovered security vulnerabilities in the DST [75]. In particular, a successful reverse engineering of the DST encryption algorithm was accomplished. First, a rough schematic of the cipher was obtained from a published Texas Instruments presentation. With the reverse engineering of the cipher, they showed that a 40-bit key length was inadequate, the cipher being not only vulnerable to brute-force attacks as known by cryptographers. The attack can be divided into three phases:

Reverse engineering: They were equipped with a DST reader and some blank DST tags. With the reader and the blank tags, the output of the encryption function, with any key and challenge, could be obtained. Using specific key/challenge pairs and centering on the schematic of the encryption, operational details of the algorithm were derived.

Key cracking: After determining the encryption algorithm, a programmed hardware "key cracker" was implemented to recover the unique cryptographic key of the DST. The cracker operated by brute force (full space of 2^{40}). Given two input-output, in about 30 minutes the secret key was recovered.

Simulation: They programmed a hardware device with the key recovered from the DST. This device could impersonate the original DST.

The research on the DST exemplifies Kerckhoffs' principles. Another significant example is the proprietary CRYPTO1 encryption algorithm used in Philips Mifare cards, which has been recently reverse engineered [76]. We recommend the publication of any algorithms. Open algorithms can be analyzed and refined by the scientific community, bolstering confidence in their security.

Back-End Database

Tag Counterfeiting and Duplication

Because of the incorporation of RFID technology in sensitive applications such as passports [77] and pharmaceutical pedigrees [78], the possibility of creating counterfeiting tags has unleashed some concerns.

Here are some arguments that may dissuade users from alarmist attitudes [79]:

1. Usually, each tag has a unique identifier (ID) that allows its unequivocal identification. To counterfeit a tag, one would have to modify the identity of an item, which generally implies tag manipulation. The tag (ID) implementation may vary in each manufacturer as well as in each product. The major manufacturers first program the tag and then lock it. So resistance to using attacks lies in the lock. In most cases, it is not possible to unlock the tag without using invasive techniques. These techniques are not commonly available to the general industry.
2. RFID tags are generally sold preprogrammed with their identifiers, this being one of the phases of the normal production process. The ID format usually accords with a standard. The nonavailability of blank tags will therefore reduce the possibility of counterfeiting.
3. Another alternative is the design of blank tags. However, even with the equipment necessary for IC fabrication, designing these kind of chips is not an easy task.

Despite the difficulty of counterfeiting tags, on some occasions tags are duplicated. It is a similar problem to that of credit card fraud, where a card is duplicated and possibly used in multiple places at the same time. As duplicate tags cannot be operatively distinguished, the back-end database should detect rare conditions. An example of a rare condition is the following: a tag cannot be in the toll gate on the Madrid-Barcelona motorway and 15 minutes later in the toll gate of the Valencia-Barcelona motorway. The design of back-end databases should be considered case by case [80].

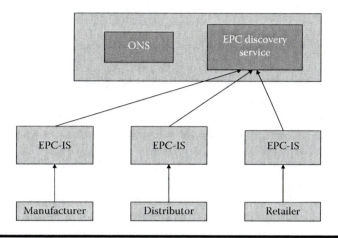

FIGURE 21.5   EPCglobal network.

EPC Network: ONS Attacks

The EPCglobal network is made up of three key elements, as displayed in Figure 21.5:

1. EPC information services (EPC-IS)
2. EPC discovery services
3. ONS

When an RFID tag is manufactured with an EPC, the EPC is registered within the ONS. The RFID tag is attached to a product and the EPC becomes a part of that product as it moves through the supply chain. The particular product information is added to the manufacturer's EPC-IS and the knowledge that this data exists within the manufacturer's EPC-IS is passed to the EPC discovery service.

The ONS is a distributed but authoritative directory service that routes request for information about EPCs. Existing or new network resources can be employed to route the requests. The ONS is similar to domain name service (DNS) both technologically and functionally. When a query is sent to the ONS including the EPC code, one or more localizations (uniform resource locator or URL), where information about items reside, are returned. The ONS service is divided in two layers. First, the Root ONS, which is the authoritative directory of manufacturers whose products may have information on the EPC network. Second, the local ONS, which is the directory of products for that particular manufacturer.

As the ONS can be considered a subset of the DNS, the same security risks are applicable. In 2004, a threat analysis of the domain name system was published as RFC 3833 [81]. Some of the principal threats identified are the following:

1. *Packet interception*: manipulating internet protocol (IP) packets carrying DNS information.
2. *Query prediction*: manipulating the query/answer schemes of the DNS protocol.
3. *Cache poisoning*: injecting manipulated information into DNS caches.
4. *Betrayal by trusted server*: attacker controlling DNS servers in use.
5. *DoS*: DNS is vulnerable to DoS as happens in any other network service. Additionally, the DNS itself might be used to attack third parties.

However, there are some risks that are particular to the ONS service [82]:

1. *Privacy*: There are many situations where the EPC of an RFID tag can be considered highly sensitive information. Sensitive information can be obtained even knowing just part of the EPC. For example, knowing only the class of the identifier, you can find out the kind of object. To obtain the information associated with a tag, the EPC-IS has to be located. Even if the connections to the EPC-IS are secured (i.e., Secure Sockets Layer [SSL]/Transport Layer Security [TLS] protocol), the initial ONS look-up process is not authenticated or encrypted in the first place. Therefore, sensitive information passes in clear on the channel (middleware-networks-DNS server).

2. *Integrity*: The correctness and the completeness of the information should be guaranteed. An attacker controlling intermediate DNS servers or launching a successful man-in-the-middle attack could forge the list of URLs (i.e., a fraudulent server). To prevent this attack, an authentication mechanism should be used for the EPC-IS.

3. *Availability*: If the adoption of the EPC network is widespread, there will be a great number of companies dependent on network services. ONS will become a service highly exposed to attacks. These could include distributed denial-of-service (DDoS) attacks that reduce the functioning of the server or its network connection by issuing countless and intense queries, or targeted exploits that shut down the server software or its operating system.

Virus Attacks

The RFID tag memory contains a unique identifier, but additional data may be stored. The data size varies from a few bytes to several kilobytes. The memory where this additional information is stored is rewritable. The information sent by the tags is implicitly trusted, which implies some security threats [80,83]:

1. *Buffer overflow*: It is one of the most frequent sources of security vulnerabilities in software. Programming languages, such as C or C++, are not memory safe. In other words, the lengths of the inputs are not checked. An attacker could introduce an input that is deliberately longer, writing out of the buffer. As program control data is often located in memory areas adjacent to data buffers, the buffer overflow may lead the program to execute an arbitrary code. As a great number of tags have severe storage limitations, resource-rich tag-simulating devices could be utilized [84].

2. *Code insertion*: An attacker might inject malicious code into an application, using any script language (i.e., common gateway interface, Java, Perl, etc.). RFID tags with data written in a script language could perform an attack of this kind. Imagine that the tags used for tracking baggage in the airport contain the airport destination in their data field. Each time a tag is read, the back-end system fires the query, "select * from location_table where airport =<tag data>." Imagine that an attacker stores in one piece of baggage "MAD;shutdown." When this data is read, the database will be shut down and the baggage system will crash.

3. *Structure Query Language (SQL) injection*: This is a type of code insertion attack, executing SQL codes in the database that were not intended. The main objectives of these attacks are the following: enumerate the database structure, retrieve authorized data, make unauthorized modifications or deletions, etc. RFID tags could contain data for a SQL injection attack. Storage limitation is not a problem, as it is possible to do a lot of harm with a very small amount of SQL. For example, the SQL "drop table <*tablename*>" will delete a specified database table.

Summarizing, an RFID tag is an unsecured and untrusted database. So the information obtained from such devices should be analyzed until there is sufficient evidence that the data is accurate. However, this is not a new concept, as in all information systems the input data should be examined to ensure that it will not cause problems.

References

1. L. Bolotnyy and G. Robins. Physically unclonable function-based security and privacy in RFID systems. In *Proceedings of PerCom'07*, pp. 211–220. IEEE Computer Society Press, Washington, DC, 2007.
2. J. Cichon, M. Klonowski, and M. Kutylowski. Privacy protection in dynamic systems based on RFID tags. In *Proceedings of PerSec'07*, pp. 235–240. IEEE Computer Society Press, Washington, DC, 2007.
3. T. Heydt-Benjamin, H.-J. Chae, B. Defend, and K. Fu. Privacy for public transportation. In *Proceedings of PET'06, LNCS*, 4258, pp. 1–19. Springer-Verlag, Cambridge, U.K., 2006.
4. T. Hjorth. Supporting privacy in RFID systems. Master thesis, Technical University of Denmark, Lyngby, Denmark, 2004.
5. A. Juels and R. Pappu. Squealing euros: Privacy protection in RFID-enabled banknotes. In *Proceedings of FC'03, LNCS*, 2742, pp. 103–121. Springer-Verlag, Guadeloupe, French West Indies, 2003.
6. S. Kinoshita, M. Ohkubo, F. Hoshino, G. Morohashi, O. Shionoiri, and A. Kanai. Privacy enhanced active RFID tag. In *Proceedings of ECHISE'05*, Munich, Germany, 2005.
7. E. Kosta, M. Meints, M. Hensen, and M. Gasson. An analysis of security and privacy issues relating to RFID enabled e-passports. In *Proceedings of Sec'07, IFIP*, 232, pp. 467–472. Springer, Sandton, South Africa, 2007.
8. D. Ranasinghe, D. Engels, and P. Cole. Security and privacy: Modest proposals for low-cost RFID systems. In *Proceedings of Auto-ID Labs Research Workshop*, Zurich, Switzerland, 2004.
9. M. Rieback, B. Crispo, and A. Tanenbaum. Uniting legislation with RFID privacy-enhancing technologies. In *Security and Protection of Information*, Brno, Czech Republic, 2005.
10. M. Rieback, G. Gaydadjiev, B. Crispo, R. Hofman, and A. Tanenbaum. A platform for RFID security and privacy administration. In *Proceedings of LISA'06*, Washington, DC, 2006.
11. S.E. Sarma, S.A. Weis, and D.W. Engels. RFID systems and security and privacy implications. In *Proceedings of CHES'02, LNCS*, 2523, pp. 454–470. Springer-Verlag, Redwood City, CA, 2002.
12. S. Spiekermann and H. Ziekow. RFID: A 7-point plan to ensure privacy. In *Proceedings of ECIS'05*, Regensburg, Germany, 2005.
13. Universal declaration of human rights, Article 12, 1948.
14. EU Directive 95/46/EC—Data Protection Directive. *Official Journal of the European Communities*, November 23, 1995.
15. M. Weiser. The computer for the 21st century. *Scientific American*, 265(3):94–104, September 1991.
16. J.-H. Hoepman, E. Hubbers, B. Jacobs, M. Oostdijk, and R. Wichers Schreur. Crossing borders: Security and privacy issues of the European e-passport. In *Proceedings of IWSEC'06, LNCS*, 4266, pp. 152–167. Springer-Verlag, Kyoto, Japan, 2006.
17. A. Juels, D. Molnar, and D. Wagner. Security and privacy issues in e-passports. In *Proceedings of SecureComm'05*. IEEE Computer Society, Athens, Greece, 2005.
18. Advanced security mechanisms for machine readable travel documents—extended access control (EAC) version. 1.0.1. Technical guideline TR-03110, Federal Office of Information Security, Bonn, Germany, 2006.
19. CASPIAN. http://www.nocards.org/, October 1, 2005.
20. FoeBuD. http://www.foebud.org/rfid, October 5, 2005.
21. Boycott Benetton. http://www.boycottbenetton.com/, April 9, 2003.
22. *RFID Journal*. Behind the benetton brouhaha. http://www.rfidjournal.com, April 14, 2003.
23. Boycott Tesco. http://www.boycotttesco.com/, January 26, 2005.
24. Boycott Guillette. http://www.boycottguillette.com/, September 2, 2003.

25. K. Albrecht and L. McIntyre. *SPYCHIPS: How Major Corporations and Government Plan to Track your Every Move with RFID*. Nelson Communications, Inc., Nashville, TN, 2005.
26. California Senate Bill 682. http://www.epic.org/privacy/rfid/, February 22, 2005.
27. What's in California's proposed RFID Bill? http://www.rfidproductsnew.com, January 20, 2006.
28. S. Garfinkel. Bill of Rights. http://www.technologyreview.com, October 2002.
29. G. Danezis, S. Lewis, and R. Anderson. How much is location privacy worth. In *Proceedings of Workshop of Economics of IS'05*, Cambridge, MA, 2005.
30. A. Beresfor and F. Stajano. Location privacy in pervasive computing. *IEEE Pervasive Computing*, 2(1):1536–1268, 2003.
31. S. Weis, S. Sarma, R. Rivest, and D. Engels. Security and privacy aspects of low-cost radio frequency identification systems. In *Proceedings of SPC'03, LNCS*, 2802, pp. 454–469. Springer-Verlag, 2003.
32. Identification cards–contactless integrated circuits cards–proximity cards. http://www.wg8.de/sdi.html, 2001.
33. Machine readable travel documments, Doc. 9303. http://www.mrtd.icao.int, July 8, 2006.
34. M. Brown, E. Zeisel, and R. Sabella. *RFID+Exam Cram*. Que Publishing, Indianapolis, IN, 2006.
35. D.C. Ranasinghe and P.H. Cole. Confronting security and privacy threats in modern RFID systems. In *Proceedings of ACSSC 06*, pp. 2058–2064, Pacific Grove, CA, 2006.
36. Z. Kfir and A. Wool. Picking virtual pockets using relay attacks on contactless smartcard systems. In *Proceedings of SecureComm'05*. IEEE Computer Society, Athens, Greece, 2005.
37. J. Atkinson. Contactless credit card consumer report. http://www.findcreditcards.org, April 3, 2006.
38. T.S Heydt-Benjamin, D.V. Bailey, K. Fu, A. Juels, and T. Ohare. Vulnerabilities in first-generation RFID-enabled credit cards. In *Proceedings of FC'07*, LNCS. Springer-Verlag, Lowlands, Scarborough, Trinidad/Tobago, 2007.
39. M. Feldhofer. A proposal for an authentication protocol in a security layer for RFID smart tags. In *Proceedings of MELECON'04*, vol. 2. IEEE Computer Society, Dubrovnik, Croatia, 2004.
40. I. Vajda and L. Buttyán. Lightweight authentication protocols for low-cost RFID tags. In *Proceedings of UBICOMP'03*, Seattle, WA, 2003.
41. M. Ohkubo, K. Suzuki, and S. Kinoshita. Cryptographic approach to "privacy-friendly" tags. In *Proceedings of RFID Privacy Workshop*, MIT, Cambridge, MA, 2003.
42. P. Peris-Lopez, J.C. Hernandez-Castro, J. Estevez-Tapiador, and A. Ribagorda. M2AP: A minimalist mutual-authentication protocol for low-cost RFID tags. In *Proceedings of UIC'06, LNCS*, 4519, pp. 912–923. Springer-Verlag, Wuhan and Three Gorges, China, 2006.
43. H.Y. Chien and C.H. Chen. Mutual authentication protocol for RFID conforming to EPC class-1 generation-2 standards. *Computer Standards and Interfaces*, 29(2):254–259, 2007.
44. A. Juels. Minimalist cryptography for low-cost RFID tags. In *Proceedings of SCN'04, LNCS*, 3352, pp. 149–164. Springer-Verlag, Amalfi, Italy, 2004.
45. D. Molnar and D. Wagner. Privacy and security in library RFID: Issues, practices, and architectures. In *Proceedings of ACM CCS'04*, pp. 210–219. ACM Press, Washington, DC, 2004.
46. ISO/IEC 9798 Information Technology—Security techniques—Entity authentication. http://www.iso.org, 1995.
47. Anti-skimming in Japan. http://www.future.iftf.org/index.html, August 10, 2005.
48. A. Laurie. RFIDIOt project. http://www.rfidiot.org, August 5, 2007.
49. Verichip corporation. http://www.verichipcorp.com, August 15, 2007.
50. Easing traveling in London's congested public transport network. http://www.mifare.net/showcases/london.asp, August 10, 2007.
51. M. Halváč and T. Rosa. A note on the relay attacks on e-passports: The case of Czech e-passports. In *Cryptology ePrint Archive, Report 2007/244*, IACR, 2007.
52. D. Carluccio, K. Lemke, and C. Paar. Electromagnetic side channel analysis of a contactless smart card: First results. In *Handout of Workshop on RFID Security*, Graz, Austria, 2006.
53. H. Welte. OpenMRTD project. http://www.openmrtd.org, August 7, 2007.
54. SoSGroup, ICIS, and Radbound University. JMRTD project. http://www.jmrtd.sourceforge.net/, August 9, 2007.
55. A. Juels. RFID security and privacy: A research survey. Manuscript, 2005.

56. S.H. Weingart. Physical security devices for computer subsystems: A survey of attacks and defenses. In *Proceedings of CHES'00, LNCS*, 1965, pp. 302–317. Springer-Verlag, Worcester, MA, 2000.

57. Class-1 Generation-2 UHF air interface protocol standard version 1.0.9: "Gen-2". http://www.epcglobalinc.org/standards/, 2005.

58. C. Lee, D. Houdeau, and R. Bergmann. Evolution of the e-passport. http://www.homelandsecurityasia.com, September 3, 2007.

59. C. Swedberg. Broadcom introduces secure RFID chip. RFID Journal. http://www.rfidjournal.com, June 29, 2006.

60. S. Malladi, S. Alves-Foss, and R. Heckendorn. On preventing replay attacks on security protocols. In *Proceedings of SM'02*, pp. 77–83, CSREA Press, Las Vegas, NV, 2003.

61. P. Syverson. A taxonomy of replay attacks. In *Proceedings of CSF'94*, pp. 187–191. IEEE Computer Society, Franconia, NH, 1994.

62. T. Aura. Strategies against replay attacks. In *Proceedings of CSF'97*. IEEE Computer Society, Rockport, MA, 1997.

63. G. Hancke. Practical attacks on proximity identification systems (short paper). In *Proceedings of SP'06*. IEEE Computer Society, Oakland, CA, 2000.

64. mCloak for RFID tags. http://www.mobilecloak.com/rfidtag/rfid.tag.html, September 10, 2005.

65. Envelope to help you do it with your security, privacy, and discretion intact. http://www.emvelope.com, August 13, 2007.

66. A. Juels, R. Rivest, and M. Szydlo. The blocker tag: Selective blocking of RFID tags for consumer privacy. In *ACM CCS'03*, pp. 103–111. ACM Press, Washington, DC, 2003.

67. A. Juels and J. Brainard. Soft blocking: Flexible blocker tags on the cheap. In *WPES'04*, pp. 1–7. ACM Press, Washington, DC, 2004.

68. RSA Laboratories. Faq on RFID and RFID privacy. http://www.rsa.com/rsalabs/node.asp?id=2120, October 4, 2007.

69. J. Collins. RFID-Zapper shoots to kill. *RFID Journal*, January 23, 2006.

70. MiniMe and Mahajivana. RFID-Zapper project. http://www.events.ccc.de/congress/2005/static/r/f/i/RFID-Zapper(EN)_77f3.html, 2006.

71. G. Karjoth and P.A. Moskowitz. Disabling RFID tags with visible confirmation: Clipped tags are silenced. In *Proceedings of WPES'05*. ACM Press, Alexandria, VA, 2005.

72. A. Kerckhoffs. La cryptographie militaire. *Journal des Sciencies*, 9:161–191, 1983.

73. Recommendation for key management. Technical Report Special Publication 800-57 Draft, National Institute of Technology, 2005.

74. Year report on algorithms and keysizes. Technical Report IST-2002-507932, ECRYPT, 2006.

75. S. Bono, M. Greem, A. Stubblefield, A. Juels, A. Rubin, and M. Syzdlo. Security analysis of a cryptographically-enabled device. In *Proceedings of SSYM'05*. Usenix Association, Alexandria, VA, 2005.

76. N. Karten and H. Plotz. Mifare little security, despite obscurity. http://events.ccc.de/congress/2007/Fahrplan/events/2378.en.html, 2007.

77. P. Prince. United States sets date for e-passports. *RFID Journal*, October 25, 2005.

78. E. Wasserman. Purdue Pharma to run pedigree pilot. *RFID Journal*, May 31, 2005.

79. M. Guillory. Analysis: Counterfeit tags. http://www.aimglobal.org, June 30, 2005.

80. F. Thornton, B. Haines, A. Das, H. Bhargava, A. Campbell, and J. Kleinschmidt. *RFID Security*. Syngress Publishing, 2006.

81. D. Atkins and R. Austein. Threat analysis of the domain name system (DNS). In *Request for Comments—RFC 3833*, Berkeley, CA, 2004.

82. B. Fabian, G. Oliver, and S. Spiekermann. Security analysis of the object name service for RFID. In *Proceedings of SecPerU'05*. IEEE Computer Society, Santorini Island, Greece, 2005.

83. M. Rieback, C. Bruno, and A. Tanenbaum. Is your car infected with a computer virus? In *Proceedings of PerCom'06*. IEEE Computer Society, Pisa, Italy, 2006.

84. B. Jamali, P.H. Cole, and D. Engels. In *Networked RFID Systems and Lightweight Cryptography, chapter RFID Tag Vulnerabilities in RFID Systems*, pp. 147–155. Springer, 2007.

CRYPTOGRAPHY

Cryptographic Concepts, Methodologies, and Practices

Chapter 22

Chapter 22

Cryptography: Mathematics vs. Engineering

Ralph Spencer Poore

Modern cryptography is all about the mathematics. The algorithms are typically based on a "hard" problem in mathematics. Tedious mathematical proofs underlay the arguments of the strength of the cryptographic algorithm. However, translating a cryptographic algorithm to an actual instantiation that can operate securely in the real world is an engineering feat approaching legerdemain. In the pure mathematics of the cryptographic algorithm, power fluctuations, electromagnetic interference, and human behavior play no role. These all play a role when a company designs and builds cryptographic equipment or when cryptographic software is written for general purpose computers.

The Math

Both symmetric key and asymmetric key cryptographic algorithms are based on decades (in some cases centuries) of mathematics associated with functions that are relatively easy to calculate in one direction but very difficult to solve in the other. The ideal function would produce ciphertext from plaintext using an encryption key, but knowing only the plaintext and ciphertext would require the testing of every possible key (called key-space exhaustion) in order to determine the correct decryption key. In such a case, the number of possible keys represents the maximum effective key strength. In symmetric key cryptography (e.g., Triple DES, AES, RC5, and IDEA) this is less than or equal to the bit length of the cryptographic key. The reason it may be less than the bit length is that the best known attack against some algorithms is not key-space exhaustion.

Feistel

The Data Encryption Standard (DES) is an iterated block cipher based on a Feistel function. An iterated block cipher is one that encrypts a plaintext block by a process that has several rounds where each round uses the same transformation or round function. This function is applied to the data using a subkey that exists only internally to the cipher. The user-provided secret key (or a key schedule) is usually used to derive the set of subkeys.

Feistel ciphers are a special class of iterated block ciphers where the ciphertext is calculated from the plaintext by repeated application of the same transformation or round function. In a Feistel cipher, the text being encrypted is split into two halves. The round function f is applied to one half using a subkey and the output of f is exclusive-ored (XOR) with the other half. The two halves are then swapped. Each round follows the same pattern, except for the last round, where there is no swap. The Feistel cipher produces encryption and decryption that are structurally identical, with the subkeys used during encryption at each round taken in reverse order during decryption. In general, the more rounds, the better the cryptographic strength.

DES has a 64-bit block size and uses a 56-bit key during encryption. It is a 16-round Feistel cipher.

It is possible to design iterative ciphers that are not Feistel ciphers, yet whose encryption and decryption (after a certain reordering or recalculation of variables) are structurally the same. One such example is International Data Encryption Algorithm (IDEA).

The Advanced Encryption Standard (AES) [1] resulted from an international competition among teams of cryptomathematicians and cryptographers. The AES algorithm is a symmetric block cipher capable of using cryptographic keys of 128, 192, and 256 bits to encrypt and decrypt data in blocks of 128 bits. AES uses a different number of rounds depending on the key length selected. It is described in detail in Federal Information Processing Standards (FIPS) 197, which is available through National Institute of Standards and Technology (NIST) at no cost.

Asymmetric Algorithms

The "hard" problems used for the basis of public-key cryptography include integer factoring, logarithms, elliptic curves, and lattice reduction. While the universe of "hard" problems appears to be enormous, only a small number of them have, as yet, shown promise as cryptosystems. Finding suitable problems and developing the appropriate cryptographic algorithms remain formidable research challenges.

The integer factorization problem (IFP) is a "hard" problem because mathematicians have not found a solution in deterministic polynomial-time (referred to as "P"). The security of many practical Public-Key Cryptosystems and Protocols, for example Rivest-Shamir-Adleman (RSA), depends on the computational intractability of IFP. By way of an oversimplified illustration, trying to find the values x and y that are relative prime factors of z when you only know z is very difficult, but creating z when you know x and y is easy: $x \times y = z$.

The discrete logarithm problem (DLP) is another hard problem. Its main idea is that calculating $h = g^x$ is easy where finding x when given g and h is very hard.

Related to the DLP is the calculation of elliptic curves. The general form for a nonsupersingular elliptic curve (i.e., one of the classes of interest to cryptography) is $y^2 + y = x^3 + a_2 x^2 + a_6$. However, not every curve has characteristics useful to a cryptosystem. Finding appropriate curves requires substantial research. Fortunately, the NIST has published well-vetted curves for use in cryptosystems [2].

The security of lattice-based cryptosystems relies on the hardness of finding approximate solutions to lattice problems. One such problem of interest in building cryptosystems is the shortest vector problem (SVP) [3]. Daniele Micciancio proves that the SVP is NP-hard (nondeterministic polynomial-time hard) to approximate to within any constant less than the square root of 2. This area of mathematics holds great promise for future cryptosystems.

Engineering

Some important characteristics of secure cryptography are not about the algorithm as much as they are about the implementation design. For example, DES was originally designed for implementation in hardware. Some argue that the engineering design was intentionally to make it inefficient in software on general purpose computers, thereby lowering the effectiveness of unauthorized export of the algorithm—which they knew was unavoidable. Controlling export of the hardware was viewed as more manageable.

From the mathematics side, the more rounds in an algorithm like DES, the better. However, from the engineering side, each round takes time, power, cooling, and perhaps even additional space on a chip. These physical factors affect cost and utility. The engineer has to ask: how secure is secure enough? It is always a trade off. Sometimes, the mathematician can help the engineer answer this question. Such analysis for Feistel-based ciphers was done by Jacques Patarin [4]. Sometimes outside factors impose a limit on the engineer (e.g., export laws, available technology, or cost). When this happens, the resulting instantiation may prove considerably less secure than the mathematics would suggest.

One example of this problem is the accessibility of intermediate results. From a crypto-mathematics perspective, the algorithm is expected to function as a "black box." That is, an adversary may have access to plaintext and to the resulting ciphertext, but not to intermediate inputs or outputs internal to the algorithm. When engineering a specific implementation, however, preventing the leakage of information from within the "black box" is not trivial. Since the algorithm itself is never assumed to be a secret, the resources it consumes in its execution—if measurable outside of the "black box"—can provide indications of what instructions are executing and how often. Each bit of leaked information contributes to a better understanding of what the underlying cryptographic key is most likely to be. For each binary bit of symmetric keying information obtained, the key is weakened by half of its key space. For asymmetric keys, depending on the cryptosystem, the impact can be even more devastating.

For cryptographic implementations, good engineering requirements can be found in FIPS 140-2 and in the Common Criteria. Components, subassemblies, and complete devices providing cryptographic services should be independently evaluated against appropriate criteria. Those who must rely on cryptographic services are rarely in a position (and rarely have the expertise) to evaluate the underlying cryptosystem.

Implementations

The most rigorously, formally proofed cryptomathematics with "perfect security" and all of the other best mathematical traits desired in a cryptosystem can come to naught through poor engineering. Certified equipment passing rigorous testing and relying on the best algorithms can also fail when put into use. It is necessary, but not sufficient, that the mathematics support the intended security functionality. It is further necessary, but not sufficient, that the product engineering produces a certifiably trustworthy cryptosystem that protects the "goodness" of the mathematics. Lastly, the implementation and operation of the cryptosystem must not result in the subversion of the engineered product.

The most important aspect of an implementation is cryptographic key management. Done well, it supports the good engineering and strong algorithms. Done poorly, it renders everything else ineffective. Several excellent treatments of cryptographic key management have appeared in earlier editions of the handbook [5].

Summary

Historically, cryptographic algorithms can and have failed when advances in cryptanalysis have discovered flaws, when new mathematical approaches have leapt ahead, and when computational capabilities have advanced to reduce the work-factor costs for brute-force attacks. Implementers need to anticipate that this is just a natural part of the life cycle of cryptographic algorithms. The need to transition to future algorithms is inevitable [6]. However, using well-vetted algorithms in certified equipment by properly trained personnel following appropriate security practices that are regularly independently assessed by qualified assessors best protects your organization's investment in cryptographic security and assures the cryptographic security has the best possibility for protecting the information assets that depend on it. The math, the engineering, and the implementation all play vital roles in cryptography.

About the Author

Ralph Spencer Poore, CISSP, CFE, CISA, CHS-III, CTGA, QSA, is president and chief cryptologist, Cryptographic Assurance Services LLC (Arlington, TX). Ralph has over thirty-five years of information technology experience with emphasis on privacy, security, audit, and control in electronic commerce, enterprise systems, and enabling technologies. An author, speaker, inventor, and instructor, he is well known in the information security profession. Ralph is a Certified Fraud Examiner (CFE), Certified Information Systems Auditor (CISA), Certified Information Systems Security Professional (CISSP), Certified in Homeland Security—Level III (CHS-III), Certified TG-3 Assessor (CTGA), PCI Qualified Security Assessor (QSA), and toastmaster (CTM/CL). www.ralph-s-poore.com.

References

1. Federal Information Processing Standards (FIPS) Publication 197, *Announcing the Advanced Encryption Standard (AES)*, U.S. DoC/NIST, 2001.
2. FIPS 186-3, *Digital Signature Standard (DSS)*. U.S. DoC/NIST, 2009.
3. Micciancio, D. and Regev, O. "Lattice-based Cryptography". *Post Quantum Cryptography*. D.J. Bernstein, J. Buchmann, and E. Dahmen (eds.), pp. 147–191, Springer, February 2009.
4. Patarin, J. "Luby-Rackoff: 7 Rounds are Enough for $2^{n(1-\varepsilon)}$ Security." *Advances in Cryptology—CRYPTO 2003*. 2003.
5. Poore, R. S. "Cryptographic Key Management Concepts." *Information Security Management Handbook*, Fifth Ed., Vol. 2, Chapter 26. Auerbach Publications. Boca Raton, FL. 2005.
6. Poore, R. S. "Guest Editorial: Cryptographic Hardware—A Short, Practical Checklist." *Information Security Journal: A Global Perspective*, 19:51–52, Taylor & Francis Group, LLC. 2010.

Additional Resources

- Koc, C. K. (ed.) *Cryptographic Engineering.* New York: Springer Science + Business Media, LLC, 2009.
- csrc.nist.gov (Computer Security Resource Center).
- www.iacr.org (International Association for Cryptologic Research).

Chapter 23

Cryptographic Message Syntax

Jeff Stapleton

Cryptographic Message Syntax

Cryptographic Message Syntax (CMS) is a data formatting scheme whereby one data object can be encapsulated within another to apply various cryptographic methods to achieve data confidentiality, data integrity, and data authenticity. CMS is essentially a tool kit that enables a designer to define secured data objects that can be used to develop a message protocol. Developers can then create systems to generate, process, and validate CMS objects. End users can then rely on the message protocols to protect the application data, whatever it might be. CMS has evolved over the past twenty years and is defined in several standards developed by just a few standards organizations. Many message protocols and data protection schemes in use today rely on CMS. A basic understanding of CMS allows users and professional practitioners to comprehend the complex diversity of cryptography and its current and future importance in protecting everyday information and safeguarding systems.

Introduction

CMS describes an "encapsulation" syntax for using cryptography methods to protect data objects. The encapsulation structures are defined using Abstract Syntax Notation One (ASN.1) or Extended Markup Language (XML). The cryptographic methods include encryption, message authentication, digital signatures, and the relevant key management methods. There have been three principal groups developing CMS standards:

- RSA Data Security developed a series of Public Key Cryptography Standards (PKCS) which included PKCS #7 CMS Standard. Today, RSA is the security division of EMC.
- Internet Engineering Task Force (IETF) developed a series of Request For Comment (RFC) specifications, which included CMS and related documents.

Accredited Standards Committee (ASC) X9 developed several American National Standards to support CMS for the financial services industry. ASC X9 is accredited by the American National

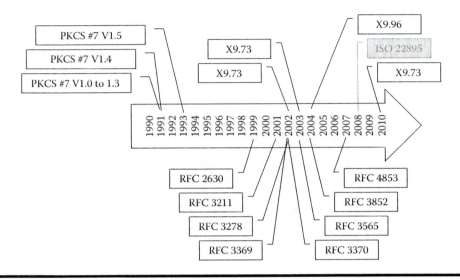

Figure 23.1   CMS timeline.

Standards Institute (ANSI) to (i) develop standards for the financial services industry, (ii) act as the United States (U.S.) Technical Advisory Group (TAG) to ISO Technical Committee 68 Financial Services, and (iii) act as the ISO TC68 secretariat.

Figure 23.1 shows the development history of the CMS. PKCS #7 was developed in the early 1990s, the IETF developed several sequential CMS specifications essentially in the 2000s, and X9 developed several CMS standards during the same time frame. ISO began developing a CMS-type standard later in 2008, which X9 liaised as the US TAG, however the ISO draft was eventually abandoned due to an overall lack of ISO member support, as an insufficient number of countries supported the effort. Consequently, the American National Standard X9.73 was revised to realign with the current IETF specification RFC 3852, including XML from X9.96, and incorporate the work achieved in the abandoned ISO 22895 draft international standard. Note that although RFC 4853 was published three years later, it provides a clarification of RFC 3852 when more than one digital signature is present, so RFC 3852 is considered to be the current IETF CMS specification.

CMS defines data objects as "content types" and for the most part all of the CMS standards are similar, however not all content types are supported in the different standards and the content types have evolved during the 20 year history of CMS. The later part of this chapter provides a CMS change history for each standard. An overview of the different content types is provided in the main part of this chapter. And since object identifiers (OID) are an essential element of CMS, an overview of OID is provided in the next section.

Object Identifiers

An OID is a sequence of one or more numbers where each position and value provides information about the corresponding object. An OID is represented by a variety of formats, for example the following illustrations all represent the same object identifier:

a. iso(1), member-iso(2), us(840), rsa-data-security(113549) pkcs(1), pkcs7(7)
b. 1.2.840.113549.1.7
c. {1 2 840 113549 1 7}

The first representation (a) includes both the definition of each value and the actual value in parentheses, whereas the second (b) and third (c) representations only provide the positional values. Representation (a) is a more formal syntax used in technical specifications. Representation (b) is a shorthand format where a period (".") is used as a delimiter between each value. Representation (c) is more of a set theory notational format using squiggly brackets with spaces between each value. Other representations may use square brackets or parentheses, and use other delimiters such as slashes. Almost any format is acceptable, so long as each positional value is clearly delineated and readable. OID are typically given names such as:

    d. id-pkcs-7 OBJECT IDENTIFIER ::= {iso(1), member-iso(2), us(840), rsa-data-security(113549) pkcs(1), pkcs7(7)}

The first position of any OID defines the standards organization for which the object identifier has been registered. There are only three assigned values: "0" is the International Telecommunication Union (ITU) Standardization Sector formerly known as the CCITT; "1" is the ISO International Organization for Standardization; and "2" is the Joint ISO and ITU. Each subsequent position has meaning based on the previous position.

The OID example provided above (1.2.840.113549.1.7) consists of six values beginning under the ISO (1) arc. The second position has several assigned values: "0" refers to standards; "1" refers to the registration authority; "2" refers to an ISO member (e.g., U.S.); and "3" refers to an organization that is not an ISO member (e.g., Department of Defense). Other secondary position values can only be assigned by ISO.

For the same OID example, the third position has the value "840," which identifies the U.S., such that only the U.S. can assign further positions under the arc (1.2.840). The fourth position with the value "113549" identifies RSA Data Security as a U.S. company. Under this arc (1.2.840.113549) only the company can assign further positions. RSA Data Security has developed a series of PKCS under the arc (1.2.840.113549.1) and assigned the OID "7" to PKCS #7 *CMS Standard*. And once an arc is named and defined, other OID can be defined using the previous definition, such as:

    a. id-signedData OBJECT IDENTIFIER ::= {id-pkcs-7 signedData(2)} or (1.2.840.113549.1.7.2)

Since each position can have an infinite value and the number of positions is likewise infinite, the OID structure is both extensible and expandable such that every OID is unique, no OID ever needs to be reused, and the world can never run out of OID.

Content Types

CMS provides for six common content types: one (data) which is a basic building block without any cryptographic protection, another (digested data) which provides data integrity, two (signed data and authenticated data) which provide data integrity and authenticity, and two (encrypted data and enveloped data) which provide data confidentiality. Any content type can be encapsulated within any other content type. This is often described as building an onion, where each layer is fully enclosed in another layer such that one can peel back the onion layers until the final content type reveals the data.

Table 23.1 CMS Content Types

Content Types	PKCS #7	IETF	X9.73	X9.96
Data	v1.5	RFC 3852	2010	2004
Signed data	v1.5	RFC 3852	2010	2004
Enveloped data	v1.5	RFC 3852	2010	2004
Signed and enveloped data	v1.5	–	–	–
Digested data	v1.5	RFC 3852	2010	2004
Encrypted data	v1.5	RFC 3852	2010	2004
Authenticated data	–	RFC 3852	2010	2004
Named encrypted data	–	–	2010	2004

Table 23.1 lists the six common types and two additional types. PKCS #7 also defined a combination type (signed and enveloped data) which was not included in the IETF or X9 standards as the enveloping nature of CMS allows this type to be recursively defined. X9.73 and X9.96 provided an additional type (named encrypted data) to reflect the key management method used throughout the financial services industry. The new type was added to avoid ambiguity with the existing CMS type (encrypted data).

The content types listed in Table 23.1 are composed of various data components. Content types providing data encryption have similar components and, correspondingly, content types providing data integrity and authenticity have comparable components. Note that all of the content types have a data component designated as "data content" but have different names (refer to the grayed rows) depending on its usage. Some of the data components are simple objects such as integers and octets (8-bit binary strings) while others are complex objects consisting of multiple simple objects. Compound objects consist of multiple complex objects and simple objects.

Table 23.2 provides a list of the data components for each content type.

Note that the PKCS #7 signed and enveloped data content type is not included in this chapter as the enveloping nature of CMS allows this type to be recursively defined. For each content type, the purpose, structure, and related key management are described. The actual ASN.1 and XML definitions are not provided but can be obtained from the respective standards.

To obtain copies of these standards and specifications, refer to the following:

■ PKCS are available at the RSA Laboratories website under its Standards Initiatives page located at http://www.rsa.com/rsalabs.
■ IETF specifications are available at its website at http://www.ietf.org.
■ ANSI standards are purchasable from the X9 Standards Store at http://www.x9.org or the ANSI Standards Store at http://webstore.ansi.org.

Data Type

The content type "data" depicted in Figure 23.2 is a complex component consisting of two simple components called the **contentType** and **content**. The component **contentType** is an OID and

Table 23.2　CMS Data Components

Data	Encrypted	NamedKey	Enveloped	Digested	Authenticated	Signed
–	version	version	version	version	version	version
–	–	–	–	digestAlgorithm	digestAlgorithm	digestAlgorithm
content	–	–	–	–	–	–
–	encryptedContentInfo	encryptedContentInfo	encryptedContentInfo	–	–	–
–	–	–	–	encryptedContentInfo	encryptedContentInfo	encryptedContentInfo
–	–	–	–	–	–	certificates
–	–	–	–	–	–	crls
–	–	–	–	–	–	singerInfos
–	–	–	originatorInfo	–	originatorInfo	–
–	unprotectedAttrs	unprotectedAttrs	unprotectedAttrs	–	unprotectedAttrs	–
–	–	–	–	digest	–	–
–	–	–	–	–	macAlgorithm	–
–	–	–	–	–	authenticated	–
–	–	–	–	–	mac	–
–	–	namedKey	–	–	–	–

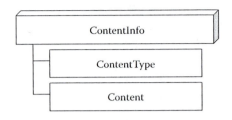

Figure 23.2   Data type.

the component **content** is an octet string containing any binary data. Figure 23.2 shows the complex component **ContentInfo** object depicted as a flat three-dimensional (3D) cube with two-dimensional (2D) boxes representing the two simple components. When the **content** is "data," the **contentType** contains the appropriate OID providing an unambiguous label that the data is unprotected. Conversely, when the **content** is a cryptographic type such as **EncryptedData**, the **contentType** contains a different and unique OID signifying that the data is encrypted using an implicit cryptographic key.

At a minimum, a CMS-encoded object contains at least one **ContentInfo** object where the **contentType** is a cryptographic type (and not the data type). When the content types are encapsulated within each other, each type is distinguishable by its OID. Other more complex data structures and cryptographic techniques can be defined using the CMS cryptographic types. The cryptographic types are discussed by order of complexity in each of the following sections.

Encrypted Data Type

The content type "Encrypted Data" depicted in Figure 23.3 is a compound component consisting of simple components, complex components, and sets of complex components. Simple components are depicted using 2D boxes. Complex components are depicted using flat 3D cubes. Sets of complex components are depicted as three sequential complex components (three 3D cubes); they are usually defined as one or more occurrences and sometimes have a maximum limit. CMS also uses sets of simple components within complex components, however none are used in this synopsis.

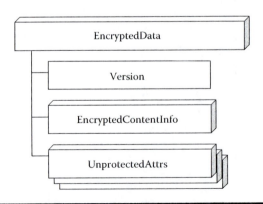

Figure 23.3   Encrypted data type.

The **EncryptedData** type consists of three components: **version**, **encryptedContentInfo**, and an optional **unprotectedAttrs**. The **version** component defines the syntax of the content type, indicating whether **unprotectedAttrs** is present (value is "2") or absent (value is "0"). The component **unprotectedAttrs** is a collection of one or more attributes that are not encrypted. The component **encryptedContentInfo** contains the encrypted data, versus the **contentType** containing unprotected data. Since no other key management information is provided, the encryption key is an implicit cryptographic key such that the management of the key is by other means outside the scope of the CMS. For more discussion about implicit cryptographic keys, refer to the Key Management section.

Named Encrypted Data Type

The content type "named encrypted data" depicted in Figure 23.4 is a compound component identical to the **EncryptedData** type with the addition of the **namedKey** simple component. **NamedKeyEncryptedData** is only defined in ANSI X9.73 for compatibility with other X9 and ISO key management standards for the financial services industry where the name of a key is explicitly included in a message. The **namedKey** component could have been added to the existing **EncryptedData** type as an optional field to eliminate the need for a separate content type, however the component is not optional for X9 and ISO standards. Implementers need to understand when an optional field is mandated and know when it is present. Adding further values for the **version** component was determined to be too complicated as two optional components (**unprotectedAttrs** and **namedKey**) would require four values and it still would not address the issue that the **namedKey** component is mandated for the financial services industry.

The **namedKey** component provides two very important features. First, it allows two communicating parties to synchronize encryption keys even when the keys are being changed without interruption of service. Each message identifies the encryption key used by the sender such that the receiver can verify it is using the correct decryption key. Second, it allows repetitive attributes to be reference by name instead of by value, thereby reducing communication overhead and some cryptanalysis attacks. The less information provided about a cryptographic system, the more difficult it is for an attacker. For more discussion about explicit named keys, refer to the Key Management section.

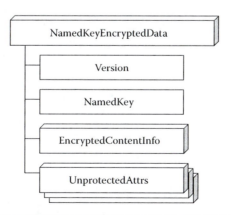

Figure 23.4   Named key encrypted data type.

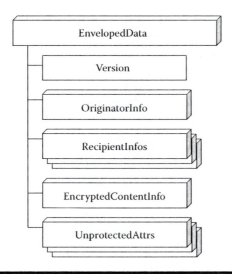

Figure 23.5   Enveloped data type.

Enveloped Data Type

The content type "enveloped data" depicted in Figure 23.5 is a compound component consisting of simple components, complex components, and sets of complex components. The **EnvelopedData** type offers the same data confidentiality protection as does the **EncryptedData** and **NamedEncryptedData** types; however, it provides more robust key establishment methods where the encryption key is randomly generated. This type also supports encryption from a sender (**originatorInfo**) to one or more receivers (**recipientInfos**), whereas the previous types were limited to a single sender and receiver.

For **EnvelopedData** the **version** component indicates whether the optional **originatorInfo** component is present, what options are used in the mandatory **recipientInfos** component, and whether the optional **unprotectedAttrs** component is present. The **originatorInfo** component may contain public key certificates and a certificate revocation list (CRL). It does not provide any pointers such as a universal resource locator (URL) to where other certificate status information can be found. The **recipientInfos** component contains key management information for each recipient. The key management information includes the encrypted content encryption key (**encryptedKey**) used to encrypt the content (**encryptedContentInfo**), the algorithm identifier (**keyEncryptionAlgorithm**) for the key encryption key (KEK) used to encrypt the content encryption key, and the key management method(s) used to establish the KEK used to recover the content encryption key. The key management methods for establishing the KEK are the following:

[0] Key transportation
[1] Key agreement
[2] KEK
[3] Password
[4] Other

For more discussion about the key management methods, refer to the Key Management section. The **encryptedContentInfo** component provides an OID field (**contentType**) to denote

Table 23.3   Enveloped Data Encryption Layers

Content being Encrypted	Key Encrypting Content	Algorithm Identifier
1. Encrypted content	Content encryption key	Content encryption algorithm
2. Encrypted content encryption key	Key encryption key	Key encryption algorithm
3. Key encryption key	Key management method	*Outside the scope of CMS*

the encrypted content (encryptedContent), an algorithm identifier field (**contentEncryption-Algorithm**) for the content encryption key, and of course a field to contain the actual encrypted content (**encryptedContent**). The component **unprotectedAttrs** is a collection of one or more attributes that are not encrypted.

Table 23.3 provides an overview of the overall encryption scheme. First, the content is encrypted using a randomly generated content encryption key whose algorithm is specified using an identifier. Second, the content encryption key is encrypted using a KEK whose algorithm might be different and thus specified using another identifier. Third, the KEK is established using one of the key management methods. The algorithm identifier for each key management method is dependent on the method and outside the scope of CMS.

Digested Data Type

The content type "digested data" depicted in Figure 23.6 is a compound component consisting of simple components and complex components. A message digest algorithm is an older term for a hash function. A hash function accepts any content of arbitrary length as its input and outputs are a fixed-length octet value. The output length is determined by the specific hash function. The smaller output value, called a digest or a hash, is a mathematical representation of the larger input value such that the same outputs provide a very high probability that the inputs were likewise the same. Hash functions by themselves cannot provide integrity or authenticity, as a new hash can be

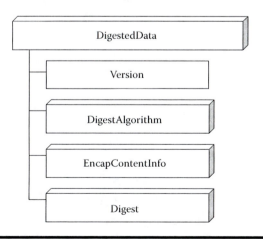

Figure 23.6   Digested data type.

generated from any modified or substituted content; however hash functions are a critical technology for digital signatures and **DigestedData** is effective when used in conjunction with the CMS encryption methods to validate data integrity of the decrypted content.

The **DigestedData** type consists of four components: **version**, **digestAlgorithm**, **encapContentInfo**, and **digest**. The **version** component identifies the data type in **encapContentInfo**. The **digestAlgorithm** component identifies the message digest algorithm (hash function) and any associated parameters used to generate the digest (hash). The **encapContentInfo** component contains the hash function input value and **digest** contains hash function output value.

Authenticated Data Type

The content type "authenticated data" depicted in Figure 23.7 is a compound component consisting of simple components, complex components, and sets of complex components. As a reminder, simple components are depicted using 2D boxes, complex components are depicted using flat 3D cubes, and sets of complex components are depicted as three sequential complex

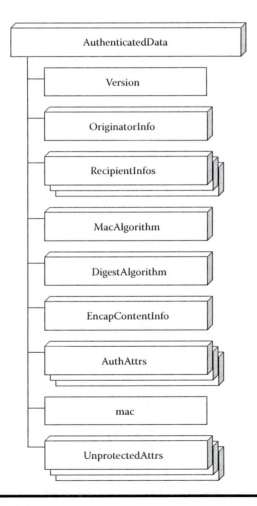

Figure 23.7 Authenticated data type.

components (three 3D cubes). The AuthenticatedData type provides data integrity and authenticity from a sender (**originatorInfo**) to one or more receivers (**recipientInfos**) using any message authentication code (MAC) algorithm or any keyed hash message authentication code (HMAC) algorithm.

For **AuthenticatedData** the **version** component indicates whether the optional **originatorInfo** component is present and what type of originator certificates or CRL are provided. Similar to **EnvelopedData**, the **originatorInfo** component may contain public key certificates and a CRL, and the **recipientInfos** component contains key management information for each recipient. The key management information includes the encrypted authentication key (**encryptedKey**) used to generate the message authentication code (**mac**), the algorithm identifier (**keyEncryptionAlgorithm**) for the KEK used to encrypt the authentication key, and the key management method(s) used to establish the KEK used to recover the authentication key. The key management methods for establishing the KEK are the same as for **EnvelopedData**:

[0] Key transportation
[1] Key agreement
[2] KEK
[3] Password
[4] Other

For more discussion about the key management methods, refer to the Key Management section. The **macAlgorithm** component is the MAC algorithm identifier. The **digestAlgorithm** component is the message digest (hash) algorithm identifier, which is only present if the optional **authAttrs** component is used. The **authAttrs** component is a collection of authenticated attributes such as providing a time stamp. The **mac** component contains the MAC of the **encapContentInfo** component. Note that if the **authAttrs** component is present then the MAC is calculated on both the **encapContentInfo** component and a message digest (hash) of the **authAttrs** component. If the **authAttrs** component is not present then the MAC is calculated on only the content of the **encapContentInfo** component. The component **unprotectedAttrs** is a collection of one or more attributes that are not authenticated.

Table 23.4 provides an overview of the overall cryptographic scheme. First, the content is authenticated using a randomly generated authentication key whose algorithm is specified using an identifier. Second, the authentication key is encrypted using a KEK whose algorithm might be different and thus specified using another identifier. Third, the KEK is established using one of the key management methods. The algorithm identifier for each key management method is dependent on the method and outside the scope of CMS.

Table 23.4   Authenticated Data Cryptography Layers

Content being Protected	Key Encrypting Content	Algorithm Identifier
1. Authenticated content	Authentication key	MAC algorithm
2. Encrypted authentication key	Key encryption key	Key encryption algorithm
3. Key encryption key	Key management method	*Outside the scope of CMS*

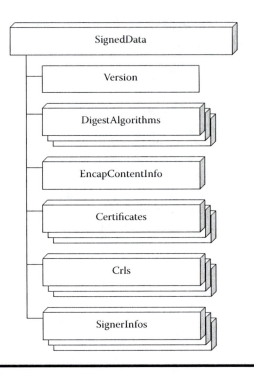

Figure 23.8   Signed data type.

Signed Data Type

The content type "signed data," depicted in Figure 23.8, is a compound component consisting of simple components, complex components, and sets of complex components. The **SignedData** type provides digital signatures for one or more signers. A digital signature is an authentication value generated by a signer's asymmetric private key whereby any relying party can validate the digital signature using the signer's asymmetric public key. The public key is preferably obtained from a public key certificate, which is a core element of a public key infrastructure (PKI).

For **SignedData** the **version** component conveys information about **certificates**, **crls**, **eContentType**, and **SignerInfo** fields. The **digestAlgorithms** component is a collection of message digest (hash) algorithm identifiers. Each **DigestAlgorithmIdentifier** element identifies the message digest algorithm, along with any associated parameters, used by each signer. The collection is intended to list the message digest (hash) algorithms employed by all of the signers, in any order, to facilitate processing.

The **encapContentInfo** component contains an **eContentType** object identifier and an optional **eContent** octet string. The optional omission of the **eContent** field makes it possible to construct "external signatures" such that the content being signed is absent from the **SignedData** type. In fact, the **eContent** field is optional in both the **encapContentInfo** components and the **encryptedContentInfo** components, enabling a method called "detached" data such that the data content is absent from the content type. For more discussion about detached data, refer to the CMS profiles section.

The **certificates** and **crls** components are the same as the public key certificates and CRL contained in the **originatorInfo** component for the **EnvelopedData** and **AuthenticatedData** types. For more discussion about certificates and CRL, refer to the Key Management section.

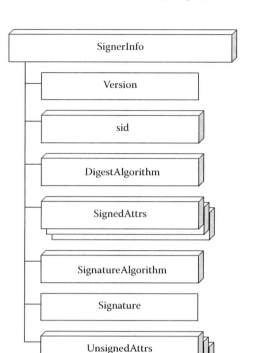

Figure 23.9   SignerInfo.

The **signerInfos** component, depicted in Figure 23.9, is a collection of information about each signer called the **SignerInfo** type. It is another compound component consisting of simple components, complex components, and sets of complex components. The data structure is sufficiently complicated that it contains its own **version** component indicating the nature of information in the signer identifier (**sid**) component. The **sid** component contains either the issuer name and serial number of the signer's certificate, or the subject key identifier of the signer's certificate. The subject key identifier is an X.509 v3 extension found in most certificates, which contains a hash of the certificate itself. The **digestAlgorithm** component is the algorithm identifier of the message digest (hash function) used by the specific signer. Note that the **digestAlgorithms** component contained in the main body of the **SignedData** type echoes the same algorithm identifier information to facilitate processing.

The **SignerInfo** type contains **signedAttrs** and **unsignedAttrs** components, which are both collections of attributes similar to the **authAttrs** component in the **AuthenticatedData** type and the **unprotectedAttrs** components in the **EncryptedData**, **NamedKeyEncryptedData**, **EnvelopedData**, and **AuthenticatedData** types. The **signatureAlgorithm** component is the algorithm identifier of the signature algorithm used by the specific signer. Unlike the **digest-Algorithm** component, the **signatureAlgorithm** component is not echoed in the main body of the **SignedData** type. And finally the **signature** component contains the digital signature of the **encapContentInfo** component in the main body of the **SignedData** type. Note again that the content may be "detached" data such that the **eContent** field in the main body of the **SignedData** type is omitted. For more discussion about detached data refer to the CMS profiles section.

Key Management

Any use of cryptography including encryption, MACs, digital signatures, and other methods requires management of the cryptographic keys in a secure manner. Key management is itself a complicated discipline and outside the scope of this chapter. In general, cryptography has two distinct categories: symmetric keys and asymmetric keys. Symmetric keys are secret values where each party has a copy of the same key. Asymmetric keys come in pairs where only the originator has a copy of the private (secret) key and recipients have a copy of the originator's public key, hence it is also called public key cryptography. There is actually a third category of one-way functions that do not use any cryptographic keys but are an essential element of cryptography which include hash functions (message digests). These three categories make up the rich mathematical world of modern cryptography.

Key management can be defined as the discipline to properly maintain the security of all cryptographic information throughout its life cycle, which includes generation, distribution, storage, usage, change, and eventually termination and archival. CMS provides some aspects of key distribution and arguably key storage when message content is encapsulated in one or more content types.

Key Transport

Symmetric keys must be established between participating parties. One method of achieving this is key transport, where an encrypted symmetric key is sent from one party to another. An encrypted symmetric key can be encrypted by another symmetric key called the KEK or an asymmetric public key. The sender uses either a previously established KEK or the public key of the recipient. The recipient can then use the previously established KEK or the corresponding private key to recover the encrypted symmetric key.

The **EnvelopedData** type actually transports the content encryption key as an encrypted object. The content encryption key is randomly generated, used to encrypt the content (**encryptedContentInfo**), and is itself encrypted using one of the key encryption methods defined in the **recipientInfos** component.

[0] Key transportation is a method whereby the content encryption key is encrypted using the asymmetric public key of the recipient.

[2] KEK is a method whereby the content encryption key is encrypted using a previously distributed symmetric key as the KEK.

The **AuthenticatedData** type also transports the content authentication key as an encrypted object. The content authentication key is randomly generated, used to generate the MAC, and is itself encrypted using one of the key encryption methods defined in the **recipientInfos** component. The methods are the same as the **EnvelopedData** type options.

Key Agreement

Another method of establishing symmetric keys between participating parties is key agreement where the parties have sufficient information to mutually generate a symmetric key without actually transporting the cryptographic key. The most common cryptographic method is for two parties to exchange public key certificates such that for some asymmetric algorithms the combination of public keys and private keys can be used to calculate a shared secret. The shared secret can then be used to derive a common symmetric key. In general, the mutually agreed upon symmetric key could be used as a data key or a KEK to exchange other symmetric keys.

The **EnvelopedData** type also supports key agreement but still transports the content encryption key as an encrypted object. For CMS the mutually agreed upon symmetric key is used as a KEK.

[1] Key agreement is a method whereby the content encryption key is encrypted using a derived KEK from a shared secret calculated from an asymmetric algorithm.

[3] Password is a method whereby the content encryption key is encrypted using a KEK generated from a pseudo random number generator using a previously established password.

The **AuthenticatedData** type likewise supports key agreement but still transports the content authentication key as an encrypted object. For CMS the mutually agreed upon symmetric key is used as a KEK. The methods are the same as the **EnvelopedData** type options.

Explicit Named Key

The **NamedKeyEncryptedData** type provides the ability to identify the content encryption key. Key management standards for the financial services industry have their own key management methods including the concept of a key set identifier (KSI). Each cryptographic key is provided a KSI such that the recipient can identify the key and its associated attributes. In this manner, a recipient can manage multiple keys with the same party and manage multiple parties using different keys.

For example, a typical debit transaction includes an authorization request transmitted from the merchant to its financial institution (acquirer) and then forwarded to the cardholder's financial institution (issuer) for authorization. The merchant's financial institution is called the "acquirer," because it acquires the payment authorization, and the cardholder's financial institution is the called the "issuer," because it issued the debit card to the cardholder. The consumer purchasing goods or services at the merchant location is called the "cardholder," because a debit card has been presented to the merchant for payment.

When standing at the merchant location, the cardholder enters their personal identification number (PIN) at the point of sale (POS), which is instantly encrypted. The debit authorization request message contains the encrypted PIN, which the issuer will use to help authenticate the cardholder. The PIN encryption key used to encrypt the PIN within the POS terminal is identified using a KSI. When the acquirer receives the authorization request from the merchant the PIN encryption key is unambiguously identified by the KSI. The acquirer translates the encrypted PIN from the POS terminal key to another PIN encryption key with a different KSI so that the authorization request can be forwarded to an intermediary financial network. The network also translates the encrypted PIN from the key shared with the acquirer to the key shared with the issuer that has another KSI. When the issuer receives the authorization request from the acquirer via the financial network the PIN encryption key is again unambiguously identified by the KSI.

The KSI not only identifies the PIN encryption key(s) used in the authorization request, it also indicates the associated attributes of the key. These attributes include the encryption algorithm, the key length, and the key owner. Further, because the KSI is present in every request message, when the PIN encryption key is changed the recipient can determine whether the previous key or the current key was used for that particular message. In this manner, the PIN encryption keys can be kept synchronized and even changed rapidly without interruption of the authorization traffic.

Implicit Cryptographic Key

The **EncryptedData** type transports encrypted data but does not provide any key management. Its content encryption key is presumed to be previously established and further presumes that no key change ever occurs. Unlike the **NamedKeyEncryptedData** type, the **EncryptedData** type does not provide any mechanism to keep encryption keys synchronized. Since the key distribution is decoupled from the actual key usage, the only practical way to change keys would be to shut down the application, establish the new keys, and then restart the application. Some systems in fact perform key changes in exactly this manner.

Certificate Management

Public key certificates bind the asymmetric public key to the subscriber's identity and the issuing certification authority (CA) by encapsulating the information by a digital signature. The content signature from a subscriber can be verified by the public key in the subscriber's certificate. The certificate signature from the CA can be verified by the public key of the CA. Typically a hierarchy of CAs is used such that the CA signing and issuing the subscriber certificate has its own public key in another certificate signed by a superior CA. Figure 23.10 depicts an example.

The scriber certificate contains the scriber's public key, which is signed by the subordinate CA. The subordinate CA signature is verified using the subordinate CA's public key. The subordinate certificate contains the subordinate's CA public key, which is signed by the root CA. The root CA signature is verified using the root CA's public key. The root CA certificate contains the root CA public key, which is signed by itself and verified by itself. Thus the root CA certificate is a trust anchor for all of the other certificates and public keys. Each entity maintains its own private key.

Certificates contain validity dates, a "not before" and a "not after" date. The certificate is not valid until after the "not before" date and is no longer valid past the "not after" date. Asymmetric keys, like any cryptographic key, have a useful lifetime and should not be used past the end of their

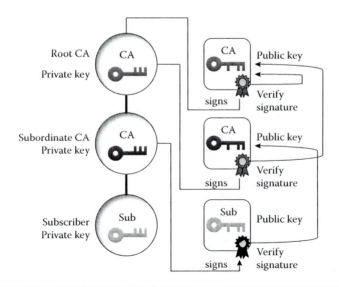

Figure 23.10   Public key infrastructure.

life cycle. However, sometimes certificates need to be revoked before their "not after" date so CAs often publish a CRL. Thus a relying party not only needs to verify the certificate digital signature and validity dates but also check the current CRL to ensure the certificate is still valid. Not every CA provides a CRL, which is considered a "negative" file. Some CAs provide certificate status using online certificate status protocol (OCSP) technology, which provides the current status of a certificate issued by that particular CA.

CMS Profiles

CMS provides several different methods for protecting data including data confidentiality, data integrity, and data authentication, not to mention the "detached" data option. Consequently CMS cannot be used "as is," but rather a profile must be developed that articulates how the CMS objects are used. Profiles define the order in which the CMS content types are encapsulated, and the rules for generating the objects by the originator (or signer) and for validating the objects by the recipients. When the objects are used within a message protocol, typically the profile will also provide use cases, operating rules, and exception handling. There are also advanced uses of CMS for other CMS objects that are not defined in CMS but where the content types can be adopted or adapted.

Common Use

Figure 23.11 depicts the encapsulation of the **EncryptedData** type within the **SignedData** type. In this example, the encrypted content is encapsulated within the **EncryptedData** object and in order to prevent an inadvertent or intentional modification of the encrypted data the **EncryptedData** object is protected by the digital signature of the **SignedData** object. This compound object is an example of a two-layer CMS onion.

The originator would first encrypt the content and create the **EncryptedData** object, then generate a digital signature of the **EncryptedData** object and create the **SignedData** object, and finally send the compound onion to the recipient. The recipient would unpeel the first layer by verifying the digital signature to validate that the content had not been altered and at the same time authenticate the signer, and then decrypt the content to recover the data.

Figure 23.12 depicts the encapsulation of the **SignedData** type within the **EncryptedData** type. In this example, the signed content is encapsulated within the **SignedData** object to provide integrity and authentication of the original content, and then to provide data confidentiality the **SignedData** object is protected by the encryption of the **EncryptedData** object. This compound object is another example of a two-layer CMS onion using the same objects as in Figure 23.11 but in a different order for different reasons and protection.

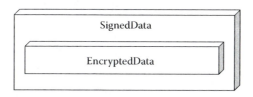

Figure 23.11   Sign encrypted data.

Figure 23.12   Encrypt signed data.

The originator would first generate the digital signature and create the **SignedData** object, then encrypt the SignedData object and create the **EncryptedData** object, and finally send the compound onion to the recipient. The recipient would unpeel the first layer by decrypting its content to reveal the **SignedData** object, and then verify the digital signature to validate that the original content had not been altered and at the same time authenticate the signer.

The difference between Figure 23.11 and Figure 23.12 is that the digital signature of Figure 23.11 provides validation of encrypted data whereas Figure 23.12 provides validation of the original content. If the signer and encryptor are not the same entity, then the protection afforded by the digital signatures represent very different assurance levels. Receiving originally signed content across an encrypted communications channel has a different trust model than receiving original content across an encrypted communications channel that happens to provide data integrity and authenticity of the encrypted data using a digital signature. Figure 23.12 provides assurance of the originality for the content, whereas Figure 23.11 cannot necessarily provide that same assurance without additional compensating controls.

Advanced Use

Suppose there is a scenario such that a sensitive data object needed to be transmitted across multiple domains that must be encrypted at all times but the domains did not share a common encryption system. Further, suppose that each domain needed to demonstrate the integrity and authenticity of the data object to every other domain wherever the object traversed that domain. To avoid creating a multiple-layered onion, the object depicted in Figure 23.13 might be used.

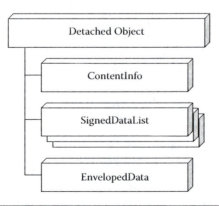

Figure 23.13   Detached object.

The original domain would generate a digital signature of the content, create a **SignedData** object as the first instance in the **SignedDataList**, encrypt the data using a key agreement scheme with the next domain, create an **EnvelopedData** object, create the detached object shown in Figure 23.13, and send it to the next domain.

Each intermediate domain would decrypt the content and verify the digital signatures of each previous domain, generate a digital signature of the content, create and append a **SignedData** object to the **SignedDataList**, encrypt the data using a key agreement scheme with the next domain, create and replace the **EnvelopedData** object, and send it to the next domain. At each domain another **SignedData** object would be added to the list, but the overall detached object would be composed of three components: **ContentInfo**, **SignedDataList**, and **EnvelopedData**.

The final domain would decrypt the content and verify the digital signatures of each previous domain where the **SignedDataList** component was essentially a verifiable audit record of which domains the object had traversed. In order for the protection of the sensitive data to be assured, each domain would have performed all of the cryptographic functions within a cryptographic hardware module such that the unencrypted content would never be disclosed except at the original and final domains.

CMS Change History

PKCS #7 Cryptographic Message Syntax Standard

Public Key Cryptography Standard (PKCS) #7 is an RSA Laboratories Technical Note. The following content types are supported: data, **signedData**, **envelopedData**, **signedAndEnvelopedData**, **digestedData**, and **encryptedData**. There were three releases of PKCS #7 listed as follows:

PKCS #7 versions 1.0–1.3
> Versions 1.0–1.3 were distributed to participants in RSA Data Security, Inc.'s Public-Key Cryptography Standards meetings in February and March 1991.

PKCS #7 Version 1.4
> Version 1.4 is part of the June 3, 1991, initial public release of PKCS. Version 1.4 was published as NIST/OSI Implementers' Workshop document SEC-SIG-91-22.

PKCS #7 Version 1.5
> Version 1.5, published in November 1993, incorporated several editorial changes, including updates to the references and the addition of a revision history. The following substantive changes were made:
> - Section 6: **CertificateRevocationLists** type is added.
> - Section 9.1: **SignedData** syntax is revised. The new version allows for the dissemination of certificate-revocation lists along with signatures. It also allows for the dissemination of certificates and certificate-revocation lists alone, without any signatures.
> - Section 9.2: **SignerInfo** syntax is revised. The new version includes a message-digest encryption process compatible with Privacy-Enhanced Mail (PEM) as specified in RFC 1423.
> - Section 9.3: Meaning of "the DER encoding of the **authenticatedAttributes** field" is clarified as "the DER encoding of the **Attributes** value."
> - Section 10.3: Padding method for content-encryption algorithms is described.

- Section 11.1: **SignedAndEnvelopedData** syntax is revised. The new version allows for the dissemination of certificate-revocation lists.
- Section 13: **Encrypted-data** content type is added. This content type consists of encrypted content of any type.
- Section 14: encryptedData object identifier is added.

IETF History

The CMS history within the Internet Engineering Task Force (IETF) includes the following technical specifications. The notes are borrowed directly from the IETF documents.

RFC 2630 Cryptographic Message Syntax, June 1999, R. Housley (Spyrus)

- The Cryptographic Message Syntax is derived from PKCS #7 version 1.5 as specified in RFC 2315 [PKCS#7]. Wherever possible, backward compatibility is preserved; however, changes were necessary to accommodate attribute certificate transfer and key agreement techniques for key management.
- Obsoleted [superseded] by RFC3369, RFC3370

RFC 3211 Password-based Encryption for CMS, December 2001, P. Gutmann (University of Auckland)

- This document provides a method of encrypting data using user-supplied passwords and, by extension, any form of variable-length keying material which is not necessarily an algorithm-specific fixed-format key. The Cryptographic Message Syntax data format does not currently contain any provisions for password-based data encryption.

RFC 3278 Use of Elliptic Curve Cryptography (ECC) Algorithms in Cryptographic Message Syntax (CMS), April 2002, S. Blake-Wilson (Certicom), D. Brown (Certicom), P. Lambert (Cosine)

- This document describes how to use Elliptic Curve Cryptography (ECC) public-key algorithms in the Cryptographic Message Syntax (CMS). The ECC algorithms support the creation of digital signatures and the exchange of keys to encrypt or authenticate content. The definition of the algorithm processing is based on the ANSI X9.62 standard, developed by the ANSI X9F1 working group, the IEEE 1363 standard, and the SEC 1 standard.

RFC 3369 Cryptographic Message Syntax (CMS), August 2002, R. Housley (RSA Labs)

- Obsoletes RFC 2630 [OLDCMS] and RFC 3211 [PWRI]. Password-based key management is included in the CMS specification, and an extension mechanism to support new key management schemes without further changes to the CMS is specified. Backward compatibility with RFC 2630 and RFC 3211 is preserved; however, version 2 attribute certificate transfer is added. The use of version 1 attribute certificates is deprecated.
- S/MIME v2 signatures [OLDMSG], which are based on PKCS#7 version 1.5, are compatible with S/MIME v3 signatures [MSG], which are based on RFC 2630. However, there are some subtle compatibility issues with signatures using PKCS#7 version 1.5 and the CMS.

■ Specific cryptographic algorithms are not discussed in this document, but they were discussed in RFC 2630. The discussion of specific cryptographic algorithms has been moved to a separate document [CMSALG]. Separation of the protocol and algorithm specifications allows the IETF to update each document independently. This specification does not require the implementation of any particular algorithms. Rather, protocols that rely on the CMS are expected to choose appropriate algorithms for their environment. The algorithms may be selected from [CMSALG] or elsewhere.

RFC 3370 Cryptographic Message Syntax (CMS) Algorithms, August 2002, R. Housley (RSA Labs)

■ Describes the conventions for using several cryptographic algorithms with the Cryptographic Message Syntax (CMS).
■ Obsoletes section 12 of RFC 2630 [OLDCMS]. RFC 3369 [CMS] obsoletes the rest of RFC 2630. Separation of the protocol and algorithm specifications allows each one to be updated without impacting the other. However, the conventions for using additional algorithms with the CMS are likely to be specified in separate documents.

RFC 3565 Use of the Advanced Encryption Standard (AES) Encryption Algorithm in Cryptographic Message Syntax (CMS), July 2003, J. Schaad (Soaring Hawk Consulting)

■ Specifies the conventions for using Advanced Encryption Standard (AES) content encryption algorithm with the Cryptographic Message Syntax [CMS] enveloped-data and encrypted-data content types.

RFC 3852 Cryptographic Message Syntax (CMS), July 2004, R. Housley (Vigil Security)

■ CMS is derived from PKCS #7 version 1.5, which is documented in RFC 2315 [PKCS#7]. PKCS #7 version 1.5 was developed outside of the IETF; it was originally published as an RSA Laboratories Technical Note in November 1993. Since that time, the IETF has taken responsibility for the development and maintenance of the CMS. Today, several important IETF standards-track protocols make use of the CMS.
■ RFC 2630 [CMS1] was the first version of the CMS on the IETF standards track. Wherever possible, backward compatibility with PKCS #7 version 1.5 is preserved; however, changes were made to accommodate version 1 attribute certificate transfer and to support algorithm independent key management. PKCS #7 version 1.5 included support only for key transport. RFC 2630 adds support for key agreement and previously distributed symmetric key-encryption key techniques.
■ RFC 3369 [CMS2] obsoletes RFC 2630 [CMS1] and RFC 3211 [PWRI]. Password-based key management is included in the CMS specification and an extension mechanism to support new key management schemes without further changes to the CMS is specified. Backward compatibility with RFC 2630 and RFC 3211 is preserved; however, version 2 attribute certificate transfer is added and the use of version 1 attribute certificates is deprecated.
■ S/MIME v2 signatures [OLDMSG], which are based on PKCS#7 version 1.5, are compatible with S/MIME v3 signatures [MSG], which are based on RFC 2630. However, there are some subtle compatibility issues with signatures based on PKCS #7 version 1.5. These issues are discussed in section 5.2.1. These issues remain with the current version of the CMS.

■ Specific cryptographic algorithms are not discussed in this document, but they were discussed in RFC 2630. The discussion of specific cryptographic algorithms has been moved to a separate document [CMSALG]. Separation of the protocol and algorithm specifications allows the IETF to update each document independently. This specification does not require the implementation of any particular algorithms. Rather, protocols that rely on the CMS are expected to choose appropriate algorithms for their environment. The algorithms may be selected from [CMSALG] or elsewhere.

RFC 4853 Cryptographic Message Syntax (CMS) Multiple Signer Clarification, April 2007, R. Housley (Vigil Security)

■ Updates the Cryptographic Message Syntax (CMS), which is published in RFC 3852. This document clarifies the proper handling of the SignedData protected content type when more than one digital signature is present.

X9 History

X9.73 Cryptographic Message Syntax (CMS) was originally published in 2002 as a CMS profile for the financial services industry with the addition of the **NamedKeyEncryptedData** content type. It was based on RFC 2630 with updated ANS.1 definitions.

X9.73 Cryptographic Message Syntax (CMS) was updated in 2003. It was aligned with RFC 3369 with updated ANS.1 definitions, but did not include XML.

X9.96 XML Cryptographic Message Syntax (XCMS) was published in 2004 as an Extended Markup Language (XML) version of X9.73 CMS.

X9.73 Cryptographic Message Syntax – ANS.1 and XML was published in 2010. It combined the Abstract Syntax Notation One (ASN.1) from X9.73 and the Extended Markup Language (XML) from X9.96, it was aligned with RFC 3852, and included the changes from the abandoned ISO 28895 effort.

About the Author

Jeff Stapleton is a vice president at the Bank of America in their global information security division. He has over 25 years of experience in the security, financial, and healthcare industries with expertise in software development, payment systems, PCI, cryptography, PKI, key management, biometrics, and trusted time stamps. Jeff holds degrees from the University of Missouri, has instructed at other universities, and is a published author, reviewer, and frequent speaker at various security conferences. He has participated in developing dozens of ANSI and ISO security standards and has been chair of the X9F4 Cryptographic Protocols and Application Security working group since 1998.

SECURITY ARCHITECTURE AND DESIGN

Principles of Computer and Network Organizations, Architectures, and Designs

Chapter 24

An Introduction to Virtualization Security

Paul Henry

A Quick Overview of Virtualization Technology

In the simplest of terms, the concept of virtualization in its most popular use today (server virtualization) is providing the ability to transparently share hardware resources across multiple operating systems as well as the respective applications that are running on top of the respective operating systems. Virtualization provides for a layer of software that is commonly referred to as a "hypervisor" that sits between the computer hardware and operating system that effectively encapsulates that hardware. This encapsulation of hardware by the hypervisor allows each of possibly many operating systems running on top of the hypervisor to believe that it has exclusive access to the underlying hardware. One of the primary functions of the hypervisor is to allow multiple operating systems to have access to the underlying hardware without collision or contention issues.

There Are Four Primary Types of Virtualization in Use Today

1. Server virtualization
   a. An entire server operating platform such as Windows server 2003 or a Linux derivative operates as a virtual image running on top of a hypervisor transparently sharing underlying computing resources with other virtualized server operating platforms. One of the benefits of current generation server virtualization platforms is that almost any commercially available operating system today can operate in a server virtualization environment without modification.
2. Application virtualization
   a. The application itself is encapsulated and operates isolated from the underlying operating system and hardware. The application is sometimes referred to as "sandboxing." A benefit of application virtualization is that if the virtualized application is compromised it does not allow direct interaction of the malware associated with the compromise and

the underlying operating system and hardware. Early on, one of the most popular forms of application virtualization was browser virtualization i.e., Microsoft Internet Explorer and Firefox. Today application virtualization includes popular Windows applications such as Microsoft Office.

3. Desktop virtualization
   a. Allows the sharing of hardware resources in a desktop environment whereby a user can operate multiple operating system environments on top of an underlying host operating system when using virtualization software. Unlike server virtualization, which operates on top of a hypervisor, desktop virtualization software operates on top of the host operating system. It is important to note that while desktop virtualization is in some respects similar to server virtualization, the simple fact that the virtualization software is running on top of a complete operating system and not a smaller and more efficient hypervisor makes the operation of desktop virtualization less efficient then server virtualization.

4. Storage virtualization
   a. The abstraction of individual physical storage devices effectively makes them location independent in such a manner that many physical storage devices appear to be a single virtual storage object. One of the primary benefits of storage virtualization is that it can allow for the easy migration of the virtual storage object to other physical storage devices without interrupting the use of the storage object by the processes that are using the storage object.

Who Are the Key Players in Today's Virtualization Marketplace?

A quick check on virtualization platforms at Wikipedia lists over 70 different virtualization products (http://en.wikipedia.org/wiki/Comparison_of_platform_virtual_machines). When considering market share, three vendors' products clearly stand out:

1. VMware
2. Citrix
3. Microsoft

In the author's opinion, VMware offers the most robust and feature-rich virtualization platform available today. However Microsoft cannot simply be counted out, as they are rapidly and continuously adding additional product features while aggressively pricing the product to gain market share. In fact, just a year after releasing their Hyper-V product, Microsoft claimed to have captured 24% of market share from VMware (http://communities.VMware.com/blogs/VMSpotlight/2009/08/04/microsoft-claims-hyperv-has-24-virtualization-market-share).

For the purposes of this chapter we will focus our attention on VMware. This is not a reflection in any way on any inherent insecurities of the VMware product offering, but is an effort to provide information to the largest segment of the virtualization community, and no one can dispute that VMware is clearly the leader in that respect.

Are Security Concerns Perhaps Hindering the Growth of Virtualization?

While there is no denying that virtualization can bring dramatic cost reduction to the enterprise, security concerns have become a significant barrier to its overall acceptance. While virtualization has been around for a number of years, by the end of 2009, according to a recent report from Neil McDonald at Gartner (http://www.outlookseries.com/N6/Security/2825_Neil_MacDonald_Gartner_virtualized_workloads_deployed_insecurely_Neil_MacDonald.htm), only 18% of enterprise data center workloads that could be had been virtualized. Further, the report goes on to predict that the number will grow to 50% or more by 2012. At the same time the report points out that through 2010 60% of virtualized servers will be less secure than the physical servers they replace. The survey data from Gartner points to six specific areas of concern summarized as follows:

1. Information security is not initially involved in the virtualization projects.
2. A compromise of the virtualization layer could result in the compromise of all hosted workloads.
3. The lack of visibility and controls on internal virtual networks created for virtual machine (VM)-to-VM communications blinds existing security policy enforcement mechanisms.
4. Workloads of different trust levels are consolidated onto a single physical server without sufficient separation.
5. Adequate controls on administrative access to the hypervisor/VMM layer and to administrative tools are lacking.
6. There is a potential loss of separation of duties for network and security controls.

The Inherent Risk of Virtualization

Most virtualization product vendors will tell a prospective customer that their product will make them inherently more secure because they are effectively adding a layer of isolation between the operating system and the underlying hardware. While this sounds great, one simply has to look at the x86 privilege levels to see the potential risk of virtualization (Figure 24.1).

In the protection rings of an x86 processor there are four privilege levels, numbered 0 with the most privilege to 3 with the least privilege. Ring 0 is commonly known as supervisor mode and most of the integral OS functions such as accessing memory and I/O occur at ring 0. Ring 3 is commonly known as user mode and does not directly access memory and I/O.

Not to oversimplify it, but with the protection rings in mind it is important to note that desktop virtualization products typically operate at ring 3, and hence have limited privilege and pose

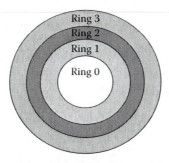

Figure 24.1   In the protection rings of an x86 processor there are 4 privilege levels numbered 0 with the most privilege to 3 with the least privilege.

limited risk. However server virtualization products often run at ring 0 and present a virtualized ring 0 to the guest's operating systems running in the virtual environment so they can perform operating system functions. A compromise of a server virtualization product operating at ring 0 can potentially expose the underlying memory and I/O to the malware. Further, it is important to note that if the server virtualization product is compromised, each and every operating system running on top of the server virtualization product is also potentially exposed to the malware.

In the simplest of terms, a vulnerability in a server virtualization product can potentially create a scenario where the underlying memory, I/O, and every guest running on top of the virtualization product are also made vulnerable and placed at risk of compromise.

Making a blanket statement that virtualization by-and-of-itself makes you more secure because of the additional layer it places between the hardware and the operating system can clearly lead to a dangerous false sense of security. Any virtualization product should be treated like any other application operating within the enterprise environment and must be properly secured. Further the virtualization software does not remove or reduce the necessity to properly harden the operating systems running on top of the server virtualization product as well as the respective applications and their add-ons that are running on top of that operating system.

Traditional Network Security Products Simply Do Not Work in Today's Virtual Realm

Traditional network security products filter traffic that is presented via the security product's respective network interface. This can be used in a virtual realm, however only with limited results. Only traffic that is placed literally "on the wire" by individual ESX/ESXi servers can be filtered (Figure 24.2).

In order to maximize the benefits of virtualization, it is not uncommon for servers operating at different levels of trust to be required to operate on the same ESX/ESXi server. This creates an issue as traditional network security products are simply incapable of seeing and acting upon intra-VM traffic and therefore can afford no security benefit within a given ESX/ESXi host.

In the physical world, all servers are cabled to a firewall (and other security devices like sensors). Consequently, all traffic is "seen" by some application that is meant to protect it (Figure 24.3).

In the virtualized environment physical servers are collapsed into a single physical host. They now exist as more or less free floating software entities inside this new container. The "traffic" that flows between these virtual machines (VMs) stays mostly inside the container and doesn't make its way to physical security (Figure 24.4).

A new capability was recently introduced as an available option within the current version of VMware in the vSphere 4 product family that affords some level of intra-VM firewalling capability called VMware vShield Zones (Figure 24.5). However it should be noted that VMware vShield Zones are limited to only applying layer 2/3 rules. Most security professionals today clearly recognize the need to filter network traffic beyond layers 2/3 all the way up through the application layer (layer 7) in the current environment.

Considerations for Securing Your Virtual Realm

When looking for potential security risks inherent to the implementation of any vendor's virtualization product, a good place to start is by reviewing that vendor's own security hardening recommendations.

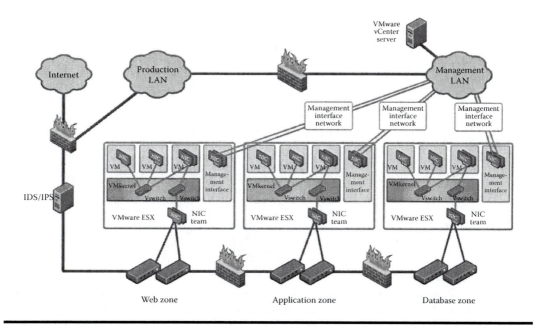

Figure 24.2   Traditional network security products filter traffic that is presented via the security products respective network interface. This can be used in a virtual realm however only with limited results. Only that traffic that is placed literally "on the wire" by individual ESX/ESXi servers can be filtered.

The purpose of this chapter is to make the point that while virtualization can potentially make security easier to implement, by-and-of-itself virtualization does not necessarily solve your enterprise security issues. In fact the implementation of virtualization undeniably actually can increase your overall threat envelope. With that being said, the author wants to make it clear that he has chosen to focus on VMware because they are the current market leader. This in no way should be

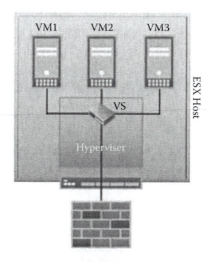

Figure 24.3   In the physical world, all servers are cabled to a firewall and other security devices like sensors. Consequently, all traffic is "seen" by some application that is meant to protect it.

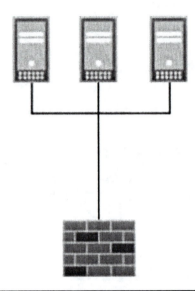

Figure 24.4 In the virtualized environment physical servers are collapsed into a single physical host. They now exist as more or less free floating software entities inside this new container. The "traffic" that flows between these virtual machines (VMs) stays mostly inside the container and does not make its way to physical security.

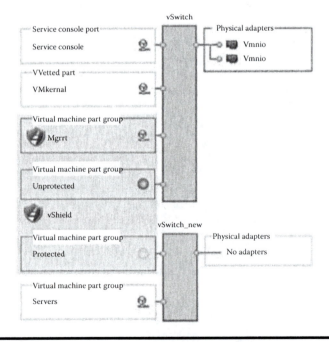

Figure 24.5 VMware vShield Zones, a new capability introduced as an available option within the current version of VMware in the vSphere 4 product family, affords some level intra-VM firewalling.

misinterpreted that VMware was chosen because it is less secure than any other vendor's virtualization product offering. In fact in the author's opinion VMware today offers the most robust and feature-rich product, with proper hardening steps—the most secure virtual solution available in today's virtualization marketplace.

VMware has gone to great lengths to provide documentation on properly hardening their virtual environment to aid in risk mitigation. The latest version of the hardening guide is titled "vSphere 4.0 Security Hardening Guide." It was released in April 2010 and can be downloaded at http://communities.VMware.com/docs/DOC-12306. In the author's opinion, it is an excellent starting point in securing a VMware virtual environment.

A summary of the recommendations of the vSphere Hardening Guide, using the short name of the guideline, along with commentary provided by the author is included below. This summary is not provided as a replacement of the official VMware hardening guide and it is provided only as a simplified overview with the author's comments to provide his personal insights to augment the actual official VMware hardening guide.

VMX01	**Prevent virtual disk shrinking**
	Unauthorized virtual disk shrinking can be used to facilitate a denial of service (DoS) attack.
VMX02	**Prevent other users from spying on administrator remote consoles**
	While an administrator is connected to a remote console a nonadministrator can log in to a remote console and view the administrator's actions.
VMX03	**Disable copy/paste to remote console**
	A virtual machine running VMware tools allows copy and paste between the guest operating system and a computer running a remote console. This copy/paste capability could potentially facilitate both the introduction of malware and unintended exposure of sensitive data.
VMX10	**Ensure unauthorized devices are not connected**
	Any connected device such as a USB or CD represents another potential channel for attack. Any unnecessary devices should be disabled to reduce the threat envelope.
VMX11	**Prevent unauthorized removal, connection, and modification of devices**
	Unprivileged users and processes have the ability by default to connect or disconnect devices such as network interfaces, etc. and to modify device settings. Risks range from an unauthorized device such as a CD drive either introducing unauthorized software or being used for removal of data/data theft. Further, disconnecting a device such as a network interface can easily cause a potential DoS.
VMX12	**Disable VM-to-VM communications through VMCI**
	Any VM connected to the VMCI interface can be seen by any other VM that is also connected to the VMCI interface. A malicious program using the VMCI interface can potentially interact with all other VMs connected to the VMCI.

VMX20   **Limit VM log file size and number**
Unlimited logging could potentially fill the data store resulting in a DoS.

VMX21   **Limit informational messages from the VM to the VMX file**
Unlimited message storage in the VMX file could potentially fill the data store resulting in a DoS.

VMX22   **Avoid using independent-nonpersistent disks**
When operating with a nonpersistent disk, a VM's activities are not logged to disk. Hence there may be no record of an attack or compromise.

VMX30   **Disable remote operations within the guest**
A malicious person could potentially use the VIX API to run unauthorized scripts within a guest OS.

VMX31   **Do not send host performance information to guests**
A malicious person could potentially use performance information as part of the typical reconnaissance phase of an attack.

VMX51   **Restrict access to VMsafe CPU/Mem APIs**
A malicious person could potentially use the VMsafe introspection channel in an attack against all VMs connected to the channel.

VMX52   **Control access to VMs through VMsafe CPU/Mem API**
The VMsafe introspection channel could potentially facilitate the compromise of a VM. If a given VM is not utilizing the VMsafe product then access to the VMsafe introspection channel should not be enabled in the respective VMX file.

VMX54   **Restrict access to VMsafe Network APIs**
A malicious person could potentially attack all VMs connected to the introspection channel.

VMX55   **Control access to VMs through VMsafe Network API**
Take advantage of the filtering capability of VMsafe to filter and control access to the VMsafe introspection channel. Not controlling access to the VMsafe introspection channel leaves a window of opportunity open to a malicious person.

VMP01   **Secure virtual machines as you would physical servers**
Moving a server to a virtual environment does not eliminate the need to follow the very same industry best practices that would be followed to secure the server in the physical realm.

VMP02   **Disable unnecessary or superfluous functions inside VMs**
In a VM, just like in a physical server, one of the best ways to reduce the threat envelope is to remove or disable unnecessary functionality. Leaving an unnecessary function or service leaves a window of opportunity open for a malicious person.

VMP03 **Use templates to deploy VMs whenever possible**

One of the many benefits of VMware is the ability to build a "Gold Master" VM that represents your best effort to harden and lock down a given VM. This VM can be converted to a template and the template can then be used to deploy new VMs that will use the work you did on the original VM as a baseline to deploy additional VMs.

VMP04 **Prevent virtual machines from taking over resources**

In the physical server world we have a tendency to commit all available resources to each stand-alone physical server—the concept of more is better is the norm. In the virtual realm it is critical to carefully manage shared resources by setting limits and shares to those that provide only that which is required for the necessary performance of each virtual server. Not configuring shares and limits will potentially cause resource exhaustion, impacting the performance of all virtual machines operating on the respective physical hardware.

VMP05 **Minimize use of the VM console**

VM Console access should only be granted when absolutely necessary. A malicious user having access to a VM Console could wreak havoc within a virtual environment, as he/she would have the ability to literally bring down a VM using the VM Console's power management and device management capabilities. Of further concern is that each VM console consumes service console resources, hence multiple VM consoles opened simultaneously potentially could exhaust all available service console resources, effectively causing a DoS.

VMP06 **Verify the integrity of software before installation**

In the current environment it is not uncommon for a malicious person to add additional unwanted functionality such as a rootkit or other malware into popular software distributions and then make the modified but otherwise seemingly legitimate software available for download on the public Internet. It is important to not only install software downloaded only from the vendor's website but to also verify the SHA1 of the downloaded software against the hash provided by the software vendor to validate the integrity of the software download.

HST01 **Ensure bidirectional CHAP authentication is enabled for iSCSI traffic**

Not implementing bidirectional CHAP could leave you wide open to a man-in-the-middle attack that could enable the malicious person to steal data. It is built in and easy to implement—take advantage of the risk mitigation available within VMware.

HST02 **Ensure the uniqueness of CHAP authentication secrets**

Unfortunately administrators have a tendency to share mutual authentication secrets across multiple hosts. If the shared secret is discovered for a single host, it puts all hosts at risk. A good practice to follow would be to create a unique shared secret for each client authenticating to the host.

HST03	**Mask and zone SAN resources appropriately**
	Zoning can help facilitate the segregation of departmental data and masking can make certain that only those VMs with a specific need to connect with a SAN resource can in fact actually see the SAN resource in the first place.
HCM01	**Do not use self-signed certificates for ESX/ESXi communications**
	The use of the self-signed certificates that are shipped with VMware can potentially make life much easier for a malicious person that desires to perform a man-in-the-middle attack. Using a commercial certificate authority or an organizational certificate authority, each with full revocation capability, can go a long way in mitigating the risk of a man-in-the-middle attack.
HCM02	**Disable managed object browser**
	The managed object browser is primarily used only for diagnostics in debugging the vSphere SDK and is not normally used for general operations. A malicious person with access to the managed object browser could make unauthorized changes or actions on the host.
HCM03	**Disable web access (ESX only)**
	There have been vulnerabilities previously found in the VMware implementation of web access and by-and-of-itself there is an inherent risk in any web interface implementation. The preferred method to manage virtual machines is through the more secure center server using the vSphere Client.
HCM04	**Ensure ESX is configured to encrypt all sessions**
	No encrypting client sessions leave the door open for a malicious person to facilitate a man-in-the-middle attack, potentially gaining valuable information that could be useful in launching further attacks.
HLG01	**Configure remote syslog**
	One of the typical first steps or actions a malicious person takes after a successful attack is to delete or alter log files to hide any trace of the attack. If the attacker has gained administrative control of the virtual server, deleting or altering any locally stored log files can be a trivial task. By enabling remote logging you are making life more difficult for the bad guy, as he would have to gain administrative rights to yet another server (the syslog server) in order to alter or delete the log files.
HLG02	**Configure persistent logging**
	The logs for ESXi are stored in the in-memory, hence a reboot would erase the logs, making it easy work for a bad guy to simply reboot the server to cover their tracks. Further, by default only one day of logs are stored and this may not be adequate when troubleshooting a complex operational issue. Enabling persistent logging and storing the logs on a remote data store is the best approach.

HLG03 **Configure NTP time synchronization**

Time synchronization across all servers and VMs within the virtual environment in the author's opinion is a necessity and makes troubleshooting issues and responding to incidents significantly easier and more accurate. Not utilizing time synchronization could, in fact, cause you to miss the fact that an incident occurred in the first place. Lastly, several VMware operations, such as vMotion, require that time be accurately synchronized across the respective hosts/guests in order for the operation to be completed successfully.

HMT01 **Control access by CIM-based hardware monitoring tools**

The rule of least privilege must be enforced in the use of CIM-based monitoring tools. A CIM application operating with root or administrative level of privilege could lead to the complete compromise of the virtual environment if the CIM application is compromised. It is important to remember that a malicious person effectively gains the application's operational level of privilege when they compromise an application. By reducing the level of privilege assigned to an application you are effectively limiting the capability of the attacker if the application is compromised.

HMT02 **Ensure proper SNMP configuration (ESXi only)**

It is important to note that ESX provides for support of SNMP versions 1, 2C, and the most secure current version 3, while ESXi only supports SNMP versions 1 and 2C. Neither of these versions of SMNP provide for encryption. Hence information disclosure via ESXi (or ESX when running a version of SNMP other than 3) with intercepted unencrypted SNMP traps is a potential issue. SNMP on ESXi only supports trap operations with its limited MIB functionality. This mitigates the risk of the configuration being modified remotely with ESXi. Consideration should be given to only sending SNMP over a trusted path with ESXi. The implementation of SNMP on ESXi also only supports trap operations in its limited MIB functionality. The normal caveats of securing SNMP such as changing the default public and private community strings still apply.

HMT03 **Establish and maintain configuration file integrity (ESXi)**

The file access API in ESXi can allow for the direct modification of the following configuration files:

- esx.conf
- hostAgentConfig.xml
- hosts
- license.cfg
- motd
- openwsman.conf
- proxy.xml
- snmp.xml

- ssl_cert
- ssl_key
- syslog.conf
- vmware_config
- vmware_configrules
- vmware.lic
- vpxa.cfg

Modification of the above files can provide for unauthorized access to the host configuration as well as related VMs. By both utilizing an automated file integrity monitoring solution and tracking authorized changes in your change control program you can continuously verify that unauthorized changes to the files exposed by the vSphere API in ESXi have not occurred.

HMT10　　**Prevent unintended use of VMsafe CPU/Mem APIs**

In an effort to reduce your threat envelope, if you are not utilizing products that specifically make use of the VMsafe Network API, it should be disabled.

HMT11　　**Prevent unintended use of VMsafe Network APIs**

In an effort to reduce your threat envelope if you are not utilizing products that specifically make use of the VMsafe Network API, it should be disabled.

HCN01　　**Ensure only authorized users have access to the DCUI**

The Direct Console User Interface is the interface available at the console on ESXi and provides for basic host configuration, network, setting of the root password, and maintenance operations such as restarting agents and restarting the host.

Enforce the rule of least privilege: only those users that require access in order to accomplish their specific job tasks and responsibilities should be granted access to the DCUI.

HCN02　　**Enable lockdown mode to restrict root access**

When ESXi hosts are managed via vCenter, the threat envelope can be reduced by enabling lockdown mode to prevent remote root access to the ESXi host other than with a vSphere Client or vCLI commands to vCenter Server, vSphere Client or vCLI commands direct to ESXi, or via the DCUI.

HCN03　　**Avoid adding the root user to local groups**

Adding a root user to a local group can override lockdown mode.

HCN04　　**Disable tech support mode**

A user logged in to tech support mode can assume complete control of a host. Tech support mode is typically only used under the direction of a VMware support consultant and you can reduce your threat envelope by disabling it. However, when disabled it greatly reduces the ability to diagnose and support the host and reenabling tech support mode may require a reboot of the host.

NAR01

Ensure vSphere management traffic is on a restricted network

The management network includes both the service console interface on ESX and the Management vmkernel interface on ESXi. Sharing this traffic with production traffic can potentially expose management information that would be valuable to an attacker during the reconnaissance phase of an attack. Further, if access to the network is gained by an unauthorized user it could provide an attacker with privileged access. It is a recognized good practice to segment the traffic either using separate switches and interfaces or through the use of VLANS.

NAR02

Ensure vMotion traffic is isolated

During a vMotion the memory contents of the VM are sent unencrypted hence could be exposed to a malicious user that is sniffing the network, thereby exposing sensitive or personally identifiable information. The vMotion traffic should be isolated using separate switches and interfaces or VLANS.

NAR03

Ensure IP-based storage traffic is isolated

IP-based storage is typically unencrypted and hence could be exposed to a malicious user that is sniffing the network, thereby exposing sensitive or personally identifiable information. The IP-based storage traffic should be isolated using separate switches and interfaces or VLANS.

NAR04

Strictly control access to management network

If an attacker gains unauthorized access to the management network, it could be used as a staging ground for further attack and penetration. Client systems should not be on the management network, only dedicated machines or remote access via VPN for use only by trusted administrators.

NCN02

Ensure that there are no unused ports on a distributed vSwitch port group

Limiting the number of available ports within a port group on a vSwitch can help to mitigate the risk of an administrator accidentally or maliciously moving a VM to an unauthorized network.

NCN03

Ensure the "MAC address change" policy is set to reject

By setting the MAC address change policy to reject, no changes can be made to the effective MAC address other than the value assigned in the initial MAC address. This mitigates the risk of an attacker using the VM operating system to impersonate an authorized network adapter MAC address when sending frames to the receiving network.

NCN04

Ensure the "forged transmits" policy is set to reject

Forged transits are set by default to allow—this permits MAC address impersonation, which can be used by a malicious person to stage an attack by using a MAC address that is permitted access to the receiving network. Forged transmits should be set to reject to mitigate the risk of this issue.

NCN05   **Ensure "promiscuous mode" policy is set to reject**

When enabled on a vSwitch, promiscuous mode allows any machine connected to the vSwitch to see all network traffic associated with all other VMs connected to the vSwitch. Promiscuous mode is set to reject by default and this is the suggested setting. A safer approach to enabling promiscuous mode for a vSwitch is to leave the default setting to reject and configure a port group for only those VMs that need to be monitored in promiscuous mode and set the port group to promiscuous mode, which allows the port group setting to override the vSwitch setting, but only for those VMs within the specific port group.

NCN06   **Ensure port groups are not configured to the value of the native VLAN**

ESX does not support the concept of a native VLAN. This is not an issue when it is only connected to VMware equipment but when connected to equipment that in fact does support native VLANS it can create compatibility issues.

NCN07   **Ensure that port groups are not configured to VLAN 4095 except for virtual guest tagging**

VLAN tag 4095 is reserved to activate virtual guest tagging where the vSwitch passes all frames to the guest VM without modifying the VLAN tags. In the simplest of terms, it is only used when the guest is expected to be handling all of the tagging operations of the VLAN.

NCN10   **Ensure that port groups are configured with a clear network label**

As your network grows and becomes more complex, using generic labels that are not associated with the use of the port group can make troubleshooting difficult at best. Choosing port group names that have a meaning associated with the use of the port group is a good practice to adopt early on in the implementation of your network.

NCN11   **Ensure that all vSwitches are configured with a clear network label**

As your network grows and becomes more complex, using generic labels that are not associated with the use of the vSwitch can make troubleshooting difficult at best. Choosing vSwitch names that have a meaning associated with the use of the vSwitch is a good practice to adopt early on in the implementation of your network.

NCN12   **Fully document all VLANs used on vSwitches**

You cannot validate the security/configuration of any network component without first documenting it. Complete vSwitch configuration details should be included in your change control and configuration documentation.

NCN13   **Ensure that only authorized administrators have access to virtual networking components**

Enforce the rule of least privilege and separation of duties for networking components by utilizing the granular role-based controls available in vSphere.

NPN01   **Ensure physical switch ports are configured with spanning tree disabled**
Virtual switches in VMware do not support the spanning tree protocol, hence not disabling the spanning tree protocol on a physical network switch port can cause potential connectivity and performance issues.

NPN02   **Ensure that the nonnegotiate option is configured for trunk links between external physical switches and virtual switches in VST mode**
When a port on physical switch that connects to a virtual switch in a VLAN trunk has the negotiate option enabled, unnecessary network traffic is generated at the vSwitch as a vSwitch does not support the dynamic trunking protocol. The nonnegotiable option should be selected to reduce unnecessary traffic across the network.

NPN03   **Ensure that VLAN trunk links are connected only to physical switch ports that function as trunk links**
An improperly configured physical switch in a VLAN with a vSwitch can cause dropped frames and potentially misdirected traffic.

VSH01   **Maintaining supported operating system, database, and hardware for vCenter**
Harden the underlying operating system to mitigate the risk of vulnerabilities. The author suggests following the Security Technical Implementation Guides (STIGS) from NIST. http://iase.disa.mil/stigs/index.html.

VSH02   **Keep vCenter Server system properly patched**
The vast majority of vulnerabilities have a vendor patch available to fully mitigate the associated risk. Not implementing a patch management program in the current environment is simply irresponsible at best.

VSH03   **Provide Windows system protection on the vCenter Server host**
Implementing antivirus and antimalware solutions can still leave you unnecessarily exposed in the current environment. The author suggests complimenting these solutions with current-generation whitelisting/application control technology. Simply put, in a virtual realm you know explicitly what should be operating on the server, hence it makes sense to only permit that software (once validated) to be able to execute.

VSH04   **Avoid user login to vCenter Server system**
Enforce the rule of least privilege and separation of duties by only allowing users with the explicit need to use the facilities of the vCenter server to log in to the server. Remember vCenter is effectively the "keys to the kingdom" in your virtual realm.

VSH05   **Install vCenter Server using a service account instead of a built-in Windows account**
A built-in administrative account in Windows simply has more privilege than is necessary for the operation of a vCenter server.

VSH06	**Restrict usage of vSphere administrator privilege** Enforce the rule of least privilege and separation of duties by only granting administrative rights to those users that actually need it to get their job done.
VSC01	**Do not use default self-signed certificates** You can mitigate a large part of the risk of a man-in-the-middle attack by simply replacing self-signed certificates with certificates from a commercial Certificate Authority (CA) or an organizational CA. This is low hanging fruit in risk mitigation and should be a prerequisite in the deployment of any virtual realm.
VSC02	**Monitor access to SSL certificates** Any nonservice account access to the directory containing SSL certificates should be logged and an alert should be generated. Unauthorized access to the SSL directory can be a first notification of a malicious person attempting to escalate their level of privilege.
VSC03	**Restrict access to SSL certificates** Any user in vCenter can access the directory that contains SSL certificates by default. Enforce the rule of least privilege by changing the Windows directory permission so that only the service account can access the directory.
VSC04	**Always verify SSL certificates** Do not simply click on the "ignore" option when presented with a dialog to validate a certificate—take the time to properly validate it.
VSC05	**Restrict network access to vCenter Server system** Reduce risk by restricting the specific IP addresses that are allowed to access vCenter—a local firewall can easily meet the need.
VSC06	**Block access to ports not being used by vCenter** Leaving ports open that are not necessary for the operation of vCenter is exposing it to unnecessary risk. Nonessential ports can easily be blocked using a local firewall.
VSC07	**Disable managed object browser** As noted in HSM02, the managed object browser is primarily used only for diagnostics in debugging the vSphere SDK and is not normally used for general operations. A malicious person with access to the managed object browser could make unauthorized changes or actions on the host.
VSC08	**Disable web access** As noted in HCM03, there have been vulnerabilities previously found in the VMware implementation of web access and by-and-of-itself there is an inherent risk in any web interface implementation.
VSC09	**Disable datastore browser** The datastore browser is a web interface and there is an inherent risk in any web interface implementation.

VSD01 **Use least privileges for the vCenter Server Database user**
Enforce the rule of least privilege by removing privileges that are otherwise only needed during the initial installation or in the upgrade of the vCenter Server Database.

VCL01 **Restrict the use of Linux-based clients**
Restrict the use of Linux-based clients that could be used to access vCenter or ESX/ESXi, as some have been known not to provide for certificate validation and hence are simply not recommended for use in managing the virtual realm.

VCL02 **Verify the Integrity of vSphere Client**
The vSphere Client allows the use of software extensions known as plug-ins. These plug-ins run at the same level of privilege as the logged-in user. Hence, it should be validated that the VSphere Client is only running approved plug-ins that are necessary in the management of vCenter from trusted and reliable sources.

VCL03 **Use least privileges for the Update Manager Database user**
Support enforcement of the rule of least privilege—the level of privilege required to install the Update Manager database is higher than that which is required for normal operation. After installation the level of privilege for the Update Manager database user should be reduced.

VUM02 **Keep Update Manager system properly patched**
The vast majority of vulnerabilities have a vendor patch available to fully mitigate the associated risk. Not implementing a patch management program in the current environment is simply irresponsible at best.

VUM03 **Provide Windows system protection on the Update Manager system**
Implementing antivirus and antimalware solutions can still leave you unnecessarily exposed in the current environment. The author suggests complimenting these solutions with current-generation white listing/application control technology. Simply put, in a virtual realm you know explicitly what should be operating on the server, hence it makes sense to only permit that software (once validated) to be able to execute.

VUM04 **Avoid user login to Update Manager system**
Enforce the rule of least privilege and separation of duties by only allowing users with the explicit need to use the facilities of the Update Manager system to log in to the server.

VUM05 **Do not configure Update Manager to manage its own VM or its vCenter Server's VM**
The process of installing any patch can potentially cause a reboot, which can inadvertently stop an update process prior to its full completion.

VUM10 **Limit the connectivity between Update Manager and public patch repositories**
Update Manager connects to the public Internet and should be limited to the specific resources it is permitted to and, just as importantly, what Internet resources are permitted to connect to it in order to reduce risk.

CON01 **Ensure ESX firewall is configured to high security**

The built-in firewall in ESX server between the service console and the network should be configured to use the high-security setting to default block all outbound connections and only allow explicitly selected inbound connections.

CON02 **Limit network access to applications and services**

The ESX service console is effectively a Linux server and like any other server should be hardened by removing unnecessary services and applications.

CON03 **Do not run NFS or NIS clients in the service console**

Turning on NFS or NIS client services in the service console effectively bypasses the firewall by opening all outbound UDP and TCP ports.

COM01 **Do not apply Red Hat patches to the service console**

The ESX console is a highly modified derivative of Red Hat Linux by VMware and only patches provided by VMware should be applied.

COM02 **Do not rely upon tools that only check for Red Hat patches**

Simply put, running a third-party patch management tool on the service console that only checks for available Red Hat patches could potentially miss patches for the service console from VMware and leave you vulnerable. Further, because of the modifications made by VMware, some software could be flagged as vulnerable when it is actually not vulnerable.

COM03 **Do not manage the service console as a Red Hat Linux host**

Because of the specialized nature of the service console in ESX, using the typical Red Hat management tools could result in misconfiguration.

COM04 **Use vSphere Client and vCenter to administer the hosts instead of service console**

Any command-line management is subject to the typical "typo" issues that could result in misconfiguration. Use of scripting or the facilities available using the vCenter client directly via vCenter can minimize these issues.

COP01 **Use a directory service for authentication**

The use of a directory service can reduce the administrative burden of user account management.

COP02 **Establish a password policy for password complexity**

Use and enforcement of a password policy can go a long way in reducing the risk of passwords being guessed or otherwise cracked.

COP03 **Establish a password policy for password history**

The repeated reuse of old passwords increases the likelihood that the password will be guessed or cracked. The password policy should address the issue of password reuse through tracking password history.

COP04 **Establish a maximum password aging policy**
Using a control to establish how long a password can be used before it is changed can go a long way in reducing the risk of passwords being guessed or otherwise cracked.

COP05 **Establish a password policy for minimum days before a password is changed**
One trick users often use is to quickly change their new password multiple times so they can override the typical password reuse constraints. This often occurs right after a mandatory password change is required where the user then quickly changes the password multiple times and returns back to a password they are familiar with. Setting a minimum period of time before a password can be changed can mitigate this issue.

COP06 **Ensure that purser auto password change in vCenter meets policy**
The vpxuser password is automatically changed every 30 days by default. Be sure this policy in fact meets with the requirements of your password policy.

COL01 **Configure syslog logging**
Using remote syslog logging can reduce administrative burden as well as reducing the risk that an attacker that compromised a given machine can easily cover their tracks by deleting or modifying the logs on the local compromised machine.

COL02 **Configure NTP time synchronization**
Time synchronization across all systems within the virtual environment in the author's opinion is a necessity and makes troubleshooting issues and responding to incidents significantly easier and more accurate. Not utilizing time synchronization could in fact cause you to miss the fact that an incident occurred in the first place. Lastly, several VMware operations, such as vMotion, require that time be accurately synchronized across the respective hosts/guests in order for the operation to be completed successfully.

COH01 **Partition the disk to prevent the root file system from filling up**
Like most Linux derivatives, if the root file system fills on ESX it can degrade the ability to manage it and, worst case, can make it unresponsive, creating a DoS.

COH03 **Establish and maintain file system integrity**
Monitoring the integrity of the configuration files could be your first indication of a security incident.

COH04 **Ensure permissions of important files and utility commands have not been changed from default**
File permissions should be checked by a thorough file integrity system as part of the overall file integrity check. Altering a files permissions can impact its ability to function and could result in a DoS.

COA01 **Prevent tampering at boot time**
The service console in ESX, like most other Linux derivatives, can allow a user to enter kernel options such as booting in to single user mode during boot. A grub password is recommended to reduce the risk of an unauthorized person from passing options to the kernel during boot.

COA02 **Require authentication for single user mode**
An additional layer of security can be provided to COA01 by also requiring a password to enter single user mode.

COA03 **Ensure root access via SSH is disabled**
You simply cannot audit specifically who is issuing commands or performing tasks when a user logs in as root via SSH. Disabling root from logging in to SSH forces the user to first log in with their own account, creating an audit trail, and then use su or sudo to elevate their level of privilege.

COA04 **Disallow console root login**
As with SSH in COA03, you simply cannot audit specifically who is issuing commands or performing tasks when a user logs in as root via the local console when using a connected screen and keyboard. Disabling root from logging in to the console locally forces the user to first log in with their own account, creating an audit trail, and then use su or sudo to elevate their level of privilege.

COA05 **Limit access to the su command**
Use of the su command dramatically increases the level of privilege for a given logged-in user and should be carefully controlled.

COA06 **Configure and use sudo to control administrative access**
Use of the sudo utility can dramatically increase the level of privilege for a given logged-in user and should be carefully controlled. The configuration files for sudo users can be configured to granularly and explicitly specify which privileged commands the user can execute when using sudo.

Other Security and Operational Considerations

The official vSphere Hardening Guide is a great place to start to harden the initial configuration of the virtual realm. However, there are several areas that are simply beyond the scope of the vSphere Hardening Guide:

- Security of the software running inside the virtual machine, such as operating system and applications, or of the traffic traveling through the virtual machine networks.
- Security of any other add-on products, such as SRM.
- Detailed operational procedures related to maintaining security, such as event monitoring, auditing, and privilege management. Guidance is provided on general areas in which to perform these important tasks, but details on exactly how to perform them are beyond the scope of the guide.

Additional valuable guidance for security in the typical SANS hands-on format can be found in the SANS course SEC577 Virtualization Security Fundamentals. Additional information can be found at http://www.sans.org/security-training/virtualization-security-fundamentals-3807-tid.

While the SEC577 Virtualization Security Fundamentals course covers many of the vSphere Hardening Guide recommendations, it also provides insight into many areas not covered in the official vSphere Hardening Guide. In the author's opinion it is a valuable and highly recommended resource.

SANS SEC577 Virtualization Security Fundamentals

- Virtualization basics and introduction
- Virtual networking
- Virtual switch security policies
- Command-line virtual network configuration and administration
- Virtual network architecture design
- vCenter security and administration
- Virtual infrastructure client security
- ESX and ESXi security
- ESX file system security
- VM guest security
- Storage considerations
- Backup and recovery
- Virtualization risk assessment
- Virtualization threats
- Virtualization vulnerabilities
- Virtualization attacks
- Virtualization audit and compliance

About the Author

Paul Henry, MCP+I, MCSE, CCSA, CCSE, CISSP-ISSAP, CISM, CISA, CIFI, CCE, ACE, GCFA, MCP+VCP, is one of the world's foremost global information security and computer forensic experts, with more than 25 years of experience managing security initiatives for Global 2000 enterprises and government organizations worldwide. Throughout his career, Henry has played a key strategic role in launching network security initiatives to meet our ever-changing threat landscape. Henry advises and consults on some of the world's most challenging high-risk information security projects, including the National Banking System in Saudi Arabia, the Reserve Bank of Australia, the U.S. Department of Defense, and government projects throughout Southeast Asia.

OPERATIONS SECURITY

Operations Controls

Chapter 25

Warfare and Security: Deterrence and Dissuasion in the Cyber Era

Samuel Chun

Introduction

Over the course of the past three or four years a new terminology has entered the information technology lexicon that has been a source of much discussion, debate, and ultimately confusion in the United States. Information security, IT security, cybercrime, cyberterrorism, cybersecurity, cyberwarfare, and cyberspace all have been used interchangeably, and with little verbal precision adding to the challenge. Also, these loosely related terms have begun to gain acceptance globally without consistency, expanding to problems beyond the U.S. policy circles in Washington. While this chapter is not intended to be a comprehensive treatise of all of the policies, doctrines, and laws regarding these terms, it is intended to be a primer on the active debate, and provide guidance and specificity on the terms used currently. As the recognition of U.S. information and communications infrastructure as a strategic national asset begins to take hold in Washington, practitioners will be required more than ever to have a fundamental understanding of these terms and the issues presented in this chapter.

What Is Cyberspace?

While the term "cyberspace" has been around for over two decades, there hasn't been a clear definition that has been accepted universally. In fact, cyberspace is a term that appears to be generally amorphous and have different meanings depending on the context. For example, for the U.S. military cyberspace is a new defined military war fighting domain in addition to land, sea, air, and space, where traditional military doctrines, campaigns, and approaches dominate. For the Department of Homeland Security, cyberspace is a critical cross-sector resource that pervades all of the 20+ critical infrastructure/key resources (CI/KR) of the United States. For most regular

U.S. citizens cyberspace is a wondrously powerful, nebulous, and oftentimes extraordinarily technical and confusing entity that they need to rely on to connect, communicate, and manage their lives. Consider the following definitions that have been quoted in the past few years:

> "a global domain within the information environment consisting of the interdependent network of information technology infrastructures, including the Internet, telecommunications networks, computer systems, and embedded processors and controllers." (US Deputy Defense Secretary, Gordon England)

> "the entire electromagnetic spectrum." (Major General William T. Lord, Provisional Commander, USAF Cyber Command)

> "a resource to be shared by all." (International Telecommunication Union, a United Nations agency)

> "composed of hundreds of thousands of interconnected computers, servers, routers, switches, and fiber optic cables that allow our critical infrastructures to work" (National Strategy to Secure Cyberspace)

> "the virtual communicative space created by digital technologies." (Cees J. Hamelink, University of Amsterdam)

Regardless of whether it is the Department of Defense or Homeland Security, civilian agencies, the private sector, or private individuals, the reliability and resilience of the information and communications infrastructures are critical in our daily lives. As globalization and internationalization of our economic and national interests continues, everyone needs to have *freedom of action* to use these information and communications infrastructures with confidence without fear of exploitation, corruption, or denial. For private citizens they need to be able to rely on the Internet for commerce, for governments to provide ever-expanding services to their constituents (faster and more efficiently), and for companies the application of technology and use of Internet serve as one of the main differentiators for successful business outcomes.

Why Is Cyberspace So Important Now for the Federal Government?

So where did the term cyberspace come from? The earliest and perhaps the most apt definition in the early cyberspace dialogue to enter the lexicon was from William Gibson's *Neuromancer* in 1984. In it he defines cyberspace as "a consensual hallucination experienced daily by billions of legitimate operators, in every nation." While that may have been closer to reality at the dawn of the Internet age in 1984, cyberspace in the modern era is more complex and real. While technological advances such as cloud computing and social networking make computing and services from the Internet ubiquitous and global, the very infrastructure that it has relied upon originates from a series of academic experiments conducted by researchers from universities and DARPA. This research experiment has exploded into what we know as the Internet and more recently cyberspace, yet the fundamental networking and routing protocols and infrastructures (TCP/IP and IPv4) are fraught with weaknesses and issues never envisioned by the original researchers. For example the Internet was built on a complete model of trust with few mechanisms that were originally thought of for identity and accountability. We have built our global information and communications infrastructures and our global economies and national strength on top of this experiment and that is where the threats lay exploiting weaknesses in hardware and software, network and applications alike. It has taken governments decades to realize (1) our cyberspace is a major strategic asset and its loss or degradation could harm national security (economic and national defense), and (2) there are weaknesses that threaten the security (both economically and militarily) of the United States.

The defense of the information, communications, and infrastructures of the United States, and ensuring the freedom of use and action within it has become over the past two administrations a national priority worthy of multiple White House directives (such as HSPD-23, Comprehensive National Cybersecurity Initiative, and the National Strategy for Online Transactions, which is currently being created) and no less than 20 specific pieces of legislation in Congress in an attempt to tackle this issue. The Obama administration was the first executive office to have a press conference dedicated to cybersecurity in 2009 and appointed the first US cybersecurity coordinator, Howard A. Schmidt, reporting to the National Security Establishment at the White House in December of 2009.

The Threats Are Clearly Real and Growing

While the traditional "hacking" of vulnerable systems on the Internet has been going on for decades, in the past five years there has been a noticeable increase in the amount, type, and sources of the attacks against technology infrastructures. While the exploitation and probing of national government systems and information infrastructures have also been targeted by national intelligence communities, there has been general consensus that, due to the comparatively low cost of these efforts (in comparison to traditional human or kinetic asset-based covert/clandestine operation), "cyber espionage" by nation states is increasing.

While it is challenging to chronicle the details of these threats, it is valuable to review and categorize the types of threats and the potential threat they pose to national interests. While there are many ways to classify the threats, the author has chosen to use individual personal motivations to describe/catalog the threats.

Curious: Due to the ease of computing today, it is extremely easy for a reasonably adept technology user to obtain access malware, root kits, and botnet "kits" on the Internet. Tools such as Zeus, SpyEye, and Eleanor offer even the most novice "future hacker" the ability to create powerful armies of botnets and malware. While the individual intent might not be malicious, curiosity does drive a subset of technically savvy folks to create cybercrime assets out of personal curiosity. While they are, in general, not a big threat, if they become more technically adept they can become motivated and experienced in the more threatening categories.

Narcissistic: The underground community is one that is highly competitive and personality driven. Personal fame in the underground community drives many to discover a vast array of technical vulnerabilities, and lethal root kits, and control of vast array of botnets. While their intent is to be the "best of the best," quest for recognition and personal fame drives many into the world of "one-upmanship" in developing malware, trading in vulnerabilities, and controlling zombies and botnets.

Greedy: The timeless motivator of greed has also been an active contributor in the growth of the threats. Entire economies have arisen in the sales of private information, financial records, product vulnerability, botnet rentals, etc. It is a thriving economy, easily exceeding that of the fast food industry, and increasing involvement by organized crime has been intimated by numerous law enforcement agencies and commercial companies. The 2009 US Cyberspace Policy Review conducted by the National Security Council's Melissa Hathaway noted that cybercrime cost, according to private industry, the nation as much as $1 trillion in losses in 2008, threatening the national economic security of the United States. To combat cybercrime, numerous anti-cybercrime bills have been introduced in Congress including the Gillibrand-Hatch Cybercrime Cooperation Act, intending to coordination efforts of the United States' international partners in fighting crime while motivating developing nations with aid to pass and enforce strict cybercrime laws.

Ideological: According to many government officials, the ugly face of extremist and ideological movements has been interested in using the Internet to commit cyberterrorism against the United States. Because it is relatively inexpensive and can be conducted remotely and with relative ease, it is reported that ideological movements such as Al Qaeda and Associated Movements (AQAM) have become increasingly focused on cyberterrorism. Unfortunately, many ideological movements have access to the large amount of resources that are needed to leverage greed-motivated threats that are increasing on the Internet.

State Motivated: State-sponsored cyberthreats are becoming increasingly active on the Internet. While the probing and exploitation of foreign nations by intelligence communities of the world are nothing new, there has been increasingly public posture by the national defense and security organizations of world governments. There are dozens of "cyber military units" globally and in the United States the military has adopted the information and communications infrastructures (both government owned and private) as a new war fighting domain to be defended and dominated in a similar fashion as Land, Sea, and Air, with doctrines and techniques being developed to integrate cyberattacks with kinetic (traditional armed combatant) ones.

Our National Responses

It is the observation of this author that the way that the United States responds to threats regardless of whether they are virtual or kinetic has generally been through organizational activities and structure. For example, in response to the tragedies of September 11, 2001, a cabinet-level department, the Department of Homeland Security, was created in response to domestic threats. Over the past 5 years units and groups within the government began to take hold across civilian, law enforcement, defense, and intelligence agencies emphasizing cybersecurity as one of their primary missions. The National Security Agency (NSA), who are recognized to have decades of expertise in communications and electronics, has naturally continued to take a leadership role in helping to defend the DoD (.mil) environment while elements of DHS's National Cyber Security Division (NCSD) are responsible for the defense and resiliency of the .gov domain and coordination across the private sectors.

A whole other book could easily be written describing the various federal organizations, their roles, and interdependences with responsibilities for cyberspace. However, it is worthwhile to briefly describe the principal organizations that have lead roles in the security of U.S. cyberspace in the United States.

Executive Office of the President (*White House*): The announcement of the appointment of Howard Schmidt as the White House cybersecurity coordinator on December 22, 2009, by the deputy national security advisor for homeland security described the coordinator's role thusly: "will have the important responsibility of orchestrating the many important cybersecurity activities across the government...will have regular access to the President and serve as a key member of his National Security Staff. He will also work closely with his economic team to ensure that our cybersecurity efforts keep the Nation secure and prosperous." While the exact details of the role that his new office would play seem somewhat nebulous according to the announcement, the role is actually described very accurately. As a matter of fact, the cybersecurity coordinator's role is consistent with the other members of the national security staff and other offices within the executive office of the president. They play largely an advisory and policy setting role rather than managing programs or implementing the various policies. The actual implementation, execution, and management of policies—such as improving the IT security posture of government or aspects of the private critical infrastructure—fall upon the dozens of agencies (executive and independent) that actually "run the business of government."

Department of Homeland Security (*DHS*): In 2003 DHS Secretary Tom Ridge created the NCSD in implementing then President Bush's National Strategy to Secure Cyberspace and Homeland Security Act of 2002. Reporting to the DHS Directorate for National Protection and Programs' (NPPD) Office of Cybersecurity and Communications (CS&C), it has the massive role of working collaboratively with private, public (including state, local, and tribal governments), and international sectors to secure U.S. cyber assets. Broadly, it has two principal objectives: build and maintain a national cyber response system (led by the National Cyber Response Coordination Group—a collection of 13 federal agencies for cyber incidents of national concern) and implement a cyber risk management program for U.S. critical infrastructure (through outreach and cyber emergency exercises such as Cyber Storm). Most importantly, DHS has the lead role in leading security for nondefense and intelligence community agencies, referred to as "civilian agencies." DHS has one of the most complex and challenging implementation roles of any agency in government due to a variety of factors such as its maturity (a relatively new cabinet agency), size (over a dozen component agencies such as Transportation Security Administration, Coast Guard, Secret Service, etc.), broad scope (private, public, and international coordination), and authorities (responder, coordinator, enforcer, and defender roles). Recently, they have expanded their efforts to enhance security awareness of the general public by sponsoring competitions and programs aimed at increasing security as a national topic of discussion.

National Institute of Standards and Technology (*NIST*): Founded in 1901, NIST is an agency of the Department of Commerce entrusted with advancing measurement science, standards, and technology to enhance US economic security. Contrary to popular misconception, NIST is not a regulatory body and does not impose its guidelines and standards on the private sector. However, select standards such as the Federal Information Processing Standards, notably FIPS 140-2 for encryption, are mandatory for implementation for federal government systems, as required by the Federal Information Security Management Act (FISMA) of 2002. NIST plays an active role in the security of the federal government, especially with civilian agencies, with its publication of its special guidelines (SPs) on security. The Special Publications 800 series, notably 800-37 and 800-53, are de facto required reading for any security practitioner in the federal government. In addition, the Computer Security Division manages the National Vulnerability Database (NVD), which is the U.S. government repository of cybersecurity vulnerabilities based on data represented using the Security Content Automation Protocol (SCAP). The NVD enables the automation of vulnerability management, measurement, and compliance with its checklists, impact metrics, and potential misconfigurations. Traditionally NIST has worked somewhat separately from the Department of Defense's NSA, which plays a similar technology standards and policy role for the national defense agencies. Recently however, NIST and NSA have been working closer in their cybersecurity standards/guideline efforts, while maintaining a distinction between a guidance role for NIST and more of a policy-setting role for the defense community at the NSA.

National Security Agency/Central Security Service: The often mischaracterized NSA is a vital member of the intelligence community managed by the Department of Defense. Based in Ft. Meade, MD, and often referred to as the "The Fort" by those in government, it has three principal missions: *information assurance*—preventing foreign adversaries from exfiltrating sensitive or classified national security information or otherwise disrupting or denying access to those national security systems; *signals intelligence*—collecting, processing, and sharing intelligence information from foreign signals for intelligence, counterintelligence, and military operations; and finally *network/cyberwarfare operations* (which will be detailed later in this chapter). While initially created as a separate agency by the Department of Defense in 1972, the Central Security Service (CSS) is a partner agency of the NSA, with the primary mission of providing cryptological support to the Service Cryptologic Elements of the armed forces. The Director of the NSA (DIRNSA) must be a commissioned officer of the military, is typically a three-star general or admiral, and also serves the dual hated role of the chief of the CSS.

Department of Defense: With nearly two million active duty and civilian employees, the Department of Defense (DoD) is the largest cabinet-level department. It has four armed services, the army, navy, marine corps, and air force, along with over a dozen noncombatant component agencies such as the NSA, Defense Logistics Agency (DLA), Business Transformation Agency, and Missile Defense Agency. There has been fierce debate publicly and privately about the role and mission of the U.S. military in cybersecurity and cyberwarfare over the past few years. In addition there have been numerous command and organizational changes that have been proposed, debated, rejected, reconsidered, and re-debated over the past 18 months. At the time of the writing of this chapter the primary role of the U.S. military in cybersecurity has been publicly acknowledged to be the confidentiality, integrity, and availability of the information and communications infrastructures of the department of defense's own technology infrastructures. While this "defensive posture" is always acknowledged by senior leaders in the DoD and armed services, they also have not categorically denied the need for offensive cyber capabilities (computer network attack, computer network exploitation, electronic warfare, etc.) of the armed forces. With the acknowledged role of the NSA in enabling network warfare on behalf of the U.S. military as described in their public website, they are likely to be the primary agency for conducting offensive operations. To coordinate the various roles within the armed forces, Secretary of Defense Robert Gates has issued an order to stand up a new subordinate unified command called United States Cyber Command (USCYBERCOM), consisting of elements from the four services that reports to the United States Strategic Command (USSTRATCOM). Each of the armed forces is in the process of organizing their own cyber assets into discrete units/commands to be the component of USCYBERCOM (i.e., US Navy's Fleet Cyber Command/10th Fleet headquarters in Ft. Meade, MD, and the 24th Numbered Air Force out of Lackland Air Force Base in Texas). The most interesting aspect of the U.S. military's cyber organization is the dual role of the DIRNSA, who is also the commander of USCYBERCOM and chief of CSS, in unifying and solidifying the prominence of the NSA for DoD in cybersecurity. On May 14, 2010, Army Lt. General Keith B. Alexander, DIRNSA, was confirmed by the senate as the first commander of USCYBERCOM.

Department of Justice: The Department of Justice has a long history of conducting Internet crime investigations (FBI) and prosecuting some of the best-known cybercriminals through their natural law enforcement duties. The National Strategy of Secure Cyberspace formalized their role by identifying them as the lead in investigations and prosecutions. They also run one of the most well-recognized public-private sector partnerships for critical infrastructure protection (which includes IT): infraguard.

Department of State: Due to the global nature of Internet infrastructures, the U.S. State Department will have an increasingly important role in working with foreign governments and international partners in combating cybercrime. "Operation Aurora," which included attacks against numerous global companies and their facilities overseas, required careful coordination and effort with the State Department's foreign missions. Attacks against IT infrastructures and individuals in overseas territories are under legal purview of the nation in which the infrastructure physically reside and global companies must engage their diplomatic channels of government often for coordination with foreign government. This process will become more of a requirement as globalization and technologies such as cloud computing take hold. In recognition, Senator Orrin Hatch and Susan Gillibrand introduced the International Cybercrime Reporting and Cooperation Act in 2010, which included provision for the State Department to assign principal individuals in foreign missions to have primary responsibility for dealing with cybersecurity issues.

It is important to note that while these agencies have key roles in securing U.S. cyberspace, there are dozens of supporting government organizations and groups that have important responsibilities in cybersecurity, starting with enhancing the security posture of their own agency/group IT infrastructures.

Cybercrime vs. Cybersecurity vs. Cyberwarfare Explained

With so many different organizations and lack of a consistent taxonomy within government IT policy arenas, it is easy to confuse cyber terms. In fact even government officials do not consistently or appropriately use terms such as cybersecurity, cybercrime, and cyberwarfare. While the goals of the U.S. government are the same when it comes to the cyber infrastructures of the United States—to ensure the freedom of action and reliable use of cyberspace to enhance economic and national security—the approaches for doing so are very different. Specifically, combating cybercrime internationally and domestically, enhancing the cybersecurity posture of the critical infrastructures of the United States, and the ability to conduct full-spectrum cyberwarfare campaigns are all approaches being implemented (at various stages) currently:

Combating Cybercrime by Investigation and Prosecution: As discussed previously, treating the investigation and prosecution of criminals who commit crime thorough the use of the Internet or other electronic means has been a law enforcement activity that the government has been involved in for quite some time. The increased rate of globalization of where technology services are delivered to and from makes combating cybercrime more challenging than ever. Cybercriminals can originate from anywhere in the globe, attacking transnational organizations across boundaries, making jurisdiction a difficult challenge. Hence the engagement of the international community with laws and treaties that can be implemented effectively to combat cybercrime requires much more than the law enforcement element of U.S. national power.

Consequently, new legislation intended to combat cybercrime (such as the Gillibrand-Hatch legislation mentioned previously) includes provisions to encourage developing nations to help battle crime through economic aid programs while admonishing those that do not do the same via potential trade sanctions. As global economic conditions continue to fluctuate, the impact of cybercrime and its resulting loss of economic output will continue to get increased scrutiny in the United States and likely abroad.

Improving Cyber Critical Infrastructures through Planning, Preparing, Protecting, and Recovering: The potential for a "Katrina-like" incident through the Internet, while remote, continues to be a growing concern. In particular, devastating attacks delivered through the Internet against the CI/KR of the United States resulting in massive economic impact or loss of lives is the ultimate "worst-case" scenario. The loss of power production, disruption of the financial system, or degradation of our critical manufacturing industry due to denial of service or disruption of data integration are all concerns that DHS as the lead agency for CI/KR must address through their NPPD directorate. Compounding the issue is that most of the CI/KRs of the United States are privately owned, making coordination a challenge. In addition, the IT infrastructures of the critical infrastructures of the United States are horizontally distributed across multiple (18 CI/KR) sectors, making improving the security posture nationwide difficult to measure and improve without a level of voluntary reporting and compliance. In unregulated CI/KR sectors (such as the IT sector), coordination activities are completely voluntary. DHS has one of the most difficult roles in improving U.S. cybersecurity in that they must lead in the creation of a plan to improve IT security across all of the diverse CI/KR sectors (many of those that are unregulated), prepare them for a potential attack, protect those that they can directly through information-sharing programs for cyber threats, and lead in the recovery in the case of an attack of national significance through its National Cyber Response Coordination Group. This is such an overwhelming, massive challenge that there is mixed opinion on whether this should be a responsibility that should be at the White House level or one that should continue to remain with the DHS. In either case the who's and how's of the planning, preparing, protecting, and helping to recover from a cyberattack of national significance will be a challenge that will continue to be urgently debated within the policy and legislative arenas of Washington, DC, for years come.

Engaging Cyberwarfare: Cyberwarfare is a topic that has been thrust into the national consciousness through a combination of real organizational activity by the U.S. government (such as the stand-up of USCYBERCOM) and continued hype and misinformation prevalent in the media about the nature, size, and scope of real cyberwarfare. While the topic of real cyberwarfare is another topic for a full-blown book, this section will provide some key insights into what cyberwarfare is and how it will likely be planned and executed through a typical U.S. military campaign plan.

As discussed previously, cyberspace has been defined as a true fifth war fighting domain by the U.S. military since approximately 2007. In effect, the U.S. military now plans for military operations across Land, Sea, Air, Space, and Cyberspace through its defined military campaign planning process. In particular the joint effects of delivering a kinetic (armed combatant) combined with a nonkinetic (attacks through the Internet and communications infrastructures) are receiving particular emphasis. While exploitations and attacks against an adversary through the Internet are pretty much a given, cyberwarfare, as it is currently defined by the U.S. military, comprises a broad spectrum of activities, which is shown below:

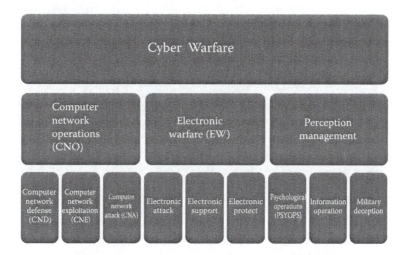

Broadly, full-spectrum cyberwarfare includes offensive and defensive actions within cybersecurity through computer network operations, which include computer network defense (traditional IT security/information assurance), computer network exploitation (exploiting adversary's cyber environment through the Internet or electronic spectrum), computer network attack (outright attacks against IT assets), perception management (use of Internet to change the perception/attitude/cognitive function of an adversary), and traditional electronic warfare (EW) against radio-frequency, millimeter wave (radar), and optical environments. In essence, cyberwarfare is an expansion of long-existing military activities of EW and psychological operations to include attacking and defending IT environments.

Big Challenges

While ensuring the freedom of action and use of cyberspace for national interests is important, there are some big challenges that put the outcome in potential doubt for the near future. Activities such as criminal prosecutions, active coordination of cyber infrastructures of critical infrastructure, and even military operations, are all currently difficult due to some very critical issues with no easy answers. There are four broad categories of "grand challenges" for national cybersecurity:

Attribution: While use of the Internet and technology has become a daily, ubiquitous activity for most people, the fundamental lack of accountability built into the Internet is unknown to most of those outside the IT industry. The ease in which TCP/IP traffic can be modified and obfuscated and commercial products exploited is one of the dark secrets of the Internet age. The simple fact is no matter who is the ultimate culprit of an attack or exploit, it is incredibly difficult using IT techniques to match the attack with the attacker. While ultimately the last IP hop can be traced, that attribution information is likely to be completely meaningless in an investigation due to the ease in which attacks can be hidden on the Internet through international hops. Currently, the best source of true attribution lies outside of technology, which needs to be fundamentally changed to significantly improve cybersecurity globally. If no identity and accountability exists on the Internet, much of the really high-impact activity (criminal prosecutions) are meaningless.

Public vs. Private vs. Global Infrastructures: One of the difficult challenges that the DHS faces in securing the cyber infrastructures of the United States is that most of the national U.S. critical infrastructures are privately owned. As the trend toward large enterprise businesses continues to be global, so will the IT infrastructures. In addition, technology and the delivery of IT itself continues to go global to harness the economic and global talent benefits available from all geographic regions. This continues to put pressure on those government organizations that need to prepare and protect these critical industries without directly regulating them (IT security CI/KR sector in particular). In addition, the diplomatic channels that have not had to take formal leadership roles in the past in helping to facilitate global business interests of transnational companies to foreign governments are just beginning to be aware of the potential for that responsibility. The appropriate level of involvement by government in this globally integrated fabric of cyberspace continues to be a challenge that has no easy answers.

International Agreements and Laws: International laws and treaties that cross boundaries to combat cybercrime continue to be sorely lacking currently. While many developed nations have laws that make certain criminal activities on the Internet illegal, they are local to that nation/jurisdiction and inconsistent in the way they are enforced. Without international and local government effort in harmonizing these activities, there are likely to be gaps between national laws that criminal elements will be able to continue to exploit.

Complexity: The issues described are deep and fundamental technical, legal, and operational issues that need intensive work that is likely be achieved only incrementally. The intersection of these issues with the day-to-day technical challenges that security practitioners face "securing cyberspace" at a national level seems so complex that it is seemingly impossible. Many argue that it is literally impossible to have that high level of assurance and that security is fundamentally a risk/loss management exercise. Regardless of the point of view, the challenges are incredibly complex, spanning legal, diplomatic, technical, and social behavioral domains. Overcoming all of them will likely take decades or even generations, so IT security practitioners should be aware of these issues and initiatives over the duration of their individual careers.

Summary: So What Can I Do Personally as an IT Security Practitioner?

Currently, there continues to be fierce debate on roles, responsibilities, and legalities on cybersecurity across the public and private policy spectrums. The maelstrom of policy debates eventually lead to concrete actions in the form of regulations (laws) and guidelines (security standards and techniques that are actually valuable to practitioners) which reverberate across the public and private sectors. For example, the bill that was introduced by Senators Rockefeller and Snowe would mandate security practitioners that work in the critical infrastructure sectors to be certified with the appropriate industry credentials like the CISSP. Individually, the author of this chapter believes that every practitioner should at minimum increase their personal awareness of the policy discussions in Washington and internationally in their respective industries, especially those that are part of the critical infrastructure sectors. In addition, in the United States there is a great need for security practitioners at all levels across civilian, defense, and intelligence communities and this is one of the most sought-after skills in government. Critical to these jobs is trustworthiness, with some of the most sensitive information and systems, so the ability to pass background checks and obtain national security clearances is essential. Regardless of the sector that the security practitioner may be working in, the real key to improving the cybersecurity posture nationally will always start with the networks that are in their direct span of control or influence personally and professionally. Cybersecurity truly begins at home!

About the Author

Samuel Chun, CISSP, is the director of the Cyber Security Practice for HP Enterprise Services U.S. Public Sector. He is responsible for the strategy, portfolio development, and industry messaging of cybersecurity services and solutions for U.S. public sector clients. He is also the lead subject matter expert for cybersecurity policy for HP Global Government Affairs. Chun is a regular speaker at industry conferences and cybersecurity policy workshops and legislative briefings in Washington, DC. He recently provided expert testimony on the "State of Federal Information Security" at a hearing before the House Subcommittee on Government Management, Organization, and Procurement.

Author's Note: All of the information provided in this chapter is based on publicly available information. On no occasion was U.S. Classified or Controlled Unclassified Information used in the writing of this chapter.

Chapter 26

Configuration, Change, and Release Management

Sean M. Price

This chapter introduces the triune concepts of configuration management, change management, and release management. The concepts can exist independently and serve an organization well. However, when they are assimilated into a centralized process the problem of managing the relentless changes in our system becomes manageable.

Many processes and tools exist for managing changes to systems. The security professional must have a good understanding of what constitutes a change and how it should be handled. The best tool for a job is the one that works. Organizations should seek to implement the most appropriate tools and processes to help manage changes to their systems. The security professional must be armed with a good foundation of the concepts needed to manage changes and their authorizations from start to finish. A conjectural process is presented as one alternative an organization could follow.

Managing and monitoring changes is often viewed as a paper exercise with little value. This is simply not the case. A wealth of actionable intelligence about the system can be obtained through changes to the system that benefit managers and the security staff.

Rising to the Challenge

Change is inevitable. Modern information technology (IT) is an extreme case of a man-made system in continuous flux. New technologies seem to emerge on a daily basis. Users continuously demonstrate an unending appetite for new and improved applications. Similarly, new vulnerabilities also become known at a rapid rate. Attackers continue to find inventive ways to keep IT managers paranoid and busy. The rate of new technology release and the appearance of novel threats continue to accelerate. System change is, therefore, unavoidable, and requires appropriate planning and management to achieve an acceptable level of stability.

A system can be defined by a manager's influence on its components and settings. System components include the hardware and software items that make up the baseline of the system. Baselines are the parts of a system. Individual system components make up its basic functionality.

However, this functionality must be put together in a meaningful way. Heaping these parts together in an incoherent mass will not prove effective. System components must be combined in a particular way to achieve the desired functionality. The ordering and settings of hardware and software define a system's configuration. The overarching IT systems management strategy is to lump the parts into a whole according to a particular configuration that achieves the desired functionality. If only IT system design and maintenance were this simple.

The relentless expansion of new solutions combined with the dreaded discovery of flaws guarantee a lifetime of management activity. The marketplace is continually flooded with new tools. Some of these tools use recently developed techniques and protocols designed to improve the user's experience and/or efficiency. Occasionally a new tool replaces an older one that is no longer supported by the vendor for technical or economic reasons. As is the case for most software tools, it is only a matter of time before the shiny exterior fades and the flaws emerge. In due course vulnerabilities emerge. These revelations are occasionally followed by a flurry of work to fix the problem. In any event, IT mangers are caught in a never-ending cycle of system change.

Change activity is best tempered with a process to make it happen in the least painful way. No one appreciates disruptions in system availability. Poorly planned or uncoordinated disruptions will inconvenience the most important users at the worst possible time. IT managers, therefore, release changes into a system in an organized fashion to minimize disruptions and hopefully eliminate unpleasant surprises.

Managing system change is primarily viewed as operational activity. Security professionals are typically involved with system changes when it's necessary to assess risk or conduct security testing. However, this limited view sells short the importance of configuration, change, and release management (CCRM) as a security management activity. CCRM is a core defense measure that can be effectively used to combat internal and external threats.

Security as Enabler

Ideally, security is a business enabler. Security controls should enable an organization to operate in hostile environments with little or no inconvenience to system users. The goals and objectives of an organization should not be impaired by the controls employed. Unfortunately, we often have to select inconvenient trade-offs to achieve the right balance with security. Sometimes the tools used impact performance or are difficult to use. This can frustrate users and disrupt the pursuit of organizational goals. In these cases security is often viewed as an obstacle. The lofty goal of security as an enabler can be difficult to achieve when the tools hinder users.

Some computing professionals may not buy into this philosophy of security as an enabler. They would say that the problem with security is that it imposes restrictions and limits. These controls seem contrary to the goal of system managers that want to make their system as flexible as possible for its users. Rigid processes often imply mountains of useless paperwork and slow productivity to a snail's pace.

Consider a moderately sized system of 200 workstations, 10 file servers, and 5 home-grown web-based application servers supported by 3 databases. Such a system would have organizational and external customers as users. It's likely that dozens of applications unique to each department exist across the enterprise. Some offices might also require specialized hardware as well. Now imagine if the entire system was swept away by a natural disaster. Server backups are common practices in most organizations, but workstations' images are not always updated. However, backups alone are not enough to efficiently recreate a system of this size. Restoration would be daunting without sufficient system documentation of all of the unique pieces and how they fit together. An organization with a comprehensive CCRM process would likely recover from this problem without significant difficulty.

Existing Methods

A number of processes exist for implementing CCRM. Some of these have been in place for many years, while others are just now emerging. Notable organizations and methods worthy of further study by the security professional include:

- *Information Technology Infrastructure Library (ITIL)*: This is a collection of best practices for IT management developed by the United Kingdom government. As of this writing, ITIL v3 is the most recent release of the library and is comprised of five volumes. Some of the ideas expressed in Service Support of ITIL v2 are incorporated in this chapter.
- *Capability Maturity Model Integration (CMMI)* is a model used by some organizations to improve their software development activities. There are maturing levels from 1, the lowest, to 5, which is the highest. CMMI is primarily concerned with exhibiting improvements as opposed to specifying a particular process. CMMI is maintained by the Carnegie Mellon Software Engineering Institute.
- *National Institute of Standards and Technology (NIST)*: The NIST continuously develops guidance to assist the U.S. federal government to meet security requirements. The recently drafted Special Publication, 800-128, Guide for Security Configuration Management of Information Systems, provides a lean CCRM process designed to exploit the Security Content Automation Protocol (SCAP). The goal is to achieve security operation efficiencies and improvements through security monitoring automation.

Standards bodies have also developed guidance related to CCRM. The International Organization for Standardization (ISO) produced *ISO 10007 Configuration Management*, while the Institute of Electrical and Electronic Engineers (IEEE) published *1042-1987 Guide to Software Configuration Management*.

Configuration Management

Systems are composed of many discrete physical and logical items. Hardware, software, and settings make up the bulk of these items and constitute the configuration of the system. Proper management of these items requires knowing the location and state of each. Physical items, such as hardware, are somewhat easier to locate and identify since they are tangible. However, accurately tracking thousands of hardware pieces in an organization that is geographically dispersed is no easy task. Logical items, such as software and settings, can easily outnumber hardware components. Automated tools are essential to identify and track all software components and system settings. But, tracking these items too can be a daunting challenge when there is a large amount of software and/or settings that are not standardized across the organization. In this regard, configuration management is the activity that seeks to identify and track the location and state of each physical and logical item within a system.

It is easy to assume that configuration management is just another term for inventory management. In fact, configuration management requires inventories as well. But, configuration management is much more than inventorying the hardware and software of a system. Good inventory systems identify unique items or classes of items according to a few attributes such as serial numbers, manufacturer, dimensions, and perhaps even location. The primary focus of inventory systems is to track the quantity of the item or class. Configuration management, on the other hand, goes beyond such counting. Comprehensive configuration management includes more attributes and the history of items as well. The state of an item, such as its particular settings, may vary across the organization. For instance, an organization may have the Print Spooler service enabled for workstations, but disabled for servers. Software components and settings can change frequently. Tracking the history of components is necessary to troubleshoot system errors. Typical inventory systems either consider changed items as a new item or ignore the change if the primary attributes are the same. Configuration management incorporates inventory management, but it is much more.

The location and state of system components is a matter of perspective. A server has both physical and logical locations. Software may reside on specific hosts and in different directories on each. State primarily refers to settings that can be tracked uniquely. Just as the logical locations of software can change from host to host, so too can state. Care must, therefore, be taken when tracking location and state to avoid making the configuration management process too complex.

Every item tracked in configuration management is referred to as a configuration item (CI). Each CI is assigned a unique identifier and includes a list of attributes that describe the item. A CI may refer to something specific or a class of things. Suppose a CI refers to a particular software setting. This CI may be applicable to all servers or only one in particular. The attributes of the CI should refer to a specific thing (or class), location, state, and other distinguishable features.

An important CI attribute that differentiates configuration management from inventory management is versioning. System changes, such as security updates, are quite common. Just as updated software modules are commonly differentiated by a version, so too should a changed CI. Using an incremental versioning scheme for each CI enables historical tracking of changes. CI versioning is a critical configuration management element.

Configuration management should be broadly applied to system management and operational activity. There are a multitude of areas beyond hardware and software that can benefit from configuration management. Much of the activity and outputs from a typical system development life cycle are configuration item candidates for organizational configuration management. These areas include the following:

- *Requirements*: Systems exist according to requirements. The design of the system is affected by the organizational mission as well as various policies and standards. Operational needs of the users also affect the system architecture and the way it is managed. Every element of a system should have traceability to one or more requirements. Requirements too can change overtime, which can impact aspects of a system. Therefore, requirements should be tracked similarly to other hardware and software to support system governance.
- *Baselines*: The actual hardware and software pieces that make up the system form its baseline. Most of the configuration items in a baseline tend to be a class. Suppose a system with 1,000 Windows XP workstations is required to host calc.exe. Rather than specify 1,000 configuration items for each instance, a single configuration item is established, identifying it as a class that applies to every Windows XP workstation in the system.
- *Inventories*: Asset accountability is best achieved through inventories. Configuration management can also be used to manage discrete assets. Inventories typically identify individual

items found in a broad baseline class. In this case, each configuration item in an inventory represents a specific asset in the organization.

■ *Configurations*: The type and quantity of settings in a system can be truly staggering. An incorrect setting may cause a system failure or compromise. Managing relevant settings is crucial to system operation and security. Settings commonly have multiple values, each establishing a particular state. Configuration items in this category are usually a class since identical settings across devices are common.

■ *Documentation*: A multitude of system operational processes require documentation. Contingency plans, system backup procedures, administration guides, and account management plans are only a few of the many documents needed to guide system management. Documents such as these should also be controlled through configuration management much the same as any other aspect of the system.

■ *Interfaces*: A graphical user interface (GUI) can have very particular requirements. Organizations may have particular needs for layout and functionality of an in-house GUI such as a web page. Usability is a critical factor for any GUI. User acceptance of a particular GUI requires continued attention to how it is designed and presented. Managing GUI requirements is needed to efficiently converge design, development, and user acceptance.

■ *Data exchanges*: Applications often interface with other applications internal as well as external to the organization. The exchange could be in the form of data sharing or in support of transaction processing. The details of these connections are needed to ensure changes accommodate and do not disrupt these exchanges. Ideally, all protocols used are matched up to those applications and services authorized for their use.

Change Management

Maintaining an up-to-date configuration of a system requires disciplined change management. Technologies like Plug and Play as well as automated software updates make it easy to forego management processes. While these automated aspects of modern systems simplify our lives, they also hamper the ability to control and track changes. Changes to system configuration items should not be made unless they are appropriately approved and tested.

Systems ultimately exist to support their users and the organization's mission. Changes should therefore be made according to the needs of the system users and the organization. Users request changes to the system to support their duties and enhance their performance. The direction of an organization compels certain changes to be made to a system. Changes in the external business environment, such as competition and customers needs, affect the course of an organization. Regulatory requirements and industry standards can also influence changes to a system. A structured change management process jointly supports users and the organization's mission.

Change management that is well defined ensures that consideration and tracking is given for system changes. Proposed changes should not be made without sufficient testing and appropriate approvals. A detailed record should be kept for each change made to the system. This record should tie the request, testing, approvals, and the change itself together. Ideally, the record is the ultimate output of the change management activity.

Poorly implemented or designed change management hinders efficient configuration management. Uncontrolled changes can quickly alter inventories and baselines. What is and what is not authorized in the system will be difficult to distinguish. In this regard, configuration management is dependent on change management.

The change management techniques employed are likely to be different from one organization to another. This is not surprising given the different cultures and management styles of organizations. However, effective change management has a few key factors in common. Elements of the change management records will in one way or another show consideration, approvals, and tracking occurred for each change. Some of these essential elements of a change management process include the following:

- *Change requests*: The change to the system was initiated by the request of a user or manager. A documented change request provides legitimacy for the change and a formal method for tracking. Those requesting the change should be kept informed of its status.
- *Requirements analysis*: Changes should align with user needs, organizational mission, and existing requirements. An analysis should be conducted to determine if the requested change aligns or conflicts with existing requirements. In most cases a change will establish new requirements for the system.
- *Development actions*: Based on the requested change and the requirements analysis the development approach should be planned. At the conclusion of the development activity the configuration items affected are recorded. Documenting the development actions is critically important to the entire process.
- *Security reviews*: At one or more points during change management security reviews are conducted. Feedback from the review provides developers with an alternate viewpoint of their activities. Likewise, security issues identified during the development activity or from the request provide management with the opportunity to make risk-based decisions before the change is made to the production system.
- *Testing*: A variety of testing methods should be used to confirm the change will not break the system, introduce a weakness, or reduce usability. Component testing ensures the change itself works. Functional testing confirms that the change performs its intended functions. Integration testing confirms the change can operate in the production environment. Regression testing ensures the change does not negatively affect other configuration items in the production system. Finally, end users are involved with acceptance testing to determine their satisfaction level and desire to use the proposed change.

Threats and vulnerabilities contribute to the rapid changes in our systems. Attackers constantly seek methods to exploit systems. Software flaws provide potential avenues for attackers to achieve their objectives. Protecting systems is a never-ending cycle of security tool updates and software patches. Automating these updates is ideal, but not without its downsides. An update may break the system or introduce another vulnerability. In this regard, testing is still essential. Likewise, automating these updates can make it difficult to associate the change with the affected configuration items. Even though a change may be vital for security, system managers should not be tempted to forego appropriate consideration, approval, and tracking of these changes, especially when automated.

Release Management

Deploying a system change requires coordination. Changes made to the system without proper coordination may end up being disruptive to the organization. Release management seeks to reduce the impact of a change to the organization through communications and scheduling.

Changes to the system must be communicated to the organization prior to release. Divergent groups using the system need to be aware of the pending change and prepared for what will come. Communication of the pending change will help the various groups prepare for the event. Some of the various groups that should be communicated with include the following:

- *Users*: Organization individuals directly affected by the change should be notified of the pending release.
- *Customers*: Individuals and organizations using the system should be informed of the change if it significantly affects how they use the system. This might be through e-mail or simply a website posting.
- *Help desk*: The support staff must have enough detail of the change to properly assess and route problems that might be related to the release.
- *Security*: Those involved with security monitoring, such as intrusion detection analysts, need to be aware of the changes to quickly rule out false positives.
- *Data interfaces*: Internal departments and external organizations interfacing with the affected system should be informed. Some of the types of interfaces to consider include those involved with data sharing, transaction processing, and work flows.

The communication sent should target the specific group. The notification should include sufficient information for the target group to respond or prepare accordingly. The communication should tell the following:

- What is changing in the system
- Why the change is needed
- When the change will be initiated
- When the change should be completed
- What actions they may need to take
- Where they can obtain training if necessary
- Who they should contact with further questions or concerns

Some changes can be quite significant and affect operations within the organization. An initial communication should be sent out well in advance to assess any perceived or actual implications for the change. Feedback received from concerned groups may affect the release schedule or the change itself. Not providing affected groups with an opportunity to voice their concerns prior to the change can jeopardize organization productivity and mission objectives.

After the initial communication a second communication should be made just prior to the release date. This provides the affected groups with one last reminder of the change before it is made. At this point the release schedule should be evident and not a total surprise to those impacted.

A change is released according to a predefined schedule. This schedule determines when and to what extent the change is made to the system. Changes involving software updates often require the affected host to be restarted. To this extent these types of changes are typically made during periods when the least number of users would be affected. Changes to hardware might also impact users and should be conducted during periods of low system usage. When practical, changes should be released in phases. Even when extensive testing is conducted prior to release it is still possible that a change may cause unexpected problems. The release schedule should include a waiting period to determine if change is stable enough to deploy to the entire organization.

In some instances problems are encountered with the change that affect normal operations. Removing the deployed change through a rollback is another aspect of release management. Rollbacks can be difficult and themselves cause problems. Although a rollback essentially returns the system to a prior state, it should be remembered that it is also a change to the system. As with all changes, rollbacks should also be communicated to the groups affected by the change.

An important part of release management is the confirmation that the change was made as intended. The process of confirming the change was successful is sometimes referred to as a configuration audit. After a release is deemed completed, the configuration audit commences. The individuals performing the configuration audit may validate the change was implemented in every target instance or a smaller sample of the population. This minimally determines if the change was deployed to the target configuration items as intended. The audit should also check closely associated configuration items and validate that they had not been incorrectly altered.

Suppose a new software package is deployed to a small group of user workstations. The configuration audit should determine that the change was made as anticipated. The validation conducted by the configuration audit is often technical and may include some specialized tools to scan the system. However, the focus of the audit should not be strictly on the results of tools. Individuals performing the audit should seek to validate the integrity of the system after the release of the changes. A well-defined configuration audit seeks to answer basic questions about the affects of the change released. Some of the questions a configuration audit should seek to answer in this case include:

- Did the change make it to each workstation?
- Was the change found on other nontarget hosts?
- Are all of the files (i.e., configuration items) expected to be included in the change on the workstation?
- Were any unexpected files or registry entries discovered?
- Are the access control lists on files and directories still set properly?
- Were any other applications removed or services disabled?

Requirements as Drivers

Far too often organizations seek to develop systems without adequately defined requirements. System management and security activity must be requirement driven. A lack of adherence to requirements results in system operations and activity that does not efficiently support the mission. Requirements must be the foundation for all activity.

Organizations require a variety of tools to support their operations. These could be simple instruments such as pencils and filing cabinets, or magnificently complex devices like satellites and aircraft. The tools selected should be cost effective and support the mission. Tools therefore exist to support the organization. The organization's core mission should not be to support the tool. The benefit of the tool should further the goals of the organization and support its continued existence through an appropriate revenue stream. Tools that overtake an organization can morph into a new and hideous life form. Organizations catering to such a monstrosity will eventually succumb to their beastly creation.

Organizations keep tools in check through requirements analysis. Simply put, if there is no compelling business need or requirement then a system change should not be pursued. Requirements provide the guideposts for system development and maintenance. They are the markers established by various authorities and their boundaries should be respected. Failure to follow requirements is a guaranteed route that diverges from acceptable system governance.

Requirements come from many sources. Many are mandatory in the form of laws and regulations and may not be negotiable. Some may be organizational policies that may provide certain latitude in their interpretation even when they are compulsory. Other requirements may be local or specific to the needs of end users.

The specificity of a requirement is often reflected by its source. This is to say that high-level requirements such as laws and regulations tend to be very general and in some cases ambiguous. Lower-level requirements generated to directly support the organization and the system are often more specific. Whenever there is ambiguity in a requirement it is best for those collecting the requirement to caveat it with an appropriate interpretation. Reducing ambiguity increases the likelihood that those relying on its specificity will apply management principles in a consistent manner.

When designing and maintaining a system it is helpful to group requirements according to how they might affect development and operations. The following categories are one way to group related requirements accordingly:

- *Business*: Laws, regulations, policies, industry guidance, and other requirements defining and affecting the organization and its mission comprise this category.
- *Security*: Promulgated guidance and best practices identifying the confidentiality, integrity, and availability security goals for a system. Methods and techniques described provide guidance for the physical, operational, and technical controls and assurances needed for the handling, processing, and storing of organizational information.
- *Operational*: Rules governing appropriate system management and acceptable usage.
- *Functional*: Items in this category establish the overall purpose, capabilities, functionalities, and major components of the system.
- *User interfaces*: Detailed descriptions and/or elements of GUIs. Some of these elements may include menu options and locations, field restrictions, range checks, and error handling.
- *Data exchanges*: Specified connections with other systems and data sharing may be established by this category. Acceptable addresses, ports and protocols for the associated services and data are examples of elements that may be included.

Designing a system based on requirements gathered is not easy or straightforward. For instance, business and security requirements are frequently written to a high level. This can introduce a degree of ambiguity, which is followed by inconsistent interpretation. A vague policy statement may result in a complete disconnect between designers, developers, administrators, and managers. Consider a statement such as, "All access to privacy information must be audited." This may seem trivial at first glance, but it is fraught with enough ambiguity to raise several arguments. Does all access apply to only people or must it include automated processes such as backup routines? Is the definition of privacy information well known and understood by all key players? Is a user account name and time of access sufficient or must the workstation name of the user also be included in the audit record? The vagueness of a policy statement is best eliminated by a concise interpretation of its meaning. The interpretation should be included with design documents for clarification.

A system design based on requirements specifies the details of what a system is and the things that it does. The design is a documented list of the system parts and how they fit together. Some of the main elements of a design include the following:

- *Hardware*: What they are and where they are physically located.
- *Software*: What they are and where they are logically located.

- *Communications*: Physical and logical connections with other systems. Detailed communication designs identify the ports and protocols used for each software item, the physical paths available, and logical termination points.
- *Configurations*: Descriptions and settings of how the pieces fit together.
- *Documentation*: Formalized descriptions of the system as well as vendor documentation.

Process Qualities

The overall goal of a CCRM process is to ensure that only appropriately requested and authorized changes are made to a system. Appropriate requests are those that support the organizational mission and requirements. Those granted authorization authority typically evaluate change requests ensuring:

- Support for the mission
- Established requirements are met
- Technically feasible
- Sufficient resource availability

Authorization authorities also approve changes implemented in the system. Each change made should be traceable to an authorization and a request. Meeting the goal requires methods to match up requests, authorizations, and changes. The process itself serves as a control and verification mechanism that can be used to assess goal alignment.

An effective CCRM process obtains its strength through design and planning that is formally communicated. It is easy for a manager to say, "We have a process," but it is much more difficult to prove it. The main elements of a process are inputs, activity, and outputs. These elements are further encapsulated with various qualities. A well-defined process will have qualities such as:

- *Goals*: The process supports the organizational mission and requirements.
- *Flows*: Something goes in and something else comes out.
- *Roles*: Particular people doing specific things.
- *Activity*: Outputs are a transformation or representation of inputs.
- *Evidence*: A record is available, tying roles and flows with activity.
- *Measurable*: Some aspect of the process can be accurately counted to support the evidence.
- *Repeatable*: Given all of the same variables, identical inputs should produce outputs that are sufficiently the same. Note that most processes introduce some level of error so it is unlikely that in every case outputs will be truly identical.
- *Verifiable*: It should be possible to compare the elements of the process itself against a standard. Generally, the standard is a detailed specification of the process elements and their relation to the various qualities.

The *verifiable* quality is often a stumbling block for organizations. To be verifiable a process needs a standard or specification. This implies the process is documented. An appropriately documented process enables a third party to assess its qualities and their effectiveness. A process without sufficient documentation is challenged to prove it contains the mentioned qualities. Furthermore, an insufficiently documented process is less likely to produce results that are consistent and in all likelihood is also inefficient. A less than adequately documented process might keep aspects of the organization going, but it is poor management nonetheless. Therefore, the elements and qualities of the CCRM process must be sufficiently documented to prove its strength.

A well-defined CCRM process will have multiple phases or steps. The qualities expressed above should be part of the flow between and integrated within the process steps. Activity within the process will touch multiple groups and affect many system management attributes. Artifacts and reports associated with the activity outcomes are essential for historical tracking. Obtaining an accurate picture of what has been requested versus what is being developed against what is deployed can be challenging. The complexity can be managed when these items are related to each other in a configuration management database (CMDB). The database should be designed to track and relate the following:

- Requirements
- Requests
- Authorizations
- Configuration item versions
- Activity reports

The CMDB should be a central repository used to track activity within the CCRM process. The database is a type of historical archive of the CCRM process. Queries against the CMDB should be capable of revealing the authorized state of configuration items for specified period of time. However, the fundamental purpose of the CMDB is to show traceability from a configuration item to its authorized request back to the foundation requirements.

Categories and Roles of Assigned Duties

Change management involves a number of people with different responsibilities within an organization. An individual will often cross duty categories and roles. For instance, the chief information officer (CIO) is not only the top manager, but is also a system user. From a high level the CCRM process requires participants from management, operations, consumers, and assurance. Within each of these categories a number of roles exist supporting change management.

Management: These roles ensure the strategic and tactical plans are carried out supporting the organization's mission.

- *Chief information officer*: The CIO has the primary duty of allocating funds, establishing requirements, and accepting risk. This individual may participate directly in the CCRM process or rely on a designated representative. The strategic perspective of the CIO is to ensure appropriate governance is applied to the system. The CIO is primarily concerned that changes support the organizational mission and meet established requirements.
- *System manager*: This person generally oversees the day-to-day management of the system. A system manager often represents the CIO and chairs the review board. Whereas the CIO is concerned with strategic use of a system, the system manager's focus is on tactical issues. A system manager approaches changes as a project management tasking.

Operations: The actual work conducted to keep the system running is performed by the roles in this category.

- *CCRM custodian*: System changes can generate a lot of activity. Tracking this activity is essential to reduce errors, ensure all requests are considered, and retain proof of governance. The CCRM custodian acts as the secretary of system change activity. This individual helps ensure the CCRM process is followed and relevant activity is sufficiently documented.
- *Analysts*: Change requests will frequently need interpretation. Analysts evaluate change requests to identify new requirements or modifications. Contact with the user requesting the change is common to better understand their needs. High-level designs are generated by the analysts based on their interpretation of the request and its impacts on existing requirements.
- *Librarian*: A copy of all changes deployed are needed to validate baselines and configurations. The librarian manages a protected repository containing historical evidence of system components and their settings. Configuration item versions are usually tracked by the librarian. Ideally, the librarian controls the movement of changes from the development environment to production.
- *Developers*: These individuals conduct diverse activities resulting in system changes. The primary focus of developers is the creation of solutions meeting the requested change. This may involve code development, documentation, changes to settings, or integration of new technology. Developers work with analysts to create a solution meeting the high-level design.
- *Testers*: Changes must be evaluated before they are deployed to the system. This role typically includes individuals from other roles that test the solution for a proposed change. A tester provides a type of quality assurance for the change. Testing assesses the functional and nonfunctional aspects of a solution.
- *Administrators*: Continued operations of the system are in the hands of the administrators. These individuals maintain the system and deploy approved changes. Their intimate knowledge of system operations is often critical to solutions considered for pending requests. Furthermore, administrators often deal with user issues and can offer other insights on proposed changes.

Consumers: The system may play a wide variety of roles, but its primary role is to support the organization's mission.

- *User representatives*: Outside of maintenance activity and mission directives from the CIO, changes are mainly driven by user requests. A system exists primarily for the purpose of its users, who are the most important customers to satisfy. User needs frequently become system requirements. Users provide an operational perspective that can foresee the operational success of a proposed change. Proposed changes reducing usability or not favored might be opposed by the user community. Therefore, user involvement during the change management process can affect the overall success and relevance of the change.

Assurance: This category exists as management's feedback mechanism for governance. The activities conducted within this category focus on audit and compliance.

- Security – Individuals in this role help ensure changes do not introduce weaknesses into the system. The security expert is often involved at all stages of the change by reviewing requirements, designs, solutions, and deployment. This activity is essential to ensure unintentional and malicious weaknesses are not introduced into the system.

Groups found within the categories of management, operations, consumers, and assurance periodically come together as the configuration control board (CCB). The purpose of the CCB is to evaluate proposed changes and decide which should be developed and/or released. The various groups have separate activities outside of the CCB regarding the proposed changes. Some group representatives may have voting rights on the board regarding changes during the various points of consideration. The CCB serves as the governing body that authorizes changes to be made to the system.

Separation of Duties

The CCRM process should be designed in such a way that it is unlikely that a fraudulent or malicious change to the system can be made without detection. This is generally easier to achieve in systems with a large staff. However, it is much more difficult to achieve separation of duties in systems with a small staff. Instances with insufficient separations are best handled by management oversight. This involves increased supervisor review and security audit of change activity. Some of the more important conflicts needing special care include:

- *Management and operations*: Managers should not be capable of invoking changes outside of the CCRM process. This separation helps ensure there is opportunity to document change decisions made versus requests.
- *Management and consumers*: Although most managers are also customers, they should not have the authority to request changes. This is needed to prevent managers from changing the system predominately to suit their own interests. Change requests should only be submitted by individuals that do not have the authority to approve requests or changes.
- *Operations and assurance*: Those assigned security duties monitor audit logs and the integrity of the system. Security folks are sometimes referred to as "the watchers." Operations are mainly comprised of developers and administrators. Security should have limited rights in a system but have sufficient ability to monitor everyone else's activity. Assigning operations and security duties to the same individual puts too much power in the hands of a single individual. Ideally, watchers should be able to observe, but not affect the configuration of the system.
- *Librarians and other operations*: Within operations, librarians should be mutually exclusive. They are essentially the integrity gatekeepers. They should not have access to developer code repositories or possess elevated privileges in the production system. This provides a means to identify unauthorized code changes and prevent them from potentially abusing the production system. Ideally, they would not have access to either development or production environments. However, this is often infeasible.
- *Developers and administrators*: Within operations these two roles must be separated. Developers should be prevented from physical and logical access to the production system. Administrators should not be deploying changes they themselves have developed. Combining these two roles enables a malicious individual to bypass existing controls, implement backdoors, or perhaps extract information using covert channels.

Conjectural Configuration, Change, and Release Management Process

The process used to control configurations, changes, and releases will vary from one organization to the next. The function of the process is to manage each of the three principle aspects of the CCRM. The design of the process should include the desired qualities providing the necessary formalization for the organization. Figure 26.1 and Figure 26.2 comprise one method that could be used to control the CCRM process. The following describes each of the steps in the figures:

Step 1. *Proceed*: The CCB receives a request and determines if it warrants further analysis or should be rejected outright. Common request types include changes that propose a fix to errors and problems; incorporate new functionality; seek improvements; update documentation; or report flaws.

Step 2. *Analysis*: The development team, consisting of analysts and developers, review the request and conduct an initial analysis of the requirement. The level of effort needed to develop and deploy the solution is estimated. An approach or design is proposed on how the request could be fulfilled. Configuration items likely to be affected by this change are reported.

Step 3. *Security impact*: The security team reviews the request and the approach proposed by the development team from Step 2. Security issues or potential risks regarding the proposed approach are reported back to the CCB.

Step 4. *Continue*: The CCB weighs the results of the analysis and security steps to determine if the request should be developed. In some cases there may be insufficient resources to develop the solution or the risk may be too great, causing the request to be rejected. Requests deemed worthy are forwarded to the development team for a solution.

Step 5. *Develop solution*: The development team creates an appropriate solution for the request. Component and integration testing is conducted by the development team on the solution. The affected configuration items are identified and associated with the change request.

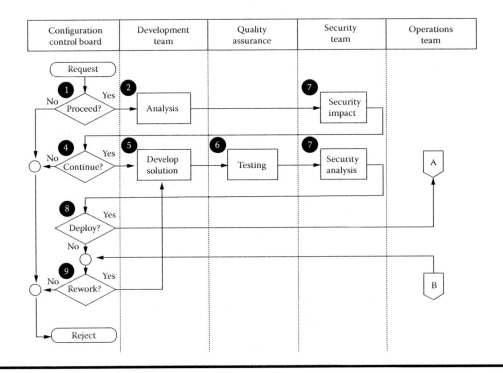

Figure 26.1   CCR Process: Part 1.

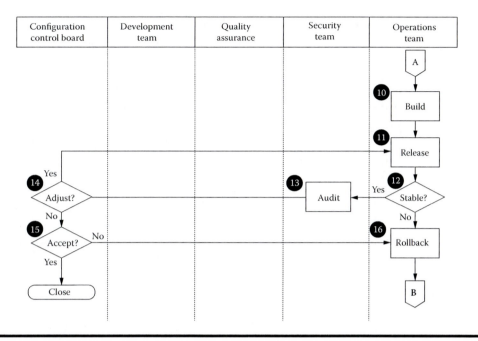

Figure 26.2　CCR Process: Part 2.

Step 6. *Testing*: A quality assurance team comprised of analysts, testers, and user representatives evaluates the solution produced by the development team. Testing is conducted in a staging environment that closely resembles the production environment. The quality assurance team usually performs acceptance, functional, and regression testing to determine if the designed change meets requirements and appears to work in the target system.

Step 7. *Security analysis*: The security team may need to conduct an in-depth review of the designed solution. Developed solutions often deviate from their original design. The team tests the solution in the staging environment according to any changes made by the developers or concerns arising from Step 3.

Step 8. *Deploy*: The CCB considers the reports from the teams in Steps 4, 5, and 6. At this point the CCB determines if the change should be rejected, reworked, or scheduled for release.

Step 9. *Rework*: Changes that need more work may require further analysis or review to determine feasibility or consider risk factors. A task force might be formed to further study the request and determine if the change is really needed and what should be done to resolve the issues. The change will either be rejected or returned to the development team with further guidance.

Step 10. *Build*: Change requests at this stage are prepared to be deployed on the production system. The librarian obtains the actual changes (i.e., configuration items) from the development team and/or quality assurance team as appropriate. The librarian retains copies of the deployment items and delivers them to the administrators for release.

Step 11. *Release*: The deployment configuration items are obtained from the librarian. Any issues identified by the CCB regarding the deployment are corrected as directed.

Step 12. *Stable*: The CCB establishes a period of time to wait and see if problems arise from the deployment. If no serious issues emerge then control is passed to Step 13; otherwise Step 16 is evoked.

Step 13. *Audit*: The security team conducts a configuration audit of the release. The team compares status of the deployed configuration items against those held by the librarian. Any issues identified are reported to the CCB.

Step 14. *Adjust*: Reported findings from the configuration audit are carefully reviewed. Minor issues are returned back to Step 11 for correction.

Step 15. *Accept*: If there are no significant issues then the change request is closed, otherwise control moves to Step 16.

Step 16. *Rollback*: The change is removed from the system and control is passed back to Step 9 to determine the next course of action.

The design of the process depicted above essentially tracks the life cycle of a change request. This approach was selected because a CCB generally concerns itself with change requests as opposed to configuration items themselves. The steps listed above are at a high level and do not consider some important aspects commonly encountered during CCRM. Some additional things to consider include:

■ *Holds*: A request may be held in place due to resource constraints or the need for clarifying information. Items held in place should be reported to the CCB and subjected to its decisions.

■ *Reports*: The output from each step should produce a report with an authorizing signature. This provides a level of accountability for the actions taken within each step of the process.

■ *CCB activity*: The CCB must be supported by a charter outlining its structure; specifying roles and responsibilities of the participants; and granting the board its appropriate authority. An agenda should be created for each meeting outlining the items to be covered. Meeting minutes summarizing the discussions and decisions made by the board are published and distributed to the CCB participants.

Benefits to the Organization

The dynamic nature of our systems challenges management strategies. Selecting a workable and repeatable CCRM process is needed to meet the constant churning of changes in the system. An organization that strives to implement a finely crafted process will reap the benefits of their effort. Some of the potential benefits include:

■ *Improved governance*: A fully documented CCRM process includes controls and approvals supporting the governance goal of accountability. The forum of the CCB provides a degree of transparency for the process. Implementing segregation of duties among the roles balances the power and thereby supports integrity of the process.

■ *Performance evaluation*: Estimates of resources needed versus what was required for development and management can be obtained from artifacts within the process. Efficiency of the system management process could be obtained by measuring the various aspects of requests and time frames of performance. Management should be able to get a sense of how well operations is meeting the demands of its users and maintaining the system.

■ *Resource tracking*: Tracking hardware devices and software packages using the configuration item paradigm is evident. However, other resource usages could also be tracked such as labor hours; hardware/software costs; as well as network connection usage. This can be done by simply including additional data points for the desired resources to be tracked.

- *User and mission focus*: The CCRM is dually focused on the needs of the users and the mission of the organization. Building these aspects into a process helps management to achieve efficiency and reduce waste by determining if changes proposed align with the needs of the organization as opposed to the frivolous desire of a few.
- *Organizational synergy*: Management by committee is never trivial. However, when the process and roles are clearly defined then the focused energy of the individuals enhances the performance of the group. Implementing a CCRM process with a motivated CCB enables the participants to make meaningful contributions to improve the system.

The ultimate boon to the organization is a well-managed system and content users. What most managers would definitely enjoy is some Teflon coating for external scrutiny. A solid CCRM process will cover a multitude of compliance issues and help keep auditors at bay.

Leveraging Security

At first glance CCRM looks like a big paperwork exercise with little value for the security professional. Indeed, configuration management is a reoccurring theme for many compliance requirements where an emphasis is on documentation. Attackers could care less about what documentation is in place and will exploit the system by any means at their disposal. However, a well-documented CCRM process contains a treasure trove of information for the astute security professional. The data generated and the process itself provide a deeper understanding and insight into the system. The CCRM process and information generated can be used to improve security in ways that might otherwise be too difficult. Some areas that can be used to improve security using the CCRM process include:

- *System life cycle integration*: Sometimes security gets left out of the development life cycle. In some instances security is brought in only at the beginning and in others at the end. Injecting security personnel into the system life cycle at multiple points provides the best possibility of detecting issues before too many resources are invested. The security professional embracing CCRM can affect system development and maintenance more efficiently. Involvement within multiple stages provides the security professional with the opportunity to ensure the security architecture is properly applied and appropriate security engineering is accomplished.
- *Vulnerability and patch management*: Security patches should flow through the CCRM process one way or another. However, vulnerabilities are frequently reported long before the patch is available. The security professional can help the organization become more proactive by submitting change requests based on the vulnerability. Usually, the CCB may elect to hold the request until the patch is released. However, this provides an opportunity to propose countermeasures to be applied before the patch is available. In either case, the CCB acknowledges the weakness and makes a decision on the course of action they deem necessary. Best of all, a record of the decision is created and would likely appease the concerns of external auditors.
- *Compliance monitoring*: The task of monitoring compliance often falls on the shoulders of the security professional. This can be a challenge when many of the items that need to be monitored are outside of their realm of responsibility. Fortunately, the components of CCRM represent a large portion of many regulatory requirements imposed on a system. A

well-defined and executed CCRM process provides sufficient evidence substantiating compliance monitoring results. The security professional may be able to more quickly determine compliance and obtain the artifacts necessary to support assessments conducted.

■ *Contingency planning*: Developing and testing a contingency plan is difficult when the details of the system are not known. Configuration items managed in the CCRM process expose the key elements that must be considered in a contingency plan. These details provide the security professional with information needed to ensure the contingency plan addresses the necessary aspects of the system. Contingency plan tests can be developed to exercise aspects of the system perceived to be weak or vulnerable during an event. The contingency plan itself should be subject to the CCRM process.

■ *Penetration testing*: System weaknesses are not always apparent. Penetration testers are used to reveal unknown system vulnerabilities. Providing testers with detailed documentation of the system helps them focus on areas that are the most concerning or likely to be weak. Details gathered by the CCRM process improve penetration testing efficiency and the relevance of their results.

■ *Incident response*: System knowledge depth affects the adequacy of the response to an incident. Insufficient knowledge of a system may result in an inadequate response failing to mitigate the threat. The CCRM process provides the security professional with a wealth of information that can be used to enhance incident response. Threat-specific countermeasures can be implemented according to the information contained in the CCRM process. In fact, a savvy security professional could define threat-specific countermeasures in advance and integrate them into incident response procedures.

■ *Intrusion detection*: The two classes of intrusion detection methods are attack signatures and anomalies. Both methods typically produce false positives, which are reduced using intrusion detection system (IDS) tuning. The security professional needs the information in the CCRM process to efficiently tune the IDS. If the information in the CCRM is insufficient or unavailable then the IDS tuning process could be substantially long-lived and may accidentally incorporate false negatives representing actual attacks.

■ *Forensic analysis*: After an incident, investigations are sometimes needed to determine the cause. Computer forensics can bring to light many puzzle pieces of files long deleted. However, it can be difficult at times to conclude if a given file was ever authorized or not when the CCRM process is lacking or nonexistent. Tracking configuration items at the file level can help forensic investigators sort through the puzzle pieces more quickly and reveal a more complete picture of the event.

■ *Insider threat*: Most compromises are facilitated by insiders. Whether a user clicks on a spam e-mail attachment, falls for spear phishing, or is exploited by an unknown zero-day browser vulnerability lurking at a legitimate website, the problem is not a matter of if but when. Insiders will unwittingly introduce malware and provide an avenue for attackers to establish a foothold in the system. A CCRM process that designates and manages all authorized software modules as configuration items provides the security professional with a strong defensive foundation to detect compromised aspects of the system. The CCRM process is one of the most powerful tools the security professional can use to detect and remove advanced persistent threats from their system.

The CCRM process may be mundane and unappealing. But, the information generated can be used to alter security in a positive way. Effectively using this information assurance weapon relies on knowledge, instead of paper, to defeat the enemy.

Conclusion

Systems change at breakneck speed. Grappling with the never-ending stream of security patches, newfangled hardware, and bleeding edge software toys is a relentless challenge. Without warning, the infant IT system everyone was proud of could quickly mutate into a freakish technological collage that might even terrorize Mary Shelley. Fortunately, we need not succumb to the rush of technology.

Order can be maintained within our systems by using a well-defined approach to introduce, approve, monitor, and deploy changes. Implementing a process with desirable qualities that join the mutual goals of users, the organization mission, and established requirements is essential. Operating the process within the oversight of a configuration control board with appropriately segregated duties can infuse accountability and integrity into the process.

The process used for configuration, change, and release management will differ from one organization to the other. Regardless of the process used, it should produce artifacts that support due diligence, accountability, and detailed information about the configuration items managed. Organizations implementing a meaningful and defined process will eventually reap the benefits of their work. As for the security professional, CCRM represents an opportunity to leverage the process and shape information generated into formidable defensive weapons of information assurance.

About the Author

Sean M. Price, CISA, CISSP, is an independent security researcher and consultant living in northern Virginia. He specializes in designing and evaluating organizational information assurance programs and system security architectures. Research interests include insider threat, information flows, and applications of artificial intelligence to information assurance problems. Prior publications include contributions to the *Information Security Management Handbook*, *Official (ISC)² Guide to the CISSP CBK*, and *IEEE Computer* magazine, as well as other journals and conferences. You can reach him at sean.price@sentinel-consulting.com.

Chapter 27

Tape Backup Considerations

Sandy Bacik

It's time for another security patch to be applied to the intranet site. This is the internal site that tracks all project work and deliverables. No problem: nothing major included in the patch. Information technology (IT) has been performing daily incremental backups and weekly full backups. IT rotates the tapes off-site on a weekly basis and keeps the quarter-end backups for two years. Due to budget restrictions, there is no test environment for the intranet. IT installs the intranet site patch; the server reboots well and comes up displaying the main internal intranet page. An internal user clicks on a link for a critical project—oops, a 404 web error, page not found. IT restores the files from a backup tape—oops, there are no files on the tape, yet all the backup jobs showed no aborts or errors. IT recalls the off-site sites for the last month: no files on any tapes. IT needed to go back two months off-site before finding a valid backup tape. IT sends out an e-mail to the user community that project files have been lost for the last two months. How many projects were lost? How many critical reports were gone? Has this ever happened to your enterprise? Has the off-site facility ever "lost" a backup set of tapes? What would happen if the application software were lost? Would the data backups be useful? If no losses, well done for the enterprise backup and recovery processes being documented and tested on a regular basis. If so, then the enterprise may want to enhance their existing processes to prevent this type of incident in the future.

What the heck are Linear Tape Open (LTO), 8mm, Digital Linear Tape (DLT), Super DLT (SDLT), and Scalable Linear Recording (SLR)? These are just a few tape types that enterprises use to back up systems. Yes, some enterprises have gone to removable disk and disk-to-disk backups. Yet, many more enterprises continue to use tape backup systems. Every enterprise understands that system and data backups are a daily requirement of business. Many of those enterprises that have implemented tape backup systems do not implement best practices for their physical and logical tape backup processes. A backup process copies important enterprise information onto magnetic tape or other devices. Backups enable the enterprise to restore anything from a single file to a complete system. Backups and restores have helped enterprises recover from data losses caused by outages, disasters, power surges, user errors, equipment failures, or viruses. Data recovery processes, tools, and services exist, but they can be limited and can be expensive. Recovery of all lost information through a system restore may be unlikely and users may have to recreate some of the data again. Enterprises need to continue the downtime during the recovery, which may also be costly. A well-designed backup system safeguards critical information by providing the most efficient and cost-effective methodology as insurance against a potentially large data loss. An information backup and recovery standard should consist of four major components:

- Enterprise critical information should be backed up.
- Information backups should be stored at a physically different location from its original creation and usage location.
- Backup test processes should be performed regularly.
- The enterprise's ability to retrieve and restore backup data should be tested and produce successful results on a regular basis.

When evaluating tape backup systems, has the enterprise looked at the physical placement of the device? Have the requirements been defined for:

- Size of the data center racks
- Dimension of the tape device
- Power supply (primary and redundant) for the tape device
- Air-flow considerations of the tape device

The enterprise knows that the device will go into the server room or data center. Wait—when were the environmental elements of the location or the devices and physical space reviewed for expansion? When a tape backup system is implemented or upgraded, the environmental and physical status needs to be evaluated. Along with the above-listed requirements, other requirements and standards the enterprise must define are as follows:

- *Power on password*: For cold and warm boots, this would prevent the use of the server/device until a password is entered. This is to prevent unauthorized access to the device setup utility and operating system. While this is a good practice, the enterprise must also remember that a staff member must then be at the console whenever the server/device boots.
- *Administrator password*: This would prevent local or remote access to a server/device after a possible automatic recovery and also prevents unauthorized changes to the server's/device's system configuration information.
- *CD-ROM/diskette drive/boot control*: This would disable the ability to read or boot from a different device, which might bypass the operating system and leave system files vulnerable to changes or deletion.
- *Serial/parallel interface control*: This would disable access by anyone walking up to the device and using the serial or parallel ports for unauthorized access.

The above are some of the basic security requirements. How does an enterprise determine the backup needs for the enterprise? Developing a successful backup strategy begins with planning a backup needs analysis or reviewing what is being backed up currently. The backup administrator needs to look at the enterprise backup needs and match those to the tape backup hardware and software. The backup administrator needs to start with the following types of questions:

- What information (systems, programs, and data) must be backed up and recoverable?
- How much information does this entail—gigabytes, terabytes?
- What format will the tapes and tape headers use? American National Standards Institute (ANSI). Does all the information being backed up qualify for ANSI backups?
- How much additional capacity is needed because of backup redundancies resulting from special, user-defined backups?
- How much time is going to be needed to perform each set of information backups?
- Are any pieces of software customized or can the enterprise use CD-ROM media for software (not data) recovery?
- How much will the information grow over the next three to five years for determining storage capacity and budget planning?
- What is our backup scheduling and archiving? Daily differentials or incrementals and a weekly full backup? Grandfather, father, son tape rotations?
- What does the enterprise want to do about remote locations?
- Does the enterprise also want the desktops and laptops backed up?
- Can the backups run unattended to reduce administrative costs? If so, how will the tapes be taken off-site?
- What is the rotation and capacity of the off-site tape storage facility?
- What is the tape return time from the off-site tape storage facility?

The enterprise has implemented a tape backup system, selected an off-site tape storage supplier, ordered the backup and replacement tapes, and is ready to start developing the formal processes for information backup and recovery. The following are the topics that should be required for documenting the information backup and recovery:

- Who is responsible for the information backups and restores?
- Who has the authority to request an information backup or restore?
- What is the step-by-step process for the information backup and restore?
- Per regulatory requirements, does the enterprise have to encrypt all or some of the backed up information on the tape?
- Are we going to compress the data on tapes to store more information per tape?
- Is the server environment virtualized? If so, besides the virtual servers, will the underlying operating system or applications be backed up?
- What is the tape retention standard for the information backed up and who owns the information that is backed up?
- What happens when an information backup or restore fails or is successful?
- How are the information backups and restores monitored and tracked?
- Which databases are backed up—production, test, development, human resources, manufacturing, and/or finance?
- Are database backups handled differently from regular file backups, e.g., are databases backed up to a flat file and the flat file backed up to tape?
- Are the database schemas backed up with the database data or separately?
- How do users back up their assigned desktop or laptop systems?

The enterprise has defined the above topics into standards, practices, guidelines, and procedures, but how do they validate that the backup tapes are still valid? If the enterprise has a business continuity and disaster recovery plan, then the backup tapes are tested on a regular basis. But what happens if the enterprise has not put the time, staff, and money into an enterprise business continuity and disaster recovery plan? The following are standards and procedures that can be put into place in the enterprise environment to validate that backup tapes contain valid and good information:

- Ensure backups are successful and checked on a daily basis.
- Document the criteria for a successful or failed back up. For example, on a full backup, if less than 20 files failed to back up, then the backup is successful, or on a full backup, if one database fails to backup, then the backup has failed.
- If incremental backups fail the first day, then do not rerun.
- If incremental backups fail two days in a row, then correct, rerun, and validate they are successful.
- If the weekly backups fail, then correct, rerun, and validate they are successful.
- As backup tapes come back onsite on a quarterly basis, perform a full system restore on a system or two that contain mission critical data, such as a financial or payroll system.

Then as the enterprise develops the business continuity and disaster recovery plans, the enterprise will want to include these tips when performing a test or performing a live disaster recovery:

- Does the disaster recovery site have the hardware and software that matches your backups and backup tapes?
- If the disaster recovery site has the tape hardware, does the enterprise disaster recovery plan contain a set of the tape backup software?
- Does the disaster recovery plan include a copy of the procedures for system and information recovery?
- Consider taking two sets of backup tapes to the event, just in case the primary set of tapes are corrupt.
- Consider taking one set of tapes on one mode of transportation and another set of tapes on another mode of transportation to the disaster recovery site.

While many of the above considerations are geared toward tape backups, the same considerations can also be used for other backup media. The table below represents a sample table backup plan template.

Purpose	The purpose of the backup plan is to establish and implement procedures to create and maintain retrievable exact copies of electronic information and related technology components that are necessary for recovery activities. This document will define the following standards for organization backup processing: to provide a standard operating procedure for backup of organization data; to provide a standard for labeling backup media; to provide a standard for data retention; to provide a standard for off-site storage and retrieval of backup media; the data backup plan enables the organization to meet the availability requirements for regulatory compliance

Table of contents	Confidentiality statement and compliance
	Plan maintenance (change history)
	Introduction
	Purpose
	Scope
	Responsibilities
	Data backup requirements
	Procedures
	Backup processing
	Daily incremental backups
	Weekly full backups
	Monthly full backups
	Quarter-end full backups
	Failed backups
	Restoration processing
	Request for restore
	Authorization for restore
	Testing for successful restore
	Failed restoration
	Backup tape testing
	Quarterly
	Regulatory
	Regular validations
	Annual: off-site contracts
	Annual: software maintenance renewals
	Annual: hardware maintenance renewals
	Quarterly: tape access authorizations
	Quarterly: tape inventory
	Tapes
	Scheduling backup media rotation
	Sending tapes off-site
	Recalling tapes back onsite
	Tape labeling
	Retention cycle
	Tape drive cleaning
	Contacts
	Backup software supplier
	Backup hardware supplier

	Off-site storage supplier
	Authorized staff to recall and send tapes
	Appendix (forms/logs/schedules)
	Tape labeling log
	Data backup schedule
	Backup job log
	Tape cleaning log

If an enterprise cannot completely implement business continuity and disaster recovery plans, strong backup controls need to be part of every enterprise environment. Without strong backup controls, an enterprise may not know that backups and backup media are good and can be used to recover operational data. In the future, the enterprise may also want to consider moving to remote backups off-site as a service.

About the Author

Sandy Bacik, CISSP-ISSMP, CISM, CGEIT, CHS-III, author and former CSO, has over 14 years of direct development, implementation, and management information security experience in the areas of audit management, disaster recovery and business continuity, incident investigation, physical security, privacy, regulatory compliance, standard operating policies and procedures, and data center operations and management. Ms. Bacik has managed, architected, and implemented comprehensive information assurance programs and managed internal, external, and contracted and outsourced information technology audits to ensure various regulatory compliance for state and local government entities and Fortune 200 companies. She has developed methodologies for risk assessments, information technology audits, vulnerability assessments, security policy and practice writing, incident response, and disaster recovery.

Chapter 28

Productivity vs. Security

Sandy Bacik

Enterprises around the globe are increasingly concerned about the risk of cyberthreats and the rising number of incidents shared publicly justifies their worries. In today's economy budgets are being reduced and technology departments are being asked to cut resources. So, risk up, budgets down. The risk realities are exploited by anyone who uses the downturn in security enforcement to step up the pace of exploitation. Disgruntled employees are also walking away with valued information assets, while businesses scale back on defense in an effort to become more productive. And it's happening at a time when an enterprise can ill afford downtime, decreased productivity, stolen data, lost sales, and a damaged enterprise reputation. This is what we call the "security paradox" or "productivity versus security." This debate is becoming harder to implement as single-point external attacks have moved toward multisource external attacks and the model of the "trusted employee" is being eroded. Information technology's (IT) primary purpose is to make the enterprise employees as productive, efficient, and effective at doing their jobs as possible. Laptops, portable memory, and even smart devices are part of that efficiency/productivity environment, allowing for work to get done on the train, plane, at a client site, or at an employee's home. Now, the top IT security purpose is at odds with that primary purpose. IT security's primary purpose is to protect company data, whether from a power outage, an inadvertent erasure, a disk glitch, or more evil efforts, such as sabotage or intentional theft. Another example, the traditional defined enterprise network perimeter around an enterprise's information assets, is no longer realistic. The enterprise mobile workforce demands that data be portable and instantly accessible from anywhere. This negates the physical barriers designed to keep information secure.

Every security professional knows that nothing we do with respect to information security will eliminate all of the risks inherent within the enterprise. At best, we can mitigate the risks and bring them down to an acceptable level. So what is an acceptable level of risk? Every asset owner needs to decide that for themselves and it will vary by industry, organization, perceived and real threats, the software in use, and many other factors. The point is that security is an ongoing balancing act. Often the balancing act is between security needs and the culture of the organization. Some enterprises have a goal of allowing the employees a great deal of freedom within the work place and that "freedom" is often extended to the network—even though the enterprise has a stated policy that the network is for business use only and that there should be no expectation of privacy for any network activity. Applications such as instant messaging (IM) and peer-to-peer services (e.g., KaZaA music downloads) are known to have security implications yet their use is allowed even though there is generally no good business reason for them. Why would an enterprise want to use software that exposes its business data to a possible security breach? Perhaps, instead, you should consider purchasing a secure version of the proper application rather than using nonsecure (albeit free) software that only approximates the right functionality—and provides a significant exposure. Wait. That points to the same balancing act about "productivity" versus security. Enterprises use software known to be security nightmares—but use them anyway, ostensibly for "user productivity."

The dilemma of productivity versus security also makes the compliance challenge a daunting obstacle for companies struggling to stay competitive. The enterprise demand for a more mobile workforce exposes the networks to increases in the risk of potential data leakage. The basic purpose of addressing security in a productivity environment is to ensure the continued effective protection of sensitive information and the system's critical processes. The adequacy of automated system security is examined through periodic audits, evaluations, risk analyses, and approval reviews. Evaluations and reviews should be performed in conjunction with follow-on tests and evaluations, self-inspections, and other required evaluations. Yet, how much security can be implemented without affecting the enterprise's productivity? Let's look at the CobIT®* model. Using the CobIT model when advancing technological implementations or trying to stay ahead of the curve for technology, the enterprise should

1. *Plan and organize*: The enterprise must perform an assessment of the existing infrastructure to determine its strengths and weaknesses. The ideal solution to satisfy these requirements should be to increase performance and productivity. Do not forget about including the enterprise security requirements.
2. *Acquire and implement*: The next step is evaluation, selection, and implementation of the solution that best matches the requirements.
3. *Deliver and support*: Hopefully, some of the requirements include security and security is part of the selected and implemented solution. Ideally, the solution adopted should protect the confidentiality, integrity, and availability of sensitive information by managing user privileges and restricting the transfer of information to users and unauthorized devices.
4. *Monitor and evaluate*: The final component of CobIT controls focuses on the ability to continuously measure the performance of an enterprise's established IT infrastructure.

To achieve the highest possible protection levels and the lowest possible risk and cost, while keeping the enterprise productive, the enterprise must consider an approach that incorporates these elements:

■ Integrated and layered defense across systems and networks
■ Real-time threat intelligence and reputational analysis
■ Centralized security management platform that provides a singular management console
■ Real-time network monitoring to ensure response times and employee productivity
■ All network monitoring and administration backed by a dedicated team of security research experts and competent administrators

---

* http://www.isaca.org/Template.cfm?Section=COBIT6&Template=/TaggedPage/TaggedPageDisplay. cfm&TPLID=55&ContentID=7981.

What is an enterprise to do when balancing productivity and security? Enterprises need to look for a cost-cutting environment opportunity to make their IT security solutions streamlined and effective. The enterprise result is fewer security breaches, less downtime and revenue loss, and less risk in tough economies.

Combining consolidated information assurance protection with centralized management is one of the best security practices. The enterprise needs to be proactive in identifying potential risks and stemming loss of productivity and revenue. When looking at technology, the enterprise must review

- *Integration*: Do not look for specifically for the one-size-fits-all product. Look at security vendors who offer integrated suites rather than siloed products.
- *Centralized management*: Gain greater visibility and increased control via a single management console and limit the required staff for monitoring.
- *Lower costs*: Integrated solutions, often, are more economical, resulting in savings in license and support costs, and more efficient administration and management.

Using this approach can extend to many types of threat vectors: e-mail, web, networks, systems, and data. In reviewing vendors, the enterprise should also ensure some form of autoupdating to ensure that the protection is current. Enterprise solutions should cover every security element: system protection beyond antivirus, web, and e-mail security, network defense with firewalls, host intrusion prevention, network access control, and data protection. With an integrated set of security offerings, centrally managed, an IT administrator can still dedicate the same number of hours per week while gaining a more proactive and comprehensive security coverage. A good practice when integrating security practices into an IT administrator's work environment is to ensure that security is part of an everyday practice and does not exceed more than 15–30 minutes of their daily activities.

Looking at productivity from an enterprise user's point of view also requires some consideration. How much security will the enterprise user tolerate? Often, what users do not know will not hurt them. Well, yes and no. Additional auditing, logging, and compliance are a requirement for many enterprise environments. Enterprise users begrudgingly accept having to perform extra steps as part of their daily duties. On the other hand, some enterprise users still challenge the concept with statements like "I am a trusted employee, why are you checking up on my work." In today's enterprise environment, the concept of the trusted employee needs to be challenged. Loss of intellectual property, mistakes in data entry, and loss of data integrity, whether accidental or deliberate, need to be evaluated within an enterprise. What are security activities that can be implemented to lower enterprise risk while not impacting enterprise user productivity? Baseline the environment. To ensure there is a balance of productivity and security, the enterprise needs to baseline the network activities. Once a baseline is completed and additional production or security is implemented on the network, the enterprise can see the impact of the activities. Once the baseline is completed, then a few additional activities and solutions for consideration are listed below:

- *Turning on auditing and logging*: But not so much as to slow network traffic and use lots of hard drive space. Ensuring there is staff to monitor those logs and/or reports.
- *Using role-based access control*: Knowing which users are accessing a network resource limits risk and administrators have an easier job maintaining access control.
- Using the role-based access control makes the authorization process more efficient, because an asset owner can review who is accessing their assets more easily and frequently.

- Using whitelisting, rather than blacklisting, with a request process for adding additional resources limits the risk, yet ensures enterprise users can still access what they need for productivity.
- Using something similar to a single sign-on for access control will assist in users being more productive in not having to use multiple user IDs and passwords for access to applications and resources.

Yes, balancing productivity and security takes careful planning and review. To tie everything together when balancing productivity and security: First, information security is not an add-on to a network, project, or application—it is something that should be considered throughout the idea, requirements, architecture, and implementation phases. Second, security takes time and some money, but, usually, not as much as some would think. Finally, a widely stated mantra in the security field is that "security is a process not a product." Even if you have the best, most comprehensive security hardware and software available, it is soon useless unless it is maintained, updated, and integrated into the larger system for productivity. When balancing productivity and security, if the enterprise gets it right, the enterprise has innovation; get it wrong and the enterprise has trouble.

About the Author

Sandy Bacik, CISSP-ISSMP, CISM, CGEIT, CHS-III, author and former CSO, has over 14 years of direct development, implementation, and management information security experience in the areas of audit management, disaster recovery and business continuity, incident investigation, physical security, privacy, regulatory compliance, standard operating policies and procedures, and data center operations and management. Ms. Bacik has managed, architected, and implemented comprehensive information assurance programs and managed internal, external, and contracted and outsourced information technology audits to ensure various regulatory compliance for state and local government entities and Fortune 200 companies. She has developed methodologies for risk assessments, information technology audits, vulnerability assessments, security policy and practice writing, incident response, and disaster recovery.

BUSINESS CONTINUITY AND DISASTER RECOVERY PLANNING

Business Continuity Planning

Chapter 29

Continuity Planning for Small- and Medium-Sized Organizations

Carl Jackson

Small Organization Continuity Planning Realities

Crisis management and continuity planning issues are just one of the primary differences between a larger, more geographically diverse organization and a smaller single or limited location enterprise. Three primary reasons for the differences in overall continuity planning approach include: (1) relative level of need; (2) staff time/dedicated personnel; and (3) budget/resource availability. A more detailed discussion of each of these three areas follows, with subsequent suggestions on how to address each of the three that could be applied to help alleviate their impact upon the small organization manager.

- *Relative Level of Need*: Smaller organizations usually "have all their eggs in one basket." Larger organizations, often mandated through regulation, commonly accepted standards, or audit oversight requirements, will ordinarily have built continuity planning measures into everyday business practices. Information technology (IT) backup and off-site storage of data and software, systems redundancy and diversity, network connectivity, and formalized emergency response and continuity plans are all typically developed to be complementary with business unit/process continuity requirements. On the other hand, smaller organizations with fewer resources may or may not have included continuity planning hooks into existing IT and business processes. Of even more significance is that the relative level of need for protection of smaller organization data/information resources that are often resident on underprotected single-location computing systems make them more vulnerable to catastrophic loss should a disaster occur. One other point here is that smaller organizations that *ARE* addressing continuity planning issues often focus the majority of their efforts on IT backup and IT continuity planning rather than focusing efforts on time-critical business process recoverability. Additionally, there is often a failure to tie the IT continuity plans into a more coordinated enterprise crisis management infrastructure that will make possible a more efficient and effective recovery when disaster does occur.

■ *Staff Time/Dedicated Personnel*: Larger organizations, by virtue of their greater size and geographical distribution, are able and even mandated in some cases to have dedicated continuity planning staff, either as part of IT or as standalone position descriptions. Smaller organizations are forced to assign continuity planning responsibilities to disparate positions within the organization, frequently with focused continuity planning energies on backup and recovery issues within those individuals' specific sphere of influence. This approach leads to patchwork recovery planning programs that allow critical cracks to emerge in the enterprise approach to recovery as well as to eventually result in an incomplete emergency response and recovery efficiencies and effectiveness.

■ *Budget/Resource Availability*: For the small organization manager, it boils down to a simple question of percent of budget allocation for dedicated continuity planning activities. A fairly common rule of thumb for larger enterprises is that three to five percent of IT budgets is typically devoted to information security, including continuity planning activities. In contrast, dedication of three to five percent of small organization IT budget for security and BCP would normally be considered out of line. Smaller organizations simply do not have the deep pockets to tackle extensive crisis management and continuity planning initiatives.

Achieving economies of scale in these areas is where the smaller organization can best do more with less to achieve a more rigorous program to address recoverability and survivability.

Before moving on to specific suggestions on how the smaller organization manager might address the challenges discussed above, what follows is a quick review of what a truly rigorous enterprise-wide continuity planning program should encompass.

Continuity Planning Program Structure

The enterprise continuity program structure is the *same no matter the size of the organization*. The structure is focused on preparations for recovery of time-critical business processes. Both large and small organizational management must be focused laser-like on the identification, classification, and recovery of time-critical business processes.

Each element of the enterprise-wide continuity program, in turn, supports the continuity program's goal of ensuring the ongoing viability of organizational time-critical business processes. Figure 29.1 is a simple illustration of how the primary components of the enterprise-wide continuity planning program must relate to one another.

The enterprise-wide continuity planning approach closely links and even overlaps three traditional continuity planning disciplines, as follows:

■ *IT Continuity Planning*: Often referred to as disaster recovery planning, IT continuity planning addresses technology-based operations (computer systems, networks, telecommunications, etc.) including IT technologies, voice and data communications, and any other automated resources that the organization relies upon to support time-critical business process recoverability.

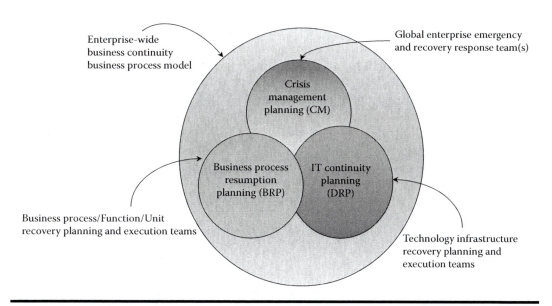

Figure 29.1 Interrelated components of the enterprise-wide continuity planning program.

- *Business Process Resumption Planning (BRP)*: Business process resumption plans address the continuity and recovery requirements of an organization's business processes (i.e., accounting purchasing, sales, patient care, customer call center, operations, etc.) should they lose access to or support of their infrastructure resources (i.e., IT, communications networks, facilities, key business partner support, etc.). The primary goal here is to understand the time-critical nature of each of the enterprise's business processes and their support components and to prioritize those processes with the most time-critical needs for access to resources.

- *Crisis Management Planning (CMP)*: Crisis management plans document the activities and tasks necessary for overall coordination of an organization's response to a crisis, in an effective and timely manner, with the goal of avoiding or minimizing damage to the organization's profitability, reputation, or ability to operate. It is the crisis management process that provides the glue that holds the organization's continuity planning business structure together. Crisis management planning focuses on the development of effective and efficient enterprise-wide emergency/disaster response capabilities. A top-down approach to crisis management ensures that open lines of communication are maintained among executive management, the business process and IT continuity teams, and with critical external entities (regulatory agencies, key business partners, customers, civil authorities, financial markets, etc.). This capability has three broad objectives: (1) The first is to provide the executive management group with a predefined organizational structure and the wherewithal to facilitate communication with continuity planning teams of the affected business units and their processes. (2) It also must be able to facilitate communication not only with the business units, but also among the various components of the continuity planning infrastructure, one-to-another (i.e., the IT continuity planning teams and the business process continuity teams). (3) The crisis management plan also addresses the issues associated with outsider communication. It aids management in effective communication with outsiders, such as civil authorities, key business partners, employees' families, regulatory agencies, audit entities, shareholder groups, the press, etc. This response capability includes forming appropriate management teams and preparing the members to react to serious disruptive emergency situations (i.e., hurricane, earthquake, flood, fire, kidnapping, systems outages caused by serious hacker or virus damage, pandemic, etc.).

Following are a number of suggestions on how the smaller organization might go about achieving a better protection posture and implement a program closer to the enterprise-wide approach discussed above.

Small Business Continuity Planning Infrastructure Suggestions

The vast majority of small organization continuity planning programs, if they even exist, do not resemble the enterprise-wide continuity planning structure model defined in Figure 29.1. If a program does exist, it is usually highly IT-centric. Where business process resumption plans exist, they rarely interface effectively (lack of mutual dependency testing, for instance) with one another. And an even more important shortcoming is the failure to interweave the IT and business resumption plans into the enterprise crisis management program, which would result in a more coordinated and efficient infrastructure.

So, what can small organization management do specifically to address existing shortcomings in their program structure? Following are a number of solutions that can be taken individually, or in combination, to assist the manager in making some headway in achieving better crisis management and continuity planning protection for their enterprise.

Recognize the Relative Level of Need: Management of smaller organizations must acknowledge the significance of the relative level of need for protection of their data/information resources. These resources are typically resident on underprotected or secure single-location computing systems, making them more vulnerable to catastrophic loss should a disaster occur. One other point here is that smaller organizations that are addressing continuity planning issues often focus the majority of their efforts on IT backup and continuity planning rather than focusing efforts on time-critical business process recoverability. What are some of the ways the manager might enhance their program in this area?

■ *Formalize a Business Impact Assessment*: Management must understand all potential losses or impacts to the organization as precisely as possible in order to allocate resources to the continuity planning process. The purpose of the business impact assessment (BIA) is twofold: (1) to identify and prioritize business processes according to their time criticality, and (2) to establish a realistic recovery time objective to which all continuity plans will be aligned. It is vital that they thoroughly understand the time-critical business processes. The BIA is where this information is gathered, analyzed, consolidated, and presented with recommendations. Another important outcome of the BIA is the mapping of time-critical processes to their constituent support resources (i.e., IT servers and applications, infrastructure and networks, facilities' space requirements, business partner connectivity, etc.).

■ *Formalize a Threat Analysis*: Small organization management would be well served to perform a threat analysis which is a high-level review that serves to identify major exposures such as physical threats (i.e., earthquakes, fire, water damage, wind damage, etc.) and man-made threats (i.e., human errors or omissions, computer viruses, software and hardware failures, hackers, etc.).

- *Recognize Continuity Planning as a Critical Internal Initiative*: Executive management support and funding, continuity program staffing commitment, enterprise continuity planning infrastructure, team structures, crisis/incident management process, and overall level of continuity planning awareness are all areas where small organization management may want to focus in order to improve readiness. (1) *Executive level policy/standards*. Develop, formalize, and articulate crisis management and continuity planning policy and supporting standards and processes. (2) *Metrics*. Establish appropriate risk management-based or standards-based measurements. You get what you measure. Failure to clearly establish and track realistic measures anywhere within an organization, not the least of which relates to crisis management and continuity planning, will inevitably sentence organization management to wandering between inefficiencies. Continuity planning is rarely the core competency of an organization. The three-phase process for facilitating continuity planning process metrics should assist the continuity planner in jumpstarting the executive justification process. Each measurement should be broken down so it can be made operational, manageable, and one from which the impacts of management decisions can be measured. Presenting a solid set of continuity planning program metrics that are clearly articulated should resonate with your executive management group. These metrics must demonstrate the value-added contribution to the enterprise that the continuity planning program brings. (3) *Awareness and Training*. Emphasizing another key component, awareness and training issues are paramount to the success of any continuity planning program. It will be the organization's people who will have to recover the enterprise following a disaster or disruption, so it only makes sense that those same people are intimately involved in the development, implementation, testing, and maintenance of the process. Once planning has been accomplished, however, it does not release the organization's people of further responsibilities. It is vital that a regular and ongoing program of continuity planning awareness and training be put into place.

Analyze Levels of Continuity Planning-Related Staff Time or Use of Dedicated Personnel (insiders or outsiders): Following are several suggestions on how smaller organization management can achieve a more focused emphasis on disparate crisis management and continuity planning activities. What are some of the ways the manager might enhance their program in this area?

- *Appoint an Internal Coordinator*: Smaller organizations can take a positive step by designating an internal position with responsibility for consolidating and coordinating the disparate crisis management and continuity planning-related activities across the organization. Given the assignment of a centralized "the buck stops here" position that reports to senior management will help focus attention and create an atmosphere where crisis management and continuity planning economies of scale can be achieved.
- *Evaluate the Need for Consulting Assistance*: Because smaller organizations have fewer resources for dedicated crisis management and/or continuity planning, the one-time or limited use of outside consultants is advisable. Consultants are especially useful for performing threat analysis, business impact assessments, documenting continuity plans, and assisting in design and implementation of processes that will tie the business process units, IT infrastructure, and crisis management processes into a coordinated enterprise-wide infrastructure.
- *Consider Outsourcing*: Another potential solution for smaller organization management is to utilize outsourced providers or servicers (IT outsourced services, human resource outsourced services, continuity planning hot-site servicers, etc.) to assist in certain crisis management and continuity planning activities. One of the advantages of interleaving continuity

planning specialists who work for outsourcers is that they can significantly supplement the efforts of internal resources already assigned continuity planning responsibilities. Utilizing the internal coordinator function mentioned above will help to focus enterprise-wide efforts to ensure economies of scale and reduce redundant initiatives to drive down overall costs.

Budget/Resource Availability: It is simply a question of percent of budget opportunities for dedicated continuity planning activities. A fairly common rule of thumb for larger enterprise is that three to five percent of IT budgets are typically devoted to information security, including crisis and continuity planning activities. In contrast, dedicating three to five percent of small organization IT budget for security and BCP would normally be considered out of line. So, while there are no real guidelines on what percentage of resources should be spent on crisis management and continuity planning, there are a number of initiatives the small organization manager can take to increase survivability. What are some of the ways the manager might enhance their program in this area?

■ *Ensure Data and Software Backup*: Lost data is LOST data. Time-critical data, once lost, is almost always either prohibitively expensive to reproduce or simply gone forever. Therefore, management must acknowledge that, first and foremost, it is data backup and offsite storage of data and software that support time-critical business processes and this is the linchpin to success when planning IT-related recovery. Companies such as Carbonite, ElephantDrive, Sharpcast, and SOS Online Backup, to name a few, specialize in offering individuals and small organizations online backup and access to time-critical data files and software. These types of companies provide the small business with a value-added service that can dramatically reduce the workload of internal or outsourced IT professionals. This approach helps ensure that minimum data and software backup is performed regularly, and rotated and stored offsite to protect it should disaster occur.

■ *Consider Turnkey Solutions*: There are a number of off-the-shelf approaches to assist smaller enterprises in the development of crisis management and continuity plans. Several vendors offer continuity planning software for sale that, when coupled with competent crisis management and/or lease continuity planning expertise, can be used to facilitate plan development. Sources for this type of solution include SunGard Availability Services' LDRPS; ErLogix's Business Continuity Planner; the BCP Generator from Disaster Recovery World; and web-based BCM software from TAMP, to name just a few. Additionally, there are web-based solutions that offer combinations of software, consulting, knowledge base, and continuity planning online community interaction to organizations that do not have full-time planning personnel or who need additional expertise and assistance in addressing crisis management and continuity planning issues. Supplementary services that might be offered include threat assessment, business impact assessment, testing assistance and oversight, data backup, hardcopy document backup and/or destruction, training and awareness services, etc. It would be wise for small organization management to not overlook this potentially valuable source of crisis management and continuity planning assistance when considering their program while also attempting to lower the costs of implementation.

■ *Reevaluate Insurance Coverage Philosophies*: Continuity planning is sometimes erroneously referred to as being "just like insurance." This philosophy implies that all the management group has to do is simply determine how much insurance they can afford, buy it, and move on. While continuity planning is a form of insurance certainly, it is not "just like insurance" in that an appropriately designed and implemented continuity plan will assist in recovery of assets and operations that are uninsurable or underinsured. For this reason, a good continuity plan can be worth its weight in gold while those organizations with a more simple insurance-only approach to continuity planning are being hampered in attempting to recover while struggling in a "replacement-cost versus original-cost versus depreciated-cost" quagmire, and that is even if the insurable cost of the data lost, for instance, can be determined.

■ *More Closely Align Crisis Management Planning*: Not only in smaller organizations, but also in larger ones, there is a lack of a closely interleaved coordination between the crisis management plans and the IT and business process resumption planning infrastructure. The primary goal of the crisis management plan is to facilitate communications of all parties. This includes the continuity planning teams on both the IT and business process sides with the crisis management team as well as with one another. The crisis management plan should also assist the executive management group in communicating with outside entities such as civil authorities like police and fire authorities, primary customers and shareholders, regulatory agencies, employees' families, unions, the press, and the like. A key advantage to a well-developed and tested crisis management plan is the ability of executive management to respond quickly with the correct actions that will facilitate rapid response and recovery of time-critical processes thereby driving down the resulting cost/impact of the incident. Members of the crisis management team, including members of executive management, are then responsible for directing recovery efforts from the top, providing needed resources and support, and for ensuring that the organization continues to operate as optimally as possible during the recovery effort. It is not enough to simply develop crisis management plans; they must be exercised or rehearsed if you will. Including the testing of the crisis management team activities during the annual testing of the continuity planning structure is imperative, making the team more efficient and effective during times of crisis. It is incumbent on executive management to ensure that as the overall continuity planning infrastructure matures, all plans and the recovery team personnel outlined in the plans understand that during times of crisis the reporting structure of the organization flows up and down through the crisis management team.

■ *Link Risk Management to Recoverability*: Tie traditional risk management disciplines (financial risk management, insurance risk management, operations risk management, etc.) to the enterprise-wide continuity planning program. More and more management groups are recognizing the need to combine control functions such as financial, operational, and insurance plus others that might include audit, legal, tax, information security, physical security, continuity planning, and the like under one overall risk management umbrella. Based on the concept that any adverse event would have some degree of impact upon enterprise value drivers (financial, customer service, shareholder, etc.), then coordinating and managing risk functions across the enterprise makes sense.

■ *Conduct Regular and Ongoing Testing*: Last but not least is the topic of regular and ongoing testing. Testing or exercising crisis and continuity plans at least annually is an absolute must. Organization staff and management must practice regularly what has been written in the plans. Regular and ongoing testing serves several purposes. Testing serves to reinforce the importance of the defined lines of communication up and down through the crisis management plan. Testing is also a basis for identifying outdated plan activities and tasks, call lists, inventory listings, offsite arrangements, etc. And finally, and most importantly, testing serves to train employees and raises overall management and staff awareness. Testing reinforces understanding of the precise measures that need to be taken immediately and subsequent to the disaster and, if done properly, allows everyone to take pause, look around, and consider what it will be like during a crisis situation and how best to carry out their roles in helping the organization survive.

While there are other measures that can be taken by the smaller organization manager to improve the effectiveness of the overall crisis management and continuity planning infrastructure, considering and thoughtfully adopting the major suggestions outlined above will help to significantly reduce the potential impact of a disaster.

Summary

The old saying that one should "never put all your eggs in one basket" is unfortunately very relevant to smaller organization managers who often have little or no choice.

Challenges facing smaller organizations are many, with priorities elsewhere drawing resources away from a coordinated approach to preparations that help ensure enterprise survivability. Crisis management and continuity planning assignments are, more often than not, informal and/or set aside for more pressing matters. And it seems that the last thing a small organization manager needs is another initiative on the plate.

Disasters do occur, and they occur every day, as a casual glance at the morning newspaper or news website will confirm. Often, smaller organization managers do not have a good appreciation for the fact that small organizations tend to suffer more than larger ones due to lack of relatively deep pockets. Smaller organizations' vital IT needs are also often centralized and lack more sophisticated physical, environmental, and information security protections, making them more vulnerable to sudden catastrophic loss.

This chapter dealt with the three primary differences between large and small organizations' approaches when dealing with crisis management and continuity planning. These included the necessity for management to appreciate their organization's relative level of need, and staffing and budget/resource availability issues. Several suggestions were discussed including conducting a formalized threat and business impact analysis, formalizing an internal coordinator position, and perhaps formalizing a crisis management and continuity planning initiative. It was also suggested that management consider evaluating the need for outside assistance, including use of consultants, service providers, and other outsourced assistance. Suggestions also included ensuring data and software backup practices are as bulletproof as possible, and reevaluating insurance coverage philosophies. From an enterprise-wide standpoint, management should take a closer look at how to align crisis management and continuity planning initiatives with one another as well as with the overall risk management process, and lastly perform regular and ongoing testing and increasing awareness and training.

Depending on the size of the organization in question, these suggestions may or may not be applicable. The bottom line is that small organizations have a lot to lose with little cushion for comfort. Taking all this into consideration, management would be well served to give these suggestions some serious thought. At the end of the day, it must surely be true that if you are forced to place all your eggs in one basket, be very certain you keep your eye on that basket!

About the Author

Carl Jackson is the former director of the Business Continuity Program at Pacific Life Insurance Company in Southern California. He has more than thirty years of experience in the areas of continuity planning, information security and information technology internal control, and quality assurance reviews and audits. He has also served with various consultancies specializing in business continuity planning and information security where their responsibilities included development and oversight of continuity methodologies, project management, tools acquisition, and ongoing testing/maintenance/training/measurement of the enterprise-wide business continuity planning.

Carl has served as chairman of the Information Systems Security Association (ISSA) international board of directors. Previously, he was a founding board member and past president of the ISSA as well as serving as a founding board member of the Houston, Texas, document of the Association of Contingency Planners (ACP). Carl is a past member and past emeritus member of the Computer Security Institute (CSI) Advisory Council and is the recipient of the 1997 CSI Lifetime Achievement Award. Carl has authored numerous reports and articles on business continuity planning and information security issues.

LEGAL, REGULATIONS, COMPLIANCE, AND INVESTIGATIONS

Information Law

Chapter 30

The Cost of Risk: An Examination of Risk Assessment and Information Security in the Financial Industry

Seth Kinnett

Since the advent of the Sarbanes–Oxley legislation, public attention has increasingly turned towards the topic of regulation within the financial industry. A number of groups find themselves vested in the outcomes and processes employed by financial institutions: government has a regulatory obligation and consumers increasingly voice concerns surrounding privacy. These consumers expect firms to take steps to mitigate risk both to assets and personal information. This chapter explores risk assessment and information security in the context of a financial services firm, including key considerations, industry differentiators, and methods for mitigating the risk present in this vertical.

The term "financial services firm" will largely be used to encompass firms involved in the transaction of securities in some way, such as mutual funds. It is necessary to make this distinction because firms performing valuations, for example, would have different fundamental concerns from a transaction-based firm. Indeed it is the process of trading—and the systems required to support and facilitate this process—that pose the greatest threats to a sound information security plan, as exposure suffered from these systems has the potential to cause legal, reputational, and financial problems, at a minimum. The term "banks" will refer largely to investment banks, though retail banks would not be excluded from this discussion and care will be taken to specify which type of bank is being referred is pertinent, as needed.

As we explore the considerations, challenges, and concerns facing the financial industry, it is important to understand how these challenges and concerns parallel as well as diverge from those of other industries. Indeed, it is useful and appropriate to examine industry-specific considerations of risk assessment and the larger topic of information security, understanding that various industries face different challenges. As Deborah Radcliff (1999) notes in an article for *Computer World*, "while the financial industry worries about integrity and customer confidence, another industry, manufacturing, must protect against theft of intellectual property. Meanwhile, the entertainment industry is wondering how to prevent piracy of its products on the Internet" (p. 38). In this example, the financial industry vertical is juxtaposed with two others, which are strikingly different, both with regard to soft issues such as public perception and hard concerns such as law and regulation.

Although all industry verticals face the threat of security breach, research suggests the evolving technology landscape has brought increasing threats to the financial industry more than other businesses. "As more transactions are conducted via the Internet, businesses face an evergrowing [*sic*] risk from hackers perpetrating crimes in cyberspace" (Turner et al., 2006). While home users remain the target most often attacked, current attacks on financial institutions have increased from 4% to 14% of total targeted attacks, "increasingly motivated by financial gain" (Elms et al., 2008, p.2).

As we explore information security, the primary focus of the discussion centers upon high-level security policies rather than specific security controls. It is useful to understand the limitations inherent in such a discussion, particularly as it does not directly reflect the realities within many business organizations. Indeed, the theory of information security "describes a state in which security 1) organically pervades the network and 2) serves the organization by measuring and managing business risk. The reality is that security today consists of isolated plugs jammed into leaky holes" (Conry-Murray, 1999, p.1). Organizations could be well served by implementing projects to ensure that the "plugs" they have used correspond with a broader information security policy. If they don't, it is necessary to rewrite the policy or change the plug. Through either process, the organization would benefit from increased education about the options before them and the manner in which they would like to create policy. In practice, it is clear that most budgets are spent on controls rather than high-level policy strategy initiatives.

> The most widely used risk management techniques in combating hackers have been loss prevention and loss control. In the financial services industry, it is estimated that individual corporations spend approximately $17.5 million to $28 million protecting their information systems from hackers (Brown, 2007). These funds are typically used to construct complicated security systems that make it harder for hackers to access sensitive information systems. (Elms et al., 2008, p.4)

The financial industry spends such sums, in part, because of the type of data they are charged with protecting. Whereas any company might be in possession of name, address, and credit card information, a financial services firm must protect a significant amount of data such as net worth, assets, and particular security positions. We will now explore how financial firms handle the issue of risk prioritization.

Considering the wealth of concerns facing every industry vertical, it is especially critical to understand how, in this case, the financial industry can prioritize its risks and concerns. Reputational risk is significant and is at stake surrounding a number of issues:

> Because consumer trust is the financial industry's biggest asset, banking and investment firms should, above all else, protect customer accounts from unauthorized funds transfers, according to Paul Raines, vice president of electronic security at the Federal Reserve Bank of New York. "Banks want to protect the assets of their customers.

There's a reputational risk if they don't," Raines explains. "If consumers felt that certain large banks can't protect their assets, they may feel the other banks can't either. So banks need to be diligent for the health of the industry as a whole." (Radcliff, 1999)

Data suggest that these concerns are warranted and financial services firms rightly must guard against this type of negative exposure. The financial industry has the unfortunate challenge of finding itself under heavy media scrutiny and even small incidents can develop into headlines, as one UK bank found in 2007. In this example, the British "Financial Services Authority fined Swindon, England-based Nationwide Building Society… for 'failing to have effective systems and controls to manage its information security risks'" (Kirk, 2007, p.18). What is particularly striking about this example is the public perception that Nationwide did not act upon the security breach immediately. The breach in this case involved a laptop which "was stolen from an employee's home during a burglary…. Nationwide, which has about 11 million customers, did not immediately realize that the stolen laptop contained customer information and waited three weeks before starting an investigation" (ibid., 18). In order to mitigate the risks to public opinion, Nationwide spent time and resources as they "informed its customers of the problem… and commissioned a review of its information security [policies]" (ibid., 18). Financial firms can learn from Nationwide by committing resources to investigations, treating every breach as critical. Of course, such a policy is resource-strapping and challenging to implement. At a minimum, firms must be diligent in their research of the plights of similar firms in this industry vertical.

A final example of the pervasive trends seen in security-related issues in the financial space occurs in a most exposed and visible organization, the Securities and Exchange Commission. Indeed, the SEC itself has come under scrutiny for its lax security measures. The Government Accountability Office issued a report which found "that the SEC has corrected or mitigated only eight of 51 weaknesses cited by the GAO in a report last year, a response the oversight office of the U.S. Congress called inadequate" (Rosencrance, 2006, p.23). One example of the lax attitude towards security surrounds two fundamental information security concepts: access control and authentication. The GAO cites that the SEC has not adequately controlled user accounts and passwords to enforce basic access control principles—namely preventing unauthorized people from accessing its systems and data. The GAO further discovered that the SEC has poor permission management and an open file system that does not make use of even rudimentary security best practices, thus "increasing the risk that the SEC's applications and sensitive financial data could be compromised. The report determined that the vulnerabilities continue to leave sensitive SEC financial information without sufficient protection against disclosure, modification or loss" (ibid., 23).

This example is particularly useful to our examination as a result of the level of detail which was publicized as a result of the security audit. Unlike private financial companies, who fear negative media attention, particularly around issues such as these, the SEC must submit to government oversight. The people, therefore, have the right to information about how governmental agencies meet or fail given benchmarks, hence the presence of the GAO report. Though not a conclusion that can be drawn by causal connection, it is reasonable to suspect that if the regulator itself is not keeping atop of its risk management issues, the companies it regulates are not either. This may or may not be due to negligence on the part of companies. Oftentimes the intentions and initiatives of a company are legitimate. In other words, their "hearts are in the right place," but they face a key challenge of translating their particular goals into actionable technical projects, or vice versa. In some cases, business risk is discussed in an ethereal state, at too high a level. "As for business risk, measurements are a kludgy mix of vulnerability data and unquantifiable gut feelings that don't satisfy financial officers and are difficult to manage" (Conry-Murray, 1999, p.1). As companies seek to cut costs, they may eliminate resources such as business analysts, who are able to translate business needs into technical language. This is a dangerous error, which will prove costly in the long term. Paradoxically, the attempt to save money in this area often backfires into additional financial—not to mention reputational—costs. To the former, studies have begun to quantify the costs experienced by companies in terms of internal expenditures and through impact to stock price in the case of publicly traded firms. One study in *Information Systems Security* magazine explained that "security incidents can cost companies between $17 and $28 million per incident or 0.5 to 1.0 percent of annual sales for the average publicly listed company. Second, investor reactions to IT breaches extend to more than the breached party; they also 'spill over' to Internet security vendors and insurance carriers" (Garg, et al. 2003, p.22). The strength of the financial industry has often been used as an indicator of the strength of the overall economy. This positioning makes our examination of particular costs associated with security particularly relevant.

Our discussion so far has focused largely upon financial services firms, their technology landscapes, their information security challenges, and the resulting investor response to firms' abilities to confront or ignore those challenges. We now turn to an issue in which ethics, public policy, consumer confidence, and corporate strategy all intersect in a powerful way: privacy. In 2006, a congressional proposal to limit the use of social security numbers as a means to identify citizens caused massive concerns for the financial services industry. Corporations, no doubt initially concerned with the impact of regulation on their bottom lines, scrambled to have their voices heard. In testimony before congress, the CEO of the American Financial Services Association, Randy Lively Jr., insisted that the proposed legislation

> could deprive banks, insurance firms, credit bureaus and other businesses of a reliable identity verification method while doing little to bolster consumer privacy. 'The Social Security number is the only unique identifier in our country that enables a [company] to be sure that the consumer they are doing business with is the correct John Smith,' Lively said. Any attempt to limit the use of the numbers in commercial transactions could disrupt the nation's economy, he argued. (Vijayan, 2006, p.22)

While this testimony sounds, at first, like typical corporate lobbyist posturing, an understanding of information security controls and implementation concerns reveals the legitimacy of Lively's concerns. From our existing analysis, we know financial firms already face a long list of information security concerns; no doubt their technology departments have projects, enhancements, and other initiatives queued up as it is. This point was underscored by "a written statement submitted at the [Congressional] hearing by the Securities Industry Association's Financial Services Coordinating Council (FSCC) [which] warned that overly broad legislation will raise the cost of credit and force 'fundamental and costly changes to internal business operating systems'" (Vijayan, 2006, p.22). Privacy is always a delicate issue for the financial services industry, and the Social Security Number (SSN) issue is something of a paradox. Indeed, Lively's case suggested that SSNs have been used as a means to *preserve* privacy. The SSN was a natural unique identifier, rarely known by individuals other than the person to which it was assigned. That it has been compromised demonstrates several points: the failure of companies (including financial services companies) to prevent identity theft via SSN.

Had financial services firms collectively made information security and privacy among their highest priorities, they may have prevented the very sort of security breaches that allowed specific

Social Security Numbers to be compromised. Ultimately, firms might have prevented the need for governmental oversight. It is important to examine the government's handling of this event. In this case it is clear, however, that the Federal Trade Commission has been cooperative rather than confrontational. "FTC Commissioner Jon Leibowitz said companies and government agencies can take other actions to reduce identity theft, such as implementing better processes for protecting data and developing better fraud detection technologies" (Vijayan, 2006, p.22). It is further useful to underscore a more important point raised by the Social Security Number example. Financial services firms* expend massive resources lobbying against governmental oversight and regulation. Their arguments vary, but often center upon the industry's ability to police itself, arguing that it will do those things in the best interests of itself and its customers, so as to preserve those customers and retain their business. It would seem reasonable to believe that placing consumer privacy as a top concern would be crucial to retaining business. As we have seen, however, consumers do not always have many options, particularly when the majority of firms in the industry are failing to take action. Firms deserve blame in this case, particularly considering the relatively lenient measures they have taken on the whole. Consumer choice is only a viable argument when a true choice is represented. In the financial services sector, where the quantity of firms performing a particular function is limited, and in which these firms typically have the resources to shield consumers from learning of firm setbacks and limitations, it is even more critical for governmental agencies to impose regulation. Fortunately, this is exactly what the Federal Trade Commission proposes to do. "The FTC itself will continue to move against companies that fail to demonstrate due diligence in protecting sensitive data, Leibowitz said in a statement posted on the commission's Web site. For example, he noted that the FTC levied a $10 million civil penalty against data aggregator ChoicePoint Inc. in January and required it to pay $5 million in restitution to victims of a data theft" (Clifford, 2010). Fortunately for consumers, it is not simply a matter of corporate responsibility—or intelligence—that should give them some degree of hope. The obligation to protect consumer privacy has been a topic of legislation. "The Gramm-Leach-Bliley Act (GLBA), along with additional regulatory guidance from financial regulators, established this obligation and mandated a set of information security best practices aimed at keeping consumers' nonpublic personal information (NPI) private" (Hietala, 2008, p.41). GLBA has shown itself to be imperfect at upholding its mandate, though legislation is only the first step in ensuring compliance.

> Despite the relative maturity of GLBA as a compliance regulation and the fact that it is taken more seriously than other regulations such as the Health Insurance Portability and Accountability Act, or HIPAA (which lacks enforcement), financial institutions are still experiencing significant data losses that compliance was supposed to mitigate. This is evidenced by the fact that numerous financial organizations have had to publicly disclose security breaches. (Hietala, 2008, p.41)

While we have already explored some examples of these breaches and the associated embarrassment they pose to firms—not to mention stock price impact—it is useful to understand exactly what GLBA had attempted to mandate. That is, what steps should firms take with regards to information security in order to comply with the regulation? The answer lies within a seamless integration of what we may call the "privacy priority" within the larger context of a robust

---

* Virtually all companies fall under the umbrella of at least one lobbying initiative. Financial services companies, due to their relative success among industries, have greater resources to pursue such initiatives.

information security program. Privacy, as we have seen, is an inherent component of an effective security program, but corporate information security is a vast landscape in which privacy may not be a central focus. For example, corporations may be focusing their information security resources on tactical initiatives other than those that would specifically support a privacy priority. Research suggests, however, that "to effectively protect access to information, financial institutions need an information privacy program that works hand in glove with the information security function" (Hietala, 2008, p.43). Once again we find that there is a decisive gap between the ends mandated by regulations, and the policies, controls, and procedures which corporations may employ in order to meet these procedures. While this has caused concern for companies in our previous examples, certainly they would not trade this freedom for additional governmental oversight. From an economic perspective, this is good for labor. Firms have little choice but to employ information security experts in order to gain insights. Executive-level buy-in is important as firms look to close the gap between policy and tactical execution. And that gap must be closed, for governmental regulations have gone global, and these regulations are not going away or showing any signs of decreasing. "Without question, with all of the security breaches that have recently been disclosed, legislators in the United States and around the world are getting more aggressive about legislating protections for consumer data" (ibid., 42). For less-savory firms, the easy solution might be to cozy up to regulators. Indeed, firms in the financial industry are often chided for what appears to be close connections to governmental agencies such as the Federal Reserve and the SEC. These examples, however, show that the relationship between governmental regulators and financial institutions is neither parasitic nor egalitarian, but rather practical and symbiotic. Our discussion of the relationship between regulation and financial corporations' information security responses continues with a look at Sarbanes–Oxley.

No discussion of the financial industry would be complete without an examination of Sarbanes–Oxley legislation and its impact on the financial sector. Sarbanes–Oxley (SOX) laid forth a new set of regulations that impact the stance firms must take with regards to confidential information and information security. Passed in 2002, SOX was purported to prevent "an assortment of ills related to corporate finance and reporting. The legislation's vehicles for accomplishing its goals were to be a series of steps designed to ensure that publicly traded corporations instituted adequate financial controls, that they documented those controls, and that they certified their accuracy" (Montana, 2007, p.48). The crux of the SOX challenge is in the ambiguity of its language. The legislation mandates what must be done, but says little to nothing about how firms can implement plans to cooperate with this legislation. In other words, the firms are given the utmost of freedom to determine how they will meet SOX requirements. At first, this would appear to be in line with exactly what firms have demanded of government, yet the evidence suggests most firms have struggled with the implementation and compliance of the legislation. The "be careful what you wish for" axiom applies to this predicament.

The result of Sarbanes–Oxley's ambiguity is a slew of initiatives surrounding financial control, reporting, internal and external communication, and general compliance. Firms have thrown resources haphazardly, in some cases, towards any project that might seem to help them stave off the wrath of SOX noncompliance. This fear-based approach was not without warrant, for "SOX enforced its goals with a very big stick: personal liability and the possibility of criminal penalties for corporate financial officers" (Montana, 2007, p.48). The results of these corporate initiatives are difficult to measure. On one hand, data exist to quantify exactly how drastically companies have been spending money.

"'The Cost of Being Public in the Era of Sarbanes–Oxley,' a study from Foley & Lardner LLP, found that since 2001, the average cost of SOX compliance for companies with under $1 billion in annual revenue has increased more than $1.7 million to about $2.8 million" (SOX Costs Sock

Small Firms, 2008, p.14). Since Sarbanes–Oxley primarily addresses the manner in which companies perform financial reporting, the information security ramifications are not always as clear and direct as they are with regards to an issue like consumer privacy. In this case, companies have the responsibility to organize and segment data as well as aggregate it. This almost certainly requires the use of technology, and the analysis of such key financial data necessitates the use of security controls, as we have already discussed. It is reasonable to believe that the initiatives upon which firms are spending such sums are aimed at this purpose. Despite the complaints of the corporate world and the frustrations on the part of lawmakers eager to see the effects of their legislation take hold, some suggest the initiative has been constructive overall.

> There have been some positive aspects of Sarbanes–Oxley. First, it did re-orient us back to first principles—an independent board, an independent auditor, a Chief Executive Officer who is willing to sign the bottom line in a certification that says, "I know what my financials mean, and what they mean is what I tell you," and then finally a CEO who is also going to be held responsible for whether or not there are adequate controls that support that certification. Those should be no-brainers. And that is Sarbanes–Oxley. (Aufhauser, 2007, p.435)

Perhaps the silver lining of the legislation is contained in this sentiment. A final interesting note about the corporate grumbling over the costs of these initiatives is that "while many [corporations] complain about the cost of SOX, no one is as yet unable to meet it" (Montana, 2007, p.53).

Through our analysis of financial services firms, we have identified issues which apply specifically to that industry vertical, along with general concerns which affect all firms, regardless of vertical. Throughout the examination, a few key results have become clear. First, firms absolutely must invest in information security initiatives, both to comply with regulations and to hedge against a loss of consumer confidence. Second, firms in all verticals, including financial firms, have done a relatively poor job to date of executing these initiatives. This point is supported by the fact that many regulations stipulate the ends which must be met, but provide few insights into the best means by which to meet them. Firms then find themselves lost, scrambling to develop strategies, struggling to implement controls, and confused as to where the budgets for these initiatives will be found. Yet if our examination has uncovered one truth, it is that firms simply cannot afford to place information security anywhere below a top priority. Some of the costs of noncompliance are understood; others have no caps and, therefore, have the potential to bankrupt or destroy firms who find themselves without measures. Risk, we see, is inevitable and universal to financial firms. The costs of prevention and mitigation are significant. But the costs of ignorance are monumental.

References

Aufhauser, D. D. (2007). Overall, Sarbanes–Oxley Good for U.S. Competitiveness. *Texas Review of Law & Politics*. Vol. 12. pp. 433–439.

Burns, J. (2008). Sarbanes–Oxley Costs for Compliance Decline. *Wall Street Journal* [New York, N.Y.] 1 May 2008, Eastern edition: C.3. *Wall Street Journal*. ProQuest. Paul V. Galvin Library, IIT, Chicago, 8 August 2008.

Clifford, S. (2010). F.T.C.: Has Internet Gone beyond Privacy Policies? *The New York Times*, 11 January, 2010. http://mediadecoder.blogs.nytimes.com/2010/01/11/ftc-has-internet-gone-beyond-privacy-policies/.

Conry-Murray, A. (2005). Security Goes to Business School. *Network*, May 1, 2005.

Elms, E. R., LaPrade, J. D., & Maurer, M. L. (2008). Hacking of Corporate Information Systems: Increasing Threats and Potential Risk Management Techniques. *CPCU Journal*. February 2008.

Garg, A., Curtis, J., & Halper, H. (2003). The Financial Impact of IT Security Breaches: What Do Investors Think? *Information Systems Security*. March/April 2003, pp. 22–33.

Hietala, J. (2008). Managing Information Privacy. *Bank Accounting and Finance*. April–May 2008, pp 41–44.

Joellen, P. (2008, April 10). Finance Firms Vow to Do Self-Cleaning. *Wall Street Journal* (Eastern Edition), p. C.2. Retrieved June 13, 2008, from *Wall Street Journal* database (Document ID: 1459634571).

Kirk, J. (2007). U.K. Bank Fined for Loss of Laptop. *ComputerWorld*, 02/19/07, p. 18.

Montana, J. J. D. (2007). The Sarbanes–Oxley Act: Five Years Later. *The Information Management Journal*. November/December 2007, pp. 48–53.

Radcliff, D. (1999). Three Industries, Three Security Needs. *ComputerWorld*. 11/29/99, p. 38.

Rosencrance, L. (2006). SEC Must Shore Up IT Security, Says GAO. *ComputerWorld*. April 10, 2006, p. 23.

SOX Costs Sock Small Firms. (2008). *The Information Management Journal*. March/April 2008.

Vijayan, J. (2006). Financial Industry Looks to Avoid ID Restrictions. *ComputerWorld*. May 22, 2006, p.22.

Chapter 31

Data Security and Privacy Legislation

Salahuddin Kamran

Introduction

The security of personal information and risks to data are paramount concerns addressed in federal and state law, legislation, and regulations. However, in the United States, no comprehensive national law yet exists that generally requires notification of security breaches involving personal information. California paved the way for data breach notification laws back with SB 1386, which took effect in 2003. Since then, forty-six states, the District of Columbia, Puerto Rico, and the Virgin Islands have enacted legislation requiring notification of security breaches involving personal data, according to the National Conference of State Legislatures. Table 31.1 lists the states and corresponding breach notification laws.

Many of the laws, including California's, make exceptions for encrypted data. The state regulations have led to a flurry of disclosures and a constant stream of breaches involving credit card numbers and other personal information.

According to the nonprofit consumer organization Privacy Rights Clearinghouse, as of late March, more than 350 million records containing sensitive personal data had been compromised since 2005. Figures 31.1 and 31.2 shows the number of incidents over time and by breach type as reported by Open Security Foundation's DataLossDB.

In this document we discuss some legislation in the Western world with a focus on the United States.

Privacy Act, 1974

The Privacy Act of 1974 established a code of fair information practice that governs the collection, maintenance, use, and dissemination of personally identifiable information (PII) about individuals that is maintained in systems of records by federal agencies. A system of records is a group of records under the control of an agency from which information is retrieved by the name of the individual or by some identifier assigned to the individual. The Privacy Act requires that agencies give the public notice of their systems of records by publication in the Federal Register.

The Privacy Act states, in part, that no agency shall disclose any record which is contained in a system of records by any means of communication to any person, or to another agency, except pursuant to a written request by, or with the prior written consent of, the individual to whom the record pertains.

Table 31.1 State Breach Notification Laws

Alaska	Alaska Stat. § 45.48.010 et seq.
Arizona	Ariz. Rev. Stat. § 44-7501
Arkansas	Ark. Code § 4-110-101 et seq.
California	Cal. Civ. Code §§ 56.06, 1785.11.2, 1798.29, 1798.82
Colorado	Colo. Rev. Stat. § 6-1-716
Connecticut	Conn. Gen Stat. 36a-701(b)
Delaware	Del. Code tit. 6, § 12B-101 et seq.
Florida	Fla. Stat. § 817.5681
Georgia	Ga. Code §§ 10-1-910, -911
Hawaii	Haw. Rev. Stat. § 487N-2
Idaho	Idaho Code §§ 28-51-104 to 28-51-107, 2010 H.B. 566
Illinois	815 ILCS 530/1 et seq.
Indiana	Ind. Code §§ 24-4.9 et seq., 4-1-11 et seq., 2009 H.B. 1121
Iowa	Iowa Code § 715C.1 (2008 S.F. 2308)
Kansas	Kan. Stat. 50-7a01, 50-7a02
Louisiana	La. Rev. Stat. § 51:3071 et seq.
Maine	Me. Rev. Stat. tit. 10 §§ 1347 et seq., 2009 Public Law 161
Maryland	Md. Code, Com. Law § 14-3501 et seq.
Massachusetts	Mass. Gen. Laws § 93H-1 et seq.
Michigan	Mich. Comp. Laws § 445.72
Minnesota	Minn. Stat. §§ 325E.61, 325E.64
Mississippi	2010 H.B. 583 (effective July 1, 2011)
Missouri	Mo. Rev. Stat. § 407.1500
Montana	Mont. Code § 30-14-1701 et seq., 2009 H.B. 155, Chapter 163
Nebraska	Neb. Rev. Stat. §§ 87-801, -802, -803, -804, -805, -806, -807

Table 31.1 (Continued)   State Breach Notification Laws

Nevada	Nev. Rev. Stat. 603A.010 et seq.
New Hampshire	N.H. Rev. Stat. §§ 359-C:19, -C:20, -C:21
New Jersey	N.J. Stat. 56:8-163
New York	N.Y. Gen. Bus. Law § 899-aa
North Carolina	N.C. Gen. Stat § 75-65
North Dakota	N.D. Cent. Code § 51-30-01 et seq.
Ohio	Ohio Rev. Code §§ 1347.12, 1349.19, 1349.191, 1349.192
Oklahoma	Okla. Stat. § 74-3113.1 and 2008 H.B. 2245
Oregon	Oregon Rev. Stat. § 646A.600 et seq.
Pennsylvania	73 Pa. Stat. § 2303
Rhode Island	R.I. Gen. Laws § 11-49.2-1 et seq.
South Carolina	S.C. Code § 39-1-90
Tennessee	Tenn. Code § 47-18-2107, 2010 S.B. 2793
Texas	Tex. Bus. & Com. Code § 521.03
Utah	Utah Code §§ 13-44-101, -102, -201, -202, -310
Vermont	Vt. Stat. tit. 9 § 2430 et seq.
Virginia	Va. Code § 18.2-186.6, 2010 H.B. 1039 (eff. 1/1/2011)
Washington	Wash. Rev. Code § 19.255.010, 2010 H.B. 1149 (eff. 7/1/2010)
West Virginia	W.V. Code §§ 46A-2A-101 et seq.
Wisconsin	Wis. Stat. § 134.98 et seq.
Wyoming	Wyo. Stat. § 40-12-501 to -502
District of Columbia	D.C. Code § 28- 3851 et seq.
Puerto Rico	10 Laws of Puerto Rico § 4051 et. seq.
Virgin Islands	V.I. Code § 2208

There are specific exceptions for the record allowing the use of personal records for (i) statistical purposes by the Census Bureau and the Bureau of Labor Statistics, (ii) routine uses within a U.S. government agency, (iii) archival purposes "as a record which has sufficient historical or other value to warrant its continued preservation by the United States Government", (iv) law enforcement purposes, (v) congressional investigations, and (vi) other administrative purposes.

The Privacy Act mandates that each U.S. Government agency has in place an administrative and physical security system to prevent the unauthorized release of personal records.

The act also provides individuals with a means by which to seek access to and amend their records, and sets forth various agency record-keeping requirements.

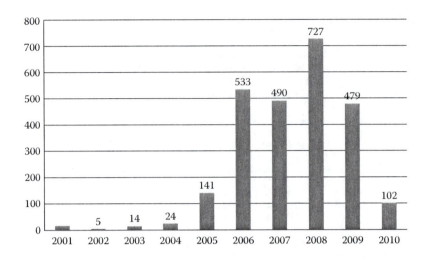

Figure 31.1   Incidents over time. (From Open Security Foundation' DataLossDB.)

Following the controversial Passenger Name Record (PNR) agreement signed with the European Union (EU) in 2007, the Bush administration provided an exemption for the Department of Homeland Security and the Arrival and Departure System (ADIS) from the U.S. Privacy Act. ADIS is intended to authorize people to travel only after PNR and Advance Passenger Information (API) data has been checked and cleared through a U.S. agency watch-list. The Automated Targeting System is also to be exempted. An important point to note is that the Privacy Act does not protect non-U.S. citizens, which is problematic for the exchange of PNR information between the United States and the European Union.

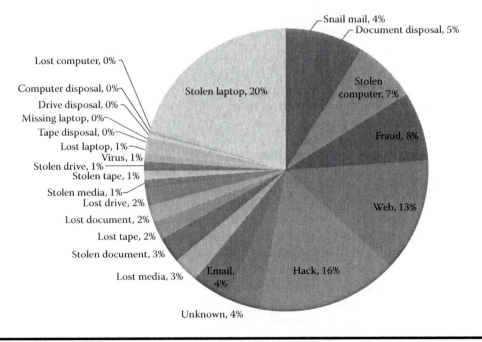

Figure 31.2   Incidents by breach type. (From Open Security Foundation' DataLossDB.)

Computer Matching and Privacy Protection Act, 1988

The Computer Matching and Privacy Protection Act of 1988 amended the Privacy Act of 1974 by adding certain protections for the subjects of Privacy Act records whose records are used in automated matching programs. These protections have been mandated to ensure procedural uniformity in carrying out matching programs, due process for subjects in order to protect their rights, and oversight of matching programs through the establishment of Data Integrity Boards at each agency engaging in matching to monitor the agency's matching activity. The Computer Matching and Privacy Protection Act is codified as part of the Privacy Act.

European Union Data Protection Directive, 1995

The Data Protection Directive is a European Union directive that regulates the processing of personal data within the European Union. It is officially called Directive 95/46/EC on the protection of individuals with regard to the processing of personal data and on the free movement of such data and is an important component of EU privacy and human rights law. The directive was implemented in 1995 by the European Commission.

The right to privacy is a highly developed area of law in Europe. All the member states of the EU are also signatories of the European Convention on Human Rights (ECHR). Article 8 of the ECHR provides a right to respect for one's "private and family life, his home and his correspondence," subject to certain restrictions. The European Court of Human Rights has given this article a very broad interpretation in its jurisprudence. In 1981 the Convention for the Protection of Individuals with regard to Automatic Processing of Personal Data was negotiated within the Council of Europe. This convention obliges the signatories to enact legislation concerning the automatic processing of personal data, which many duly did.

It is necessary to understand how and why EU and U.S. perspectives on data protection and privacy are different. The United States prefers what is called a "sectoral" approach to data protection legislation, relying on a combination of legislation, regulation, and self-regulation, rather than overarching governmental regulations. Former U.S. President Bill Clinton and former Vice President Al Gore explicitly recommended in their "Framework for Global Electronic Commerce" that the private sector should lead and companies should implement self-regulation in reaction to issues brought on by Internet technology. As mentioned earlier, to date, the United States has no single, overarching privacy law comparable to the EU directive. Privacy legislation in the United States tends to be adopted on an "as-needed" basis, with legislation arising when certain sectors and circumstances require. Therefore, while certain sectors may already satisfy the EU directive, at least in part, most do not.

The reasoning behind this approach probably has as much to do with American laissez-faire economics as with different social perspectives. The First Amendment of the United States Constitution guarantees the right to free speech. While free speech is an explicit right guaranteed by the United States Constitution, privacy is an implicit right guaranteed by the Constitution as interpreted by the United States Supreme Court. Europeans are acutely familiar with the dangers associated with uncontrolled use of personal information from their experiences under World War II-era fascist governments and postwar communist regimes, and are highly suspicious and fearful of unchecked use of personal information. In addition, Europe has experienced atrocities directly related to privacy and the release of personal information inconceivable to most Americans. In the age of computers, Europeans' guardedness of secret government files has translated into a distrust of corporate databases and governments in Europe took decided steps to protect personal information from abuses in the years following World War II. Germany and France, in particular, set forth comprehensive data protection laws.

In 1980, in an effort to create a comprehensive data protection system throughout Europe, the Organization for Economic Cooperation and Development (OECD) issued its "Recommendations of the Council Concerning Guidelines Governing the Protection of Privacy and Trans-Border Flows of Personal Data." The OECD guidelines, however, were nonbinding, and data privacy laws still varied widely across Europe. The United States, meanwhile, while endorsing the OECD's recommendations, did nothing to implement them within the United States. However, all seven principles were incorporated into the EU directive.

The European Commission realized that diverging data protection legislation in the EU member states would impede the free flow of data within the EU zone. Therefore, the European Commission decided to harmonize data protection regulation and proposed the directive on the protection of personal data.

The EU directive regulates the processing of personal data, regardless of whether the processing is automated or not. It requires that personal data not be processed at all, except when certain conditions are met. These conditions fall into three categories: transparency, legitimate purpose, and proportionality. The data subject has the right to be informed when his personal data are being processed. The controller must provide his name and address, the purpose of processing, the recipients of the data, and all other information required to ensure the processing is fair. Personal data can only be processed for specified explicit and legitimate purposes and may not be processed further in a way incompatible with those purposes. The data subject even has the right to demand the rectification, deletion, or blocking of data that is incomplete, inaccurate, or isn't being processed in compliance with the data protection rules. Personal data may be processed only insofar as it is adequate, relevant, and not excessive in relation to the purposes for which they are collected and/or further processed. When sensitive personal data is being processed, extra restrictions apply. The data subject may object at any time to the processing of personal data for the purpose of direct marketing.

The directive requires that each member state must set up a supervisory authority, an independent body that monitors the data protection level in that member state, give advice to the government about administrative measures and regulations, and start legal proceedings when data protection regulation has been violated. Individuals may lodge complaints about violations to the supervisory authority or in a court of law.

EU directives are addressed to the member states and aren't legally binding for citizens in principle. The member states are required to transpose the directive into internal law. Directive 95/46/EC on the protection of personal data had to be transposed by the end of 1998. All member states have enacted their own data protection legislation.

Health Insurance Portability and Accountability Act, 1996

The Health Insurance Portability and Accountability Act of 1996 (HIPAA) was passed by Congress to safeguard patient identities, medical records, health insurance activities, and other protected health information (PHI). The regulation mandates that healthcare plans, clearinghouses, and providers take steps to ensure the standardization of electronic patient data, assign unique health identifiers to patients and others, and implement security standards regarding the confidentiality and integrity of patient data.

The HIPAA Security Standards Rule requires healthcare-covered entities to maintain administrative, technical, and physical safeguards to ensure the confidentiality, integrity, and availability of electronic-protected health information; to protect against any reasonably anticipated threats or hazards to the security or integrity of such information; and to protect against any unauthorized uses or disclosures of such information.

United Kingdom Data Protection Act, 1998

The Data Protection Act 1998 (DPA) is a United Kingdom Act of Parliament which defines UK law on the processing of data on identifiable living people. It is the main piece of legislation that governs the protection of personal data in the UK. Although the act itself does not mention privacy, it was enacted to bring UK law into line with the European directive of 1995, which required member states to protect people's fundamental rights and freedoms and in particular their right to privacy with respect to the processing of personal data. In practice it provides a way for individuals to control information about themselves. Most of the act does not apply to domestic use, for example keeping a personal address book. Anyone holding personal data for other purposes is legally obliged to comply with this act, subject to some exemptions.

The 1998 act replaced and consolidated earlier legislation such as the Data Protection Act 1984 and the Access to Personal Files Act 1987. At the same time it aimed to implement the European Data Protection Directive. In some aspects, notably electronic communication and marketing, it has been refined by subsequent legislation. The Privacy and Electronic Communications (EC Directive) Regulations 2003 altered the consent requirement for most electronic marketing to "positive consent," such as an opt-in box. Exemptions remain for the marketing of "similar products and services" to existing customers and enquirers, which is still allowed on an opt-out basis.

The act covers any data about a living and identifiable individual. Anonymized or aggregated data is not regulated by the act, providing the anonymization or aggregation has not been done in a reversible way. Individuals can be identified by various means including their name and address, telephone number, or e-mail address. The act applies only to data that is held, or intended to be held, on computers, or held in a "relevant filing system."

The Data Protection Act creates rights for those who have their data stored, and responsibilities for those who store, process, or collect personal data. The person who has their data processed has the right to view the data an organization holds on them, for a small fee, known as a "subject access fee," or request that incorrect information be corrected. If the company ignores the request, a court can order the data to be corrected or destroyed, and in some cases compensation can be awarded; to require that data is not used in any way that may potentially cause damage or distress; and to require that their data is not used for direct marketing.

The act is structured such that all processing of personal data is covered by the act, while providing a number of exceptions. Notable exceptions are national security, crime, and taxation and domestic purposes.

Children's Online Privacy Protection Act, 1998

The Children's Online Privacy Protection Act of 1998 (COPPA) was enacted in 1998 and applies to the online collection of personal information by persons or entities under U.S. jurisdiction from children under 13 years of age. It requires an owner or operator of a website or online service directed to children, or any operator that collects or maintains personal information from a child, to establish and maintain reasonable procedures to protect the confidentiality, security, and integrity of personal information collected from children. It also details what a website operator must include in a privacy policy when and how to seek verifiable consent from a parent or guardian, and what responsibilities an operator has to protect children's privacy and safety online including restrictions on marketing to those under 13. While children under 13 can legally give out personal information with their parents' permission, many websites altogether disallow underage children from using their services due to the amount of paperwork involved.

Gramm–Leach–Bliley Act, 1999

The Gramm–Leach–Bliley Act (GLBA), also known as the Financial Services Modernization Act of 1999, was enacted to allow commercial and investment banks, securities firms, and insurance companies to consolidate. The law includes three requirements to protect personal data controlled by financial institutions:

■ They must securely store personal financial information.
■ They must advise consumers of their policies on sharing of personal financial information.
■ They must give consumers the option to decline some sharing of personal financial information.

The FTC's Safeguards Rule, issued to implement provisions of the GLBA, requires financial institutions to have an information security plan that contains administrative, technical, and physical safeguards to protect the security, confidentiality, and integrity of personal consumer information.

Interagency guidance issued by the federal banking regulators to implement provisions of the GLBA requires covered entities to implement information security programs to ensure the security and confidentiality of customer information, protect against anticipated threats or hazards to the security or integrity of such information, and protect against unauthorized access to or use of such information that could result in substantial harm or inconvenience to any customer.

In addition to banks, securities firms, and insurance companies, GLBA affects any organization that services consumer loans, transfers money, prepares tax returns, or provides financial advice. GLBA noncompliance can lead to severe civil and criminal penalties, including fines of up to $100,000 per violation and imprisonment.

Federal Information Security Management Act, 2002

The Federal Information Security Management Act of 2002 (FISMA) was enacted in 2002 as Title III of E-Government Act of 2002. The act requires each federal agency to develop, document, and implement an agency-wide program to provide information security for the information and information systems that support the operations and assets of the agency, including those provided or managed by another agency, contractor, or other source.

FISMA brought attention within the federal government to cybersecurity and explicitly emphasized a "risk-based policy for cost-effective security." It requires agency program officials, chief information officers, and inspectors general to conduct annual reviews of the agency's information security program and report the results to the Office of Management and Budget (OMB). OMB uses this data to assist in its oversight responsibilities and to prepare this annual report to Congress on agency compliance with the act. In FY 2008, federal agencies spent $6.2 billion securing the government's total information technology investment of approximately $68 billion or about 9.2% of the total information technology portfolio.

FISMA assigns specific responsibilities to federal agencies, the National Institute of Standards and Technology (NIST), and OMB in order to strengthen information system security. In particular, FISMA requires the head of each agency to implement policies and procedures to cost-effectively reduce information technology security risks to an acceptable level. According to FISMA, the term *information security* means protecting information and information systems from unauthorized access, use, disclosure, disruption, modification, or destruction in order to provide integrity, confidentiality, and availability.

As a key element of the FISMA Implementation Project, NIST also developed an integrated risk framework, which effectively brings together all of the FISMA-related security standards and guidance to promote the development of comprehensive and balanced information security programs by agencies.

California Security Breach Information Act, 2002

California Security Breach Information Act of 2002 (SB1386) is a California law regulating the privacy of personal information. The act has specific and restrictive privacy breach reporting requirements. SB 1386 requires companies that collect and hold personal information on California residents—whether customers, employees, or individuals involved in some facet of the business—to notify immediately each person on their database should an information security breach occur or if one is suspected. (Encrypted data is excluded from this requirement.)

SB 1386 is applicable to all organizations—state government agencies and nonprofit organizations—as well as companies of all sizes, regardless of geographic location, that hold personal data on persons living in California. SB 1386 requires these organizations to disclose any unauthorized access of computerized data files containing personal information.

SB 1386 gives consumers the right to sue businesses in civil court for damages incurred through the compromise of such information. The costs and penalties of civil litigation, coupled with a tarnished public image, can cause untold long-term damage to the organization.

Massachusetts 201 CMT 17.00 LAW, 2010

The Massachusetts Data Protection Regulations took effect on March 1, 2010. Any person or business with personal information about a Massachusetts resident must comply with a new regulatory scheme intended to protect that information from improper use or disclosure. The Office of Consumer Affairs and Business Regulations originally promulgated the regulations in fall 2008, mandating that those holding personal information about Massachusetts residents devise and implement specific, detailed policies to protect the security and integrity of that information. Virtually all Massachusetts businesses are covered and the regulations also apply to entities outside the Commonwealth that hold Massachusetts residents' Social Security Numbers, credit card numbers, driver's license numbers, or financial account numbers.

The regulations apply to both paper and electronic records, and can cover such commonplace items as benefits records, payroll files, invoices evidencing customer payments, and databases that use Social Security Numbers as unique identifiers. Virtually any business with a Massachusetts employee falls under the regulations' scope.

The regulatory requirements are extensive and detailed, and demand the adoption and maintenance of a written information security plan and designation of an individual to be responsible for it. The information security plan must:

1. Identify reasonably foreseeable risks to records containing personal information.
2. Address policies regarding the storage and transportation of records outside of business premises.
3. Mandate disciplinary measures for violations.
4. Prevent access to personal information by former employees.
5. With respect to third-party service providers with access to personal information, it must provide for due diligence and appropriate contractual terms to ensure that the contract will treat such information in a manner consistent with regulatory mandates.
6. Require physical records containing personal information to be kept in locked containers or facilities.
7. Provide for regular monitoring of the plan, and for updates when circumstances merit.
8. Establish procedures for postincident actions in the event of a data breach.
9. Require secure user authentication protocols with respect to computer equipment that can access personal information.
10. Impose access control measures such that only those individuals with a need can access electronic personal information records.
11. Require the encryption of any personal information that is transmitted over the Internet, transmitted over an unsecured wireless network, stored on a laptop, or stored on a portable device such as a BlackBerry.
12. Provide for up-to-date antivirus software, operating system security patches, and firewall patches with respect to any computers that can access personal information.
13. Establish regular education and training of employees on the proper use of computer security systems and the importance of personal information security.

While the regulations are directly enforceable by the Attorney General, a business's failure to comply with them may leave it exposed to civil litigation, jeopardize insurance coverage, and put it at risk of breaching contractual representations and commitments.

Nevada Law SB227, 2010

Senate Bill No. 227 was signed into law on May 29, 2009, and went into effect on January 1, 2010. This law repealed data protection law NRS 597.970, which had been in effect for less than a year. Among other things, the new law requires data collectors to use cryptographic key technology that meets established industry standards and, if they accept credit or debit cards, to comply with the Payment Card Industry Data Security Standard (PCI DSS) with respect to those transactions.

In late 2007 Nevada became one of two states in the country (the other being Massachusetts) to depart from a technology-neutral regulatory standard and specifically require the use of encryption to protect certain data transfers. The original Nevada data protection law, which became effective on October 1, 2008, provided that businesses could not electronically transmit "any personal information of a customer" (other than by fax) "outside of the secure system of the business" unless encryption was used to ensure the security of the transmission.

Personal information is defined as information consisting of an individual's last name and first name (or first initial), combined with his or her Social Security Number, driver's license or identification card number, or financial account number plus password or access code.

However, encryption was very loosely defined as "the use of any protective or disruptive measure [including cryptography] to: 1. Prevent, impede, delay or disrupt access to any data, information, image, program, signal or sound; 2. Cause or make any data, information, image, program, signal or sound unintelligible or unusable; or 3. Prevent, impede, delay or disrupt the normal operation or use of any component, device, equipment, system or network."

By this standard, simply requiring a user to input a password to open a file would have been sufficient for compliance. The statute prescribed no specific penalties or remedies for violators.

Senate Bill 227 applies more rigorous technical standards to "data collectors" who do business in the state. A data collector is any organization (including a nonprofit or agency) that "handles, collects, disseminates or otherwise deals with nonpublic personal information." Any organization with customers, employees, or operations in Nevada must comply.

The centerpiece of the new law is its requirement that data collectors must comply with the most current applicable PCI DSS with respect to their payment card transactions and, with respect to all other matters, must encrypt personal information transmitted "through an electronic, non-voice transmission other than a facsimile" outside of the data collector's secure system. Personal information covered by the statute includes employee and other noncustomer data. Encryption is now explicitly defined as the protection of data by means of a technology that renders the data indecipherable without the use of cryptographic keys.

The encryption technology must have been adopted by an established standards-setting body, including, but not limited to, the standards issued by the NIST. It must also incorporate "appropriate management and safeguards of cryptographic keys to protect the integrity of the encryption," using guidelines issued by an established standards-setting body. Data collectors must also encrypt personal information stored on any device or medium (including any portable device or medium such as a laptop, thumb drive, mobile phone, CD, or magnetic tape) that is moved "beyond the logical or physical controls" of the data collector or its data storage vendor. This requirement imposes a clear obligation to monitor and enforce compliance by vendors. If a vendor is to be entrusted with personal information, the data collector needs to review the vendor's information security program beforehand to verify compliance with the encryption requirement and should include this requirement in its contract with the vendor. It should also reserve the right to audit the vendor's information security practices for ongoing compliance.

The new law contains exemptions for telecommunications providers and certain payment processing and account activities conducted through a secure, private channel, as well as for fax transmissions. As might be expected, telecommunications providers are not required to encrypt communications when they are acting solely in the role of conveying the communications for third parties. Also exempt are data transmissions over a secure, private communication channel for approval or processing of negotiable instruments, electronic fund transfers or similar payment methods, or for issuance of account closure reports.

Like its predecessor, Senate Bill 227 does not spell out the consequences of violation. The law effectively creates what is known as a statutory standard of care, meaning that a failure to utilize the required encryption resulting in unauthorized access or interception of unencrypted data may render the data collector liable for negligence. The statute provides a safe harbor where compliance will insulate a data collector from liability for damages for a data breach, unless the data breach is caused by the gross negligence or intentional misconduct of the data collector or its officers, employees, or agents.

Like Massachusetts's regulation 201 CMR 17.00, which requires encryption as part of a comprehensive written information security program, Senate Bill 227 signals a more top-down regulatory approach that leaves businesses less discretion to choose their methodologies for managing information security risk.

H.R. 2221 Data Accountability and Trust Act (DATA)

The House of Representatives approved the new Data Accountability and Trust Act (DATA) on December 8, 2009. If passed, the act would preempt many state breach notification laws and introduce a federal notification requirement. The DATA is a comprehensive federal data security law that explicitly preempts state law—including state breach notice laws passed in approximately 46 U.S. states. If passed in its current form, it will likely have a significant impact on a substantial majority of companies handling personal information of U.S. residents.

The act addresses three main areas:

1. Information security requirements for personal information in general.
2. Information security requirements for personal information for "information brokers."
3. Breach notice obligations. This article focuses on the act's breach notice obligations.

In many respects, DATA's breach notice obligations include the same or similar elements as the breach notice laws currently in place in most states. The following elements are common—but perhaps not exactly the same—in both DATA and many state breach notice laws:

■ The person or entity that "owns or possesses" personal information has the primary obligation to notify the affected individuals. Third-party agents and service providers maintaining or processing data on behalf of the data owner/possessor have an obligation to notify the owner/possessor of a security breach.
■ Delay of notification is permitted if law enforcement determines that notification would impede a criminal or civil investigation.
■ The primary means of notice is via written notification or by e-mail but only if e-mail is the primary means of communication and the consent requirements of the ESIGN Act (15 U.S.C. 7001) have been satisfied.
■ Substitute notice is allowed under certain circumstances, including e-mail notification, notice via a website, and notification in print and broadcast media.
■ Notice is required only if a risk of harm threshold has been met. DATA's harm threshold is higher than that in many state breach notice laws.
■ Encrypted personal data may allow entities to avoid notice obligations, although DATA provides a "presumption" of no harm rather than a strict encryption "safe harbor."
■ Notification is triggered by unauthorized access to or acquisition of data in electronic form.
■ The definition of personal information is first name/initial and last name in combination with one or more data elements typically listed in state breach notice laws (e.g., Social Security Number, driver's license/ID card, or financial account/payment card number and required security/access code).

If passed in its current form, the breach notice provisions of DATA will include some significant variations from most current state breach notice laws. Based on the preemption provisions in the act, these differences could change the breach notice landscape relative to existing state laws:

- Notice must be provided within 60 days after the discovery of a breach of security (some states do impose specified deadlines for notice—the Florida notice deadline is 45 days).
- Notice must be provided to the Federal Trade Commission (FTC) in addition to affected individuals and the FTC has the option, at its discretion, to post the notice letter on its website (many state laws require a notice to state attorneys general).
- For breaches involving more than 5,000 affected individuals, notice must be provided without unreasonable delay to the major credit-reporting agencies.
- The notices must include a toll-free number that affected individuals can call to receive information about the breach (e.g., a call center).
- The entity must offer affected individuals, free of charge, two years of credit monitoring services or access to their credit reports on a quarterly basis.
- Notice can be delayed if a federal national security agency determines that notification would threaten U.S. national security.
- The risk of harm threshold provides that notice is required unless there is no reasonable risk of identity theft, fraud, or other unlawful conduct.
- Civil penalties of up to $11,000 per violation are possible, with an aggregate cap of $5 million per breach of security. Each failure to send the required notification is treated as a separate violation.
- The act explicitly does not provide a private right of action (many states' breach notice laws don't provide a private right of action, although some are less explicit than others).

DATA's breach notice obligations have the potential to significantly alter the breach notice landscape in the United States. Following is a brief discussion of some of the potential material impacts of DATA if passed in its current form.

Preemption

One of the most significant DATA impacts arises out of its preemption clause, which appears to fully preempt state law. Unlike the HIPAA, DATA does not preempt only those state laws that are "less stringent" or "contrary to" the act. Rather, DATA "supersedes any provision of a statute, regulation, or rule of a State...that expressly...requires notification to individuals of a breach of security resulting in unauthorized access to or acquisition of data in electronic form containing personal information." However, there is one significant caveat with respect to preemption: the act does not apply to every person or entity in the United States. Rather, DATA only applies to those entities over which the FTC has authority pursuant to section 5(a)(2) of the Federal Trade Commission Act. As such, DATA would not appear to apply to financial institutions, insurance companies, governmental bodies, or common carriers (e.g., telecommunications companies or transportation companies). Those entities would still be required to comply with state breach notice laws, even if DATA is passed.

Risk of Harm

The trigger for state breach notice laws often comes down to the risk of harm posed to personal information by the security breach. On one end of the spectrum are those laws that are triggered by a reasonable belief of unauthorized access to personal information, while others require a likelihood of "harm" or "misuse" of personal information. Assuming DATA is passed and fully preempts state laws, all of these competing standards would be eliminated. Instead, notice would be required only if the breached entity determines there is a "reasonable risk of identity theft, fraud or other unlawful conduct." This risk of harm standard arguably falls on the higher end of the spectrum. For example, in the case of a lost laptop, without evidence that the laptop fell into the hands of wrongdoers, there may not be a reasonable risk of identity theft, fraud, or unlawful conduct. In contrast, if the notice trigger was a reasonable belief of unauthorized acquisition, notice to affected individuals of the missing laptop might be required. The overall impact of this change is likely to be less reporting of breaches.

Enforcement

The act directs the FTC to create rules for destroying obsolete nonelectronic data in addition to requiring data brokers to submit their security policies to the FTC in conjunction with a security breach notification or on FTC request. If a breach does occur, the FTC is ordered to conduct a security audit of the data broker. However, it is interesting to note that the FTC's jurisdiction does not extend to a number of organizations, including nonprofit organizations, government agencies, and depository institutions.

While the trigger for DATA may be relatively higher, the enforcement provisions of the act could act as a counterbalance. Even though the act does not provide for a private right of action, it does provide for potentially significant civil penalties in the event the act is not complied with. Under the act, the FTC can impose civil penalties of up to $11,000 per violation and each failure to send the required notification to an affected individual is treated as a separate violation. However, civil penalties are limited to $5 million per breach of security. The magnitude of the potential expenses that arise out of a breach covered under DATA represent a major change from state breach notice laws. Ironically, they also may encourage companies to avoid reporting breaches in order to avoid substantial expenses, acting as a counterforce to the civil penalties under the act.

Conclusion

The Massachusetts and Nevada laws have changed the way the state and federal governments will deal with personal data protection. It appears to be a fact of life that organizations that handle protected data in whatever form (health care, financial, or identity) need to maintain formal security and compliance programs. While the formality and extent of the programs are allowed to be structured according to the size and resources of a given organization and geared to risk of compromise, it is unlikely that the courts will look favorably on any organization that does not implement a formal security program. It is important for organizations to recognize that the time and expense involved in complying with new state data protection laws will produce benefits over time, reducing the likelihood of compromise while at the same time avoiding costly noncompliance penalties. The release of personal data—whether through human error or criminal activities—is both disruptive and costly and can be disastrous for customers and the organizations that serve them.

About the Author

Salahuddin Kamran, CISSP, CISA, CISM, CFE, EnCE, has more than 20 years of experience in IT security, computer forensics, electronic discovery, and litigation consulting. He also has significant experience in regulatory compliance audits. He currently is a senior director at Alvarez & Marsal's Forensic Technology and Security practice of DA&F and provides litigation consulting and electronic discovery services. He previously worked in the IT security and high-tech investigations group at Aon Corporation; prior to that he worked at Kroll Worldwide and Marsh & McLennan Companies. He has spoken at conferences on topics such as electronic discovery, privacy, and data spoliation. He has consulted numerous Fortune 100 companies on projects, including network architecture, litigation consulting, and regulatory compliance.

Incident Handling

Chapter 32

Discovery of Electronically Stored Information

Salahuddin Kamran

Introduction

Discovery is the pretrial exchange of information by parties in a case. E-discovery refers to the discovery of all electronically stored information (ESI)—information such as e-mail messages, web pages, instant messages, voice mails, cell phone and pager text messages, websites, call logs, word processing documents, databases, digital photos, spreadsheets, and virtually any information that is stored on a computer or other electronic device, as well as backup and archived copies of that same information. Technically, information is "electronic" if it exists in a medium that can be read through the use of computers or other digital devices. Such media include random access memory, magnetic disks (such as computer hard drives or floppy disks), optical disks (such as DVDs or CDs), and magnetic tapes. Electronic discovery can be distinguished from "paper discovery," which refers to the discovery of writings on paper that can be read without the aid of electronic devices.

As businesses have begun to keep most records as electronically stored information (ESI), scholars and practitioners have debated how liberal electronic discovery (e-discovery) standards should be. Amendments to the Federal Rules of Civil Procedure (the Rules) have sought to reduce the "uncertainty, expense, delays and burdens" created by discovering volumes of electronic data. Reformers amended the discovery Rules in 1983, 1993, and 2000 to limit abuses that developed under the traditional presumption favoring free discovery. In 2006, further amendments focused on e-discovery and introduced a new but undefined category of electronic evidence that is "not reasonably accessible." The amended Rule 26 requires the requesting party to make certain showings before being granted discovery. Even then, a court may shift the costs of discovery, compelling the party requesting the documents to pay some or all of the costs of production. Cost-shifting existed before 2006 as a matter of judicial discretion, but the commentary to the amended Rules expressly incorporates the term for the first time, which may encourage using cost-shifting to limit e-discovery inappropriately.

Electronically stored information is not only wide-ranging, but is now a fundamental and integral part of American life. By all accounts, more than 90% of the information developed today is created and stored electronically, and most will never be printed out. Moreover, the volume of information being created is staggering: for example, it is estimated that American businesses exchange about 2.5 trillion e-mails annually, and 75% of those e-mails are believed to contain proprietary information. In an increasing number of disputes, information relevant to the parties' claims and defenses is no longer in a filing cabinet but on a hard drive.

E-discovery is a complex and difficult process and requires a very high degree of collaboration between technical, legal, and business people.

How Are Electronic Documents Different from Paper Documents?

Electronically stored information presents unique opportunities and problems for document production. These subtle, but sometimes profound, differences can be grouped into six broad categories.

Large Volume and Ease of Duplication

Electronically stored information is created at much greater rates than paper documents and, therefore, there are vastly more electronic documents than paper documents. Today, the great majority of households and businesses in the United States are connected to the Internet. The dramatic increase in e-mail usage and electronic file generation poses special problems for large corporations. A single large corporation can generate and receive millions of e-mails and electronic files each day. Ninety-two percent of new information is stored on magnetic media, primarily hard disks, compared to 0.01% for paper. Not surprisingly, the proliferation of the use of electronic data in corporations has resulted in vast accumulations of data. While a few thousand paper documents fill a file cabinet, a single computer tape or disk drive the size of a small book can hold the equivalent of millions of printed pages. Organizations often accumulate thousands of such disks and tapes as data is stored, transmitted, copied, replicated, backed up, and archived.

Electronic documents are more easily duplicated than paper documents. For example, e-mail users frequently send the same e-mail to many recipients. These recipients, in turn, often forward the message, and so on. At the same time, e-mail software and the systems that are used to transmit the messages automatically create multiple copies as the messages are sent and re-sent. Similarly, other business applications are designed to periodically and automatically make copies of data. Examples of these applications include web pages that are automatically saved and file data that is routinely backed up to protect against inadvertent deletion or system failure.

Persistence

Electronic documents are more difficult to dispose of than paper documents. Despite the attempt to delete electronic documents, information may remain on an electronic storage device until it is overwritten by new data. Meanwhile it may still be available for discovery. In Prism Hospital Software Inc. v. The Hospital Records Institute, the defendants produced a quantity of magnetic media from which the plaintiff was able to locate a series of files that, though "deleted," continued to exist. This persistence of electronically stored information compounds the rate at which it accumulates in places hidden from custodians who may have no idea that the information is still available on their computers. Due to the difficulty of fully deleting electronically stored information, software is sold that purports to completely erase or "wipe" the data by repeatedly overwriting the data numerous times.

Metadata

Electronic documents contain information known as "metadata," which is information created by the operating system or application about a file that allows the operating system or application to store and retrieve the file at a later date. Much metadata is not accessible by the computer user without special tools.

Metadata includes information on file designation, creation and edit dates, authorship, and edit history, as well as hundreds of other pieces of information used in system administration. For instance, e-mail metadata elements include the dates that mail was sent, received, replied to, or forwarded, blind carbon copy ("bcc") information, and sender address book information. Internet documents contain hidden data that allow for the transmission of information between an Internet user's computer and the server on which the document is located. So-called "meta tags" allow search engines to locate websites responsive to specified search criteria. "Cookies" are embedded codes that can be placed on a computer (without user knowledge) that can, among other things, track usage and transmit information back to the originator of the cookie.

Metadata presents unique issues for the preservation and production of documents in litigation. On the one hand, it is easy to conceive of situations where metadata is necessary to authenticate a document or establish facts material to a dispute, such as when a file was accessed in a suit involving theft of trade secrets. There is also a real danger that information recorded by the computer may be inaccurate. For example, when a new employee uses a word processing program to create a memorandum by using a memorandum template created by a former employee, the metadata for the new memorandum may incorrectly identify the former employee as the author. E-mail, on the other hand, may have some very useful metadata that can be extracted and used to generate the to:, from:, date:, and cc: fields for use in the review or litigation support tool. Unlike the possibly erroneous information that might be transferred from a template, some e-mail metadata is generally accurate, and capturing it automatically can save time and money. Deciding what metadata needs to be specifically preserved and produced represents one of the biggest challenges in electronic document production.

Dynamic, Changeable Content

Unlike paper documents, electronic documents have dynamic features that may change over time, often without the user even being aware of the changes taking place. Databases are constantly being updated with new information, most often through direct user input, but also automatically through other systems. For example, a store with fourteen locations may have the accounting system at each location update a main system with daily sales information. Because the stores may be located in several time zones, the updated data will appear at various times throughout the day. Under this scenario, deciding which "version" of the database is the appropriate one to preserve for discovery may be problematic.

Standard office applications like electronic mail, word processors, or spreadsheets also have dynamic features. Opening an electronic mail message can change dates and times. Metadata elements change to reflect new dates and times each time a spreadsheet or word processed document is copied. Files that have other files linked with them, or embedded within them, may change whenever the related file changes. The move towards sharing application data files among many users ("virtual" work groups) further compounds discovery problems as the data within the file can change without any particular custodian being aware of the change.

In the course of discovery, managing the dynamic nature of electronically stored information is an ongoing challenge.

Electronic Data Often Need a Computer Program, Which May Become Obsolete

Electronic data, unlike paper data, may be incomprehensible when separated from the working environment. For example, information in a database is organized into structured fields interpreted by an application. Without the application, the raw data in the database will appear as a long list of undefined characters. To make sense of the data, a viewer needs the context, including labels, columns, report formats, and other information. Existing or customized "reports" based on queries of the database can be generated without producing the entire database. It is normal for an organization to upgrade its systems every few years, but technological change and obsolescence can create unique issues for recovering "legacy data" not present in the recovery of paper documents. Neither the personnel familiar with the obsolete systems nor the technological infrastructure necessary to restore the out-of-date systems may be available when this "legacy" data needs to be accessed. In a perfect world, electronically stored information that has continuing value for business purposes or litigation would be converted for use in successor systems, and all other data would be discarded. In reality, such migrations are rarely flawless.

Electronic Documents Are Searchable and May Be Dispersed in Many Locations

While paper documents will often be consolidated in a handful of boxes or filing cabinets, employees' electronically stored information could reside in numerous locations, such as desktop hard drives, laptop computers, network servers, handheld digital devices, floppy disks, CDs, and backup tapes. Many of these electronic documents may be identical copies. Others may be earlier versions drafted by a single employee, or by other employees working on a shared network.

The ease of transmission, routine modification, and a multiuser editing process may obscure the origin of a document. Electronic files are often stored in shared network folders that may have departmental or functional designations rather than author information. In addition, there is growing use of collaborative software that allows for group editing of electronically stored information, rendering the determination of authorship far more difficult. Finally, while electronically stored information may be stored on a single drive, it may also be found on high-capacity, undifferentiated backup media, or on network servers not under the custodianship of the individual who may have created the document.

Counterbalancing the dispersed nature of electronically stored information is the fact that some forms and media can be searched quickly and fairly accurately by automated methods. For these types of electronically stored information, lawyers may be able to search through far more documents than they could hope to review manually.

Electronic Discovery Lifecycle

The concept of an e-discovery work flow is a comprehensive concept that will help guide the e-discovery practitioner through the various stages of the process. The Electronic Discovery Reference Model Project—a team of service and software providers, corporations, and legal organizations who came together to create standards for the practice of e-discovery—provides the most widely accepted outline of the e-discovery work flow. This Electronic Discovery Reference Model is shown in Figure 32.1.

The EDRM work flow creates a flexible conceptual framework for e-discovery. It begins on the left with an immense amount of ESI (represented by the yellow "volume" portion of the graphic) with only a small percentage of relevant data (represented by the orange "relevance" portion). The end result of following the work flow is a small amount of overall data, with a large percentage of relevant, useful information ready for production, settlement conferences, and/or trial.

Each step of the work flow represents a discrete task with a set of specific goals. The overall goal is to progress from left to right along the work flow, but it might become necessary to revisit stages along the way. For example, while conducting an analysis of the collected data, new issues may arise that will require identification and preservation of additional ESI. Participants in the process should return to the identification stage to locate appropriate ESI, which will in turn require new preservation, collection, and analysis.

Information Management

The e-discovery work flow begins with the document retention policies of the organization. Companies should have a document retention policy that must be actively enforced and audited. Although the case law may appear to mandate keeping everything for an indefinite period of time, recent decisions have indicated that even companies in continuous litigation are not required to keep every "shred of paper, every email or electronic document and every backup tape … Such a requirement would cripple large corporations" (*Zubulake IV*). Thus, outside of industry regulations and any litigation hold requirement, a company need only keep electronic information as

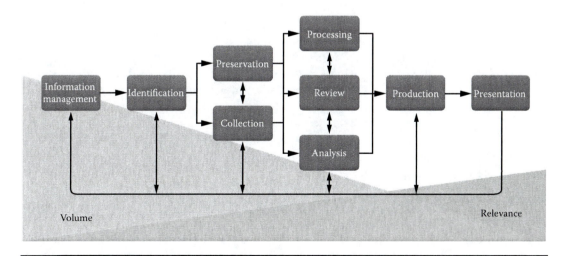

Figure 32.1 Electronic discovery reference model. (Copyright EDRM [edrm.net].)

long as necessary for business purposes—but no longer than that. If a document retention policy limits how long information is kept, companies will have less information to search and review if served with a document request. For example, if a company's policy is to hold on to documents for two years, then once a litigation hold is in place, there should only be two years of stored information that must be searched in order to find relevant documents. This can save a company time and money in the long run, as the most expensive part of any discovery phase is the attorney time spent reviewing documents.

Under the amendments to the Federal Rules of Civil Procedure, only electronic information that is "reasonably accessible due to undue burden or cost" is discoverable. If the proposed amendments are adopted, a good policy will put a company in control of what is available and discoverable under the new federal rules.

A good document retention policy can also be used as a litigation preparedness tool and will give in-house and outside counsel a roadmap to finding documents in the event of a document request. In order to create a workable policy, companies must know where all of their documents and information are kept and how that information is stored. *Coleman Holdings* can be seen as a cautionary tale of a corporation (Morgan Stanley) that did not know where it stored and kept all of its electronic data. After the company was found guilty of discovery abuses stemming primarily from its lack of knowledge about the location of its discoverable information, a jury awarded the plaintiff $1.4 billion in compensatory and punitive damages. A comprehensive document retention policy would have directed the company to its relevant documents.

Any policy should also state the names of the custodians of the information and should list the types of servers and backup tapes that are used. Creating a policy will also require counsel to become familiar with their client's IT systems, which will be necessary if a court ever requires an explanation. In fact, some local federal rules, such as the U.S. District Court of New Jersey, currently require attorneys to understand these systems before an F.R.C.P. 26(f) conference. The amendments to the Federal Rules also require attorneys have a working knowledge of their clients' IT systems. Pairing with a client's IT department early can also prevent problems later on. Many corporate IT departments are not equipped to handle the volume of document retrieval that is often involved in litigation or government inquiries. Knowledge of the capabilities of an IT department will allow a corporation to hire outside vendors who can help archive data so that it is searchable later if needed.

In the end, when it comes down to litigation or a government information request, the most important reason for a company to have a workable and active document retention policy is that it can persuade a court that documents that no longer exist were purged pursuant to a policy and not willfully destroyed and spoliated. Courts do not have a lot of patience for companies that mismanage or delete documents on an inconsistent basis. The amendments to the Federal Rules even contain a "safe harbor" for companies who fail to provide electronically stored information lost as a result of the routine, good faith operation of an electronic information system. If a company's policy is comprehensive and routinely audited, it can provide the court with assurance that a company has all of the information it is required to keep and knows how to find it, which can go a long way to protecting a corporation in the long run.

Identification

Once an event occurs that puts a client in reasonable anticipation of litigation, it becomes vitally important to identify the location of all relevant information. During this stage, attorneys and clients will need to list the custodians of the data, determine the time frames involved, identify the types of documents, map the client's information systems, and decide whether or not forensic data retrieval is necessary.

One of the biggest problems with preservation is the unknown. One of the reasons that in-house lawyers should lead the preservation process is the fact that they know a lot more about who and what should be subject to a legal hold than an outside lawyer or consultant could possibly know. But in many organizations the in-house lawyers still cannot know all the custodians and systems that might be relevant to a particular matter. As such, corporations should have a preservation process that includes immediate meetings with IT and a few key people who have knowledge about the facts of the case to discuss what should be preserved. The team should also identify the key systems and databases that are likely to come up regularly in litigation and discuss specific ways for preserving that data (Figure 32.2).

Preservation and Collection

During this crucial stage, attorneys must first ascertain when exactly the duty to preserve arises. Then, they must begin the process of saving and collecting all relevant data in all relevant formats in all relevant locations. This quickly amounts to a mammoth store of information from points around the globe. The Federal Rules stress reasonableness in this area, and mandate a meet and confer between opposing counsel to establish preservation approaches and definitions for what may be considered relevant material. This can help corral e-discovery costs and ensure a more efficient pretrial process (Figure 32.3).

The plan for preservation is an integral part of a successful process. Without proper preservation, the risk of a spoliation claim increases dramatically. On the other hand, preserving too much can lead to higher costs throughout the process. Corporations must be mindful of ways to control the volume at every stage and thus control the costs. Plans for preservation need to include the following:

■ *Communicate a litigation hold to individual employees*: Most companies create a standard form that includes the name of the matter, what it is about, and the types of documents that need to be held. Employees should be required to respond and confirm whether or not they have responsive documents and whether they are holding those documents. The employees should also be given training and instruction on why legal holds are important, the consequences to them and the company for noncompliance, and how and where to hold documents. The

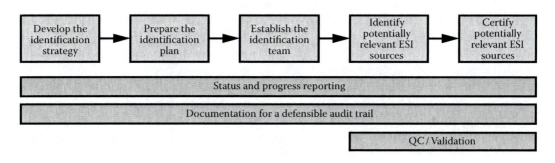

Figure 32.2   Identification process flow. (Copyright EDRM [edrm.net].)

Figure 32.3   Preservation process flow. (Copyright EDRM [edrm.net].)

legal department should issue the hold, but based on the size of the organization, help may be needed from the business units to distribute the notices to the appropriate individuals and collect their responses. Working with IT, compliance, and records management allows corporations to integrate the legal hold process into other compliance and records management processes.

■ *Communicate with IT*: The IT team plays a key role in preserving much of the data needed for a case. A clear process is required for requesting a hold of particular data, including who is authorized to make the request and who should receive it, a time frame in which IT will respond, and a method for IT to confirm compliance. IT also needs to ensure that the data cannot be accidentally deleted, and there should be a clear process for lifting the hold. Because preservation often comes at some cost, such as in additional server space, extra backup tapes, etc., corporations should also determine how those costs will be covered.

■ *Document the process*: When a litigation matter comes in, teams will need to document the decisions and steps it took to ensure proper preservation. In case the process is questioned, a protocol should be put into place to ensure that the documentation is kept in one place so it can be quickly converted into an affidavit. An in-house paralegal or litigation support manager is usually a good person to lead the preservation effort and document the steps. Teams should make sure that the thoroughness and reasonableness of the process are documented in case something is missing at some point.

■ *Issue preservation reminders*: The process should also include a way to issue periodic reminders to custodians and IT about the legal hold. Reminders that come too often lose their effectiveness, but quarterly or every six months is a good guideline. Deciding whether to send specific reminders to individuals or general reminders to all employees will depend on the cases and the company culture.

Backup tapes probably represent the most difficult preservation decision in any matter. Before deciding how to handle it, e-discovery teams need a process in place that ensures the quick preservation of tapes. As an initial matter, a clear policy is needed to establish that backup tapes will only be used for disaster recovery. As part of enforcing that policy, tapes should be rotated at reasonable intervals (15–45 days is customary) and should not be restored unless doing so is necessary for disaster recovery. By using tapes to find information, corporations run the risk of a court deciding they are utilizing an archive system deemed reasonably accessible under the new Federal Rules. Teams should work with IT to make sure tape retention policies are enforced and that proper storage of backup tapes is in place. The stories about unmarked backup tapes in closets or under floorboards are real (just ask Morgan Stanley). Before backup tapes can be taken out of rotation, approval should be required from a specially selected legal team member. IT and legal should keep an inventory of what tapes are subject to a legal hold and why, and a very detailed description of the tape content should be included in the inventory.

Preserving backup tapes over the life of a case can be quite expensive, particularly for corporations that have many tapes and many lawsuits. This struggle is one of the reasons companies have gone to e-mail archiving. They know that e-mail will be an issue for years so they might as well keep it all in a place and format that they can control. In making the decision, think hard about whether the backup tapes are likely to have relevant data that cannot be retrieved elsewhere. Determine if the hold can be limited to just a few tapes: for instance, in the *Zubulake* case, the court stated that the backup tapes holding the e-mail of the few key witnesses should have been kept.

Accurate records need to be kept of what has been preserved, how it has been communicated, the responses that were received, and the reminders that were provided. Companies can either utilize specialized software to assist in the preservation process or develop their own ways of recording processes through a spreadsheet or database. Decisions about e-mail archiving and hardware backup that might be needed for preservation also fall into this category (Figure 32.4).

Collection is another key stage to reducing volume and saving on costs. If the number of custodians and the amount of data collected from each custodian can be limited, the team will be better off. At the planning stage, consider what resources will be needed for collection. There are several enterprise solutions that allow for remote data collection from servers, desktops, and laptops. These solutions can be used for litigation as well as internal investigations and security reviews. However, they all have limitations, and manual collection will probably be necessary. The need for an enterprise solution will also depend on the frequency and volume of collection. As with data identification, corporations need to work with the IT team to determine what resources can be brought in-house and what makes sense to outsource. If the company plans to outsource a portion of the process, it is better to select a service provider or service providers who will be ready when the need arises. Regardless of how collections are handled, corporations need a process for documenting the collections and ensuring that the metadata has been preserved and the data is authentic.

During collection, the owners of the ESI should gather it in a manner that is "comprehensive, maintains its content integrity and preserves its form." Collection of metadata may also

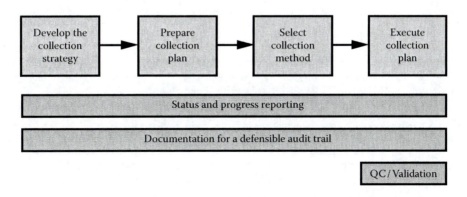

Figure 32.4 Collection process flow. (Copyright EDRM [edrm.net].)

be required, and some authentication and chain-of-custody measures should be put in place. Normally, it is assumed that documents will be collected in their native formats (e.g., an Excel spreadsheet rather than a PDF reproduction).

Processing, Review, and Analysis

This is the stage where the raw data is converted into a format that conforms to the law firm's requirements. The ESI is then reviewed and marked for relevance. Irrelevant or useless data is culled, and the relevant data moves on to be analyzed according to the legal theories and needs of the case. Document review is essential, time-consuming, and expensive, but vendors are constantly improving storage, sorting, and search capabilities to streamline the process and cut down on the amount of time and money spent on document review. Once the data is reviewed, attorneys can then begin to formulate strategy and apply evidence to the legal issues before them (Figure 32.5).

Processing refers to the technical steps necessary to put data in a reviewable format. Processing is also where duplicates are removed and techniques such as near-de-duplication and other culling take place. Effective processing can significantly reduce the amount of data that needs to be reviewed (typical numbers range from 50% to 80% reduction). Good processing requires technical ability, problem-solving skills, and excellent customer service. These are some of the traits that companies should look for when selecting a service provider (Figure 32.6).

By far the most significant cost in the e-discovery process comes from review, the stage in which lawyers (billing at an hourly rate) examine the company's collected documents to determine if they are relevant to the matter, privileged, etc. For the Fortune 1000 companies that are handling hundreds of legal matters a year, it is not uncommon for them to spend millions of dollars on each case, and review is often a big component of that cost. Not only is review the most expensive stage of e-discovery, it is also the most important since review enables the legal team to get into the heart of the matter, find "smoking gun" e-mails, and develop case strategy.

The cost of review correlates to the volume of data and the speed in which the data can be reviewed. Even with effective processing, a high-quality review tool is needed to cut the huge costs and time required for review. But more importantly, the review tool is needed to make sure the important documents are found quickly. Different review tools require different data formats. It will be important to assess the costs and efficiencies that flow from using a tool that keeps the data in native format for review or one that requires the documents to be in Tagged Image File Format (TIFF) (Figure 32.7).

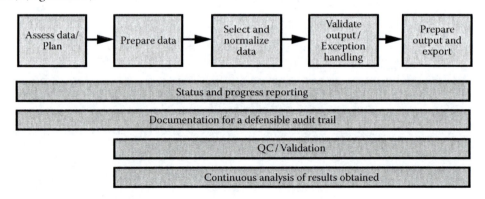

Figure 32.5 Processing process flow. (Copyright EDRM [edrm.net].)

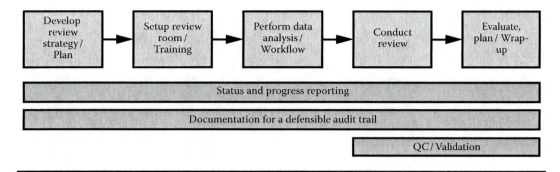

Figure 32.6   Review process flow. (Copyright EDRM [edrm.net].)

Based on and concurrent to the document review, an analysis of the documents is performed. Steps are taken for enhancing search terms and review performance. Quality assurance is also performed in this stage.

Production

Production is the final step in the e-discovery process. Some choose to use the same tool for review and production, while others use specialized tools. Concordance and Summation, for example, have been around a long time, and many lawyers are comfortable using these tools to build the witness files and hot document notebooks following production. Different tools may be appropriate for different cases and different companies. However, when evaluating processing and review tools,

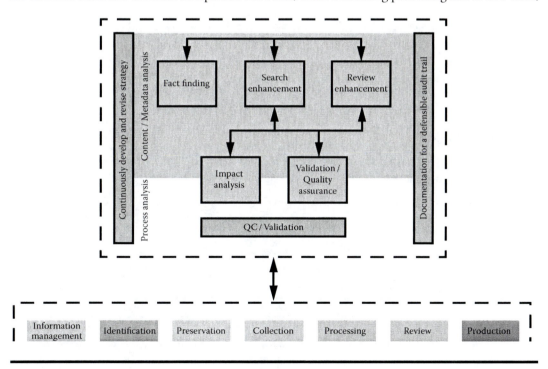

Figure 32.7   Iterative review process. (Copyright EDRM [edrm.net].)

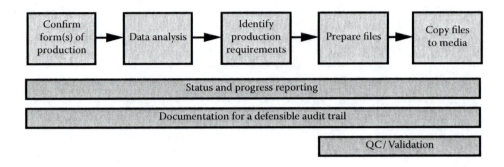

Figure 32.8   Production process flow. (Copyright EDRM [edrm.net].)

teams need to also consider how they plan to produce and work with these documents. Production format is something that will be discussed with opposing counsel early in cases, so corporations should be prepared with a preferred approach (Figure 32.8).

This is a stage fraught with peril: undetected metadata can sink a case, and privileged information can be given to the opposing party inadvertently. Fortunately, litigants have a chance to make sure the playing field is level. Rule 26(f) expects parties to establish methods and formats for production of ESI early on in litigation, and Rule 26(b)(5)(B) contains responses to the mistaken release of privileged information.

Presentation

Finally, it all comes together at trial or in settlement negotiations. Making good use of all that information can be tricky, especially when arguing in front of a jury. Keeping the material simple and easy to follow is essential to making a successful case, as is ensuring that presentation technology operates as it should. Everything from the readability of graphs to the number of power outlets in the courtroom should be considered at this stage (Figure 32.9).

Project Management

In addition to understanding the concepts that form an effective e-discovery process, practitioners should also consider the impact that project management principles can have on the e-discovery

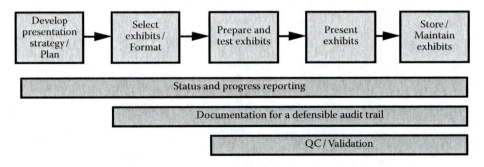

Figure 32.9   Presentation process flow. (Copyright EDRM [edrm.net].)

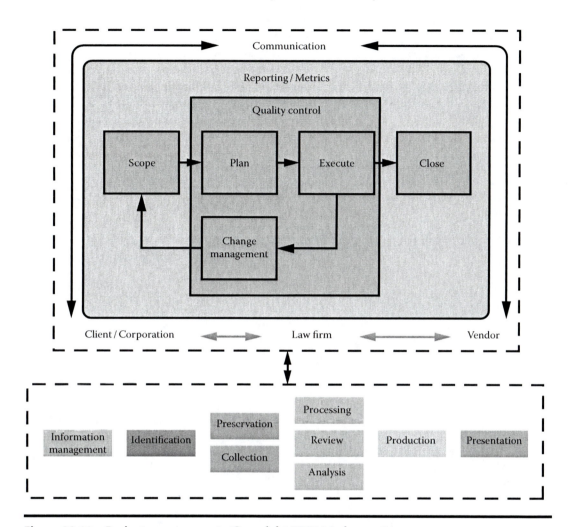

Figure 32.10   Project management. (Copyright EDRM [edrm.net].)

process. By applying project management processes to the e-discovery work flow, firms can establish key efficiencies, cut costs, and effectively monitor the successes and failures of the e-discovery work flow in each case. One of the key advantages of establishing a project management system to oversee the e-discovery process is the creation of institutional knowledge. With a project management sector firmly established, the loss of one or more e-discovery experts in the firm will only minimally impact the firm's e-discovery capabilities. Project management specialists within the firm can then transmit knowledge of the e-discovery process to new or inexperienced attorneys in order to increase the wealth of knowledge at the firm (Figure 32.10).

Conclusion

In 2002 former Defense Secretary Donald Rumsfeld said "There are known knowns. These are things we know that we know. There are known unknowns. That is to say, there are things that we know we don't know. But there are also unknown unknowns. There are things we don't know we don't know."

A streamlined electronic discovery work flow avoids or minimizes the "unknown unknowns." The key to a good discovery process is for all the parties involved to work closely together to leverage the power of supply-chain integration and improved process. There is a real power when stakeholders get together to solve problems. By using the process described in this article, organizations and attorneys can avoid the possibility of sanctions while saving their money.

PHYSICAL (ENVIRONMENTAL) SECURITY

Elements of Physical Security

Chapter 33

The Layered Defense Model and Perimeter Intrusion Detection

Leo Kahng

Introduction

When discussing topics of information protection, physical (or environmental) security is one of the top considerations in today's highly networked information technology environments. Additionally, the creation, distribution, and storage of sensitive and classified information are prolific practices designed to facilitate the rapid and accurate sharing of mission-critical information. Coupled with ever-increasing threats to information integrity and increases in terrorist activity, physical security measures have become highly developed to deter prospective attackers from accessing facilities, physical assets, or the information itself. Physical security plays a critical role in information security practices by providing defensive barriers as well as alerts to potential threats and attempts to compromise an entity and its resources. Preventing an attacker from even getting to the information has proved to be one of the most effective elements in maintaining the security and integrity of sensitive assets. When optimally deployed, networked physical security technologies are a highly effective force multiplier, allowing existing security officers and staff to cover and reach many more locations, and respond immediately to threats that are occurring, or strike preemptively to prevent a breach.

With respect to the information security industry, the primary drivers for physical (environmental) security arise from a need to alleviate common pain points experienced by information security professionals. From a largely physical perspective, many professionals are concerned with (but not limited to these items):

- Personal and employee safety
- Physical damage to buildings and facilities
- Loss of valuable assets

- Vandalism
- Site-specific shooting incidents
- Natural disasters
- Electrical outages
- Fire damage
- Terrorism
- Biological threats

From an information security perspective, many pain points stem from:

- Protecting existing technology investments and data integrity during migrations
- Loss of physical assets that house sensitive and/or classified information (laptops, storage drives, removable media, etc.)
- Loss of time and revenue dollars due to interruptions in operations
- Improving threat detection and incident response
- Improving surveillance coverage
- Centralizing physical security controls and administration

In this chapter, we will cover two main topic areas that define prominent best practices and methodologies for implementing physical security. They are the layered defense model and perimeter intrusion detection. In layered defense (sometimes referred to as layered security or defense in depth), we will look at multithreaded security strategies that promote resiliency through the deployment of security practices for physical facilities and information assets.

Progressing to perimeter intrusion detection, we will review several popular methods of detecting and reporting physical access threats, and how these perimeter intrusion detection technologies have improved the efficiency of security officers and their teams in day-to-day operations through the benefits of integration and internetworking.

Layered Defense Model

Layered defense can trace its roots to military strategies that involve multiple lines of defense designed to resist rapid penetration by an opposing force. More archaic military methods often concentrated defensive forces at the front line, but if that line is overpowered, the defenders become highly susceptible to being completely compromised. Employing multiple layers, or groups, of defenders, and subsequently placing defensive units in strategic locations behind the front line affords defenders a much higher probability of resisting the opposition, or suppressing them completely by diminishing their presence and containing the threat, without leaving any positions unguarded. In modern military terminology, this is referred to as "defense in depth."

These same principles are applied to the physical and information security world where multiple lines of defense are employed to protect assets and information. This segment of the chapter will explore some of the more popular layered defense techniques which are emphasized in the physical (environmental) security segment of the common body of knowledge (CBK) as defined per the CISSP certification for security professionals, and discuss how these multiple lines of defense may be used to complement each other. Figure 33.1 depicts a layered defense model for a physical structure.

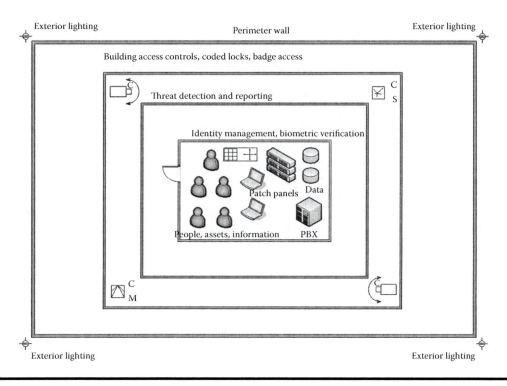

Figure 33.1 Layered defense example.

This defense-in-depth model employs an outside-in approach where physical deterrents are installed to thwart malicious behavior.

Exterior Facility Elements and Construction

Lighting: Lighting is a very effective tool for the prevention of physical breaches. The threat of simply being seen is often all that is needed to discourage a trespasser or attacker. Providing enough lighting coverage can virtually eliminate "dead spots" in the immediate perimeter of a facility and provide 360-degree coverage. Linking lighting systems with notification tools and video surveillance can provide a great deal of insight into the behavior of trespassers and attackers on the premises.

Barriers: A physical barrier such as a wall or fence, or a combination of the two, adds a level of difficulty to access to the facility. Depending on the importance of the assets in question, armed guards and dogs trained specifically for protection duty can be hugely effective in discouraging an attacker. Locked and/or guarded gates for access to the premises funnel entering traffic to the facility in a controlled area which can be closely monitored and fortified for protection detail.

Location: Stepping backward a bit, it can also be argued that proactive selection of the actual location for a facility is a security measure. For example, choosing a low-crime area to build in can reduce the possibility of break-ins, vandalism, and asset thefts. Choosing a less secure neighborhood may be advantageous for real state costs, but more funds will be spent protecting your facility, its assets, and most importantly the people occupying that facility.

- Is the area where you wish to locate a facility, or facilities, prone to a high occurrence of natural disasters?
- Is the location convenient to emergency services such as medical first responders and law enforcement officers?
- Is the location highly visible from a distance, or does the surrounding environment provide cover for concealment?

Construction: Aside from the building construction guidelines that are recommended for CISSP compliance, other elements to consider are:

- Should certain areas of the facility be "hardened" to repel or delay forced entry?
- Are ceilings and floors robust enough to prevent traversal of walls of locked doors by accessing crawl spaces?
- Can ventilation systems that pass through sensitive areas of the facility be easily breached?
- Is fire resistance robust enough to prevent a total facility loss, or weakening of structures to allow an attacker to gain access to restricted areas?

Building Access

Continuing to the next layer of security, if the exterior of the premise is compromised, we then rely on building/facility access controls to defend against our attacker(s), and identify who is entering and leaving.

Entry Points: Limiting the number of entry points to the facility can provide for fewer positions to monitor. This also aids in the rapid identification of where a breach may be occurring. Manning the main entry points can serve to improve response times to threats.

Access Restrictions: Physical locks act as an effective deterrent, but if they are overcome, employing card readers for badge access can add extra security and another locking mechanism (electromechanical) to pass before gaining access to the interior of the facility. Electronic lock systems also allow the possibility of monitoring who specifically entered/exited the building and when.

Biometric Verification: For additional authentication to gain access to a facility, biometrics can be used in the form of fingerprint scanners, retinal scanners, and other alternative methods to verify identity and access privileges.

Threat Detection and Notification

If an attacker has been able to breach the facility and gain access to the interior, being alerted to their presence and their activities is critical for risk mitigation. Continuing to follow the defense-in-depth methodology, utilizing detection and notification tools that address one's most crucial threats can help provide mission-critical information sooner.

Forced Entry Alarms: Door breach alarms, glass breakage sensors, and motion detectors can provide instantaneous notification of forced entry.

Video Surveillance: Video is a hugely popular security tool which will be discussed in detail in the next segment, on perimeter intrusion detection, but leveraging video coverage easily multiplies manpower by providing visual coverage of virtually anywhere in the facility. With the advent of video analytics, surveillance systems can also be used as motion detectors, "trip wires," loitering alarms, tailgating (following a badged employee into a facility, for example) alarm, and location tracking devices.

Biometric Sensors: Sensing and actuation devices can be implemented to detect the presence of a living being within certain parts of a facility.

Biological Sensors: Chemical sensors have been very popular for defense against biological threats. Deployed throughout populated areas of the facility, water delivery systems, and HVAC systems, they can be an effective notification tool for biological threats and terrorist activity, as well as outbreaks of highly toxic matter.

Seismic Sensors: Seismic sensors can alert to hostile activity or attempts to breach portions of the facility with force. Seismic sensors can also be used to alert security teams of human presence in a particular area.

Internal Asset Protection

If an attacker has managed to overcome all physical access security measures, countermeasures must come into play which prevent assets and information from leaving the facility. If an attacker manages to remove resources from the facility, additional measures need to be activated to protect that information and reduce the impact of data loss.

Network and Data Center Security: We will only highlight methods and measures in network security and access control, since they are covered in detail in other chapters of this publication. In layered defense (sometimes referred to as layered security or defense in depth), we can categorize network and data center security into two main focus areas:

- *Inclusion Measures*: This is the practice of restricting access to assets and resources based on establishing credentials or passage through a barrier once identity has been established and confirmed. For instance, technologies for inclusion may consist of access control lists (ACL), firewall services, web application firewall (WAF) services, network admission control (NAC), role-based access control (RBAC), identity management, wireless network control, and port-level authentication/authorization.

- *Exclusion Measures*: These are developed to prevent access or unlawful intrusion by blocking unauthorized penetration attempts. These measures could be intrusion detection and/or prevention systems (IDS/IPS), endpoint security (HIDS, security agents), rogue wireless endpoint detection and quarantine, antivirus (host and network based), antispyware, antispam filters, patch management, and security monitoring.

Asset Tracking: If physical media exits the facility, devices such as RFID tags can be planted on high-value assets for tracking purposes. GPS locators can provide real-time monitoring of location and movement.

Data Protection: Information rights can be managed to only allow access by authenticated and authorized users. Also, file and document protection programs can "expire" sensitive information if it is not accounted for in a set period of time, in addition to encryption best practices.

Segment Summary

A scenario that is often top of my mind is laptop or storage media theft, where devices storing data at rest could be housing very sensitive or sometimes classified information. For example, we were all made aware of public incidents of laptop theft when news flashes alerted us to the missing laptop from the Veterans Administration that supposedly contained personnel records of millions of military veterans. A very similar incident was publicized when a laptop was stolen in early 2008 from the National Institutes of Health, which contained private medical information for nearly 2,000 people. In each of these cases and similar incidents around the globe it was unclear until well after the fact as to how these thefts took place virtually unnoticed and in most cases the information was not encrypted beyond password-protected access to the laptop itself.

If we were to apply a layered defense strategy to the prevention of information loss, we could employ tactics such as physical barriers and smart building access technologies to repel or restrict access to facilities. With perimeter security devices and surveillance technologies, organizations have a much better chance of detecting attackers and thieves before they get to high-value assets, should they breach the outer defenses of a facility. Once intruders have penetrated the facility, adding security to sensitive areas can deter attacks. Enhancing network security with tactics like authentication/authorization, port-level security, ACL, and a whole host of other network access and admission controls can make it nearly impossible for the attacker to be exposed to any information at all. If the media is captured and removed from the facility, it can be tracked via RFID tags and/or GPS locators. If for any reason the assets become lost, data-at-rest encryption and rights management utilities can be employed to essentially render those devices useless after their theft becomes known, or after a predetermined "expiration" period.

With its roots in the military, its tactics and strategies widely deployed by military and commercial organizations around the globe, layered defense has become a widely used best-practice among security professionals in both information security and physical (environmental) security.

Perimeter Intrusion Detection

Being well informed and informed well in advance often gives those in the know a tremendous advantage when it comes to physical (environmental) security. Perimeter intrusion detection can provide the necessary alerting and notification to warn of a potential attack or when an attack commences. In modern information security practices, leveraging the reach and access of the network is a force multiplier for the security professional, allowing him or her to be informed immediately of security incidents, regardless of location. Leveraging the network for perimeter security also allows security teams to do more with less, and we will explore some key examples of how this is implemented in this chapter segment. Again, we owe much of our knowledge of perimeter intrusion detection to the military and law enforcement community, whose lives depend on accurate early detection processes to maintain situational awareness and being alerted to threats that are present in the immediate vicinity. In this chapter segment we will focus on three areas of interest with respect to perimeter security:

- Sensing and actuation
- Physical access control
- Video surveillance and analysis

Sensing and Actuation

Sensor: A detector is a device that detects an action or the presence of some object or entity in real-time.

Actuator: This is a device that performs a specific action, in response to an input or instruction. Can turn things on or off, and can be networked and operated remotely.

Sensing and actuation plays a significant role in the realm of physical security. Effective sensing and actuation fulfills the response needed to deal with threats immediately and mitigate the losses that may occur from security attacks. Additionally, when optimally deployed, sensing and actuation allows alerting of threats to happen rapidly, provision of critical information to security professionals, and taking action without having to rely on deployed human resources. Effective sensing and actuation can provide:

- The consolidation of information from different types of sensors, converting the data to a standardized and/or normalized format that multiple entities can interpret
- Analysis and fusion of information from multiple sources to create intelligence and rapidly deduce the necessary actions to be taken
- Automated activation of actuators to respond to a particular type of threat
- IP networking of sensors and actuators to accelerate detection of threats, improve situational awareness, improve the response time to mitigate threats, and force multiply the effectiveness of a security team to develop a common operational picture and resolution to all threats

To add additional perspective, one may break down sensing and actuation into several components that cover key functions. They include, but are not limited to:

Qualitative and Quantitative Sensors

Qualitative sensors report on the presence or absence of objects, people, patterns, or certain activities. These can be devices such as motion sensors, audio sensors, sound navigation and ranging (SONAR), video analytics, "electric eyes," and light sensors.

Quantitative sensors measure physical properties and associated changes relative to an acceptable range or other reference point. Examples include proximity sensors, temperature sensors, humidity sensors, barometric sensors, seismic sensors, accelerometers, flow sensors, and sensors specific to chemical, biological, radiological, nuclear, and explosive materials.

Human Identification (biometric) and Object Identification

Human identification, or biometric, sensors recognize human presence through tools that detect human characteristics such as heartbeat and thermal presence, but they can now recognize individuals based on intrinsic physical or behavioral traits. Voiceprinting is one such method. Biometric readers for building access not only provide entry based on fingerprint, signature, retinal scans, and other methods, but when integrated with information systems, they can alert to the presence of specific individuals within a known area. Facial recognition solutions can augment security practices by preventing identity fraud and adding another layer of defense for secure access to facilities and controlled assets.

Object identification involves the collection of information from multiple sensors, then analyzing that data to determine whether something is where it should be, has been moved, has gone missing, or is being tampered with. RFID tags provide an alerting method if something is removed from a monitored area. Bar codes are widely used for managing inventory. Optical character recognition (OCR) can be employed to verify markings and text of tracked items. GPS locators are sometimes employed to provide real-time tracking of assets as they are transported.

Actuators

An actuator is a device that can turn a device on or off, move an object, or invoke some other action to accomplish a desired result. Network-connected actuators remotely lock or unlock doors, gates, or other physical barriers. They can turn on or off fire control sprinklers, activate ventilation components to flush a space of its existing air, or shut off HVAC systems to prevent the spread of airborne contagions. Actuators can activate or deactivate lighting, raise or lower temperature, activate video surveillance cameras, sound alarms, or provide notification to security personnel. Actuators respond to sensors to invoke these actions based on response scenarios that are determined ahead of time by security teams through a well-defined operational policy.

Sensor Fusion, Correlation, and Base Lining

Traditional methods for monitoring sensor output are focused on analyzing the information from each individual sensor, then manually correlating that data. Combining inputs can give a more complete picture of the event. For example, in a building security scenario, physical barrier sensors and actuators are linked and correlated with activity reported from chemical and temperature sensors throughout the building. Additionally, the data from those sensors is fused with video surveillance information and asset tagging mechanisms. Individual sensor readings may not be so alarming, like simply detecting the presence of a person outside of a secure room, or that a piece of storage media has moved may not be compelling. However, if an unauthorized person has entered the building, a person was seen via video analysis to be very close to a secured room where sensitive storage media is kept, then that room's temperature increased slightly due to the presence of a human being, and an asset moved outside of the room, this could be correlated to alert of a high probability of suspicious or malignant activity.

The value of the sensor fusion, correlation, and base lining component includes the detection of anomalous conditions, such as asset movement, extra bodies in a physical space, and people loitering near secure rooms, by analyzing data and correlating it with information from other sensors. We can also reduce the occurrence of false positives and false negatives, for more actionable intelligence, by using diverse sensing technologies. Monitoring system health so that you know when a sensor has failed can be an effective indicator of an attack, or simply a sensor malfunction. Leveraging the reach and power of an IP network can provide immediate and accurate information as to what is failing and where. Security operations can also establish the automated notification of appropriate personnel based on inputs from diverse sensors, devices, and systems.

Legacy Integration

A security operation may already have a significant investment in hundreds, if not thousands, of sensors and actuators. Many of these may be connected to proprietary or closed networks or may be simply operating alone. A team can increase the value of these existing legacy assets by connecting them to the IP network and having an integrated view and reporting mechanism for existing and updated sensing platforms.

Physical Access Control (Concept)

Physical access control refers to the practice of electronically monitoring and controlling barriers like doors and gates, by managing locks and card/badge readers from a centralized management platform. Networked physical access control is a solution that provides electronic access control (EAC) while taking advantage of the benefits provided by an IP network. In traditional EAC architectures, a central controller or access panel was used to connect via serial interface to each individual door. Additionally, those door-locking mechanisms all required their own power supply on a separate circuit to operate the locking hardware. Another cumbersome property of traditional EAC architectures is the difficulty in adding additional doors to monitor and control. Again, each additional door would need to be added, wired all the way back to the controller, the controller would need to be expanded or completely replaced, and power considerations would come back into play for running a dedicated circuit for the door-locking hardware.

In a networked physical access control solution, both hardware and software components are implemented on an IP network to take advantage of the reach and scalability that is inherent in the networking foundation. For example, use of network services such as DHCP, DNS, NTP, etc., are leveraged to ease deployment and the addition of doors to the controller/gateway. Power over Ethernet (PoE) can be used to lower deployment costs and power consumption. This also brings with it a greater degree of convenience now that dedicated electrical circuits are no longer needed for every barrier. Using a distributed architecture over IP improves scalability greatly and does not limit the access management solution to one singular point of centralization.

Additionally, using an IP-based system of physical access control allows ease of integration with other physical security systems to take advantage of the richness of information that is gathered when multiple systems are integrated and the output information is correlated to paint an overall operational picture of the physical security environment. For example, the movement of a classified laptop is detected by RFID asset tags activating sensors in various parts of a building, showing a path headed toward an exit. With an integrated security solution, this could trigger actuators that correspond with the physical access control system to lock down all doors, windows, and elevator control systems to prevent anything or anyone from physically leaving the facility.

Video Surveillance and Analysis

One very innovative and important advent in the evolution of perimeter intrusion detection and video surveillance is that of video content analysis (VCA), which is more commonly referred to today as video analytics. Performance studies have shown that the effectiveness of persons tasked with monitoring live video feeds, or reviewing recorded video footage, can dramatically decrease in as little as 22 minutes. If you consider the prospect of staring at monitors in 8–12 hour shifts, or viewing hours upon hours of recorded footage to spot an intruder, there is a huge window of opportunity for human error to miss detecting the threat. Video analytics leverages automated algorithms and detection parameters to identify movement, anomalies, or behavior patterns within a particular field of view. For example, Figure 33.2 depicts an IP surveillance camera tracking movement within the field of view in a parking garage, where a person is spending time around a particular vehicle, or set of vehicles that may be considered high-value assets.

Using video analytics, human intervention can be greatly reduced, dramatically reducing the number of fatigue-related errors, while allowing more efficient management of the video surveillance system. Video analytics provides customizable real-time analysis and detection of security events from many different cameras, simultaneously, identifying events as they occur, and providing tools to analyze those situations and actuate responses, such as notifications, alerts, and alarms, and physical

Figure 33.2 Sample video analytics for motion or loitering.

security actions, such as locking doors, starting or stopping HVAC systems, and activating lighting in strategic locations. Some of the most common algorithms and behavior detection scenarios are:

- *Motion Detection*: An object, animal, or person crossing a particular field of view.
- *Video Tripwire*: Alert based on detection of a breach of a defined boundary. This can be as simple as motion detection, or identifying movement or the presence of an entity in just a portion of the camera's field of view. Also, video tripwires can be utilized to trigger loitering alarms where a suspicious person may be lurking by a secure door waiting to enter a facility as someone from inside is leaving.
- *Erratic/Suspicious Behavior*: Spending an unusual amount of time within one area or a repeated pattern of movement around vehicles in a parking garage.
- *Congestion Detection*: Too many people in a particular space.
- *Abandoned Object Detection*: Parcels or luggage left unattended at an airport, for example.
- *Opposing Flow*: Objects or persons moving opposite the normal direction of flow, e.g., a car going the wrong way down a one-way street.
- *Shape-Based Detection*: Automobile detection, detection of persons or animals, unusual size objects in the field of view.
- *Missing Object Detection*: Detection of something removed from a scene.
- *Character Recognition*: Detecting specific characters, text, or patterns.
- *License Plate Recognition*: Identifying vehicles or state of license plate registration.
- *Facial Recognition*: Identifying specific individuals via facial recognition programs that reference intrinsic human characteristics that are unique identifiers.

When we approach video surveillance and analysis from an IP standpoint, we immediately begin to incorporate features and utilities in the network infrastructure to augment the physical security enhancements that video monitoring enables. For instance:

- *Enable the use of wired and wireless video surveillance cameras*: Anytime, anywhere coverage. Allows one to overcome the challenges associated with cabling where it is prohibitively difficult or costly to place a surveillance camera.

- *Taking advantage of an existing infrastructure*: IP-based physical security leverages the network, which often already exists, and provides a physical infrastructure that can be adapted and/or easily expanded to present more video camera coverage options.
- *Leverage network security features*: Use the authentication, authorization, and access control features native to the network security platforms in place. Monitor rogue device implantation in real time and implement policy-based countermeasures.
- *Digitally record video*: Provide immediate access to recorded events and enable real-time incident response, investigation, and resolution.
- *Ability to distribute management and recording of video*: Eliminates the "silo" effect and prevents systems from becoming a single point of failure.
- *Monitoring and controls can be transferred to any point in the network*: No longer does one have to be physically colocated with the video surveillance infrastructure to manipulate and manage the video system. Provides true remote access to video streams, camera control, system management, and recorded video.
- *Integration with other physical (environmental) security tools and systems*: As we have explored in the layered defense model, sensing and actuation, and physical access control, the fusion of security technologies and corresponding their respective data can provide a greater and more detailed operational picture for security teams.

When deploying an IP-based video surveillance and analysis solution, we now turn to an IP network to provide the communications infrastructure. With this in mind, some key best practices and network design considerations for IP video surveillance have been developed by Cisco Systems, who are beginning to challenge the traditional physical security brands by approaching this market from a networking perspective. Much of this segment, and those following immediately after, will be based on the design guidance set forth by Cisco Systems.

With a focus on the IP network, several factors come into consideration. Some of the most significant elements will be discussed in this section of the chapter.

The Nature of Video Surveillance Traffic: Surveillance traffic imposes demands on the networking infrastructure in the form of constant as well as variable bit-rate video, which have different implications for bandwidth utilization. Constant bit-rate video defines bandwidth for each video stream, which can be useful for capacity planning and storage, but can also occasionally waste bandwidth. Variable bit-rate video changes as differences in the video stream are captured. Typically this results in lower overall bandwidth consumption, but traffic can be bursty, which makes it difficult to plan for capacity. To put this into perspective, let's examine Table 33.1, which depicts constant bit-rate metrics based on video resolution.

To put video resolution into perspective, Table 33.2 outlines respective resolution figures, represented as pixel measurements of width and height.

Video is also categorized into live video and prerecorded video. Live video is clearly delay sensitive and quality of service (QoS) is very important in maintaining the integrity of live video streams. In most cases, transport is typically UDP (best effort). Recorded video is not adversely affected by delay and reviews of the recorded video streams can be scheduled or ad hoc. Typically, transport is TCP based and the location of recording devices is of importance to understand where the information should be retrieved.

Performance and Storage Considerations: When addressing video performance, parameters such as resolution and frame rate have a direct impact on both bandwidth and storage requirements. For

Table 33.1   Constant Bit-Rate Bandwidth Consumption Guidelines

CBR Rate Guidelines by Resolution and Frame Rate			
	Resolution		
Frame Rate	*CIF*	*2CIF*	*4CIF or D1*
1.5	155,000	230,000	450,000
2	200,000	315,000	600,000
3	260,000	410,000	770,000
3.75	300,000	475,000	935,000
5	330,000	525,000	1,050,000
7.5	400,000	750,000	140,000
10	530,000	900,000	1,700,000
15	60,000	1,100,000	2,200,000
30	850,000	1,600,000	3,000,000

Note: All values in bits per second.

instance, if we consider a video capture practice like dual-streaming, where live viewing locally and remotely need to be facilitated, one would be best served by using high resolution and frame rates for local live viewing, while remote viewing can be adjusted to lower frame rates depending on available bandwidth. Also, especially for storage of captured video streams, the two leading methods are as follows.

■ *Centrally Located*: Centralized storage is typically deployed in a single environmentally controlled facility with close proximity to personnel who provide the technical support and

Table 33.2   Video Resolution Represented in Pixels

Resolution	*PAL*	*NTSC*
QCIF	176×144	176×120
VGA	640×480	640×480
SVGA	800×600	800×600
XGA	1024×768	1024×768
CIF	352×288	352×240
2 CIF	704×288	704×240
4 CIF	704×576	704×480
D1	720×576	720×480

management of the surveillance and storage systems. Often, these centralized storage models provide the advantage of potentially reducing operational costs due to only having a single location where the video is stored. However, in order to pass on video to other locations, or collect video from multiple locations in a central storage facility, there is likely more video (data) flowing across WAN links.

■ *Distributed Storage*: A distributed model for the storage of video surveillance streams positions storage to be located where events are happening, and within close proximity to local surveillance teams who can monitor and react to events in real time. Scalability can be achieved by using multiple smaller systems and there is not a single point of failure. Distributed storage also reduces the bandwidth requirements on the LAN and WAN links, however there are downsides like economies of scale—the cost per hour of storage with multiple smaller systems may be higher. Also, overall operational costs can be higher due to the required maintenance of more devices.

Multicast: Just for a quick recap:

■ *Unicast*: Communications between one source address and one destination host address.
■ *Broadcast*: Communication from one host address, typically to all hosts on a network segment or broadcast destination.
■ *Multicast*: Communications where one host sends one copy of each packet being sent to a special address that is then used by several hosts interested in receiving this information. The receiving hosts are members of a designated multicast group and can join or leave the group dynamically, be members of one or multiple groups, and can be located anywhere on the network.
  Multicast is often desirable for IP video surveillance applications, since increased efficiencies can be realized. For instance, lower CPU utilization is often observed since senders and receivers only receive requested data. Obviously, network utilization is optimal when compared to replicating multiple streams. However, the nature of multicast relies on UDP, rather than TCP, for transport, thus drops can occur and are often expected since there is not a built-in receipt mechanism, or congestion avoidance.

Quality of Service and Network Design Principles: QoS is a critical technology that must be employed to maintain the integrity and efficacy of IP video surveillance. QoS when employed in IP networks allows a systems administrator to prioritize and protect video surveillance traffic from all other types of traffic that traverse the network. Also, proper deployment of QoS prevents degradation of service events like packet loss, latency, and jitter, which represent the effects of mismanaged traffic congestion and will often result in poor video quality and sometimes a complete loss of video. Let's consider some of the impacts of these congestion events as they pertain to IP video surveillance.

■ *Packet Loss*: Video surveillance decoders may be able to tolerate some degree of packet loss, but the quality of the image will degrade. However, since surveillance video is often required to reconstruct critical information, there is not a specific amount of packet loss that can be deemed as "acceptable." IP video surveillance packet loss may represent itself as shown in Figure 33.3.
■ *Latency*: This measure of delay represents the time required to encode, transmit, buffer, and decode the video. This delay sensitivity can be more critical for Pan/Tilt/Zoom (PTZ) cameras due to their movement. A popular best-practice metric is to optimize total end-to-end delay to less than 500 ms, with encoding and decoding best done under 250 ms, leaving 1–50 ms for LAN transport and 100–150 ms for WAN transport.

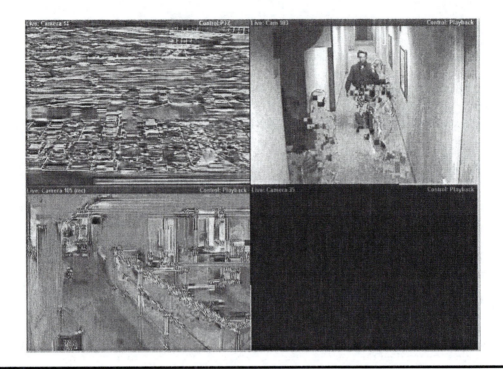

Figure 33.3 Examples of video surveillance packet loss.

■ *Jitter*: Represented as delay variation, accounts for differences in the end-to-end delay for IP packets for a given video surveillance stream. Packets can over- or under-run the available buffer space, affecting the quality of playback. This effect can cause additional frames to be stored in the decoder's buffer, potentially reordering the frame sequence and introducing latency, and can result in dropped packets. Jitter is often recommended to be kept under 10 ms whenever possible.

QoS implementation for IP video surveillance traffic requires classification, marking, queuing, and scheduling provisions. The access layer defines the edge of the network, or the ingress point, where traffic must be classified and marked for further treatment in the architecture. The edge devices may be able to rely on configurable Differentiated Services Code Point (DiffServ Code Point, or DSCP) markings that originate from the end devices themselves, i.e., video surveillance cameras. Access layer switches are then configured to trust these markings and preserve them upon ingress.

When looking at the actual classification and markings, the preferred methods for marking packets are Class of Service (CoS) marking, which is performed at Layer 2 of the OSI model, and DiffServ Code Point (DSCP) marking, which is conducted at Layer 3. Let us briefly examine CoS marking at Layer 2 (Figure 33.4).

An Ethernet frame can be marked at Layer 2 (trunked) with their relative importance by setting the 802.1p User Priority bits of the 802.1Q header. Since only 3 bits are available for 802.1p marking, 8 classes of service can be marked 0–7.

If we now examine a DSCP marking at Layer 3, we see where several key pieces of information are coded into the packet (Figure 33.5).

Here we see information written into the Type of Service (ToS) byte. The three most significant bits of the ToS byte are called IP Precedence (IPP). The six most significant bits of the ToS

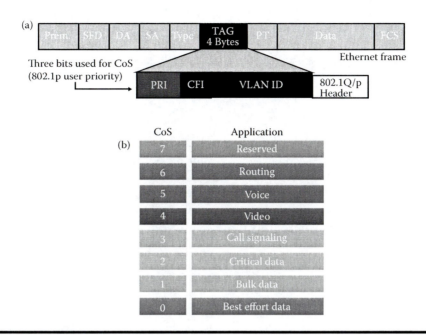

Figure 33.4   Class of service marking.

byte are called the DSCP, with the remaining two bits left for flow control. IPP values define eight levels of marking, which some find too restrictive and much prefer the 6-bit/64-value DSCP model.

We must also consider the implications for WAN traffic. QoS for video surveillance across the wide-area network primarily accounts for queuing and scheduling, in particular, Priority or Low Latency Queuing (LLQ) and Class-Based Weighted Fair Queuing (CBWFQ). LLQ is employed to immediately service the highest-priority traffic to minimize delay and prevent bandwidth starvation. CBWFQ will sort traffic based on markings and weight them for servicing, while also providing traffic shaping for events like recorded video bursts across the WAN. For example, delay-, loss-, and jitter-sensitive traffic such as live video and audio surveillance and PTZ camera control will use a LLQ algorithm. Traffic that is more tolerant of fluctuations like recorded video and system administration can use CBWFQ algorithms.

With respect to network design for IP video surveillance, QoS, when implemented properly, can greatly increase efficiencies and the performance of surveillance systems, whether traffic is traversing the LAN and/or WAN. QoS is not a substitute for the proper provisioning of adequate

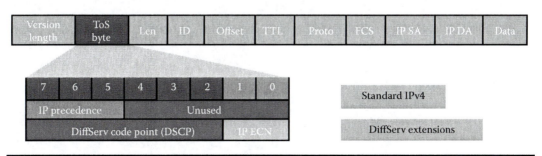

Figure 33.5   IP Precedence and DiffServ Code Points.

link speeds, but, conversely, provisioning a high level of bandwidth on a link is also not a replacement for properly configuring QoS on the network. When balanced in concert, these elements of networking work well together to provide optimal performance while not wasting bandwidth or network resources.

Segment Summary

Sensing and actuation, physical access control, and video surveillance/analysis are key technologies among many available and developing solutions for providing perimeter intrusion detection for security professionals and their respective teams. It can also be shown that when we leverage the reach and robustness of IP-based networks to aid in the integration of disparate systems, then correlate separate sets of data output, perimeter intrusion detection technologies act as a highly effective force multiplier to allow security teams to cover far, wide, and deep, yet respond immediately to security threats and attempts to acquire sensitive protected information.

Summary

In closing, whether an entity deals specifically with protecting people, protecting assets, or is mitigating business risks that can be realized through physical damage and losses, employing a well thought out physical (environmental) security solution can greatly reduce threats to an organization, with the obvious goal of eliminating them altogether. Among the first steps in protecting people and assets is to be sure they can't be reached. As technological advances continue to develop at breakneck speeds, and networked solutions increase the effective range of physical security, the line between physical security and information security continues to become more blurred. When we make perimeter intrusion detection part of an already robust layered defense model, we add yet another highly effective layer of security to established defense-in-depth methods that have been proven to reduce business losses, asset theft, information corruption, and threats to personal safety and security.

About the Author

Leo Kahng is a senior technical consultant with over 15 years of progressive technology industry experience in architecture design and implementation best-practices. Kahng currently consults for Cisco's U.S.-Canada Public Sector practice, focusing on the K-12 & Higher Education verticals, targeting communications and collaboration architectures.

Index

A

Access management reviews
  ACF2 and RACF, 293–294
  automated and sustainable process, 298
  back-end and user interface code, 300
  centralized solution, 293–294
  CoBIT, 293
  commercial products, 295
  detective controls, 295
  directory technologies, 293
  effectiveness, affecting factors, 299
  infrastructure, spanning, 294
  integrated tests, 297
  job profiling, 297
  level minimization, 298
  mainframe computing platforms, 294–295
  manager notification, 298–300
  periodic manager reviews, 298–299
  preventive controls, 296
  process, 296
  relationships, 294
  requirements, 298
  security practitioners challenge, 293
  terminated users identification, 297
  transferred users, 298
  user and profile relationships, 297
  XML-based representation, 295
Access requirement matrix. *See also* Unstructured data
  ABAC method, 223–224
  content category access, 224–225
  DAC method, 226
  determining questions, 223
  for IT department, 224–225
  MAC method, 224–225
  sensitivity handling levels and information, 224
  vertical and horizontal access levels, 223–224
Access review process, 296
Accredited Standards Committee (ASC), 343
Active tag, 25
Actuator, 495–496

Adult education principles. *See* Security awareness
    programs, adult education principles in
Advanced Encryption Standard (AES), 338, 363
Against the Gods: The Remarkable Story of Risk, 234
AIM. *See* Application identity manager (AIM)
Analyzer. *See also* Automated predictive analysis
  actions in, 276–277
  database, 278
  function, 277–278
  issue-by-issue tracking, 278
  predictive analysis engine
      specific information, 278
      targeted scanning, 278
Antivirus solutions, 5
APM. *See* Automated password management (APM)
Application identity manager (AIM), 43
Application vulnerability assessment. *See also* Software as
    a service (SaaS)
  availability, 309
  backup, 309
  data security
      assessments test, 308
      unauthorized access, 308
  identity management and sign-on process, 309–310
  network security, 308–309
ASC. *See* Accredited Standards Committee (ASC)
Asset Reporting Format (ARF), 88
Attribute-based access control (ABAC), 219–220
Authenticated data types, 352
  authAttrs and digestAlgorithm, 353
  cryptography layers, 353
  macAlgorithm and KEK, 353
  originatorInfo and recipientInfos, 353
  unprotectedAttrs, 353
  version, 353
Authentication in RFID system
  cryptographic check function, 321
  entity, 321
  mechanisms, 321–322
  tokens, 321

505

Automated password management (APM), 47
Automated predictive analysis
    data collection, 273
    external scan system, 276–277
    functional implementation, 274
    objectives, 273–274
    physical architecture elements, 274
        analyzer, 276–278
        logical architecture, 279–280
        network/host and application vulnerability
            scanners, 276
        network inventory database interface, 279
        scan manager, 275–276
        system and application inventory database
            interface, 279
        trouble ticketing system interface, 279
        web interface, 279
    predictive analysis engine, 278
    process, 274

B

Back-end database of RFID system
    EPC network
        ONS and services, 329–330
        tag counterfeiting and duplication, 328
Beacon Point Sensor (BPS) outpost, 69
*Beyond Fear: Thinking Sensibly about Security in an
    Uncertain World,* 167
Blacklisting
    access control, 15
    approach, 4–5
    whitelists
        advantages and disadvantages, 16
        comparison, 16–17
Boyd model. *See also* Risk management
    act and decide stage, 250
    information security, 249–250
    IS unit, size basis, 250–251
    military warfare strategy, 248–249
    observe and orient stage, 250
    OODA loop, 249
Bulletin boards, 56
Business associate (BA) security and privacy programs
    clearinghouses, 154
    compliance management
        automated CEs and drawbacks, 160
        effective and cost-efficient, 161
        ongoing monitoring capabilities, 161
    of covered entities (CEs), types, 153–154
    HHS Breach Notice Rule, statistics, 154
    HIPAA/HITECH compliant
        breach notice requirements, 158–159
        HHS announcement, 159–160
        HITECH Act Enforcement Interim
            Final Rule, 158–159
        violations and penalty amounts, 158–159
    indicators and problems
        assigned security/privacy responsibility, 156
        business continuity and disaster recovery plans, 158
        company responses, 157
        encryption use, 157
        incomplete response, 156
        mobile computing controls, 157
        policy and response, inconsistencies, 156
        prior breaches, corrective actions, 158
        subcontracting, 157
    services, 154–156
Business process resumption planning (BRP), 437

C

CA access control. *See also* Identity and access
        management suites
    IAM suite component, 45
    operating systems, access controls, 45
    PUPM
        entitlements reports, 46
        UNAB, 46
California Security Breach Information Act, 2002, 463
Call-based whitelisting, 6
Capability maturity model integration (CMMI), 405
CCB. *See* Configuration control board (CCB)
CCERT. *See* Countywide computer emergency response
        team (CCERT)
CCRM. *See* Configuration, change, and release
        management (CCRM)
Certificate Revocation List (CRL), 350
Change management
    elements of process, 408
    plug and play technologies, 407
    system users and organization, 407
Children's Online Privacy Protection Act, 1998,
    461–462
CI/KR. *See* Critical infrastructure/key resources (CI/KR)
Class-Based Weighted Fair Queuing (CBWFQ)
    algorithms, 503
Cloning and physical attacks of RFID system
    attacks, 323–324
    hash and encryption function, 323
    symmetric-key cryptography, 323
    tags, 324
    tamper-resistant microprocessors and
        devices, 323–324
Cloud Security Alliance (CSA), 307
CMDB. *See* Configuration Management Database
    (CMDB)
CMMI. *See* Capability Maturity Model
    Integration (CMMI)
CMS change history
    cryptographic message syntax standard
        PKCS #7 versions 1.0–1.3, 361
        PKCS #7 versions 1.4, 361
        PKCS #7 versions 1.5, 361

IETF history
    AES, 363
    ECC, 362
    password based key management, 363–364
    RFC, 362–364
X9 history
    NamedKeyEncryptedData, 364
    RFC, 364
    XCMS, 364
CND, Computer Network Defense (CND)
CoBIT. *See* Common objectives for information
      technology (CoBIT)
Collaborative risk management
    executive-based unit, 241–242
    human factor
      information resource, 242
      threats and vulnerabilities sources, 242
    organizational financial data, protecting, 241
    organizational responsibilities (*see* Organizational
      responsibilities)
    process, 241
Collection process flow, 481
Combined Standards Glossary, 238
Commercial off-the-shelf (COTS), 102
Common Configuration Enumeration (CCE), 82
Common Configuration Scoring System (CCSS), 89
Common Misuse Scoring System (CMSS), 89
Common objectives for information technology
    (CoBIT), 293, 295
Common Platform Enumeration (CPE), 82–83
    specification and dictionary, 79–80
Common vulnerability and exposures
    (CVE), 78, 82–83
Computer Emergency Response Team
    (CERT), 38–39, 170–171
Computer Matching and Privacy Protection
    Act, 1988, 459
Computer network attack (CNA), 399
Computer network defense (CND), 399
Computer network exploitation (CNE), 399
Computer network operations (CNO), 399
Confidentiality, integrity and availability (CIA), 102
    triad, 314–315
Configuration, change, and release management
    (CCRM), 404
Configuration Control Board (CCB), 414
Configuration management
    automated tools, 405–406
    baselines, 406
    CCR process, 416–418
    elements
      change requests, 408
      development actions, 408
      requirements analysis, 408
      security reviews, 408
      testing, 408
    systems, 407

Configuration Management Database (CMDB), 413
Content management systems
    component, 217
    effectiveness, 218
    fundamental issue with, 218
    Microsoft Office SharePoint popularity, 217–218
    policy framework development, 218
    unstructured data access policy building, 218
ContentType data types of CMS, 346–348
Continuity planning program structure
    BRP, 437
    CMP
      objectives, 437–438
      top down approach, 437
    interrelated components, 437
    IT Continuity Planning, 436–437
Core RBAC model, 255–256
Countywide computer emergency response team
    (CCERT), 174
Crisis management planning (CMP), 437
Critical infrastructure/key resources (CI/KR), 391–392
Cryptographic message syntax (CMS)
    ASC and PKCS standards, 343–344
    content data types, 346–347
      authenticated, 352–354
      digested, 351–352
      encrypted, 348–349
      enveloped, 350–351
      signed, 354–355
    key management
      agreement and transport, 356–357
      and certificate management, 358–359
      implicit and explicit, 357–358
    object identifiers (OID), ISO and ITU, 345
    profiles
      advanced use, 360–361
      common use, 359–360
    timeline, 344
Cryptography
    asymmetric algorithms
      DLP and IFP, 338
      NIST and SVP, 338–339
    engineering
      black box, 339
      secure cryptography, 339
    Feistel ciphers
      AES, 338
      DES and FIPS, 337–338
    implementations
      cryptomathematics, 339
      cryptosystem, 339–340
      key management, 340
    math
      key-space exhaustion, 337
      symmetric key and asymmetric key, 337
    vulnerabilities of RFID system
      DST, 327–328
      key cracking, 328

reverse engineering, 328
  simulation, 328
  tags, 327
CSA. *See* Cloud Security Alliance (CSA)
Cyber-Ark PIM suite
  AIM and PSM, 43
  EPV, 43 (*See also* Privileged user management)
Cybercrime/cybersecurity/cyberwarfare
  CNA and CND, 399
  CNO and CNE, 399
  infrastructures
    CI/KR, 398
    DHS, 398
  investigation and prosecution, 397–398

D

DAC. *See* Discretionary access control (DAC)
Data Encryption Standard (DES), 337–338
Data governance
  categories and focus, 220–221
  compliance requirements enforcement, 220–221
  concept, 220
  information security, 220
  purpose, 221
Data security and privacy legislation
  breach type, 455, 458
  California Security Breach Information
    Act, 2002, 463
  Children's Online Privacy Protection
    Act, 1998, 461–462
  Computer Matching and Privacy Protection
    Act, 1988, 459
  European Union Data Protection
    Directive, 1995, 459–460
  Federal Information Security Management
    Act, 2002, 462–463
  Gramm–Leach–Bliley Act, 1999, 462
  Health Insurance Portability and Accountability
    Act, 1996, 460–461
  H.R. 2221 DATA (*see* H.R. 2221 Data
    Accountability and Trust Act (DATA))
  Massachusetts 201 CMT 17.00 Law, 2010, 463–464
  Nevada Law SB227, 2010, 464–466
  over time, incidents, 455, 458
  Privacy Act, 1974, 455–458
  state breach notification laws, 455–457
  United Kingdom Data Protection Act, 1998, 461
Department of Homeland Security (DHS), 394
Deployment, 11
Digested data types
  digestAlgorithm, 351–352
  encapContentInfo, 351–352
  hash function, 351–352
  version, 351–352
Digital linear tape (DLT), 423
Discrete logarithm problem (DLP), 338

Discretionary access control (DAC), 218–219
Distributed Threat Database (DTDB), 70
Domain Name System (DNS) server system, 7

E

Eavesdropping attacks
  range classification
    backward and forward channel range, 320
    malicious scanning range, 320
    operating range, 320
  reasons for problems, 320
ECC. *See* Elliptic curve cryptography (ECC)
e-DMZ TPAM suite. *See also* Privileged user management
  application password management module, 42
  modular solution, 41
  privileged command management module, 43
  privileged session management module, 43
Electronically stored information (ESI), 473
  electronic discovery lifecycle, 477
  identification, 478
    preservation process, 479
    process flow, 479
  information management
    document retention policy, 478
    e-discovery work flow, 477–478
    litigation/government information request, 478
  paper documents and
    computer program, 475–476
    dynamic, changeable content, 475–476
    large volume and duplication, 474
    metadata, 475
    persistence, 474–475
    searchable and dispersed, 476
  presentation, process flow, 484
  preservation and collection
    backup tapes, 480–481
    e-mail archiving and hardware backup, 481
    issue preservation reminders, 480
    with IT, 480
    litigation hold, communication, 479–480
    metadata, 481–482
    process flow, 479–481
  processing, review and analysis
    document review, 482
    e-discovery process, cost, 482
    iterative process, 482–483
    process flow, 482–483
    quality assurance, 483
    raw data, format, 482
  production
    concordance and summation, 483–484
    peril, fraught with, 484
    process flow, 483–484
  project management
    advantages, 484–485
    e-discovery process, impact on, 484–485

Electronic discovery lifecycle
  e-discovery work flow, 477
  goal, 477
  reference model, 477
Electronic discovery reference model, 477
Elliptic curve cryptography (ECC), 362
Encrypted data types
  components, 348–349
  encryptedContentInfo, 349
  unprotectedAttrs, 349
  version, 349
Enterprise password vault (EPV), 43
Enterprise subsystem
  analytic systems and middleware, 26
  function, 25–26
  network infrastructure, 27
Enveloped data types
  encryption layers, 351
  KEK, 350–351
  recipientInfos and originatorInfo, 350
  version, 350
European Convention on Human Rights (ECHR), 459
European Union Data Protection Directive, 1995
  ECHR, 459
  EU directives, 460
eXtensible Configuration Checklist Description Format (XCCDF), 81
eXtensible Markup Language (XML), 295

F

Federal Information Processing Standards (FIPS), 338
Federal Information Security Management
      Act, 2002, 462
  management and budget, 463
  National Institute of Standards and
      Technology, 463
Federal Trade Commission (FTC), 451
Feistel ciphers, 337–338
File-based whitelisting, 6–8
Financial industry and cost of risk. *See also* Sarbanes–
      Oxley (SOX) legislation
  banks, 447
  concern and challenges, 447–448
  consumer privacy protection, 451
  in financial services firm, 447, 451
  FTC proposal, 451
  GLBA legislation, 451–452
  governmental oversight, 450–451
  hackers, risk management techniques, 448
  high-level security policies, 448
  information security
    experts, employment, 452
    theory, 448
  legislation, key results, 453
  media scrutiny, 449
  negative exposure type, 449

privacy, 450
  priority, 451–452
proposed legislation for, 450
reputational risk, 448–449
risk prioritization issue, 448
Sarbanes–Oxley legislation, 447
  compliance, average cost, 452–453
  impact, 452
in SEC, 449
  private financial companies, 450
security breach threat, 448
SSN, limited use, 450
FIPS. *See* Federal Information Processing
      Standards (FIPS)
FTC. *See* Federal Trade Commission (FTC)

G

GLBA. *See* Gramm–Leach–Bliley Act (GLBA)
Global Information Grid (GIG), 69–70, 103–105
Global Information Systems Transformation (GIST), 69
Governance and regulatory compliance (GRC), 307
Gramm–Leach–Bliley Act (GLBA), 451–452, 462
GRC. *See* Governance and regulatory compliance (GRC)
Guide to the Project Management Body of Knowledge, 238
Government off-the shelf (GOTS) software, 102

H

Health Information Technology for Economic and
      Clinical Health Act (HITECH). *See* Business
      associate (BA) security and privacy programs
Health Insurance Portability and Accountability Act
      (HIPAA), 153–160, 216
  1996
    regulations, 460
    requirements, 461
Hiding of RFID system
  active and passive jamming, 326
  Faraday cage, 325
Host-based Intrusion Prevention System (HIPS), 6
H.R. 2221 Data Accountability and Trust Act (DATA)
  areas, 466
  breach notice obligations, 466
  enforcement, 468
  preemption and variations, 467
  risk of harm, 467–468

I

Identification process flow, 479
Identity and access management suites. *See also*
      Privileged user management
  BeyondTrust Privilege Manager and PowerKeeper
    APM solution, 47
    client libraries, 48
    physical and virtual solutions, 48

security, multiple layers, 47
Windows-only solution, 46
CA access control (*see* CA access control)
Lieberman software products
Enterprise Random Password Manager, 49
I.D.E.A. process, 48
Novell Privileged User Manager (*See* Novell
Privileged User Manager)
ScriptLogic Privilege Authority, 48
Verdasys privileged user management, 50
Identity management (IdM) and SSO model of SaaS
advantages/disadvantages and security
challenges, 306
credential synchronization, 305
federated IdM, 305
independent IdM stack, 305
Identity management system (IDMS), 101
IF-MAP servers, 70, 97
base use case, 105
adoption of SCAP/IF-MAP, 109–114
relevant OVAL capabilities, 106–108
standards, 108–109
contractor access, 100–101
guest access, conference room
business requirements, 100
operations, 98–99
production network
business requirements, 99–100
security use case, 101–105
Information security and RFID systems
for other parts
cloning and corrupted drivers, 36
gateway interface misuse, 36
reader-gateway communication, 36
tag-borne attacks, 35
for reader
corrupted drivers, 34
gateway communication and interface misuse, 34
ID falsifying, 33, 35
tag-borne attacks, 33
for tags
contents falsification, 31
deactivation and detaching, 32, 34
ID falsification and contents, 34
physical destruction, 32, 34
for wireless interface
blocking, 32, 35
eavesdropping, 32, 35
jamming, 32, 35
relay attack, 32–33, 35
Information security governance, 179
board of directors' role
and compliance, state, 185
internal audit department, 185
risk appetite, 184–185
C-level suite role, 185–186
end users' security role

administrative assistants, 189
business continuity planner, 188
data custodian and business owners, 188
help desk administrator, 189–190
individuals purpose, 187
physical security, 189
responsibility, 187
systems administrator, 188–189
technology professionals, 188–189
goal, 180
origin and meaning, 180
roles defining
access, 180–181
profile content, recertification, 181
security department, 180
standardized set and profile, 181
security officer's role, 181
planning, 183–184
reporting relationships, 182–183
senior/middle management role
assets, protection, 186
council, establishment, 186
investment decisions, 186
steering committee/council role
grassroots support and benefits, 186–187
managerial and technical representatives,
186–187
unambiguous roles, establishing
benefits, 190
team effort, 190–191
Information security organization. *See also*
Organizational governance
CCERT, 174
DISO responsibilities, 173–174
ISSC responsibilities and security triangle, 173
in local government, 173
strategic framework, 174
Information Security Steering Committee (ISSC), 173
Information Technology Infrastructure Library (ITIL),
405
Integer factorization problem (IFP), 338
Integrative Document and Content Management, 218
International Organization for Standardization (ISO),
405
International Telecommunication Union (ITU), 345
Internet Protocol version 4 (IPv4)
address space problems, 121–122
attack methods, 119–121
IPv6, similarity with, 122–123
Internet Protocol version 6 (IPv6)
address space, 124
autoconfiguration/stateful and stateless, 126
efficiency, 124–125
features and benefits, 123–124
IP header, 124
IPsec, integrated, 126
IPv4, similarity with, 122–123

misunderstandings, 123

mitigations, 130

mobility, 125

proposed implementation, 132

QoS, 125

reconnaissance, 129

renumbering, 126–127

routing/protocol

    issues, 128–129

    recommendations, 130–131

security issues, 127

software hardware support recommendations, 132

training

    lack, 129

    provide, 131

transition methods, 127–128

viruses/worms, 130

Irdeto cloakware password authority, 43–44. *See also* Privileged user management

external directory (LDAP) integration, 43

passwords, life-cycle management, 43

server-based component architecture, 44

ISSC. *See* Information Security Steering Committee (ISSC)

Iterative review process, 483

ITIL. *See* Information Technology Infrastructure Library (ITIL)

IT/IS vulnerabilities management. *See also* Risk management

act

    hardware and software technology, 263

    IR team, 263

    IS practices, 262–263

core RBAC, 256

decide stage

    human resource, 258–259

    incident response, 262

    software environment, 261–262

    technology infrastructure, 259–261

observe stage

    earlier stages feedback, 263

    IS program, dual foundation, 263–264

orient stage

    human resource, 251–253

    incident response, 257–258

    software environment, 254–257

    technology infrastructure, 253–254

plan, areas, 251

ITU. *See* International Telecommunication Union (ITU)

K

Kernel-hooking malware, 11

Key encryption key (KEK), 350

Key management of CMS

certificate management

    certification authority (CA), 358–359

    CRL, 359

    public key infrastructure, 358–359

explicit named key

    acquirer and cardholder, 357

    issuer, 357

    KSI, PIN and POS, 357

    NamedKeyEncryptedData, 357

implicit cryptographic key

    EncryptedData, 358

    NamedKeyEncryptedData, 358

key agreement

    EnvelopedData, 357

    password, 357

    public and private keys, 357

key transport

    AuthenticatedData, 356

    EnvelopedData, 356

    recipientInfos and KEK, 356

Key set identifier (KSI), 357

Kiribati Digital Modernization Program (KDMP), 69

L

LAN. *See* Local area network (LAN)

Lattice-based cryptosystems, 338–339

Layered defense model

building access

    biometric verification, 492

    entry points, 492

    restrictions, 492

example, 490–491

exterior facility elements and construction

    barriers and lighting, 491

    CISSP compliance, 492

    location, 491–492

information loss, prevention, 494

internal asset protection

    data, 493

    network and data center security, 493

    tracking, 493

laptop/storage media theft scenario, 493–494

roots, 490

threat detection and notification

    biological sensors, 493

    biometric sensors, 493

    forced entry alarms, 492

    seismic sensors, 493

    video surveillance, 492

Linear tape open (LTO), 423

Local area network (LAN), 16

"Luddite Group" (LG), 69–70

M

MAC. *See* Mandatory access control (MAC)

Malware life cycle, 3–4

under whitelisting, 7

Mandatory access control (MAC), 219

Manual analysis process, 272–273

Manual predictive analysis
    generalities, deal in, 272–273
    process, 272–273
Massachusetts 201 CMT 17.00 law, 2010, 463
    plan, 464
Multi-State Information Sharing and Analysis Center
        (MS-ISAC), 72

N

Named encrypted data type
    namedKey, 349
    version, 349
National Checklist Program (NCP)
    checklists, 88
    goals of, 87–88
National Cyber Security Division (NCSD), 394
National Institute of Standards and Technology
        (NIST), 76, 338, 395, 405
National Vulnerability Database (NVD), 84
Network vulnerability assessment. *See also* Software as a
        service (SaaS)
    availability, DoS testing, 310
    SaaS deployment model, 310
Nevada Law SB227, 2010
    payment card industry data security standard, 464
    personal information, 465
    Senate Bill 227, 465–466
NIST. *See* National Institute of Standards and
        Technology (NIST)
North Carolina Identity Theft Act, 240
Novell Privileged User Manager. *See also* Identity and
        access management suites
    business-defined rules utilization, 50
    compliance auditor, 51
    graphical interface, 50
    process workflow, 51
    supported platforms, 51
    UNIX SUPM system, 50
    user
        management and tracking., 52
        and operating system, 50

O

"Observe," "Orient," "Decide," "Act," (OODA)
        loop, 249–250
Official Vendor Statements on CVE
        vulnerabilities, 85
Online social networks
    case about privacy, 57–59
    identity-related threats
        information leakage, 63
        phishing, 63
        profile squatting, 63
    implications, privacy, 60–61

network and information security threats
    aggregators, 63
    cross site scripting/viruses and worms, 63
    spamming, 62
privacy-related threats
    complete account deletion, difficulty, 62
    content-based image retrieval, 62
    face recognition, 62
    image tagging and cross-profiling, 62
    personal information, digital dossier, 61–62
    revelation, 59–60
security exposure
    benefits, 195
    blocking, 198
    communications types, 193
    definition and structure, 193
    employee use, control, 195
    enterprise guidance information, 197–198
    implications, 193–194
    malicious people and social engineering attack, 194
    policy/standard/guideline questions, 196–197
    policy statement for enterprise employees, 196
    privacy/security issues and threats, 194–195
    professional networks, 195
    recommendations, 195–196
    user ID and password, 194
social threats
    corporate espionage, 64
    stalking, 63–64
    technology and privacy, 65
    users and privacy, 64–65
structure and evolution, 56
Websites in United States, 59
Open and closed RFID systems, 28
"Open API," 72
Open Checklist Interactive Language
        (OCIL) 2.0, 81–82
Open Checklist Reporting Language (OCRL), 88–89
open source community, 78
Open Vulnerability and Assessment Language
        (OVAL), 78
    capabilities, 92
    definition classes, 93
    definition file, 81
    format, 92–93
    schemas, 90–91
    system inventory
        malware and threat indicator sharing, 96
        relevant OVAL capabilities, 96
    use cases
        auditing and centralized audit validation, 95
        patch management, 94
        relevant OVAL capabilities, 94–96
        security advisory distribution, 93–94
        SIMS, 95
Organizational culture, 167
Organizational governance

federated organizational structure, 165–166
five-member board, 165
information security, strategic framework, 165
information security executive
    business-related risk consideration, 170
    CERT, 170–171
    effective CISOs features, 169
    group/team evolution stages, 170–171
    matrix reporting structure, 169
    relationships, establishing, 169
    security function advantages and
        disadvantages, 169–170
    SET, 170
    staff managing, 170
public sector/private sector/corporate
    organizations, 165–166
security triangle, 165–166
Organizational responsibilities. *See also* Collaborative
    risk management
executives
    collaborative model decisions, 242–243
    decision makers, 242
general business units
    high-level processes, 243
    internal threats and vulnerabilities, 243–244
    workforce training and users, 244
IS/IT/physical security
    collaboration basis, 245–246
    IS and IT units, 244–245
    PS/S unit, 245
    units role, 244
risk management unit
    functions, 243
    single purpose entity, 243
Organization culture awareness and information security
    program. *See also* Organizational governance
components of, 171
culture and behavior
    difference in, 168
    prescriptive aphorisms outcomes, 168
    public sector, 167
    rational-utilitarian institutions, 167
    reshaping, 168
    security and people, 167
    as social energy, 167
    stakeholders desired behavior, 168
data breach/press and media release, 164–165
establishment, 163
five-level model, hierarchy, 163
government social services programs, 163–164
guidelines, 172
"Lucky 7," 164
policy
    resources and writing style, 173
procedures and standard, 172
Organization for Advancement of Structured
    Information Standards (OASIS), 256

P

Passenger name record (PNR), 458
Passive tag, 24
Payment card industry act (PCI), 216
PCI. *See* Payment card industry act (PCI)
Perimeter intrusion detection
    physical access control
        IP-based system, use, 497
        networked, 496–497
    sensing and actuation, 494
        actuators, 496
        effective, 495
        human and object identification, 495
        legacy integration, 496
        physical security realm, 495
        qualitative and quantitative sensors, 495
        sensor fusion, correlation, and base lining, 496
    video surveillance and analysis (*See* Video
        surveillance and analysis)
Personal identification number (PIN), 357
PIM. *See* Privileged identity management (PIM)
PKCS. *See* Public key cryptography standards (PKCS)
Point of sale (POS), 357
Predictive analysis engine, 278
Predictive vulnerability analysis
    analysis tools types, 269
    attack types, CSI/FBI data, 268–269
    automated
        data collection, 273
        functional implementation, 274
        objectives, 273–274
        physical architecture, 274–275
        process, 274
    computer security, 268
    concept, 270–272
    environment, cursory assessment, 272
    information sources, 270
    manual
        generalities, deal in, 272–273
        process, 272–273
    network vulnerability analysis, 269
    solution designing
        enterprise network elements, 272
        network security controls, 272
        security management strategies, 272
    systems
        knowledge, 270–271
        scanning, factors affecting, 270
Preservation process flow, 480
Priority or Low Latency Queuing (LLQ) algorithms, 503
Privacy Act, 1974
    automated targeting system, 458
    fair information practice code, 455–456
    personal records, use, 457
    PNR agreement, 458
    statement, 456

Privacy of RFID system
Bill 682 and 768, 316–317
consumers right, 317
data-processing systems, 315
tags and technology, 316
Privileged identity management (PIM), 43
Privileged session manager (PSM), 43
Privileged user management, 37–39
audit solutions
DirectAudit, 40
IBM Tivoli Compliance Insight Manager, 40–41
control solutions
Cyber-Ark PIM suite, 43
e-DMZ TPAM suite, 41–43
IRDETO cloakware password authority, 43–44
NETWRIX privileged account manager, 44–45
identity and access management suites
BeyondTrust Privilege Manager and PowerKeeper, 47–48
CA access control, 45–46
Lieberman software products, 48–50
Novell Privileged User Manager, 50–52
ScriptLogic Privilege Authority, 48
Verdasys privileged user management, 50
Privileged user password management (PUPM), 45
Processing process flow, 482
Product cycle and threat cycle, 74
Productivity and security
baseline
blacklisting, 432
turning on auditing and logging, 431
using role-based access control, 431
CoBIT® model
acquire and implement, 430
deliver and support, 430
monitor and evaluate, 430
plan and organize, 430
dilemma, 430
enterprise reviews
centralized management, 431
integration, 431
lower costs, 431
information technology (IT)
administrator, 431
primary purpose, 429
security purpose, 429
protection levels approach, 430
security element, 431–432
threat vectors, 431
Profiles of CMS
advanced use
ContentInfo, 361
EnvelopedData, 361
SignedDataList, 361
common use
digital signatures, 359–360
EncryptedData, 359–360
SignedData, 359–360

PSM. *See* Privileged session manager (PSM)
Public key cryptography standards (PKCS), 343
PUPM. *See* Privileged user password management (PUPM)

R

RACF. *See* Resource access control facility (RACF)
Radio frequency identification (RFID) system
applications, 28–29
attack on
targets, 314
tracking/data manipulation, 314
automated identification, 21
CIA triad, 314–315
components, 313
history, 22–23
information security measures (*see* Information security and RFID systems)
information security threats (*see* Information security and RFID systems)
operating frequencies and reading distances
microwaves tags, 319
UHF, HF and LF tags, 319
privacy aspects, 29
at backend, 30–31
tag-reader system, 30
purpose, 21
replay and relay attacks
clock synchronization, 324
ghost and leech, 325
risks, 29
security concerns
privacy, 315–317
tracking, 317–318
skimming
nonauthentication, 322
password authentication, 322–323
system components, 21
tags, 21–22
technology
enterprise subsystem, 25–27
interenterprise subsystem, 27
open and closed, 28
RF subsystem, 23–25
RBAC. *See* Role-based access control (RBAC)
Release management
CCR process, 416–418
changes, 408–409
configuration audit, 410
configuration item (CI), 406
data
exchanges, 407
interfaces, 409
documentation, 407
hardware and software, 405–406
help desk, 409

inventories, 406–407
requirements, 406
rollbacks, 410
security, 409
Replay and relay attacks, 324–325
Request for comment (RFC), 343
Resource access control facility (RACF), 293–295
Review process flow, 483
RF subsystem
mobile handheld reader, 25, 27
reader antennas and portal, 25–26
tags, 23–25
Risk management. *See also* IT/IS vulnerabilities
management
assessment
classic, 247–248
discipline, 246
information security context, 248
collaborative
executive-based unit, 241–242
human factor, 242
organizational financial data, 241
organizational responsibilities, 242–246
process, 241
definitions
characterizations, 235
components, 235–237
decision/process, 235
financial activities, 233–234
goal, 235
harmful consequences, 234
historical perspective, 234–235
information security
assets, monetary loss, 240–241
breach, 240
business risk characterizations, 239
resources management, 239
threats, 239–240
measuring
components, characterization, 237
as formula, 237–238
risk analysis, 238–239
organizations list, 230–231
Role-based access control (RBAC), 219

S

Sarbanes–Oxley (SOX) legislation, 452
SCADA systems, 70
Scalable linear recording (SLR), 423
ScriptLogic Privilege Authority, 48
Secure Configuration Management ver.1, 103–105
Secure Content Automation Protocol (SCAP)
approach, 80
design, purpose and flow, 79–80
enumerations
CCE, 82
CPE 2.2, 82–83

languages, 81
ARF, 88
OCIL, 81–82
OCRL, 88–89
XCCDF and OVAL, 81
metrics
CCSS and CMSS, 89
CVSS 2.0, 85–86
real-world use case
NCP, 87–88
standards, 79
vulnerability assessment
using XCCDF and OVAL, 86–87
Securities and Exchange Commission (SEC), 449
Security awareness programs, adult education
principles in
application
behaviors and actions decisions, 208
business perspective points, 209
effectiveness, 207–208
tripartite model, 208
users, attitudes and belief systems, 208
difference
content, focus, 211
emotional state effect, 210
evaluation, 211–212
Hansche's model, 211
learned and unlearned behavior, 210
objective and principles, 210
program, delivery phase, 211
visual and auditory learners, 211
formal education, 209
goal, 207
informal education, 210
nonformal education, 209
training formats, 209
Security engineering teams (SET), 170
Security Information Management Systems (SIMS), 95
Security outsourcing
business risk managing, 283
cons of, 284–285
contractual agreement
business issues, 287–288
SLA and SLO, 287
cost decision, 283
direction establishment, 283–284
enterprise due diligence
customers and employees interests, 285
process metrics, 286
risks and related benefits analysis, 285–286
service-level items, 286
technical metrics, 286
threats, 286–287
key things, 288–289
pros/benefits, 284
services, 284

Security paradox. *See* Productivity and security
Semiactive and semipassive tags, 25
Sensor, 494
Service-level agreement (SLA), 287
Service-level objective (SLO), 287
SET. *See* Security engineering teams (SET)
"Shepherd Collector Servers" (SCS), 70
Shortest vector problem (SVP), 338
Signed data type
    certificates, 354
    DigestAlgorithmIdentifier, 354
    digestAlgorithms, 354–355
    eContent and eContentType, 354–355
    encapContentInfo, 354
    sid, 354–355
    signatureAlgorithm, 355
    signedAttrs and unsignedAttrs, 355
    signerInfos, 355
    version, 354–355
Signer identifier (sid), 355
Simple Object Access Protocol (SOAP), 97
Small business continuity planning infrastructure
      suggestions
    budget/resource availability
      align crisis management planning, 441
      conduct regular and ongoing testing, 441–442
      data and software backup, 440
      insurance coverage philosophies, 440–441
      link risk management, 441
      turnkey solutions, 440
    dedicated personnel
      internal coordinator, 439
      need for consulting assistance, 439
      outsourcing, 439–440
    relative level of need, 438
      BIA, 438
      continuity planning, 439
      threat analysis, 438
Small organization continuity planning realities
    budget/resource availability, 436
    relative level of need, 435–436
    staff time/dedicated personnel, 436
Social media, security risks. *See* Social networking,
      security risks
Social networking, security risks
    availability
      site access type, 205
      slashdot effect, 205
      URLs, 205
      Websites, referencing, 205
    civility, 206
    confidentiality
      aggregated information issue, 200
      anonymous account, 201
      company, social engineering attack, 200
      corporate, 201–202
      ego search, 202

      friends and family information, 202
      information, improper disclosure, 200
      location information, 200
      privacy laws, 202
      usage agreements, 200
    Facebook and Twitter, corporate purpose, 199
    integrity
      company and personal information, 204
      research, 202–204
      system, 204–205
    social engineering, 199
Social Security numbers (SSNs), 450–451
Software as a service (SaaS)
    high-level security
      availability, 304–305
      backup, 305
      data security, 303
      data segregation, 304
      IdM and sign-on process, 305–306
      network security, 304
      regulatory compliance, 304
      SaaS deployment model, 302–303
    on-demand licensing, 301
    securing applications
      deployment, 307
      GRC audits, 307
      product engineering, 306–307
      third-party SaaS security assessment, 307–308
    security challenges
      cloud provider, 302
      enterprise data, 302
      on-premise model, 302
      SaaS stack, 302–303
    software deployment model, 301
    vendors, 301–302
SOX. *See* Sarbanes–Oxley (SOX) legislation
Spanning, 294
SPYCHIPS: How Major Corporations and Government
      Plan to Track Your Every Move with
      RFID, 316
SSN. *See* Social Security numbers (SSNs)
Standard Autonomic Field Engagement One
      (SAFE1), 69
Standard Secure Configuration Management
      (S2CM), 78–79
State Breach Notification Laws, 456–457
Super user privilege management (SUPM), 50
SVP. *See* Shortest vector problem (SVP)
System call-based whitelisting, 6–8
System management and security activity
    categories and roles of assigned duties
      assurance, 414
      CCB, 414–415
      CIO, 413
      consumers, 414
      operations, 413–414
      system manager, 413

challenge
    attackers, 403
    CCRM, 404
    change activity, 404
    IT, 403–404
leveraging security
    CCRM, 419
    compliance monitoring, 419–420
    contingency planning, 420
    forensic analysis, 420
    incident response, 420
    insider threat, 420
    intrusion detection, 420
    penetration testing, 420
    system life cycle integration, 419
    vulnerability and patch management, 419
methods
    CMMI and ISO, 405
    ITIL and NIST, 405
organization benefits, 418
    governance, 418
    organizational synergy, 419
    performance evaluation, 418
process qualities
    activity and goals, 412
    CCRM and CMDB, 412–413
    evidence and flows, 412
    measurable and repeatable, 412
    verifiable, 412–413
requirements as drivers
    business, 411
    data exchanges, 411
    designs, 411–412
    high-level and lower-level requirements, 411
    operational, 411
    tools, 410
    user interfaces, 411
resource tracking, 418
security as enabler, 404–405
separation of duties
    CCRM, 415
    developers and administrators, 415
    librarians and other operations, 415
    management and consumers, 415
    management and operations, 415
    operations and assurance, 415
user and mission focus, 419

T

Tags and readers of RFID system
    authentication, 321
    cloning and physical attacks, 323–324
    cryptographic vulnerabilities, 327–328
    deactivating, 326
    eavesdropping, 320–321
    hiding, 325–326

    operating frequencies and reading distances, 318–319
    replay and relay attacks, 324–325
    skimming, 321–323
Tape backup considerations
    administrator questions, 424–425
    enterprise requirements and standards
        administrator password, 424
        boot control, 424
        power on password, 424
        serial/parallel interface control, 424
    information backup and recovery, 424–425
    information technology (IT), 423
    live disaster recovery, 426
    plan template
        appendix, 428
        contacts, 427–428
        procedures, 427
        purpose, 426–427
        tapes, 427
    procedures
        incremental backups, 426
        weekly backups, 426
    SLR, DLT and LTO, 423
TCP and OSI reference model, 118–119
Technology dis-innovation life cycle, 73
Technology of RFID systems
    enterprise subsystem
        analytic systems and middleware, 26
        function, 25–26
        network infrastructure, 27
    interenterprise subsystem, 27
    open and closed, 28
    RF subsystem
        mobile handheld reader, 25, 27
        reader antennas and portal, 25–26
        tags, 23–25
    supply chain application, 23
Threats
    cyber espionage, 393
    hacking, 393
    identity-related
        information leakage and phishing, 63
        profile squatting, 63
    motivations for, 393–394
    network and information security
        aggregators, 63
        cross site scripting/viruses and worms, 63
        spamming, 62
    privacy-related
        complete account deletion, difficulty, 62
        content-based image retrieval, 62
        face recognition, 62
        image tagging and cross-profiling, 62
        personal information, digital dossier, 61–62
    social
        corporate espionage, 64
        privacy, protecting, 64

stalking, 63–64
technology and privacy, 65
users and privacy, 64–65
Total privileged access management (TPAM), 41–43
Tracking of RFID system
components, 317
e-passports, 318
GPS functionality, 317
individual product packaging, 318
location information and privacy, 317
risks, 317–318
Wal-Mart, 318
Traditional security assessment
audit and assessment techniques, 267
enhanced assessment processes, elements, 268
requirements from, 267
security controls, 267
Trusted Computing Group (TCG), 76–77
Trusted Network Connect (TNC) working group, 77
Trusted Open Group (TOG), 76

U

UNAB. *See* Unix authentication broker (UNAB)
Uniform Resource Identifiers (URI), 82
United Kingdom Data Protection Act, 1998, 461
United States Computer Emergency Readiness Team
(US-CERT) Technical Cyber Security
Alerts, 84–85
Unix authentication broker (UNAB), 46
Unstructured data
access policy
automated and manual process, 226
complexity limiting, 223–224
content categories, 221–222
data governance, 221
department representatives, 222
document retention series, 221–222
essential deliverables, 221
framework, 226
information, 222
IT department, 222–223
overall organizer, 221
primary goal, 226–227
project manager, 226
requirement matrix, 223–226
sensitivity handling levels and procedures, 222
situations, 222
strategy development, 226–227
writing, 226
access problem
chain-of-custody verification, 216
control, lack of, 216
legal standpoint issues, 216
PCI and HIPAA, 216
Sarbanes–Oxley act, 216
security standpoint, 217

amount estimation, 215–216
available access solutions
ABAC, 219–220
content management systems, 217–218
DAC, 218–219
data governance concept, 220–221
MAC and RBAC, 219
policy guidance, 218
structuring methods, 220
technology solutions, 217
context dependence, 215
defined, 215
User Datagram Protocol (UDP), 7

V

Verdasys privileged user management, 49–50
Video content analysis (VCA), 497
Video surveillance and analysis
algorithms and behavior detection scenarios, 497–498
CBR consumption guidelines, 499–500
communications infrastructure, 499
IP precedence and DiffServ code points, 502–503
IP standpoint and, 498–499
network
design, 503–504
security features, 499
packets
loss, 501–502
marking methods, 502–503
performance and storage considerations, 499–501
QoS and network design principles, 501–502
resolution in pixels, 499–500
sample video analytics, 497–498
service marking class, 502–503
traffic nature, 499
VCA, 497
WAN traffic, implications, 503
Virtualization
benefits
dynamic load balancing, 138–139
information security, 139–140
server consolidation, 138
inherent risk
protection rings, 369–370
server, vulnerability, 370
software, 370
x86 privilege levels, 369
marketplace, key players
Citrix, 368
Microsoft, 368
VMware, 368
risk mitigation approaches
air-gapped networks, 144
malicious code research, 144
security, leverage, 144
VMs on same physical machine, 144

security risks, 368–369, 386–387
    data storage-related, 142
    hyperjacking, 141
    malicious code, 142
    mechanisms, uniformity, 143
    network defense controls, 141
    patching barriers, 143
    physical security, 142–143
    products, vulnerabilities in, 141–142
    service denial, 142
    sniffing-related, 141
    time synchronization, 143
    VMs, 140–141, 143
technology, 367
traditional network security products
    ESX/ESXi server, 370
    physical servers, 370–372
    security product's respective network
        interface, 370
    traffic filtration, 370–371
    VMware vShield zones, 370–372
types
    application, 367–368
    application and network, 138
    desktop, 368
    server and storage, 138, 367–368
virtual realm, securing
    implementation, 371, 373
    vendor's virtualization product, 370
    vSphere Hardening Guide, 373–386
Virtualized environments, securing
  approach
    configuration standards and tools, 145
    VMs physical security, 145
  controls, selection and implementation
    technical control measures, 146
    VM OS, 146
  deployment questions, 144–145
  policies and standards
    areas address, 145–146
    trusted virtualized server library, 145–146
  security, 144
  VM
    auditing, 148
    COS, 147
    data security, 147
    patching and updating, 147–148
    VM backup, 147
    VM deployment, 147
    VMkernel, 146–147
    VM networks, 146
    VM-server to VM-server traffic and VMkernel
        traffic, 147
Virus attacks of RFID system
  buffer overflow, 330
  code insertion, 330
  SQL injection, 330–331

Virus Bulletin, 5
VirusTotal, 5
Vulnerability search engine, 84

W

Warfare and security
  challenges
    attribution, 399
    complexity, 400
    global infrastructures, 400
    international agreements and laws, 400
  cybercrime/cybersecurity
    and cyberwarfare, 398–399
    infrastructures, 398
    investigation and prosecution, 397–398
  cyberspace
    CI/KR, 391–392
    freedom of action, 392
    global domain, 392
    national strategy, 392
    virtual communicative space, 392
  federal government, 392–393
  national responses
    Central Security Service, 396
    Department of Defense, 396
    Department of Justice, 397
    Department of State, 397
    Executive Office of President, 394–395
    NCSD and NSA, 394
    NIST and DHS, 394–396
  threats
    cyber espionage, 393
    hacking, 393
    motivations, 393–394
Web 1.0 and 2.0, 56–57
Web 2.0, security risks
  availability
    site access type, 205
    slashdot effect, 205
    URLs, 205
    Websites, referencing, 205
  civility, 206
  confidentiality
    aggregated information issue, 200
    anonymous account, 201
    company, social engineering attack, 200
    corporate, 201–202
    ego search, 202
    friends and family information, 202
    information, improper disclosure, 200
    location information, 200
    privacy laws, 202
    usage agreements, 200

Facebook and Twitter, corporate purpose, 199
integrity
    company and personal info, 204
    research, 202–204
    system, 204–205
social engineering, 199
Whitelisting, 3
    access control, 15
    blacklists
        advantages and disadvantages, 16
        comparison, 16–17
    deployment, 8–9
    forms of
        file-based and system call-based, 6–8

implementing, 8, 17
and malware life cycle, 7
postdeployment challenges to, 9–10
products of, 11–12
types
    application, 16
    e-mail, 15
    LAN, 16
    program, 16
users and user environments, 10–11
using, 17

X

XML cryptographic message syntax (XCMS), 364

Information Security Management Handbook, Sixth Edition: Comprehensive Table of Contents

Domain 1   Access Control

Title	Vol. 1	Vol. 2	Vol. 3	Vol. 4	Vol. 5
1.1 Access Control Techniques					
A Look at RFID Security, Ben Rothke	x				
New Emerging Information Security Technologies and Solutions, Tara Chand	x				
Sensitive or Critical Data Access Controls, Mollie E. Krehnke and David Krehnke	x				
An Introduction to Role-Based Access Control, Ian Clark	x				
Smart Cards, Jim Tiller	x				
A Guide to Evaluating Tokens, Joseph T. Hootman	x				
Controlling FTP: Providing Secured Data Transfers, Chris Hare	x				
Authentication Tokens, Paul A. Henry		x			
Authentication and the Role of Tokens, Jeff Davis		x			

(continued)

Domain 1 (continued) Access Control

Title	Vol. 1	Vol. 2	Vol. 3	Vol. 4	Vol. 5
Expanding PKI-Based Access Control Capabilities with Attribute Certificates, Alex Golod			x		
Whitelisting for Endpoint Defense, Rob Shein					x
Whitelisting, Sandy Bacik					x
1.2 Access Control Administration					
Back to the Future, Paul A. Henry				x	
End Node Security and Network Access Management: Deciding among Different Strategies, Franjo Majstor	x				
Identity Management: Benefits and Challenges, Lynda L. McGhie	x				
Blended Threat Analysis: Passwords and Policy, Daniel D. Houser	x				
Accountability, Dean R. Bushmiller		x			
Five Components to Identity Management Systems, Kevin Castellow			x		
RFID and Information Security, Salahuddin Kamran					x
Privileged User Management, Georges J. Jahchan					x
Privacy in the Age of Social Networking, Salahuddin Kamran					x
1.3 Identification and Authentication Techniques					
Enhancing Security through Biometric Technology, Stephen D. Fried	x				
Single Sign-On for the Enterprise, Ross A. Leo	x				
1.4 Access Control Methodologies and Implementation					
Centralized Authentication Services (RADIUS, TACACS, DIAMETER), Bill Stackpole	x				
An Introduction to Secure Remote Access, Christina M. Bird	x				

Domain 1 (continued)   Access Control

Title	Vol. 1	Vol. 2	Vol. 3	Vol. 4	Vol. 5
1.5 Methods of Attack					
Hacker Tools and Techniques, Ed Skoudis	x				
A New Breed of Hacker Tools and Defenses, Ed Skoudis	x				
Breaking News: The Latest Hacker Attacks and Defenses, Ed Skoudis	x				
Counter-Economic Espionage, Craig A. Schiller	x				
Rootkits: The Ultimate Malware Threat, E. Eugene Schultz and Edward Ray		x			
Security Weaknesses of System and Application Interfaces Used to Process Sensitive Information, Sean Price			x		
1.6 Monitoring and Penetration Testing					
Insight into Intrusion Prevention Systems, Gildas Deograt-Lumy	x				
Penetration Testing, Stephen D. Fried	x				

Domain 2   Telecommunications and Network Security

Title	Vol. 1	Vol. 2	Vol. 3	Vol. 4	Vol. 5
2.1 Communications and Network Security					
Adaptive Threats and Defenses, Sean Price				x	
Achieving Global Information Systems Transformation (GIST) through Standards: Foundations for Standards-Based Network Visibility via IF-MAP and Beyond, David O'Berry				x	
A Primer on Demystifying U.S. Government Networks, Samuel W. Chun				x	
Network Security Utilizing an Adaptable Protocol Framework, Robby Fussell	x				

(continued)

Domain 2 (continued)   Telecommunications and Network Security

Title	Vol. 1	Vol. 2	Vol. 3	Vol. 4	Vol. 5
The *Five W's and Designing a Secure, Identity-Based, Self-Defending Network (5W Network)*, Samuel W. Chun	x				
Maintaining Network Security: Availability via Intelligent Agents, Robby Fussell	x				
PBX Firewalls: Closing the Back Door, William A. Yarberry, Jr.	x				
Network Security Overview, Bonnie A. Goins and Christopher A. Pilewski	x				
Putting Security in the Transport: TLS, Chris Hare	x				
WLAN Security Update, Franjo Majstor	x				
Understanding SSL, Chris Hare	x				
Packet Sniffers and Network Monitors, James S. Tiller and Bryan D. Fish	x				
Secured Connections to External Networks, Steven F. Blanding	x				
Security and Network Technologies, Chris Hare	x				
Wired and Wireless Physical Layer Security Issues, James Trulove	x				
Network Router Security, Steven F. Blanding	x				
What's Not So Simple about SNMP? Chris Hare	x				
Network and Telecommunications Media: Security from the Ground Up, Samuel Chun	x				
Security and the Physical Network Layer, Matthew J. Decker	x				
Wireless LAN Security Challenge, Frandinata Halim and Gildas Deograt	x				
ISO/OSI and TCP/IP Network Model Characteristics, George G. McBride	x				
Facsimile Security, Ben Rothke		x			
Mobile Data Security, George McBride			x		

Domain 2 (continued)   Telecommunications and Network Security

Title	Vol. 1	Vol. 2	Vol. 3	Vol. 4	Vol. 5
Integrated Security through Open Standards: A Path to Enhanced Network Visibility, David O'Berry			x		
IF-MAP as a Standard for Security Data Interchange, David O'Berry					x
2.2 Internet, Intranet, Extranet Security					
VoIP Security Issues, Anthony Bruno	x				
An Examination of Firewall Architectures, Paul A. Henry	x				
Voice over WLAN, Bill Lipiczky	x				
Spam Wars: How to Deal with Junk E-Mail, Al Bredenberg	x				
Secure Web Services: Holes and Fillers, Lynda L. McGhie	x				
IPSec Virtual Private Networks, James S. Tiller	x				
Internet Security: Securing the Perimeter, Douglas G. Conorich	x				
Application-Layer Security Protocols for Networks, Bill Stackpole	x				
Application Layer: Next Level of Security, Keith Pasley	x				
Security of Communication Protocols and Services, William Hugh Murray	x				
An Introduction to IPSec, Bill Stackpole	x				
VPN Deployment and Evaluation Strategy, Keith Pasley	x				
Comparing Firewall Technologies, Per Thorsheim	x				
Cookies and Web Bugs: What They Are and How They Work Together, William T. Harding, Anita J. Reed, and Robert L. Gray	x				
Security for Broadband Internet Access Users, James Trulove	x				
Network Content Filtering and Leak Prevention, Georges J. Jahchan		x			

(continued)

Domain 2 (continued) Telecommunications and Network Security

Title	Vol. 1	Vol. 2	Vol. 3	Vol. 4	Vol. 5
Web Application Firewalls, Georges J. Jahchan			x		
Understating the Ramifications of IPv6, Foster Henderson					x
2.3 E-Mail Security					
Instant Messaging Security Issues, William Hugh Murray	x				
2.4 Secure Voice Communications					
Voice Security, Chris Hare	x				
Secure Voice Communications, Valene Skerpac	x				
2.5 Network Attacks and Countermeasures					
Deep Packet Inspection Technologies, Anderson Ramos	x				
Wireless Penetration Testing: Case Study and Countermeasures, Christopher Pilewski	x				
Auditing the Telephony System: Defenses against Communications Security Breaches and Toll Fraud, William A. Yarberry, Jr.	x				
Insecurity by Proxy, Micah Silverman	x				
Wireless Security, Charles R. Hudson and Chris R. Cunningham	x				
Packet Sniffers: Use and Misuse, Steve A. Rodgers	x				
ISPs and Denial-of-Service Attacks, K. Narayanaswamy	x				
The Ocean Is Full of Phish, Todd Fitzgerald		x			
Botnets, Robert M. Slade			x		
Antispam: Bayesian Filtering, Georges J. Jahchan				x	
Managing Security in Virtual Environments, E. Eugene Schultz and Edward Ray					x

Domain 3   Information Security and Risk Management

Title	Vol. 1	Vol. 2	Vol. 3	Vol. 4	Vol. 5
3.1 Security Management Concepts and Principles					
Bits to Bytes to Boardroom, Micki Krause	x				
Information Security Governance, Todd Fitzgerald	x				
Corporate Governance, David Krehnke	x				
IT Governance Institute (ITGI) Overview, Molly Krehnke	x				
Top Management Support Essential for Effective Information Security, Kenneth J. Knapp and Thomas E. Marshall	x				
Managing Security by the Standards: An Overview and Primer, Bonnie A. Goins	x				
Information Security for Mergers and Acquisitions, Craig A. Schiller	x				
Information Security Governance, Ralph Spencer Poore	x				
Belts and Suspenders: Diversity in Information Technology Security, Jeffrey Davis	x				
Building Management Commitment through Security Councils, Todd Fitzgerald	x				
Validating Your Business Partners, Jeff Misrahi	x				
Measuring ROI on Security, Carl F. Endorf	x				
The Human Side of Information Security, Kevin Henry	x				
Integrated Threat Management, George G. McBride		x			
Understanding Information Security Management Systems, Tom Carlson		x			
Security Management, Ken Buszta	x				
It Is All about Control, Chris Hare	x				
Collaborating Information Security and Privacy to Create Effective Awareness and Training, Rebecca Herold			x		

(continued)

Domain 3 (continued)   Information Security and Risk Management

Title	Vol. 1	Vol. 2	Vol. 3	Vol. 4	Vol. 5
Security Information and Event Management (SIEM) Technology, E. Eugene Schultz			x		
Managing Mobile Device Security, E. Eugene Schultz and Gal Shpantzer				x	
Establishing an Information Security Program for Local Government, Robert Pittman				x	
Do Your Business Associate Security and Privacy Programs Live Up to HIPAA and HITECH Requirements? Rebecca Herold					x
Organization Culture Awareness Will Cultivate Your Information Security Program, Robert Pittman					x
3.2 Change Control Management					
Patch Management 101: It Just Makes Good Sense! Lynda McGhie	x				
Security Patch Management Process, Felicia M. Nicastro	x				
Configuration Management: Charting the Course for the Organization, Mollie E. Krehnke and David C. Krehnke	x				
3.3 Data Classification					
Understanding Information Risk Management, Tom Carlson and Nick Halvorson				x	
Information Classification: A Corporate Implementation Guide, Jim Appleyard	x				
Ownership and Custody of Data, William Hugh Murray	x				
Developing and Conducting a Security Test and Evaluation, Sean M. Price	x				
Enterprise Security Management, George McBride	x				
A Matter of Trust, Ray Kaplan	x				
Trust Governance in a Web Services World, Daniel D. Houser	x				

Domain 3 (continued)   Information Security and Risk Management

Title	Vol. 1	Vol. 2	Vol. 3	Vol. 4	Vol. 5
3.4 Risk Management					
The Role of Information Security in the Enterprise Risk Management Structure, Carl Jackson and Mark Carey	x				
Technology Convergence and Security: A Simplified Risk Management Model, Ken M. Shaurette	x				
Using Quasi-Intelligence Resources to Protect the Enterprise, Craig A. Schiller		x			
Information Risk Management: A Process Approach to Risk Diagnosis and Treatment, Nick Halvorson		x			
Department-Level Transformation, R. Scott McCoy		x			
Setting Priorities in Your Security Program, Derek Schatz		x			
Why and How Assessment of Organization Culture Shapes Security Strategies, Don Saracco		x			
Information Security Risk Assessment, Samantha Thomas Cruz	x				
Risk Management and Analysis, Kevin Henry	x				
New Trends in Information Risk Management, Brett Regan Young	x				
Cyber-Risk Management: Technical and Insurance Controls for Enterprise-Level Security, Carol A. Siegel, Ty R. Sagalow, and Paul Serritella	x				
A Look Ahead, Samantha Thomas		x			
The Insider Threat: A View from the Outside, Todd Fitzgerald			x		
Pod Slurping, Ben Rothke			x		
The USB (Universal Security Burden) Nightmare: Pod-Slurping and Other High Storage Capacity Portable Device Vulnerabilities, Kenneth F. Belva			x		

(continued)

Domain 3 (continued)   Information Security and Risk Management

Title	Vol. 1	Vol. 2	Vol. 3	Vol. 4	Vol. 5
Diary of a Security Assessment: "Put That in Your Pipe and Smoke It!" Ken M. Shaurette			x		
Role-Based Information Security Governance: Avoiding the Company Oil Slick, Todd Fitzgerald					x
Social Networking Security Exposure, Sandy Bacik					x
Social Networking, Social Media, and Web 2.0 Security Risks, Robert M. Slade					x
Applying Adult Education Principles to Security Awareness Programs, Chris Hare					x
3.5 Policies, Standards, Procedures, and Guidelines					
Committee of Sponsoring Organizations (COSO), Mignona Cote	x				
Toward Enforcing Security Policy: Encouraging Personal Accountability for Corporate Information Security Policy, John O. Wylder	x				
The Security Policy Life Cycle: Functions and Responsibilities, Patrick D. Howard	x				
People, Processes, and Technology: A Winning Combination, Felicia M. Nicastro	x				
Building an Effective Privacy Program, Rebecca Herold	x				
Establishing an E-Mail Retention Policy: Preventing Potential Legal Nightmares, Stephen Fried	x				
Ten Steps to Effective Web-Based Security Policy Development and Distribution, Todd Fitzgerald	x				
Roles and Responsibilities of the Information Systems Security Officer, Carl Burney	x				
Organizing for Success: Some Human Resources Issues in Information Security, Jeffrey H. Fenton and James M. Wolfe	x				

Domain 3 (continued) Information Security and Risk Management

Title	Vol. 1	Vol. 2	Vol. 3	Vol. 4	Vol. 5
Information Security Policies from the Ground Up, Brian Shorten	x				
Policy Development, Chris Hare	x				
Training Your Employees to Identify Potential Fraud and How to Encourage Them to Come Forward, Rebecca Herold	x				
Planning for a Privacy Breach, Rebecca Herold		x			
A Business Case for ISO 27001 Certification, Tom Carlson and Robert Forbes				x	
Achieving PCI DSS Compliance: A Compliance Review, Bonnie A. Goins and Christopher A. Pilewski				x	
The Sarbanes–Oxley Revolution: Hero or Hindrance? Seth Kinnett				x	
Leveraging IT Control Frameworks for Compliance, Todd Fitzgerald				x	
Rats in the Cellar and Bats in the Attic, "Not Enough Depth to My Security", Ken M. Shaurette				x	
Security Outsourcing, Sandy Bacik					x
3.6 Security Awareness Training					
Measuring Information Security and Privacy Training and Awareness Effectiveness, Rebecca Herold				x	
Change That Attitude: The ABCs of a Persuasive Security Awareness Program, Sam Chun	x				
Maintaining Management's Commitment, William Tompkins	x				
Making Security Awareness Happen, Susan D. Hansche	x				
Beyond Information Security Awareness Training: It Is Time to Change the Culture, Stan Stahl	x				

(*continued*)

Domain 3 (continued)   Information Security and Risk Management

Title	Vol. 1	Vol. 2	Vol. 3	Vol. 4	Vol. 5
3.7 Security Management Planning					
The Outsourcing of IT: Seeing the Big Picture, Foster Henderson				x	
Overview of an IT Corporate Security Organization, Jeff Davis	x				
Make Security Part of Your Company's DNA, Ken M. Shaurette	x				
Building an Effective and Winning Security Team, Lynda McGhie	x				
When Trust Goes beyond the Border: Moving Your Development Work Offshore, Stephen Fried	x				
Maintaining Information Security during Downsizing, Thomas J. Bray	x				
The Business Case for Information Security: Selling Management on the Protection of Vital Secrets and Products, Sanford Sherizen	x				
How to Work with a Managed Security Service Provider, Laurie Hill McQuillan	x				
Considerations for Outsourcing Security, Michael J. Corby	x				
Achieving NERC Compliance: A Compliance Review, Bonnie Goins Pilewski and Christopher A. Pilewski			x		
Controlling the Emerging Data Dilemma: Building Policy for Unstructured Data Access, Anne Shultz					x
Governance and Risk Management within the Context of Information Security, James C. Murphy					x
Improving Enterprise Security through Predictive Analysis, Chris Hare					x
3.8 Ethics					
The Ethical and Legal Concerns of Spyware, Janice C. Sipior, Burke T. Ward, and Georgina R. Roselli	x				
Ethics and the Internet, Micki Krause	x				
Computer Ethics, Peter S. Tippett	x				

Domain 4 Application Development Security

Title	Vol. 1	Vol. 2	Vol. 3	Vol. 4	Vol. 5
4.1 Application Issues					
Application Service Provider Security: Ensuring a Secure Relationship for the Client and the ASP, Stephen D. Fried	x				
Stack-Based Buffer Overflows, Jonathan S. Held	x				
Web Application Security, Mandy Andress	x				
Security for XML and Other Metadata Languages, William Hugh Murray	x				
XML and Information Security, Samuel C. McClintock	x				
Application Security, Walter S. Kobus, Jr.	x				
Covert Channels, Anton Chuvakin	x				
Security as a Value Enhancer in Application Systems Development, Lowell Bruce McCulley	x				
Open Source versus Closed Source, Ed Skoudis	x				
A Look at Java Security, Ben Rothke	x				
Neural Networks and Information Assurance Uses, Sean M. Price		x			
Information Technology Infrastructure Library and Security Management Overview, David McPhee		x			
Adaptation: A Concept for Next-Generation Security Application Development, Robby S. Fussell		x			
Quantum Computing: Implications for Security, Robert M. Slade		x			
Mashup Security, Mano Paul			x		
Format String Vulnerabilities, Mano Paul			x		
4.2 Databases and Data Warehousing					
Reflections on Database Integrity, William Hugh Murray	x				

(*continued*)

Domain 4 (continued)   Application Development Security

Title	Vol. 1	Vol. 2	Vol. 3	Vol. 4	Vol. 5
Digital Signatures in Relational Database Applications, Mike R. Prevost	x				
Security and Privacy for Data Warehouses: Opportunity or Threat? David Bonewell, Karen Gibbs, and Adriaan Veldhuisen	x				
4.3 Systems Development Controls					
Data Loss Prevention Program, Powell Hamilton				x	
Data Reliability: Trusted Time Stamps, Jeff Stapleton				x	
Security in the .NET Framework, James D. Murray				x	
Building and Assessing Security in the Software Development Lifecycle, George G. McBride	x				
Avoiding Buffer Overflow Attacks, Sean Price	x				
Secure Development Life Cycle, Kevin Henry	x				
System Development Security Methodology, Ian Lim and Ioana V. Bazawan	x				
Software Engineering Institute Capability Maturity Mode, Matt Nelson	x				
Enterprise Security Architecture, William Hugh Murray	x				
Certification and Accreditation Methodology, Mollie E. Krehnke and David C. Krehnke	x				
System Development Security Methodology, Ian Lim and Ioana V. Carastan	x				
Methods of Auditing Applications, David C. Rice and Graham Bucholz	x				
The Effectiveness of Access Management Reviews, Chris Hare					x
Securing SaaS Applications: A Cloud Security Perspective for Application Providers, Pradnyesh Rane					x
Attacking RFID Systems, Pedro Peris-Lopez, Julio Cesar Hernandez-Castro, Juan M. Estevez-Tapiador, and Arturo Ribagorda					x

Domain 4 (continued)   Application Development Security

Title	Vol. 1	Vol. 2	Vol. 3	Vol. 4	Vol. 5
4.4 Malicious Code					
Fast Scanning Worms, Paul A. Henry			x		
Organized Crime and Malware, Michael Pike			x		
Net-Based Malware Detection: A Comparison with Intrusion Detection Models, Robert M. Slade		x			
Malware and Computer Viruses, Robert M. Slade	x				
An Introduction to Hostile Code and Its Control, Jay Heiser		x			
A Look at Java Security, Ben Rothke	x				
4.5 Methods of Attack					
Hacking Methods, Georges J. Jahchan	x				
Enabling Safer Deployment of Internet Mobile Code Technologies, Ron Moritz	x				

Domain 5   Cryptography

Title	Vol. 1	Vol. 2	Vol. 3	Vol. 4	Vol. 5
5.1 Use of Cryptography					
Auditing Cryptography: Assessing System Security, Steve Stanek	x				
Three New Models for the Application of Cryptography, Jay Heiser		x			
5.2 Cryptographic Concepts, Methodologies, and Practices					
Cryptography: A Unifying Principle in Compliance Programs, Ralph Spencer Poore				x	
Cryptographic Transitions, Ralph Spencer Poore	x				
Blind Detection of Steganographic Content in Digital Images Using Cellular Automata, Sasan Hamidi	x				
An Overview of Quantum Cryptography, Ben Rothke	x				

(continued)

Domain 5 (continued)   Cryptography

Title	Vol. 1	Vol. 2	Vol. 3	Vol. 4	Vol. 5
Elliptic Curve Cryptography: Delivering High-Performance Security for E-Commerce and Communications, Paul Lambert	x				
Cryptographic Key Management Concepts, Ralph Spencer Poore	x				
Message Authentication, James S. Tiller	x				
Fundamentals of Cryptography and Encryption, Ronald A. Gove	x				
Steganography: The Art of Hiding Messages, Mark Edmead	x				
An Introduction to Cryptography, Javek Ikbal	x				
Hash Algorithms: From Message Digests to Signatures, Keith Pasley	x				
A Look at the Advanced Encryption Standard (AES), Ben Rothke	x				
Message Digest, Ralph Spencer Poore			x		
Quantum Computing: The Rise of the Machine, Robby Fussell			x		
Cryptography: Mathematics vs. Engineering, Ralph Spencer Poore					x
Cryptographic Message Syntax, Jeff Stapleton					x
5.3 Private Key Algorithms					
Principles and Applications of Cryptographic Key Management, William Hugh Murray	x				
5.4 Public Key Infrastructure (PKI)					
Preserving Public Key Hierarchy, Geoffrey C. Grabow	x				
PKI Registration, Alex Golod	x				
Encryption Key Management in Large-Scale Network Deployments, Franjo Majstor and Guy Vancollie		x			

Domain 5 (continued) Cryptography

Title	Vol. 1	Vol. 2	Vol. 3	Vol. 4	Vol. 5
5.5 System Architecture for Implementing Cryptographic Functions					
Implementing Kerberos in Distributed Systems, Joe Kovara and Ray Kaplan	x				
5.6 Methods of Attack					
Methods of Attacking and Defending Cryptosystems, Joost Houwen	x				

Domain 6 Security Architecture and Design

Title	Vol. 1	Vol. 2	Vol. 3	Vol. 4	Vol. 5
6.1 Principles of Computer and Network Organizations, Architectures, and Designs					
Enterprise Assurance: A Framework Explored, Bonnie A. Goins	x				
Creating a Secure Architecture, Christopher A. Pilewski and Bonnie A. Goins	x				
Common Models for Architecting an Enterprise Security Capability, Matthew J. Decker	x				
The Reality of Virtual Computing, Chris Hare	x				
Service-Oriented Architecture and Web Services Security, Glenn J. Cater		x			
Analysis of Covert Channels, Ralph Spencer Poore		x			
Security Architecture of Biological Cells: An Example of Defense in Depth, Kenneth J. Knapp and R. Franklin Morris, Jr.		x			
ISO Standards Draft Content, Scott Erkonen		x			
Security Frameworks, Robert M. Slade		x			
Information Flow and Covert Channels, Sean Price			x		
Securing Data at Rest: From Smartphones to Tapes Defining Data at Rest, Sam Chun and Leo Kahng			x		
Best Practices in Virtualization Security, Shanit Gupta				x	

(continued)

Domain 6 (continued)   Security Architecture and Design

Title	Vol. 1	Vol. 2	Vol. 3	Vol. 4	Vol. 5
Everything New Is Old Again, Robert M. Slade				x	
An Introduction to Virtualization Security, Paul Henry					x
6.2 Principles of Security Models, Architectures, and Evaluation Criteria					
Formulating an Enterprise Information Security Architecture, Mollie E. Krehnke and David C. Krehnke	x				
Security *Architecture and Models,* Foster J. Henderson and Kellina M. Craig-Henderson	x				
The Common Criteria for IT Security Evaluation, Debra S. Herrmann	x				
6.3 Common Flaws and Security Issues: System Architecture and Design					
Common System Design Flaws and Security Issues, William Hugh Murray	x				

Domain 7   Operations Security

Title	Vol. 1	Vol. 2	Vol. 3	Vol. 4	Vol. 5
7.1 Concepts					
Security Considerations in Distributed Computing: A Grid Security Overview, Sasan Hamidi	x				
Managing Unmanaged Systems, Bill Stackpole and Man Nguyen	x				
Storage Area Networks Security Protocols and Mechanisms, Franjo Majstor	x				
Operations: The Center of Support and Control, Kevin Henry	x				
Why Today's Security Technologies Are So Inadequate: History, Implications, and New Approaches, Steven Hofmeyr	x				
Operations Security and Controls, Patricia A.P. Fisher	x				

Domain 7   Operations Security

Title	Vol. 1	Vol. 2	Vol. 3	Vol. 4	Vol. 5
7.2 Resource Protection Requirements					
The Nebulous Zero Day, Rob Slade	x				
Understanding Service Level Agreements, Gilbert Held	x				
Physical Access Control, Dan M. Bowers	x				
7.3 Auditing					
Auditing the Electronic Commerce Environment, Chris Hare	x				
7.4 Intrusion Detection					
Improving Network-Level Security through Real-Time Monitoring and Intrusion Detection, Chris Hare		x			
Intelligent Intrusion Analysis: How Thinking Machines Can Recognize Computer Intrusions, Bryan D. Fish	x				
7.5 Operations Controls					
Directory Security, Ken Buszta	x				
Patch Management 101: It Just Makes Good Sense! Lynda McGhie		x			
Security Patch Management: The Process, Felicia M. Nicastro		x			
Validating Tape Backups, Sandy Bacik			x		
A Brief Summary of Warfare and Commercial Entities, Rob Shein				x	
Information Destruction Requirements and Techniques, Ben Rothke				x	
Warfare and Security: Deterrence and Dissuasion in the Cyber Era, Samuel Chun					x
Configuration, Change, and Release Management, Sean M. Price					x
Tape Backup Considerations, Sandy Bacik					x
Productivity vs. Security, Sandy Bacik					x

(continued)

Domain 8   Business Continuity and Disaster Recovery Planning

Title	Vol. 1	Vol. 2	Vol. 3	Vol. 4	Vol. 5
Section 8.1 *Business Continuity Planning*					
Developing Realistic Continuity Planning Process Metrics, Carl B. Jackson	x				
Building Maintenance Processes for Business Continuity Plans, Ken Doughty	x				
Identifying Critical Business Functions, Bonnie A. Goins	x				
Selecting the Right Business Continuity Strategy, Ken Doughty	x				
Contingency Planning Best Practices and Program Maturity, Timothy R. Stacey	x				
Reengineering the Business Continuity Planning Process, Carl B. Jackson	x				
The Role of Continuity Planning in the Enterprise Risk Management Structure, Carl Jackson	x				
Determining Business Unit Priorities in Business Continuity Management, Kevin Henry			x		
Continuity Program Testing, Maintenance, Training and Awareness, Carl Jackson			x		
Integrated Business Continuity Planning, James C. Murphy				x	
CERT/BERT: Community and Business Emergency Response, Carl B. Jackson				x	
Continuity Planning for Small- and Medium-Sized Organizations, Carl Jackson					x
Section 8.2 *Disaster Recovery Planning*					
Contingency at a Glance, Ken M. Shaurette and Thomas J. Schleppenbach	x				
The Business Impact Assessment Process and the Importance of Using Business Process Mapping, Carl Jackson	x				
Testing Business Continuity and Disaster Recovery Plans, James S. Mitts	x				

Domain 8 (continued) Business Continuity and Disaster Recovery Planning

Title	Vol. 1	Vol. 2	Vol. 3	Vol. 4	Vol. 5
Restoration Component of Business Continuity Planning, John Dorf and Martin Johnson	x				
Business Resumption Planning and Disaster Recovery: A Case History, Kevin Henry	x				
Business Continuity Planning: A Collaborative Approach, Kevin Henry	x				
Section 8.3 Elements of Business Continuity Planning					
The Business Impact Assessment Process, Carl B. Jackson	x				

Domain 9 Legal, Regulations, Compliance, and Investigations

Title	Vol. 1	Vol. 2	Vol. 3	Vol. 4	Vol. 5
Section 9.1 Information Law					
Sarbanes–Oxley Compliance: A Technology Practitioner's Guide, Bonnie A. Goins	x				
Health Insurance Portability and Accountability Act Security Rule, Lynda L. McGhie	x				
Jurisdictional Issues in Global Transmissions, Ralph Spencer Poore	x				
An Emerging Information Security Minimum Standard of Due Care, Robert Braun and Stan Stahl	x				
ISPs and Accountability, Lee Imrey		x			
The Case for Privacy, Michael J. Corby	x				
Liability for Lax Computer Security in DDoS Attacks, Dorsey Morrow	x				
Compliance Assurance: Taming the Beast, Todd Fitzgerald		x			
The Cost of Risk: An Examination of Risk Assessment and Information Security in the Financial Industry, Seth Kinnett					x
Data Security and Privacy Legislation, Salahuddin Kamran					x

(continued)

Domain 9 (continued)   Legal, Regulations, Compliance, and Investigations

Title	Vol. 1	Vol. 2	Vol. 3	Vol. 4	Vol. 5
Section 9.2 Investigations					
Operational Forensics, Michael J. Corby	x				
Computer Crime Investigation and Computer Forensics, Thomas Welch	x				
What Happened? Kelly J. Kuchta	x				
Section 9.3 Major Categories of Computer Crime					
Potential Cyber Terrorist Attacks, Chris Hare	x				
The Evolution of the Sploit, Ed Skoudis	x				
Computer Crime, Christopher A. Pilewski	x				
Phishing: A New Twist to an Old Game, Stephen D. Fried	x				
It's All about Power: Information Warfare Tactics by Terrorists, Activists, and Miscreants, Gerald L. Kovacich, Andy Jones, and Perry G. Luzwick	x				
Bluesnarfing, Mano Paul			x		
Cyberstalking, Micki Krause Nozaki				x	
Section 9.4 Incident Handling					
Social Engineering: The Human Factor in Information Assurance, Marcus K. Rogers	x				
Privacy Breach Incident Response, Rebecca Herold	x				
Security Event Management, Glenn Cater	x				
DCSA: A Practical Approach to Digital Crime Scene Analysis, Marcus K. Rogers	x				
What a Computer Security Professional Needs to Know about E-Discovery and Digital Forensics, Larry R. Leibrock	x				
How to Begin a Non-Liturgical Forensic Examination, Carol Stucki	x				
Honeypot Essentials, Anton Chuvakin	x				
Managing the Response to a Computer Security Incident, Michael Vangelos	x				
Cyber-Crime: Response, Investigation, and Prosecution, Thomas Akin	x				

Domain 9 (continued) Legal, Regulations, Compliance, and Investigations

Title	Vol. 1	Vol. 2	Vol. 3	Vol. 4	Vol. 5
Enterprise Incident Response and Digital Evidence Management and Handling, Marcus K. Rogers		x			
Security Information Management Myths and Facts, Sasan Hamidi		x			
Virtualization and Digital Investigations, Marcus K. Rogers and Sean C. Leshney			x		
Is Software Write Blocking a Viable Alternative to Hardware Write Blocking in Computer Forensics? Paul A. Henry				x	
Discovery of Electronically Stored Information, Salahuddin Kamran					x

Domain 10 Physical (Environmental) Security

Title	Vol. 1	Vol. 2	Vol. 3	Vol. 4	Vol. 5
10.1 Elements of Physical Security					
Perimeter Security, R. Scott McCoy	x				
Melding Physical Security and Traditional Information Systems Security, Kevin Henry	x				
Physical Security for Mission-Critical Facilities and Data Centers, Gerald Bowman	x				
Physical Security: A Foundation for Information Security, Christopher Steinke	x				
Physical Security: Controlled Access and Layered Defense, Bruce R. Matthews	x				
Computing Facility Physical Security, Alan Brusewitz	x				
Closed-Circuit Television and Video Surveillance, David Litzau	x				
Mantraps and Turnstiles, R. Scott McCoy		x			

(continued)

Domain 10 (continued) Physical (Environmental) Security

Title	Vol. 1	Vol. 2	Vol. 3	Vol. 4	Vol. 5
Halon Fire Suppression Systems, Chris Hare			x		
Crime Prevention through Environmental Design, Mollie Krehnke			x		
Data Center Site Selection and Facility Design Considerations, Sandy Bacik			x		
Protection of Sensitive Data, Sandy Bacik				x	
Water Leakage and Flooding, Sandy Bacik				x	
Site Selection and Facility Design Considerations, Sandy Bacik				x	
An Overview of IP-Based Video Surveillance, Leo Kahng				x	
The Layered Defense Model and Perimeter Intrusion Detection, Leo Kahng					x
10.2 Technical Controls					
Types of Information Security Controls, Harold F. Tipton	x				
10.3 Environment and Life Safety					
Workplace Violence: Event Characteristics and Prevention, George Richards	x				
Physical Security: The Threat after September 11, 2001, Jaymes Williams	x